**3rd edition**

# Nolo's Encyclopedia of Everyday Law

## Answers to Your Most Frequently Asked Legal Questions

**edited by Attorneys Shae Irving
and Kathleen Michon**

# Keeping Up to Date

To keep its books up to date, Nolo issues new printings and new editions periodically. New printings reflect minor legal changes and technical corrections. New editions contain major legal changes, major text additions or major reorganizations. To find out if a later printing or edition of any Nolo book is available, call Nolo at 510-549-1976 or check our website at http://www.nolo.com.

To stay current, follow the "Update" service at our website: http://www.nolo.com/update. In another effort to help you use Nolo's latest materials, we offer a 35% discount off the purchase of the new edition of your Nolo book when you turn in the cover of an earlier edition. (See the "Special Upgrade Offer" in the back of the book.)

This book was last revised in: August 2001.

*Third Edition*

| | |
|---|---|
| *Third Printing* | *August 2001* |
| Editors | *Shae Irving & Kathleen Michon* |
| Cover | *Jaleh Doane* |
| Book Design | *Linda Marie Wanczyk & Jackie Mancuso* |
| Production | *Susan Putney & Sarah Hinman* |
| Index | *Nancy Mulvany* |
| Proofreader | *Kristin Barendsen* |
| Printer | *Bertelsmann Services, Inc.* |

Nolo's encyclopedia of everyday law : answers to your most frequently asked legal questions / [edited by Kathleen A. Michon].- -3rd ed.
        p.   cm.
  Includes index.
  ISBN 0-87337-609-9
  1. Law- -United States- -Popular works. 2. Law- -United States- -Miscellanea. I. Title: Everyday Law Book. II. Michon, Kathleen A., 1966-
KF387.N65  2001
349.73- -DC21             00-056242

QUANTITY SALES: FOR INFORMATION ON BULK PURCHASES OR CORPORATE PREMIUM SALES, PLEASE CONTACT THE SPECIAL SALES DEPARTMENT.

FOR ACADEMIC SALES OR TEXTBOOK ADOPTIONS, ASK FOR ACADEMIC SALES. 800-955-4775, Nolo, 950 PARKER ST., BERKELEY, CA, 94710.

# Dedication

*For Edward F. Dolan*

# Acknowledgments

First things first—thanks to Jake Warner for thinking up the project and providing the support to get it done. And thanks to all the Nolo editors who kept us (and the book) on track, particularly Robin Leonard, for rising above the call of duty, Mary Randolph for her eminent good judgment and Steve Elias for his relentless and contagious enthusiasm.

For diligent research help, we'd like to thank Ella Hirst, Naomi Starkman and Peri Pakroo. For helping manage the changes through draft after draft of the earlier editions, thanks go to Susan Cornell and Stephanie Harolde.

Jackie Mancuso made the book look great. Jaleh Doane, Susan Putney and Linda Marie Wanczyk brought their sharp minds and good humor to the design process, and made the whole thing even easier.

Finally, we're grateful to every Nolo author and editor whose fine work has shaped these pages. You'll find many of these talented folks listed in the Contributors section on the following page. But we want to give special thanks to:

Paul Bergman and Sara Berman-Barrett, authors of *Represent Yourself in Court* and *The Criminal Law Handbook*

David W. Brown, author of *How to Change Your Name* and *Beat Your Ticket: Go to Court and Win!*

Stephen Colwell and Ann Shulman, authors of *Trouble Free Travel…And What to Do When Things Go Wrong*

Frederick W. Daily, author of *Stand Up to the IRS, Tax Savvy for Small Business* and *Surviving an Audit.*

James Evans, author of *Law on the Net* and *Government on the Net*

Cora Jordan, author of *Neighbor Law: Fences, Trees, Boundaries and Noise* and co-author (with Denis Clifford) of *Plan Your Estate*

Mimi E. Lyster, author of *Child Custody: Building Agreements That Work*

Joseph Matthews, author of *How to Win Your Personal Injury Claim* and co-author (with Dorothy Matthews Berman) of *Social Security, Medicare and Pensions*

Tanya Starnes, author of *Mad at Your Lawyer*

Fred S. Steingold, author of *The Legal Guide for Starting and Running a Small Business* and *The Employer's Legal Handbook.*

# Contributors

**Denis Clifford** (Estate and Gift Taxes). Denis is the author of several Nolo books, including *Nolo's Will Book, The Quick and Legal Will Book, Plan Your Estate* (with Cora Jordan) and *The Partnership Book* (with Ralph Warner). A graduate of Columbia Law School, where he was an editor of *The Columbia Law Review,* Denis has practiced law in various ways, and is convinced that people can do much of their own legal work.

**Amy DelPo** (Workplace Rights, Travel, Retirement Plans). Amy has been an editor at Nolo since January 2000. She specializes in workers' rights, sexual harassment law, employment law, criminal law and civil litigation. She brings more than six years of criminal and civil litigation experience to her work at Nolo, having litigated cases in all levels of state and federal courts, including the California Supreme Court and the United States Supreme Court. Amy received her law degree with Honors from the University of North Carolina at Chapel Hill.

**Stephen R. Elias** (Patents, Copyrights, Trademarks, Criminal Law, Legal Research). Steve received a law degree from Hastings College of the Law in 1969. He has practiced law in California, Vermont and New York, working for a variety of programs delivering legal services to the poor. In 1980, he discovered Nolo and, referring to himself as a recovering lawyer, has never looked back. Steve has authored, co-authored or edited over 30 Nolo titles covering such topics as family law, patents, copyrights, trademarks and bankruptcy.

**Lisa Guerin** (Employers' Rights and Responsibilities). During her years as a law student at Boalt Hall School of Law at the University of California at Berkeley, Lisa worked for Nolo as a research and editorial assistant. After a stint as a staff attorney at the U.S. Court of Appeals for the Ninth Circuit, Lisa has worked primarily in the field of employment law, in both government and private practice. Lisa recently rejoined the staff at Nolo, where she is the co-author of *Nolo's Pocket Guide to California Law.*

**Shae Irving** (Durable Powers of Attorney for Finances, Wills and Estate Planning). Shae graduated from Boalt Hall School of Law at the University of California at Berkeley in 1993 and began working for Nolo in 1994. She has written extensively on durable powers of attorney and other estate planning issues. She edits many other Nolo titles, including *Plan Your Estate* and *Make Your Own Living Trust.*

**Bethany K. Laurence** (Small Businesses). Beth graduated from Hastings College of the Law at the University of California in 1993. She spent several years working for a corporate legal publisher before coming to Nolo. She joined Nolo's editorial staff in 1997 and has never been happier. Beth is the co-author of Nolo's *How to Create a Buy-Sell Agreement and Control the Destiny of Your Small Business* and the editor of several Nolo publications, including *The Small Business Start-Up Kit, Nolo's California Quick Corp* and *Nolo's Quick LLC.*

**Robin Leonard** (Your Money, Cars and Driving, Traveling, Spouses and Partners, Dealing With Your Lawyer). Robin specializes in debt, credit, bankruptcy and family law. She earned her law degree from Cornell Law School in 1985. Robin is the author (or co-author) of many Nolo books, including *Money Troubles: Legal Strategies to Cope With Your Debts, How to File for Bankruptcy, Nolo's Pocket Guide to Family Law, Take Control of Your Student Loans* and *Credit Repair.*

*Deanne Loonin* (Your Money). Deanne works with Nolo on debt and credit issues. She is also a staff attorney with the National Consumer Law Center (NCLC) in Boston. Prior to joining Nolo and NCLC, she directed Bet Tzedek Legal Service's senior consumer fraud unit in Los Angeles. Deanne is the co-author of *Surviving Debt: A Guide for Consumers* (NCLC) and *Money Troubles* (Nolo).

*Peter Lovenheim* (Mediation). A 1979 graduate of Cornell Law School, Peter has been an active mediator since 1986 and is founder and president of a private dispute resolution service. He is the author of *Mediate, Don't Litigate* (McGraw-Hill), *Reading Between the Lines: New Stories From the Bible,* with co-editor David Katz (Jason Aronson), and *Mediate Your Dispute* (Nolo). Peter lives in Rochester, New York, with his wife and three children.

*Anthony Mancuso* (Nonprofit Corporations). Tony is a California attorney and the author of Nolo's best-selling corporate law series, including *How to Form Your Own Corporation* (California, Texas, New York and computer editions). He is also the author of Nolo's *Taking Care of Your Corporation* series and the book *How to Form a Nonprofit Corporation.* Tony is a jazz guitarist and a licensed helicopter pilot.

*Beth McKenna* (Criminal Law and Procedure, Changing Your Name). Beth

received her law degree from Stanford Law School. Before coming to Nolo, she worked as a public defender for five years, concentrating in appellate and habeas corpus law. She is Nolo's criminal law editor and is responsible for Nolo's best-selling *Willmaker.*

*Kathleen Michon* (Cars and Driving, Legal Research Retirement Plans). Kathleen graduated cum laude from Northwestern University School of Law in 1993. Prior to joining Nolo's editorial staff, Kathleen was the Directing Attorney of Public Counsel's Consumer Rights Project. She is the editor of Nolo's debt and credit books, including *Credit Repair* and *Money Troubles,* and is a co-author of *How to File for Chapter 7 Bankruptcy.*

*Shannon Miehe* (Small Businesses, Dealing With the IRS). Shannon graduated from the University of Southern California Law School. She then spent several years representing small and mid-size entrepreneurial companies in connection with mergers, acquisitions and business formation issues. At Nolo, Shannon edits small business products, including *Legal Forms for Starting and Running a Small Business, The Partnership Book* and *How to Form Your Own California Corporation.*

*Janet Portman* (Landlords and Tenants). Janet received undergraduate and graduate degrees from Stanford University and a law degree from the University of Santa Clara. She was a public defender before coming to Nolo. Janet is Nolo's Publisher and the editor of several Nolo books, including *Legal Research: How to Find and Understand the Law* and *The Criminal Records Book.* She is the co-author of Nolo's *Every Landlord's Legal Guide, Every Tenant's Legal Guide* and *Renters' Rights.*

**Mary Randolph** (Deeds, Neighbors, Wills and Estate Planning). Mary has been editing and writing Nolo books and software for more than a decade. She earned her law degree from Boalt Hall School of Law at the University of California at Berkeley, and her undergraduate degree at the University of Illinois. She is the author of *Dog Law, The Deeds Book, 8 Ways to Avoid Probate* and other Nolo materials.

**Barbara Kate Repa** (Workplace Rights, Employers' Rights and Responsibilities, Funeral Planning and other Final Arrangements, Body and Organ Donations, Healthcare Directives, Older Americans, Traffic Accidents). Barbara Kate, a lawyer, has written several books for Nolo, including *Your Rights in the Workplace,* and *Sexual Harassment on the Job.*

**Linda Robayo** (Spouses and Partners, Parents and Children). Linda graduated from Boston College in 1989 and Seton Hall University School of Law in 1995. Linda practiced law with the Community Health Law Project and Ocean-Monmouth Legal Services in New Jersey for three years, representing clients in family law, landlord-tenant and Social Security cases, with a concentration in domestic violence. Linda has written articles for Nolo and has been published in national publications such as *Good Housekeeping* and *Mademoiselle.*

**Spencer Sherman** (Older Americans). Spencer is the editor of several Nolo books, including *Beat Your Ticket, Fight Your Ticket*

(California Edition), *How to Get a Green Card* and *U.S. Immigration Made Easy.* A journalist for many years before joining Nolo, he reported on legal issues in California and from the U.S. Supreme Court.

**Marcia Stewart** (Houses, Landlords and Tenants). Marcia is an expert on landlord-tenant law, buying and selling houses and other issues of interest to consumers. She is the co-author of Nolo's *Every Landlord's Legal Guide, Every Tenant's Legal Guide, Renters' Rights, Leases & Rental Agreements* and editor of Nolo's *LeaseWriter* software for landlords.

**Richard Stim** (Patents, Copyrights, Trademarks). Rich graduated from the University of San Francisco Law School in 1984 and worked in private practice for 16 years until joining Nolo as an editor in 2000. He is the author of *License Your Invention, Getting Permission, Music Law,* and is the co-author with David Pressman of *Nolo's Patents For Beginners.*

**Ralph Warner** (Courts and Mediation). Ralph is the co-founder and Publisher of Nolo. He is the author (or co-author) of a number of Nolo books, including *Every Landlord's Legal Guide, Everybody's Guide to Small Claims Court, The Partnership Book* and *Get a Life: You Don't Need a Million to Retire Well.* Ralph is a lawyer who became fed up with the legal system and as a result has dedicated his professional life to making law more accessible and affordable to all Americans.

# Table of Contents

## About This Book

## Houses

1.2    **Buying a House**

1.9    **Selling Your House**

1.14   **Deeds**

1.16   **Home Safety**

## Neighbors

2.2    **Boundaries**

2.3    **Fences**

2.4    **Trees**

2.6    **Views**

2.8    **Noise**

## Landlords and Tenants

3.2    **Leases and Rental Agreements**

3.4    **Tenant Selection**

3.4    **Housing Discrimination**

3.6    **Rent and Security Deposits**

3.8    **Tenants' Privacy Rights**

3.9    **Repairs and Maintenance**

3.12   **Landlord Liability for Criminal Acts and Activities**

3.14   **Landlord Liability for Lead Poisoning**

3.15   **Insurance**

3.17   **Resolving Disputes**

## Workplace Rights

4.2    **Fair Pay and Time Off**

4.9    **Workplace Health and Safety**

4.12   **Workers' Compensation**

4.17   **Age Discrimination**

4.21   **Sexual Harassment**

4.25   **Disability Discrimination**

4.29   **Losing or Leaving Your Job**

## Small Businesses

5.2    **Before You Start**

5.8    **Legal Structures for Small Businesses**

5.15   **Nonprofit Corporations**

5.18   **Small Business Taxes**

5.24   **Home-Based Businesses**

5.29   **Employers' Rights and Responsibilities**

**6**

## Patents

6.2 *Qualifying for a Patent*

6.7 *Obtaining a Patent*

6.9 *Enforcing a Patent*

6.12 *Putting a Patent to Work*

6.14 *How Patents Differ from Copyrights and Trademarks*

**7**

## Copyrights

7.2 *Copyright Basics*

7.4 *Copyright Ownership*

7.6 *Copyright Protection*

7.10 *Copyright Registration and Enforcement*

**8**

## Trademarks

8.2 *Types of Trademarks*

8.5 *Trademark Protection*

8.8 *Using and Enforcing a Trademark*

8.11 *Conducting a Trademark Search*

8.14 *Registering a Trademark*

8.18 *How Trademarks Differ From Patents and Copyrights*

**9**

## Your Money

9.2 *Purchasing Goods and Services*

9.7 *Using Credit and Charge Cards*

9.10 *Using an ATM or Debit Card*

9.12 *Strategies for Repaying Debts*

9.18 *Dealing With the IRS*

9.22 *Debt Collections*

9.25 *Bankruptcy*

9.29 *Rebuilding Credit*

**10**

## Cars and Driving

10.2 *Buying a New Car*

10.7 *Leasing a Car*

10.10 *Buying a Used Car*

10.12 *Financing a Vehicle Purchase*

10.13 *Insuring Your Car*

10.16 *Your Driver's License*

10.19 *If You're Stopped by the Police*

10.21 *Drunk Driving*

10.23 *Traffic Accidents*

## 11 Traveling

11.2 *Airlines*

11.9 *Rental Cars*

11.14 *Hotels and Other Accommodations*

11.19 *Travel Agents*

11.23 *Travel Scams*

## 12 Wills and Estate Planning

12.2 *Wills*

12.8 *Probate*

12.9 *Executors*

12.13 *Avoiding Probate*

12.15 *Living Trusts*

12.18 *Estate and Gift Taxes*

12.22 *Funeral Planning and Other Final Arrangements*

12.25 *Body and Organ Donations*

## 13 Healthcare Directives and Powers of Attorney

13.2 *Healthcare Directives*

13.7 *Durable Powers of Attorney for Finances*

13.10 *Conservatorships*

## 14 Older Americans

14.2 *Social Security*

14.8 *Medicare*

14.13 *Pensions*

14.20 *Retirement Plans*

## 15 Spouses and Partners

15.2 *Living Together—Gay and Straight*

15.6 *Premarital Agreements*

15.8 *Marriage*

15.14 *Divorce*

15.22 *Domestic Violence*

15.27 *Changing Your Name*

## 16 Parents and Children

16.2 *Adopting a Child*

16.11 *Stepparent Adoptions*

16.13 *Adoption Rights: Birthparents, Grandparents and Children*

16.17 *Child Custody and Visitation*

16.24 *Child Support*

16.30 *Guardianship of Children*

## 17

# Courts and Mediation

17.2   *Representing Yourself in Court*

17.13  *Small Claims Court*

17.21  *Mediation*

17.27  *Dealing With Your Lawyer*

## 18

# Criminal Law and Procedure

18.2   *Criminal Law and Procedure: An Overview*

18.9   *If You Are Questioned by the Police*

18.10  *Searches and Seizures*

18.14  *Arrests and Interrogations*

18.17  *Bail*

18.20  *Getting a Lawyer*

# Appendix: Legal Research

# Glossary

# About this Book

Whether we like it or not, the law touches our personal lives in many ways each day. We may not think much about the laws that affect us as we carry out simple tasks such as driving a car, making a telephone call or buying milk at the corner grocery store. But every now and again, we're sure to need an answer to a common legal question that arises in the course of daily life:

*What can I do about my noisy neighbor?*

WHAT ARE MY RIGHTS IF I'M FIRED FROM MY JOB?

*Do I really need to make a will?*

What should I do if I can't pay the child support I owe?

And so on.

This book provides answers to frequently asked questions about more than 100 subjects you might encounter in your personal life—topics that range from buying a house to getting a divorce, from paying your debts to starting and running a small business. Obviously, we can't answer every question on a particular subject, but we've answered many common ones to get you started. Throughout each chapter, you'll find resource boxes listing sources for more information about a particular subject.

In addition, for those of you who are computer savvy, each chapter contains a list of online sites that will help you learn more about a particular area of the law. Look for the "Online Help" icon as you read. And if you need more information about finding the law, The Legal Research Appendix contains a section that shows you how to do basic legal research—with a focus on searching the Internet.

Think of this book as a desk reference—a little encyclopedia that unpacks the law and puts it in your hands in a language you can understand. But remember that the law changes constantly as legislatures pass new laws and courts hand down their rulings. We will publish new, revised editions of this book periodically, but it will never be perfectly current. It's always your responsibility to be sure a law is up to date before you rely on it. Check the Legal Update Service on our website at http://www.nolo.com/update.html for the most current legal information affecting Nolo books & software.

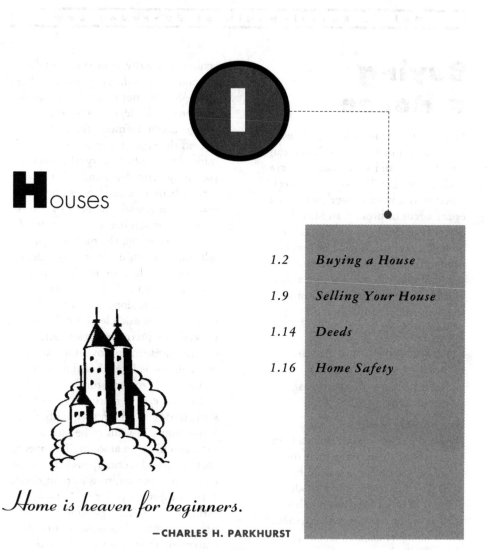

# **H**ouses

1.2   *Buying a House*

1.9   *Selling Your House*

1.14   *Deeds*

1.16   *Home Safety*

*Home is heaven for beginners.*

**—CHARLES H. PARKHURST**

**B**uying or selling a house is a major undertaking. To do it right, you need to understand how houses are priced, financed and inspected; how to find and work with a real estate agent; how to protect your interests when negotiating a contract; and how legal transfer of ownership takes place. Once you own a home, you want to keep it safe and secure. This chapter covers many of the basic issues that buyers, sellers and owners need to know.

# Buying a House

Before you look for a house, it's essential to determine how much you can afford to pay and what your financing options are. You'll also need to decide whether you want to work with a real estate agent or broker, and finally, even if you think you've found your dream home, you'll need to master the ins and outs of house inspections. This section gives you some answers that will help you find your way through the house-buying maze—and to your new front door.

## I'm a first-time home buyer. Is there any easy way to determine how much house I can afford?

As a broad generalization, most people can afford to purchase a house worth about three times their total (gross) annual income, assuming a 20% down payment and a moderate amount of other long-term debts, such as car or student loan payments. With no other debts, you can probably afford a house worth up to four or even five times your annual income.

The most accurate way to determine whether you can afford a particular house is to total up the estimated monthly principal and interest payments plus one-twelfth of the yearly bill for property and homeowner's insurance. Now compare that to your gross monthly income.

Lenders normally want you to make all monthly housing payments with 28%-38% of your monthly income—the percentage depends on the amount of your down payment, the interest rate on the type of mortgage you want, your credit history, the level of your long-term debts and other factors. A bank or other lender can give you the paperwork you need to determine how much house you can afford.

Or you can run the numbers yourself, using an online mortgage calculator such as those on the Websites listed at the end of this chapter.

Once you've done the basic calculations, you can ask a lender or loan broker for a prequalification letter saying that loan approval for a specified amount is likely based on your income and credit history.

In competitive markets, you will want to do more than prequalify for a loan—you will want to be guaranteed for a specific loan amount. This means that the lender actually evaluates your financial situation, runs a credit check and preapproves you for a loan—rather than giving a general prequalification based on your own statement about your income and debts. Having lender preapproval for a loan makes you more attractive financially to sellers than simple loan prequalification and is crucial in competitive markets.

## How important is my credit history in getting loan approval?

Your credit history has an important effect on the type and amount of loan lenders offer you. When reviewing loan applications and making financing decisions, lenders typically request your credit risk score from the credit bureaus. This score is a statistical summary of the information in your credit report and includes:

- your history of paying bills on time
- the level of your outstanding debts
- how long you've had credit
- your credit limit
- the number of inquiries for your credit report (too many can lower your score), and
- the types of credit you have.

The higher your credit score, the easier it will be to get a loan. If you routinely pay your bills late, you can expect a lower score, in which case a lender may either reject your loan application altogether or insist on a very large down payment or high interest rate to lower the lender's risk.

To avoid problems, always check your credit report and clean up your file if necessary—before, not after, you apply for a mortgage. For information on how to order your credit report, what to do if you find mistakes in your report and how to rebuild good credit, see *Rebuilding Credit* in Chapter 9, *Your Money*.

## How can I find the best home loan or mortgage?

Many entities, including banks, credit unions, savings and loans, insurance companies and mortgage bankers make home loans. Lenders and terms change frequently as new companies appear, old ones merge and market conditions fluctuate. To get the best deal, compare loans and fees with at least a half-dozen lenders. Fortunately, mortgage rates and fees are usually published in the real estate sections of metropolitan newspapers.

Many online services also provide mortgage rate information. While these services don't provide information on all the loans available, they offer a great way to get a good sense of market rates, points and terms and useful advice on choosing a mortgage. And even if you are considering a loan you found via more traditional approaches, you can check the Internet to see if you have been offered the best terms. See the list of recommended websites at the end of this chapter.

Because many types of home loans are standardized to comply with rules established by the Federal National Mortgage Association (Fannie Mae), Federal Home Loan Mortgage Corporation (Freddie Mac) and other quasi-governmental corporations that purchase loans from lenders, comparison shopping is not difficult. You can also work with a loan broker, someone who specializes in matching house buyers with an appropriate mortgage lender. Loan brokers usually collect their fee from the lender.

You may also be eligible for a government-guaranteed loan, offered by:

- the Federal Housing Administration (FHA), an agency of the Department of Housing and Urban Development (HUD) (see http://www.hud.gov/buyhome.html)
- the U.S. Department of Veterans Affairs (see http://www.va.gov), or
- a state or local housing agency.

Government loans usually have low down payment requirements and sometimes offer better-than-market interest rates as well.

Also, ask banks and other private lenders about any "first-time buyer programs" that offer low down payment plans and flexible qualifying guidelines to low and moderate income buyers with good credit.

Finally, don't forget private sources of mortgage money—parents, other relatives, friends or even the seller of the house you want to buy. Borrowing money privately is usually the most cost-efficient mortgage of all.

## What's the difference between a fixed and an adjustable rate mortgage?

With a fixed rate mortgage, the interest rate and the amount you pay each month remain the same over the entire mortgage term, traditionally 15, 20 or 30 years. A number of variables are available, including five- and seven-year fixed rate loans with balloon payments at the end.

With an adjustable rate mortgage (ARM), the interest rate fluctuates as the interest rates in the economy fluctuate. Initial interest rates of ARMs are usually offered at a discounted ("teaser") rate which is lower than those for fixed rate mortgages. Over time, however, initial discounts are filtered out and ARM rates fluctuate as general interest rates go up or down. To avoid constant and drastic changes, ARMs typically regulate (cap) how much and how often the interest rate and/or payments can change in a year and over the life of the loan. A number of variations are available for adjustable rate mortgages, including hybrids that change from a fixed to an adjustable rate after a period of years.

A good loan officer or loan broker will walk you through all mortgage options and tradeoffs such as higher fees (or points) for a lower interest rate.

## How do I decide whether to choose a fixed or an adjustable rate mortgage?

Because interest rates and mortgage options change often, your choice of a fixed or an adjustable rate mortgage should depend on the interest rates and mortgage options available when you're buying, your view of the future (generally, high inflation will mean that ARM rates will go up and lower inflation means that they will fall), and how willing you are to take a risk. Very risk-averse people usually prefer the certainty of a fixed rate mortgage, rather than take a chance that an ARM might be cheaper in the long run.

Keep in mind that lenders not only lend money to purchase homes; they also lend money to refinance homes. If you take out a loan now, and several years from now interest rates have dropped, refinancing may be an option.

## What's the best way to find and work with a real estate agent or broker?

Get recommendations from people who have purchased a house in the past few years and whose judgment you trust. Don't work with an agent you meet at an open house or find in the Yellow Pages or on the Internet unless and until you call references and thoroughly check the person out. The agent or broker you choose should be in the full-time business of selling real estate and should have the following five traits: integrity, business sophistication, experience with the type of services you need, knowledge of the area where you want to live and sensitivity to your tastes and needs.

All states regulate and license real estate agents and brokers. You may have different options as to the type of legal relationship you have with an agent or broker; typically, the seller pays the commission of the real estate salesperson who helps the buyer locate the seller's house. The commission is a percentage (usually 5% to 7%) of the sales price of the house. What this means is that your agent or broker has a built-in conflict of interest: Unless you've agreed to pay her separately, she won't get paid until you buy a home, and the more you pay for a house, the bigger her cut.

In short, when you evaluate the suitability of a house, it's not wise to rely principally on the advice of a person with a significant financial stake in your buying it. You need to be knowledgeable about the house-buying process, your ideal affordable house and neighborhood, your financing needs and options, your legal rights and how to evaluate comparable prices.

## What's the best way to get information on homes for sale and details about the neighborhood?

Thanks to the Internet, you no longer have to rely solely on a real estate agent for information about homes for sale. You can scan online listings to see which homes are worth a visit, how much they cost and what amenities they offer. Virtual visits to new homes often include floor plans and photographs.

Once you identify a house you like, you can e-mail the address or identification number to your agent, the listing agent or the owner (if it's a listing by a FSBO—For Sale By Owner) to obtain additional information or to set up an appointment to see the home in person.

The list of websites at the end of this chapter has some of the major national real estate listing sites. Your state or regional realty association or multiple listing service (MLS) may also have a website listing homes for sale. Major real estate companies, including ERA, RE/MAX, Coldwell Banker, Prudential and others often offer lists on their websites. Finally, virtually all online editions of newspapers offer a homes-for-sale classifieds section that works much like an online listing site. Check the Newspapers Association of America (http://

www.naa.org) for a link to your news-paper. (Click on "Hot Links.")

Advice on relocation decisions and details about your new community and its services are also readily available online. For valuable information about cities, communities and neighborhoods, including schools, housing costs, demographics, crime rates and jobs, see the websites listed at the end of this chapter.

## My spouse and I want to buy a $300,000 house. We have good incomes and can make high monthly payments, but we don't have $60,000 to make a 20% down payment. Are there other options?

Assuming you can afford (and qualify for) high monthly mortgage payments and have an excellent credit history, you should be able to find a low (10% to 15%) down payment loan for a $300,000 house. However, you may have to pay a higher interest rate and loan fees (points) than someone making a higher down payment. In addition, a buyer who puts less than 20% down should be prepared to purchase private mortgage insurance (PMI), which is designed to reimburse a mortgage lender up to a certain amount if a buyer defaults and the foreclosure sale price is less than the amount owed the lender (the mortgage plus the costs of the foreclosure sale).

PMI premiums are usually paid monthly and typically cost less than one-half of one percent of the mortgage loan. With the exception of some government and older loans, you can drop PMI once your equity in the house reaches 22% and you've made timely mortgage payments.

## I want to buy a newly built house. Is there anything special I need to know?

The most important factor in buying a newly built house is not what you buy (that is, the particular model), but rather from whom you buy. Shop for an excellent builder—someone who builds quality houses, delivers on time and stands behind his or her work. To check out a particular builder, talk to existing owners in the development you're considering, or ask an experienced contractor to look at other houses the developer is building.

Many developers of new housing will help you arrange financing; some will also pay a portion of your monthly mortgage or subsidize your interest payments for a short period of time (called a "buydown" of the mortgage). As with any loan, be sure you comparison shop before arranging financing through a builder.

Also, be sure to negotiate the prices of any add-ons and upgrades, such as a spa or higher quality carpet. These can add substantially to the cost of a new home.

## Is there anything else I need to know before buying a home in a development run by a homeowners' association?

When you buy a home in a new subdivision or planned unit development, chances are good that you also automatically become a member of an exclusive club—the homeowners' association, whose members are the people who own homes in the same development. The homeowners' association will probably exercise a lot of control over how you use your property.

Deeds to houses in new developments almost always include restrictions on how the property can be used—from the colors you can paint your house to the type of front yard landscaping you can do to where (and what types of vehicles) you can park in your driveway. Usually, these restrictions, called covenants, conditions and restrictions (CC&Rs), put decision-making rights in the hands of a homeowners' association. Before buying, study the CC&Rs carefully to see if they're compatible with your lifestyle. If you don't understand something, ask for more information and seek legal advice if necessary.

Usually, getting relief from overly restrictive CC&Rs after you move in isn't easy. You'll likely have to submit an application (with fee) for a variance, get your neighbors' permission and possibly go through a formal hearing. And if you want to make a structural change, such as building a fence or adding a room, you'll probably need formal permission from the association in addition to complying with city zoning rules.

## How can I make sure that the house I'm buying is in good shape?

In some states, you may have the advantage of a law that requires sellers to disclose considerable information about the condition of the house. (See *Selling Your House*, below.) Regardless of whether the seller provides disclosures, however, you should have the property inspected for defects or malfunctions in the building's structure.

Start by conducting your own inspection. There are several useful do-it-yourself inspection books available to help you learn what to look for. Ideally, you should inspect a house before you make a formal written offer to buy it so that you can save yourself the trouble should you find serious problems.

If a house passes your inspection, hire a general contractor to check all major house systems from top to bottom, including the roof, plumbing, electrical and heating systems and drainage. This will take two or three hours and cost you anywhere from $200 to $500 depending on the location, size, age and type of home. You should accompany the inspector during the examination so that you can learn more about the maintenance and preservation of the house and get answers to any questions you may have, including which problems are important and which are relatively minor. Depending on the property, you may want to arrange specialized inspections for pest damage, hazards from floods, earthquakes and other natural disasters and environmental health hazards such as asbestos and lead.

Professional inspections should be done after your written purchase offer has been accepted by the seller. (Your offer should be contingent upon the house passing one or more inspections). To avoid confusion and disputes, be sure you get a written report of each inspection.

If the house is in good shape, you can proceed, knowing that you're getting what you paid for. If an inspector discovers problems—such as an antiquated plumbing system or a major termite infestation—you can negotiate with the seller to have him pay for necessary repairs and provide a home warranty (see Selling Your House, below). Finally, you can back out of the deal if an inspection turns up problems, assuming your contract is properly written to allow you to do so.

### I'm making an offer to buy a house, but I don't want to lock myself into a deal that might not work out. How can I protect myself?

Real estate offers almost always contain contingencies—events that must happen within a certain amount of time (such as 30 days) in order to finalize the deal. For example, you may want to make your offer contingent on your ability to qualify for financing, the house passing certain physical inspections or even your ability to sell your existing house first. Be aware, however, that the more contingencies you place in an offer, the less likely the seller is to accept it. See Selling Your House, below, for more on real estate offers.

## Strategies for Buying an Affordable House

To find a good house at a comparatively reasonable price, you must learn about the housing market and what you can afford, make some sensible compromises as to size and amenities and, above all, be patient. Here are some proven strategies to meet these goals:

**1**
Buy a fixer-upper cheap.

**2**
Buy a small house (with remodeling potential) and add on later.

**3**
Buy a house at an estate or probate sale.

**4**
Buy a house subject to foreclosure (when a homeowner defaults on his mortgage).

**5**
Buy a shared-equity house, pooling resources with someone other than a spouse or partner.

**6**
Rent out a room or two in the house.

**7**
Buy a duplex, triplex or house with an in-law unit.

**8**
Lease a house you can't afford now with an option to buy later.

**9**
Buy a limited-equity house built by a nonprofit organization.

**10**
Buy a house at an auction.

## More Information About Buying a Home

*100 Questions Every First-Time Home Buyer Should Ask*, by Ilyce R. Glink (Times Books), is a substantial book designed to help first-time buyers through the maze of buying a house.

*Your New House: The Alert Consumer's Guide to Buying and Building a Quality Home*, by Alan & Denise Fields (Windsor Peak Press), offers valuable advice for those who want to buy or build a new home.

*The Home Inspection Troubleshooter*, by Robert Irwin (Dearborn), shows how to inspect a house in order to discover major problems such as a bad foundation, leaky roof or malfunctioning fireplace.

*How to Buy a House in California*, by Ralph Warner, Ira Serkes and George Devine (Nolo), explains all the details of the California house-buying process and contains tear-out contracts and disclosure forms.

# Selling Your House

If you're selling a home, you need to time the sale properly, price the home accurately and understand the laws, such as disclosure requirements, that cover house transactions. These questions and answers will get you started.

I'm trying to decide whether to put my house on the market or wait a while. What are the best and worst times to sell?

Too many people rush to sell their houses and lose money because of it. Ideally, you should put your house on the market when there's a large pool of buyers—causing prices to go up. This may occur in the following situations:

- Your area is considered especially attractive—for example, because of the schools, low crime rate, employment opportunities, weather or proximity to a major city.
- Mortgage interest rates are low.
- The economic climate of your region is healthy and people feel confident about the future.
- There's a jump in house buying activity, as often occurs in spring.

Of course, if you have to sell immediately—because of financial reasons, a divorce, a job move or an imperative health concern—and you don't have any of the advantages listed above, you may have to settle for a lower price, or help the buyer with financing, in order to make a quick sale.

I want to save on the real estate commission. Can I sell my house myself without a real estate broker or agent?

Usually, yes. This is called a FSBO (pronounced "fizzbo")—For Sale By Owner. You must be aware, however, of the legal rules that govern real estate transfers in your state, such as who must sign the papers, who can conduct the actual transaction and what to do if and when any problems arise that slow down the transfer of ownership. You also need to be aware of any state-mandated disclosures as to the physical condition of your house. (See the discussion below.)

If you want to go it alone, be sure you have the time, energy and ability to handle all the details—from setting a realistic price to negotiating offers and closing the deal. Also, be aware that FSBOs are usually more feasible in hot or sellers' markets where there's more competition for homes, or when you're not in a hurry to sell. For more advice on FSBOs, including the involvement of attorneys and other professionals in the house transaction, contact your state department of real estate. Also, check online at http://www.owners.com for useful advice on selling a home without an agent.

If you're in California, check out *For Sale by Owner* by George Devine (Nolo). This book provides step-by-step advice on handling your own sale in California, from putting the house on the market to negotiating offers to transferring title.

## Is there some middle ground where I can use a broker on a more limited (and less expensive) basis?

You might consider doing most of the work yourself—such as showing the house—and using a real estate broker's help with such crucial tasks as:

- setting the price of your house
- advertising your home in the local multiple listing service (MLS) of homes for sale in the area, published by local boards of realtors, and

- handling some of the more complicated paperwork when the sale closes.

If you work with a broker in a limited way, you may be able to negotiate a reduction of the typical 5%-7% broker's commission, or you may be able to find a real estate agent who charges by the hour for specified services such as reviewing the sales contract.

## How much should I ask for my house?

The key is to determine how much your property is actually worth on the market—called "appraising" a house's value. The most important factors used to determine a house's value are recent sales prices of similar properties in the neighborhood (called "comps").

Real estate agents have access to sales data for the area ("comp books") and can give you a good estimate of what your house should sell for. Many real estate agents will offer this service free, hoping that you will list your house with them. You can also hire a professional real estate appraiser to give you a documented opinion as to your house's value. Public record offices, such as the county clerk or recorder's office, may also have information on recent house sales. A few private companies offer detailed comparable sales prices online for many areas of the country, based on information from County Recorder's Offices and property assessors. See the list of recommended websites at the end of this chapter.

Finally, asking prices of houses still on the market can also provide guidance (adjusting for the fact that asking prices are typically 10% or more above the usual sales price). To find out asking prices, go to open houses and check newspaper real estate classified ads and online listings of homes for sale.

## *Preparing Your House for Sale*

Making your house look as attractive as possible may put several thousand dollars in your pocket. Sweep the sidewalk; mow the lawn; clean the windows; fix chipped or flaking paint. Clean and tidy up all rooms; be sure the house smells good— hide the kitty litter box and bake some cookies. Check for loose steps, slick areas or unsafe fixtures, and deal with everything that might cause injury to a prospective buyer. Take care of real eyesores, such as a cracked window or overgrown front yard. Don't overlook small but obvious problems, such as a leaking faucet or loose doorknob. Find ways to improve the look of your house without spending much money—a new shower curtain and towels might really spruce up your bathroom.

## Do I need to take the first offer that comes in?

Offers, even very attractive ones, are rarely accepted as written. More typically, you will respond with a written counteroffer accepting some, maybe even most, of the offer terms, but proposing certain changes. Most counteroffers correspond to these provisions of an offer:

- price—you want more money
- financing—you want a larger down payment
- occupancy—you need more time to move out
- buyer's sale of current house—you don't want to wait for this to occur
- inspections—you want the buyer to schedule them more quickly.

A contract is formed when either you or the buyer accept all of the terms of the other's offer or counteroffer in writing within the time allowed.

## What are my obligations to disclose problems about my house, such as a basement that floods in heavy rains?

In most states, it is illegal to fraudulently conceal major physical defects in your property, such as your troublesome basement. And states are increasingly requiring sellers to take a pro-active role by making written disclosures on the condition of the property. California, for example, has stringent disclosure requirements. California sellers must give buyers a mandatory disclosure form listing such defects as a leaky roof, faulty plumbing, deaths that occurred within the last three years on the property, even the presence of neighborhood nuisances, such as a dog that barks every night. In addition, California sellers must disclose potential hazards from floods, earthquakes, fires, environmental hazards and other problems in a Natural Hazard Disclosure Statement. California sellers must also alert buyers to the availability of a database maintained by law enforcement authorities on the location of registered sex offenders.

Generally, you are responsible for disclosing only information within your personal knowledge. While it's not usually required, many sellers hire a general contractor to inspect the property. The information will help you determine which items need repair or replacement and will assist you in preparing any required disclosures. An inspection report is also useful in pricing your house and negotiating with prospective buyers.

Full disclosure of any property defects will also help protect you from legal problems from a buyer who seeks to rescind the sale or sues you for damages suffered because you carelessly or intentionally withheld important information about your property.

Check with your real estate broker or attorney, or your state department of real estate, for disclosures required in your state and any special forms you must use. Also, be aware that real estate brokers are increasingly requiring that sellers complete disclosure forms, regardless of whether it's legally required.

## Sellers Must Disclose Lead-Based Paint and Hazards

If you are selling a house built before 1978, you must comply with the federal Residential Lead-Based Paint Hazard Reduction Act of 1992 (U.S.Code § 4852d), also known as Title X (Ten). You must:

- disclose all known lead-based paint and hazards in the house
- give buyers a pamphlet prepared by the U.S. Environmental Protection Agency (EPA) called *Protect Your Family From Lead in Your Home*
- include certain warning language in the contract, as well as signed statements from all parties verifying that all disclosures (including giving the pamphlet) were made
- keep signed acknowledgments for three years as proof of compliance, and
- give buyers a ten-day opportunity to test the housing for lead.

If you fail to comply with Title X, the buyer can sue you for triple the amount of damages suffered—for example, three times the cost of repainting a house previously painted with lead-based paint.

For more information, contact the National Lead Information Center, 800-424-LEAD (phone) or http://www.epa.gov/lead/nlic.htm.

## What are home warranties, and should I buy one?

Home warranties are service contracts that cover major housing systems—electrical wiring, built-in appliances, heating, plumbing and the like—for one year from the date the house is sold. Most warranties cost $300-$500 and are renewable. If something goes wrong with any of the covered systems after escrow closes, the repairs are paid for (minus a modest service fee)—and the new buyer saves money. Many sellers find that home warranties make their house more attractive and easier to sell.

Before buying a home warranty, be sure you don't duplicate coverage. You don't need a warranty for the heating system, for example, if your furnace is just six months old and still covered by the manufacturer's three-year warranty.

Your real estate agent or broker can provide more information on home warranties.

## What is the "house closing"?

The house closing is the final transfer of the ownership of the house from the seller to the buyer. It occurs after both you and the buyer have met all the terms of the contract and the deed is recorded. (See *Deeds*, below). Closing also refers to the time when the transfer will occur, such as "The closing on my house will happen on January 27 at 10:00 a.m."

## Do I need an attorney for the house closing?

This varies depending on state law and local custom. In some states, attorneys are not typically involved in residential property sales, and an escrow or title company handles the entire closing process. In many other states, par-

ticularly in the eastern part of the country, attorneys (for both buyer and seller) have a more active role in all parts of the house transaction; they handle all the details of offer contracts and house closings. Check with your state department of real estate or your real estate broker for advice.

## I'm selling my house and buying another. What are some of the most important tax considerations?

The 1997 Taxpayer Relief Act contained a big break for homeowners. If you sell your home, you may exclude up to $250,000 of your profit (capital gain) from tax. For married couples filing jointly, the exclusion is $500,000.

The law applies to sales after May 6, 1997. To claim the whole exclusion, you must have owned and lived in your residence an aggregate of at least two of five years before the sale. You can claim the exclusion once every two years.

Even if you haven't lived in your home a total of two years out of the last five, you are still eligible for a partial exclusion of capital gains if you sold because of a change in employment, health or unforeseen circumstances. You get a portion of the exclusion, based on the percentage of the two-year period you lived in the house. To calculate it, take the number of months you lived there before the sale and divide it by 24.

For example, if you're an unmarried taxpayer who's lived in your home for 12 months, and you sell it for a

$100,000 profit, the entire amount would be excluded from capital gains. Because you lived in the house for half of the two-year period, you could claim half the exclusion, or $125,000. (12/24 x $250,000 = $125,000.) That's enough to exclude your entire $100,000 gain.

For more information on current tax laws involving real estate transactions, contact the IRS at 800-829-1040 or check their website at http://www.irs.gov. Ask for Form 2119, *Sale of Your Home*, and the general instructions for this form. If you're claiming the exclusion, you must file Form 2119 with your tax return.

# Deeds

*Castles in the air are the only property you can own without the intervention of lawyers. Unfortunately, there are no title deeds to them.*

**—J. FEIDOR REES**

Remember playing Monopoly as a kid, where amassing deeds to property—those little color-coded cards—was all-important? Real-life deeds aren't nearly so colorful, but they're still very, very important. Here are some questions commonly asked about deeds.

## What is a deed?

A deed is the document that transfers ownership of real estate. It contains the names of the old and new owners and a legal description of the property, and is signed by the person transferring the property.

## Do I need a deed to transfer property?

Almost always. You can't transfer real estate without having something in writing. In some situations, a document other than a deed is used—for example, in a divorce, a court order may transfer real estate from the couple to just one of them.

## I'm confused by all the different kinds of deeds—quitclaim deed, grant deed, warranty deed. Does it matter which kind of deed I use?

Probably not. Usually, what's most important is the substance of the deed: the description of the property being transferred and the names of the old and new owners. Here's a brief rundown of the most common types of deeds:

A *quitclaim* deed transfers whatever ownership interest you have in the property. It makes no guarantees about the extent of your interest. Quitclaim deeds are commonly used by divorcing couples; one spouse signs over all his rights in the couple's real estate to the other. This can be especially useful if it isn't clear how much of an interest, if any, one spouse has in property that's held in another spouse's name.

A *grant deed* transfers your ownership and implies certain promises—that the title hasn't already been transferred to someone else or been encumbered, except as set out in the deed. This is the most commonly used kind of deed, in most states.

A *warranty deed* transfers your ownership and explicitly promises the buyer that you have good title to the property. It may make other promises as well, to address particular problems with the transaction.

## Does a deed have to be notarized?

Yes. The person who signs the deed (the person who is transferring the property) should take the deed to a notary public, who will sign and stamp it. The notarization means that a notary public has verified that the signature on the deed is genuine. The signature must be notarized before the deed will be accepted for recording (see the next question).

## After a deed is signed and notarized, do I have to put it on file anywhere?

Yes. You should "record" (file) the deed in the land records office in the county where the property is located. This office goes by different names in different states; it's usually called the County Recorder's Office, Land Registry Office or Register of Deeds. In most counties, you'll find it in the courthouse.

Recording a deed is simple. Just take the signed, original deed to the land records office. The clerk will take the deed, stamp it with the date and some numbers, make a copy and give the original back to you. The numbers are usually book and page numbers, which show where the deed will be found in the county's filing system. There will be a small fee, probably about $5 a page, for recording.

## What's a trust deed?

A trust deed (also called a deed of trust) isn't like the other types of deeds; it's not used to transfer property. It's really just a version of a mortgage, commonly used in some states.

A trust deed transfers title to land to a "trustee," usually a trust or title company, which holds the land as security for a loan. When the loan is paid off, title is transferred to the borrower. The trustee has no powers unless the borrower defaults on the loan; then the trustee can sell the property and pay the lender back from the proceeds, without first going to court.

More
Information
About Deeds

*The Deeds Book,*
by Mary Randolph (Nolo),
contains tear-out deed forms and
instructions for transferring
California real estate.
For information about deeds
in other states, check your
local law library.

# Home Safety

Most burglars prefer to enter an empty house and get in and out quickly. Here are ten ways to avoid making your house an easy target.

### Burglar-proof your house.

If you've been meaning to get better locks, an alarm system, metal bars on windows or motion sensor lights, do it now. Cut down shrubbery that gives burglars a hiding place. Pay special attention to back doors and windows, where burglars often find the easiest entry. See if a police department representative will evaluate your home's security and recommend improvements.

### Lock up.

Half of all burglaries occur through unlocked doors and windows. Don't hide keys in obvious places, such as under a doormat or flowerpot, on top of the door frame or under a plant. If you have to hide a key, put it in the spot where it is least likely to be discovered.

### Have a trusted person house-sit.

Or ask a friend, relative or neighbor to keep an eye on things. Some police departments provide security checks for vacationers.

### Give your house a lived-in look.

An overstuffed mailbox and yellowing newspapers signal that no one is home; have someone pick up your mail and newspapers, or have deliveries put on hold.

Arrange to have the lawn mowed, garden watered, leaves raked or snow shoveled. You may even want to have your neighbor put garbage in your garbage cans.

### *Put lights on automatic timers.*

Inexpensive timers turn lights and radios on and off at set times. For instance, a radio and lamp in the living room might be on in the early evening, and then a bedroom lamp could be on from 9:30 to midnight. You might also consider installing motion sensor lights for your back yard or back entrance, or other spots where someone might hide.

### *Leave drapes and shades the way you normally have them.*

If you can, have someone open drapes during the day and shut them at night. A house that's shuttered up tight looks unoccupied.

### *Put valuables out of sight.*

Don't leave valuables such as jewelry, art and electronic equipment in sight, close to windows. Even simple steps to hide your property may be effective if an intruder does manage to get in. A dusty hatbox in the top of a closet, empty food containers, a laundry hamper or a toy box are all places to stash valuables. As an extra precaution, consider leaving some valuables with a trusted neighbor, friend or relative—if that house is secure and someone will be home the entire time you're gone.

### *Consider a safe.*

If you need to protect very expensive property, consider getting a safe deposit box or buying a good fireproof safe.

### *Make a home inventory.*

If your home is burglarized, an up-to-date home inventory will make it easier to deal with police and your insurance company. Without one, you'll have to create a list of all your property from memory. (An inventory is also very useful if you lose property as a result of a fire, earthquake, flood or other natural disaster.)

Fortunately, making a home inventory isn't an onerous task. And doing so not only prepares you for possible losses—it can also help you prevent the loss itself. As you inventory your possessions, you'll become more aware of their vulnerability, and you can take steps to secure them.

Start by walking through your house with a pad of paper and a still or video camera. Take pictures and jot down a list of any items worth more than $50 or so. Go room by room, and don't forget the garage, attic and basement. Be sure to include jewelry, clothing, stamp or coin collections, CD and record collections, silver, tools and electronic equipment. Then take a little time to formalize your inventory. Insurance companies often supply inventory forms. Making and updating an inventory can be even easier if you own a computer.

Keep your written and photographic inventory in a safe place, such as a fire-resistant file cabinet or safe, the freezer or a safe deposit box. Keep at least one copy away from home. If you take a long vacation, give a copy to a friend or neighbor; that way, if your house is broken into while you're gone, that person can determine what's missing and report it to the police.

**Buy adequate insurance.**
Homeowner's insurance covers your house and protects furnishings and other personal items, as well as any other structures on the property, such as a pool. It also covers some types of personal liability—if the mail carrier trips over your kid's skateboard, your policy will pay for his medical expenses and other losses.

You will want to purchase additional insurance if your house is in a high-risk area for fire, floods, earthquakes or other natural disasters or you have expensive art or business equipment at home.

For more information on homeowner's insurance, see http://www.insure.com/home.

# What to Include in a Home Inventory

Your home inventory should include the following key information about each item:

- Complete description, including whether or not the item is marked with a serial number or an ID number such as your driver's license number. (You can buy an electric engraving pen for $20 or so at a hardware store.) ID and serial numbers will help police identify stolen goods. Also, remember to record the make and model of the item; this will help you justify its estimated value to your insurance company.

- Location. This will help you identify what you've lost if only one area, such as the garage, is hit.

- Location of ownership documents, receipts, owner's manuals and repair bills.

- Purchase price, current value and replacement cost. For most items, your best estimate will do. For antiques or other difficult-to-price items, such as a stamp collection, you may need a professional appraisal.

## More Information About Home Security

*Nolo's Personal RecordKeeper* (Nolo) (software for Windows or Macintosh), allows you to create a complete home inventory on your computer.

### http://www.nolo.com

*Nolo offers self-help information on a wide variety of legal topics, including real estate matters. The website also has several real estate calculators, including a Home Affordability calculator.*

### http://www.homefair.com/home

*Homefair offers lots of information and calculators that will help you move amd make relocation decisions. It's especially useful if you're deciding where to live based on home prices, schools, crime, salaries and other factors.*

### http://www.homeadvisor.com

*Home Advisor helps with all aspects of buying or selling a home—from listings and financing to home improvements.*

### http://www.ashi.com

*The American Society of Home Inspectors offers information on buying a home in good shape, including referrals to local home inspectors.*

### http://www.inman.com/

*Real estate columnist Brad Inman provides the latest real estate news.*

### http://www.realtylocator.com

*Realty Locator provides over 100,000 real estate links nationwide, including property listings, agents, lenders, neighborhood data, real estate news and resources on everything from home improvement to mortgage calculators.*

### http://www.homepath.com

*Fannie Mae, the nation's largest source of home mortgage loans, offers several useful home affordability mortgage calculators. It also provides a wide range of consumer information.*

### http://www.iOwn.com

*iOwn allows you to compare rates from various lenders, prequalify and apply for a home loan. It includes detailed advice on choosing the best type of mortgage, determining how much house you can afford, selecting a real estate broker and evaluating the value of a house. Similar online mortgage sites are available at http://www.e-loan.com and http://homeadvisor.com.*

**http://www.hsh.com**

*HSH Associates publishes detailed information on mortgage loans available from lenders across the U.S. A similar service is available at http://www.bankrate.com.*

**http://www.realtor.com**

*The official Website of the National Association of Realtors lists over one million homes for sale throughout the United States and provides links to real estate broker websites and a host of related realty services.*

**http://www.homebuilder.com**

*The National Association of Homebuilders' website lists new homes and developments in major metropolitan areas.*

**http://www.owners.com**

*This site lists homes sold without a broker, also known as FSBOs (for sale by owner). It also provides useful information for anyone considering selling their home without a real estate agent.*

**http://www.homegain.com**

*HomeGain is geared toward home sellers. It provides an Agent Evaluator service to help you find a real estate agent, a Home Valuation tool to help price your home, calculators for a wide variety of tasks and other resources.*

**http://www.dataquick.com/ consumer**

*For a modest fee, Dataquick.com (click on the "Neighborhood Report Center") provides details on houses—including purchase price, sales date, address, number of bedrooms and baths, square footage and property tax information. Similar information is available at http:// www.experian.com (check out "Real estate reports" in the "Products and Services" area).*

**http://www.monstermoving.com**

*Monstermoving offers a wealth of information for people who are relocating, including links to demographics data, building and construction activity, city guides, government agencies, parenting resources and schools.*

# **N**eighbors

2.2   *Boundaries*

2.3   *Fences*

2.4   *Trees*

2.6   *Views*

2.8   *Noise*

*People have discovered that they can fool
the devil, but they can't fool the neighbors.*
**—EDGAR WATSON HOWE**

**Y**ears ago, problems between neighbors were resolved informally, perhaps with the help of a third person respected by both
sides. These days, neighbors—who may not know each other well,
if at all—are quicker to head for court. Usually, of course, lawsuits only exacerbate bad feelings and cost everyone money, and
the courthouse should be the place of last, not first, resort. But
knowing the legal ground rules is important; you may prevent
small disputes from turning into big ones.

# Boundaries

Most of us don't know, or care, exactly where our property boundaries are located. But if you or your neighbor wants to fence the property, build a structure or cut down a tree close to the line, you need to know where it actually runs.

## How can I find the exact boundaries of my property?

You can hire a licensed land surveyor to survey the property and place official markers on the boundary lines. A simple survey usually costs about $500; if no survey has been done for a long time, or if the maps are unreliable and conflicting, be prepared to spend up to $1,000.

## My neighbor and I don't want to pay a surveyor. Can't we just make an agreement about where we want the boundary to be?

You and the neighbor can decide where you want the line to be, and then make it so by signing deeds that describe the boundary. If you have a mortgage on the property, consult an attorney for help in drawing up the deeds. You may need to get the permission of the mortgage holder before you give your neighbor even a tiny piece of the land.

Once you have signed a deed, you should record (file) it at the county land records office, usually called the County Recorder's Office, Land Registry Office or something similar.

Deeds are discussed in more detail in Chapter 1.

## What can I do if a neighbor starts using my property?

If a neighbor starts to build on what you think is your property, do something immediately. If the encroachment is minor—for instance, a small fence in the wrong place—you may think you shouldn't worry. But you're wrong. When you try to sell your house, a title company might refuse to issue insurance because the neighbor is on your land.

Also, if you don't act promptly, you could lose part of your property. When one person uses another's land for a long enough time, he can gain a legal right to continue to do so and, in some circumstances, gain ownership of the property.

Talk to your neighbor right away. Most likely, a mistake has been made because of a conflicting description in the neighbor's deed or just a mistaken assumption about the boundary line. If your neighbor is hostile and insists on proceeding, state that you will sue if necessary. Then send a firm letter— or have a lawyer send one on his or her letterhead. If the building doesn't stop, waste no time in having a lawyer get a judge's order to temporarily stop the neighbor until you can bring a civil lawsuit for trespass before the judge.

## A Little Common Sense

If you are having no trouble with your property and your neighbors, yet you feel inclined to rush out to determine your exact boundaries just to know where they are, please ask yourself a question. Have you been satisfied with the amount of space that you occupy? If the answer is yes, then consider the time, money and hostility that might be involved if you pursue the subject.

If a problem exists on your border, keep the lines of communication open with the neighbor, if possible. Learn the law and try to work out an agreement. Boundary lines simply don't matter that much to us most of the time; relationships with our neighbors matter a great deal.

# Fences

Local fence ordinances are usually strict and detailed. Most regulate height and location, and some control the material used and even appearance. Residents of planned unit developments and subdivisions are often subject to even pickier rules. On top of all this, many cities require you to obtain a building permit before you begin construction.

Fence regulations apply to any structure used as an enclosure or a partition. Usually, they include hedges and trees.

## How high can I build a fence on my property?

In residential areas, local rules commonly restrict artificial (constructed) backyard fences to a height of six feet. In front yards, the limit is often four feet.

Height restrictions may also apply to natural fences—fences of bushes or trees—if they meet the ordinance's general definition of fences. Trees that are planted in a row and grow together to form a barrier are usually considered a fence. When natural fences are specifically mentioned in the laws, the height restrictions commonly range from five to eight feet.

If, however, you have a good reason (for example, you need to screen your house from a noisy or unsightly neighboring use, such as a gas station), you can ask the city for a one-time exception to the fence law, called a variance. Talk to the neighbors before you make your request, to explain your problem and get them on your side.

## My neighbor is building a fence that violates the local fence law, but nothing's happening. How can I get the law enforced?

Cities are not in the business of sending around fence inspection teams, and as long as no one complains, a nonconforming fence may stand forever.

Tell the neighbor about the law as soon as possible. She probably doesn't know what the law is, and if the fence is still being built, may be able to modify it at a low cost. If she suggests that you mind your own business, alert the city. All it takes in most circumstances is a phone call to the planning or zoning department or the city attorney's office. The neighbor will be ordered to conform; if she doesn't, the city can fine her and even sue.

## My neighbor's fence is hideous. Can I do anything about it?

As long as a fence doesn't pose a threat of harm to neighbors or those passing by, it probably doesn't violate any law just because it's ugly. Occasionally, however, a town or subdivision allows only certain types of new fences—such as board fences—in an attempt to create a harmonious architectural look. Some towns also prohibit certain materials—for example, electrically charged or barbed wire fences.

Even without such a specific law, if a fence is so poorly constructed that it is an eyesore or a danger, it may be prohibited by another law, such as a blighted property ordinance. And if the fence was erected just for meanness—it's high, ugly and has no reasonable use to the owner—it may be a "spite fence," and you can sue the neighbor to get it torn down.

## The fence on the line between my land and my neighbor's is in bad shape. Can I fix it or tear it down?

Unless the property owners agree otherwise, fences on a boundary line belong to both owners when both are using the fence. Both owners are responsible for keeping the fence in good repair, and neither may remove it without the other's permission.

A few states have harsh penalties for refusing to chip in for maintenance after a reasonable request from the other owner. Connecticut, for example, allows one neighbor to go ahead and repair, and then sue the other owner for double the cost.

Of course, it's rare that a landowner needs to resort to a lawsuit. Your first step should be to talk to the neighbor about how to tackle the problem. Your neighbor will probably be delighted that you're taking the initiative to fix a fence that's already an eyesore and might deteriorate into a real danger.

# Trees

WOODMAN, SPARE THAT TREE.

TOUCH NOT A SINGLE BOUGH:

IN YOUTH IT SHELTERED ME,

AND I'LL PROTECT IT NOW.

**—GEORGE POPE MORRIS**

We human beings exhibit some complicated, often conflicting, emotions over our trees. This is especially true when it comes to the trees in our own yards. We take ownership of our trees and their protection very seriously in this country, and this is reflected in the law.

### Can I trim the branches of the neighbor's tree that hang over my yard?

You have the legal right to trim tree branches up to the property line. But you may not go onto the neighbor's property or destroy the tree itself.

## Deliberately Harming a Tree

In almost every state, a person who intentionally injures someone else's tree is liable to the owner for two or three times the amount of actual monetary loss. These penalties protect tree owners by providing harsh deterrents to would-be loggers.

### Most of a big oak tree hangs over my yard, but the trunk is on the neighbor's property. Who owns the tree?

Your neighbor. It is accepted law in all states that a tree whose trunk stands wholly on the land of one person belongs to that person.

If the trunk stands partly on the land of two or more people, it is called a boundary tree, and in most cases it belongs to all the property owners. All the owners are responsible for caring for the tree, and one co-owner may not remove a healthy tree without the other owners' permission.

### My neighbor dug up his yard, and in the process killed a tree that's just on my side of the property line. Am I entitled to compensation for the tree?

Yes. The basic rule is that someone who cuts down, removes or hurts a tree without permission owes the tree's owner money to compensate for the harm done. You can sue to enforce that right—but you probably won't have to, once you tell your neighbor what the law is.

### My neighbor's tree looks like it's going to fall on my house any day now. What should I do?

You can trim back branches to your property line, but that may not solve the problem if you're worried about the whole tree coming down.

City governments often step in to take care of, or make the owner take care of, dangerous trees. Some cities have ordinances that prohibit maintaining any dangerous condition—including a hazardous tree—on private property. To enforce such an ordinance, the city can demand that the owner remove the tree or pay a fine. Some cities will even remove such a tree for the owner. To check on your city's laws and policies, call the city attorney's office.

You might also get help from a utility company, if the tree threatens its equipment. For example, a phone company will trim a tree that hangs menacingly over its lines.

If you don't get help from these sources, and the neighbor refuses to take action, you can sue. The legal theory is that the dangerous tree is a "nuisance" because it is unreasonable for the owner to keep it and it interferes with your use and enjoyment of your property. You can ask the court to order the owner to prune or remove the tree. You'll have to sue in regular court (not small claims court) and have proof that the tree really does pose a danger to you.

# V i e w s

The privilege of sitting in one's home and gazing at the scenery is a highly prized commodity. And it can be a very expensive one. Potential buyers, sometimes overwhelmed by a stunning landscape, commit their life savings to properties, assuming that the view is permanent. Sometimes it is not.

## If a neighbor's addition or growing tree blocks my view, what rights do I have?

Unfortunately, you have no right to light, air or view, unless it has been granted in writing by a law or subdivision rule. The exception to this general rule is that someone may not deliberately and maliciously block another's view with a structure that has no reasonable use to the owner.

This rule encourages building and expansion, but the consequences can be harsh. If a view becomes blocked, the law will help only if:
• a local law protects views
• the obstruction violates private subdivision rules, or
• the obstruction violates some other specific law.

## How can a view ordinance help?

A few cities that overlook the ocean or other desirable vistas have adopted view ordinances. These laws protect a property owner from having his view (usually, the view that he had when he bought the property) obstructed by growing trees. They don't cover buildings or other structures that block views.

The ordinances allow someone who has lost a view to sue the tree owner for a court order requiring him to restore the view. A neighbor who wants to sue must first approach the tree owner and request that the tree be cut back. The complaining person usually bears the cost of trimming or topping, unless the tree was planted after the law became effective, or the owner refuses to cooperate.

Some view ordinances contain extensive limitations that take most of the teeth out of them. Some examples:

- Certain species of trees may be exempt, especially if they grew naturally.
- A neighbor may be allowed to complain only if the tree is within a certain distance from his or her property.
- Trees on city property may be exempt.

## Cities Without View Ordinances

If, like most cities, your city doesn't have a view ordinance, you might find help from other local laws. Here are some laws that may help restore your view:

**Fence Height Limits.** If a fence is blocking your view, it may be in violation of a local law. Commonly, local laws limit artificial (constructed) fences in back yards to six feet high and in front yards to three or four feet. Height restrictions may also apply to natural fences, such as hedges.

**Tree Laws.** Certain species of trees may be prohibited—for example, trees that cause allergies or tend to harm other plants. Laws may also forbid trees that are too close to a street (especially an intersection), to power lines or even to an airport.

**Zoning Laws.** Local zoning regulations control the size, location and uses of buildings. In a single-family area, buildings are usually limited to 30 or 35 feet. Zoning laws also usually require a certain setback, or distance between a structure and the boundary lines. They also limit how much of a lot can be occupied by a structure. For instance, many suburban cities limit a dwelling to 40% to 60% of the property.

## I live in a subdivision with a homeowners' association. Will that help me in a view dispute?

Often, residents of subdivisions and planned unit developments are subject to a detailed set of rules called Covenants, Conditions and Restrictions (CC&Rs). They regulate most matters that could concern a neighbor, including views. For example, a rule may state that trees can't obstruct the view from another lot, or simply limit tree height to 15 feet.

If someone violates the restrictions, the homeowners' association may apply pressure (for example, removing the privilege of using a swimming pool) or even sue. A lawsuit is costly and time-consuming, however, and the association may not want to sue except for serious violations of the rules.

If the association won't help, you can take the neighbor to court yourself, but be prepared for a lengthy and expensive experience.

I want to buy a house with a great view. Is there anything I can do to make sure I won't ever lose the view—and much of my investment?

First, ask the property owner or the city planning and zoning office if the property is protected by a view ordinance. Then check with the real estate agent to see if neighbors are subject to restrictions that would protect your view. Also, if the property is in a planned unit development, find out whether a homeowners' association actively enforces the restrictions.

Check local zoning laws for any property that might affect you. Could the neighbor down the hill add a second-story addition?

Finally, look very closely from the property to see which trees might later obstruct your view. Then go introduce yourself to their owners and explain your concerns. A neighbor who also has a view will probably understand your concern. If someone is unfriendly and uncooperative, you stand warned.

## How to Approach a View Problem

Before you approach the owner of a tree that has grown to block your view, answer these questions:

- Does the tree affect the view of other neighbors? If it does, get them to approach the tree owner with you. Trimming costs may be divided among you.
- Which part of the tree is causing view problems for you—one limb, the top, one side of it?
- What is the least destructive action that could be taken to restore your view? Maybe the owner will agree to a limited and careful pruning.
- How much will the trimming cost? Be ready to pay for it. Remember that every day you wait and grumble is a day for the trees to grow and for the job to become more expensive. The loss of your personal enjoyment is probably worth more than the trimming cost, not to mention the devaluation of your property (which can be thousands of dollars).

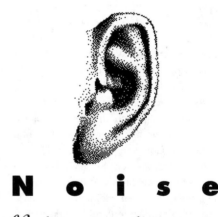

# N o i s e

*Nothing so needs reforming as other people's habits.*

**—MARK TWAIN**

If you are a reasonable person and your neighbor is driving you wiggy with noise, the neighbor is probably violating a noise law.

## Do I have any legal recourse against a noisy neighbor?

You bet. The most effective weapon you have to maintain your peace and quiet is your local noise ordinance. Almost every community prohibits excessive, unnecessary and unreasonable noise, and police enforce these laws.

Most laws designate certain "quiet hours"—for example, from 10 p.m. to 7 a.m. on weekdays, and until 8 or 9 a.m. on weekends. So running a power mower may be perfectly acceptable at 10 a.m. on Saturday, but not at 7 a.m. Many towns also have decibel level noise limits. When a neighbor complains, they measure the noise with electronic equipment. To find out what your town's noise ordinance says, ask at the public library or the city attorney's office.

If your neighbor keeps disturbing you, you can also sue, and ask the court for money damages or to order the neighbor to stop the noise ("abate the nuisance," in legal terms). For money damages alone, you can use small claims court. For a court order telling somebody to stop doing something, you'll have to sue in regular court.

Of course, what you really want is for the nuisance to stop. But getting a small claims court to order your neighbor to pay you money can be amazingly effective. And suing in small claims court is easy and inexpensive, and it doesn't require a lawyer.

Noise that is excessive and deliberate may also be in violation of state criminal laws against disturbing the peace or disorderly conduct. This means that, in very extreme circumstances, the police can arrest your neighbor. Usually, these offenses are punishable by fines or short jail sentences.

## The neighbor in the apartment next to mine is very noisy. Isn't the landlord supposed to keep tenants quiet?

In addition to the other remedies all neighbors have, you have another arrow in your quiver: You can lean on the landlord to quiet the neighbor. Standard rental and lease agreements contain a clause entitled "Quiet Enjoyment." This clause gives tenants the right to occupy their apartments in peace, and also imposes upon them the responsibility not to disturb their neighbors. It's the landlord's job to enforce both sides of this bargain.

If the neighbor's stereo is keeping you up every night, the tenants are probably violating the rental agreement, and could be evicted. Especially if several neighbors complain, the landlord will probably order the tenant to comply with the lease or face eviction. For more information about your rights as a tenant, see Chapter 3.

## Tips for Handling a Noise Problem

- Know the law and stay within it.
- Be reasonably tolerant of your neighbors.
- Assert your rights.
- Communicate with your neighbors—both the one causing the problem and others affected by it.
- Ask the police for help when it is appropriate.
- Use the courts when necessary.

### My neighbor's dog barks all the time, and it's driving me crazy. What can I do?

Usually, problems with barking dogs can be resolved without resorting to police or courts. If you do eventually wind up in court, however, a judge will be more sympathetic if you made at least some effort to work things out first. Here are the steps to take when you're losing patience (or sleep) over a neighbor's noisy dog:

*1. Ask your neighbor to keep the dog quiet.* Sometimes owners are blissfully unaware that there's a problem. If the dog barks for hours every day—but only when it's left alone—the owner may not know that you're being driven crazy.

If you can establish some rapport with the neighbor, try to agree on specific actions to alleviate the problem: for example, that your neighbor will take the dog to obedience school or consult with an animal behavior specialist, or that the dog will be kept inside after 10 p.m. After you agree on a plan, set a date to talk again in a couple of weeks.

*2. Try mediation.* Mediators, both professional and volunteers, are trained to listen to both sides, identify problems, keep everyone focused on the real issues and suggest compromises. A mediator won't make a decision for you, but will help you and your neighbor agree on a resolution.

Many cities have community mediation groups which train volunteers to mediate disputes in their own neighborhoods. Or ask for a referral from:

- the small claims court clerk's office
- the local district attorney's office—the consumer complaint division, if there is one
- radio or television stations that offer help with consumer problems, or
- a state or local bar association.

For more information on mediation, see Chapter 17, *Courts and Mediation*.

*3. Look up the law.* In some places, barking dogs are covered by a specific state or local ordinance. If there's no law aimed specifically at dogs, a general nuisance or noise ordinance makes the owner responsible. Local law may forbid loud noise after 10 p.m., for example, or prohibit any "unreasonable" noise. And someone who allows a dog to bark after numerous warnings from police may be arrested for disturbing the peace.

To find out what the law is where you live, go to a law library and check the state statutes and city or county ordinances yourself. Look in the index under "noise," "dogs," "animals" or "nuisance." For more information on how to do this, see the Legal Research Appendix. Or call the local animal control agency or city attorney.

*4. Ask animal control authorities to enforce local noise laws.* Be persistent. Some cities have special programs to handle dog complaints.

*5. Call the police, if you think a criminal law is being violated.* Generally, police aren't too interested in barking dog problems. And summoning a police cruiser to a neighbor's house obviously will not improve your already-strained relations. But if nothing else works, and the relationship with your neighbor is shot anyway, give the police a try.

### More Information About Neighbor Law

*Neighbor Law: Fences, Trees, Boundaries and Noise,* by Cora Jordan (Nolo), explains laws that affect neighbors and shows how to resolve common disputes without lawsuits.

*Dog Law,* by Mary Randolph (Nolo), is a guide to the laws that affect dog owners and their neighbors.

http://www.nolo.com
*Nolo offers self-help information about a wide variety of legal topics, including neighbor law.*

# Landlords and Tenants

| 3.2 | Leases and Rental Agreements |
| 3.4 | Tenant Selection |
| 3.4 | Housing Discrimination |
| 3.6 | Rent and Security Deposits |
| 3.8 | Tenants' Privacy Rights |
| 3.9 | Repairs and Maintenance |
| 3.12 | Landlord Liability for Criminal Acts and Activities |
| 3.14 | Landlord Liability for Lead Poisoning |
| 3.15 | Insurance |
| 3.17 | Resolving Disputes |

*Property has its duties as well as its rights.*

**–THOMAS DRUMMOND**

Thirty years ago, custom, not law, controlled how most landlords and tenants interacted with each other. This is no longer true. Today, whether you focus on leases and rental agreements; habitability; discrimination; the amount, use and return of security deposits; how and when a landlord may enter a rental unit; or a dozen other issues, both landlord and tenant must understand their legal rights and responsibilities.

Because landlord-tenant laws vary significantly depending on where you live, remember to check your state and local laws for specifics. A list of state landlord-tenant statutes is included at the end of this chapter. You can read the state status of all but one state (Louisiana) online. (See "Can I find statutes on the Internet?" in Chapter 19.)

# Leases and Rental Agreements

It's important to carefully read—and fully understand—the terms of your lease or rental agreement. This piece of paper is the contract that forms the legal basis for the landlord-tenant relationship.

## Why is it important to sign a lease or rental agreement?

The lease or rental agreement is the key document of the tenancy, setting out important issues such as:

- the length of the tenancy
- the amount of rent and deposits the tenant must pay
- the number of people who can live on the rental property
- who pays for utilities
- whether the tenant may have pets
- whether the tenant may sublet the property
- the landlord's access to the rental property, and
- who pays attorney fees if there is a lawsuit.

Leases and rental agreements should always be in writing, even though oral agreements for less than a year are enforceable in most states. While oral agreements may seem easy and informal, they often lead to disputes. If a tenant and landlord later disagree about key agreements, such as whether or not the tenant can sublet, the end result is all too likely to be a court argument over who said what to whom, when and in what context.

## What's the difference between a rental agreement and a lease?

The biggest difference is the period of occupancy. A written rental agreement provides for a tenancy of a short period (often 30 days). The tenancy is automatically renewed at the end of this period unless the tenant or landlord ends it by giving written notice, typically 30 days. For these month-to-month rentals (meaning the rent is paid monthly), the landlord can change the terms of the agreement with proper written notice, subject to any rent control laws. This notice is usually 30 days, but can be shorter in some states if the rent is paid weekly or bi-weekly or if the landlord and tenant agree. In some states, the rental period is longer.

A written lease, on the other hand, gives a tenant the right to occupy a rental unit for a set term—most often for six months or a year, but sometimes longer—if the tenant pays the rent and complies with other lease provisions. Unlike a rental agreement, when a lease expires it does not usually automatically renew itself. A tenant who stays on with the landlord's consent will generally be considered a month-to-month tenant.

In addition, with a fixed-term lease, the landlord cannot raise the rent or change other terms of the tenancy during the lease, unless the changes are specifically provided for in the lease or the tenant agrees.

## What happens if a tenant breaks a long-term lease?

As a general rule, a tenant may not legally break a lease unless the landlord significantly violates its terms—for example, by failing to make necessary repairs, or by failing to comply with an important law concerning health or safety. A few states have laws that allow tenants to break a lease because health problems or a job relocation require a permanent move.

A tenant who breaks a lease without a legally recognized cause will be responsible for the remainder of the

rent due under the lease term. In most states, however, a landlord has a legal duty to try to find a new tenant as soon as possible—no matter what the tenant's reason for leaving—rather than charge the tenant for the total remaining rent due under the lease. At that point, the old tenants' responsibility for the rent will stop.

## When can a landlord legally break a lease and end a tenancy?

Usually, a landlord may legally break a lease if a tenant significantly violates its terms or the law—for example, by paying the rent late, keeping a dog in violation of a no-pets clause in the lease, substantially damaging the property or participating in illegal activities on or near the premises, such as selling drugs.

Usually a landlord must first send the tenant a notice stating that the tenancy has been terminated. State laws set out very detailed requirements as to how a landlord must write and deliver (serve) a termination notice. Depending on what the tenant has done wrong, the termination notice may state that the tenancy is over and warn the tenant that he or she must vacate the premises or face an eviction lawsuit. Or, the notice may give the tenant a few days to clean up his or her act—for example, pay the rent or find a new home for the dog. If the tenant fixes the problem or leaves as directed, no one goes to court. If a tenant doesn't comply with the termination notice, the landlord can file a lawsuit to evict the tenant.

# Tenant Selection

Choosing tenants is the most important decision any landlord makes. To do it well, landlords need a reliable system that helps weed out tenants who will pay their rent late, damage the rental unit or cause legal or practical problems later.

## What's the best way for landlords to screen tenants?

Savvy landlords should ask all prospective tenants to fill out a written rental application that includes the following information:
- employment, income and credit history
- Social Security and driver's license numbers
- past evictions or bankruptcies, and
- references.

Before choosing tenants, landlords should check with previous landlords and other references; verify income, employment and bank account information; and obtain a credit report. The credit report is especially important because it will indicate whether a particular person has a history of paying rent or bills late, has gone through bankruptcy, has been convicted of a crime or has ever been evicted.

## How can a landlord avoid discrimination lawsuits when choosing a tenant?

Fair housing laws specify clearly illegal reasons to refuse to rent to a tenant. (For details, see *Housing Discrimination*, below.) Landlords are legally free to choose among prospective tenants as long as their decisions comply with these laws and are based on legitimate business criteria. For example, a landlord is entitled to reject someone with a poor credit history, insufficient income to pay the rent or past behavior—such as damaging property—that makes the person a bad risk. A legally recognized occupancy policy limiting the number of people per rental unit—one that is clearly tied to health and safety—can also be a legal basis for refusing tenants.

# Housing Discrimination

Not so long ago, a landlord could refuse to rent to an applicant, or could evict a tenant, for almost any reason. If a landlord didn't like your race or religion, or the fact that you had children, you might find yourself out on the street. But times have changed. To protect every American's right to be treated fairly and to help people find adequate housing, Congress and state legislatures passed laws prohibiting discrimination, most notably the federal Fair Housing Acts.

## What types of housing discrimination are illegal?

The federal Fair Housing Act and Fair Housing Amendments Act prohibit landlords from choosing tenants on the basis of a group characteristic such as:

- race
- religion
- ethnic background or national origin
- sex
- age
- the fact that the prospective tenant has children (except in certain designated senior housing), or
- a mental or physical disability.

In addition, some state and local laws prohibit discrimination based on a person's marital status or sexual orientation. And some cities and counties have added other criteria, such as one's personal appearance.

On the other hand, landlords are allowed to select tenants using criteria that are based on valid business reasons, such as requiring a minimum income or positive references from previous landlords, as long as these standards are applied equally to all tenants.

## Examples of Housing Discrimination

The Fair Housing Act and Amendments prohibit landlords from taking any of the following actions based on race, religion or any other protected category:

- advertising or making any statement that indicates a preference based on group characteristic, such as skin color
- falsely denying that a rental unit is available
- setting more restrictive standards, such as higher income, for certain tenants
- refusing to rent to members of certain groups
- refusing to accommodate the needs of disabled tenants, such as allowing a guide dog, hearing dog or service dog
- setting different terms for some tenants, such as adopting an inconsistent policy of responding to late rent payments, or
- terminating a tenancy for a discriminatory reason.

## How does a tenant file a discrimination complaint?

A tenant who thinks that a landlord has broken a federal fair housing law should contact the U.S. Department of Housing and Urban Development (HUD), the agency which enforces the Fair Housing Act. To find the nearest office, call HUD's Fair Housing Information Clearinghouse at (800) 343-3442, or check the HUD Website at www.hud.gov. HUD will provide a complaint form and will investigate and decide the merits of the claim. A tenant must file his or her complaint within one year of the alleged discriminatory act. HUD will typically appoint a mediator to negotiate with the landlord and reach a settlement (called a "conciliation"). If a settlement can't be reached, the fair housing agency will hold an administrative hearing to determine whether discrimination has occurred.

If the discrimination is a violation of a state fair housing law, the tenant may file a complaint with the state agency in charge of enforcing the law. In California, for example, the Department of Fair Employment and Housing enforces the state's two fair housing laws.

Also, instead of filing a complaint with HUD or a state agency, tenants may file lawsuits directly in federal or state court. If a state or federal court or housing agency finds that discrimination has taken place, a tenant may be awarded damages, including any higher rent he or she had to pay as a result of being turned down, and damages for humiliation or emotional distress.

# Rent and Security Deposits

Landlords may charge any dollar amount for rent, except in certain areas covered by rent control. Many states do, however, have rules as to when and how rent must be paid and how it may be increased.

Security deposits are more strictly regulated by state law. Most states dictate how much money a landlord can require, how the funds can be used—for example, to cover unpaid rent—and when and how the deposit must be returned.

## What laws cover rent due dates, late rent and rent increases?

By custom, leases and rental agreements usually require rent to be paid monthly, in advance. Often rent is due on the first day of the month. However, it is legal for a landlord to require rent to be paid at different intervals or on a different day of the month. Unless the lease or rental agreement specifies otherwise, there is no legally-recognized grace period— in other words, if a tenant hasn't paid the rent on time, the landlord can usually terminate the tenancy the day after it is due. Some landlords charge fees for late payment of rent or for bounced checks; these fees are usually legal if they are reasonable. The laws on late fees can be found in your state's landlord-tenant statutes, listed at the end of this chapter.

For month-to-month rentals, the landlord can raise the rent (subject to any rent control laws) with proper written notice, typically 30 days. With a fixed-term lease, the landlord may not raise the rent during the lease, unless the increase is specifically called for in the lease or the tenant agrees.

## How Rent Control Works

Communities in only five states—California, the District of Columbia, Maryland, New Jersey and New York—have laws that limit the amount of rent landlords may charge. Rent control ordinances (also called rent stabilization, maximum rent regulation or a similar term) limit the circumstances and times rent may be increased. Many rent control laws require landlords to have a legal or just cause (that is, a good reason) to terminate a tenancy—for example, if the tenant doesn't pay rent or if the landlord wants to move a family member into the rental unit. Landlords and tenants in New York City, Newark, San Francisco and other cities with rent control should be sure to get a current copy of the ordinance and any regulations interpreting it. Check the phone book for the address and phone number of the local rent control board, or contact the mayor or city manager's office.

### How much security deposit can a landlord charge?

All states allow landlords to collect a security deposit when the tenant moves in; the general purpose is to assure that the tenant pays rent when due and keeps the rental unit in good condition. Half the states limit the amount landlords can charge, usually not more than a month or two worth of rent—the exact amount depends on the state.

Many states require landlords to put deposits in a separate account, and some require landlords to pay tenants the interest on deposits.

### What are the rules for returning security deposits?

The rules vary from state to state, but landlords usually have a set amount of time in which to return deposits, usually 14 to 30 days after the tenant moves out—either voluntarily or by eviction.

Landlords may normally make certain deductions from a tenant's security deposit, provided they do it correctly and for an allowable reason. Many states require landlords to provide a written itemized accounting of deductions for unpaid rent and for repairs for damages that go beyond normal wear and tear, together with payment for any deposit balance.

A tenant may sue a landlord who fails to return his or her deposit when and how required, or who violates other provisions of security deposit laws such as interest requirements; often these lawsuits may be brought in small claims court. If the landlord has intentionally and flagrantly violated the ordinance, in some states, a tenant may recover the entire deposit—sometimes even two or three times this amount—plus attorney fees and other damages.

The rules for the keeping and return of security deposits can be found in state landlord-tenant statutes, listed at the end of this chapter.

# Tenants' Privacy Rights

In most states, the tenant's duty to pay rent is conditioned on the landlord's proper repair and maintenance of the premises. This means that landlords have a legal responsibility to keep fairly close tabs on the condition of the property. To balance landlords' responsibilities with tenants' rights to privacy in their homes, laws in many states set rules about when and how landlords may legally enter rented premises.

## Under what circumstances may a landlord enter rental property?

Typically, a landlord has the right to legally enter rented premises in cases of emergency, in order to make needed repairs (in some states, just to determine whether repairs are necessary) or to show the property to prospective new tenants or purchasers.

Several states allow landlords the right of entry during a tenant's extended absence (often defined as seven days or more) to maintain the property as necessary and to inspect for damage and needed repairs. In most cases, a landlord may not enter just to check up on the tenant and the rental property.

## Must landlords provide notice of entry?

States typically require landlords to provide advance notice (usually 24 hours) before entering a rental unit. Without advance notice, a landlord or manager may enter rented premises while a tenant is living there only in an emergency, such as a fire or serious water leak, or when the tenant gives permission.

To find out how much notice a landlord must give a tenant before entering, check your state's landlord-tenant statutes, listed at the end of this chapter.

## Is it legal for a landlord to answer questions about a tenant's credit?

Creditors, banks and prospective landlords may ask a landlord to provide credit or other information about a current or former tenant. A landlord who sticks to the facts that are relevant to the tenant's creditworthiness (such as whether the tenant paid rent on time) is allowed to respond to these inquiries. To be extra careful, some landlords insist that tenants sign a release giving the landlord permission to respond to such requests.

# Repairs and Maintenance

In 1863, an English judge wrote that "Fraud apart, there is no law against letting [leasing] a tumble-down house." But in 20th century America, it's no longer legal to be a slumlord. Landlords must repair and maintain their rental property or face financial losses and legal problems from tenants—who may withhold rent and pursue other legal remedies—and from government agencies that enforce housing codes.

## What are the landlord's repair and maintenance responsibilities?

Under most state and local laws, rental property owners must offer and maintain housing that satisfies basic habitability requirements, such as adequate weatherproofing; available heat, water and electricity; and clean, sanitary and structurally safe premises. Local building or housing codes typically set specific standards, such as the minimum requirements for light, ventilation and electrical wiring. Many cities require the installation of smoke detectors in residential units and specify security measures involving locks and keys.

To find out more about state laws on repair and maintenance responsibilities, check your state's landlord-tenant statutes listed at the end of this chapter. Your local building or housing authority, and health or fire department, can provide information on local housing codes and penalties for violations.

## What are a tenant's rights if the landlord refuses to maintain the property?

If a landlord doesn't meet his or her legal responsibilities, a tenant usually has several options, depending on the state. These options include:
- paying less rent
- withholding the entire rent until the problem is fixed
- making necessary repairs or hiring someone to make them and deducting the cost from the next month's rent
- calling the local building inspector, who can usually order the landlord to make repairs, or
- moving out, even in the middle of a lease.

A tenant can also sue the landlord for a partial refund of past rent, and in some circumstances can sue for the discomfort, annoyance and emotional distress caused by the substandard conditions.

Tenants should check state and local laws and understand remedies available before taking any action such as withholding rent.

## What must tenants do to keep the rental property in good shape?

All tenants have the responsibility to keep their own living quarters clean and sanitary. And a landlord can usually delegate his repair and maintenance tasks to the tenant in exchange for a reduction in rent. If the tenant fails to do the job well, however, the landlord is not excused from his responsibility to maintain habitability. In addition, tenants must carefully use common areas and facilities, such as lobbies, garages and pools.

## Is a landlord liable if a tenant or visitor is injured on the rental property?

A landlord may be liable to the tenant—or others—for injuries caused by dangerous or defective conditions on the rental property. In order to hold the landlord responsible, the tenant must prove that the landlord was negligent, and that the landlord's negligence caused an injury. To do this, the tenant must show that:

- the landlord had control over the problem that caused the injury
- the accident was foreseeable
- fixing the problem (or at least giving adequate warnings) would not have been unreasonably expensive or difficult
- a serious injury was the probable consequence of not fixing the problem

- the landlord failed to take reasonable steps to avert the accident
- the landlord's failure—his negligence—caused the tenant's accident, and
- the tenant was genuinely hurt.

For example, if a tenant falls and breaks his ankle on a broken front door step, the landlord will be liable if the tenant can show that:

- It was the landlord's responsibility to maintain the steps (this would usually be the case, because the steps are part of the common area, which is the landlord's responsibility).
- An accident of this type was foreseeable (falling on a broken step is highly likely).
- A repair would have been easy or inexpensive (fixing a broken step is a minor job).
- The probable result of a broken step is a serious injury (a fall certainly qualifies).
- The landlord failed to take reasonable measures to maintain the steps (this will be easy to prove if the step was broken for weeks, or even days, but less so if the step broke five minutes earlier and showed no previous signs of weakening).
- The broken step caused the injury (this is easy to prove if the tenant has a witness to the fall, but might be hard if there are no witnesses and the landlord claims that the tenant really injured himself somewhere else and is attempting to pin the blame on the landlord), and

- He is really hurt (in the case of a broken bone, this is easy to establish).

A tenant can file a personal injury lawsuit for medical bills, lost earnings, pain and other physical suffering, permanent physical disability and disfigurement and emotional distress. A tenant can also sue for property damage that results from faulty maintenance or unsafe conditions.

### More Information on Personal Injury Lawsuits

*How to Win Your Personal Injury Claim,* by Joseph L. Matthews (Nolo), provides step-by-step details on how to understand what a claim is worth, prepare a claim for compensation, negotiate a fair settlement and manage a case even if a lawyer is not involved.

## How can property owners minimize financial losses and legal problems related to repairs and maintenance?

Landlords who offer and maintain housing in excellent condition can avoid many problems. Here's how:
- Clearly set out responsibilities for repair and maintenance in the lease or rental agreement.

- Use a written checklist to inspect the premises and fix any problems before new tenants move in.
- Encourage tenants to immediately report plumbing, heating, weatherproofing or other defects or safety or security problems—whether in the tenant's unit or in common areas such as hallways and parking garages.
- Keep a written log of all tenant complaints and repair requests with details as to how and when problems were fixed.
- Handle urgent repairs as soon as possible. Take care of major inconveniences, such as a plumbing or heating problem, within 24 hours. For minor problems, respond in 48 hours. Always keep tenants informed as to when and how the repairs will be made, and the reasons for any delays.

- Twice a year, give tenants a checklist on which to report potential safety hazards or maintenance problems that might have been overlooked. Use the same checklist to inspect all rental units once a year.

# Landlord Liability for Criminal Acts and Activities

Can a law-abiding citizen end up financially responsible for the criminal acts of a total stranger? Yes—if it's a landlord who owns rental property where an assault or other crime occurred. Rental property owners are being sued with increasing frequency by tenants injured by criminals, with settlements and jury awards typically ranging from $100,000 to $1 million. What are the landlord's responsibilities for tenant safety and security?

Property owners are responsible for keeping their premises safe for tenants and guests. Landlords in most states now have at least some degree of legal responsibility to protect their tenants from would-be assailants and thieves and from the criminal acts of fellow tenants. Landlords must also protect the neighborhood from their tenants' illegal activities, such as drug dealing. These legal duties stem from building codes, ordinances, statutes and, most frequently, court decisions.

## How can a landlord limit responsibility for crime committed by strangers on the rental property?

Effective preventive measures are the best response to possible liabilities from criminal acts and activities. The following steps will not only limit the likelihood of crime, but also reduce the risk that the property owner will be found responsible if a criminal assault or robbery does occur. A landlord should:

- Meet or exceed all state and local security laws that apply to the rental property, such as requirements for deadbolt locks on doors, good lighting and window locks.
- Realistically assess the crime situation in and around the rental property and neighborhood and design a security system that provides reasonable protection for the tenants—both in individual rental units and common areas such as parking garages and elevators. Local police departments, the landlord's insurance company and private security professionals can all provide useful advice on security measures. If additional security requires a rent hike, the landlord should discuss the situation with his or her tenants. Many tenants will pay more for a safer place to live.
- Educate tenants about crime problems in the neighborhood, and describe the security measures provided and their limitations.
- Maintain the rental property and conduct regular inspections to spot and fix any security problems, such as broken locks or burned out exterior flood lights. Asking tenants for their suggestions as part of an ongoing repair and maintenance system is also a good idea.
- Handle tenant complaints about dangerous situations, suspicious

activities or broken security items immediately. Failing to do this may saddle a landlord with a higher level of legal liability should a tenant be injured by a criminal act after a relevant complaint is made.

## The Costs of Crime

The money a landlord spends today on effective crime-prevention measures will pale in comparison to the costs that may result from crime on the premises. The average settlement paid by landlords' insurance companies for horrific crimes such as rape and assault is $600,000, and the average jury award (when cases go to trial) is $1.2 million.

## What kind of legal trouble do landlords face from tenants who deal drugs on the property?

Drug-dealing tenants can cause landlords all kinds of practical and legal problems:

- It will be difficult to find and keep good tenants and the value of the rental property will plummet.
- Anyone who is injured or annoyed by drug dealers—be it other tenants or people in the neighborhood—may sue the landlord on the grounds that the property is a public nuisance that seriously threatens public safety or morals.
- Local, state or federal authorities may levy stiff fines against the landlord for allowing the illegal activity to continue.

- Law enforcement authorities may seek criminal penalties against the landlord for knowingly allowing drug dealing on the rental property.
- In extreme cases, the presence of drug dealers may result in the government confiscating the rental property.

## How can a property owner avoid legal problems from tenants who deal drugs or otherwise break the law?

There are several practical steps landlords can take to avoid trouble from tenants and limit their exposure to any lawsuits that are filed:

- Screen tenants carefully and choose tenants who are likely to be law-abiding and peaceful citizens. Weed out violent or dangerous individuals to the extent allowable under privacy and anti-discrimination laws that may limit questions about a tenant's past criminal activity, drug use or mental illness.
- Keep the results of background checks that show that the tenants' rent appeared to come from legitimate sources (jobs and bank accounts).
- Don't accept a cash deposit or rental payments.
- Do not tolerate tenants' disruptive behavior. Include an explicit provision in the lease or rental agreement prohibiting drug dealing and other illegal activity and promptly evict tenants who violate the clause.

- Be aware of suspicious activity, such as heavy traffic in and out of the rental premises.
- Respond to tenant and neighbor complaints about drug dealing on the rental property. Get advice from police immediately upon learning of a problem.
- Consult with security experts to do everything reasonable to discover and prevent illegal activity on the rental property.

## Protecting Tenants From the Manager

Rental property owners should be particularly careful hiring a property manager—the person who interacts with all tenants and has access to master keys. Landlords should scrupulously check a manager's background to the fullest extent allowed by law, and closely supervise his or her job performance. A tenant who gets hurt or has property stolen or damaged by a manager could sue the property owner for failing to screen the manager properly. If tenants complain about illegal acts by a manager, landlords should pay attention. Finally, property owners should make sure their insurance covers illegal acts of their employees.

# Landlord Liability for Lead Poisoning

Landlords are increasingly likely to be held liable for tenant health problems resulting from exposure to lead and other environmental toxins, even if the landlord didn't cause—or even know about—the danger.

## What are a landlord's legal responsibilities regarding lead in rental property?

Because of the health problems caused by lead poisoning, the Residential Lead-Based Paint Hazard Reduction Act was enacted in 1992. This law is commonly known as Title X (ten). Environmental Protection Agency (EPA) regulations implementing Title X apply to rental property built before 1978.

Under Title X, before signing or renewing a lease or rental agreement, a landlord must give every tenant the EPA pamphlet, *Protect Your Family From Lead in Your Home,* or a state-approved version of this pamphlet. Both the landlord and tenant must sign an EPA-approved disclosure form to prove that the landlord told the tenants about any known lead-based paint or hazards on the premises. Property owners must keep this disclosure form as part of their records for three years from the date that the tenancy begins.

A landlord who fails to comply with EPA regulations faces penalties of up to $10,000 for each violation. And a landlord who is found liable for tenant injuries from lead may have to pay three times what the tenant suffered in damages.

### More Information on Lead Hazard Resources

Information on the evaluation and control of lead dust, and copies of *Protect Your Family From Lead in Your Home* may be obtained by calling the National Lead Information Center at 800-424-LEAD, or checking its website at http://www.epa.gov/oppintr/lead/nlic.htm. In addition, state housing departments have information on state laws and regulations governing the evaluation and control of lead hazards.

### Are there any rental properties exempt from Title X regulations?

These properties are not covered by Title X:
- housing for which a construction permit was obtained, or on which construction was started, after January 1, 1978
- housing certified as lead-free by a state-accredited lead inspector
- lofts, efficiencies and studio apartments
- short-term vacation rentals of 100 days or less

- a single room rented in a residential dwelling
- housing designed for persons with disabilities, unless any child less than six years old lives there or is expected to live there
- retirement communities (housing designed for seniors, where one or more tenants is at least 62 years old), unless children under the age of six are present or expected to live there.

## Landlord's Liability for Exposure to Asbestos

In addition to lead, property owners may be liable for tenant health problems caused by exposure to other environmental hazards, such as asbestos. Regulations issued by the Occupational Safety and Health Administration (OSHA) set strict standards for the testing, maintenance and disclosure of asbestos in buildings constructed before 1981. For information call the nearest OSHA office or check OSHA's website at http://www.osha.gov.

# Insurance

Both tenants and landlords need insurance to protect their property and bank accounts. Without adequate insurance, landlords risk losing hundreds of thousands of dollars of property from fire or other hazards. While tenants may not have as much at stake financially, they also need insurance—especially tenants with expensive personal belongings. Tenant losses from fire or theft are not covered by the landlord's insurance.

## How can insurance help protect a rental property business?

A well-designed insurance policy can protect rental property from losses caused by many perils, including fire, storms, burglary and vandalism. (Earthquake and flood insurance are typically separate.) A comprehensive policy will also include liability insurance, covering injuries or losses suffered by others as the result of defective conditions on the property.

Equally important, liability insurance covers the cost (mostly lawyer's bills) of defending personal injury lawsuits.

Here are some tips on choosing insurance:

- Purchase enough coverage to protect the value of the property and assets.
- Be sure the policy covers not only physical injury but also libel, slander, discrimination, unlawful and retaliatory eviction and invasion of privacy suffered by tenants and guests.
- Carry liability insurance on all vehicles used for business purposes, including the manager's car or truck if he or she will use it on the job.
- Make sure your policy is "occurence based," not "claims based." Here's the difference: under a claims-based policy, your policy must be in effect on the date you make the claim—

even if it was in place when the incident leading to the claim occurred. Under an occurance-based arrangement, you can make the claim after the policy has ended—which is obviously to your advantage.

If you need more information, *The Legal Guide for Starting and Running a Small Business*, by Fred S. Steingold (Nolo), contains a detailed discussion of small business law, including how to insure your rental property.

## What does renter's insurance cover?

The average renter's policy covers tenants against losses to their belongings occurring as a result of fire and theft, up to the amount stated on the face of the policy, such as $25,000 or $50,000.

Most renter policies include deductible amounts of $250 or $500. This means that if a tenant's apartment is burglarized, the insurance company will pay only for the amount of the loss over and above the deductible amount.

In addition to fire and theft, most renter's policies include personal liability coverage ($100,000 is a typical amount) for injuries or damage caused by the tenant—for example, if a tenant's garden hose floods the neighbor's cactus garden, or a tenant's guest is injured on the rental property due to the tenant's negligence.

Renter's insurance is a package of several types of insurance designed to cover tenants for more than one risk. Each insurance company's package will be slightly different—types of coverage offered, exclusions, the dollar amounts specified and the deductible will vary. Tenants who live in a flood or earthquake-prone area will need to pay extra for coverage. Policies covering flood and earthquake damage can be hard to find; tenants should shop around until they find the type of coverage that they need.

# Resolving Disputes

Legal disputes—actual and potential—come in all shapes and sizes for landlords and tenants. Whether it's a disagreement over a rent increase, responsibility for repairs or return of a security deposit, rarely should lawyers and litigation be the first choice for resolving a landlord-tenant dispute.

## How can landlords and tenants avoid disputes?

Both landlords and tenants should follow these tips to avoid legal problems:

- Know your rights and responsibilities under federal, state and local law.
- Make sure the terms of your lease or rental agreement are clear and unambiguous.
- Keep communication open. If there's a problem—for example, a disagreement about the landlord's right to enter a tenant's apartment—see if you can resolve the issue by talking it over, without running to a lawyer.

- Keep copies of any correspondence and make notes of conversations about any problems. For example, a tenant should ask for repairs in writing and keep a copy of the letter. The landlord should keep a copy of the repair request and note when and how the problem was repaired.

## We've talked about the problem and still don't agree. What should we do next?

If you can't work out an agreement on your own, but want to continue the rental relationship, consider mediation by a neutral, third party. Unlike a judge, the mediator has no power to impose a decision but will simply work to help find a mutually acceptable solution to the dispute. Mediation is often available at little or no cost from a publicly-funded program.

### *More Information About Mediation*

For information on local mediation programs, call your mayor's or city manager's office, and ask for the staff member who handles "landlord-tenant mediation matters" or "housing disputes." That person should refer you to the public office, business or community group that handles landlord-tenant mediations.

You can learn more about mediation by reading Chapter 17 of this book, *Courts and Mediation.*

## If mediation doesn't work, is there a last step before going to a lawyer?

If you decide not to mediate your dispute, or mediation fails, it's time to pursue other legal remedies. If the disagreement involves money, such as return of the security deposit, you can take the case to small claims court. A few states use different names for this type of court (such as "Landlord-Tenant Court"), but traditionally the purpose has been the same: to provide a speedy, inexpensive resolution of disputes that involve relatively small amounts of money.

Keep in mind that your remedy in small claims court may be limited to an award of money damages. The maximum amount you can sue for varies from $3,000 to $7,500, depending on your state.

You can find more information about small claims court in Chapter 17, *Courts and Mediation*.

## Landlord-Tenant Statutory Codes

Here are some of the key statutes pertaining to landlord-tenant law in each state.

**ALABAMA**
Ala. Code §§ 35-9-1 to -100

**ALASKA**
Alaska Stat. §§ 34.03.010 to .380

**ARIZONA**
Ariz. Rev. Stat. Ann. §§ 12-1171 to -1183; §§ 33-1301 to -1381

**ARKANSAS**
Ark. Code Ann. §§ 18-16-101 to -306

**CALIFORNIA**
Cal. [Civ.] Code §§ 1925-1954, 1961-1962.7, 1995.010-1997.270

**COLORADO**
Colo. Rev. Stat. §§ 38-12-101 to -104, -301 to -302

**CONNECTICUT**
Conn. Gen. Stat. Ann. §§ 47a-1 to 50a

**DELAWARE**
Del. Code. Ann. tit. 25, §§ 5101-7013

**DISTRICT OF COLUMBIA**
D.C. Code Ann. §§ 45-1401 to -1597, -2501 to -2593

**FLORIDA**
Fla. Stat. Ann. §§ 83.40-.66

**GEORGIA**
Ga. Code Ann. §§ 44-7-1 to -81

**HAWAII**
Haw. Rev. Stat. §§ 521-1 to -78

**IDAHO**
Idaho Code §§ 6-301 to -324 and §§ 55-201 to -313

**ILLINOIS**
765 Ill. Comp. Stat. 705/0.01-740/5

**INDIANA**
Ind. Code Ann. §§ 32-7-1-1 to 37-7-9-10

**IOWA**
Iowa Code Ann. §§ 562A.1-.36

**KANSAS**
Kan. Stat. Ann. §§ 58-2501 to -2573

**KENTUCKY**
Ky. Rev. Stat. Ann. §§ 383.010-.715

**LOUISIANA**
La. Rev. Stat. Ann. §§ 9:3201-:3259; La. Civ. Code Ann. art. 2669-2742

**MAINE**
Me. Rev. Stat. Ann. tit. 14, §§ 6001-6046

**MARYLAND**
Md. Real Prop. Code Ann. §§ 8-101 to -604

**MASSACHUSETTS**
Mass. Gen. Laws Ann. ch. 186 §§ 1-21

**MICHIGAN**
Mich. Comp. Laws Ann. § 554.601-640

**MINNESOTA**
Minn. Stat. Ann. §§ 504B.001 to 504B.471

**MISSISSIPPI**
Miss. Code Ann. §§ 89-8-1 to -27

**MISSOURI**
Mo. Ann. Stat. §§ 441.005 to 441.880; and §§ 535.150-.300

**MONTANA**
Mont. Code Ann. §§ 70-24-101 to -25-206

**NEBRASKA**
Neb. Rev. Stat. §§ 76-1401 to -1449

**NEVADA**
Nev. Rev. Stat. Ann. §§ 118A.010-.520

**NEW HAMPSHIRE**
N.H. Rev. Stat. Ann. §§ 540:1 to 540:29; 540-A:1 to 540-A:8

**NEW JERSEY**
N.J. Stat. Ann. §§ 46:8-1 to -49

**NEW MEXICO**
N.M. Stat. Ann. §§ 47-8-1 to -51

**NEW YORK**
N.Y. Real Property Law "Real Prop. L." §§ 220-238; Real Property Actions and Proceedings Law ("RPAPL") §§ 701-853; Multiple Dwelling Law ("MDL") all; Multiple Residence Law ("MRL") all; General Obligations Law ("GOL") §§ 7-103-108

**NORTH CAROLINA**
N.C. Gen. Stat. §§ 42-1 to 42-14.2; 42-25-6 to 42-76

**NORTH DAKOTA**
N.D. Cent. Code §§ 47-16-01 to -41

**OHIO**
Ohio Rev. Code Ann. §§ 5321.01-.19

**OKLAHOMA**
Okla. Stat. Ann. tit. 41, §§ 1-136

**OREGON**
Or. Rev. Stat. §§ 90.100-.450

**PENNSYLVANIA**
Pa. Stat. Ann. tit. 68, §§ 250.101-.510-B

**RHODE ISLAND**
R.I. Gen. Laws §§ 34-18-1 to -57

**SOUTH CAROLINA**
S.C. Code Ann. §§ 27-40-10 to -910

**SOUTH DAKOTA**
S.D. Codified Laws Ann. §§ 43-32-1 to -29

**TENNESSEE**
Tenn. Code Ann. §§ 66-28-101 to -520

**TEXAS**
Tex. Prop. Code Ann. §§ 91.001-92.354

**UTAH**
Utah Code Ann. §§ 57-17-1 to -5, -22-1 to -6

**VERMONT**
Vt. Stat Ann. tit. 9, §§ 4451-4468

**VIRGINIA**
Va. Code Ann. §§ 55-218.1 to -248.40

**WASHINGTON**
Wash. Rev. Code Ann. §§ 59.04.010-.900, .18.010-.911

**WEST VIRGINIA**
W. Va. Code §§ 37-6-1 to -30

**WISCONSIN**
Wis. Stat. Ann. §§ 704.01-.45

**WYOMING**
Wyo. Stat. §§ 1-21-1201 to 1-21-1211; 34-2-128 to -129

*More Information About Landlord-Tenant Law*

## From the landlord's point of view:

*Every Landlord's Legal Guide*, by Marcia Stewart, Ralph Warner and Janet Portman (Nolo). This 50-state book provides extensive legal and practical information on leases, tenant screening, rent, security deposits, privacy, repairs, property managers, discrimination, roommates, liability, tenancy termination and much more. It includes more than 25 legal forms and agreements as tear-outs and on disk.

*Lease Writer* (Nolo)(CD-ROM for Windows/Macintosh). This software program generates a customized legal residential lease or rental agreement, plus more than a dozen key documents and forms every landlord and property manager needs. It includes a database to track tenants and rental properties, and a log for rental payments, repairs and problems. The program gives you instant access to state-specific landlord-tenant information, and extensive online legal help.

## From the tenant's point of view:

*Every Tenant's Legal Guide*, by Janet Portman and Marcia Stewart (Nolo). This book gives tenants in all 50 states the legal and practical information they need to deal with their landlords and protect their rights when things go wrong. It covers all important issues of renting, including signing a lease, getting a landlord to make needed repairs, fighting illegal discrimination, protecting privacy rights, dealing with roommates, getting the security deposit returned fairly, moving out and much more.

*Renters' Rights*, by Janet Portman and Marcia Stewart (Nolo). A concise, highly accessible guide for tenants in every state, loaded with tips and strategies.

### For both landlords and tenants:

*Everybody's Guide to Small Claims Court*, by Attorney Ralph Warner (National and California Editions)(Nolo). The book explains how to evaluate your case, prepare for court and convince a judge you're right. It also tells you what remedies (money only, or enforcement of the lease) are available in your state.

*How to Mediate Your Dispute*, by Peter Lovenheim (Nolo), explains how to choose a mediator, prepare a case and navigate the mediation process.

Additionally, tenants' unions and rental property owners' associations are good sources of advice. Look in your telephone book's white pages for names of these organizations.

**http://www.nolo.com**
*Nolo offers self-help information about a wide variety of legal topics, including landlord-tenant law and provides links to federal and state statutes.*

**http://tenant.net/main.html**
*TenantNet provides information about landlord-tenant law, with a focus on tenants' rights. TenantNet is designed primarily for tenants in New York City, but the site offers information about the law in many other states. The site also provides the text of the federal fair housing law.*

**http://www.spl.org/govpubs/ municode.html**
*The Seattle Public Library has links to many cities that have posted their ordinances (and often their rent control laws) online.*

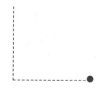

# **W**orkplace Rights

| | |
|---|---|
| 4.2 | *Fair Pay and Time Off* |
| 4.9 | *Workplace Health and Safety* |
| 4.12 | *Workers' Compensation* |
| 4.17 | *Age Discrimination* |
| 4.21 | *Sexual Harassment* |
| 4.25 | *Disability Discrimination* |
| 4.29 | *Losing or Leaving Your Job* |

I LIKE WORK; IT FASCINATES ME.

I CAN SIT AND LOOK AT IT FOR HOURS.

—JEROME K. JEROME

**I**f you're like most workers, you have experienced occasional job-related problems or have questions about whether you are being fairly and legally treated on the job. Here are several common problems:

- You were not hired for a job and you have good reason to suspect it was because of your race, age, sex, sexual orientation or because you are disabled.
- Your employer promoted a less-qualified person—perhaps someone who is younger than you are—to fill a position you were promised.
- You are regularly forced to work overtime but are not given extra pay. Or, you are paid for working extra hours, but you do not receive a premium rate, such as time-and-a-half.
- You need to take a leave of absence from your job to care for a sick parent, but you are concerned that this will jeopardize your job or your eligibility for a promotion.
- You have been called to serve on a jury and wonder if your employer must pay you for this time.
- You have just been laid off and you want to know whether, if business at your company picks up in the future, you have any right to get your job back. You also want to know whether you're entitled to unemployment payments, or whether your employer owes you severance pay.

It is reassuring for many workers to learn that they do not face these issues alone. In recent years, a number of laws have been passed to protect your rights in the workplace. Federal laws now establish some basic guarantees for most workers—such as the right to be paid fairly and on time and to work free from discrimination. And state laws may place their own twists on your workplace rights—giving more protection than federal law, for example, or regulating whether or not you are entitled to time off work to vote or to care for a sick child.

# Fair Pay and Time Off

*I do not like work even when someone else does it.*

**—MARK TWAIN**

These days, most of us spend at least half of our waking hours working. Ideally, this time will be spent on jobs that are fulfilling. But whether or not we enjoy our work, the bottom line for almost all of us is to be paid fairly and on time. Fortunately, both state and federal laws protect this right.

## I suspect my employer is bending some of the rules on paying employees. What are the legal controls on pay for work?

The most important and far-reaching law guaranteeing a worker's right to be paid fairly is the federal Fair Labor Standards Act or FLSA. The FLSA:
- defines the 40-hour workweek
- covers the federal minimum wage (currently $5.15 per hour)
- sets requirements for overtime, and
- places restrictions on child labor.

The FLSA is the single law most often violated by employers. But employers must also comply with other local, state or federal workplace laws that sometimes set higher standards. So in addition to determining whether you are being paid properly under the FLSA, you may need to check other laws that apply to your situation. For example, many states have a higher minimum wage than mandated by federal law. Your employer must comply with whichever minimum wage is higher.

To learn about state and local labor laws that might apply to you, contact the local office of your state department of labor, which should be able to supply you with written materials setting forth your legal rights.

### What is the current minimum wage?

The federal minimum wage is currently $5.15 per hour. But many states have their own minimum wage laws that require a higher rate of pay. For example, Rhode Island's minimum wage is $6.15 per hour. Employers must pay whichever minimum wage rate—federal or state—is higher. To find out the minimum wage rates in the 50 states, the District of Columbia, Puerto Rico and Guam, visit the U.S. Department of Labor's website at http://www.dol.gov/dol/esa/public/minwage/america. You can also contact your local labor department for information.

**My boss says that because I'm a supervisor, I am not legally entitled to overtime pay. Is this true?**

It may be. Some employees are exempt from the overtime requirements of the FLSA—and the biggest and most abused exemption is for executive, administrative and professional workers. To qualify as an exempt executive, the employee must, among other things, supervise two full-time employees (or the equivalent). The definitions of administrative and professional employees have their own quirks. For example, employees categorized as professionals must perform work that is primarily intellectual. The definitions also change with the employee's salary level. For example, if the weekly salary of the executive, administrative or professional employee exceeds a certain minimum, fewer factors are required to qualify for the exemption.

Determining whether you truly are exempt from overtime requirements becomes even more complex when you factor in state law requirements. If you have a question about whether your particular job is exempt, it may be worth your while to go to the nearest law library and carefully read the Fair Labor Standards Act, 29 U.S.C. §§ 201 and following. You can also read this law online by visiting the U.S. Department of Labor site at http://www.dol.gov.

To learn about overtime laws in your state, contract your state department of labor.

## I put in more than forty hours on the job each week, without overtime pay. Am I entitled to time off to compensate for this?

Most workers are familiar with compensatory or comp time—the practice of offering employees time off from work in place of cash payments for overtime. What comes as a shock to many is that the practice is illegal in most situations. Under the FLSA, only state or government agencies may legally allow their employees time off in place of wages (29 U.S.C. § 207(o)). Even then, comp time may be awarded only:

- according to the terms of an agreement arranged by union representatives, or
- if the employer and employee agree to the arrangement before work begins.

When compensatory time is allowed, it must be awarded at the rate of one and one-half times the overtime hours worked—and comp time must be taken during the same pay period that the overtime hours were worked.

Some states do allow private employers to give employees comp time instead of cash. But there are complex, often conflicting laws controlling how and when it may be given. A common control, for example, is that employees must voluntarily request in writing that comp time be given instead of overtime pay—before the extra hours are worked. Check with your state's labor department for special laws on comp time in your area.

Many employers and employees routinely violate the rules governing the use of compensatory time in place of cash overtime wages. However, such violations are risky. Employees can find themselves unable to collect money due them if a company goes out of business or they are fired. And employers can end up owing large amounts of overtime pay to employees as the result of a labor department prosecution of compensatory time violations.

## Can my boss force me to work overtime?

Under the FLSA (which, you'll recall, is a federal law) your employer can force you to work overtime and can even fire you if you refuse to do so.

The FLSA does not limit the number of hours in a day or days in a week that an employer can schedule an employee to work. It only requires employers to pay non-exempt employees overtime (time and a half the worker's regular rate of pay) for any hours over 40 that the employee works in a week.

However, your state law may provide additional rights. Contact your state labor department to learn more.

## Does my employer have to pay me overtime if I work more than eight hours in a day?

Under the FLSA, your employer does not have to pay you overtime if you work more than eight hours in any given day. The federal law is interested only in weeks, not days, so as long as you work less than 40 hours in a week, you aren't entitled to overtime.

In this area, however, it's definitely worth checking to see what your state law has to say on the subject. Some states, such as California, do require employers to pay overtime to employees who work more than eight hours in a day. Your employer must comply with whichever law—federal or state—is most beneficial to you.

## I work as a waitress and make good tips. My boss says that because I get this extra money at work, he can pay me a wage that is lower than the hourly minimum wage. Is this true?

It depends on how much money you make in tips. Employers must pay all employees not less than the minimum wage.

But the matter of minimum wage becomes tricky when an employee routinely receives at least $30 per month in tips. Under federal law, employers are allowed to credit half of those tips against the minimum wage requirement, which, under federal law, is currently $5.15 per hour. So, they can credit up to $2.12 an hour of the tips received toward their wage obligation and actually pay you only $2.13 an hour. However, the employer's offset must not exceed the tips the employee actually receives.

### EXAMPLE

*Alphonse is employed as a waiter and earns more than $10 per hour in tips. Denis, the restaurant's owner, is required to pay Alphonse at least $2.13 per hour on top of his tips for the first 40 hours worked in each week.*

*If business slows and Alphonse's tips dip to, say, $1 an hour, Denis may credit the tip amount toward Alphonse's hourly minimum wage. Denis must pay the additional salary required to make up the full amount of minimum wage Alphonse is owed: $5.15 an hour.*

I am required to carry a beeper 24 hours a day, every day of the week for my job. I am occasionally called on my vacation, holidays and other days off. Am I entitled to be paid anything for on-call time?

Under federal law, vacation days, holidays and other paid days off work should be just that—days off work—and you are entitled to enjoy them free from the reins of your beeper. When your employer requires you to be on-call but does not require you to stay on the company's premises, the following two rules generally apply:

- On-call time that you control and use for your own enjoyment or benefit is not counted as payable time.
- On-call time over which you have little or no control and which you cannot use for your own enjoyment or benefit is payable time.

Disputes usually boil down to the slipperiness in the definition of control and use of time. If the occasional beep beckons you only to call in to give advice, but you are otherwise free to spend your time any way you want, your employer need only pay for the time you spend answering the beeper. However, if your employer insists that you be available to return to work on demand and puts constraints on your behavior between beeper calls—you cannot consume alcohol, or you must stay within a certain radius of work, for example—you may be entitled to compensation for your on-call time.

Similarly, if you receive five or six beeper calls on every day off, and if each of those beeps require you to come into the office or be in a specific place, then a court will likely see that your time isn't your own and will require that your employer compensate you.

And—as always—be sure to check with your state labor department to see if your state has different rules.

## Independent Contractors Are Exempt

The Fair Labor Standards Act covers only employees, not independent contractors, who are considered independent business people. Whether a person is an employee for purposes of the FLSA, however, generally turns on whether that worker is employed by a single employer, and not on the sometimes more lax Internal Revenue Service definition of an independent contractor.

If nearly all of your income comes from one company, a court would probably rule that you are an employee of that company for purposes of the FLSA, regardless of whether other details of your worklife would appear to make you an independent contractor.

The FLSA was passed to clamp down on employers who cheated workers of their fair wages. As a result, employee status is broadly interpreted so that as many workers as possible come within the protections of the law. In recent cases determining close questions of employment status, growing numbers of courts have found workers to be employees rather than independent contractors.

Courts are more likely to find that workers are employees when:

- the relationship appears to be permanent
- the worker lacks bargaining power with regard to the terms of his or her employment, and
- the individual worker is economically dependent upon the business to which he or she gives service.

## What laws ensure my right to take vacations?

Here's a surprising legal truth that most workers would rather not learn: No law requires employers to pay you for time off, such as vacation or holidays. This means that if you receive a paid vacation, it's because of custom, not law.

And just as vacation benefits are discretionary with each employer, so is the policy of how and when they accrue. For example, it is perfectly legal for an employer to require a certain length of employment—six months or a year are common—before an employee is entitled to any vacation time. It is also legal for employers to prorate vacations for part-time employees, or to deny them the benefit completely. Employers are also free to set limits on how much paid

time off employees may store up before it must be taken or is lost.

If your employer does have a policy of offering employees paid time off, however, it cannot discriminate in offering it—all employees must be subject to the same rules.

## If I lose or leave my job, when will I receive my final paycheck?

Unfortunately, there is no easy answer to this question. Many state laws, but not all, mandate that a worker who is fired must be paid all accrued wages and promised vacation pay immediately. Furthermore, state laws often set short limits—generally 72 hours—as the time in which this payment must be made if an employee quits. But you'll need to check with your state's deparment of labor to learn the details of the law that applies to you.

## Am I entitled to take time off from work if I get sick?

No law requires an employer to offer paid time off for illness. As with paid vacation time, however, an employer who offers paid sick time to some workers cannot discriminate by denying it to others.

Though you may not be entitled to paid time off, the Family and Medical Leave Act (FMLA), a federal law passed in 1993, gives workers some rights to unpaid leave for medical reasons. Under the FMLA, you may be eligible for up to 12 weeks of unpaid sick leave during any 12-month period. Your employer can count your accrued paid benefits—vacation, sick leave and personal leave days—toward the 12 weeks of leave allowed under the law. But many employers give employees the option of deciding whether or not to include paid leave time as part of their 12 weeks of sick leave.

The FMLA applies to all private and public employers with 50 or more employees—an estimated one-half of the workforce. To be covered under the law, you must have:

- been employed at the same workplace for a year or more, and
- worked at least 1,250 hours (about 24 hours a week) during the year preceding the leave.

There are a number of loopholes in the FMLA. Companies with fewer than 50 employees working at offices within a 75-mile radius are exempt from the FMLA—this means that small regional companies of even the largest corporations may not need to comply with the Act. The law also allows companies to exempt the highest paid 10% of employees. And finally, schoolteachers and instructors who work for educational agencies and private elementary or secondary schools may have restrictions on their FMLA leave.

Note, however, that a number of states have passed their own versions of family leave laws—and most of them give workers more liberal leave rights. A number of laws apply, for example, to smaller workplaces and

extend to workers who have been on the job only a short time. Check with your state's department of labor for more information.

## What if a member of my family gets sick—can I take time off to care for him or her?

Possibly. Workers' rights under the Family and Medical Leave Act (FMLA)—or under your state's version of it—also apply if a member of your close family gets sick, or if you give birth to or adopt a child. The rights for new parents apply to both mothers and fathers in all situations—birth or adoption.

## My employer refused to grant me the time off for sick leave guaranteed by the FMLA. What can I do?

The FMLA is enforced by the U.S. Department of Labor. If you have specific questions about this law, including how to file a claim against your employer for failing to comply, contact your local Department of Labor office. You should be able to find a listing under U.S. Government, Department of Labor, in the phone book. You can also find a list of local offices of the U.S. Department of Labor by visiting the agency's website at http://www.dol.gov.

You generally must file a claim under the FMLA within two years of an employer's violation. If the violation was willful (intentional), you'll have up to three years to file.

## More Information About Wages, Hours and Time Off

You can check into your employer's wage and payment policies by calling the local U.S. Labor Department, Wage and Hour Division office, listed in the federal government section of your telephone directory.

Most of the exemptions to FLSA coverage are listed in federal statute, 29 U.S.C. §213. The most direct way to become familiar with these exemptions is to read about them in an annotated edition of the U.S. Code, which is what your local law library (or even a large public library) is most likely to have. You can also find this law through Nolo's Legal Research Center at http://www.nolo.com/research/index.html.

Also, the United States Department of Labor, 200 Constitution Avenue, NW, Washington, DC 20210, 202-219-7316, offers pamphlets describing federal wage and hours laws and the Family Medical Leave Act. Or, visit the agency's website at http://www.dol.gov.

# Workplace Health and Safety

Over the past 20 years, workers have pushed strongly for laws to protect their health and safety on the job. And they have been somewhat successful. Several laws now establish basic safety standards aimed at reducing the number of illnesses, injuries and deaths in workplaces. Because most workplace safety laws rely for their effectiveness on employees who are willing to report job hazards, most laws also prevent employers from firing or discriminating against employees who report unsafe conditions to proper authorities.

## Do I have any legal rights if I feel that my workplace is unsafe or unhealthy?

The main federal law covering threats to workplace safety is the Occupational Safety and Health Act of 1970 (OSHA). OSHA requires employers to provide a workplace that is free of dangers that could physically harm employees.

The law quite simply requires that your employer protect you from "recognized hazards" in the workplace. It does not specify or limit the types of dangers covered. Instead, it includes everything from equipment that might cause a serious cut or bruise to the unhealthy effects of long-term exposure to radiation, chemicals or airborne pollutants.

Basically, to prove an OSHA violation, you must produce evidence that:
- your employer failed to keep the workplace free of a hazard, and
- the particular hazard was recognized as being likely to cause death or serious physical injury.

Most states now have their own OSHA laws, most of which offer protections similar to the federal law. State laws typically concentrate on protecting workers who complain about safety violations from being demoted or fired. A few states, including California, require all employers to fashion workplace safety plans. And Texas, big in its approach to most everything, has instituted a 24-hour hotline to receive complaints; the state prohibits employers from discriminating against those who call in.

## How do I assert my rights to a safe workplace?

If you feel that your workplace is unsafe, your first action should be to make your supervisor aware of the danger. If your employer doesn't take prompt action, follow up in writing. Then, if you are still unsuccessful in getting your company to correct the safety hazard, you can file a complaint at the nearest OSHA office. Look under the U.S. Labor Department in the federal government section of your local telephone directory. You can also file a complaint online at http://www.osha.gov/as/opa/worker/index.html.

If you feel that a workplace hazard poses an imminent danger (which is a danger that could immediately cause death or serious physical harm), you should act immediately and call the agency's hotline at 800-321-OSHA.

## Preventing Additional Injuries

Workplace hazards often become obvious only after they cause an injury. For example, an unguarded machine part that spins at high speed may not seem dangerous until someone's clothing or hair becomes caught in it. But even after a worker has been injured, employers sometimes fail—or even refuse—to recognize that something that hurt one person is likely to hurt another.

If you have been injured at work by a hazard that should be eliminated before it injures someone else, take the following steps as quickly as possible after obtaining the proper medical treatment:
- Immediately file a claim for workers' compensation benefits so that your medical bills will be paid and you will be compensated for your lost wages and injury. In some states, the amount you receive from a workers' comp claim will be larger if a violation of a state workplace safety law contributed to your injury. (For more information about workers' compensation, see the next series of questions in this chapter.)

- Point out to your employer that a continuing hazard or dangerous condition exists. As with most workplace safety complaints, the odds of getting action will be greater if other employees join in your complaint.
- If your employer does not eliminate the hazard promptly, file a complaint with OSHA and any state or local agency that you think may be able to help. For example, if your complaint is about hazardous waste disposal, you may be able to track down a specific local group that has been successful in investigating similar complaints in the past.

## Does OSHA protect against the harmful effects of tobacco smoke in the workplace?

OSHA rules apply to tobacco smoke only in rare and extreme circumstances, such as when contaminants created by a manufacturing process combine with tobacco smoke to create a dangerous workplace air supply that fails OSHA standards.

Workplace air quality standards and measurement techniques are so technical that typically only OSHA agents or consultants who specialize in environmental testing are able to determine when the air quality falls below allowable limits.

## If OSHA won't protect me from secondhand tobacco smoke at work, is there anything I can do to limit or avoid exposure?

If your health problems are severely aggravated by co-workers' smoking, there are a number of steps you can take.

*Check local and state laws.* A growing number of local and state laws prohibit smoking in the workplace. Most of them also set out specific procedures for pursuing complaints. Your state's labor department should have up-to-date information about these. If you can't find local laws that prohibit smoking in workplaces, check with a national nonsmokers' rights group, such as Americans for Nonsmokers Rights, 2530 San Pablo Avenue, Suite J, Berkeley, CA 94702, 510-841-3032, http://www.no-smoke.org.

*Ask your employer for an accommodation.* Successful accommodations to smoke-sensitive workers have included installing additional ventilation systems, restricting smoking areas to outside or special rooms and segregating smokers and nonsmokers.

*Consider income replacement programs.*
If you are unable to work out a plan to resolve a serious problem with workplace smoke, you may be forced to leave the workplace. But you may qualify for workers' compensation or unemployment insurance benefits. See *Losing or Leaving Your Job*, below.

### More Information About Workplace Health and Safety

The Occupational Safety and Health Administration, 200 Constitution Avenue, NW, Washington, DC 20210, 202-693-1999, publishes pamphlets about workplace safety laws. You can also visit OSHA online at http://www.osha.gov.

# Workers' Compensation

If you are injured on the job—or suffer a work-related illness or disease that prevents you from working—you are eligible to receive benefits from your state workers' compensation program. You are also entitled to free medical care. If your disability is classified as permanent or results in death, additional benefits are available to you and your family. In exchange for workers' compensation coverage, you—as the worker—lose your right to sue your employer for the injury.

## Who pays workers' compensation benefits?

In most states, employers are required to purchase insurance for their employees from a workers' compensation insurance company—also called an insurance carrier. In some states, larger employers who are clearly solvent are allowed to self-insure or act as their own insurance companies, while smaller companies (with fewer than three or four employees) are not required to carry workers' compensation insurance at all. When a worker is injured, her claim is filed with the insurance company—or self-insuring employer—who pays medical and disability benefits according to a state-approved formula.

## Are all on-the-job injuries covered by workers' compensation?

Most are. The workers' compensation system is designed to provide benefits to injured workers no matter whether an injury is caused by the employer's or employee's negligence. But there are some limits. Generally, injuries caused because an employee is intoxicated or using illegal drugs are not covered by workers' compensation. Coverage may also be denied in situations involving:

- self-inflicted injuries (including those caused by a person who starts a fight)
- injuries suffered while a worker was committing a serious crime
- injuries suffered while an employee was not on the job, and
- injuries suffered when an employee's conduct violated company policy.

## Does an injury have to have a definite date of onset in order to be covered?

Not necessarily. Your injury does not need to be caused by an accident—such as a fall from a ladder. Many workers, for example, receive compensation for repetitive stress injuries, including carpal tunnel syndrome and back problems, that are caused by overuse or misuse over a long period of time. You may also be compensated for some illnesses and diseases that are the gradual result of work conditions—for example, heart conditions, lung disease and stress-related digestive problems.

## Are You Covered by Workers' Compensation?

Most workers are eligible for workers' compensation coverage, but every state excludes some workers. Exclusions often include:

- business owners
- independent contractors
- casual workers
- domestic employees in private homes
- farm workers
- maritime workers
- railroad employees, and
- unpaid volunteers.

Check the workers' compensation law of your state to see whether these exclusions affect you.

Federal government employees are also excluded from state workers' compensation coverage, but they receive workers' compensation benefits under a separate federal law.

Employees who aren't covered by workers' compensation usually must sue the employer for damages or, in some cases, they can sue the maker of a faulty piece of equipment.

## Do I have to be injured at my workplace to be covered by workers' compensation?

No. As long as your injury is job-related, it's covered. For example, you'll be covered if you are injured while traveling on business, doing a work-related errand or even attending a required, business-related social function.

## How do I claim workers' compensation benefits?

First, promptly report the work-related injury or sickness to your employer. Most states require that this be done within two to 30 days following an injury. If an injury occurs over time (for example, a breathing problem or carpal tunnel syndrome), you must report your condition soon after you discover it and realize that it is caused by your work.

Next, get the medical treatment you need and follow the doctor's instructions exactly. (This may include an "off-work order" or a "limited-duties work order.") Finally, file a claim with your workers' compensation carrier. Necessary forms must be provided by your employer. Ask someone in the personnel or benefits department.

Finally, make sure you save copies of all correspondence with your employer, its insurance carrier and your doctor concerning your workers' compensation claim.

## What kind of benefits will I receive?

The workers' compensation system provides replacement income, medical expenses and sometimes vocational rehabilitation benefits—that is, on the job training, schooling or job placement assistance. The benefits paid through workers' compensation, however, are almost always limited to relatively modest amounts.

If you become temporarily unable to work, you'll usually receive two-thirds of your average wage up to a fixed ceiling. But because these payments are tax-free, if you received decent wages prior to your injury, you'll fare reasonably well in most states. You will be eligible for these wage-loss replacement benefits as soon as you've lost a few days of work because of an injury or illness that is covered by workers' compensation.

If you become permanently unable to do the work you were doing prior to the injury, or unable to do any work at all, you may be eligible to receive long-term or lump-sum benefits. The amount of the payment you may be entitled to receive varies greatly with the nature and extent of your injuries. If you anticipate a permanent work disability, contact your local workers' compensation office as soon as possible; these benefits are rather complex and may take a while to process.

## Social Security Benefits for the Permanently Disabled

If you're permanently unable to return to work, you may qualify for Social Security Disability benefits. Social Security will, over the long run, provide more benefits than workers' compensation—but be forewarned that these benefits are hard to get. They are reserved for seriously injured workers. To qualify, your injury or illness:

- must prevent you from doing any "substantial gainful work," and
- must be expected to last at least twelve months, or to result in death.

If you think you may meet the above requirements, contact your local Social Security office. For more information about Social Security benefits, see Chapter 14.

## Can I be treated by my own doctor and, if not, can I trust a doctor provided by my employer?

In some states, you have a right to see your own doctor if you make this request in writing before the injury occurs. More typically, however, injured workers are referred to a doctor or health plan recruited and paid for by their employer.

Your doctor's report will have a big impact upon the benefits you receive. While it's crucial that you tell the doctor the truth about both your injury and your medical history (your benefits may be denied based on fraud if you don't), be sure to clearly identify all possible job-related medical problems and sources of pain. In short, this is no time to downplay or gloss over the presence of a pain.

Keep in mind that a doctor paid for by your employer's insurance company is not your friend. The desire to get future business may motivate a doctor to minimize the seriousness of your injury or to identify it as a pre-existing condition. For example, if you injure your back and the doctor asks you if you have ever had back problems before, it would be unwise to treat the doctor to a 20-year history of every time you suffered a minor pain or ache. Just say "no" unless you really have suffered a significant previous injury or chronic condition.

## If I am initially treated by an insurance company doctor, do I have a right to see my own doctor at some point?

State workers' compensation systems establish technical and often tricky rules in this area. Often, you have the right to ask for another doctor at the insurance company's expense if you clearly state you don't like the one the insurance company provides, although there is sometimes a waiting period before you can get a second doctor. Also, if your injury is serious, you usually have the right to a second opinion. And in some states, after you are treated by an insurance company's doctor for a certain period (90 days is typical), you may have the automatic right to transfer your treatment to your own doctor or health plan—with the cost being paid for by the workers' comp insurance company.

To understand your rights, get a copy of your state's rules—or, if necessary, research your state workers' compensation laws and regulations in the law library. Chapter 19 contains information about how to do your own legal research.

## Suppose I suffer an injury to a part of my body that had been injured previously—will I still be covered?

If the previous injury was also work-related, workers' compensation should provide full coverage. If it wasn't, you may receive lower-level benefits.

If your earlier injury occurred at a former job, it's generally up to your current employer's insurance company and your former employer to sort out who's responsible for paying your benefits—sometimes they will split the costs between them.

## How do I find a good workers' compensation lawyer—and how much will it cost?

You usually don't need a lawyer unless you suffer a permanent disability, or all or part of your workers' compensation claim is denied. If one of these situations occurs, you'll probably want to do some research to familiarize yourself with your rights and duties. For example, many claims are denied based on a doctor's report claiming that you are not injured. If you dispute this, you may have a right to obtain a second doctor's opinion paid for by the workers' compensation insurer.

If your claim is denied, consider hiring an experienced workers' compensation lawyer to help you navigate the appeals process. The best way to find a good lawyer is often through word of mouth—talk to other injured workers or check with a local union or other workers' organization.

In most states, fees for legal representation in workers' compensation cases are limited to between 10% and 15% of any eventual award. Because these fees are relatively modest, workers' compensation lawyers customarily take on many clients and, as a result, do not have time to provide much individual attention. Most of your contacts with your attorney's office

will be with paralegals and other support personnel. This is not a bad thing in itself, if the office is well run by support staff. Be sure that the office is able to stay on top of paperwork and filing deadlines, and that a knowledgeable person is available to answer your questions clearly and promptly.

## What to Do When the Insurance Company Won't Pay

Some workers' compensation carriers take an aggressive stance and deny legitimate claims for workers' compensation. When this happens, it's often because the insurer claims you haven't been injured or, if you have, that it's not serious enough to qualify you for temporary or total disability. Commonly, this is done after a private investigator hired by the insurance company follows you and obtains photographs showing you engaging in fairly strenuous physical activity, such as lifting a box or mowing the lawn, despite claiming a back injury.

If your legitimate benefits are denied, you should immediately file an appeal with your state appeals agency—called the industrial accidents board, the workers' compensation appeals board or something similar. You may also want to hire an attorney to help you press your claim.

## If I receive workers' compensation, can I also sue my employer in court?

Generally, no. The workers' compensation system was established as part of a legal trade-off. In exchange for giving up the right to sue an employer in court, you get workers' compensation benefits no matter who was at fault. Before the workers' compensation system was passed, if you went to court, you stood to recover a large amount of money, but only if you could prove the injury was caused by your employer.

Today, you may be able to sue in court if your injury was caused by someone other than your employer (a visitor or outside contractor, for example) or if it was caused by a defective product (such as a flaw in the construction of the equipment you were working with).

## What if my employer tells me not to file a workers' compensation claim or threatens to fire me if I do?

In most states, it is a violation of the workers' compensation laws to retaliate against an employee for filing a workers' compensation claim. If this happens, immediately report it to your local workers' compensation office.

### More Information About Workers' Compensation

*How to Handle Your Workers' Compensation Claim*, by Christopher Ball (Nolo), includes all forms and instructions for filing a workers' compensation claim in California. The book is also useful for people who live elsewhere, given the absence of self-help resources for other states; it provides a good overview of how the system works.

# Age Discrimination

*Young men think old men are fools, but old men* know *young men are fools.*

**—GEORGE CHAPMAN**

Unfortunately, rather than value older workers' intelligence, experience and work ethic, some employers assume that older workers are "out of touch" or set in their ways. And, because older workers often earn higher salaries and have higher healthcare premiums than younger workers, some employers think they are too "expensive." For these reasons, some employers try to get rid of their more seasoned workers and are reluctant to hire older workers.

Fortunately, federal and state laws afford some protection to older workers who face discrimination in the workplace—and also help protect their pension rights when they leave.

## My employer has just cut the workforce in half, singling out older workers. Is there any legal protection for us?

Possibly. The federal Age Discrimination in Employment Act (ADEA) provides that workers over the age of 40 cannot be arbitrarily discriminated against because of age in any employment decision. Perhaps the single most important rule under the ADEA is that no worker can be forced to retire.

Under the ADEA, there has to be a valid reason—not related to age—for all employment decisions, especially lay-offs. Examples of valid reasons would be poor job performance by the employee or an employer's economic trouble. If lay-offs have been announced or are in the wind, talk with other affected workers. If most people who are laid off are 40 or older, and the majority of workers kept on are younger, you may have the basis for an ADEA complaint or lawsuit. This is especially likely if the employer has hired younger workers to take the places of workers over 40.

## Does the ADEA protect all workers from age discrimination?

Unfortunately not; there are limits on both the employees and the employers who are covered. The ADEA applies only to employees age 40 and older—and only to workplaces with 20 or more employees. The ADEA applies to federal employees, private sector employees and labor union employees. It does not, however, cover state employees.

There are several other exceptions to the broad protection of the ADEA:

- Executives or people "in high policy-making positions" can be forced to retire at age 65 if they would receive annual retirement pension benefits worth $44,000 or more.

- There are special exceptions for police and fire personnel, tenured university faculty and certain federal employees having to do with law enforcement and air traffic control. If you are in one of these categories, check with your personnel office or benefits plan office for details.

- An additional exception to the federal age discrimination law is made when age is an essential part of a particular job—referred to by the legal jargon of a "bona fide occupational qualification" (BFOQ). For example, if an employer who sets age limits on a particular job can prove that the limit is necessary because a worker's ability to adequately perform the particular job does, in fact, diminish after the age limit is reached, it's okay to discriminate. However, it has become more difficult for employers to prove a BFOQ because the law protects workers as young as age 40.

## If I'm not protected by the ADEA, is an employer free to discriminate against me because of my age?

That depends on where you live. All states except Alabama and South Dakota have laws against age discrimination in employment, and those state laws often provide greater protection than the federal law. For example, several states provide age discrimination protection to workers before they reach age 40, and other states protect against the actions of employers with fewer than 20 employees. In addition, state laws against age discrimination do protect state employees, unlike the federal ADEA.

To find out more about the laws of your own state, contact your state labor department.

## I've noticed a pattern where I work: Older workers tend to be laid off just before their pension rights lock in or vest. Is that legal?

Using various ploys like this one to cheat workers out of their promised pensions is a technique some employers use to save money. But it's not legal. The federal Older Workers Benefit Protection Act forbids

- using an employee's age as the basis for discrimination in benefits, and
- targeting older workers for their staff cutting programs.

## Can my employer force me to take early retirement?

No employer can require you to retire because of your age. An early retirement plan is legal only if it gives you a choice between two options: keeping things as they are or choosing to retire under a plan that leaves you better off than you previously were. This choice must be a genuine one; you must be free to reject the offer. In addition, if either choice leaves you worse off, the offer violates the Older Workers Benefit Protection Act.

## How can I enforce my rights under the laws that protect against age discrimination?

If you believe that an employer has discriminated against you because of your age, you can file a complaint with the federal Equal Employment Opportunity Commission (EEOC) just as you would against any other workplace discrimination. Call 800-669-4000 to find the EEOC office nearest you. You can also find a list of EEOC regional offices on the agency's website at http://www.eeoc.gov. If the EEOC does not resolve your complaint to your satisfaction, you can consult an attorney for advice about filing a lawsuit.

In addition, you can file a complaint under your state age discrimination law, if your state has one. Contact your state labor department or fair employment office for details.

Like all fair employment laws, age discrimination laws require you to file a complaint within a specified amount of time, usually 180 days. Therefore, it is important for you to act as soon as you realize that you might be the victim of age discrimination. If you wait too long, you might lose your rights.

## Out From Under the Golden Parachute

A growing number of employers ask older workers to sign waivers—also called releases or agreements not to sue. In return for signing the waivers, the employer offers the employee an incentive to leave the job voluntarily, such as a significant amount of severance pay. The Older Workers Benefit Protection Act places a number of restrictions on such waivers:

- Your employer must make the waiver understandable to the people who are likely to use it.

- The waiver may not cover any rights or claims that you discover are available after you sign it, and it must specify that it covers your rights under the ADEA.
- Your employer must offer you something of value (such as severance pay)—over and above what is already owed to you—in exchange for your signature on the waiver.
- Your employer must advise you, in writing, that you have the right to consult an attorney before you sign the waiver.
- If the offer is being made to a group or class of employees, your employer must inform you in writing how the class of employees is defined; the job titles and ages of all the individuals to whom the offer is being made; and the ages of all the employees in the same job classification or unit of the company to whom the offer is not being made.
- You must be given a fixed time in which to make a decision on whether or not to sign the waiver.

### More Information About Age Discrimination

Several organizations offer help and information on age discrimination in employment. Among the most helpful are:

American Association of Retired Persons
601 E Street, NW
Washington, DC  20049
800-424-3410
http://www.aarp.org

AARP is a nonprofit membership organization of older Americans open to anyone age 50 or older. It offers a wide range of publications on retirement planning, age discrimination and employment-related topics. Networking and direct services are available through local chapters.

Older Women's League
666 Eleventh Street, NW, Suite 700
Washington, DC 20001
202-783-6686

The Older Women's League provides advice on discrimination and other issues facing elderly men and women.

# Sexual Harassment

Sexual harassment on the job took a dramatic leap into public awareness in October 1991, when Professor Anita Hill made known her charges against Judge Clarence Thomas after his nomination to the U.S. Supreme Court. Many other incidents have erupted since then, including investigations into the Navy after the Tailhook incident and into government officials after Senator Bob Packwood was accused of harassing several female staffers. Paula Jones dominated headlines for months with her claim that President Clinton harassed her while a conventioneering governor. And more recently, Mitsubishi Motors agreed to pay a record $34 million settlement to hundreds of women harassed at its auto assembly plant.

Enforcement of the laws prohibiting sexual harassment has been stepped up in the last few years. But in workplaces across America, the issue is far from settled. Sexual harassment is still a daily problem for many workers, especially women.

## What is sexual harassment?

In legal terms, sexual harassment is any unwelcome sexual advance or conduct on the job that creates an intimidating, hostile or offensive working environment. In real life, sexually harassing behavior ranges from repeated offensive or belittling jokes to a workplace full of offensive pornography to an outright sexual assault.

## Are there laws that protect against sexual harassment on the job?

Yes. But surprisingly, those laws are fairly new. In 1980, the Equal Employment Opportunity Commission (EEOC) issued regulations defining sexual harassment and stating it was a form of sex discrimination prohibited by the Civil Rights Act, which had been originally passed in 1964. In 1986, the U.S. Supreme Court first ruled that sexual harassment was a form of job discrimination—and held it to be illegal.

Today, there is greater understanding that the Civil Rights Act prohibits sexual harassment at work. In addition, most states have their own fair employment practices laws that prohibit sexual harassment—many of them more strict than the federal law.

To find out more about the federal prohibition against sexual harassment, contact the EEOC office nearest you. For a list of EEOC regional offices, call the main EEOC office at 800-669-4000 or refer to the agency's website at http://www.eeoc.gov.

To learn more about state laws prohibiting sexual harassment, contact your state labor department or state fair employment office. In addition, your local EEOC office should be able to give you information about the laws in your state.

## Can a man be sexually harassed?

Yes, a man can be sexually harassed. The laws prohibiting sexual harassment on the job protect all workers, male and female, from being harassed on the basis of their gender.

But in the overwhelming majority of cases of sexual harassment, it's a male co-worker or supervisor who is harassing a female worker. No one is sure why this is so. Socialization probably plays a part: Men are more likely than women to find sexual advances flattering, women more likely to be perceived as the gatekeepers of sexual conduct. Economics probably enter, too. There are simply more women in the workforce than ever before—and at least some male workers feel the influx as a threat to their own livelihoods. Finally, sexual harassment is usually a power ploy, a way to keep some workers in lower-paid, less respected positions—or force them out of the workplace altogether.

## Are gays and lesbians protected by the laws against sexual harassment?

Whether federal civil rights laws protect gays and lesbians is a hot question these days. The U.S. Supreme Court has not addressed the issue, so there is no definitive word on whether gays and lesbians can find shelter under the federal prohibition against sexual harassment in the workplace. A number of lower federal courts have considered the issue, however, and they have proven to be quite hostile to the protection of gays and lesbians.

If you are gay or lesbian, you might find protection under a state law or a local ordinance. In addition, you might live in an area where the federal courts are more receptive to granting protection. To find out about what laws might protect you in your geographical area, contact the Lambda Legal Defense and Education Fund at 202-809-8585 or http://www.lambdalegal.org.

## I'm being sexually harassed at work. What is the first thing should I do?

Tell the harasser to stop. Surprisingly often—some experts say up to 90% of the time—this works.

When confronted directly, harassment is especially likely to end if it is at a fairly low level: off-color jokes, inappropriate comments about your appearance, tacky cartoons tacked onto the office refrigerator or repeated requests for dates after you have said no.

But clearly saying you want the offensive behavior to stop does more than let the harasser know that the behavior is unwelcome. It is also a crucial first step if you later decide to take more formal action against the harasser, whether through your company's complaint procedure or through the legal system. And be sure to document what's going on by keeping a diary or journal; your case will be stronger if you can later prove that the harassment continued after you confronted the harasser.

## What if the harassment doesn't stop even after I've confronted the harasser?

If confronting the harasser doesn't work, complain, complain, complain. Talk to your supervisor. Talk to the harasser's supervisor. If that doesn't work, talk to their supervisors, and so on. If your company has a complaint procedure in place, follow it. If your company has a human resources department, talk to someone there. And every step of the way, document your complaints. Save copies of all letters and e-mails. Take notes of all conversations. You have a right to a work environment free of sexual harassment, and you must be assertive about making that right work for you.

Of course, there will be times when you are afraid to complain about harassment, perhaps because the harasser is your supervisor or because the harasser has made threats against you. The laws against sexual harassment prohibit your employer from retaliating against you for complaining about sexual harassment. Although this fact might be cold comfort if you fear for

your job or your safety, the fact is that the law can protect you only if you let someone with power at your workplace know about your problem. Be creative. If your supervisor is the one harassing you, go to his supervisor or go to a supervisor in another department.

Collect as much detailed evidence as possible about the harassment. Be sure to save any offensive letters, photographs, cards or notes you receive. And if you were made to feel uncomfortable because of jokes, pin-ups or cartoons posted at work, confiscate them—or at least make copies. An anonymous, obnoxious photo or joke posted on a bulletin board is not anyone else's personal property, so you are free to take it down and keep it as evidence. If that's not possible, photograph the workplace walls. Note the dates the offensive material was posted—and whether there were hostile reactions when you took it down or asked another person to do so.

Also, keep a detailed journal. Write down the specifics of everything that feels like harassment. Include the names of everyone involved, what happened, and where and when it took place. If anyone else saw or heard the harassment, note that as well. Be as specific as possible about what was said and done—and how it affected you, your health or your job performance.

If your employer has conducted periodic evaluations of your work, make sure you have copies. In fact, you may want to ask for a copy of your entire personnel file—before you tip your hand that you are considering taking action against a harassing co-worker. Your records will be particularly persuasive evidence if your evaluations have been good but after you complain, your employer retaliates by trying to transfer or fire you, claiming poor job performance.

## If You're Afraid of Offending

The super-cautious advice—don't talk with co-workers about anything but business—is surely overkill. The better approach is to use common sense. There is plenty of room to be friendly and personable without behaving in a way that is likely to offend workers of either gender.

Some rough guides for evaluating your own workplace behavior:

- If you wouldn't say or do something in front of your spouse or parents, it's probably a poor idea to say or do it at work.
- Would you say or do it in front of a colleague of the same gender?
- How would you feel if your mother, wife, sister or daughter were subjected to the same words or behavior?
- How would you feel if a co-worker said or did the same things to you?
- Does it need to be said or done at all?

If you are truly concerned that your words or conduct may be offensive to a co-worker, there is one surefire way to find out: ask.

## If the harassment still doesn't stop, what are my options short of filing a lawsuit or a complaint with a government agency?

If the harasser has ignored your oral requests to stop, or you are uncomfortable making the request, write a succint letter demanding an end to the behavior. If that doesn't end the harassment, you may want to take more forceful action. Consider giving a copy of your letter to the harasser's supervisor—along with a memo explaining that the behavior has become more outrageous.

If the harassment still does not abate—or if you believe the supervisor is sympathetic to the harassment or the harasser—send the letter to the next-ranked worker or official at your workplace. Include a cover letter in which you offer your own remedy for the situation—something realistic that might help end the discomfort, such as transferring the harasser to a more distant worksite. If it's your own supervisor who has been harassing you, consider asking to be assigned a different supervisor.

These days, most workplaces have specific written policies prohibiting sexual harassment. If you have followed the steps that seem reasonable to you but the harassment continues, your next option is to pursue any procedure your company has established for handling harassment.

## What legal steps can I take to end the harassment?

If all investigation and settlement attempts fail to produce satisfactory results, one option is to file a civil lawsuit for damages either under the federal Civil Rights Act or under a state fair employment practices statute.

Even if you intend right from the beginning to file such a lawsuit, you sometimes must first file a claim with a government agency. For example, an employee pursuing a claim under the Civil Rights Act must first file a claim with the federal EEOC, and a similar complaint procedure is required under some state laws. The EEOC or state agency may decide to prosecute your case on its own, but that happens only occasionally.

More commonly, at some point, the agency will issue you a document referred to as a "right-to-sue" letter that allows you to take your case to court. When filing an action for sexual harassment, you will almost always need to hire a lawyer for help.

***More Information About Sexual Harassment***

*Sexual Harassment on the Job*, by William Petrocelli and Barbara Kate Repa (Nolo), explains what sexual harassment is and how to stop it.

9to5, National Association of Working Women
614 Superior Avenue, NW
Cleveland, OH 44113
216-566-9308 (general information)
800-522-0925 (hotline)
http://www.9to5.org

9to5 is a national nonprofit membership organization for working women. It provides counseling, information and referrals for problems on the job, including family leave, pregnancy disability, termination, compensation and sexual harassment. 9to5 also offers a newsletter and publications. There are local chapters throughout the country.

# Disability Discrimination

Many individuals fortunate enough to be healthy in mind and body—and to be employed—lament the difficulties a workplace can impose. But for those with physical or mental disabilities, many workplaces can be truly daunting. Fortunately, the federal Americans with Disabilities Act (ADA), has helped to level the playing field a bit.

## What laws protect disabled workers from workplace discrimination?

The Americans with Disabilities Act (ADA) prohibits employment discrimination on the basis of workers' disabilities. Generally, the ADA prohibits employers from:

- discriminating on the basis of virtually any physical or mental disability
- asking job applicants questions about their past or current medical conditions
- requiring job applicants to take medical exams, and
- creating or maintaining worksites that include substantial physical barriers to the movement of people with physical disabilities.

The ADA covers companies with 15 or more employees. Its coverage broadly extends to private employers, employment agencies and labor organizations. A precursor of the ADA, the Vocational Rehabilitation Act, prohibits discrimination against disabled workers in state and federal government.

In addition, many state laws protect against discrimination based on physical or mental disability.

## Exactly whom does the ADA protect?

The ADA's protections extend to disabled workers—defined as people who:

- have a physical or mental impairment that substantially limits a major life activity
- have a record of impairment, or
- are regarded as having an impairment.

An impairment includes physical disorders, such as cosmetic disfigurement or loss of a limb, as well as mental and psychological disorders.

The ADA protects job applicants and employees who, although disabled as defined above, are still qualified for a particular job. In other words, they would be able to perform the essential functions of a job with some form of accommodation, such as wheelchair access, a voice-activated computer or a customized workspace. As with other workers, whether a disabled worker is deemed qualified for a given job depends on whether he or she has appropriate skill, experience, training or education for the position.

## If I am disabled, how do I get my employer to accommodate my disability?

The first step is simple, but often skipped: Ask. The ADA places the burden on you, the employee, to inform the employer that you have a disability and that you need an accommodation for it. Indeed, the ADA forbids employers from asking employees whether they have a disability.

When you ask for an accommodation, you do not need to use formal legal language or even do it in writing (though it's always a good idea to document your request). Just tell your employer what your disability is and why you need an accommodation. If you aren't comfortable going to your employer and making this request yourself, you can ask a friend, family member, or representative to do it for you.

Once you request the accommodation, your employer should engage in an informal process of determining whether it can accommodate you and, if so, how. Remember that your employer may be concerned about cost or worried that other employees may incorrectly view you as getting "special treatment." The more helpful and understanding you can be during this process, the more likely it is that your employer will find a way to accommodate you.

As part of this process, your employer is allowed to ask you for documentation, or proof, of your disability. It is important that you comply with this request to the best of your ability; if you don't, then you will lose your right to an accommodation.

If an accommodation is not "reasonable" (see below for more explanation), your employer does not have to provide it. Nor does your employer have to provide you with the accommodation that you want, as long as it provides another one that is effective.

You don't have to accept a particular accommodation, but be prepared to defend your choice on the grounds that the accommodation isn't effective. If a court decides that the offered accommodation was reasonable, you may no longer be qualified for the job, and your employer can terminate you.

## Accommodations Don't Need to Cost a Bundle

According to ergonomic and job accommodation experts, the cost of accommodating a particular worker's disability is often surprisingly low.

- 31% of accommodations cost nothing.
- 50% cost less than $50.
- 69% cost less than $500.
- 88% cost less than $1,000.

The Job Accommodation Network (JAN), which provides information about how to accommodate people with disabilities, gives the following examples of inexpensive accommodations:

- Glare on a computer screen caused an employee with an eye disorder to get eye fatigue. The problem was solved with a $39 antiglare screen.
- A deaf medical technician couldn't hear the buzz of a timer, which was necessary for laboratory tests. The problem was solved with an indicator light at a cost of $26.95.

To contact JAN, call 1-800-526-7234 or visit its website at http://www.janweb.icdi.wvu.edu.

### How can I tell if a particular accommodation offered by my employer is reasonable?

The ADA points to several specific accommodations that are likely to be deemed reasonable—some of them changes to the physical set-up of the workplace, some of them changes to how or when work is done. They include:

- making existing facilities usable by disabled employees—for example, by modifying the height of desks and equipment, installing computer screen magnifiers or installing telecommunications devices for the deaf
- restructuring jobs—for example, allowing a ten-hour/four-day workweek so that a worker can receive weekly medical treatments
- modifying exams and training materials—for example, allowing more time for taking an exam, or allowing it to be taken orally instead of in writing
- providing a reasonable amount of additional unpaid leave for medical treatment
- hiring readers or interpreters to assist an employee, and
- providing temporary workplace specialists to assist in training.

These are just a few possible accommodations. The possibilities are limited only by an employee's and employer's imaginations—and the reality that might make one or more of these accommodations financially impossible in a particular workplace.

## When can an employer legally claim that a particular accommodation is simply not feasible?

The ADA does not require employers to make accommodations that would cause them an undue hardship—a weighty concept defined in the ADA only as "an action requiring significant difficulty or expense."

The Equal Employment Opportunity Commission (EEOC), the federal agency responsible for enforcing the ADA, has set out some of the factors that will determine whether a particular accommodation presents an undue hardship on a particular employer:
- the nature and cost of the accommodation
- the financial resources of the employer (a large employer may be expected to foot a larger bill than a mom-and-pop business)
- the nature of the business (including size, composition and structure of the workforce), and
- accommodation costs already incurred in the workplace.

It is not easy for employers to prove that an accommodation is an undue hardship, as financial difficulty alone is not usually sufficient. Courts will look at other sources of money, including tax credits and deductions available for making some accommodations, as well as the disabled employee's willingness to pay for all or part of the costs.

## Taking Action Under the ADA

The ADA is enforced by the Equal Employment Opportunity Commission (EEOC). To start an investigation of your claim, file a complaint at the local EEOC office. Call 800-669-4000 to find the office nearest you. Or refer to the agency's website at http://www.eeoc.gov.

If you live in a state with laws that protect workers against discrimination based on physical or mental disability, you can choose to file a complaint under your state's law, the ADA or both. To find out about state laws, contact your state labor department or fair employment office.

For additional information on the ADA, contact:

Office of the Americans
with Disabilities Act
Civil Rights Division
U.S. Department of Justice
P.O. Box 66118
Washington, DC 20035-6118
Hotline:
800-514-0301 (voice)
800-514-0383 (TTY)
http://www.usdoj.gov/
crt/ada/adahom1.htm

# Losing or Leaving Your Job

*Nothing is really work unless you would rather be doing something else.*

—SIR JAMES A. BARRIE

The possibility of being laid off or fired looms large in the list of fears of most workers. Employers have traditionally had a free hand to hire and fire, but a number of recent laws and legal rulings restrict these rights.

## For what reasons can I be fired?

Unfortunately, the answer to this question is: "It depends." Generally, the reasons for which you can be fired depend in large part on whether you have a contract for employment.

Determining whether you have an employment contract can be tricky. A contract can be oral or written, express or implied. Sometimes, a contract is a document labeled "Contract for Employment" that has a number of provisions and that is signed by you and your employer. Other times, it is an oral promise that your employer makes to you when you are hired that you will only be fired if you perform your job incompetently. Still other times, it is something that is implied from the peculiar circumstances of your employment, such as the amount of time you have worked for your employer, the way that your employer has treated other employees and provisions in your employee handbook.

If you do have a contract for employment, that generally (but not always) means that you can be fired only for "good cause," a legal concept that includes such things as incompetence, excessive absences and violation of work rules.

If you don't have a contract for employment (which is likely since the majority of employees in this country do not have employment contracts), then your employer can terminate you for any reason that isn't illegal (see below). For example, your employer can terminate you simply because she doesn't like you or because your work style does not fit in with the company or because you and your supervisor disagree too much on how your job should be done. Be aware, however, that sometimes these sorts of superficial reasons, such as "I just didn't like her" or "She didn't fit in with the rest of the office," can mask the real reason behind the termination, which is an illegal one.

Whether or not you have an employment contract, the law does place limits on your employer's ability to fire you. For example, employers do not have the right to discriminate against you illegally or to violate state or federal laws, such as those controlling wages and hours. Most state discrimination laws are quite broad. In addition to protecting against the traditional forms of discrimination

based on race, color, religion, national origin and age, many also protect against discrimination based on sexual orientation, physical and mental disability, marital status and receiving public funds.

Separate state laws protect workers from being fired or demoted for taking advantage of laws protecting them from discrimination and unsafe workplace practices. And there are a number of other more complex reasons that may make it illegal for an employer to fire you—all boiling down to the fact that an employer must deal with you fairly and honestly.

## I've just received a warning from my employer, and I suspect I will be fired soon. What should I do?

If you find yourself on the receiving end of a disciplinary notice you consider to be unfair, there are several steps you should take to avoid losing your job.

First, be sure you understand exactly what work behavior is being challenged. Check your company handbook to see if there is a clear policy against what you've done. If you are unclear, ask for a meeting with your supervisor or human resources staff to discuss the issue more thoroughly.

If you think that there might be some truth to what you are told, find out what you can do to improve the situation. Arrange a meeting with your supervisor and ask her what you can do to improve. Or you can make your own suggestions. For example, if your employer is unhappy with your performance, consider requesting training or educational materials. If your employer thinks that you talk too much on company time, ask to move your workstation to a place where you won't be quite so tempted to talk. Make sure you document any meeting or communication with your supervisor regarding the discipline, your performance and strategies you can pursue to improve.

If you disagree with allegations that your work performance or behavior is poor, you may want to ask for the assessment in writing. You can then write a clarification and ask that it be inserted in your personnel file. But do this only if you feel your employer's assessment is clearly inaccurate; otherwise you may risk escalating a minor verbal reprimand into a more major incident that will be permanently recorded in your file. Before you sit down to write, take some time to reflect and perhaps discuss your situation with friends.

If you think you are likely to be fired, see if any policy in the employee handbook will buy you time—for example, the right to file an appeal—so the controversy can die down and, if necessary, you can change your work habits.

Finally, read between the lines to see whether your employer's action may be discriminatory or in other ways unfair. Look particularly at the timing. For example, if you were let go shortly before your rights in the company pension plan were permanently locked in or vested, the company may be guilty of age discrimina-

tion. Look also at uneven applications of discipline: Are women more often given substandard performance reviews or fired before they could be elevated to supervisor?

## What can I do to protect any legal rights I might have before leaving my job?

Even if you decide not to challenge the legality of your firing, you will be in a much better position to enforce all of your workplace rights if you keep careful written records of everything that happens. For example, if you apply for unemployment insurance benefits and your former employer challenges that application, you will probably need to prove that you were dismissed for reasons that were not related to your misconduct.

There are a number of ways to document events. The easiest is to keep an employment diary where you record and date each significant work-related event such as performance reviews, commendations or reprimands, salary increases or decreases and even informal comments your supervisor makes to you about your work. Note the date, time and location for each event, which members of management were involved and whether or not witnesses were present. Whenever possible, back up your log with materials issued by your employer, such as copies of the employee handbook, memos, brochures, employee orientation videos and any written evaluations, commendations or criticisms of your work. In addition, if a problem develops, ask to see your personnel file and make a copy of all reports and reviews in it.

## Am I entitled to severance pay if I'm fired?

No law requires an employer to provide severance pay. Nevertheless, some employers voluntarily offer one or two months' salary to employees who are laid off. A few are more generous to long-term employees, basing severance pay on a formula such as one month's pay for every year an employee worked for the company.

An employer may be legally obligated to give you some severance pay if you were promised it, as evidenced by:

- a written contract stating that severance will be paid
- a promise in an employee handbook of severance pay
- a long history of the company paying severance to other employees in your position, or
- an oral promise to pay you severance—although you may run into difficulties proving the promise existed.

## My biggest concern about losing my job is losing health insurance coverage. Do I have any rights?

Ironically, workers have more rights to health insurance coverage after they lose their jobs than while employed. This is because of a 1986 law, the Consolidated Omnibus Budget Reconciliation Act (COBRA). Under COBRA, employers with 20 or more employees must offer them the option of continuing to be covered by the company's group health insurance plan at the workers' own expense for a specific period—often 18 months—

after employment ends. Family coverage is also included. In some other circumstances, such as the death of the employee, that employee's dependents can continue coverage for up to 36 months.

Another federal law, the Health Insurance Act, makes it easier for employees to change jobs without the fear of losing insurance coverage—and makes it easier for many employees to get coverage in the first place. The law imposes some restrictions on group health plans, including HMOs. Under this law:

- Employees with preexisting conditions may not be denied coverage under a new health insurance plan if they have been continuously covered for 12 months under another plan. Employees who do not have this prior coverage may be denied coverage based on a preexisting condition for only one year.
- No group health plan may discriminate in eligibility for coverage or premiums based on health status, physical or mental condition, claims experience, receipt of healthcare, medical history, genetic information, evidence of insurability or disability of the individual or dependents seeking coverage.

# Getting Money When You're Out of Work

If you've lost your job, you may be desperately seeking income. It's best to act quickly to apply for unemployment and other possible benefits, as there is often a delay—in a few states, as long as six weeks—between the time you apply and the date on which you actually receive a check.

Here is a brief breakdown of what is covered by each of the three major income replacement programs.

**Unemployment insurance.** This program may provide some financial help if you lose your job, temporarily or permanently, through no fault of your own. Benefits will be less than your former pay and temporary—often lasting for about 26 weeks.

**Workers' compensation.** When you cannot work because of a work-related injury or illness, this program is designed to provide you with prompt replacement income. It may also pay the medical bills resulting from a workplace injury or illness; compensate you for a permanent injury, such as the loss of a limb; and provide death benefits to the survivors of workers who die from a workplace injury or illness. For more information, see the questions and answers on workers' compensation that appear earlier in this chapter.

**Social Security disability insurance.** This is intended to provide income to adults who, because of injury or illness, cannot work for at least 12 months. Unlike the workers' compensation program,

it does not require that your disability be caused by a workplace injury or illness.

Also consider possible income from a private disability insurance program if you were paying for it through payroll withholdings, or if your employer paid for such premiums.

In addition, a few states offer disability benefits as part of their unemployment insurance programs. Typical program requirements mandate that you submit your medical records and show that you requested a leave of absence from your employer. Some may also require proof that you intend to return to your job when you recover. Call the local unemployment insurance and workers' compensation insurance offices to determine whether your state is one that maintains this kind of coverage.

**http://www.nolo.com**
*Nolo offers self-help information about a wide variety of legal topics, including workplace rights.*

**http://www.eeoc.gov**
*The U.S. Equal Employment Opportunity Commission is the federal agency responsible for enforcing federal fair employment laws, including Title VII (which outlaws discrimination in employment based on*

race, gender, religion and national origin), the Equal Pay Act, the Age Discrimination in Employment Act and the Americans with Disabilities Act. The agency's website is a gold mine of information about these fair employment laws. Among other things, it includes information on your workplace rights, the text of the fair employment laws and instructions on how to file a charge against your employer.

### http://www.dol.gov

The U.S. Department of Labor enforces many of the laws that govern your relationship with your employer, including wage and hour laws, health and safety laws and benefits laws. This website offers information about your rights under all of the laws enforced by the department, and it contains links to state labor department websites.

### http://www.law.cornell.edu

The Legal Information Institute at Cornell Law School provides information about discrimination in the workplace, including relevant codes and regulations.

### http://www.ahipubs.com

The Alexander Hamilton Institute serves up common sense packaged as FAQs about many aspects of employment, from benefits to safety and health concerns. The information is aimed at managers, but it's helpful for employees, too.

# **S**mall Businesses

5.2     *Before You Start*

5.8     *Legal Structures
        for Small Businesses*

5.15    *Nonprofit Corporations*

5.18    *Small Business Taxes*

5.24    *Home-Based Businesses*

5.29    *Employers' Rights and
        Responsibilities*

*Business is never so healthy as when, like a chicken, it must do a certain amount of scratching for what it gets.*

**—HENRY FORD**

**F**or all sorts of personal and economic reasons, more Americans are starting and running their own businesses today than ever before. This trend has been helped by the increasing availability of powerful and affordable data storage and communications equipment, most notably the personal computer and the Internet. Because of this accessible technology, today's savvy small-time operator can often accomplish tasks that just a few decades ago could be tackled only by large corporations.

But not all change has been positive. When it comes to the law, the relatively informal world of just 40 years ago—where deals were often sealed with a handshake—has given way to a world where legal rules affect almost every small business relationship, including organizing the business, dealing with co-owners, hiring and supervising employees and relating to customers and suppliers. Staying on top of all these rules is as necessary as it is challenging. Fortunately, by using affordable, good quality self-help legal resources and getting additional help from a knowledgeable small business lawyer, you can master the laws you need to know to keep your business healthy.

# Before You Start

*Your imagination is your preview of life's coming attractions.*

**—ALBERT EINSTEIN**

No matter what type of business you're thinking of starting, there are some practical and legal issues you'll face right away, including choosing a name and location for your business, deciding whether or not to hire employees, writing a business plan, choosing a legal structure (sole proprietorship, partnership, corporation or limited liability company), establishing a system for reporting and paying taxes and adopting policies to deal with your customers. This section addresses many of these concerns. As you read, don't be discouraged by the details. If you have chosen a business that you will truly enjoy and, after creating a tight business plan, are confident you'll make a decent profit, your big jobs are done. Furthermore, many people and affordable sources of information are available to help you cope with the practical details we discuss here.

## I'm thinking of starting my own business. What should I do first?

Be sure you are genuinely interested in what the business does. If you aren't, you are unlikely to succeed in the long run—no matter how lucrative your work turns out to be. Yes, going into business with a firm plan to make a good living is important, but so, too, is choosing a business that fits your life goals in an authentic way. Here are a few things you might want to consider before you take the leap:

• Do you know how to accomplish the principal tasks of the business? (Don't open a transmission repair shop if you hate cars, or a restaurant if you can't cook.)

- If the business involves working with others, do you do this well? If not, look into the many opportunities to begin a one-person business.
- Do you understand basic business tasks, such as bookkeeping and how to prepare a profit-and-loss forecast and cash-flow analysis? If not, learn before—not after—you begin.
- Does the business fit your personality? If you are a shy introvert, stay away from businesses that require lots of personal selling. If you are easily bored, find a business which will allow you to deal with new material on a regular basis (publishing a newsletter, for example).

## What should I keep in mind when choosing a name for my business?

First, assume that you will have competitors and that you will want to market your products or services under the name you choose. (This will make your name a trademark.) For marketing purposes, the best names are those that customers will easily remember and associate with your business. Also, if the name is memorable, it will be easier to stop others from using it in the future.

Most memorable business names are made-up words, or are somehow fanciful or surprising, such as Exxon and Kodak (made-up words), Double Rainbow ice cream and Penguin Books. And some notable names are cleverly suggestive, such as The Body Shop (a store that sells personal hygiene products) and Accuride tires.

Names that tend to be forgotten by consumers are common names (names of people), geographic terms and names that literally describe some aspect of a product or service. For instance, Steve's Web Designs may be very pleasing to Steve as a name, but it's not likely to help Steve's customers remember his company when faced with competitors such as Sam's Web Designs and Sheri's Web Designs. Similarly, names like Central Word Processing Services or Robust Health Foods are not particularly memorable.

Of course, over time even a common name can become memorable through widespread use and advertising, as with Ben and Jerry's Ice Cream. And unusual names of people can sometimes be very memorable indeed, as with Fuddrucker's (restaurants and family entertainment centers).

## Choosing a Domain Name

If your business will have a website, part of choosing your business name will be deciding on a domain name. Using all or part of your business name in your domain name will make your website easier for potential customers to find. But many domain names are already taken, so you'll want to see what's available before you settle on a business name. See *Conducting a Trademark Search* in Chapter 8, *Trademarks*, for more information on conducting name searches.

## How do I find out whether I'm legally permitted to use the business name I've chosen?

Your first step depends on whether you plan to incorporate your business. If you do, you should check with the Secretary of State's office in your state to see whether your proposed name is the same or confusingly similar to an existing corporate name in your state. If it is, you'll have to choose a different name.

If you don't plan to incorporate, check with your county clerk to see whether your proposed name is already on the list maintained for fictitious or assumed business names in your county. In the few states where assumed business name registrations are statewide, check with your Secretary of State's office. (The county clerk should be able to tell you whether you'll need to check the name at the state level.) If you find that your chosen name (or a very similar name) is listed on a fictitious or assumed name register, you shouldn't use it.

## If my proposed business name isn't listed on a county or state register, am I free to use it however I like?

Not necessarily. Even if you are permitted to use your chosen name as a corporate or assumed business name in your state or county, you might not be able to use the name as a trademark or service mark. To understand what all this is about, consider the potential functions of a business name:

- A business name may be a tradename that describes the business for purposes of bank accounts, invoices and taxes.
- A business name may be a trademark or servicemark used to identify and distinguish products or services sold by the business (for example, Ford Motor Co. sells Ford automobiles, and McDonald's Corporation offers McDonald's fast food services).

While your corporate or assumed business name registration may legally clear the name for the first purpose, it doesn't speak to the second. For example, if your business is organized as a limited liability company (LLC) or corporation, you may get the green light from your Secretary of State to use IBM Toxics as your business name (if no other corporation of LLC in your state is using it or something confusingly similar), but if you try to use that name out in the marketplace, you're asking for a claim of trademark violation from the IBM general counsel's office.

To find out whether you can use your proposed name as a trademark or servicemark, you will need to do what's known as a trademark search. See Chapter 8, *Trademarks*.

## I've found out that the name I want to use is available. What do I need to do to reserve it for my business?

If you are forming a corporation or an LLC, every state has a procedure—operated by the Secretary of State's office—under which a proposed name can be reserved for a certain period of time, usually for a fee. Additional reservation periods can usually be purchased for additional fees. (For more information about corporations, see *Legal Structures for Small Businesses*, below.)

If you are not forming a corporation or an LLC, then you may need to file a fictitious or assumed business name statement with the agency who handles these registrations in your state (usually the county clerk, but sometimes the Secretary of State). Generally speaking, you need to file a ficticious business name statement only if your business name does not include the legal names of all the owners.

If you plan to use your business name as a trademark or servicemark, and your service or product will be marketed in more than one state (or across territorial or international borders), you can file an application with the U.S. Patent and Trademark Office to reserve the name for your use. See Chapter 8, *Trademarks*.

## What should I keep in mind when choosing a location for my business?

Commercial real estate brokers are fond of saying the three most important factors in establishing a business are location, location and location. While true for a few types of businesses—such as a retail sandwich shop that depends on lunchtime walk-in trade—for most, locating in a popular, high-cost area is a mistake. For example, if you design computer software, repair tile, import jewelry from Indonesia or do any one of ten thousand other things that don't rely on

foot traffic, your best bet is to search out convenient, low-cost, utilitarian surroundings. And even if yours is a business that many people will visit, consider the possibility that a low-cost, offbeat location may make more sense than a high-cost, trendy one.

## What about zoning and other rules which restrict where a business may locate?

Never sign a lease without being absolutely sure you will be permitted to operate your business at that location. If the rental space is in a shopping center or other retail complex, this involves first checking carefully with management, because many have contractual restrictions (for example, no more than two pizza restaurants in the Mayfair Mall). If your business will be located in a non-shopping center area, you'll need to be sure that you meet applicable zoning rules, which typically divide a municipality into residential, commercial, industrial and mixed-use areas.

You'll also need to find out whether any other legal restrictions will affect your operations. For example, some cities limit the number of certain types of business—such as fast food restaurants or coffee bars—in certain areas, and others require that a business provide off-street parking, close early on weeknights, limit advertising signs or meet other rules as a condition of getting a permit. Fortunately, many cities have business development offices that help small business owners understand and cope with restrictions.

## What is a business plan, and do I need to write one?

A business plan is a written document that describes the business you want to start and how it will become profitable. The document usually starts with a statement outlining the purpose and goals of your business and how you plan to realize them, including a detailed marketing plan. It should also contain a formal profit-and-loss projection and cash-flow analysis designed to show that if the business develops as expected, it will be profitable.

Your business plan enables you to explain your business prospects to potential lenders and investors in a language they can understand. Even more important, the intellectual rigor of creating a tight business plan will help you see whether the business you hope to start is likely to meet your personal and financial goals. Many times when budding entrepreneurs take an honest look at their financial numbers, they see that hoped-for profits are unlikely to materialize. Or, put another way, one of the most important purposes of writing a good business plan is to talk yourself out of starting a bad business.

## I plan to sell products and services directly to the public. What do I need to know to comply with consumer protection laws?

Many federal and state laws regulate the relationship between a business and its customers. These laws cover such things as advertising, pricing, door-to-door sales, written and implied warranties and, in a few states, layaway plans and refund policies. You can find out more about consumer protection laws by contacting the Federal Trade Commission, 6th and Pennsylvania Avenue, NW, Washington DC 20850, 202-326-2222, http://www.ftc.gov, and by contacting your state's consumer protection agency.

Although it's essential to understand and follow the rules that protect consumers, most successful businesses regard them as only a foundation for building friendly customer service policies designed to produce a high level of customer satisfaction. For example, many enlightened businesses tell their customers they can return any purchase for a full cash refund at any time for any reason. Not only does this encourage existing customers to continue to patronize the business, but it can be a highly effective way to get customers to brag about the business to their friends.

# Selling Goods and Services on Consignment

Many small business people, especially those who produce art, crafts and specialty clothing items, sell on consignment. In a consignment agreement, the owner of goods (in legal jargon, the consignor) puts the goods in the hands of another person or business—usually a retailer (the consignee)—who then attempts to sell them. If the goods are sold, the consignee receives a fee, which is usually a percentage of the purchase price, and the rest of the money is sent to the consignor. For example, a sculptor (the consignor) might place his or her work for sale at an art gallery (the consignee) with the understanding that if the artwork sells, the gallery keeps 50% of the sale price. Or a homeowner might leave old furniture with a resale shop that will keep one-third of the proceeds if the item sells. Typically, the consignor remains the owner of the goods until the consignee sells them.

As part of any consignment of valuable items, the consignor (owner) wants to be protected if the goods are lost or stolen while in the consignee's possession. The key here is to establish that the consignee has an insurance policy which will cover any loss. When extremely valuable items are being consigned, it's often appropriate to ask to be named as a co-insured so that you can receive a share of the insurance proceeds if a loss occurs.

If you're a consignee, check your insurance coverage. Before you accept the risk of loss or theft, make sure your business insurance policy covers you for loss of "personal property of others" left in your possession—and that the amount of coverage is adequate. Getting full reimbursement for the selling price of consigned goods may require an added supplement (called an endorsement) to your insurance policy. Check with your insurance agent or broker.

## More Information About Starting Your Small Business

*Legal Guide for Starting and Running a Small Business,* by Fred S. Steingold (Nolo), provides clear, plain-English explanations of the laws that affect business owners every day. It covers partnerships, corporations, limited liability companies, leases, trademarks, contracts, franchises, insurance, hiring and firing and much more.

*Legal Forms for Starting and Running a Small Business,* by Fred S. Steingold (Nolo), contains the forms and instructions you need to accomplish many routine legal tasks, such as borrowing money, leasing property and contracting for goods and services.

*The Small Business Start-Up Kit,* by Peri H. Pakroo (Nolo), shows you how to choose from among the basic types of business organizations, write an effective business plan, file the right forms in the right place, acquire good bookkeeping and accounting habits and get the proper licenses and permits.

*Small Time Operator,* by Bernard Kamoroff, C.P.A. (Bell Springs Publishing), is the best single source of practical information on getting a small business off the ground—from business licenses, to taxes, to basic accounting. It includes ledgers and worksheets to get you started.

*Running a One-Person Business*, by Claude Whitmyer and Salli Rasberry (Ten Speed Press), covers the nuts and bolts of doing business on your own: finances, time management, marketing and more.

*How to Write a Business Plan*, by Mike McKeever (Nolo), shows you how to write the business plan and loan package necessary to finance your business and make it work. It includes up-to-date sources of financing.

*Guerrilla Marketing*, by Jay Conrad Levinson (Houghton Mifflin), contains hundreds of ideas and strategies to help you market your business.

*Marketing Without Advertising*, by Michael Phillips and Salli Rasberry (Nolo), shows you how to generate sales and encourage customer relations without spending a lot of money on advertising.

# Legal Structures for Small Businesses

There is no one legal structure that's best for all small businesses. Whether you're better off starting as a sole proprietor or choosing one of the more complicated organizational structures, such as a partnership, corporation or limited liability company (LLC), usually depends on several factors, including the size and profitability of your business, how many people will own it and whether it will entail liability risks not covered by insurance.

## If I'm the only owner, what's the easiest way to structure my business?

The vast majority of small business people begin as sole proprietors, because it's cheap, easy and fast. With a sole proprietorship, there's no need to draft an agreement or go to the trouble and expense of registering a corporation or limited liability company (LLC) with your state regulatory agency. All it usually entails is getting a local business license, and unless you are doing business under your own name, filing and possibly publishing a fictitious name statement.

## If it's so simple, why aren't all businesses sole proprietorships?

There are several reasons why doing business as a sole proprietor is not appropriate for everyone. First, the owner of a sole proprietorship is personally responsible for all business debts, whereas limited liability companies and corporations normally shield their owners' assets from such debts. Second, a sole proprietorship is possible only when a business is owned by one person or, in some cases, a husband and wife. And finally, unlike a corporation (or a partnership or LLC that elects to be taxed as a corporation), which is normally taxed separately from its owners (something that can result in lower taxes for many small businesses—see below), a sole proprietor and her business are considered to be the same legal entity for tax purposes. This means you'll report all of the business's income, expenses and deductions on your individual tax return.

## I'm starting my business with several other people. What are the advantages and disadvantages of forming a general partnership?

One big advantage of a general partnership is that you usually don't have to register it with your state and pay an often-hefty fee, as you do to establish a corporation or limited liability company. And because a partnership is normally a "pass through" tax entity (the partners, not the partnership, are taxed on the partnership's profits), filing income tax returns is easier than it is for a regular corporation, where separate tax returns must be filed for the corporate entity and its owners. But because the business-related acts of one partner legally bind all others, it is essential that you go into business with a partner or partners you completely trust. It is also essential that you prepare a written partnership agreement establishing, among other things, each partner's share of profits or losses, day-to-day duties and what happens if one partner dies or retires.

Finally, a major disadvantage of doing business as a partnership is that all partners are personally liable for business debts and liabilities (for example, a judgment in a lawsuit). While it's true that a good insurance policy can do much to reduce lawsuit worries and that many small, savvy

businesses do not face debt problems, it's also true that businesses which face significant risks in either of these areas should probably organize themselves as a corporation or LLC in order to benefit from the limited liability these business structures provide.

## What exactly is "limited liability" — and why is it so important?

Some types of businesses—corporations and limited liability companies are the most common—shield their owners from personal responsibility for business debts. That is, if the business goes bankrupt, its owners are not usually required to use their personal assets to make good on business losses—unless they voluntarily assume responsibility. Other types of business—sole proprietorships and general partnerships—do not provide this shield, which means their owners are personally responsible for business liabilities. To see how this works, assume someone obtains a large court judgment against an incorporated business. Because corporate stockholders are not personally liable for business debts, their houses and other personal assets can't be taken to pay the judgement, even if the corporation files for bankruptcy. By comparison, if a sole proprietorship or partnership gets into the same kind of trouble, the houses, bank accounts and other valuable personal assets of the business's owners (and possibly their spouses) can be attached and used to satisfy the debt.

## Why do so many small business owners choose not to take advantage of limited liability protection?

Many small businesses simply don't have major debt or lawsuit worries, so they don't need limited liability protection. For example, if you run a small service business (perhaps you are a graphic artist, management consultant or music teacher), your chances of being sued or running up big debts are low. And when it comes to liability for many types of debts, creating a limited liability entity makes little practical difference for newly formed businesses. Often, if you want to borrow money from a commercial lender or establish credit with a vendor, you will be required to pledge your personal assets or personally guarantee payment of the debt (waive limited liability status) should your business be unable to pay.

Finally, even if your business faces serious and predictable financial risks (for instance, the risk that a customer may trip and fall on your premises or that your products may malfunction), organizing your business to achieve limited liability status is no substitute for purchasing a good business insurance policy. After all, without insurance, if a serious injury occurs, all the assets of your business—which will probably amount to a large portion of your net worth—can be grabbed to satisfy any resulting court judgment. It follows that even if you operate your business as a sole proprietorship, if you purchase comprehensive business insurance, your personal assets are not at significant risk and you may therefore sensibly conclude you don't need limited liability status.

## Given all its limitations, when is it wise for a small business person to seek limited liability status?

You should consider limited liability status if:

- your business subjects you to a risk of lawsuits in an area where insurance coverage is unaffordable or incomplete, or
- your business is well established and has a good credit rating so that you no longer need to personally guarantee every loan or credit application.

The easiest and most popular way to gain limited liability status is to form a corporation or a limited liability company (LLC).

## SMALL BUSINESS STRUCTURES: AN OVERVIEW

| Type of Entity | Main Advantages | Main Drawbacks |
| --- | --- | --- |
| Sole Proprietorship | Simple and inexpensive to create and operate | Owner personally liable for business debts |
| | Owner reports profit or loss on his or her personal tax return | |
| General Partnership | Simple and inexpensive to create and operate | Owners (partners) personally liable for business debts |
| | Owners (partners) report their share of profit or loss on their personal tax returns | Must prepare and file seperate partnership tax return |
| Limited Partnership | Limited partners have limited personal liability for business debts as long as they don't participate in management | General partners personally liable for business debts |
| | General partners can raise cash without involving outside investors in management of business | More expensive to create than general partnership |
| | | Suitable mainly for companies that invest in real estate |
| Regular Corporation | Owners have limited personal liability for business debts | More expensive to create than partnership or sole proprietorship |
| | Fringe benefits (such as health insurance and pension plans) can be deducted as business expense | Paperwork can seem burdensome to some owners |
| | Owners can split corporate profit among owners and corporation, paying lower overall tax rate | Separate taxable entity that must prepare and file a separate corporate tax |
| S Corporation | Owners have limited personal liability for business debts | More expensive to create than partnership or sole proprietorship |
| | Owners report their share of corporate profit or loss on their personal tax returns | More paperwork than for a limited liability company, which offers similar advantages |
| | Owners can use corporate loss to offset income from other sources (such as another business in which they are active) | Income must be allocated to owners in proportion to their ownership interests |
| | | Fringe benefits limited for owners who own more than 2% of shares |
| Professional Corporation | Owners have no personal liability for malpractice of other owners | More expensive to create than partnership or sole proprietorship |
| | | Paperwork can seem burdensome to some owners |
| | | All owners must generally belong to, and often be licensed to practice in, the same profession |
| Nonprofit Corporation | Corporation doesn't pay income taxes | Full tax advantages available only to groups organized for charitable, scientific, educational, literary or religious purposes |
| | Contributions to charitable corporation are tax-deductible | |
| | Fringe benefits can be deducted as business expense | Property transferred to corporation stays there; if corporation ends, property must go to another nonprofit |

| Type of Entity | Main Advantages | Main Drawbacks |
|---|---|---|
| Limited Liability Company | Almost all states now allow LLCs to be organized with only one member | More expensive to create than partnership or sole proprietorship |
| | Owners have limited personal liability for business debts even if they participate in management | |
| | Profit and loss can be allocated differently than ownership interests | State laws for creating LLCs may not reflect latest federal tax changes |
| | IRS rules now allow LLCs to choose between being taxed as partnership or corporation | |
| Professional Limited Liability Company | Same advantages as a regular limited liability company | Same as for a regular limited liability company |
| | Gives state-licensed professionals a way to enjoy those advantages | Members must all belong to the same profession |
| | | At least one state (CA) does not permit professionals to organize as an LLC |
| Limited Liability Partnership | Mostly of interest to partners in old line professions such as, law, medicine and accounting | Unlike a limited liability company or a professional limited liability company, owners (partners) remain personally liable for many types of obligations owed to business creditors, lenders and landlords |
| | Owners (partners) aren't personally liable for the malpractice of other partners | |
| | Owners report their share of profit or loss on their personal tax returns | Not available in all states |
| | | Often limited to a short list of professions |

## Is forming a corporation difficult?

No. As long as you and close associates and family members will own all stock and none will be sold to the public, the necessary documents—principally your Articles of Incorporation and corporate bylaws—can usually be prepared in a few hours. The first step is to check with your state's corporate filing office (usually either the Secretary of State or Department of Corporations) and conduct a trademark search to be sure the name you want to use is legally available. You then fill in blanks in a preprinted form (available from commercial publishers or your state's corporate filing office or website) listing the purpose of your corporation, its principal place of business and the number and type of shares of stock. You'll file these documents with the appropriate office, along with a registration fee which will usually be between $200 and $1,000, depending on the state.

You'll also need to complete, but not file, corporate bylaws. These will outline a number of important corporate housekeeping details, such as when annual shareholder meetings will be held, who can vote and the manner in which shareholders will be notified if there is need for an additional "special" meeting.

Fortunately, good self-help books exist in many states which make it easy and safe to incorporate your business without a lawyer.

## What about operating my corporation? Aren't ongoing legal formalities involved?

Assuming your corporation has not sold stock to the public, conducting corporate business is remarkably straightforward and uncomplicated. Often it amounts to little more than recording key corporate decisions (for example, borrowing money or buying real estate) and holding an annual meeting. Even these formalities can often be done by written agreement and don't usually necessitate a face-to-face meeting.

## Doesn't forming a corporation mean income will be taxed twice—once at the corporate level and then again when dividends are paid to the corporation's owners (shareholders)?

Taxation of business is complicated; we'll be able to cover only the main points here. First, understand that most types of businesses—sole proprietorships and corporations that have qualified for subchapter S status, as well as partnerships and limited liability companies that have not elected to be taxed as regular, or C corporations—are known as pass-through tax entities, meaning that all business profits and losses are re-flected on the individual tax returns of the owners. For example, if a sole proprietor's convenience store turns a yearly profit of $85,000, this amount goes right on his personal tax return. By contrast, a regular profit corporation (and any partnership or LLC that elects to be taxed like a corporation) is a separate tax entity—meaning that the business files a tax return and pays its own taxes.

But the fact that a corporation is taxed separately from its owners doesn't always mean that profits will be taxed twice. That's because owners of most incorporated small businesses are also employees of those businesses; the money they receive in the form of salaries and bonuses is tax-deductible to the corporation as an ordinary and necessary business expense. After paying surplus money to owners in the form of salaries, along with bonuses and other fringe benifits, a corporation often shows no profit and therefore pays no corporate income tax.

## Are there tax advantages to forming a corporation?

Frequently, yes. Corporations pay federal income tax at a far lower rate than do most individuals for the first $75,000 of their profits—15% of the first $50,000 of profit, and 25% of the next $25,000. By contrast, in a sole proprietorship or partnership, where the business owner(s) pay taxes on all profits, up to 39.6% could be subject to federal income tax.

A corporation can often reduce taxes by paying its owner-employees a decent salary (which, of course, is tax-deductible to the corporation but taxable to the employee), and then retaining additional profits in the business (say, for future expansion). Under IRS rules, however, the maximum amount of profits most corporations are allowed to retain is $250,000, and some professional corporations are limited to $150,000.

## Recently I've heard a lot about limited liability companies. How do they work?

For many years, small business people have been torn between operating as a sole proprietor (or, if several people are involved, as a partnership) or incorporating. On the one hand, many owners are attracted to the tax reporting simplicity of being a sole proprietor or partner. On the other, they desire the personal liability protection offered by incorporation. Until the mid 1990s it was possible to safely achieve these dual goals only by forming a corporation at the state level and then complying with a number of technical rules to gain S-corp status from the IRS. Then the limited liability company (LLC) was introduced and slowly gained full IRS acceptance. LLCs can have many of the most popular attributes of both partnerships (pass-through tax status) and corporations (limited personal liability for the owners). You can establish an LLC by filing a document called Articles or a Certificate of Organization with your state's corporate filing office (often the Secretary or Department of State).

## Can any small business register as a limited liability company?

Most can, because limited liability companies are recognized by all states. And almost all states (except Massachusetts and the District of Columbia) now permit one-owner LLCs, which means that sole proprietors can easily organize their business as an LLC to obtain both limited liability and pass-through tax status.

## Are there any drawbacks to forming a limited liability company?

Very few, beyond the fact that LLCs require a moderate amount of paperwork at the outset. You must file Articles of Organization with your state's Secretary of State, along with a filing fee that will range from a few hundred dollars in some states to almost $1,000 in others.

### *More Information About Choosing a Structure for Your Small Business*

*Legal Guide to Starting and Running a Small Business,* by Fred S. Steingold (Nolo), explains what you need to know to choose the right form for your business and shows you what to do to get started.

*Legal Forms for Starting and Running a Small Business,* by Fred S. Steingold (Nolo), provides all the forms you'll need to get your business up and running, no matter what ownership structure you choose.

*LLC Maker,* by Anthony Mancuso (Nolo), is interactive software containing all the information and forms you'll need to set up an LLC on your own.

*Form Your Own Limited Liability Company,* by Anthony Mancuso (Nolo), explains how to set up an LLC in any state, without the aid of an attorney.

*How to Form Your Own Corporation (California, New York and Texas editions),* by Anthony Mancuso (Nolo), offers state-specific instructions and forms for creating a corporation in those states.

# Nonprofit Corporations

*In the long run you hit only what you aim at. Therefore, though you should fail immediately, you had better aim at something high.*

**—HENRY DAVID THOREAU**

A nonprofit corporation is a group of people who join together to do some activity that benefits the public, such as running a homeless shelter, an artists' performance group or a low-cost medical clinic. Making a profit from these activities is allowed under legal and tax rules, but the primary purpose of the organization should be to do good work, not make money. Nonprofit goals are typically educational, charitable or religious.

## How are nonprofit organizations structured?

Most nonprofits start out as small, loosely-structured organizations. Volunteers perform the work, and the group spends what little money it earns to keep the organization afloat. Because there is no profit, the group does not file tax returns. Formal legal papers (such as a nonprofit charter or bylaws) are rarely prepared in the beginning. Legally, groups of this sort are considered nonprofit associations, and each member can be held personally liable for organizational debts and liabilities.

Once a nonprofit association gets going and starts to make money, or wishes to obtain a tax exemption to attract public support and qualify for grant funds, the members will formalize its structure. Usually the members decide to incorporate, but forming a nonprofit association by adopting a formal association charter and operating bylaws is an alternative. Most groups form a nonprofit corporation because it is the traditional form—the IRS and grant agencies are very familiar with it. Also, once incorporated, the individual members of the nonprofit are not personally liable for debts of the organization—a big legal advantage of the corporate form over the unincorporated association.

## Will my association benefit from becoming a nonprofit corporation?

Here are some circumstances that might make it worth your while to incorporate and get tax-exempt status:

- *You want to solicit tax-deductible contributions.* Contributions to nonprofits are generally tax deductible for those who make them. If you want to solicit money to fund your venture, you'll make it more attractive to potential donors if their contribution is tax-deductible.
- *Your association makes a taxable profit from its activities.* If your association will generate any kind of income from its activities, it's wise to incorporate so that you and your associates don't have to pay income tax on this money.
- *You want to apply for public or private grant money.* Without federal tax-exempt status, your group is unlikely to qualify for grants.
- *Your members want some protection from legal liability.* By incorporating your association, you can generally insulate your officers, directors and members from liability for the activities they engage in on behalf of the corporation
- *Your advocacy efforts might provoke legal quarrels.* If, for instance, your association is taking aim at a powerful industry (such as tobacco companies) it might be worth incorporating so that your association's officers and directors will have some protection from the spurious lawsuits that are sure to come—and also receive compensation for their legal fees.

Forming a nonprofit corporation brings other benefits as well, such as lower nonprofit mailing rates and local real and personal property tax exemptions.

## Is forming a nonprofit corporation difficult?

Legally, no. To form a nonprofit corporation, one of the organization's founders prepares and files standard Articles of Incorporation—a short legal document that lists the name and directors of the nonprofit plus other basic information. The Articles are filed with the Secretary of State's office for a modest filing fee. After the Articles are filed, the group is a legally recognized nonprofit corporation.

## Is there more to forming a nonprofit than this simple legal task?

Taxwise, there is more. In addition to filing your Articles, you will want to apply for and obtain a federal and state nonprofit tax exemption. If the formation of your organization depends on its nonprofit status, you'll likely want to know whether you'll qualify for tax exemption at the outset. Unfortunately, your corporation must be formed before you submit your federal tax exemption application. Why? Because the IRS requires that you submit a copy of your filed Articles with the exemption application. This means you must carefully review the tax exemption application before you submit your corporation papers. Doing so will give you a good idea of whether your organization will qualify or not.

## What type of tax exemption do most nonprofits get?

Most organizations obtain a federal tax exemption under Section 501(c)(3) of the Internal Revenue Code for charitable, education, religious, scientific or literary purposes. States typically follow the federal lead and grant state tax-exempt status to nonprofits recognized by the IRS as 501(c)(3)s.

## How can my organization get a 501(c)(3) tax exemption?

You'll need to get the IRS Package 1023 exemption application. This is a lengthy and technical application with many references to the federal tax code. Most nonprofit organizers need help in addition to the IRS instructions that accompany the form. But you can do it on your own if you have a good self-help resource by your side such as Nolo's *How to Form Your Own Nonprofit Corporation*, by Anthony Mancuso, which shows you, line by line, how to complete your application.

## Are there any restrictions imposed on 501(c)(3) nonprofits?

You must meet the following conditions to qualify for a 501(c)(3) IRS tax exemption:

- The assets of your nonprofit must be irrevocably dedicated to charitable, educational, religious or similar purposes. If your 501(c)(3) nonprofit dissolves, any assets it owns must be transferred to another 501(c)(3) organization. (You don't have to name the specific organization that will receive your assets—a broad dedication clause will do.)
- Your organization cannot campaign for or against candidates for public office, and political lobbying activity is restricted.
- If your nonprofit makes a profit from activities unrelated to its exempt-purposes activities, it must pay taxes on the profit (but up to $1,000 of unrelated income can be earned tax-free).

### More Information About Nonprofit Corporations

*How to Form a Nonprofit Corporation*, by Anthony Mancuso (Nolo), shows you how to form a tax-exempt corporation in all 50 states. In California, look for *How to Form a Nonprofit Corporation in California*, also by Anthony Mancuso (Nolo).

*The Law of Tax Exempt Organizations*, by Bruce Hopkins (Wiley), is an in-depth guide to the legal and tax requirements for obtaining and maintaining a 501(c)(3) tax exemption and public charity status with the IRS.

# Small Business Taxes

THE MAN WHO IS
ABOVE HIS BUSINESS
MAY ONE DAY FIND HIS
BUSINESS ABOVE HIM.

**—SAMUEL DREW**

Taxes are a fact of life for every small business. Those who take the time to understand and follow the rules will have little trouble with tax authorities. By contrast, those who are sloppy or dishonest are likely to be dogged by tax bills, audits and penalties. The moral is simple: Meeting your obligations to report business information and pay taxes is the cornerstone of operating a successful business.

## I want to start my own small business. What do I have to do to keep out of trouble with the IRS?

Start by learning a new set of "3 Rs"—recordkeeping, recordkeeping and (you guessed it) recordkeeping. IRS studies show that poor records—not dishonesty—cause most small business people to lose at audits or fail to comply with their tax reporting obligations, with resulting fines and penalties. Even if you hire someone to keep your records, you need to know how to supervise him—if he goofs up, you'll be held responsible.

## I don't have enough money in my budget to hire a business accountant or tax preparer. Is it safe and sensible for me to keep my own books?

Yes, if you remember to keep thorough, current records. Consider using a check register-type computer program such as Quicken (Intuit) to track your expenses, and if you are doing your own tax return, use Intuit's companion program, Turbotax for Business. To ensure that you're on the right track, it's a good idea to run your bookkeeping system by a savvy small business tax pro. With just a few hours of work, she should help you avoid most common mistakes and show you how to dovetail your bookkeeping system with tax filing requirements.

When your business is firmly in the black and your budget allows for it, consider hiring a bookkeeper. He can do your day-to-day payables and receivables. And hire an outside tax pro to handle your heavy duty tax work—not only are his fees a tax-deductible business expense, but chances are your business will benefit if you put more of your time into running it and less into completing routine paperwork.

## Recordkeeping Basics

Keep all receipts and canceled checks for business expenses. It will help if you separate your documents by category, such as:

- auto expenses
- rent
- utilities
- advertising
- travel
- entertainment, and
- professional fees.

Organize your documents by putting them into individual folders or envelopes, and keep them in a safe place. If you are ever audited, the IRS is most likely to zero in on business deductions for travel and entertainment, and car expenses. Remember that the burden will be on

you—not the IRS—to explain your deductions. If you're feeling unsure about how to get started or what documents you need to keep, consult a tax professional familiar with recordkeeping for small businesses.

## I've been operating my own business for several years, but I'm still often confused as to what is—and isn't—a tax-deductible business expense. Can you help me?

Just about any "ordinary, necessary and reasonable" expense that helps you earn business income is deductible. This term reflects the purpose for which the expense is made. For example, buying a computer, or even a sound system, for your office or store is an "ordinary and necessary" business expense, but buying the same items for your family room obviously isn't. In the latter case, the computer and stereo would be nondeductible personal expenses. The property must be used in a "trade or business," which means it is used with the expectation of generating income.

In addition to the "ordinary and necessary" rule, a few things are specifically prohibited by law from being tax deductable—for instance, you can't deduct a bribe paid to a public official. Other deduction no-nos are traffic tickets, your home telephone line and clothing you wear on the job, unless it is a required uniform. As a rule, if you think it is necessary for your business, it is probably deductible. Just be ready to explain it to an auditor.

### Business Costs That Are Never Deductible

A few expenses are not deductible even if they are business related, because they violate public policy (IRC §162). These expenses include:

- any type of government fine, such as a tax penalty paid to the IRS, or even a parking ticket
- bribes and kickbacks
- any kind of payment made for referring a client, patient or customer, if it is contrary to a state or federal law, and
- expenses for lobbying and social club dues.

Thankfully, very few other business expenses are affected by these rules.

### If I use my car for business, how much of that expense can I write off?

You must keep track of how much you use your car for business in order to figure out your deduction. (You'll also need to produce these records if you're ever audited.) Start by keeping a log showing the miles for each business use, always noting the purpose of the trip. Then, at the end of the year, you will usually be able to figure your deduction by using either the "mileage method" (as of 2001 you can take 34.5¢ per mile deduction for business usage) or the "actual expense" method (you can take the total you pay for gas and repairs plus depreciation according to a tax code schedule, multiplied by the percentage of business use). Figure the deduction both ways and use the method that benefits you most.

### Can I claim a deduction for business-related entertainment?

You may deduct only 50% of expenses for entertaining clients, customers or employees, no matter how many martinis or Perriers you swigged. (Yes, this is a change. In the old days you could write off 100% of every entertainment expense, and until a few years ago, 80%.) The entertainment must be either directly related to the business (such as a catered business lunch) or "associated with" the business, meaning that the entertainment took place immediately before or immediately after a business discussion. Qualified business entertainment includes taking a client to a ball game, a concert or dinner at a fancy restaurant, or just inviting a few of your customers over for a Sunday barbecue at your home.

Parties, picnics and other social events you put on for your employees and their families are an exception to the 50% rule—such events are 100% deductible. Keep in mind that if you are audited, you must be able to show some proof that it was a legitimate business expense. So, keep a guest list and note the business (or potential) relationship of each person entertained.

# Commonly Overlooked Business Expenses

Despite the fact that most people keep a sharp eye out for deductible expenses, it's not uncommon to miss a few. Some overlooked routine deductions include:

- advertising giveaways and promotion
- audio and video tapes related to business skills
- bank service charges
- business association dues
- business gifts
- business-related magazines and books (like the one in your hand)
- casual labor and tips
- casualty and theft losses
- charitable contributions
- coffee service
- commissions
- consultant fees
- credit bureau fees
- education to improve business skills
- interest on credit cards for business expenses
- interest on personal loans used for business purposes
- office supplies
- online computer services related to business
- parking and meters
- petty cash funds
- postage
- promotion and publicity
- seminars and trade shows
- taxi and bus fare
- telephone calls away from the business

## I've heard that some types of business supplies and equipment can be fully deducted in the year they are purchased, but the purchase price of others must be deducted over several years. Is this true?

Current expenses, which include the everyday costs of keeping your business going, such as office supplies, rent and electricity, can be deducted from your business's total income in the year you incurred them. But expenditures for things that will generate revenue in future years—for example, a desk, copier or car—must be "capitalized," that is, written off or "amortized" over their useful life—usually three, five or seven years—according to IRS rules. There is one important exception to this rule, discussed next.

## I want to purchase a new computer system for my business. Does this mean that, even if I buy the entire system this year, I must spread the deduction over a period of five years?

Not necessarily. Normally the cost of "capital equipment"—usually equipment that has a useful life of more than one year—must be deducted over a number of years, but there is one major exception. In 2001, Internal Revenue Code § 179 allows you to deduct up to $24,000 worth of capital assets in any one year against your business income. Even if you buy the computer on credit, with no money down, you can still qualify for this deduction.

## New Law: Increasing § 179 Deductions to $25,000

The annual limit on expensing of business assets under IRC § 179 increases as follows: 2001: $24,000; 2002: $24,000; 2003: $25,000.

## Business Assets That Must Be Capitalized

Buildings

Cellular phones and beepers

Computer components and software

Copyrights and patents

Equipment

Improvements to business property

Inventory

Office furnishings and decorations

Small tools and equipment

Vehicles

Window coverings

## A friend told me that corporations get the best tax breaks of any type of business, so I am thinking of incorporating my startup. What do you recommend?

There's a seed of truth in what your friend told you, but keep in mind that most tax benefits flow to profitable, established businesses, not to startups in their first few years. For example, corporations, and LLCs which elect to be taxed like corporations, can offer more tax-flexible pension plans and greater medical deductions than sole proprietors or partnerships, but few startups have the cash flow needed to take advantage of this tax break. Similarly, the ability to split income between a corporation and its owners—thereby keeping income in lower tax brackets—is only effective if the business is solidly profitable. And incorporating adds a lot of state fees, as well as legal and accounting charges, to your expense load. So unless you are sure that substantial profits will begin to roll in immediately, hold off.

For more information about choosing the right structure for your business, see Legal Structures for Small Businesses, above.

## I am thinking about setting up a consulting business with two of my business associates. Do we need to have partnership papers drawn up? Does it make any difference tax-wise?

If you go into business with other people and split the expenses and profits, under the tax code you are in partnership whether you have signed a written agreement or not. (The only exception to this rule is for a husband and wife, who have a choice: they can be a sole proprietorship or a partnership.) This means that you will have to file a partnership tax return every year, in addition to your individual tax return.

Even though a formal partnership agreement doesn't affect your tax status, it's essential to prepare one to establish all partners' rights and responsibilities vis-à-vis each other, as well as to provide for how profits and losses will be allocated to each partner. For more information about partnerships, see Legal Structures for Small Businesses, above.

## I am a building contractor with a chance to land a big job. If I get it, I'll need to hire people quickly. Should I hire independent contractors or employees?

If you will be telling your workers where, when and how to do their jobs, you should treat them as employees, because that's how the IRS will classify them. Generally, you can treat workers as independent contractors only if they have their own businesses and offer their services to several contractors—for example, a specialty sign painter with his own shop who you hire to do a particular job.

If in doubt, err on the side of treating workers as employees. While misclassifying your workers might save you money in the short run (you wouldn't have to pay the employer's share of payroll taxes or have an accountant keep records and file payroll tax forms), it may get you into big trouble if the IRS later audits you. (The IRS is very aware of the tax benefits of misclassifying an employee as an independent contractor and regu-

larly audits companies who hire large numbers of independent contractors.) If your company is audited, the IRS may reclassify your "independent contractors" as employees—with the result that you are assessed hefty back taxes, penalties and interest.

## I've heard that I can no longer claim a deduction for an office in my home. But I also see that the IRS has a form for claiming home office expenses. What's the story?

It's not as confusing as it sounds. A while back, the Supreme Court told a doctor who was taking work home from the hospital that he couldn't take a depreciation deduction for the space used at his condo. But this is quite different from maintaining a home-based business. If you run a business out of your home, and you devote most of the time you dedicate to that business working in your home office, you can claim a deduction for the portion of the home used for business. Also, you can deduct related costs—utilities, insurance, remodeling—whether you own or rent.

For more information about running a home-based business, see the next section.

## I am planning a trip to Los Angeles to attend a trade show. Can I take my family along for a vacation and still be able to deduct the expenses?

If you take others with you on a business trip, you can deduct business expenses for the trip no greater than if you were traveling alone. If on the trip your family rides in the back seat of the car and stays in one standard motel room, then you can fully deduct your automobile and hotel expenses. You can also fully deduct the cost of air tickets even if they feature a two-for-one or "bring along the family" discount. You can't claim a deduction for your family's meals or jaunts to Disneyland or Universal Studios, however. And if you extend your stay and partake in some of the fun after the business is over, the expenses attributed to the nonbusiness days aren't deductible, unless you extended your stay to get discounted airfare (the "Saturday overnight" requirement). In this case, your hotel room and your own meals would be deductible.

### More Information About Small Business Taxes

*Tax Savvy for Small Business*, by Frederick W. Daily (Nolo), tells small business owners what they need to know about federal taxes and shows them how to make the right tax decisions.

*Hiring Independent Contractors: The Employer's Legal Guide*, by Stephen Fishman (Nolo), explains who qualifies as an independent contractor, describes applicable tax rules and shows employers how to set up effective working agreements with independent contractors.

*Working for Yourself: Law and Taxes for the Self-Employed*, by Stephen Fishman (Nolo), is designed for the estimated 20 million Americans who are self-employed and offer their services on a contract basis.

# Home-Based Businesses

As technology advances, it becomes more and more convenient and economical to operate a business from home. Depending on local zoning rules, as long as the business is small, quiet and doesn't create traffic or parking problems, it's usually legal to do so. But as with any other business endeavor, it pays to know the rules before you begin.

### Is a home-based business legally different from other businesses?

No. The basic legal issues, such as picking a name for your business and deciding whether to operate as a sole proprietorship, partnership, limited liability company or corporation, are the same. Similarly, when it comes to signing contracts, hiring employees and collecting from your customers, the laws are identical whether you run your business from home or the top floor of a high-rise.

## Are there laws that restrict a person's right to operate a business from home?

Municipalities have the legal right to establish rules about what types of activities can be carried out in different geographical areas. For example, they often establish zones for stores and offices (commercial zones), factories (industrial zones) and houses (residential zones). In some residential areas—especially in affluent communities—local zoning ordinances absolutely prohibit all types of business. In the great majority of municipalities, however, residential zoning rules allow small nonpolluting home businesses, as long as any home containing a business is used primarily as a residence and the business activities don't negatively affect neighbors.

## How can I find out whether residential zoning rules allow the home-based business I have in mind?

Get a copy of your local ordinance from your city or county clerk's office, the city attorney's office or your public library, and read it carefully. Zoning ordinances are worded in many different ways to limit business activities in residential areas. Some are extremely vague, allowing "customary home-based occupations." Others allow homeowners to use their houses for a broad—but, unfortunately, not very specific—list of business purposes (for example, "professions and domestic occupations, crafts or ser-

vices"). Still others contain a detailed list of approved occupations, such as "law, dentistry, medicine, music lessons, photography, cabinet making." If you read your ordinance and still aren't sure whether your business is okay, you may be tempted to talk to zoning or planning officials. But until you figure out what the rules and politics of your locality are, it may be best to do this without identifying and calling attention to yourself. (For example, have a friend who lives nearby make inquiries.)

## The business I want to run from home is not specifically allowed or prohibited by my local ordinance. What should I do to avoid trouble?

Start by understanding that in most areas zoning and building officials don't actively search for violations. The great majority of home-based businesses that run into trouble do so when a neighbor complains—often because of noise or parking problems, or even because of the unfounded fear that your business is doing something illegal such as selling drugs. It follows that your best approach is often to explain your business activities to your neighbors and make sure that your activities are not worrying or inconveniencing them. For example, if you teach piano lessons or do physical therapy from your home and your students or clients will often come and go, make sure your neighbors are not bothered by noise or losing customary on-street parking spaces.

Will the local ordinance regulating home-based businesses include rules about specific activities, such as making noise, putting up signs or having employees?

Quite possibly. Many ordinances—especially those which are fairly vague as to the type of business you can run from your home—restrict how you can carry out your business. The most frequent rules limit your use of on-street parking, prohibit outside signs, limit car and truck traffic and restrict the number of employees who can work at your house on a regular basis (some prohibit employees altogether). In addition, some zoning ordinances limit the percentage of your home's floor space that can be devoted to the business. Again, you'll need to study your local ordinance carefully to see how these rules will affect you.

## If Municipal Officials Say No to Your Home-Based Business

In many cities and counties, if a planning or zoning board rejects your business, you can appeal—often to the city council or county board of supervisors. While this can be an uphill battle, it is likely to be less so if you have the support of all affected neighbors. You may also be able to get an overly restrictive zoning ordinance amended by your municipality's governing body. For example, in some communities, people are working to amend ordinances that prohibit home-based businesses entirely or only allow "traditional home-based businesses" to permit those that rely on the use of computers and other high tech equipment—businesses that are usually unobtrusive, but far from traditional.

I live in a planned development that has its own rules for home-based businesses. Do these control my business activities or can I rely on my city's home-based business ordinance, which is less restrictive?

In an effort to protect residential property values, most subdivisions, condos and planned unit developments create special rules—typically called Covenants, Conditions and Restrictions (CC&Rs)—that govern many aspects of property use. Rules pertaining to home-based businesses are often significantly stricter than those found in city ordinances. But so long as the rules of your planned development are reasonably clear and consistently enforced, you must follow them.

I sell my consulting services to a number of businesses. Does maintaining a home office help me establish independent contractor status with the IRS?

No. An independent contractor is a person who controls both the outcome of a project and the means of accomplishing it, and who offers services to a number of businesses or individual purchasers. Although having an office or place of business is one factor the IRS looks at in determining whether an individual qualifies as an independent contractor, it makes no difference whether your office is located at home or in a traditional business setting.

### Are there tax advantages to working from home?

Almost all ordinary and necessary business expenses (everything from wages to computers to paper clips) are tax deductible, no matter where they are incurred—in a factory or office, while traveling or at home. In addition, if you operate your business from home and qualify under IRS rules, you may be able to deduct part of your rent from your income taxes—or if you own your home, take a depreciation deduction.

Finally, you may also be eligible to deduct a portion of your total utility, home repair and maintenance, property tax and house insurance costs, based on the percentage of your residence you use for business purposes. To qualify for the home-office deduction, the IRS requires that two legal tests be met:

- you must use your business space regularly and exclusively for business purposes, and

- your home office must the be the principal place where you conduct your business. This rule is satisfied if your office is used for administrative or managerial activities, as long as these activities aren't often conducted at another business location.

Note that, the amount of your deduction can't exceed your home-based business's total profit.

## Insuring Your Home-Based Business

It's a mistake to rely on a homeowner's or renter's insurance policy to cover your home-based business. These policies often exclude or strictly limit coverage for business equipment and injuries to business visitors. For example, if your computer is stolen or a client or business associate trips and falls on your steps, you may not be covered.

Fortunately, it's easy to avoid these nasty surprises. Sit down with your insurance agent and fully disclose your planned business operation. You'll find that it's relatively inexpensive to add business coverage to your homeowner's policy—and it's a tax-deductible expense. But be sure to check prices—some insurance companies provide special cost-effective policies designed to protect both homes and home-based businesses.

## How big will my home-office tax deduction be if my business qualifies under IRS rules?

To determine your deduction, you first need to figure out how much of your home you use for business as compared to other purposes. Do this by dividing the number of square feet used for your home business by the total square footage of your home. The resulting percentage of business usage determines how much of your rent (or, if you are a homeowner, depreciation), insurance, utilities and other expenses are deductible. But remember, the amount of the deduction can't be larger than the profit your home-based business generates. (Additional technical rules apply to calculating depreciation on houses you own to allow for the fact that the structure, but not the land, depreciates.) For more information, contact the IRS to order Publication 587, *Business Use of Your Home,* or view the publication online at http://www.irs.gov.

## Do I need to watch out for any tax traps when claiming deductions for my home-office?

Claiming a home-office deduction increases your audit risk slightly, but this needn't be a big fear if you carefully follow the rules.

Keep in mind that if you sell your house, all of the home-based office deductions you have previously taken will be subject to income tax in that year, whether you made a profit or not. And you can't use the $250,000 per person "exclusion of profits" on the sale of a home to offset this tax. For example, if your home office deductions total $15,000 for the last seven years, you will be taxed on this amount in the year you sell your house. Despite this tax, it's generally wise to continue to take your home office deductions each year. Especially for people who don't plan to sell their houses anytime soon, it's usually beneficial to receive a tax break today that you won't have to repay for many years. You can use your tax savings to help your business grow.

## I have a full-time job, but I also operate a separate part-time business from home. Can I claim a tax deduction for my home-based business expenses?

Yes, as long as your business meets certain IRS rules. It makes no difference that you work only part-time at your home-based business or that you have another occupation. But your business must be more than a disguised hobby—it has to pass muster with the IRS as a real business.

The IRS defines a business as "any activity engaged in to make a profit." If a venture makes money—even a small amount—in three of five consecutive years, it is presumed to possess a profit motive. (IRC §183(d).) However, courts have held that some activities that failed to meet this three-profitable-years-out-of-five test still qualify as a business if they are run in a businesslike manner. When determining whether a nonprofitable venture qualifies for a deduction, courts may look at whether you kept thorough business records, had a separate business bank account, prepared advertising or other marketing materials and obtained any necessary licenses and permits (a business license from your city, for example).

### More Information About Home-Based Business

*The Best Home Businesses for the 21st Century,* by Paul & Sarah Edwards (J.P. Tarcher), profiles 95 workable home-based businesses, including information about how each business works and what sets of skills and opportunities are necessary to succeed.

*Working for Yourself: Law and Taxes for Freelancers, Independent Contractors & Consultants,* by Stephen Fishman (Nolo), shows independent contractors how to meet business start-up requirements, comply with strict IRS rules and make sure they get paid in full and on time.

# Employers' Rights & Responsibilities

At some point during your business venture, you may need to hire people to help you manage your workload. When you do, you'll be held accountable to a host of state and federal laws that regulate your relationship with your employees. Among the things you'll be expected to know and understand:

- proper hiring practices, including how to write appropriate job descriptions, conduct interviews and respect privacy rights
- wage and hour laws, as well as the laws that govern retirement plans, healthcare benefits and life insurance benefits
- workplace safety rules and regulations
- how to write an employee handbook and conduct performance reviews, including what you should and shouldn't put in an employee's personnel file
- how to avoid sexual harassment as well as discrimination based on gender, age, race, pregnancy, sexual orientation and national origin, and
- how to avoid trouble if you need to fire an employee.

This section provides you with an overview of your role as an employer. And you can find more guidance elsewhere in this book. Employee's rights—including questions and answers about wages, hours and workplace safety—are discussed in Chapter 4; pension plans are covered in Chapter 14.

First things first. How can I write advertisements that will attract the best pool of potential employees—without getting in legal hot water?

Many small employers get tripped up when summarizing a job in an advertisement. This can easily happen if you're not familiar with the legal guidelines. Nuances in an ad can be used as evidence of discrimination against applicants of a particular gender, age or marital status.

**There are a number of pitfalls to avoid in job ads:**

| DON'T USE | USE |
| --- | --- |
| Salesman | Salesperson |
| College Student | Part-time Worker |
| Handyman | General Repair Person |
| Gal Friday | Office Manager |
| Married Couple | Two-Person Job |
| Counter Girl | Retail Clerk |
| Waiter | Wait Staff |
| Young | Energetic |

Also, requiring a high school or college degree may be discriminatory in some job categories. You can avoid problems by stating that an applicant must have a "degree or equivalent experience."

Probably the best way to write an ad that meets legal requirements is to stick to the job skills needed and the basic responsibilities. Some examples:

"Fifty-unit apartment complex seeks experienced manager with general maintenance skills."

"Mid-sized manufacturing company has opening for accountant with tax experience to oversee interstate accounts."

"Cook trainee position available in new vegetarian restaurant. Flexible hours."

Help Wanted ads placed by federal contractors must state that all qualified applicants will receive consideration for employment without regard to race, color, religion, sex or national origin. Ads often express this with the phrase, "An Equal Opportunity Employer." To show your intent to be fair, you may want to include this phrase in your ad even if you're not a federal contractor.

Any tips on how to conduct a good, forthright interview—and again, avoid legal trouble?

Good preparation is your best ally. Before you begin to interview applicants for a job opening, write down a set of questions focusing on the job duties and the applicant's skills and experience. For example:

"Tell me about your experience in running a mailroom."

"How much experience did you have in making cold calls on your last job?"

"Explain how you typically go about organizing your workday."

"Have any of your jobs required strong leadership skills?"

By writing down the questions and sticking to the same format at all interviews for the position, you reduce the risk that a rejected applicant will later complain about unequal treatment. It's also smart to summarize the applicant's answers for your files—but don't get so involved in documenting the interview that you forget to listen closely to the applicant. And don't be so locked in to your list of questions that you don't follow up on something significant that an applicant has said, or try to pin down an ambiguous or evasive response.

To break the ice, you might give the applicant some information about the job—the duties, hours, pay range, benefits and career opportunities. Questions about the applicant's work history and experience that may be relevant to the job opening are always appropriate. But don't encourage the applicant to divulge the trade secrets of a present or former employer—especially a competitor. That can lead to a lawsuit. And be cautious about an applicant who volunteers such information or promises to bring secrets to the new position; such an applicant will probably play fast and loose with your own company's secrets, given the chance.

## I've heard horror stories about employers who get sued for discriminating—both by employees and even by people they've interviewed but decided not to hire. What's the bottom line?

Federal and state laws prohibit you from discriminating against an employee or applicant because of race, color, gender, religious beliefs, national origin, physical disability—or age if the person is at least 40 years old. Also, many states and cities have laws prohibiting employment discrimination based on marital status or sexual orientation.

A particular form of discrimination becomes illegal when Congress, a state legislature or a city council decides that a characteristic—race, for example—bears no legitimate relationship to employment decisions. As an employer, you must be prepared to show that your hiring and promotion decisions have been based on objective criteria and that the more qualified applicant has always succeeded.

Still, when hiring, you can exercise a wide range of discretion based on business considerations. You remain free to hire, promote, discipline and fire employees and to set their duties and salaries based on their skills, experience, performance and reliability—factors that are logically tied to valid business purposes.

The law also prohibits employer practices that seem neutral, but may have a disproportionate impact on a particular group of people. Again, a policy is legal only if there's a valid business reason for its existence. For example, refusing to hire people who don't meet a minimum height and weight is permissible if it's clearly related to the physical demands of the particular job—felling and hauling huge trees, for instance. But applying such a requirement to exclude applicants for a job as a cook or receptionist wouldn't pass legal muster.

## How can I check out a prospective employee without violating his or her right to privacy?

As an employer, you likely believe that the more information you have about job applicants, the better your hiring decisions will be. But make sure any information you seek will actually be helpful to you. It's often a waste of time and effort to acquire and review transcripts and credit reports—although occasionally they're useful. If you're hiring a bookkeeper, for example, previous job experience is much more important than the grades the applicant received in a community college bookkeeping program 10 years ago. On the other hand, if the applicant is fresh out of school and has never held a bookkeeping job, a transcript may yield some insights. Similarly, if you're hiring a switchboard operator, information on a credit report would be irrelevant. But if you're filling a job for a bar manager who will be handling large cash receipts, you might want to see a credit report to learn if the applicant is in financial trouble.

To avoid claims that you've invaded a prospective employee's privacy, always obtain the applicant's written consent before you contact a former employer, request a credit report or send for high school or college transcripts.

Finally, it's usually not wise to resort to screening applicants through personality tests; laws and court rulings restrict your right to use them in most states.

# Protection for Recovering Addicts

With drug and alcohol use on the rise—along with increased pressure to make solid hiring decisions—many employers are resorting to drug and blood tests in an attempt to weed out problem employees before they're hired.

The Americans with Disabilities Act (ADA) prohibits you from discriminating against people because of past drug or alcohol problems. This includes people who no longer use drugs illegally and are receiving treatment for drug addiction or who have successfully recovered from an addiction.

To make sure that drug use isn't recurring, however, you may request evidence that a person is participating in a drug rehab program. You may also ask for the results of a drug test.

You can refuse to hire someone with a history of alcoholism or illegal drug use if you can show that the person poses a direct threat to health or safety. You must show that there's a high probability that the person will return to the illegal drug use or alcohol abuse, and a high probability of substantial harm to the person or others—harm that you can't reduce or eliminate through what the ADA deems a reasonable accommodation, such as changing the employee's job duties to eliminate working with toxic chemicals or heavy machinery.

## How do I avoid legal problems when giving employee evaluations?

Be honest and consistent with your employees. If a fired employee initiates a legal action against you, a judge or jury will analyze not only your evaluations, but other actions regarding that employee as well. For example, a jury will sense that something is wrong if you consistently rate a worker's performance as poor or mediocre—but continue to hand out generous raises or perhaps even promote the person. The logical conclusion: You didn't take seriously the criticisms in your evaluation report, so you shouldn't expect the employee to take them seriously, either.

It's just as damaging to give an employee glowing praise in report after report—perhaps to make the employee feel good—and then to fire him or her for a single infraction. That strikes most people as unfair. And unfair employers often lose court fights, especially in situations where a sympathetic employee appears to have been treated harshly.

If your system is working, employees with excellent evaluations should not need to be fired for poor performance. And employees with poor performance shouldn't be getting big raises.

## As a small employer, what should I keep in personnel files—and what right do employees have to see what's inside?

Create a file for each employee in which you keep all job-related information, including:
- job description
- job application
- offer of employment
- INS form I-9, the Employment Eligibility Verification, and supporting documents
- IRS form W-4, the Employee's Withholding Allowance Certificate
- receipt for employee handbook
- periodic performance evaluations
- sign-up forms for employee benefits
- complaints from customers and co-workers
- awards or citations for excellent performance
- warnings and disciplinary actions, and
- notes on an employee's attendance or tardiness.

# Special Rules for Medical Records

The Americans with Disabilities Act (ADA) imposes very strict limitations on how you must handle information obtained from post-offer medical examinations and inquiries. You must keep the information in medical files that are separate from nonmedical records, and you must store the medical files in a separate locked cabinet. To further guarantee the confidentiality of medical records, designate a specific person to have access to those files.

The ADA allows very limited disclosure of medical information. Under the ADA, you may:

- inform supervisors about necessary restrictions on an employee's duties and about necessary accommodations
- inform first aid and safety workers about a disability that may require emergency treatment and about specific procedures that are needed if the workplace must be evacuated, and
- provide medical information required by government officials and by insurance companies that require a medical exam for health or life insurance.

Otherwise, don't disclose medical information about employees. Although the confidentiality provisions of the ADA protect only some disabled workers, some states laws also require confidential handling of medical records. The best policy is to treat all medical information about all employees as confidential.

Many states have laws giving employees—and former employees—access to their own personnel files. How much access varies from state to state. Typically, if your state allows employees to see their files, you can insist that you or another supervisor be present to make sure nothing is taken, added or changed. Some state laws allow employees to obtain copies of items in their files, but not necessarily all items. For example, a law may limit the employee to copies of documents that he or she has signed, such as a job application. If an employee is entitled to a copy of an item in the file or if you're inclined to let the employee have a copy of any document in the file, you—rather than the employee—should make the copy.

Usually, you won't have to let the employee see sensitive items such as information assembled for a criminal investigation, reference letters and information that might violate the privacy of other people. In a few states, employees may insert rebuttals to information in their personnel files with which they disagree.

## Am I required to offer my employees paid vacation, disability, maternity or sick leave?

No law requires you to offer paid vacation time or paid sick or disability leave to your employees. You could choose to offer none—although a policy like this could make it tough to attract high-quality employees in a competitive market. If you decide to adopt a policy that gives your employees paid vacation or sick time, you must apply the policy consistently to all employees. If you offer some employees a more attractive package than others, you are opening yourself up to claims of unfair treatment.

The same rules apply to pregnancy and maternity leave. No law requires employers to provide paid leave for employees during their pregnancy or immediately after they give birth. However, if you choose to offer paid vacation, sick or disability leave, you must allow pregnant women and women who have just given birth to make use of these policies. For example, a new mother who is physically unable to work following the birth of her child must be allowed to use paid disability leave if such leave is available to other employees.

## Must I offer my employees unpaid leave?

There are two situations in which you might be legally required to offer unpaid leave to your employees. First, if the employee requesting leave qualifies as disabled under the Americans with Disabilities Act (see below for an explanation of the ADA), and requests the leave as a reasonable accommodation for the disability, you may be required to grant the leave request. For example, an employee who needs time off to undergo surgery or treatment for a disabling condition is probably entitled to unpaid leave, unless you can show that providing the leave would be an undue hardship to your business.

Second, your employees might be entitled to unpaid leave under the Family and Medical Leave Act (FMLA) or a similar state statute. See Chapter 4, *Workplace Rights*, for an explanation of when you must provide leave under the FMLA.

## I hear a lot about disabled workers being protected by the Americans with Disabilities Act (ADA), but the law is long and hard to understand. How can I make sure I comply?

The ADA states that when making hiring and employment decisions, it's illegal to discriminate against anyone because of a disability. If a person is qualified to do the work, or to do it once a reasonable accommodation is made, you must treat that person the same as all other applicants and employees. Although the concept is simple, the ADA requirements are immensely complicated—primarily because the statute is poorly drafted.

Many of the legal battles involving the ADA are waged over this imprecise language—particularly the meaning of "reasonable accommodation." The idea is quite simple: You may have to make some changes to help a disabled person do a job. This can take a number of forms, such as changing the job, an employment practice or the work environment. And you need not be psychic. Generally, the person with the disability needs to ask an employer to make the change.

The added twist is that the ADA doesn't require you to accommodate a disabled applicant or employee if it would place an undue hardship on the business—that is, if it would require significant difficulty or expense.

For employers, the ADA has its heaviest impact on the hiring process. For example, you must:

- write job descriptions that focus on essential tasks so that a person with a disability isn't eliminated because he or she can't perform a marginal job duty
- avoid questions in job applications and interviews that focus on possible disabilities, and
- defer pre-employment medical exams and inquiries until after you've made a conditional offer of employment.

See *Disability Discrimination*, in Chapter 4 for more information about the ADA.

## ADA Coverage Is Broad

Under the ADA, you can't discriminate against a person with a disability in any aspect of employment, including:

- applications
- interviews
- testing
- hiring
- job assignments
- evaluations
- disciplinary actions
- training
- promotion
- medical exams
- layoffs

- firing
- compensation
- leave, and
- benefits.

In addition, you can't deny a job to someone or discriminate against an employee because that person is related to or associates with a person who has a disability. For example, you can't:

- refuse to hire someone because that person's spouse, child or other dependent has a disability
- refuse to hire someone because that person's spouse, child or other dependent has a disability that's not covered by your current health insurance plan or that may cause increased healthcare costs, or
- fire an employee because that the employee has a roommate or close friend who has AIDS, or because the employee does volunteer work for people who have AIDS.

## One of my employees just told me that she was sexually harassed by a coworker. What should I do?

Most employers feel anxious when faced with complaints of sexual harassment. And with good reason: such complaints can lead to workplace tension, government investigations and even costly legal battles. If the complaint is mishandled, even unintentionally, an employer may unwittingly put itself out of business.

Here are some basics to keep in mind if you receive a complaint:

- *Educate yourself.* Do some research on the law of sexual harassment— learn what sexual harassment is, how it is proven in court, and what your responsibilities are as an employer. An excellent place to start is *Sexual Harassment on the Job,* by William Petrocelli and Barbara Kate Repa (Nolo).

- *Follow established procedures.* If you have an employee handbook or other documented policies relating to sexual harassment, follow those policies. Don't open yourself up to claims of unfair treatment by bending the rules.

- *Interview the people involved.* Start by talking to the person who complained. Then talk to the employee accused of harassment and any witnesses. Get details: what was said or done, when, where and who else was there.

- *Look for corroboration or contradiction.* Usually, the accuser and accused offer different versions of the incident, leaving you with no way of knowing who's telling the truth. Turn to other sources for clues. For example, schedules, time cards and other attendance records (for trainings, meetings, and so on) may help you determine if each party was where they claimed to be. Witnesses may have seen part of the incident. And in some cases, documents will prove one side right. It's hard to argue with an X-rated email.

- *Keep it confidential.* A sexual harassment complaint can polarize a workplace. Workers will likely side with either the complaining employee or the accused employee, and the rumor mill will start working overtime. Worse, if too many

details about the complaint are leaked, you may be accused of damaging the reputation of the alleged victim or alleged harasser—and get slapped with a defamation lawsuit. Avoid these problems by insisting on confidentiality, and practicing it in your investigation.

- *Write it all down.* Take notes during your interviews. Before the interview is over, go back through your notes with the interviewee, to make sure you got it right. Write down the steps you have taken to learn the truth, including interviews you have conducted and documents you have reviewed. Document any action taken against the accused, or the reasons for deciding not to take action. This written record will protect you later, if your employee claims that you ignored her complaint or conducted a one-sided investigation.

- *Cooperate with government agencies.* If the accuser makes a complaint with a government agency (either the federal Equal Employment Opportunity Commission (EEOC) or an equivalent state agency), that agency may investigate. Try to provide the agency with the materials it requests, but remember that the agency is gathering evidence that could be used against you later. This is a good time to consider hiring a lawyer to advise you.

- *Don't retaliate.* It is against the law to punish someone for making a sexual harassment complaint. The most obvious forms of retaliation are termination, discipline, demotion, pay cuts or threats of any of these actions. More subtle forms of retaliation may include changing the shift hours or work area of the accuser, changing the accuser's job responsibilities or reporting relationships and isolating the accuser by leaving her out of meetings and other office functions.

- *Take appropriate action against the harasser.* Once you have gathered all the information available, sit down and decide what you think really happened. If you conclude that some form of sexual harassment occurred, figure out how to discipline the harasser appropriately. Once you have decided on an appropriate action, take it quickly, document it and notify the accuser.

## My employees' religious differences are causing strife in the workplace. What am I required to do?

This is a tricky area. An increasing number of employees are claiming religious discrimination. And unfortunately, the law in this delicate area is unclear.

First, make sure you aren't imposing your religious beliefs on others. You have the legal right to discuss your own religious beliefs with an employee, if you're so inclined, but you can't persist to the point that the employee feels you're being hostile, intimidating or offensive. So if an employee objects to your discussion of religious subjects or you get even an inkling that your religious advances are unwelcome, back off. Otherwise,

you may find yourself embroiled in a lawsuit or administrative proceeding.

If employees complain to you that a co-worker is badgering them with religious views, you have a right—if not a duty—to intervene, although you must, of course, use the utmost tact and sensitivity.

While you may feel that the best way to resolve these knotty problems is to simply banish religion from the workplace, that's generally not a viable alternative. You're legally required to accommodate the religious needs of employees—for example, allowing employees to pick and choose the paid holidays they would like to take during the year. You don't, however, need to do anything that would cost more than a minimum amount or that would cause more than minimal inconvenience.

## Some of my employees insist they have a right to smoke during breaks and at lunch, and another group claims they'll quit if I allow smoking on the premises. I'm caught in the middle. What should I do?

It's well established that second hand tobacco smoke can harm the health of nonsmokers. Consequently, in many states and municipalities, employers are legally required to limit smoking in the workplace. And a number of locales have specific laws that ban or limit smoking in public places; if your workplace falls within the legal definition of a public place—a bar, restaurant or hotel, for example—your legal rights and responsibilities will be clearly spelled out in the law.

A rule proposed by the Occupational Health and Safety Administration (OSHA) would allow only two choices: you'd have to either prohibit smoking in the workplace, or limit it to areas that are enclosed and ventilated directly to the outdoors. Under the rule, you couldn't require employees to enter the smoking areas when performing their normal job duties. This proposal is till under consideration.

Given the scientific facts and the general direction in which the law is moving, your safest legal course is to restrict smoking in the workplace—and a total ban may be the only practical solution. That's because in many modern buildings, it's too expensive—maybe even impossible—to provide a separate ventilation system for a smokers' room.

In addition to meeting the specific requirements of laws and regulations that limit or prohibit smoking in the workplace, be aware that you may be legally liable to nonsmoking employees if you don't take appropriate actions on their complaints.

## It's been a bad year for my business—and it looks as though I may have to lay off some workers. Are there legal problems to avoid?

Generally, you're free to lay off or terminate employees because business conditions require it. But if you do cut back, don't leave your business open to claims that the layoffs were really a pretext for getting rid of employees for illegal reasons.

Be sensitive to how your actions may be perceived. If the layoff primarily affects workers of a particular race, or women or older employees, someone may well question your motives. It's better to spread the pain around; don't let the burden fall on just one group of employees.

## How can I make sure that my employees don't reveal my company's trade secrets to a competitor—especially after they leave the company?

You should take two steps to protect your trade secrets from disclosure by former employees: always treat your trade secrets as confidential, and require any employee who will come in contact with your trade secrets to sign a nondisclosure agreement.

A trade secret is any information that provides its owner with a competitive advantage in the market, and is treated as a secret—that is, handled in a manner that can reasonably be expected to prevent others from learning about it. Examples of trade secrets might include recipes, manufacturing processes, customer or pricing lists and ideas for new products. If you own a trade secret, you have the legal right to prevent anyone from disclosing, copying or using it, and can sue anyone who violates these rights to your disadvantage.

Always keep your trade secrets confidential. For example, you should mark documents containing trade secrets "confidential" and limit their circulation, disclose trade secret material only to those employees with a real need to know, keep materials in a safe place and have a written policy which makes it clear that trade secrets are not to be revealed to outsiders.

In addition to taking steps to keep your trade secrets confidential, you should also require any employee who will come in contact with your trade secrets to sign a nondisclosure agreement, or NDA. An NDA is a contract in which the parties promise to keep confidential any trade secrets disclosed during the employment relationship. You can find more information and sample NDA forms in *Nondisclosure Agreements* by Stephen Fishman (Nolo).

## What are my legal obligations to an employee who is leaving the company?

Surprisingly, your responsibility to your employees doesn't necessarily end when the employment relationship ends. Even after an employee quits or is fired, you must:

- Provide the employee's final paycheck in accordance with state law. Most states require that an employee receive this check fairly quickly, sometimes just a day or two after the last day of work.
- Provide severance pay. No law requires employers to provide severance pay (although a few states require employers to pay severance to workers fired in a plant closure). But if you promise it, you must pay it to all employees who meet your policy's requirements.
- Give information on continuation of health insurance, under a federal law

called the Consolidated Omnibus Budget Reconciliation Act (CO-BRA). If you offer your employees health insurance, and your company has twenty or more employees, you must offer departing employees the option of continued coverage under the company's group health insurance plan, at the worker's expense, for a specified period.

- Allow former employees to view their personnel files. Most states provide employees and former employees with the legal right to see their personnel file, and to receive copies of some of the documents relating to their job. State laws vary as to how long employers must keep these records for former employees.

## I have to give a reference for a former employee I had to fire. I don't want to be too positive about him, but I am also afraid he might sue me for unflattering remarks. Advice?

The key to protecting yourself is to stick to the facts and act in good faith. You'll get in trouble only if you exaggerate or cover up the truth—or are motivated by a desire to harm your former employee.

Former employees who feel maligned can sue for defamation—called slander if the statements were spoken or libel if they were written. To win a defamation case, a former employee must prove that you intentionally gave out false information and that the information harmed his or her reputation. If you can show that the information you provided was true, the lawsuit will be dismissed.

And even if it turns out that the information provided is untrue, employers in most states are entitled to some protection in defamation cases. This protection is based on a legal doctrine called "qualified privilege." To receive the benefits, you must show that:

- you made the statement in good faith
- you and the person to whom you disclosed the information shared a common interest, and
- you limited your statement to this common interest.

The law recognizes that a former employer and a prospective employer share a common interest in the attributes of an employee. To get the protection of the qualified privilege, your main task is to stick to facts that you've reasonably investigated and to lay aside your personal feelings about the former employee.

A practical policy—and one that gives you a high degree of legal protection—is simply not to discuss an employee with prospective employers if you can't say something positive. Just tell the person inquiring that it's not your policy to comment on former workers.

Where an employee's record is truly mixed, it's usually possible to accent the positive while you try to put negative information into a more favorable perspective. If you do choose to go into detail, don't hide the bad news. In very extreme cases (in which the former employee committed a se-rious crime or engaged in dangerous wrongdoing), you could be sued by the new employer for conceding this information.

## Do I have the same legal obligations to independent contractors as I do to employees?

Generally, an employer has more obligations, both legally and financially, to employees than to independent contractors. The workplace rights guaranteed to employees do not protect independent contractors, for the most part. And an employer must make certain contributions to the government on behalf of its employees, while independent contractors are expected to make these payments themselves.

Here are a number of rules that apply only to employees:

- *Anti-discrimination laws.* Most laws prohibiting employers from discriminating against employees or applicants for employment based such characteristics as race, gender, national origin, religion, age or disability do not protect independent contractors.
- *Wage and hour laws.* Independent contractors are not covered by laws governing the minimum wage, overtime pay and the like.
- *Medical and parental leave laws.* You are not required to offer independent contractors medical or parental leave.
- *Workers' compensation laws.* You do not have to provide workers' compensation for independent contractors.

- *Unemployment insurance.* You do not have to contribute to unemployment insurance for independent contractors.
- *Social Security contributions.* You are not required to make any Social Security payments on behalf of independent contractors.
- *Wage withholding.* You are not required to withhold state or federal income tax, or state disability insurance payments (where applicable) from the paychecks of independent contractors.

## When can I classify a worker as an independent contractor?

Different government agencies use different tests to decide whether workers should be classified as independent contractors or employees. Generally, these tests are intended to figure out whether an independent contractor is truly a self-employed businessperson offering services to the general public. The more discretion a worker has to decide how, when and for whom to perform work, the more likely that the worker is an independent contractor. For example, an independent contractor might do similar work for other companies, provide the tools and equipment to do the job, decide how to do the job (including when, where, and in what order to do the work) and hire employees or assistants to help out with big jobs. On the other hand, a worker who works only for you, under conditions determined by you, is more likely to be classified as an employee.

### More Information About Employers' Rights and Responsibilities

*The Employer's Legal Handbook,* by Fred Steingold (Nolo), explains employers' legal rights and responsibilities in detail.

*Firing Without Fear,* by Barbara Kate Repa (Nolo), offers employers' advice on firing workers legally .

*Avoid Employee Lawsuits,* by Barbara Kate Repa (Nolo), provides information on hiring, managing and firing employees.

*Reference Checking Handbook,* published by the Society for Human Resource Management, provides helpful information about the Ps and Qs of checking references. Call 612-885-5588 for price and ordering information.

In a concise publication called *Credit Reports: What Employers Should Know About Using Them,* the Federal Trade Commission offers examples to illustrate situations where it is and is not a good idea to check job applicants' credit records. To order, call the FTC's Office of Consumer and Business Education at 202-326-3650.

Many state trade associations publish newsletters or magazines to help keep their members informed of changes in employment law. Your state chamber of commerce may also have helpful publications on this subject.

Information on independent contractors can be found in *Hiring Independent Contractors* by Stephen Fishman (Nolo).

## General Sites for Small Businesses

### http://www.nolo.com

*Nolo offers free self-help information and small business books, software and forms on a wide variety of subjects, including starting and running your small business.*

### http://www.americanexpress. com/smallbusiness

*The American Express Small Business Exchange helps you find information, resources and customers for your small business.*

### http://www.nfibonline.com/

*The National Federation of Independent Business provides news, workshops and action alerts for small business owners. The NFIB is the nation's largest advocacy organization for small and independent businesses.*

### http://www.smalloffice.com

*Smalloffice.com offers useful tips on marketing, sales and financing, as well as advice on how to use software, computers and other technology to help your business.*

### http://www.sbaonline.sba.gov/

*The Small Business Administration provides information about starting, financing and expanding your small business.*

### http://www.yahoo.com/business/small_business_information

*Yahoo offers an abundance of links to resources for small business people.*

## Sites for Nonprofit Corporations

### http://www.igc.org

*The Institute for Global Communication offers an extensive list of links to resources for activism and nonprofit development.*

### http://www.ncnb.org

*The National Center for Nonprofit Boards provides information and publications to help you run a successful nonprofit organization.*

## Sites for Independent Contractors and Home-Based Businesses

### http://www.hoaa.com/

*The Home Office Association of America is a national association for home-based business people. It offers resources, ideas and benefits to help you run a more profitable business from home. The site also contains an extensive list of links to other sites of interest to the self-employed.*

### http://www.ssa.gov/

*The Social Security Administration provides lots of information on regulations and benefits for self-employed people.*

# **P**atents

6.2    *Qualifying for a Patent*

6.7    *Obtaining a Patent*

6.9    *Enforcing a Patent*

6.12    *Putting a Patent to Work*

6.14    *How Patents Differ from Copyrights and Trademarks*

*To invent, you need a good imagination and a pile of junk.*

**—THOMAS EDISON**

**M**any of us muse about the million-dollar idea: the invention that will make life easier for others and more lucrative for us. Most of these ideas never get off the ground, however; we decide it's not really worth the time and effort to create the perfect dog toothbrush, clothes hanger or juice squeezer. But every now and then we may hit on a winner—an idea worth developing, marketing and protecting. In these cases, we must turn to the patent laws for help.

This chapter addresses the basic legal issues that arise in the patent area, answering questions such as:

- What is a patent?
- When does a particular invention qualify for a patent?
- How do you get a patent in the U.S. or abroad?
- How are patent rights enforced?
- How can you profit from your patent?

# Qualifying for a Patent

THERE IS NOTHING WHICH

PERSEVERING EFFORT AND UNCEASING

AND DILIGENT CARE CANNOT

ACCOMPLISH.

— SENECA

A patent is a document issued by the U.S. Patent and Trademark Office (PTO) that grants a monopoly for a limited period of time on the manufacture, use and sale of an invention.

## What types of inventions can be patented?

The PTO issues three different kinds of patents: utility patents, design patents and plant patents.

Design patents last for 14 years from the date the patent issues. Plant and utility patents last for 20 years from the date of filing.

To qualify for a utility patent—by far the most common type of patent—an invention must be:

- a process or method for producing a useful, concrete and tangible result (such as a genetic engineering procedure, an investment strategy or computer software)
- a machine (usually something with moving parts or circuitry, such as a cigarette lighter, sewage treatment system, laser or photocopier)
- an article of manufacture (such as an eraser, tire, transistor or hand tool)
- a composition of matter (such as a chemical composition, drug, soap or genetically altered life form), or
- an improvement of an invention that fits within one of the first four categories.

Often, an invention will fall into more than one category. For instance, a laser can usually be described both as a process (the steps necessary to produce the laser beam) and a machine (a device that implements the steps to produce the laser beam). Regardless of the number of categories into which a particular invention fits, it can receive only one utility patent.

If an invention fits into one of the categories described above, it is known as "statutory subject matter" and has passed the first test in qualifying for a patent. But an inventor's creation must overcome several additional hurdles before the PTO will issue a patent. The invention must also:

- have some utility, no matter how trivial
- be novel (that is, it must be different from all previous inventions in some important way), and

- be nonobvious (a surprising and significant development) to somebody who understands the technical field of the invention.

For design patents, the law requires that the design be novel, nonobvious and nonfunctional. For example, a new shape for a car fender, bottle or flashlight that doesn't improve its functionality would qualify.

Finally, plants may qualify for a patent if they are both novel and nonobvious. Plant patents are issued less frequently than any other type of patent.

## More Examples of Patentable Subject Matter

The following items are just some of the things that might qualify for patent protection: biological inventions; carpet designs; new chemical formulas, processes or procedures; clothing accessories and designs; computer hardware and peripherals; computer software; containers; cosmetics; decorative hardware; electrical inventions; electronic circuits; fabrics and fabric designs; food inventions; furniture design; games (board, box and instructions); housewares; jewelry; laser light shows; machines; magic tricks or techniques; mechanical inventions; medical accessories and devices; medicines; methods of doing business; musical instruments; odors; plants; recreational gear; and sporting goods (designs and equipment).

## What types of inventions are not eligible for patent protection?

Some types of inventions will not qualify for a patent, no matter how interesting or important they are. For example, mathematical formulas, laws of nature, newly discovered substances that occur naturally in the world, and purely theoretical phenomena—for instance, a scientific principle like superconductivity without regard to its use in the real world—have long been considered unpatentable. This means, for example, that you can't patent a general mathematical approach to problem solving or a newly discovered pain killer in its natural state.

In addition, the following categories of inventions don't qualify for patents:

- processes done entirely by human motor coordination, such as choreographed dance routines or a method for meditation
- most protocols and methods used to perform surgery on humans
- printed matter that has no unique physical shape or structure associated with it
- unsafe new drugs
- inventions useful only for illegal purposes, and
- nonoperable inventions, including "perpetual motion" machines (which are presumed to be nonoperable because to operate they would have to violate certain bedrock scientific principles).

## Can computer software qualify for patent protection?

Yes. Even though you can't get a patent on a mathematical formula per se, you may be able to get protection for a specific application of a formula. Thus, software may qualify for a patent if it produces a useful, concrete and tangible result. For example, the PTO will not issue a patent on the complex mathematical formulae that are used in space navigation, but will grant a patent for the software and machines that translate those equations and make the space shuttle go where it's supposed to go.

## Can a business method qualify for a utility patent?

A business method is a series of steps that express some business activity, for example, a method of calculating an interest rate or a system for evaluating employee performance. Before 1988, the PTO rarely granted patents for methods of doing business. Then, in 1988, the United States Court of Appeals for the Federal Circuit changed this. (*State Street Bank & Trust Co. v. Signal Financial Group, Inc.* 149 F.3d 1368 (Fed. Cir. 1998).) The court ruled that patent laws were intended to protect business methods, so long as the method produced a "useful, concrete and tangible result."

In the six months following the *State Street* ruling, patent filings for business methods increased by 40%. In response to the development of these new methods, the PTO created a new classification for such applications: "Data processing: financial, business practice, management or cost/price determination."

## Is it possible to obtain a patent on forms of life?

Forms of life, from bacteria to cows, that are genetically altered to have new and useful characteristics or behaviors may qualify for utility patents. Also patentable are sequences of DNA that have been created to test genetic behaviors and the methods used to accomplish this sequencing. With the advent of cloning techniques and the ability to mix genes across species—for example, the human immune system genetic code transplanted into a mouse for testing purposes—the question of what life forms can and cannot be patented promises to be a subject of fierce debate for years to come.

## What makes an invention novel?

In the context of a patent application, an invention is considered novel when it is different from all previous inventions (called "prior art") in one or more of its constituent elements. When deciding whether an invention is novel, the PTO will consider all prior art that existed as of the date the inventor files a patent application on the invention, or if necessary, as of the date the inventor can prove he or she first built and tested the invention. If prior art is uncovered, the invention may still qualify for a patent if the inventor can show that he or she conceived of the invention before the prior art existed and was diligent in building and testing the invention or filing a patent application on it.

An invention will flunk the novelty test if it was described in a published document or put to public use more than one year prior to the date the patent application was filed. This is known as the one-year rule.

## When is an invention considered nonobvious?

To qualify for a patent, an invention must be nonobvious as well as novel. An invention is considered nonobvious if someone who is skilled in the particular field of the invention would view it as an unexpected or surprising development.

For example, in August of 2000, Future Enterprises invents a portable high quality virtual reality system. A virtual reality engineer would most likely find this invention to be truly surprising and unexpected. Even though increased portability of a computer-based technology is always expected in the broad sense, the specific way in which the portability is accomplished by this invention would be a breakthrough in the field and thus unobvious. Contrast this with a bicycle developer who uses a new, light but strong metal alloy to build his bicycles. Most people skilled in the art of bicycle manufacturing would consider the use of the new alloy in the bicycle to be obvious, given that lightness of weight is a desirable aspect of high-quality bicycles.

Knowing whether an invention will be considered nonobvious by the PTO is difficult because it is such a subjective exercise—what one patent examiner considers surprising, another may not. In addition, the examiner will usually be asked to make the nonobviousness determination well after the date of the invention, because of delays inherent in the patent process. The danger of this type of retroactive assessment is that the examiner may unconsciously be affected by the intervening technical improvements. To avoid this, the examiner generally relies only on the prior-art references (documents describing previous inventions) that existed as of the date of invention.

As an example, assume that in 2003, Future Enterprises' application for a patent on the 2000 invention is being examined in the Patent and Trademark Office. Assume further that by 2003, you can find a portable virtual reality unit in any consumer electronics store for under $200. The patent examiner will have to go back to the time of the invention to fully appreciate how surprising and unexpected it was when it was first conceived, and ignore the fact that in 2003 the technology of the invention is very common.

## What makes an invention useful?

Patents may be granted for inventions that have some type of usefulness (utility), even if the use is humorous, such as a musical condom or a motorized spaghetti fork. However, the invention must work—at least in theory. Thus, a new approach to manufacturing superconducting materials may qualify for a patent if it has a sound theoretical basis—even if it hasn't yet been shown to work in practice. But a new drug that has no theoretical basis and which hasn't been tested will not qualify for a patent.

Remember that to qualify for a design or plant patent, the other two types of patents obtained in the U.S., the inventor need not show utility

# Are You the First?

As discussed previously, patents are awarded only on new and nonobvious inventions. How can an inventor find out whether his or her invention is really new? The place to start is to see whether it has ever been patented. Although a number of great inventions have never received a patent, most have. A quick spin through the patent database can provide a good headstart on finding out just how innovative an invention really is.

The Internet can be used for free access to patents issued since 1971. The U.S. Patent and Trademark Office (http://.uspto.gov) provides free online databases where you simply type in words which describe your invention—called keywords.

Commercial fee-based databases often offer more choices than the free USPTO site. Below are some fee-based patent databases and a brief description of their contents.

- **Corporate Intelligence Corp** (http://www.1790.com). You can search U.S. patents from 1945 to the present. CIC also provides copies of patents dating back to 1790 by mail, fax or email.
- **Micropatent** (http:// www.micropatent.com). You can search U.S. and Japanese patents from 1976 to the present, International patents issued under the Patent Cooperation Treaty (PCT) from 1983 and European patents from 1988.
- **Delphion** (http:// www.delphion.com). You can search U.S patents from 1971 to the present and full-text patents from the European

Patent Office, the World Intellectual Property Organization PCT collection and abstracts from Derwent world patent index.

- **LEXPAT** (http://www.lexis-nexis.com). You can search U.S. patents from 1971 to the present. In addition, the LEXPAT library offers extensive prior-art searching capability of technical journals and magazines.
- **QPAT** (http://www.qpat.com) and **Questel/Orbit** (http:// www.questel.orbit.com). You can search U.S. patents from 1974 to the present and full-text European patents from 1987 to the present.

Sometimes an inventor needs to search for patents issued before 1971. All patents since the founding of the United States count when deciding whether an invention is sufficiently new to deserve a patent. And if the invention involves time-less technology (another way to core an apple), these pre-1971 patents are as important as those that were issued later.

A great resource for complete patent searching—from the first patent ever issued to the latest—is a network of special libraries called Patent and Trade-mark Depository Libraries (PTDLs). Every state but Connecticut has at least one. While a complete patent search can be done for free in these libraries, many of them also offer computer searches for a reasonable fee. Consult the PTO website at http://www.uspto.gov to find the PTDL nearest you.

# Obtaining a Patent

*Many times a day I realize how much my own outer and inner life is built upon the labors of my fellow men, both living and dead, and how earnestly I must exert myself in order to give in return as much as I have received.*

**—ALBERT EINSTEIN**

Because a patent grants the inventor a monopoly on his or her invention for a relatively long period of time, patent applications are rigorously examined by the Patent and Trademark Office (PTO). Typically, a patent application travels back and forth between the applicant and the patent examiner until both sides agree on which aspects of an invention the patent will cover, if any. This process typically takes between one and two years.

If an agreement is reached, the PTO "allows" the application and publishes a brief description of the patent in a weekly publication called the *Official Gazette.* If no one objects to the patent as published, and the applicant pays the required issuance fee, the PTO provides the applicant with a document called a patent deed, which we colloquially refer to as a patent. The patent deed consists primarily of the information submitted in the patent application, as modified during the patent examination process.

## What information is typically included in a patent application?

There is no such thing as an automatic patent through creation or usage of an invention. To receive patent protection, an inventor must file an application, pay the appropriate fees and obtain a patent. To apply for a U.S. patent, the inventor must file the application with a branch of the U.S. Department of Commerce known as the U.S. Patent and Trademark Office, or PTO. A U.S. patent application typically consists of:

• an Information Disclosure Statement—that is, an explanation of why the invention is different from all previous and similar developments (the "prior art")

• a detailed description of the structure and operation of the invention (called a patent specification) that teaches how to build and use the invention

• a precise description of the aspects of the invention to be covered by the patent (called the patent claims)

• all drawings that are necessary to fully explain the specification and claims

• a Patent Application Declaration—a statement under oath that the information in the application is true, and

• the filing fee.

In addition, small inventors often include a declaration asking for a reduction in the filing fee.

## Understanding the Provisional Patent Application

Often inventors want to have a patent application on file when they go out to show their invention to prospective manufacturers because it will discourage ripoffs. Also, inventors like to get their invention on record as early as possible in case someone else comes up with the same invention. To accomplish both these goals, an inventor may file what is known as a Provisional Patent Application (PPA). The PPA need only contain a complete description of the structure and operation of an invention and any drawings that are necessary to understand it—it need not contain claims, formal drawings, a Patent Application Declaration or an Information Disclosure Statement.

An inventor who files a regular patent application within one year of filing a PPA can claim the PPA's filing date for the regular patent application. If the regular patent application includes any new matter (technical information about the invention) that wasn't in the PPA, the inventor won't be able to rely on the PPA's filing date for the new matter. The PPA's filing date doesn't affect when the patent on the invention will expire; it still expires 20 years from the date the regular patent application is filed. So, the PPA has the practical effect of delaying examination of a regular patent application and extending—up to one year—the patent's expiration date.

## What happens if there are multiple applications for the same invention?

If a patent examiner discovers that another pending application involves the same invention and that both inventions appear to qualify for a patent, the patent examiner will declare that a conflict (called an interference) exists between the two applications. In that event, a hearing is held to determine who is entitled to the patent.

Who gets the patent depends on such variables as who first conceived the invention and worked on it diligently, who first built and tested the invention and who filed the first provisional or regular patent application. Because of the possibility of a patent interference, it is wise to document all invention-related activities in a signed and witnessed inventor's notebook so that you can later prove the date the invention was conceived and the steps you took to build and test the invention or quickly file a patent application.

## How are U.S. patents protected abroad?

Patent rights originate in the U.S. Constitution and are implemented exclusively by federal laws passed by Congress. These laws define the kinds of inventions that are patentable and the procedures that must be followed to apply for, receive and maintain patent rights for the duration of the patent.

All other industrialized countries offer patent protection as well. While patent requirements and rules differ from country to country, several international treaties (including the Patent Cooperation Treaty and the Paris Convention) allow U.S. inventors to obtain patent protection in other countries that have adopted the treaties if the inventors take certain required steps, such as filing a patent application in the countries on a timely basis and paying required patent fees.

# Enforcing a Patent

Once a patent is issued, it is up to the owner to enforce it. If friendly negotiations fail, enforcement involves two basic steps:
- making a determination that the patent is being illegally violated (infringed), and
- filing a federal court action to enforce the patent.

Because enforcing a patent can be a long and expensive process, many patent infringment suits that could have been filed, aren't. Instead, the patent owner often settles with the infringer. Frequently, an infringer will pay a reasonable license fee that allows the infringer to continue using the invention.

## What constitutes infringement of a patent?

To decide whether an inventor is violating a patent, it is necessary to carefully examine the patent's claims (most patents contain more than one of these terse statements of the scope of the invention) and compare the elements of each claim with the elements of the accused infringer's device or process. If the elements of a patent claim match the elements of the device or process (called "reading on" or "teaching" the device or process), an infringement has occurred. Even if the claims don't literally match the infringing device, it is possible that a court would find an infringement by applying what's known as the "doctrine of equivalents," that is, the invention in the patent and the allegedly infringing device or process are sufficiently equivalent in what they do and how they do it to warrant a finding of infringement.

For example, Steve invents a tennis racket with a score keeper embedded in the racket handle's end. The invention is claimed as a tennis racket handle that combines grasping and score keeping functions. Steve receives a patent on this invention. Later, Megan invents and sells a tennis racket with a transparent handle that provides a more sophisticated score keeping device than Steve's racket. Even though Megan's invention improves on Steve's invention in certain respects, it will most likely be held to be an infringement of Steve's invention, for one of two reasons:

• Megan's invention teaches the same elements as those claimed in Steve's patent (a tennis racket handle with two functions), or

• when considering what it is and how it works, Megan's invention is the substantial equivalent of Steve's invention (the doctrine of equivalents).

## What remedies are available for patent infringement?

A patent owner may enforce his patent by bringing a patent infringement action (lawsuit) in federal court against anyone who uses his invention without permission. If the lawsuit is successful, the court will take one of two approaches. It may issue a court order (called an injunction) preventing the infringer from any further use or sale of the infringing device, and award damages to the patent owner. Or, the court may work with the parties to hammer out an agreement under which the infringing party will pay the patent owner royalties in exchange for permission to use the infringing device.

Bringing a patent infringement action can be tricky, because it is possible for the alleged infringer to defend by proving to the court that the patent is really invalid (most often by showing that the PTO made a mistake in issuing the patent in the first place). In a substantial number of patent infringement cases, the patent is found invalid and the lawsuit dismissed, leaving the patent owner in a worse position than before the lawsuit.

## When does patent protection end?

Patent protection usually ends when the patent expires. For all utility patents filed before June 8, 1995, the patent term is 17 years from date of issuance. For utility patents filed on or after June 8, 1995, the patent term is 20 years from the date of filing. For design patents, the period is 14 years from date of issuance. For plant patents, the period is 17 years from date of issuance.

A patent may expire if its owner fails to pay required maintenance fees. Usually this occurs because attempts to commercially exploit the underlying invention have failed and the patent owner chooses to not throw good money after bad.

Patent protection ends if a patent is found to be invalid. This may happen if someone shows that the patent application was insufficient or that the applicant committed fraud on the PTO, usually by lying or failing to disclose the applicant's knowledge about prior art that would legally prevent issuance of the patent. A patent may also be invalidated if someone shows that the inventor engaged in illegal conduct when using the patent—such as conspiring with a patent licensee to exclude other companies from competing with them.

Once a patent has expired, the invention described by the patent falls into the public domain: It can be used by anyone without permission from the owner of the expired patent. The basic technologies underlying television and personal computers are good examples of valuable inventions that are no longer covered by in-force patents.

The fact that an invention is in the public domain does not mean that subsequent developments based on the original invention are also in the public domain. Rather, new inventions that improve public domain technology are constantly being conceived and patented. For example, televisions and personal computers that roll off today's assembly lines employ many recent inventions that are covered by in-force patents.

## The Life of an Invention

Although most inventors are concerned with the rights a patent grants during its monopoly or in-force period (from the date the patent issues until it expires), the law actually recognizes five "rights" periods in the life of an invention. These five periods are as follows:

1. Invention conceived but not yet documented. When an inventor conceives an invention but hasn't yet made any written, signed, dated and witnessed record of it, the inventor has no rights whatsoever.

2. Invention documented but patent application not yet filed. After making a proper signed, dated and witnessed documentation of an invention, the inventor has valuable rights against any inventor who later conceives the same invention and applies for a patent. The invention may also be treated as a "trade secret"—that is, kept confidential. This gives the inventor the legal right to sue and recover damages against anyone who immorally learns of the invention—for example, through industrial spying.

3. Patent pending (patent application filed but not yet issued). During the

patent pending period, including the one-year period after a provisional patent application is filed, the inventor's rights are the same as they are in Period 2, above, with one exception. Effective December 2000, if the patent owner intends to also file for a patent abroad, the PTO will publish the application 18 months after the earliest claimed filing date. Under the new 18-month publication statute, an inventor whose application is published prior to issuance may obtain royalties from an infringer from the date of publication, provided the application later issues as a patent and the infringer had actual notice of the published application. Otherwise, the inventor has no rights whatsoever against infringers—only the hope of a future monopoly, which doesn't commence until a patent issues. By law, the PTO must keep all patent applications secret until the application is published or the patent issues, whichever comes first. The patent pending period usually lasts from one to three years.

4. In-force patent (patent issued but hasn't yet expired). After the patent issues, the patent owner can bring and maintain a lawsuit for patent infringement against anyone who makes, uses or sells the invention without permission. The patent's in-force period lasts from the date it issues until it expires. Also, after the patent issues, it becomes a public record or publication that prevents others from getting patents on the same or similar inventions—that is, it becomes "prior art" to anyone who

files a subsequent patent application.

5. Patent expired. After the patent expires, the patent owner has no further rights, although infringement suits can still be brought for any infringement that occurred during the patent's in-force period as long as the suit is filed within the time required by law. An expired patent remains a valid "prior-art reference" forever.

# Putting a Patent to Work

OUR ASPIRATIONS ARE OUR

POSSIBILITIES.

—ROBERT BROWNING

On its own, a patent has no value. Value arises only when a patent owner takes action to realize commercial gain from his or her monopoly position. There are several basic approaches to making money from a patent.

## How can an inventor make money with a patent?

Some inventors start new companies to develop and market their patented inventions. This is not typical, however, because the majority of inventors would rather invent than run a business. More often, an inventor makes arrangements with an existing company to develop and market the invention. This arrangement usually takes the form of a license (contract) under which the developer is authorized to commercially exploit the invention in exchange for paying the patent owner royalties for each invention sold. Or, in a common variation of this arrangement, the inventor may sell all the rights to the invention for a lump sum.

## What does it mean to license an invention?

A license is written permission to use an invention. A license may be exclusive (if only one manufacturer is licensed to develop the invention) or nonexclusive (if a number of manufacturers are licensed to develop it). The license may be for the duration of the patent or for a shorter period of time.

The developer itself may license other companies to market or distribute the invention. The extent to which the inventor will benefit from these sub-licenses depends on the terms of the agreement between the inventor and the developer. Especially when inventions result from work done in the course of employment, the employer-business usually ends up owning the patent rights, and receives all or most of the royalties based on subsequent licensing activity. (See the next question.)

In many cases, a developer will trade licenses with other companies—called cross-licensing—so that companies involved in the trade will benefit from each other's technology. For example, assume that two computer

companies each own several patents on newly developed remote-controlled techniques. Because each company would be strengthened by being able to use the other company's inventions as well as its own, the companies will most likely agree to swap permissions to use their respective inventions.

## Can inventors who are employed by a company benefit from their inventions?

Typically, inventor-employees who invent in the course of their employment are bound by employment agreements that automatically assign all rights in the invention to the employer. While smart research and development companies give their inventors bonuses for valuable inventions, this is a matter of contract rather than law.

If there is no employment agreement, the employer may still own rights to an employee-created invention under the "employed to invent" doctrine. How does this rule apply? If an inventor is employed—even without a written employment agreement—to accomplish a defined task, or is hired or directed to create an invention, the employer will own all rights to the subsequent invention.

If there is no employment agreement and the inventor is not employed to invent, the inventor may retain the right to exploit the invention, but the employer is given a nonexclusive right to use the invention for its internal purposes (called shop rights). For example, Robert is a machinist in a machine shop and invents a new process for handling a particular type of metal. If Robert isn't employed to invent and hasn't signed an employment agreement giving the shop all rights to the invention, Robert can patent and exploit the invention for himself. The shop, however, would retain the right to use the new process without having to pay Robert.

# How Patents Differ From Copyrights and Trademarks

While it is possible to invent definitions that draw clear lines between the areas of patent, copyright and trademark (the three major types of intellectual property protection), there are complications when it comes to certain innovative designs. In some cases, a design may be subject to patent, trademark and copyright protection all at the same time.

## How do patents differ from copyrights?

With the exception of innovative designs, patents are closely associated with things and processes which are useful in the real world. Almost at the opposite end of the spectrum, copy-right applies to expressive arts such as novels, fine and graphic arts, music, phonorecords, photography, software, video, cinema and choreography. While it is possible to get a patent on technologies used in the arts, it is copyright that keeps one artist from stealing another artist's creative work.

An exception to the general rule that patents and copyright don't overlap can be found in product designs. It is theoretically possible to get a design patent on the purely ornamental (nonfunctional) aspects of the product design and also claim a copyright in this same design. For example, the stylistic fins of a car's rear fenders may qualify for both a design patent (because they are strictly ornamental) and copyright (as to their expressive elements). In practice, however, a product is usually granted one type of protection or the other—not both.

For more information about copyright law, see Chapter 7.

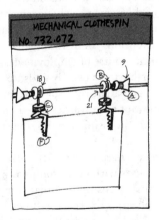

## What's the difference between patent and trademark?

Generally speaking, patents allow the creator of certain kinds of inventions that contain new ideas to keep others from making commercial use of those ideas without the creator's permission. Trademark, on the other hand, is not concerned with how a new technology is used. Rather, it applies to the names, logos and other devices—such as color, sound and smell—that are used to identify the source of goods or services and distinguish them from their competition.

Generally, patent and trademark laws do not overlap. When it comes to a product design, however—say, jewelry or a distinctively shaped musical instrument—it may be possible to obtain a patent on a design aspect of the device while invoking trademark law to protect the design as a product identifier. For example, a surfboard manufacturer might receive a patent for a surfboard design that mimics the design used in a popular surfing film. Then, if the design is intended to be—and actually is—used to distinguish the particular type of surfboard in the marketplace, trademark law may kick in to protect the appearance of the board.

For more information about trademarks, see Chapter 8.

### More Information About Patents

*Patent It Yourself,* by David Pressman (Nolo), takes you step by step through the process of getting a patent without hiring a patent lawyer. Patent It Yourself software (for Windows) is also available.

*Patent Searching Made Easy,* by David Hitchcock (Nolo), shows you how to search the U.S. Patent Database on the internet and in the library.

*How to Make Patent Drawings Yourself* by Jack Lo and David Pressman (Nolo), takes you step by step through the process of making your own patent drawing.

*License Your Invention* by Richard Stim (Nolo), walks you through the process of realizing your invention's commercial potential.

*Patent, Copyright and Trademark,* by Stephen Elias and Richard Stim (Nolo), provides concise definitions and examples of the important words and phrases commonly used in patent law.

*Nolo's Patents for Beginners,* by David Pressman and Richard Stim (Nolo), is a primer that explains all of the essential patent principles in plain English.

### http://www.nolo.com

*Nolo offers self-help information about a wide variety of legal topics, including patent law.*

### http://www.uspto.gov

*The U.S. Patent and Trademark Office is the place to go for recent policy and statutory changes and transcripts of hearings on various patent law issues. The U.S. Patent and Trademark Office maintains a seachable electronic database of the front page of all patents issued since 1971. This site is an excellent way to initiate a search for relevant patents. Also, the USPTO has announced that it is putting the full U.S. patent database online for free searching near the end of 1998.*

### http://www.inventionconvention.com

*The National Congress of Inventor Organizations (NCIO) maintain this invention website that includes links, trade show information, and advice for inventors.*

### http://www.patentcafe.com

*The Patent Café is an inventor resource that provides software, inventor kits and advice on patent searching, patent attorneys and marketing.*

### http://www.sci3.com

*Sc{I}³ provides in-depth patent searching services, patent-related products and seminars.*

### http://www.spi.org

*The Software Patent Institute lets you search for previous software developments that may affect whether your software qualifies for a patent.*

# Copyrights

7.2     *Copyright Basics*

7.4     *Copyright Ownership*

7.6     *Copyright Protection*

7.10    *Copyright Registration and Enforcement*

*People seldom improve when they have no other model but themselves to copy after.*

**—OLIVER GOLDSMITH**

It has long been recognized that everyone benefits when creative people are encouraged to develop new intellectual and artistic works. When the United States Constitution was written in 1787, the framers took care to include a copyright clause (Article I, Section 8) giving Congress the power to "promote the Progress of Science and useful Arts" by passing laws that give creative people exclusive rights in their own artistic works for a limited period of time.

Copyright laws are not designed to enrich creative artists, but to promote human knowledge and development. These laws encourage artists in their creative efforts by giving them a mini-monopoly over their works—called a copyright. But this monopoly is limited when it conflicts with the overriding purpose of encouraging people to create new works of scholarship or art.

This chapter introduces you to copyright law and guides you through the first steps of creating, owning and protecting a copyright. To learn about how copyrights differ from—and work with—patents and trademarks, see Chapters 6 and 8.

# Copyright Basics

IT IS NECESSARY TO ANY ORIGINALITY

TO HAVE THE COURAGE TO BE AN

AMATEUR.

**—WALLACE STEVENS**

Copyright is a legal device that gives the creator of a work of art or literature, or a work that conveys information or ideas, the right to control how that work is used. The Copyright Act of 1976—the federal law providing for copyright protection—grants authors a bundle of exclusive rights over their works, including the right to reproduce, distribute, adapt or perform them.

An author's copyright rights may be exercised only by the author—or by a person or entity to whom the author has transferred all or part of her rights. If someone wrongfully uses the material covered by a copyright, the copyright owner can sue and obtain compensation for any losses suffered.

## What types of creative work does copyright protect?

Copyright protects works such as poetry, movies, CD-ROMs, video games, videos, plays, paintings, sheet music, recorded music performances, novels, software code, sculptures, photographs, choreography and architectural designs.

To qualify for copyright protection, a work must be "fixed in a tangible medium of expression." This means that the work must exist in some physical form for at least some period of time, no matter how brief. Virtually any form of expression will qualify as a tangible medium, including a computer's random access memory (RAM), the recording media that capture all radio and television broadcasts and the scribbled notes on the back of an envelope that contain the basis for an impromptu speech.

In addition, the work must be original—that is, independently created by the author. It doesn't matter if an author's creation is similar to existing works, or even if it is arguably lacking in quality, ingenuity or aesthetic merit. So long as the author toils without copying from someone else, the results are protected by copyright.

Finally, to receive copyright protection, a work must be the result of at least some creative effort on the part of its author. There is no hard and fast rule as to how much creativity is enough. As one example, a work must be more creative than a telephone book's white pages, which involve a straightforward alphabetical listing of telephone numbers rather than a creative selection of listings.

## Does copyright protect an author's creative ideas?

No. Copyright shelters only fixed, original and creative expression, not the ideas or facts upon which the expression is based. For example, copyright may protect a particular song, novel or computer game about a romance in space, but it cannot protect the underlying idea of having a love affair among the stars. Allowing authors to monopolize their ideas would thwart the underlying purpose of copyright law, which is to encourage people to create new work.

For similar reasons, copyright does not protect facts—whether scientific, historical, biographical or news of the day. Any facts that an author discovers in the course of research are in the public domain, free to all. For instance, anyone is free to use information included in a book about how the brain works, an article about the life and times of Neanderthals or a TV documentary about the childhood of President Clinton—provided that they express the information in their own words.

Facts are not protected even if the author spends considerable time and effort discovering things that were previously unknown. For example, the author of the book on Neanderthals takes ten years to gather all the necessary materials and information for her work. At great expense, she travels to hundreds of museums and excavations around the world. But after the book is published, any reader is free to use the results of this ten-year research project to write his or her own book on Neanderthals—without paying the original author.

## How long does a copyright last?

For works published after 1977, the copyright lasts for the life of the author plus 70 years. However, if the work is a work for hire (that is, the work is done in the course of employment or has been specifically commissioned) or is published anonymously or under a pseudonym, the copyright lasts between 95 and 120 years, depending on the date the work is published.

All works published in the United States before 1923 are in the public domain. Works published after 1922, but before 1964, are protected for 95 years from the date of publication if a renewal was filed with the Copyright Office during the 28th year after publication. If no renewal was filed, such works are in the public domain in the U.S. Works published during 1964-1977 are protected for 95 years whether or not a renewal was filed. If the work was created, but not published, before 1978, the copyright lasts for the life of the author plus 70 years. However, even if the author died over 70 years ago, the copyright in an unpublished work lasts until December 31, 2002. And if such a work is published before 2003, the copyright lasts until December 31, 2047.

## Is the Work Published?

In the complicated scheme of copyright laws, which law applies to a particular work depends on when that work is published. A work is considered published when the author makes it available to the public on an unrestricted basis. This means that it is possible to distribute or display a work without publishing it if there are significant restrictions placed on what can be done with the work and when it can be shown to others. For example, Andres Miczslova writes an essay called "Blood Bath" about the war in Bosnia, and distributes it to five human rights organizations under a non exclusive license that places restrictions on their right to disclose the essay's contents. "Blood Bath" has not been "published" in the copyright sense. If Miczslova authorizes posting of the essay on the Internet, however, it would likely be considered published.

# Copyright Ownership

HE WHO CAN COPY, CAN DO.

**—LEONARDO DA VINCI**

A copyright is initially owned by a creative work's author or authors. But under the law, a person need not actually create the work to be its "author" for copyright purposes. A protectible work created by an employee as part of his or her job is initially owned by the employer—that is, the employer is considered to be the work's author. Such works are called "works made for hire." Works created by nonemployees (independent contractors) may also be works made for hire if they sign written agreements to that effect and the work falls within one of eight enumerated categories.

Like any other property, a copyright can be bought and sold. Transfers of copyright ownership are unique in one respect, however: Authors or their heirs have the right to terminate any transfer of copyright ownership 35 to 40 years after it is made.

## What are the exceptions to the rule that the creator of a work owns the copyright?

Copyrights are generally owned by the people who create the works of expression, with some important exceptions:

- If a work is created by an employee in the course of his or her employment, the employer owns the copyright.
- If the work is created by an independent contractor and the independent contractor signs a written agreement stating that the work shall be "made for hire," the commissioning person or organization owns the copyright only if the work is (1) a part of a larger literary work, such as an article in a magazine or a

poem or story in an anthology; (2) part of a motion picture or other audiovisual work, such as a screenplay; (3) a translation; (4) a supplementary work such as an afterword, an introduction, chart, editorial note, bibliography, appendix or index; (5) a compilation; (6) an instructional text; (7) a test or answer material for a test; or (8) an atlas. Works that don't fall within one of these eight categories constitute works made for hire only if created by an employee within the scope of his or her employment.

- If the creator has sold the entire copyright, the purchasing business or person becomes the copyright owner.

## Who owns the copyright in a joint work?

When two or more authors prepare a work with the intent to combine their contributions into inseparable or interdependent parts, the work is considered joint work and the authors are considered joint copyright owners. The most common example of a joint work is when a book or article has two or more authors. However, if a book is written primarily by one author, but another author contributes a specific chapter to the book and is given credit for that chapter, then this probably wouldn't be a joint work because the contributions aren't inseparable or interdependent.

The U.S. Copyright Office considers joint copyright owners to have an equal right to register and enforce the copyright. Unless the joint owners make a written agreement to the contrary, each copyright owner has the right to commercially exploit the copyright, provided that the other copyright owners get an equal share of the proceeds.

## Can two or more authors provide contributions to a single work without being considered a joint authors?

Yes. If at the time of creation, the authors did not intend their works to be part of an inseparable whole, the fact that their works are later put together does not create a joint work. Rather, the result is considered a collective work. In this case, each author owns a copyright in only the material he or she added to the finished product. For example, in the 1950s, Vladimir writes a famous novel full of complex literary allusions. In the 1980s, his publisher issues a student edition of the work with detailed annotations written by an English professor. The student edition is a collective work. Vladimir owns the copyright in the novel, but the professor owns the annotations.

## What rights do copyright owners have under the Copyright Act?

The Copyright Act of 1976 grants a number of exclusive rights to copyright owners, including:

- reproduction right—the right to make copies of a protected work
- distribution right—the right to sell or otherwise distribute copies to the public

- right to create adaptations (called derivative works)—the right to prepare new works based on the protected work, and
- performance and display rights—the rights to perform a protected work (such as a stageplay) or to display a work in public.

This bundle of rights allows a copyright owner to be flexible when deciding how to realize commercial gain from the underlying work; the owner may sell or license any of the rights.

### Can a copyright owner transfer some or all of his specific rights?

Yes. When a copyright owner wishes to commercially exploit the work covered by the copyright, the owner typically transfers one or more of these rights to the person or entity who will be responsible for getting the work to market, such as a book or software publisher. It is also common for the copyright owner to place some limitations on the exclusive rights being transferred. For example, the owner may limit the transfer to a specific period of time, allow the right to be exercised only in a specific part of the country or world or require that the right be exercised only through certain media, such as hardcover books, audiotapes, magazines or computers.

If a copyright owner transfers all of his rights unconditionally, it is generally termed an "assignment." When only some of the rights associated with the copyright are transferred, it is known as a "license." An exclusive

license exists when the transferred rights can be exercised only by the owner of the license (the licensee), and no one else—including the person who granted the license (the licensor). If the license allows others (including the licensor) to exercise the same rights being transferred in the license, the license is said to be nonexclusive.

The U.S. Copyright Office allows buyers of exclusive and non-exclusive copyright rights to record the transfers in the U.S. Copyright Office. This helps to protect the buyers in case the original copyright owner later tries to transfer the same rights to another party.

# Copyright Protection

Probably the most important fact to grasp about copyright protection is that it automatically comes into existence when the protected work is created. However, the degree of protection that copyright laws extend to a protected work can be influenced by later events.

### What role does a copyright notice play?

Until 1989, a published work had to contain a valid copyright notice to receive protection under the copyright laws. But this requirement is no longer in force—works first published after March 1, 1989 need not include a copyright notice to gain protection under the law.

But even though a copyright notice is not required, it's still important to include one. When a work contains a valid notice, an infringer cannot claim in court that he or she didn't know it was copyrighted. This makes it much easier to win a copyright infringement case and perhaps collect enough damages to make the cost of the case worthwhile. And the very existence of a notice might discourage infringement.

Finally, including a copyright notice may make it easier for a potential infringer to track down a copyright owner and legitimately obtain permission to use the work.

### What is a valid copyright notice?

A copyright notice should contain:
- the word "copyright"
- a "c" in a circle (©)
- the date of publication, and
- the name of either the author or the owner of all the copyright rights in the published work.

For example, the correct copyright for the fourth edition of *The Copyright Handbook*, by Stephen Fishman (Nolo), is *Copyright © 1998 by Stephen Fishman.*

# International Copyright Protection

Copyright protection rules are fairly similar worldwide, due to several international copyright treaties, the most important of which is the Berne Convention. Under this treaty, all member countries—and there are more than 100, including virtually all industrialized nations—must afford copyright protection to authors who are nationals of any member country. This protection must last for at least the life of the author plus 50 years, and must be automatic, without the need for the author to take any legal steps to preserve the copyright.

In addition to the Berne Convention, the GATT (General Agreement on Tariffs and Trade) treaty contains a number of provisions that affect copyright protection in signatory countries. Together, the Berne Copyright Convention and the GATT treaty allow U.S. authors to enforce their copyrights in most industrialized nations, and allow the nationals of those nations to enforce their copyrights in the U.S.

### When can I use a work without the author's permission?

When a work becomes available for use without permission from a copyright owner, it is said to be "in the public domain." Most works enter the public domain because their copyrights have expired.

To determine whether a work is in the public domain and available for use without the author's permission, you first have to find out when it was published. Then you can apply the periods of time set out earlier in this chapter. (See *How long does a copyright last?*, above.) If the work was published between 1923 and 1963, however, you must check with the U.S. Copyright Office to see whether the copyright was properly renewed. If the author failed to renew the copyright, the work has fallen into the public domain and you may use it.

The Copyright Office will check renewal information for you, at a charge of $65 per hour. (Call the Reference & Bibliography Section at 202-707-6850.) You can also hire a private copyright search firm to see if a renewal was filed. Finally, you may be able to conduct a renewal search yourself. The renewal records for works published from 1950 to the present are available online at http://lcweb.loc.gov/copyright. Renewal searches for earlier works can be conducted at the Copyright Office in Washington DC or by visiting one of the many government depository libraries throughout the country. Call the Copyright Office for more information.

With one important exception, you should assume that every work is protected by copyright unless you can establish that it is not. As mentioned above, you can't rely on the presence or absence of a copyright notice (©) to make this determination, because a notice is not required for works published after March 1, 1989. And even for works published before 1989, the absence of a copyright notice may not affect the validity of the copyright—

for example, if the author made diligent attempts to correct the situation.

The exception is for materials put to work under the "fair use rule." This rule recognizes that society can often benefit from the unauthorized use of copyrighted materials when the purpose of the use serves the ends of scholarship, education or an informed public. For example, scholars must be free to quote from their research resources in order to comment on the material. To strike a balance between the needs of a public to be well informed and the rights of copyright owners to profit from their creativity, Congress passed a law authorizing the use of copyrighted materials in certain circumstances deemed to be "fair"—even if the copyright owner doesn't give permission.

Often, it's difficult to know whether a court will consider a proposed use to be fair. The fair use statute requires the courts to consider the following questions in deciding this issue:

- Is it a competitive use? If the use potentially affects the sales of the copied material, it's probably not fair.

- How much material was taken compared to the entire work of which the material was a part? The more someone takes, the less likely it is that the use is fair.

- How was the material used? Did the defendant change the original by adding new expression or meaning? Did the defendant add value to the original by creating new information, new aesthetics, new insights and understandings? If the use was transformative, this weighs in favor of a fair use finding. Criticism, comment, news reporting, research, scholarship and nonprofit educational uses are also likely to be judged fair uses. Uses motivated primarily by a desire for a commercial gain are less likely to be fair use.

As a general rule, if you are using a small portion of somebody else's work in a noncompetitive way and the purpose for your use is to benefit the public, you're on pretty safe ground. On the other hand, if you take large portions of someone else's expression for your own purely commercial reasons, the rule usually won't apply.

## If You Want to Use Material on the Internet

Each day, people post vast quantities of creative material on the Internet—material that is available for downloading by anyone who has the right computer equipment. Because the information is stored somewhere on an Internet server, it is fixed in a tangible medium and potentially qualifies for copyright protection. Whether it does, in fact, qualify depends on other factors that you would have no way of knowing about, such as when the work was first published (which affects the need for a copyright notice), whether the copyright in the work has been

renewed (for works published before 1964), whether the work is a work made for hire (which affects the length of the copyright) and whether the copyright owner intends to dedicate the work to the public domain.

As a general rule, it is wise to operate under the assumption that all materials are protected by either copyright or trademark law unless conclusive information indicates otherwise. A work is not in the public domain simply because it has been posted on the Internet (a popular fallacy) or because it lacks a copyright notice (another fallacy). As a general rule permission is needed to reproduce copyrighted materials including photos, text, music and artwork. It's best to track down the author of the material and ask for permission.

The most useful sources for finding information and obtaining permission are copyright collectives or clearinghouses. These are organizations that organize and license works by their members. For example, the Copyright Clearinghouse (http://www.copyright.com), icopyright (http://www.icopyright.com) and Contentville (http://www.contentville.com) provide permissions for written materials. You can use an Internet search engine to locate other collectives for music, photos and artwork.

The only exception to this advice is for situations where you want to use only a very small portion of text for educational or nonprofit purposes. (See the previous question for a discussion of the "fair use rule.")

# Copyright Registration and Enforcement

Although every work published after 1989 is automatically protected by copyright, you can strengthen your rights by registering your work with the U.S. Copyright Office. This registration makes it possible to bring a lawsuit to protect your copyright if someone violates (infringes) it. The registration process is straightforward and inexpensive, and can be done without a lawyer.

## Why register your work with the U.S. Copyright Office?

You must register your copyright with the U.S. Copyright Office before you are legally permitted to bring a lawsuit to enforce it.

You can register a copyright at any time, but filing promptly may pay off in the long run. "Timely registration"—that is, registration within three months of the work's publication date or before any copyright infringement actually begins—makes it much easier to sue and recover money from an infringer. Specifically, timely registration creates a legal presumption that your copyright is valid, and allows you to recover up to $100,000 (and possibly lawyer's fees) without having to prove any actual monetary harm.

## How do you register a copyright?

You can register your copyright by filing a simple form and depositing one or two samples of the work (depending on what it is) with the U.S. Copyright Office. There are different forms for different types of works— for example, form TX is for literary works while form VA is for a visual art work. Forms and instructions may be obtained from the U.S. Copyright Office by telephone, (202) 707-9100, or online at http://www.loc.gov/copyright. Registration currently costs $30 per work. If you're registering several works that are part of one series, you may be able to save money by registering the works together (called "group registration").

## How are copyrights enforced? Is going to court necessary?

If someone violates the rights of a copyright owner, the owner is entitled to file a lawsuit in federal court asking the court to:

- issue orders (restraining orders and injunctions) to prevent further violations
- award money damages if appropriate, and
- in some circumstances, award attorney fees.

Whether the lawsuit will be effective and whether damages will be awarded depends on whether the alleged infringer can raise one or more legal defenses to the charge. Common legal defenses to copyright infringement are:

- too much time has elapsed between the infringing act and the lawsuit (the statute of limitations defense)
- the infringement is allowed under the fair use doctrine (discussed above)
- the infringement was innocent (the infringer had no reason to know the work was protected by copyright)
- the infringing work was independently created (that is, it wasn't copied from the original), or
- the copyright owner authorized the use in a license.

If someone has good reason to believe that a use is fair—but later finds herself on the wrong end of a court order—she is likely to be considered an innocent infringer at worst. Innocent infringers usually don't have to pay any damages to the copyright owner, but do have to cease the infringing activity or pay the owner for the reasonable commercial value of that use.

### More Information About Copyrights

*The Copyright Handbook: How to Protect and Use Written Works*, by Stephen Fishman (Nolo), is a complete guide to the law of copyright. The book includes forms for registering a copyright.

*Copyright Your Software*, by Stephen Fishman (Nolo), explains copyright protection for computer software and include all the forms and instructions necessary for registering a software copyright.

*Patent, Copyright and Trademark*, by Stephen Elias and Richard Stim (Nolo), provides concise definitions and examples of the important words and phrases commonly used in copyright law.

*Getting Permission: How to License and Clear Copyrighted Materials Online & Off*, by Richard Stim (Nolo), spells out how to obtain permission to use art, music, writing or other copyrighted works and includes a variety of permission and licensing agreements.

*The Public Domain: How to Find and Use Copyright-Free Writings, Music, Art and More*, by Stephen Fishman (Nolo), is an authoritative book devoted to what is and is not protected by copyright law.

### http://www.nolo.com

Nolo offers self-help information about a wide variety of legal topics, including copyright law.

### http://lcweb.loc.gov/copyright

The U.S. Copyright office offers regulations, guidelines, forms and links to other helpful copyright sites.

### http://fairuse.stanford.edu

This is one of the leading websites for measuring fair use. It provides academic fair use links and guidelines.

### http://www.benedict.com

The Copyright Website has articles, good links and slick design. Best of all, you can examine actual examples from real cases.

### http://www.ipmall.fplc.edu

The Intellectual Property Mall provided by the Franklin Pierce Law Center is a source of ever-changing links and information about copyrights, trademarks and patents.

# **T**rademarks

| | |
|---|---|
| 8.2 | *Types of Trademarks* |
| 8.5 | *Trademark Protection* |
| 8.8 | *Using and Enforcing a Trademark* |
| 8.11 | *Conducting a Trademark Search* |
| 8.14 | *Registering a Trademark* |
| 8.18 | *How Trademarks Differ From Patents and Copyrights* |

*A good name lost is seldom regained.*
**—JOEL HAWES**

**M**ost of us encounter many trademarks each day; we might eat Kellogg's cornflakes for breakfast, drive our Ford car to work and sit down at an IBM computer. But as we go about our daily tasks, we rarely think about the laws behind the familiar words and images that identify the products and services we use.

Trademark law consists of the legal rules that govern how businesses may:

- distinguish their products or services in the marketplace to prevent consumer confusion, and
- protect the means they've chosen to identify their products or services against use by competitors.

This chapter will introduce you to trademark law and answer common questions about choosing, using and protecting a trademark.

# Types of Trademarks

The term trademark is commonly used to describe many different types of devices that label, identify and distinguish products or services in the marketplace. The basic purpose of all these devices is to inform potential customers of the origin and quality of the underlying products or services.

## What is a trademark?

A trademark is a distinctive word, phrase, logo, graphic symbol, slogan or other device that is used to identify the source of a product and to distinguish a manufacturer's or merchant's products from others. Some examples are Nike sports apparel, Gatorade beverages and Microsoft software. In the trademark context, "distinctive" means unique enough to help customers recognize a particular product in the marketplace. A mark may either

be inherently distinctive (the mark is unusual in and of itself, such as Milky Way candy bars) or may become distinctive over time because customers come to associate the mark with the product or service (for example, Beef & Brew restaurants).

Consumers often make their purchasing choices on the basis of recognizable trademarks. For this reason, the main thrust of trademark law is to make sure that trademarks don't overlap in a manner that causes customers to become confused about the source of a product. However, in the case of trademarks that have become famous—for example, McDonald's—the courts are willing to prohibit a wider range of uses of the trademark (or anything close to it) by anyone other than the famous mark's owner. For instance, McDonald's was able to prevent the use of the mark McSleep by a motel chain because McSleep traded on the McDonald's mark reputation for a particular type of service (quick, inexpensive, standardized). This type of sweeping protection is authorized by federal and state statutes (referred to as antidilution laws) designed to prevent the weakening of a famous mark's reputation for quality.

## What is a servicemark?

For practical purposes, a servicemark is the same as a trademark—but while trademarks promote products, servicemarks promote services and events. As a general rule, when a business uses its name to market its goods or services in the yellow pages, on signs or in advertising copy, the name qualifies as a servicemark. Some familiar servicemarks: Jack in the Box (fast food service), Kinko's (photocopying service), ACLU (legal service), Blockbuster (video rental service), CBS's stylized eye in a circle (television network service) and the Olympic Games' multicolored interlocking circles (international sporting event).

## What is a certification mark?

A certification mark is a symbol, name or device used by an organization to vouch for products and services provided by others—for example, the "Good Housekeeping Seal of Approval." This type of mark may cover characteristics such as regional origin, method of manufacture, product quality and service accuracy. Some other examples of certification marks: Stilton cheese (a product from the Stilton locale in England), Carneros wines (from grapes grown in the Carneros region of Sonoma/Napa counties) and Harris Tweeds (a special weave from a specific area in Scotland).

## What is a collective mark?

A collective mark is a symbol, label, word, phrase or other mark used by members of a group or organization to identify goods, members, products or services they render. Collective marks are often used to show membership in a union, association or other organization.

The use of a collective mark is restricted to members of the group or organization that owns the mark. Even the group itself—as opposed to its members—cannot use the collective mark on any goods it produces. If the group wants to identify its product or service, it must use its own trademark or servicemark.

### EXAMPLE

*The letters "ILGWU" on a shirt label is the collective mark that identifies the shirt as a product of a member of the International Ladies Garment Workers Union. If, however, the ILGWU wanted to start marketing its own products, it could not use the ILGWU collective mark to identify them; the union would have to get a trademark of its own.*

## What is trade dress?

In addition to a label, logo or other identifying symbol, a product may come to be known by its distinctive packaging—for example, Kodak film or the Galliano liquor bottle—and a service by its distinctive decor or shape, such as the decor of Gap clothing stores. Collectively, these types of identifying features are commonly termed "trade dress." Because trade dress often serves the same function as a trademark or service-mark—the identification of goods and services in the marketplace—trade dress can be protected under the federal trademark laws and in some cases registered as a trademark or servicemark with the Patent and Trademark Office.

## What kinds of things can be considered trademarks or service marks?

Most often, trademarks are words or phrases that are clever or unique enough to stick in a consumer's mind. Logos and graphics that become strongly associated with a product line or service are also typical. But a trademark or servicemark can also consist of letters, numbers, a sound, a smell, a color, a product shape or any other nonfunctional but distinctive aspect of a product or service that tends to promote and distinguish it in the marketplace. Titles, character names or other distinctive features of movies, television and radio programs can also serve as trademarks or servicemarks when used to promote a service or product. Some examples of unusual trademarks are the pink color of housing insulation manufactured by Owens-Corning and the shape of the Absolut vodka bottle.

## What's the difference between a business name and a trademark or servicemark?

The name that a business uses to identify itself is called a "trade name." This is the name the business uses on its stock certificates, bank accounts, invoices and letterhead. When used to identify a business in this way—as an entity for nonmarketing purposes—the business name is given some protection under state and local corporate and fictitious business name registration laws, but it is not considered a trademark or entitled to protection under trademark laws.

If, however, a business uses its name to identify a product or service produced by the business, the name will then be considered a trademark or servicemark and will be entitled to protection if it is distinctive enough. For instance, Apple Computer Corporation uses the trade name Apple as a trademark on its line of computer products.

Although trade names by themselves are not considered trademarks for purposes of legal protection, they may still be protected under federal and state unfair competition laws against a confusing use by a competing business.

## If my trade name is registered with the Secretary of State as a corporate name, or placed on a fictitious business name list, can I use it as a trademark?

Not necessarily. When you register a corporate name with a state agency or place your name on a local fictitious business name register, there is no guarantee that the name has not already been taken by another business as a trademark. It is only the trade name aspect of the name that is affected by your registration. This means that before you start using your business name as a trademark, you will need to make sure it isn't already being used as a trademark by another company in a context that precludes your using it. For more information about trademark searches, see *Conducting a Trademark Search,* below.

# Trademark Protection

If a trademark or servicemark is protected, the owner of the mark can:

- prevent others from using it in a context where it might confuse consumers, and
- recover money damages from someone who used the mark knowing that it was already owned by someone else.

Trademark law also protects famous marks by allowing owners to sue to prevent others from using the same or similar mark, even if customer confusion is unlikely.

Not all marks are entitled to an equal amount of protection, however—and some aren't entitled to any protection at all.

## What laws offer protection to trademark owners?

The basic rules for resolving disputes over who is entitled to use a trademark come from decisions by federal and state courts (the common law). These rules usually favor the business that first used the mark where the second use would be likely to cause customer confusion. A number of additional legal principles used to protect owners against improper use of their marks derive from federal statutes known collectively as the Lanham Act (Title 15 U.S.C. §§ 1051 to 1127). And all states have statutes that govern the use and protection of marks within the state's boundaries.

In addition to laws that specifically protect trademark owners, all states have laws that protect one business against unfair competition by another business, including the use by one business of a name already used by another business in a context that's likely to confuse customers.

## What types of marks are entitled to the most legal protection?

Trademark law grants the most legal protection to the owners of names, logos and other marketing devices that are distinctive—that is, memorable because they are creative or out of the ordinary, or because they have become well known to the public through their use over time or because of a marketing blitz.

## Inherently Distinctive Marks

Trademarks that are unusually creative are known as inherently distinctive marks. Typically, these marks consist of:

- unique logos or symbols (such as the McDonald's Golden Arch and the IBM symbol)
- made-up words or words that have no dictionary meaning such as *Exxon* or *Kodak* (called "fanciful" or "coined" marks)
- words that are surprising or unexpected in the context of their usage, such as Time Magazine or Diesel for a bookstore (called "arbitrary marks"), and

- words that cleverly connote qualities about the product or service, such as Slenderella diet food products (called "suggestive or evocative marks").

## Which marks receive the least protection?

Trademarks and servicemarks consisting of common or ordinary words are not considered inherently distinctive and receive less protection under federal and state laws. Typical examples of trademarks using common or ordinary words are:

- people's names, such as Pete's Muffins or Smith Graphics
- geographic terms, such as Northern Dairy or Central Insect Control, and
- descriptive terms—that is, words that attempt to literally describe the product or some characteristic of the product, such as Rapid Computers, Clarity Video Monitors or Ice Cold Ice Cream.

However, nondistinctive marks may be come distinctive through use over time or through intensive marketing efforts.

## What about Ben and Jerry's Ice Cream? Even though Ben and Jerry are common names, isn't the Ben and Jerry's trademark entitled to maximum protection?

Absolutely. Even if a mark is not inherently distinctive, it may become distinctive if it develops great public recognition through long use and exposure in the marketplace. A mark that becomes protected in this way is said to have acquired a "secondary

meaning." In addition to Ben and Jerry's, examples of otherwise common marks that have acquired a secondary meaning and are now considered to be distinctive include Sears (department stores) and Park 'n Fly (airport parking services.)

## What cannot be protected under trademark law?

There are five common situations in which there is no trademark protection. In any of these situations the intended trademark cannot be registered and the owner has no right to stop others from using a similar name. Generally, when speaking of what *cannot* be protected under trademark law, we are referring to the standards established under the Lanham Act (the federal statute that provides for registration of marks and federal court remedies in case a mark is infringed).

- *Nonuse.* An owner may lose trademark protection if she "abandons" a trademark. This can happen in many ways. The most common is when the mark is no longer used in commerce and there is sufficient evidence that the owner intends to discontinue its use. Under the Lanham Act, a trademark is presumed to be abandoned after three years of nonuse. But, if the owner can prove that she intended to resume commercial use of the mark, she will not lose trademark protection.

- *Generics and genericide.* A generic term describes a type of goods or services; it is not a brand name. Examples of generic terms are "computer," "eyeglasses" and "eBook." Consumers are used to seeing a generic term used in conjunction with a trademark (for example, Avery labels or Hewlett-Packard printers). On some occasions, a company invents a new word for a product (for example, Kleenex for a tissue) that functions so successfully as a trademark that the public eventually comes to believe that it is the name of the goods. This is called genericide. When that happens, the term loses its trademark protection. Other famous examples of genericide are "aspirin," "yo-yo," "escalator," "thermos" and "kerosene".

- *Confusingly similar marks.* A mark will not receive trademark protection if it is so similar to another existing trademark that it causes confusion among consumers. This standard, known as likelihood of confusion, is a foundation of trademark law. Many factors are weighed when considering "likelihood of confusion." The most important are: the similarity of the marks, the similarity of the goods, the degree of care exercised by the consumer when making the pur-

chase, the intent of the person using the similar mark and any actual confusion that has occurred.

- *Weak marks.* A weak trademark will not be protected unless the owner can prove that consumers are aware of the mark. There are three types of weak marks: descriptive marks, geographic marks that describe a location and marks that are primarily surnames (last names). When an applicant attempts to register a weak mark, the PTO will permit the applicant to submit proof of distinctiveness or to move the application from the Principal Register to the Supplemental Register. (See Registering a Trademark, below, for more information about the different benefits offered these registers.)

- *Functional features.* Trademark law, like copyright law, will not protect functional features. Generally, a functional feature is something that is necessary for the item to work. The issue usually arises with product packaging or shapes. For instance, the unique shape of the Mrs. Butterworth bottle is not a functional feature because it is not necessary for the bottle to work. Therefore, it is eligible for trademark protection.

## Are Internet domain names— names for sites on the World Wide Web—protected by trademark law?

Domain name registration, by itself, does not permit you to stop another business from using the same name for its business or product. Instead, it gives you only the right to use that specific Internet address. To protect your domain name as a trademark, the name must meet the usual trademark standards. That is, the domain name must be distinctive or must achieve distinction through customer awareness, and you must be the first to use the name in connection with your type of services or products. An example of a domain name that meets these criteria and has trademark protection is Amazon.com. Amazon.com was the first to use this distinctive name for online retail sales and the name has been promoted to customers through advertising and sales.

# Using and Enforcing a Trademark

Generally, a trademark is owned by the business that first uses it in a commercial context—that is, attaches the mark to a product or uses the mark when marketing a product or service. A business may also obtain trademark protection if it files for trademark registration before anyone else uses the mark. (Trademark registration is discussed in more detail in the series of questions, *Registering a Trademark,* below.)

Once a business owns a trademark, it may be able to prevent others from using that mark, or a similar one, on their goods and services.

## More specifically, what does it mean to "use" a trademark?

In trademark law, "use" means that the mark is at work in the marketplace, identifying the underlying goods or services. This doesn't mean that the product or service actually has to be sold, as long as it is legitimately offered to the public under the mark in question. For example, Robert creates a website where he offers his new invention—a humane mousetrap—for sale under the trademark "MiceFree." Even if Robert doesn't sell any traps, he is still "using" the trademark as long as "MiceFree" appears on the traps or on tags attached to them and the traps are ready to be shipped when a sale is made. Similarly, if Kristin, a trademark attorney, puts up a website to offer her services under the servicemark Trademark Queen, her servicemark will be in use as long as she is ready to respond to customer requests for her advice.

## How can a business reserve a trademark for future use?

It is possible to acquire ownership of a mark by filing an "intent-to-use" (ITU) trademark registration application with the U.S. Patent and Trademark Office before someone else has actually started using the mark. The filing date of this application will be considered the date of first use of the mark if the applicant actually uses the mark within the required time limits—six months to three years after the PTO approves the mark, depending on whether the applicant seeks and pays for extensions of time.

For more information about trademark registration, see *Registering a Trademark*, below.

## When can the owner of a trademark stop others from using it?

Whether the owner of a trademark can stop others from using it depends on such factors as:

- whether the trademark is being used on competing goods or services (goods or services compete if the sale of one is likely to affect the sale of the other)
- whether consumers would likely be confused by the dual use of the trademark, and
- whether the trademark is being used in the same part of the country or is being used on related goods (goods that will probably be noticed by the same customers, even if they don't compete with each other).

In addition, under federal and state laws known as "antidilution statutes," a trademark owner may go to court to prevent its mark from being used by someone else if the mark is famous and the later use would dilute the mark's strength—that is, weaken its reputation for quality (called tarnishment) or render it common through overuse in different contexts.

Antidilution statutes can apply even if there is no way customers would be likely to confuse the source of the goods or services designated by the later mark with the famous mark's owner. For instance, consumers would not think that Microsoft Bakery is associated with Microsoft, the software company, but

Microsoft Bakery could still be forced to choose another name under federal and state antidilution laws.

## How does a trademark owner prevent others from using the mark?

Typically, the owner will begin by sending a letter, called a "cease and desist letter," to the wrongful user, demanding that it stop using the mark. If the wrongful user continues to infringe the mark, the owner can file a lawsuit to stop the improper use. The lawsuit is usually filed in federal court if the mark is used in more than one state or country, and in state court if the dispute is between purely local marks. In addition to preventing further use of the mark, a trademark owner can sometimes obtain money damages from the wrongful user.

## When can a trademark owner get money from someone who has infringed the owner's mark?

If a trademark owner proves in federal court that the infringing use is likely to confuse consumers and that it suffered economically as a result of the infringement, the competitor may have to pay the owner damages based on the loss. And if the court finds that the competitor intentionally copied the owner's trademark, or at least should have known about the mark, the competitor may have to give up the profits it made by using the mark as well as pay other damages, such as punitive damages, fines or attorney fees. On the other hand, if the trademark's owner has not been damaged, a court has discretion to allow the competitor to continue to use the trademark under limited circumstances designed to avoid consumer confusion.

## Do people have the right to use their last names as marks even if someone else is already using them for a similar business?

It depends on the name. A mark that is primarily a surname (last name) does not qualify for protection under federal trademark law unless the name becomes well known as a mark through advertising or long use. If this happens, the mark is said to have acquired a "secondary meaning."

If a surname acquires a secondary meaning, it is off limits for all uses that might cause customer confusion, whether or not the name is registered. Sears, McDonald's, Hyatt, Champion, Howard Johnson's and Calvin Klein are just a few of the hundreds of surnames that have become effective and protected marks over time.

Also, a business that tries to capitalize on the name of its owner to take advantage of an identical famous name being used as a trademark may be forced, under the state or federal antidilution laws, to stop using the name. This may happen if the trademark owner files a lawsuit.

## "TM" and ®: What do they mean?

Many people like to put a "TM" (or "SM" for servicemark) next to their mark to let the world know that they are claiming ownership of it. However, it is not legally necessary to provide this type of notice; the use of the mark itself is the act that confers ownership.

The "R" in a circle ( ® ) is a different matter entirely. This notice may not be put on a mark unless it has been registered with the U.S. Patent and Trademark Office—and it should accompany a mark after registration is complete. Failure to put the notice on a registered trademark can greatly reduce the possibility of recovering significant damages if it later becomes necessary to file a lawsuit against an infringer.

# Conducting a Trademark Search

If you want to find out whether the trademark you've chosen for your products or services is available, you'll need to conduct a trademark search—an investigation to discover potential conflicts between your desired mark and any existing marks. Ideally, the search should be done before you begin to use a mark; this will help you avoid the expensive mistake of infringing a mark belonging to someone else.

## Why do I need to conduct a trademark search?

The consequences of failing to conduct a reasonably thorough trademark search may be severe, depending on how widely you intend to use your mark and how much it would cost you to change it if a conflict later develops. If the mark you want to use has been federally registered by someone else, a court will presume that you knew about the registration—even if you did not. You will be precluded from using the mark in any context where customers might become confused. And if you do use the mark improperly, you will be cast in the role of a "willful infringer." Willful infringers can be held liable for large damages and payment of the registered owner's attorney fees; they can also be forced to stop using the mark altogether.

## My business is local. Why should I care what name or mark someone else in another part of the country is using?

Most small retail or service-oriented business owners well know the mantra for success: location, location, location. But as the Internet takes firm hold in the late 1990s, the concept of location, while still central to business success, takes on a whole new meaning. Instead of being rooted in physical space, businesses are now required to jockey for locations in the virtual or electronic space known as the Internet.

Vast numbers of businesses—even local enterprises—are putting up their own websites, creating a new potential for competition (and confusion) in the marketplace. Because of this, every business owner must pay attention to whether a proposed name or mark has already been taken by another business, regardless of the location or scope of that business.

## Can I do my own trademark search?

Yes. Although the most thorough trademark searches are accomplished by professional search firms such as Thomson & Thomson, it is also possible to conduct a preliminary online trademark search to determine if a trademark is distinguishable from other federally registered trademarks. You can accomplish this with the PTO's trademark databases (http://www.uspto.gov), which provide free access to records of federally registered marks or marks that are pending. In addition, privately owned fee-based online trademark databases often provide more current PTO trademark information. Below are some private fee-based online search companies:

*Saegis* (http://www.thomson-thomson.com). Provides access to all Trademarkscan databases (state, federal and international trademark databases), domain name databases, common law sources on the Internet and access to newly filed United States federal trademark applications. Saegis also provides access to Dialog services, discussed next.

*Dialog* (http://www.dialog.com). Provides access to Trademarkscan databases including state and federal registration and some international trademarks and provides common law searching of news databases.

*Micropatent* (http://www.micropatent.com). Provides access to federal and state trademarks.

*Corporate Intelligence* (http://www.trademarks.com). Provides ac-

cess to current federal registration information.

*Trademark Register* (http://www.trademarkregister.com). Provides access to current federal registration information.

*Marks on Line* (http://www.marksonline.com). This is a comprehensive trademark link site providing access to federal registration information and a listing of state and international trademark offices.

*LEXIS/NEXIS* (http://www.lexis-nexis.com). LEXIS provides access to federal and state registrations. You can also search for non-registered trademarks through its NEXIS news services. The PTO uses NEXIS to evaluate descriptive and generic terms.

You can also visit one of the Patent and Trademark Depository Libraries available in every state. These libraries offer a combination of hardcover directories of federally registered marks and an online database of both registered marks and marks for which a registration application is pending. To find the Patent and Trademark Depository Library nearest you, consult the PTO website at http://www.uspto.gov.

You should also search for marks that have not been registered.

This is important because an existing mark, even if it's unregistered, would preclude you from:

- registering the same or a confusingly similar mark in your own name, and
- using the mark in any part of the country or commercial transaction where customers might be confused.

You can search for unregistered marks in the Patent and Trademark Depository Libraries and on the Internet. In the libraries, use the available product guides and other materials. On the Internet, look for online shopping websites and review the inventory for items similar to yours. For example, go to eToys (http://www.etoys.com) to find hundreds of trademarked toys. You can also search for unregistered marks by using an Internet search engine. Enter your proposed name in the search field of an Internet search engine (such as Alta Vista). You will get a report of every instance that the name appears on Web pages indexed by that engine. Because no search engine is 100% complete, you should do this same search on a several different search engines.

## How can I find out whether a mark I want to use is already being used as a domain name (the name of a site on the World Wide Web)?

Every website is identified by a unique phrase known as a "domain name." For example, the domain name for Nolo is Nolo.com. Because so much business is now being done online, most people will want to be able to use their proposed mark as a domain name so that their customers can easily locate them on the Web.

The easiest way to find out if a domain name is already in use is to check with one of the dozens of online companies that have been approved to register domain names. You can access a listing of these registrars through InterNIC's site at http://www.internic.net or ICANN's site at http://www.icann.org. ICANN is the organization that oversees the process of approving domain name registrars.

## Would it be better to have a professional firm conduct my trademark search?

Many people do prefer to pay a professional search firm to handle a trademark search. This can make sense if your financial plans justify an initial outlay of several hundred dollars, the minimum cost for a thorough professional search for both registered and unregistered marks. Depending on the search firm, you may also get a legal opinion as to whether your proposed mark is legally safe to use in light of existing registered and unregistered marks. Obtaining a legal opinion may provide important protection down the road if someone later sues you for using the mark.

## How do I find a professional search firm?

There are many trademark search services in the United States. Here are three of the most well known:

*The Sunnyvale Center on Innovation, Invention and Ideas* (Sc[i]3) (http://www.sci3.com). Sc[i]3 (pronounced "sigh-cubed") is one of three Patent and Trademark Depository Libraries—the others are in Detroit and Houston—that have formed partnerships with the U.S. Patent and Trademark Office. Under this partnership,

Sc[i]3 is encouraged to offer a variety of information services—including trademark searches—for very reasonable fees.

*Trademark Express* (http://www.tmexpress.com). Trademark Express is a private company that, in addition to other trademark-related services, offers a full choice of trademark searches.

*Thomson & Thomson* (http://www.thomson-thomson.com). Thomson & Thomson is the trademark search service of choice for the legal professional.

If you don't like doing business at a distance, you can find trademark search services in your area by looking in the Yellow Pages of the nearest good-sized city under "trademark consultants" or "information brokers." If that yields nothing, consult the advertisements in a local legal journal or magazine. Finally, you can find a good list of trademark search firms at http://www.ggmark.com.

# Registering a Trademark

It is possible to register certain types of trademarks and servicemarks with the U.S. Patent and Trademark Office (PTO). Federal registration puts the rest of the country on notice that the trademark is already taken, and makes it easier to protect a mark against would-be copiers.

## How does a mark qualify for federal registration?

To register a trademark with the PTO, the mark's owner first must put it into use "in commerce that Congress may regulate." This means the mark must be used on a product or service that crosses state, national or territorial lines or that affects commerce crossing such lines—for example, a catalog business or a restaurant or motel that caters to interstate or international customers. Even if the owner files an intent-to-use (ITU) trademark application (ITU applications are discussed in the previous set of questions), the mark will not actually be registered until it is used in commerce.

Once the PTO receives a trademark registration application, the office must answer the following questions:

- Is the trademark the same as or similar to an existing mark used on similar or related goods or services?
- Is the trademark on the list of prohibited or reserved names?
- Is the trademark generic—that is, does the mark describe the product itself rather than its source?
- Is the trademark too descriptive (not distinctive enough) to qualify for protection?

If the answer to each question is "no," the trademark is eligible for registration and the PTO will continue to process the application.

I know the PTO won't register a mark if it's not distinctive or already in use. But are there other types of marks that are ineligible for federal registration?

Yes. The PTO won't register any marks that contain:

- names of living persons without their consent
- the U.S. flag
- other federal and local governmental insignias
- the name or likeness of a deceased U.S. President without his widow's consent
- words or symbols that disparage living or deceased persons, institutions, beliefs or national symbols, or
- marks that are judged immoral, deceptive or scandalous.

As a general rule the PTO takes a liberal view of the terms immoral and scandalous and will rarely refuse to register a mark on those grounds.

## If the PTO decides that a mark is eligible for federal registration, what happens next?

Next, the PTO publishes the trademark in the *Official Gazette* (a publication of the U.S. Patent and Trademark Office). The *Gazette* states that the mark is a candidate for registration; this provides existing trademark owners with an opportunity to object to the registration. If someone objects, the PTO will schedule a hearing to resolve the dispute.

Is it possible to federally register a mark made up of common or ordinary words?

Yes, if the combination of the words is distinctive. But even if the entire mark is judged to lack sufficient distinctiveness, it can be placed on a list called the Supplemental Register. (Marks that are considered distinctive—either inherently or because they have become well known—are placed on a list called the Principal Register.) Marks on the Supplemental Register receive far less protection than do those on the Principal Register. The benefits granted by each type of registration are discussed in more detail in the next question.

## What are the benefits of federal trademark registration?

It depends on which register carries the mark. Probably the most important benefit of placing a mark on the Principal Register is that anybody who later initiates use of the same or a confusingly similar trademark may be presumed by the courts to be a "willful infringer" and therefore liable for large money damages.

Placing a trademark on the Supplemental Register produces significantly fewer benefits, but still provides notice of ownership. This notice makes it far less likely that someone will use that identical mark; the fear of being sued for damages should keep potential infringers away. Also, if the trademark remains on the Supplemental Register for five years—meaning that the registration isn't canceled for some reason—and the mark remains in use during that time, it may be moved to the Principal Register under the secondary meaning rule (secondary meaning will be presumed).

Even if a mark is not registered, it is still possible for the owner to sue the infringer under a federal statute which forbids use of a "false designation of origin" (Title 15 U.S.C. § 1125). It is usually much easier to prove the case and collect large damages, however, if the mark has been registered.

## How long does federal registration last?

Once a trademark or servicemark is placed on the Principal Register, the owner receives a certificate of registration good for an initial term of ten years. The registration may lapse before the ten-year period expires, however, unless the owner files a form within six years of the registration date (called the Section 8 Declaration) stating that the mark is either still in use in commerce or that the mark is not in use for legitimate reasons.

The Section 8 Declaration is usually combined with a Section 15 Declaration, which effectively renders the trademark incontestable except for limited reasons.

The original registration may be renewed indefinitely for additional ten-year periods if the owner files the required renewal applications (called a Section 9 Affidavit) with the U.S. Patent and Trademark Office. A Section 8 Declaration must also be filed at the time of trademark renewal.

Failure to renew a registration does not void all rights to the mark, but if the owner fails to re-register, the special benefits of federal registration will be lost.

## What happens if there is a conflict between an Internet domain name and an existing trademark?

The answer depends on the nature of the conflict. There are three reasons why a conflict may develop between the owner of a trademark and the owner of a domain name:

*The domain name registrant is a cybersquatter.* If a domain name is registered in bad faith—for example, the name is registered with the intent of selling it back to a company with the same name—the domain name can be taken away under federal law or under international arbitration rules for domain name owners. A victim of cybersquatting in the U.S. can now sue under the provisions of the Anticybersquatting Consumer Protection Act (ACPA) or can fight the cybersquatter using an international arbitration system created by the Internet Corporation of Assigned Names and Numbers (ICANN). The ICANN arbitration system is usually faster and less expensive than suing under the ACPA. In addition, it does not require an attorney. For information on the ICANN policy visit the organization's website at http://www.icann.org.

*The domain name infringes an existing trademark.* If a domain name is likely to confuse consumers because it is similar to an existing trademark, the owner of the federally owned trademark can sue for infringement in federal court. For example, it's likely that the Adobe company, makers of graphics software, would be able to prevent another software company from using the domain name of www.adoobie.com.

***The domain name dilutes a famous trademark.*** If a domain name dilutes the power of a famous trademark, the trademark owner can sue under federal laws to stop the continued use. Dilution occurs when the domain name blurs or tarnishes the reputation of a famous trademark. For example, Gucci could probably prevent a company from using the domain name "guccigoo.com" for the purpose of selling baby diapers.

## Can a business register its mark at the state level?

It is possible to register a mark with the state trademark agency, although the state registration does not offer the same level of protection provided by federal law. The main benefit of state registration is that it notifies anyone who checks the list that the mark is owned by the registrant. This fact will lead most would-be users of the same mark to choose another one rather than risk a legal dispute with the registered mark's owner. If the mark is also federally registered, this notice is presumed and the state registration isn't necessary. If, however, the mark is used only within the state and doesn't qualify for federal registration, state registration is a good idea.

## How to Register Your Trademark

For most trademarks already in use, federal registration is a relatively straightforward process. You use a simple two-sided form provided by the PTO to:

- describe your mark
- state when it was first used
- describe the products or services on which the mark will be used, and
- suggest the classification under which the mark should be registered (there are approximately 40 classifications for goods and services; the PTO can help you figure out which one is right for your mark).

In addition, your form must be accompanied by:

- a "drawing" of your mark (for word marks, this simply involves setting the mark out in the middle of a page in capital letters)
- samples of how your proposed mark is being used, and
- the registration fee—currently $325.

On its website, http://www.uspto.gov, the PTO offers two electronic registration options. PrinTEAS lets you fill in the form online but requires you to print out and mail in a hardcopy. eTEAS lets you both fill in and file the form online.

If you are applying to register your mark on the basis of its intended use (See *How can a business reserve a trademark for future use?*, above), then you needn't provide the samples or the date of first use, but you can't complete your registration until you put your mark into actual use and file some additional paperwork with the PTO.

The PTO offers a free booklet containing plain English instructions for filling out this form, and also provides help on its website: www.uspto.com. For more information about registering your trademark, see the resource list at the end of this chapter.

# How Trademarks Differ From Patents and Copyrights

Trademarks are often mentioned in the same breath as copyrights and patents. While they do sometimes apply to the same thing, they're more often defined by their differences. It's important to understand how trademark law differs from other laws protecting creative works (collectively called "intellectual property laws"); rules and benefits depend on the type of intellectual property at issue.

## How does trademark differ from copyright?

Copyright protects original works of expression, such as novels, fine and graphic arts, music, phonorecords, photography, software, video, cinema and choreography by preventing people from copying or commercially exploiting them without the copy-

right owner's permission. But the copyright laws specifically do not protect names, titles or short phrases. That's where trademark law comes in. Trademark protects distinctive words, phrases, logos, symbols, slogans and any other devices used to identify and distinguish products or services in the marketplace.

There are, however, areas where both trademark and copyright law may be used to protect different aspects of the same product. For example, copyright laws may protect the artistic aspects of a graphic or logo used by a business to identify its goods or services, while trademark may protect the graphic or logo from use by others in a confusing manner in the marketplace. Similarly, trademark laws are often used in conjunction with copyright laws to protect advertising copy. The trademark laws protect the product or service name and any slogans used in the advertising, while the copyright laws protect the additional creative written expression contained in the ad.

For more information about copyright law, see Chapter 7, *Copyrights*.

## What's the difference between patent and trademark?

Patents allow the creator of certain kinds of inventions that contain new ideas to keep others from making commercial use of those ideas without the creator's permission. For example, Tom invents a new type of hammer that makes it very difficult to miss the nail. Not only can Tom keep others from making, selling or using the precise type of hammer he invented, but he may also be able to apply his patent monopoly rights to prevent people from making commercial use of any similar type of hammer during the time the patent is in effect (20 years from the date the patent application is filed).

Generally, patent and trademark laws do not overlap. When it comes to a product design, however—say, jewelry or a distinctively shaped musical instrument—it may be possible to obtain a patent on a design aspect of the device while invoking trademark law to protect the design as a product identifier. For instance, an auto manufacturer might receive a design patent for the stylistic fins that are part of a car's rear fenders. Then, if the fins were intended to be—and actually are—used to distinguish the particular model car in the marketplace, trademark law may kick in to protect the appearance of the fins.

For more information about patent law, see Chapter 6, *Patents*.

### More Information About Trademarks

*Trademark: Legal Care for Your Business and Product Name,* by Stephen Elias (Nolo), shows you how to choose a legally strong business and product name, register the name with state and federal agencies and sort out any name disputes that arise.

*Patent, Copyright and Trademark,* by Stephen Elias and Richard Stim (Nolo), provides concise definitions and examples of the important words and phrases commonly used in trademark law.

*Domain Names: How to Choose & Protect a Great Name for Your Website,* by Stephen Elias & Patricia Gima (Nolo). This how-to book provides information on selecting, registering and protecting a domain name.

*McCarthy on Trademarks and Unfair Competition,* by J. Thomas McCarthy (Clark Boardman Callaghan), is a book intended for lawyers that provides an exhaustive treatment of trademark law.

*Trademark Law—A Practitioners Guide,* by Siegrun D. Kane (Practicing Law Institute), is a good overview of trademark law written for lawyers.

*Trademark Registration Practice,* by James E. Hawes (Clark Boardman Callaghan), a book for trademark lawyers, provides the ins and outs of registering a trademark with the U.S. Patent and Trademark Office.

The following associations of trademark lawyers offer a number of helpful publications. Write or call for a list of available materials.

International Trademark Association (INTA)
1133 Avenue of the Americas
New York, NY 10036
(212) 768-9887
http://www.inta.org/

American Intellectual Property Law Association (AIPLA)
2001 Jefferson Davis Highway, Suite 203
Arlington, VA 22202
(703) 415-0780
http://www.aipla.org/

## http://www.nolo.com

*Nolo Press offers self-help information about a wide variety of legal topics, including trademarks.*

## http://www.marksonline.com

*This comprehensive trademark site provides trademark searching services, news and links as well as domain name information. It's easy to navigate, contains lots of practical information for trademark owners and includes links to state and federal trademark offices.*

## http://www.inta.org

*The International Trademark Association (INTA) provides trademark services, publications and online resources.*

## http://www.uspto.gov

*The U.S. Patent and Trademark Office provides new trademark rules and regulations and, as of August 1998, is expected to put the federal registered trademark database online.*

## http://www.sci3.com

*The Sunnyvale Center for Invention, Innovation and Ideas (a Patent and Trademark Depository Library), provides information about their excellent, low-cost trademark search service conducted by the Center's librarians.*

## http://www.ggmark.com/

*This site, maintained by a trademark lawyer, provides basic trademark information and a fine collection of links to other trademark resources.*

# **Y**our Money

9.2 **Purchasing Goods and Services**

9.7 **Using Credit and Charge Cards**

9.10 **Using an ATM or Debit Card**

9.12 **Strategies for Repaying Debts**

9.18 **Dealing With the IRS**

9.22 **Debt Collections**

9.25 **Bankruptcy**

9.29 **Rebuilding Credit**

*Too many people spend money they haven't earned, to buy things they don't want, to impress people they don't like.*

**—WILL ROGERS**

America's economy is driven by consumer spending. When we open any newspaper or magazine, turn on the radio or television, or take a drive across town, we're bombarded with ads urging us to spend our hard-earned dollars. And so we do. We pull out our cash, checks, credit cards, and increasingly, debit cards.

What the ads don't tell you is what to do when things go wrong—for example, when the item you buy is defective, when you lose your credit card, when you need extra time to pay or when you fall behind and the bill collectors start calling.

Fortunately, many federal (and some state) laws give you rights as a consumer; this chapter describes some of those that are most important. While no law substitutes for common sense, comparison shopping and avoiding offers that sound too good to be true, there are solutions to most of the problems you're likely to face as an American consumer.

# Purchasing Goods and Services

*I did not have three thousand pairs of shoes: I had one thousand and sixty.*

**—IMELDA MARCOS**

While 19th century business relationships were governed by the doctrine "caveat emptor" or "let the buyer beware," the notion that a buyer-seller arrangement should be fair gained ground in the 20th century. As a result, you now have a right to receive nondefective goods—and services that meet a minimum standard.

## When I buy something, is it covered by a warranty?

Generally, yes. A warranty (also called a guarantee) is an assurance about the quality of goods or services you buy, and is intended to give you recourse if something you purchase fails to live up to what you were promised.

Some warranties are implied and some are expressed. Virtually everything you buy comes with two implied warranties—one for "merchantability" and one for "fitness." The implied warranty of merchantability is an assurance that a new item will work if you use it for a reasonably expected purpose. For used items, the warranty of merchantability is a promise that the product will work as expected, given its age and condition. The implied warranty of fitness applies when you buy an item with a specific (even unusual) purpose in mind. If you related your specific needs to the seller, the implied warranty of fitness assures you that the item will fill your need.

Most expressed warranties state something such as "the product is warranted against defects in materials or workmanship" for a specified time. Most either come directly from the manufacturer or are included in the sales contract you sign with the seller. But an expressed warranty may be a feature in an advertisement or on a sign in the store ("all dresses 100% silk"), or it may even be an oral description of a product's features.

## How long does a warranty last?

In most states, an implied warranty lasts forever. In a few states, however, the implied warranty lasts only as long as any expressed warranty that comes with a product. In these states, if there is no expressed warranty, the implied warranty lasts forever.

## Can a seller avoid a warranty by selling a product "as is"?

The answer depends on whether the warranty is express or implied (see the previous questions for an explanation of implied and express warranties) and in what state you live. Sellers cannot avoid express warranties by claiming the product is sold "as is." On the other hand, if there is no express warranty, sellers can sometimes avoid an

implied warranty by selling the item "as is." Some states prohibit all "as is" sales. And in all states, the buyer must know that the item is sold "as is" in order for the seller to avoid an implied warranty.

## How do I enforce a warranty if something is wrong with what I bought?

Most of the time, a defect in an item will show up immediately and you can ask the seller or manufacturer to fix or replace it. If he won't, or if he tries only once and the fixed or replaced item is still defective, you can withhold payment (or refuse to pay a credit card charge). If you are uncomfortable doing this or have already paid for the item, call the seller and try to work out an arrangement. If he refuses, try to mediate the dispute through a community or Better Business Bureau mediation program. (For more information about mediation, see Chapter 17.)

If you can't get anywhere informally, you can sue. In most states, you must sue the seller or manufacturer within four years of when you discovered the defect, if the seller or manufacturer won't make good under a warranty.

## Do I have any recourse if the item breaks after the warranty expires?

Usually not. But in most states, if the item gave you some trouble while it was under the warranty (and you had it repaired by someone authorized by the manufacturer to make repairs), the manufacturer must extend your original warranty for the amount of time the item sat in the shop. Call the manufacturer and ask to speak to the department that handles warranties.

You may have other options as well. If your product was trouble-free during the warranty period, the manufacturer may offer a free repair for a problem that arose after the warranty expired if the problem is a widespread one. Many manufacturers have secret "fix it" lists—items with defects that don't affect safety and therefore don't require a recall, but that the manufacturer will repair for free. It can't hurt to call and ask.

## I just bought a stereo system and the salesclerk tried to sell me an extended warranty contract. Should I have bought it?

Probably not. Merchants encourage you to buy extended warranties (also called service contracts) because they are a source of big profits for stores, which pocket up to 50% of the amount you pay.

Rarely will you have the chance to exercise your rights under an extended warranty. Name-brand electronic equipment and appliances usually don't break down during the first few years (and if they do they're covered by the original warranty), and often have a lifespan well beyond the length of the extended warranty.

## I think I was the victim of a scam. Can I get my money back?

Federal and state laws prohibit "unfair or deceptive trade acts or practices." If you think you've been cheated, *immediately* let the appropriate government offices know. Although any government investigation will take some time, these agencies often have the resources to go after unscrupulous merchants. Law enforcement in the consumer fraud area is not great in some parts of the country, but many hardworking investigators do their jobs superbly. The more agencies you notify, the more likely someone will take notice of your complaint and act on it.

Unfortunately, government agencies are rarely able to get you your money back. If the business is a reputable one, however, it may refund your money when a consumer fraud law enforcement investigator shows up. It certainly can't hurt you to complain.

If you can't get relief from a government agency, consider suing the company in small claims court. *Everybody's Guide to Small Claims Court*, by Ralph Warner (Nolo), provides extensive information on how to sue in small claims court.

# How to File a Complaint for Fraud

The National Fraud Information Center, a project of the National Consumer's League, can help you if you've been defrauded. NFIC provides:

- assistance in filing a complaint with appropriate federal agencies
- recorded information on current fraud schemes
- tips on how to avoid becoming a fraud victim, and
- direct ordering of consumer publications in English or Spanish.

You can contact NFIC, P.O. Box 65868, Washington, DC 20035, 800-876-7060 (voice), 202-835-0767 (fax), 202-737-5084 (TTD), 202-347-3189 (electronic bulletin board), http://www.fraud.org.

If you want to contact a federal agency directly but aren't sure which one, contact the U.S. Department of Commerce's Office of Consumer Affairs, (202) 482-5001 or caffairs@doc.gov. Also contact your local prosecutor to find out if it investigates consumer fraud complaints. Finally, contact any local newspaper, radio station or television station "action line." Especially in metropolitan areas, these folks often have an army of volunteers ready to pursue every consumer complaint.

## I received some unordered merchandise in the mail and now I'm getting billed. Do I have to pay?

You don't owe any money if you receive an item you never ordered—it's considered a gift. If you get bills or collection letters from a seller who sent you something you never ordered, write to the seller stating your intention to treat the item as a gift. If the bills continue, insist that the seller send you proof of your order. If this doesn't stop the bills, notify the state consumer protection agency in the state where the merchant is located.

If you sent for something in response to an advertisement claiming a "free" gift or "trial" period, but are now being billed, be sure to read the fine print of the ad. It may say something about charging shipping and handling; or worse, you may have inadvertently joined a club or subscribed to a magazine. Write the seller, offer to return the merchandise and state that you believe the ad was misleading.

## I just signed a contract to have carpeting installed in my house and I changed my mind. Can I cancel?

Possibly. Under the Federal Trade Commission's "Cooling Off Rule," you have until midnight of the third business day after a contract was signed to cancel either of the following:

- door-to-door sales contracts for more than $25, or
- a contract for more than $25 made anywhere other than the seller's normal place of business—for instance, at a sales presentation at a hotel or restaurant, outdoor exhibit, computer show or trade show (other than public car auctions and craft fairs).

## Do I have the right to cancel any other kinds of contracts?

The federal Truth in Lending Act lets you cancel some loans up until midnight of the third business day after you signed the contract. It applies only to loans for which you pledged your home as security, as long as the loan is not a first mortgage. For example, the Act applies to home improvement loans and second mortgages. If the lender never notified you of the three-day right to cancel, you have even longer to cancel your loan.

In addition, many states have laws that allow you to cancel written contracts covering the purchase of certain goods or services within a few days of signing, including contracts for dance or martial arts lessons, credit repair services, health club memberships, dating services, weight loss programs, time share properties and hearing aids. In a few states, you can also cancel a contract if you negotiated the transaction in a language other than English but the seller did not give you a copy of the contract in that language. Call your state consumer protection agency (check directory assistance in your state capital) to find out what contracts, if any, are covered in your state.

## I ordered some clothes through a catalogue and there's a delay in shipping. Can I cancel my order?

If you order goods by mail, phone, computer or fax (other than photo development, magazine subscriptions, seeds or plants), the Federal Trade Commission's "Mail or Telephone Order Rule" requires that the seller ship to you within the time promised or, if no time was stated, within 30 days.

If the seller cannot ship within those times, the seller must send you a notice with a new shipping date and offer you the option of canceling your order and getting a refund, or accepting the new date. If you opt for the second deadline, but the seller can't meet it, you must be sent a notice requesting your signature to agree to yet a third date. If you don't return the notice, your order must be automatically canceled and your money refunded. The seller must issue the refund promptly—within seven days if you paid by check or money order and within one billing cycle if you charged your purchase.

## Do I have the right to a cash refund after I make a purchase?

Generally, no. A seller isn't required to offer refunds or exchanges, though many do.

But at least four states do have laws governing refund policies:

- *California*. Sellers who do not allow a full cash or credit refund (or an equal exchange) within seven days of purchase must post the store's refund-credit-exchange policy. If the seller fails to post the policy, you may return the goods, for a full refund, within 30 days of your purchase.
- *Florida*. If the seller has no refund policy, such a statement must be posted in the store. If a statement isn't posted, you may return unused and unopened goods within seven days for a full refund.
- *New York*. Sellers with a cash refund policy must post the policy and give the refund within 20 days. If a seller offers both refunds and exchanges, you may decide which you'd prefer.
- *Virginia*. Sellers must post their refund or exchange policies unless they give a full cash refund (or full credit) within 20 days after purchase.

### *More Information About Purchasing Goods and Services*

*Everybody's Guide to Small Claims Court*, by Ralph Warner (Nolo), has extensive information on pursuing your rights in the event a seller or manufacturer won't make good on a warranty.

The Direct Marketing Association is a membership organization made up of mail-order companies and other direct marketers. If you have a complaint about

a particular company, contact Mail-Order Action Line, c/o DMA, 1111 19th Street, NW, Suite 1100, Washington, DC 20036, 202-955-5030, 202-955-0085 (fax). DMA may contact the mail-order company and try to resolve your problem.

# Using Credit and Charge Cards

American adults hold approximately two billion total credit and charge cards—an average of nine cards per person. Buying on credit has become a cornerstone of the American economy. But buying on credit can be very expensive—the interest rate on bank credit cards averages about 18%; on gasoline company and department store cards, it's over 20%. Only charge cards (also called travel and entertainment cards), such as American Express and Diners Club, don't generally impose interest. Of course, charge cards usually require that you pay off the entire balance each month.

## My credit card debt is consuming my life. How can I cut credit card costs?

If you have more than one card, pay down the balances with the highest interest rates and then use (or obtain) a card with a low rate. Because there is great competition among credit card issuers, you might get a rate reduction simply by calling your current bank and asking.

## Which Cards Should You Keep?

When you think about the costs of using your credit cards, you may decide that you're better off canceling most of them. If so, you'll have to choose which cards to keep. If you don't carry a monthly balance, keep a card with no annual fee, but make sure it has a grace period. If you carry a balance each month, get rid of the cards that come with the worst of the following features:

- High interest rates.
- Unfair interest calculations. Avoid cards that charge interest on the average daily balance, not the balance due. Here's why. Let's say you pay $1,200 of your $1,500 balance in January. If your bank uses the average daily balance method, in February it will charge you interest on the $1,500 average daily balance from January, not on the $300 you still owe.
- No grace periods. This means you pay interest from the time of purchase until the time of payment even if you pay your balance in full.
- Nuisance fees. Get rid of cards with late payment fees, over-the-limit fees, inactivity fees, fees for not carrying a balance or for carrying a balance under a certain amount or a flat monthly fee that's a percentage of your credit limit.

I'm always getting credit card offers with low interest rates in the mail. Should I sign up and transfer the balance from my current card to the new card?

It depends. Check the fine print of the offer. Many credit card companies offer a "teaser" rate—a low rate that lasts for a short period of time. Once the "teaser" period is over, a much higher rate kicks in. Also be sure to consider any annual fees, grace periods and nuisance fees (see Which Cards Should You Keep?, above) before you switch.

I can't afford the minimum payment required on my statement. Can I pay less?

Most card companies insist that you make the monthly minimum payment, which is usually 2% to 2.5% of the outstanding balance. If you can convince the card issuer that your financial situation is desperate, the issuer may cut your payments in half. In some cases, the issuer may waive payments altogether for a few months. This courtesy is usually extended only to people who have never been late with payments.

Bear in mind that paying nothing or very little on your credit card should be only a temporary solution. The longer you pay only a small amount, the quicker your balance will increase due to interest charges.

## My checking account and Visa card are from the same bank. Can the bank take money out of my checking account to cover my missed credit card payments?

No. A bank that takes money out of a deposit account to cover a missed credit card payment violates the federal Truth in Lending Act. You can sue for damages—the amount taken out of your account and any other damages you suffer, such as lost interest or bounced-check fees.

## My wallet was stolen. Will I have to pay charges that the thief made using my credit cards?

No. Federal law limits your liability for unauthorized charges made on your credit or charge card after it has been lost or stolen. If you notify the card issuer within a reasonable time after you discover the loss or theft (usually 30 days), you're not responsible for any charges made after the notification, and are liable for only the first $50 of charges made before you notified the card issuer. In practice, card issuers rarely even charge the $50.

## I purchased an item using my credit card and it fell apart. Can I refuse to pay?

Maybe. Under federal law, you must first attempt in good faith to resolve the dispute with the merchant. If that fails, you can withhold payment only if the purchase was for more than $50 and was made within your home state or within 100 miles of your home. (This limitation applies only if you used a card not issued by the seller, such as a MasterCard. There is no $50, 100-mile or in-state limitation if you use a seller's card, such as your Sears card.)

The 100-mile limitation is easy to calculate when purchases are made in person. But if you order through the mail, over the telephone or using your computer, the law is unclear as to where the purchase took place. Your best bet is to claim that the purchase was made in the state where you live (even if the catalogue company is on the other side of the country) because you placed the order from home.

## My credit card billing statement contains an error. What should I do?

Immediately write a letter to the customer service department of the card issuer. Give your name, account number, an explanation of the error and the amount involved. Enclose copies of supporting documents, such as receipts showing the correct amount of the charge. You must act quickly—the issuer must receive your letter within 60 days after it mailed the bill to you.

Under the federal Fair Credit Billing Act, the issuer must acknowledge receipt of your letter within 30 days, unless it corrects the bill within that time. Furthermore, the issuer must, within two billing cycles (but in no event more than 90 days), correct the error or explain why it believes the amount to be correct.

During the two-billing-cycle/90-day period, the issuer cannot report the amount to credit bureaus or other creditors as delinquent. The issuer can charge you interest on the amount you dispute during this period, but if it later agrees that you were correct, it must drop the interest accrued.

### Must I give my phone number when I use a credit card?

Most often, no. Several states, including California, Delaware, Georgia, Kansas, Massachusetts, Minnesota, Nevada, New Jersey, New York, Oregon, Pennsylvania, Rhode Island and Wisconsin, bar merchants from recording personal information when you use a credit card. Furthermore, merchants agreements with Visa and MasterCard prohibit them from requiring a customer to furnish a phone number when paying with Visa or MasterCard.

### I took out a cash advance using my credit card, and feel I was gouged. What are all those fees?

Cash advances usually come with the following fees:
- *Transaction fees.* Most banks charge a transaction fee of up to 4% for taking a cash advance.
- *Grace period.* Most banks charge interest from the date the cash advance is posted, even if you pay it back in full when your bill comes.
- *Interest rates.* The interest rate is often higher on cash advances than it is on ordinary credit card charges.

# Using an ATM or Debit Card

*A bank is a place where they lend you an umbrella in fair weather and ask for it back when it begins to rain.*

**—ROBERT FROST**

Banks issue ATM cards to allow customers to withdraw money, make deposits, transfer money between accounts, find out their balances, get cash advances and even make loan payments at all hours of the day or night.

Debit cards combine the functions of ATM cards and checks. Debit cards are issued by banks, but can be used at stores. When you pay with a debit card, the money is automatically deducted from your checking account. Many merchants accept ATM cards as debit cards.

### What are the advantages to using an ATM or debit card?

There are generally two advantages:
- You don't have to carry your checkbook and identification, but you can make purchases directly from your checking account.
- You pay immediately—without running up interest charges on a credit card bill.

### Are there disadvantages?

Yes. You don't have the 20- to 25-day delay in paying the bill. Also, you don't have the right to withhold payment (the money is immediately removed from the account) in the event of a dispute with the merchant over the goods or services paid for. Finally, many banks charge transaction fees when you use an ATM or debit card at locations other than those owned by the bank.

## Do I have to pay if there's a mistake on my statement or receipt?

Although ATM statements and debit receipts don't usually contain errors, mistakes do happen. If you find an error, you have 60 days from the date of the statement or receipt to notify the bank. Always call first and follow up with a letter. If you don't notify the bank within 60 days, it has no obligation to investigate the error and you're out of luck.

The bank has ten business days from the date of your notification to investigate the problem and tell you the result. If the bank needs more time, it can take up to 45 days, but only if it deposits the disputed amount of money into your account. If the bank later determines that there was no error, it can take the money back, but it must first send you a written explanation.

# If Your ATM Card Is Lost or Stolen

If your ATM or debit card is lost or stolen (never, never, never keep your personal identification number—PIN—near your card), call your bank immediately, and follow up with a confirming letter. Under the federal Electronic Fund Transfers Act, your liability is:

- $0—after you report the card missing
- up to $50—if you notify the bank within two business days after you realize the card is missing (unless you were on extended travel or in the hospital)
- up to $500—if you fail to notify the bank within two business days after you realize the card is missing (unless you were on extended travel or in the hospital) , but do notify the bank within 60 days after your bank statement is mailed to you listing the unauthorized withdrawals
- unlimited—if you fail to notify the bank within 60 days after your bank statement is mailed to you listing the unauthorized withdrawals.

In response to consumer complaints about the possibility of unlimited liability, Visa and MasterCard now cap the liability on debit cards at $50. A few states (Iowa, Kansas, Massachusetts, Minnesota, New Mexico and Wisconsin) have capped the liability for unauthorized withdrawals on an ATM or debit card at $50 as well. And some large debit card issuers won't charge you anything if unauthorized withdrawals appear on your statement.

### More Information About Credit, Charge, ATM and Debit Cards

*Money Troubles: Legal Strategies to Cope With Your Debts*, by Robin Leonard (Nolo Press), contains extensive information on credit, charge, ATM and debit card laws and practical usage tips.

The Federal Deposit Insurance Corporation, 1730 Pennsylvania Avenue, NW, Washington, DC 20429, 800-934-3342, 202-942-3427 (fax), 800-925-4618 (TDD), http://www.fdic.gov, publishes free pamphlets, including *Fair Credit Billing*.

The Federal Trade Commission, 6th & Pennsylvania Avenue, NW, Washington, DC 20850, 202-326-2222, 202-326-2050 (fax), http://www.ftc.gov, publishes free pamphlets, including *Billing Errors*, *Fair Credit Billing*, *Lost or Stolen Credit and ATM Cards* and *Solving Credit Problems*.

# Strategies for Repaying Debts

*If you think nobody cares if you're alive, try missing a couple of car payments.*

—EARL WILSON

These days, everyone talks about how strong the American economy is. But this may be news to you. The real story is that many people have been left out of this economic boom. Many people are working harder than ever, earning less, saving little and struggling with debt. If this story sounds familiar to you, you're not alone. Here are some specific suggestions for dealing with debts.

## I feel completely overwhelmed by my debts and don't know where to begin. What should I do?

Take a deep breath and realize that for the most part, your creditors want to help you. Whether you're behind on your bills or are afraid of getting behind, call your creditors. Let them know what's going on—job loss, reduction in hours, medical problem or whatever—and ask for help. Suggest possible solutions such as a temporary reduction of your payments, skipping a few payments and tacking them on at the end of a loan, skipping a few payments and paying them off over a few months, dropping late fees and other charges or even rewriting a loan. If you need help negotiating with your creditors, consider contacting a nonprofit debt counseling organization, such as Debt Counselors of America (http://www.dca.org) or a local Consumer Credit Counseling Service office.

## I'm afraid I might miss a car payment—should I just let the lender repossess?

No. Before your car payment is due, call the lender and ask for extra time.

If you're at least a few months into the loan and haven't missed any payments, the lender will probably let you miss one or two months' payments and tack them on at the end. If you don't pay or make arrangements with the lender, the lender can repossess without warning, although many will warn you and give you a chance to pay what's due.

If your car is repossessed, you can get it back by paying the entire balance due and the cost of repossession or, in some cases, by paying the cost of the repossession and the missed payments, and then making payments under your contract. If you don't get the car back, the lender will sell it at an auction for far less than it's worth. You'll owe the lender the difference between the balance of your loan and what the sale brings in. The amount is usually in the thousands.

If you are far behind on your car payments and can't catch up, the truth is that you may not be able to afford the car. Think about voluntarily "surrendering" your car before the dealer has a chance to repossess it. This can save you expensive repossession costs and attorneys' fees. Because it also makes life easier for the dealer, try to negotiate a deal. Many dealers will agree to waive any deficiency balance or promise not to report the default or repossession to credit bureaus.

## How soon after I miss a house payment will the bank begin foreclosure proceedings?

This varies from state to state and lender to lender, but most lenders don't start foreclosure proceedings until you've missed four or five payments. Before taking back your house, a lender would usually rather rewrite the loan, suspend principal payments for a while (have you pay interest only), reduce your payments or even let you miss a few payments and spread them out over time.

If your loan is owned by one of the giant U.S. government mortgage holders, Fannie Mae or Freddie Mac, foreclosure could come even more slowly. Fannie Mae and Freddie Mac have been working with homeowners to avoid foreclosure when a loan is delinquent.

If your loan is insured by a federal agency such as the Department of Housing and Urban Development (HUD), the Federal Housing Administration (FHA), the Veterans Administration (VA) or the Farmers Home Administration (FmHA), the lender may be required to try to help you avoid foreclosure. Contact the federal agency to find out more about your rights.

## Might I be better off just selling my house?

You're certainly better off selling the house than having it go to foreclosure. If you can find a buyer who will offer to pay at least what you owe your lender, take the offer. If the offer is for less than what you owe your lender, your lender can block the sale. But many lenders will agree to a "short sale"—where the sale brings in less than you owe the lender and the lender agrees to forego the rest. Some lenders require documentation of any financial or medical hardship you are experiencing before agreeing to a short sale.

## Can I just walk away from the house?

If you get no offers for your house or the lender won't approve a short sale, you can walk away from your house. Call the lender and ask if it will accept your deed in lieu of foreclosing. If the lender won't, prepare what's called a quitclaim deed—you "quit" your interest in the property—transferring ownership to your lender. You write DEED IN LIEU OF FORECLOSURE in block capital letters across the top of the deed, pay any transfer fee, record the quitclaim deed where you recorded your ownership deed and mail a copy of the recorded quitclaim deed to the lender. This means that you no longer own the house.

## Beware of the IRS

IRS regulations could cost you money if you settle a debt or if a creditor writes off money you owe. The rules state that if a creditor agrees to forego a debt you owe, you must treat the amount you didn't pay as income. Similarly, if a creditor ceases collection efforts, declares the debt uncollectible and reports it as a tax loss to the IRS—including the amount owed after a house foreclosure or property repossession, or on a credit card bill—you must treat the write-off amount as income.

The rule applies to any bank, credit union, savings and loan or other financial institution that forgives or writes off a debt or part of a debt for $600 or more. The institution must send you and the IRS

a Form 1099-C at the end of the tax year. These forms are for the report of income, which means that when you file your tax return for the tax year in which your debt was forgiven, the IRS will make sure that you report the amount on the Form 1099-C as income.

There are five exceptions stated in the Internal Revenue Code, three of which apply to consumers. So even if the financial institution issues a Form 1099-C or 1099-A, you do not have to report the income if:

- the cancellation of the debt is intended as a gift (this would be unusual)
- you discharge the debt in bankruptcy, or
- you were insolvent before the creditor agreed to waive the debt.

The Internal Revenue Code does not define what is meant by insolvent. Generally it means that your debts exceed the value of your assets. To figure out whether or not you are insolvent, you will have to total up your assets and your debts, including the debt that was forgiven or written off.

Let's say your assets are worth $35,000 and your debts total $45,000. You are insolvent to the tune of $10,000. If a creditor forgives or writes off debts up to that amount, you will not have to include the Form 1099-C income on your tax return.

On the other hand, let's say your assets and debts are still $35,000 and $45,000 respectively, but your creditor forgives or writes off a $14,000 debt. Now, you can ignore $10,000 of the Form 1099-C income (the amount you are insolvent), but you will have to report $4,000 on your tax return.

## My utility bill was huge because of a very cold winter. Do I have to pay it all at once?

Maybe not. Many utility companies offer customers an amortization program. This means that if your bills are higher in certain months than others, the company averages your yearly bills so you can spread out the large bills. Also, if you are elderly, disabled or low income, you may be eligible for reduced rates—ask your utility company.

## I'm swamped with student loans and can't afford my payments. What can I do to avoid default?

First, know that you're right to do all you can to avoid default, rather than ignoring your loans and hoping they'll just go away. If you default, the amount you owe will probably skyrocket because the government can add a collections fee of up to 25% of the principal.

To avoid default, contact the companies that service your student loans and tell them why you can't make your payments. You may be eligible for a deferment or forbearance—ways of postponing repayment. In very limited circumstances, you may be able to cancel a loan. Also talk to your loan holders about flexible payment options—many now offer payments geared to borrowers' incomes.

In addition, consider consolidating your student loans. You can consolidate federal student loans through the government's direct lending program or through a private loan servicing company, such as Sallie Mae or USA Group. With loan consolidation, you can lower your monthly payments by

extending your repayment period; you may also be able to lower your interest rate. Most loan consolidators offer flexible repayment options based on your income, and you may be able to consolidate even if one or more of your loans is in default. Types of loans eligible for consolidation, repayment options and interest rates vary slightly from lender to lender. Contact loan servicers for more information:

- Federal Direct Consolidation Loan Center: 800-557-7392, http://www.ed.gov/offices/OSFAP/DirectLoan/consolid.html
- Sallie Mae: 800-524-9100, http://www.Salliemae.com
- USA Group: 800-382-4506, http://www.usagroup.com

Finally, if you can prove that repayment would cause you extreme hardship, you may be able to discharge your student loans in bankruptcy.

## I defaulted on a student loan a long time ago and I just received collection letters. I can't afford very much, but I can pay something. Any suggestions?

The Higher Education Act allows you to rehabilitate your student loan by making "reasonable and affordable" payments based on your income and expenses. The holder cannot insist on a monthly minimum. If you make six consecutive monthly payments on time, you will become eligible to apply for new federal student loans or grants if you want to return to school. You must continue to make the monthly payments, however, until you make at least 12 consecutive payments. Then your loans will come out of default. The default notation will come off your credit report, and if you return to school, you can apply for an in-school deferment to postpone your payments.

If you do not return to school, after you make 12 consecutive monthly payments, the holder of your loan will sell it back to a regular loan servicing company. (This is called loan rehabilitation.) Your new loan servicer will put you on a standard ten-year repayment plan, which may cause your monthly payments to increase dramatically. If you can't afford them, you will need to apply for a deferment (if you are eligible) or request a flexible repayment option.

### I paid off my student loan a long time ago, but the Department of Education recently wrote me saying I still owe it. Help!

You need documentation. First, contact your school and ask for its Department of Education report showing the loan's status. Then, think about ways you can show that you paid the loan: Do you have canceled checks or old bank statements? Can you get microfiche copies of checks from your

bank or a government regulatory agency if your bank is out of business? Does an old roommate remember seeing you write a check every month? Can you get old credit reports (check with lenders from whom you've borrowed in years past) which may show a payment status on an old loan? Get old tax returns (from the IRS, if necessary) showing that you itemized the interest deduction on student loan payments back when that was permitted. The last holder of the loan might have a copy of the signed promissory note. Any of these things will help you prove to the Department of Education that you paid your loan.

To find out more about the status of your loan, visit the Department of Education's website at http://www.ed.gov or the National Student Loan Data System's website at http://www.nslds.ed.gov. Or call 800-4-FED-AID or the student loan ombudsman at 877-557-2575.

### When can a creditor garnish my wages, place a lien on my house, seize my bank account or take my tax refund?

For the most part, a creditor must sue you, obtain a court judgment and then solicit the help of a sheriff or other law enforcement officer to garnish wages. Even then, the maximum the creditor can take is 25% of your net pay—and you can protest that amount in court if you can't live on only 75% of your wages.

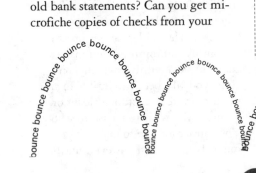

In two situations your wages may be garnished without your being sued:

- Most federal administrative agencies (including the IRS and the Department of Education) can garnish your wages to collect debts owed to that agency.
- Up to 50% of your wages can be garnished to pay child support or alimony (even more if you don't currently support any dependents or if you are in arrears).

To place a lien on your house or empty your bank account, almost all creditors must first sue you, get a judgment and then use a law enforcement officer. A few creditors, such as an unpaid contractor who worked on your house, can put a lien on your house without suing. And again, the IRS is an exception—it can place a lien or empty your bank account without suing first.

Your tax refund can never be taken unless the Treasury Department receives such a request from the IRS, the Department of Education or a child support collection agency.

## If You Bounce a Check

In every state, writing a bad check is a crime. Aggressive district attorneys don't hesitate to prosecute, especially given that an estimated 450 million rubber checks are written each year. If you are prosecuted, you may be able to avoid a trial if your county has a "diversion" program where you attend classes for bad check writers. You must pay the tuition and make good on the bad checks you wrote.

Even if you escape criminal prosecu-

tion, you'll be charged a bad check "processing" fee by your bank. Many banks charge as much as $20 or $30. In addition, most creditors who receive a bad check can sue for damages. Before suing you, the creditor usually must first make a written demand that you make good on the bad check. If you don't pay up within approximately 30 days, the creditor can sue you. Damages recoverable by the merchant vary from state to state, but are often a minimum of $50, and in most states more like a few hundred or a thousand dollars.

## Can I go to jail for not paying my debts?

Debtor's prisons were eliminated in the U.S. by 1850. In a few unusual situations, however, you could be jailed: you willfully violate a court order, especially an order to pay child support; you are convicted of willfully refusing to pay income taxes; or you are about to conceal yourself or your property to avoid paying a debt for which a creditor has a judgment against you.

### More Information About Repaying Debts

*Money Troubles: Legal Strategies to Cope with Your Debts*, by Robin Leonard (Nolo), explains your legal rights and offers practical strategies for dealing with debts and creditors.

*Take Control of Your Student Loans*, by Robin Leonard (Nolo), provides strategies for repaying your loans, dealing with loan collectors and getting out of default.

*The Ultimate Credit Handbook*, by Gerri Detweiler (Penguin Books), provides tips on doubling your credit and cutting your debt.

*Surviving Debt: A Guide for Consumers*, by Gary Klein, Deanne Loonin and Jonathan Sheldon (National Consumer Law Center), contains tips on dealing with debt collectors and repaying debts.

Debt Counselors of America, 800-680-3328, http://www.dca.org, offers free publications, recommended books, a forum for posting your debt questions, information on obtaining your credit report and special programs to help you get out of debt.

Consumer Credit Counseling Service, 800-388-2227, can put you in contact with the CCCS office located nearest you.

The Federal Student Aid Information Center, P.O. Box 84, Washington, DC 20044, 800-433-3243, http://www.ed.gov/prog_info/SFA/Student Guide provides information about federal student loan programs.

The Federal Trade Commission, 6th & Pennsylvania Avenue, NW, Washington, DC 20850, 202-326-2222, 202-326-2050 (fax), http://www.ftc.gov, publishes nearly 50 free pamphlets on debts and credit; call or write and ask for a complete list.

# Dealing With the IRS

*Of all debts men are least willing to pay the taxes.*

**—RALPH WALDO EMERSON**

No three letters bring more fear to the average American than IRS. Yet, at one time or another in our lives, nearly everyone will owe a tax bill they can't pay, need extra time to file a tax return or even get audited. This section suggests several strategies for dealing with the government's largest bureaucracy.

## How long should I keep my tax papers?

Keep anything related to your tax return—W-2 and 1099 forms, receipts and canceled checks for deductible items—for at least three years after you file. The IRS usually has three years from the day you file your return to audit you. For example, if you filed your 1997 tax return on April 15, 1998, keep those records until at least April 16, 2001. To be completely safe, you should keep your records for six years. The reason is that the IRS can audit up to six years after you file if the IRS believes you underreported your income by 25% or more.

One last caution: Keep records showing purchase costs and sales figures for real estate, stocks or other investments for at least three years after you sell these assets. This is because you must be able to show your taxable gain or loss to an auditor.

## If I can't pay my taxes, should I file a return anyway?

Absolutely. The consequences of filing and not paying (as opposed to simply not filing) are less severe. If you don't file a tax return, the IRS will assess a penalty of up to 25% of the tax due. In addition, the IRS could (although it isn't likely to) criminally charge you for failing to file a return. By contrast, if you file a return but can't pay, you'll only be on the hook for interest and penalties on any amounts you owe. You will bring an IRS collector into your life, but a collector is easier to deal with if she doesn't have to hunt you down for nonfiling, too.

## Who has access to my IRS files?

The federal Privacy Act of 1976 declares tax files to be "confidential." This was an attempt by Congress to correct the abuses of power uncovered in the Watergate scandal. Even IRS officials cannot rummage willy-nilly through your tax files unless they are involved in some kind of case involving you and your taxes. Consequently, individuals, businesses and credit reporting agencies do not have access to your tax information unless you authorize its release to the IRS in writing.

The privacy law has exceptions, however, and IRS security is sometimes lax. Your IRS files are shared with other federal and state agencies if they can demonstrate a "need to know." This usually means an investigation into your affairs by a law enforcement agency. In fairness to the IRS, most leakage of information is the result of sloppiness by other federal or state agencies granted access to IRS files. Furthermore, computer hackers have broken into IRS and government databases and retrieved private tax information. While violation of the Privacy Act is a crime, violators are rarely prosecuted.

## Do many people cheat on their taxes? And what will happen to me if I cheat on mine?

No one really knows how many people cheat the IRS, but several years ago an independent poll found that 20% of Americans admitted to cheating. This is somewhat in line with government studies showing that 82% of us faithfully file and pay our taxes every year. The IRS claims that most cheating is by self-employed small business people who do not have taxes withheld by their employers. Arguably, cheating by the self-employed approaches 100% if you count small violations like mailing a personal letter with a business-bought stamp.

If you are caught in some major cheating, the government can (but rarely does) throw you in jail. Fewer than 1,500 individuals are jailed in the U.S. for tax crimes each year, many of whom also are charged with drug crimes. That is really not many people, considering there are about 180,000,000 American adults. The

IRS would much prefer collecting money to putting anyone in prison. More likely, you'll be assessed heavy penalties, and will probably be audited for several years.

## I am faced with a tax bill that I can't pay. Am I completely at the IRS's mercy, or do I have some options?

There are six ways to deal with a tax bill you unquestionably owe:

- Borrow from a financial institution, family or friends and pay it in full.
- Negotiate a monthly payment plan with the IRS. (This will include interest and penalty charges.)
- File for Chapter 13 bankruptcy to set up a payment plan for your debts, including your taxes.
- Find out whether you can wipe out the debt in a Chapter 7 bankruptcy.
- Make an offer in compromise. (That is, ask the IRS to accept less than the full amount due.)
- Ask the IRS to designate your debt (temporarily) uncollectible if you are out of work or your income is very low. This will buy you time to get back on your feet before dealing with the IRS. Interest and penalties will continue to accrue.

## Tax Avoidance Schemes Don't Work

Dozens of tax avoidance schemes emerge every decade. Some promoters are very persuasive, particularly if you are predisposed to believing that it's possible to opt out of the tax system. Sad to say, these promoters are all snake-oil salesmen, the most successful of whom make millions peddling their products at expensive "seminars" and through underground publications. One recent scheme involves holding your assets in multiple family trusts, limited partnerships and offshore banks. While these artifices may put your assets beyond the reach of your creditors, they won't beat the IRS.

## I made a mistake on my tax return and am now being billed for the taxes, plus interest and penalties. Do I have to pay it all?

Maybe not. The IRS must charge you interest on your tax bill, but penalties are discretionary. The IRS abates (cancels) one-third of all penalties it charges. The trick is to convince the IRS that you had "reasonable cause" (a good excuse) for failing to observe the tax law. Examples that might work include:

- serious illness or a death in the family
- destruction of your records by a flood, fire or other catastrophe
- wrong advice from the IRS over the phone
- bookkeeper or accountant error, or
- your being in jail or out of the country at the time the tax return was due.

You can ask anyone at the IRS to cancel a penalty, in person or over the phone. And, you can ask for the penalty to be canceled even if you already paid it. The best way to get the IRS's attention is to use IRS Form 843, Claim for Refund and Request for Abatement. You can also write a letter to your IRS Service center (the Adjustments/Correspondence branch) requesting an abatement and providing the reasons why you need one. In either case, try to enclose payment for the underlying tax, if possible. Paying the tax stops the accrual of interest on that balance.

## Can the IRS take my house if I owe back taxes?

The IRS can seize just about anything you own—including your home and pension plans. There is a list of items exempt by federal law from IRS seizures, but it is hardly generous, and doesn't include your residence. Moreover, state homestead protection laws don't apply to the IRS. With that said, the good news is that the federal Taxpayer Bill of Rights discourages the IRS from taking homes of people who owe back taxes. In addition, the IRS doesn't like the negative publicity generated when it takes a home, unless of course it is the home of a notorious public enemy.

Nevertheless, if the IRS collection division has tried—and failed—to get any cooperation from a tax debtor (for example, if the debtor has not answered correspondence or returned phone calls, or has made threats, lied about her income or hidden her assets), the IRS may go after a residence as a last resort. A tax collector can't make the decision on his own—it must come from top IRS personnel.

If the IRS lets you know that it plans to take your house, your Congressperson may be able to intervene and put some pressure on the IRS to stop the seizure. And, if the seizure would add you and your family to the ranks of the homeless, you can contact your local IRS Problems Resolution Office to plead that the seizure would create a substantial hardship.

In the unhappy event the IRS does seize your home, all may not be lost. The IRS must sell the home at public auction, usually held about 45 days after the seizure. Then, the high bidder at auction must wait 180 days to get clear title. In this interim period you have the right to redeem (buy back) the home by coming up with the bid price plus interest.

## What are my chances of getting through an audit without owing additional taxes?

Although only about 1% of all tax returns are audited, the IRS has a pretty high success rate. Fewer than 15% of all IRS audit victims make a clean getaway. This is primarily because the IRS's sophisticated computer selection process makes it likely that the agency will audit returns in which "adjustments" are almost a certainty.

If you receive an audit notice, focus on limiting the damage rather than getting off scot-free. Most adjustments made following an audit result from poor taxpayer records, so make sure you have organized documentation to back up your deductions, exemptions and other claims. Ignore the tales about dumping a box of receipts on the auditor's desk in the hope that she will throw up her hands and let you off rather than go through the mess. It doesn't work like that. If you have any significant worries, get a tax pro to represent you or to help you navigate through the perilous audit waters.

### Can I challenge the IRS if I get audited and don't agree with the result?

You do not have to accept any audit report. In most cases, you can appeal by sending a protest letter to the IRS within 30 days after receiving the audit report. If you request an appeals consideration, you will be granted a meeting with an Appeals Officer who is not part of the IRS division that performed your audit.

If your appeal fails, you still can file a petition in Tax Court. This is a fairly inexpensive and simple process if the audit bill is for less than $50,000. If it's for more, you will most likely need the help of a tax attorney.

Generally, it pays to contest an audit report by appealing and going to court. About half the people who challenge their audit report succeed in lowering their tax bill (at least partially).

### More Information About Dealing With the IRS

*Stand Up to the IRS*, by Frederick W. Daily (Nolo), explains your legal rights and offers practical strategies for dealing with the IRS.

*Surviving an Audit*, by Frederick W. Daily (Nolo), provides a wealth of information for minimizing the damage when you are audited.

# Debt Collections

Laws prohibit debt collectors from using abusive or deceptive tactics to collect a debt. Unfortunately, many collectors ignore the rules and don't play fair. In addition, creditors and debt collectors have powerful collection tools once they have won a lawsuit for the debt. Here are some frequently asked questions and answers to help you deal with debt collectors.

### Collection agencies have been calling me all hours of the day and night. Can I get them to stop contacting me?

It's against the law for a bill collector who works for a collection agency (as opposed to working in the collections department of the creditor itself) to call you at an unreasonable time. The law presumes that calls before 8 a.m. or after 9 p.m. are unreasonable. But other hours may be unreasonable too, such as daytime hours for a person who works nights. The law, the federal Fair Debt Collection Practices Act (FDCPA), also bars collectors from calling you at work if you ask them not to, harassing you, using abusive language, making false or misleading statements, adding unauthorized charges and many other practices. Under the FDCPA, you can demand that the collection agency stop contacting you, except to tell you that collection efforts have ended or that the creditor or collection agency will sue you. You must put your request in writing.

## I'm also getting calls from the collections department of a local merchant I did business with. Can I tell that collector to stop contacting me?

Usually not. The FDCPA applies only to bill collectors who work for collection agencies. While many states have laws prohibiting all debt collectors—including those working for the creditor itself—from harassing, abusing or threatening you, these laws don't give you the right to demand that the collector stop contacting you. There is at least one exception: Residents of New York City can use a local consumer protection law to write any bill collector and say, "Leave me alone." A few states, including Colorado and Massa-

chusetts, prohibit all collectors from calling you at work if you tell them not to.

## A bill collector insisted that I wire the money I owe through Western Union. Am I required to do so?

No, and it could add a lot to your debt if you do. Many collectors, especially when a debt is more than 90 days past due, will suggest several "urgency payment" options, including:

- *Sending money by express or overnight mail.* This will add at least $10 to your bill; a first class stamp is fine.
- *Wiring money through Western Union's Quick Collect or American Express's Moneygram.* This is another $10 waste.
- *Putting your payment on a credit card not charged to its maximum.* You'll never get out of debt if you do this.

*You Can Run, But You Can't Hide*

In this technological age, it's easy to run from collectors—but hard to hide. Collectors use many different resources to find debtors. They may contact relatives, friends, neighbors and employers, posing as long-lost friends to get these people to reveal your new whereabouts. In addition, collectors often get information from post office change of address forms, state motor vehicle registration information, voter registration records, former landlords and banks.

## Can a collection agency add interest to my debt?

In most cases, yes. But only if either:
- the original agreement allows for additional interest during collection proceedings, or
- state law authorizes the addition of interest.

Virtually all states do allow this interest.

## A collection agency sued me and won. Will I still be called and sent letters demanding payment?

Probably not. Before obtaining a court judgment, a bill collector generally has only one way of getting paid: demand payment. This is done with calls and letters. You can ignore the phone calls and throw out your mail, and the collector can't do much else short of suing you. Once the collector (or creditor) sues and gets a judgment, however, you can expect more aggressive collections actions. If you have a job, the collector will try to garnish up to 25% of your net wages. The collector may also try to seize any bank or other deposit accounts you have. If you own real property, the collector will probably record a lien, which will have to be paid when you sell or refinance your property. Even if you're not currently working or have no property, you're not home free. Depending on the state,

court judgments can last up to 20 years and, in many states, can be renewed.

## What can I do if a bill collector violates the FDCPA?

Document the violation as soon as it occurs. Write down what happened, when it happened and who witnessed it. In some states, you can tape record phone conversations with debt collectors without their knowledge. But beware. In about a dozen states, this is illegal. Instead, try to have a witness present (or on another phone extension) the next time you talk to the collector.

Then file a complaint with the Federal Trade Commission (the address and phone number are at the end of this section). Next, complain to your state consumer protection agency. Finally, send a copy of your complaint to the creditor who hired the collection agency. If the violations are severe enough, the creditor may stop the collection efforts.

Also, you can sue a collection agency (and the creditor that hired the agency) in small claims court for violating the FDCPA. You are less likely to win if you can prove only a few minor violations. If the violations are outrageous, you can sue the collection agency and creditor in regular civil court. One Texas jury awarded a debtor $11 million when a debt collector made death and bomb threats against her and her husband that frightened them so much they moved out of the county.

*More Information
About Debt Collections*

*Money Troubles: Legal Strategies to Cope With Your Debts*, by Robin Leonard (Nolo), explains your legal rights and offers practical strategies for dealing with debts and creditors.

The Federal Trade Commission, 6th & Pennsylvania Avenue, NW, Washington, DC 20850, 202-326-2222, 202-326-2050 (fax), http://www.ftc.gov/, publishes free pamphlets on debts and credit, including a couple on the Fair Debt Collections Practices Act. It also takes complaints about collection agencies.

# Bankruptcy

*Where everything is bad it
must be good to know the worst.*

**—FRANCIS HERBERT BRADLEY**

If you are seriously in debt, you might consider filing for bankruptcy. Here are some common questions and answers designed to help you understand the bankruptcy process and what bankruptcy can and cannot do for you.

## What exactly is bankruptcy?

Bankruptcy is a federal court process designed to help consumers and businesses eliminate their debts or repay them under the protection of the bankruptcy court. Bankruptcy's roots can be traced to the Bible. (Deuteronomy 15:1-2 —"Every seventh year you shall practice remission of debts. This shall be the nature of the remission: Every creditor shall remit the due that he claims from his neighbor; he shall not dun his neighbor or kinsman.")

## Aren't there different kinds of bankruptcy?

Yes. Bankruptcies can generally be described as "liquidation" or "reorganization."

Liquidation bankruptcy is called Chapter 7. Under Chapter 7 bankruptcy, a consumer or business asks the bankruptcy court to wipe out (discharge) the debts owed. Certain debts cannot be discharged—these are discussed below. In exchange for the discharge of debts, the business's assets or the consumer's nonexempt property is sold—that is, liquidated—and the proceeds are used to pay off creditors. The property a consumer might lose is discussed below.

There are several types of reorganization bankruptcy. Consumers with secured debts under $871,550 and unsecured debts under $290,525 can file for Chapter 13. Family farmers can file for Chapter 12. Consumers with debts in excess of the Chapter 13 debt limits or businesses can file for Chapter 11—a complex, time-consuming and expensive process. In any reorganization bankruptcy, you file a plan with the bankruptcy court proposing how you will repay your creditors. Some debts must be repaid in full; others you pay only a percentage; others aren't paid at all. Some debts you have to pay with interest; some are paid at the beginning of your plan and some at the end.

## What generally happens in consumer bankruptcy cases?

In a Chapter 7 case, you file several forms with the bankruptcy court listing income and expenses, assets, debts and property transactions for the past two years. The cost to file is $200, which may be waived for people who receive public assistance or live below the poverty level. A court-appointed person, the trustee, is assigned to oversee your case. About a month after filing, you must attend a "meeting of creditors" where the trustee reviews your forms and asks any questions. Despite the name, creditors rarely attend. If you have any nonexempt property, you must give it (or its value in cash) to the trustee. The meeting lasts about five minutes. Three to six months later, you receive a notice from the court that "all debts that qualified for discharge were discharged." Then your case is over.

Chapter 13 is a little different. You file the same forms plus a proposed repayment plan, in which you describe how you intend to repay your debts over the next three, or in some cases five, years. The cost to file is $185 (it cannot be waived but it can be paid in installments), and a trustee is assigned to oversee the case. Here, too, you at-

tend the meeting of creditors, but often one or two creditors attend this meeting, especially if they don't like something in your plan. After the meeting of the creditors, you attend a hearing before a bankruptcy judge who either confirms or denies your plan. If your plan is confirmed, and you make all the payments called for under your plan, you often receive a discharge of any balance owed at the end of your case.

## Nondischargeable Debts

The following debts are nondischargeable in both Chapter 7 and Chapter 13. If you file for Chapter 7, these will remain when your case is over. If you file for Chapter 13, these debts will have to be paid in full during your plan. If they are not, the balance will remain at the end of your case:

- debts you forget to list in your bankruptcy papers, unless the creditor learns of your bankruptcy case
- child support and alimony
- debts for personal injury or death caused by your intoxicated driving
- student loans, unless it would be an undue hardship for you to repay
- fines and penalties imposed for violating the law, such as traffic tickets and criminal restitution, and
- recent income tax debts and all other tax debts.

In addition, the following debts may be declared nondischargeable by a bankruptcy judge in Chapter 7 if the creditor challenges your request to discharge them. These debts may be discharged in

Chapter 13. You can include them in your plan—at the end of your case, the balance is wiped out:

- debts you incurred on the basis of fraud, such as lying on a credit application
- credit purchases of $1,150 of more for luxury goods or services made within 60 days of filing
- loans or cash advances of $1,150 or more taken within 60 days of filing
- debts from willful or malicious injury to another person or another person's property
- debts from embezzlement, larceny or breach of trust, and
- debts you owe under a divorce decree or settlement unless after bankruptcy you would still not be able to afford to pay them or the benefit you'd receive by the discharge outweighs any detriment to your ex-spouse (who would have to pay them if you discharge them in bankruptcy).

## What property might I lose if I file for bankruptcy?

You lose no property in Chapter 13. In Chapter 7, you select property you are eligible to keep from either a list of state exemptions or exemptions provided in the federal Bankruptcy Code. Most debtors use the exemptions provided by their state.

Exemptions are generally as follows:
- *Equity in your home, called a homestead exemption.* Under the Bankruptcy Code, you can exempt up to $17,425. Some states have no homestead exemption; others allow debtors to protect all or most of the equity in their home.
- *Insurance.* You usually get to keep the cash value of your policies.
- *Retirement plans.* Pensions which qualify under the Employee Retirement Income Security Act (ERISA) are fully protected in bankruptcy. So are many other retirement benefits; often, however, IRAs and Keoghs are not.
- *Personal property.* You'll be able to keep most household goods, furniture, furnishings, clothing (other than furs), appliances, books and musical instruments. You may be limited up to $1,000 or so in how much jewelry you can keep. Most states let you keep a vehicle with more than $2,400 of equity. And many states give you a "wild card" amount of money—often $1,000 or more—that you can apply toward any property.
- *Public benefits.* All public benefits, such as welfare, Social Security and unemployment insurance, are fully protected.
- *Tools used on your job.* You'll probably be able to keep up to a few thousand dollars worth of the tools used in your trade or profession.
- *Wages.* In most states, you can protect at least 75% of earned but unpaid wages.

## Why choose Chapter 13 over Chapter 7?

Although the overwhelming number of people who file for bankruptcy choose Chapter 7, there are several reasons why people select Chapter 13:
- You cannot file for Chapter 7 bankruptcy if you received a Chap-

ter 7 or Chapter 13 discharge within the previous six years.

- You have valuable nonexempt property.
- You're behind on your mortgage or car loan. In Chapter 7, you'll have to give up the property or pay for it in full during your bankruptcy case. In Chapter 13, you can repay the arrears through your plan, and keep the property by making the payments required under the contract.
- You have debts that cannot be discharged in Chapter 7.
- You have codebtors on personal (nonbusiness) loans. In Chapter 7, the creditors will go after your codebtors for payment. In Chapter 13, the creditors may not seek payment from your codebtors for the duration of your case.
- You feel a moral obligation to repay your debts, you want to learn money management or you hope new creditors might be more inclined to grant you credit after a Chapter 13 than they would after a Chapter 7.

### More Information About Bankruptcy

*How to File for Chapter 7 Bankruptcy*, by Stephen Elias, Albin Renauer and Robin Leonard (Nolo), is a complete guide to filing for Chapter 7 bankruptcy, including all the forms you need.

*Nolo's Law Form Kit: Personal Bankruptcy*, by Stephen Elias, Albin Renauer, Robin Leonard and Lisa Goldoftas (Nolo), contains all the forms and instructions necessary for filing a Chapter 7 bankruptcy.

*Chapter 13 Bankruptcy: Repay Your Debts*, by Robin Leonard (Nolo), contains the forms and instructions necessary to file your own Chapter 13 bankruptcy or successfully work with a lawyer.

*Bankruptcy: Is It the Right Solution to Your Debt Problems*, by Robin Leonard (Nolo), provides tools to help you decide if filing for bankruptcy is for you and, if so, which type is best.

## Bankruptcy Law to Change for the Worse

The United States Congress recently passed legislation that makes sweeping changes to bankruptcy law. Although the legislation is tied up in committee, experts anticipate that it will eventually become law. Once that happens, the new rules will take effect 180 days later.

The legislation is very unfriendly to debtors. Among other things, it would prohibit some people from filing for bankruptcy, add to the list of debts that people cannot get rid of in bankruptcy and make it harder for people to come up with manageable repayment plans.

To learn more about the legislation, check Legal Updates on Nolo's website (http://www.nolo.com).

# Rebuilding Credit

People who have been through a financial crisis—bankruptcy, repossession, foreclosure, history of late payments, IRS lien or levy or something similar—may think they will never get credit again. Not true. Following some simple steps, you can rebuild your credit in just a couple of years.

## What's the first step in rebuilding credit?

To avoid getting into financial problems in the future, you must understand your flow of income and expenses. Some people call this making a budget. Others find the term budget too restrictive and use the term "spending plan." Whatever you call it, spend at least two months writing down every expenditure. At each month's end, compare your total expenses with your income. If you're overspending, you have to cut back or find more income. As best you can, plan how you'll spend your money each month. If you have trouble putting together your own budget, consider getting help from a nonprofit group, such as Debt Counselors of America or Consumer Credit Counseling Service, which provides budgeting help for free or at a low cost.

## Okay, I've made my budget. What do I do next?

Now it's time to clean up your credit report. Credit reports are compiled by credit bureaus—private, for-profit companies that gather information about your credit history and sell it to banks, mortgage lenders, credit unions, credit card companies, department stores, insurance companies, landlords and even a few employers.

Credit bureaus get most of their data from creditors. They also search court records for lawsuits, judgments and bankruptcy filings. And they go through county records to find recorded liens (legal claims against property).

To create a credit file for a given person, a credit bureau searches its computer files until it finds entries that match the name, Social Security number and any other available identifying information. All matches are gathered together to make the report.

Noncredit data made part of a credit report usually includes names you previously used, past and present addresses, Social Security number, employment history, marriages and divorces. Your credit history includes the names of your creditors, type and number of each account, when each account was opened, your payment history for the previous 24–36 months, your credit limit or the original amount of a loan, and your current balance. The report will show if an account has been turned over to a collection agency or is in dispute.

# How to Get Your Credit Report

There are three major credit bureaus—Equifax, Trans Union and Experian. The federal Fair Credit Reporting Act (FCRA) entitles you to a copy of your credit report, and you can get one for free if any of the following are true:

- you were denied credit because of information in your credit report and you request a copy within 60 days of being denied credit
- you receive public assistance
- you are unemployed and plan to apply for a job within 60 days, or
- you believe your file contains errors due to fraud.

Residents of Colorado, Georgia, Maryland, Massachusetts, New Jersey and Vermont are entitled to a free copy of their report once a year from each credit bureau.

If you don't qualify for a free report, you'll have to pay about $8,50 (less in some states) to obtain one. Write to Equifax (P.O. Box 740241, Atlanta, GA 30374 or http://www.equifax.com), Trans Union (Consumer Disclosure Center, P.O. Box 1000, Chester, PA 19022 or http://www.transunion.com) or Experian (P.O. Box 2104, Allen, TX 75013-2104 or http://www.experian.com).

Send the following information:

- your full name (including generations such as Jr., Sr., III)
- your birth date
- your Social Security number
- your spouse's name (if relevant)
- your telephone number, and
- your current address and addresses for the previous five years.

## What should I do if I find mistakes in my report?

As you read through your report, make a list of everything out of date:

- Lawsuits, paid tax liens, accounts sent out for collection, late payments and any other adverse information older than seven years.
- Bankruptcies older than ten years from the discharge or dismissal. (Credit bureaus often list Chapter 13 bankruptcies for only seven years, but they can stay for as many as ten.)
- Credit inquiries (requests by companies for a copy of your report) older than two years.

Next, look for incorrect or misleading information, such as:

- incorrect or incomplete name, address, phone number, Social Security number or employment information
- bankruptcies not identified by their specific chapter number
- accounts not yours or lawsuits in which you were not involved
- incorrect account histories—such as late payments when you paid on time
- closed accounts listed as open—it may look as if you have too much open credit, and
- any account you closed that doesn't say "closed by consumer."

After reviewing your report, complete the "request for reinvestigation" form the credit bureau sent you or send a letter listing each item that is incorrect or too old to be reported. Once the credit bureau receives your request, it must investigate the items you dispute and contact you within 30 days. If you don't hear back within 30 days, send a follow-up letter.

If you are right, or if the creditor who provided the information can no longer verify it, the credit bureau must remove the information from your report. Often credit bureaus will remove an item on request without an investigation if rechecking the item is more bother than it's worth.

If the credit bureau insists that the information is correct, call the bureau to discuss the problem:
- Experian: 888-397-3742
- Trans Union: 800-888-4213
- Equifax: 800-685-1111

If you don't get anywhere with the credit bureau, contact the creditor directly and ask that the information be removed. Write to the customer service department, vice president of marketing and president or CEO. If the information was reported by a collection agency, send the agency a copy of your letter, too.

If the creditor will not remove the information, remind the creditor that under the 1997 amendments to the Fair Credit Reporting Act, the creditor must do the following:
- refrain from reporting information they know is incorrect

- refrain from ignoring information they know contradicts what they have on file, and
- provide credit bureaus with correct information when that information becomes available.

If a credit bureau is including the wrong information in your report, or you want to explain a particular entry, you have the right to put a 100-word statement in your report. The credit bureau must give a copy of your statement—or a summary—to anyone who requests your report. Be clear and concise; use the fewest words possible.

## I've been told that I need to use credit to rebuild my credit. Is this true?

Yes. The one type of positive information creditors like to see in credit reports is credit payment history. If you have a credit card, use it every month. (Make small purchases and pay them off to avoid interest charges.) If you don't have a credit card, apply for one. If your application is rejected, try to find a cosigner or apply for a secured card—where you deposit some money into a savings account and then get a credit card with a line of credit around the amount you deposited. But beware. You shouldn't apply for new credit before getting back on your feet. Defaulting on new credit will only make matters worse.

## What else can I do to rebuild my credit?

After you've cleaned up your credit report, the key to rebuilding credit is to get positive information into your record. Here are two suggestions:

- If your credit report is missing accounts you pay on time, send the credit bureaus a recent account statement and copies of canceled checks showing your payment history. Ask that these be added to your report. The credit bureau doesn't have to add anything, but often will.
- Creditors like to see evidence of stability, so if any of the following information is not in your report, send it to the bureaus and ask that it be added: your current employment, your previous employment (especially if you've been at your current job fewer than two years), your current residence, your telephone number (especially if it's unlisted), your date of birth and your checking account number. Again, the credit bureau doesn't have to add these, but often will.

## How long does it take to rebuild credit?

If you follow the steps outlined above, it will take about two years to rebuild your credit so that you won't be turned down for a major credit card or loan. After around four years, you may be able to qualify for a mortgage.

### *More Information About Rebuilding Your Credit*

*Credit Repair*, by Robin Leonard (Nolo), is a quick guide to lawfully rebuilding your credit. It contains several strategies for improving credit, sample credit reports with explanations on how to read them and the text of the federal and many state credit reporting laws.

*Money Troubles: Legal Strategies to Cope With Your Debts*, by Robin Leonard (Nolo), explains your legal rights and offers practical strategies for dealing with debts and creditors, including rebuilding your credit.

The Federal Trade Commission, 6th & Pennsylvania Avenue, NW, Washington, DC 20850, 202-326-2222, 202-326-2050 (fax), http://www.ftc.gov, publishes free pamphlets on debts and credit, including *Building a Better Credit Record*, *Cosigning a Loan*, *Fair Credit Reporting* and *Fix Your Own Credit Problems and Save Money*.

The Federal Deposit Insurance Corporation, 1730 Pennsylvania Avenue, NW, Washington, DC 20429, 800-934-3342, 202-942-3427 (fax), 800-925-4618 (TDD), http://www.fdic.gov, publishes free pamphlets about credit, including *Fair Credit Reporting*.

## http://www.nolo.com
Nolo offers self-help information about a wide variety of legal topics, including advice about consumer law, debts and credit.

## http://www.fraud.org
The National Fraud Information Center helps you file a complaint with federal agencies if you've benn defrauded. It also offers information on how to avoid becoming the victim of a scam.

## http://www.financenter.com
The FinanCenter provides financial advice and includes a calculator to help you compare various financing alternatives when you're making a budget or considering a major purchase, such as a home or automobile. The cool graphics alone make visiting this site worthwhile.

## http://www.bbb.org
The Better Business Bureau provides general information on their programs and services, including alerts, warnings and updates about businesses. You can also find information about filing a complaint against a business and using the BBB's dispute resolution program.

## http://law.etext.org
The Internet Law Library provides the texts of finance, economic and consumer protection laws including the federal bankruptcy code and bankruptcy rules, banking laws, Federal Trade Commission publications and selected state consumer protection laws.

## http://www.pueblo.gsa.gov
The Consumer Information Center provides the latest in consumer news as well as many publications of interest to consumers, including the Consumer Information Catalog.

## http://www.fdic.gov
## http://www.ftc.gov
Both the Federal Deposit Insurance Corporation and the Federal Trade Commission offer consumer protection rules, guides and publications.

## http://www.irs.ustreas.gov
The Internal Revenue Service provides tax information, forms and publications.

## http://www.agin.com/lawfind
This site provides an extensive list of online bankruptcy-related materials, including other online bankruptcy sites.

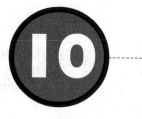

# **C**ars and Driving

10.2     *Buying a New Car*

10.7     *Leasing a Car*

10.10     *Buying a Used Car*

10.12     *Financing a Vehible Purchase*

10.13     *Insuring Your Car*

10.16     *Your Driver's License*

10.19     *If You're Stopped by the Police*

10.21     *Drunk Driving*

10.23     *Traffic Accidents*

WHEN SOLOMON SAID THAT THERE WAS
A TIME AND A PLACE FOR EVERYTHING
HE HAD NOT ENCOUNTERED THE PROBLEM
OF PARKING AN AUTOMOBILE.

**—BOB EDWARDS**

Together, Americans own more than 137 million automobiles—that's at least one car for every 1.7 people in the country. It is not surprising that this average is well above that for the rest of the world, where there is approximately one car for every 12 people. Plainly, Americans love their cars—or at least the mobility they provide. For the privilege of owning and operating a vehicle, we pay an average of more than $3,000 per year. We also expend plenty of time and energy figuring out which cars to buy, how to insure and maintain them, and how to keep out of trouble on the road. This chapter provides answers to many of your questions about owning a car and driving responsibly.

# Buying a New Car

These days, the average new car costs almost $20,000. For that amount of money, you would hope for a hassle-free buying experience and a safe and reliable product. Unfortunately, new car buyers are frequently overwhelmed with the pressure to buy immediately or spend more than planned, and worse—the product you bring home might be plagued with problems ranging from annoying engine "pings," to frequent stalls, to safety hazards such as poor acceleration or carbon monoxide leaks.

## I want to get a good deal on a new car. What make and model should I buy?

There are several good resources to help you comparison shop when you're looking for a new car. *Consumer Reports* magazine publishes an annual car-buying issue that compares price, features, service history, resale value and reliability. Other helpful sources of information are *Motor Trend* magazine and *The Car Buyer's Art*, by Darrell Parrish (Book Express). Finally, many websites provide price and feature information. To start, try http://www.autosite.com, http://www.carwizard.com or http://www.carprices.com.

When deciding which car to buy, resist the urge to buy more car than you can afford—and don't talk yourself into a more expensive car by financing it for four or five years. You'll pay a bundle in interest that way.

## Do you have any tips for negotiating with a car dealer?

Negotiating price with a dealer is almost never a pleasant experience. And, if you don't do it well, you are likely to pay hundreds or thousands of dollars more for a car. Here are some tips for getting the best deal.
• Know which car you want (or a few you are interested in), which features you want and what you can afford to pay before you walk into the dealership. Then, stick to your guns.

- Know the dealer's cost for the car before you start negotiating. Then, use this figure as the starting point from which you negotiate up. The dealer invoice price is how much the dealer paid for the car. Many websites list dealer invoice prices. But the dealer's final cost is often even lower, because manufacturers offer dealers behind-the-scenes financial incentives. To find out the car's true cost to the dealer, you can order a report from *Consumer Reports* (http://www.consumerreports.org or 800-888-8275) for about $12.

- Don't buy in a hurry. You need time to compare prices. And usually, the longer you take and the more times you walk away, the lower the price will go.

- Order your new car if the one you want is not on the lot. Cars on the lot frequently have options you don't want, which jack up the price.

- Don't make a deposit on a vehicle before the dealership has accepted your offer.

- If a rebate is offered, negotiate the price as if the rebate didn't exist. And have the rebate sent to your home—don't allow the dealership to "apply" it to the amount you owe. Rebates come from the manufacturer and shouldn't be a reason to pay the dealer more for the car.

- Don't discuss the possibility of a trade-in until you fix the price for your new car.

- Don't trade in your old vehicle without doing your homework. A dealer will give you the low *Kelley Blue Book* value, at most. (The *Kelley Blue Book* lists wholesale and retail prices for cars by year and model. You can find it in libraries, bookstores or online at http://www.kbb.com.) Take a look at classified ads to get an idea of how much you could get if you sold your car yourself. Or, order a used car price report from *Consumer Reports* magazine (http://www.consumerreports.org or 800-258-1169). Don't accept less than what you can get on the street. Or, forget the trade-in and sell your old car yourself.

- You might want to read up on the sales tactics dealerships use to get you to pay top dollar. Armed with this information, you will be better able to deflect the tactics and get a good deal. There are lots of books on this subject. Two of the best are *Don't Get Taken Every Time* by Remar Sutton (Penguin Books) and *So...You Wanna Buy a Car* by Bruce Fuller and Tony Whitney (Self-Counsel Press).

## What other information do I need to know before I buy my new car?

Be sure you know the following before you sign any contract:

- what the warranty covers and how long it lasts
- how you might lose warranty coverage (such as driving off-road)
- whether an extended warranty is available to you, and if so, the following:
  - what it will cost
  - what it covers
  - how long it lasts
  - whether it duplicates coverage provided by the manufacturer's warranty
  - how likely it is that you'll need it (whether the covered parts have a history of problems)
- the vehicle's estimated miles per gallon for city and highway driving, and
- the dealer's suggested maintenance schedule.

## Is there anything I should do when my new car is delivered?

Yes. Before signing a receipt and paying for your new vehicle, do the following:

- Check the vehicle against your order, item by item. Make sure all features are included.
- Inspect the vehicle for damage. Some new vehicles are damaged during manufacturing or in transit. For this reason, never take delivery of a new vehicle at night. Even in good artificial light, it's hard to see nicks or dents. You'll also miss subtle changes in paint that may indicate the car was damaged in transit and needed repainting.
- Test drive the vehicle and pay attention to odd noises, smells or vibrations.
- Make sure the warranty matches what the dealer agreed to.

## If I change my mind after I buy a new car, do I have the right to cancel the contract?

No. Unfortunately, many people think they have a right to change their mind, drive the car back to the dealer a day or two after buying, and cancel the contract. But the truth is, the dealer doesn't have to take the car back and probably won't, and you'll be stuck with a car you no longer want or cannot afford. Never buy a car unless you are absolutely certain you want it and can afford it.

This misunderstanding is so widespread that one state—California—requires the following to be included in new car contracts:

*California law does not provide for a "cooling off" or other cancellation period for vehicle sales. Therefore, you cannot later cancel this contract simply because you change your mind, decide the vehicle costs too much, or wish you had acquired a different vehicle. After you sign below, you may only cancel this contract with the agreement of the seller or for legal cause, such as fraud.*

**Soon after I brought my new car home, it started having problems. How do I know if it's a lemon?**

An estimated 150,000 vehicles each year (or 1% of new cars) are lemons. Although the precise definition of a

lemon varies by state, in general, a new car is a lemon if a number of attempts have been made to repair a "substantial defect" and the car continues to have this defect. A substantial defect is one that impairs the car's use, value or safety, such as faulty brakes or turn signals. Minor defects, such as loose radio and door knobs, don't qualify.

In all states, the defect must occur within a certain period of time (usually 1 or 2 years) or within a certain number of miles (usually 12,000 or 24, 000). And you must usually meet one of the following standards for repair attempts:

- the defect is a serious safety defect involving brakes or steering and remains unfixed after one repair attempt
- the defect is not a serious safety defect and remains unfixed after three or four repair attempts (the number depends on the state), or

- the vehicle is in the shop for a certain number of days (usually 30) in a one year period.

## How to Find Your State's Lemon Law

If you want to find out if your car qualifies as a lemon in your state, get a copy of your state's lemon law. If you have access to the Internet, http://www.autopedia.com has links to each state's lemon law. Or, see this book's Appendix on Legal Research for information on how to find the law in the library. For a summary of each state's lemon law, check out *Return to Sender*, by Nancy Barron (National Consumer Law Center). You can order the book from NCLC at http://www.consumerlaw.org or (617) 523-8089.

## What should I do if my new car is a lemon?

If your new car meets the lemon law requirements for your state (see the previous question), every state gives you the right to obtain a refund or replacement vehicle from the manufacturer. The process for getting this relief is different in each state. In all states, you must first notify the manufacturer of the defect. If you're not offered a satisfactory settlement, most states require you to go to arbitration before going to court. Automakers use the following types of arbitration programs:

- in-house programs run by the auto makers
- programs set up by the Better Business Bureau's Auto Line
- programs run by the American Automobile Association or the National Automobile Dealer's Association, and
- programs run through a state consumer protection agency.

You probably won't get to choose which program to use—the manufacturer selects it. If you do have a choice, however, know that consumers who appear before a state consumer protection agency usually fare much better than those who use a manufacturer's in-house program or a private arbitration program run by the BBB, AAA or NADA.

## What happens at a lemon law arbitration?

At the arbitration hearing, the arbitrator hears both sides of the dispute. The arbitrator has approximately 60 days to decide if your car is a lemon and if you're entitled to a refund or a replacement. Consumers who bring substantial documentation to the hearing tend to do better than those with little evidence to back up their claims. The types of documentation that can help include:

- brochures and ads about the vehicle —an arbitration panel is likely to make the manufacturer live up to its claims

- vehicle service records showing how often you took the car into the shop, and
- any other documents showing your attempts to get the dealer to repair your car, including old calendars and phone records.

It is important to take the arbitration seriously and be as prepared as possible. Although usually you can appeal a bad arbitration decision in court, the decision can greatly influence your case. For example, the manufacturer may be able to use the decision as evidence against you.

## If I continue to drive my car while I wait for a decision, will it hurt my case?

Because it often takes a long time to get relief, most lemon laws allow you to keep using your car while pursuing a claim. But keep in mind that some courts may look less favorably on your case if you are able to drive your car. And of course, you should never drive your car if it is unsafe to do so.

## *"Secret Warranties"*

Many automobile manufacturers have "secret warranty," or warranty adjustment, programs. Under these programs, a manufacturer makes repairs for free on vehicles with persistent problems after a warranty expires in order to avoid a recall and bad press. According to the Center for Auto Safety, at any given time there are a total of 500 secret warranty programs available through automobile manufacturers. The Center for Auto Safety's website, at http://www.autosafety.org, has information about many of these programs.

Unfortunately, consumers aren't told of these secret warranties unless they come forward after the warranty has expired, complain about a problem and demand that the manufacturer repair it.

A few states, including California, Connecticut, Virginia and Wisconsin, require manufacturers to tell eligible consumers when they adopt a secret warranty program, usually within 90 days of adopting the program.

## What if I don't like the arbitrator's decision?

If you don't like the ruling, you can usually sue the manufacturer in court. You may want to do this if you have substantial "consequential" damages—that is, damages that resulted from owning the lemon, such as the cost of renting a car while your lemon was in the shop or time off from work every time your car broke down.

### *More Information About Lemons*

If you think your new car is a lemon, an excellent book to help you sort out your rights and remedies is *Return to Sender*, by Nancy Barron (National Consumer Law Center). You can order the book from NCLC at http://www.consumerlaw.org or (617) 523-8089.

# Leasing a Car

More than one-third of new car owners lease, rather than purchase, their vehicles. Although leasing isn't for everyone, some people swear by it. Before you sign on the dotted line, be sure you know what you're getting into.

## What are the advantages of leasing a new car?

There are three main reasons people lease, rather than buy, a new vehicle:
- People who like to drive a new car every few years will pay much less by leasing than if they buy. They also don't have to deal with getting rid of their old car—they just turn it in at the end of the lease period.
- Lease payments are lower than loan payments for any given car.
- Leasing gives people the opportunity to drive a more expensive car than they could afford to buy.

## Are there any obvious disadvantages to leasing?

Yes—there are many.
- If you continually lease your cars, you will have never-ending car payments. If you look forward to paying off your car and owning it free and clear, don't lease.
- If you decide to buy the car at the lease-end, you'll pay several thousands of dollars more than if you had bought initially. For example, if you buy a car, paying $500 a month for four years, you'll pay a total of $24,000. You might be able to lease it for only $400 a

month (total payments of $19,200), but you'll probably have to pay another $8,000 to keep it—and if you finance that $8,000, you'll pay even more.

- Most leases charge you as much as 25¢ a mile if you exceed the annual mileage limit—usually between 12,000 and 15,000 miles. If you do or plan to do extensive driving, leasing probably isn't for you.

- It's very, very expensive to break a lease early. If you no longer want, or can afford, to keep your car—for example, because you lost your job or your financial situation changed—you are stuck.

- If you lease a lemon, the leasing company has to do the complaining (remember, you don't own the car) in order to get redress.

## Are all leasing costs disclosed up front?

Not necessarily. While the federal Consumer Leasing Act requires lease agreements to include a statement of costs (such as the number and amount of regular payments), terms such as insurance requirements and the penalty for defaulting, and whether you are obligated to pay only the monthly payments or whether you'll have a balloon payment at the end, many lease agreements are ambiguously drafted, with key provisions buried in the fine print.

Even the revised regulations—which strengthened the existing disclosures and added others—do not eliminate all of the abuses. For example, the revised law does not obli-

gate a dealer to disclose the interest rate that's been built into your payments. If you want to lease, you'll have to be a diligent consumer willing to read all the fine print—ask a lot of questions and demand that the answers be put in writing.

## Is there any way to find out the interest rate on a lease?

Yes. Ask the dealer for something called the "leasing factor." Multiply that factor by 24 and you'll get the approximate interest rate.

## Are there any good leasing deals?

Yes—especially those heavily advertised by car manufacturers. Those deals usually offer low monthly payments or a high value for the vehicle at the end (so that you're not paying for a lot of depreciation during the lease term), and offer to lock-in the price you'd have to pay at lease-end if you want to keep the vehicle.

To get these good deals, you cannot deviate from the advertised terms. If you want air conditioning, a larger engine or any other feature that's not in the ad, the dealer will throw out the entire lease offer and you'll wind up paying a bundle.

Another way to get a good deal is to explore financing your lease through someone other than the dealer. A number of independent companies offer leases—look for these companies in your telephone Yellow Pages under "Automotive—Leasing." Also, if you belong to a credit union or AAA, ask about the possibility of financing your lease through them. Such deals are still in their infancy, but are catching on.

## When buying a new car, I usually shop in the fall when dealers are trying to get rid of old inventory. Does this strategy work for leasing?

In general, no. Because dealers have lost money on cars sitting in their lots, they often increase the monthly lease payments to make up for lost revenue.

## If I do lease a vehicle, who pays for maintenance and repairs?

Your lease agreement will specify who must pay. In addition, the agreement should come with a manufacturer's warranty. Ideally, it will cover the entire length of the lease and the number of miles you are likely to drive.

Most lease agreements obligate you to pay for "excessive wear and tear." This means that when you return the vehicle at lease-end, the dealer could charge you to fix anything deemed "excessive." You should insist that the dealer specify in writing exactly what is meant by "excessive" before you sign the lease contract.

Finally, look for a deal that includes "gap" insurance. If the vehicle is stolen or totaled, gap insurance will pay the difference between what you owe under the lease and what the dealer can recover on the vehicle (assuming it's not stolen)—a difference that could amount to thousands of dollars.

## Can I cancel my lease agreement early?

Probably not, unless you're willing to pay a substantial penalty. If you want to cancel your lease, look carefully at the provision describing what happens if you default or want to terminate the lease early. The provision may include a claim that you'll owe an enormous sum of money, or may use a complex formula to calculate what you owe.

While the federal Consumer Leasing Act gives you the right to cancel the lease if the termination formula is so complex that you can't easily figure out how much you owe, this will be hard for you to assert with success. Because of successful consumer lawsuits, lawyers for car manufacturers have rewritten lease contracts to avoid most of the ambiguities.

Even so, if you can't understand the formula, write to the dealer stating that you want to terminate the lease early but that the termination provision of the lease agreement is ambiguous. State further that you know you are entitled to sue for damages because of the dealer's failure to use a reasonable formula. Finally, state that you are willing to waive your right to sue if the dealer will waive the balance you owe. Because the dealer probably won't back off, consider hiring a lawyer to write some letters for you.

If you can't get the dealer to drop his claim that you owe money, you can try to negotiate to reduce your payments or to extend them over time.

***More Information About
Leasing a Car***

Both the Federal Trade Commission (at
http://www.ftc.gov) and the Federal
Reserve Board (at http://
federalreserve.gov) publish brochures to
help you understand your rights when
leasing a car.

# Buying a Used Car

HORSEPOWER WAS A WONDERFUL

THING WHEN ONLY HORSES HAD IT.

**—ANONYMOUS**

While buying a used car might be the
only way you can afford a new set of
wheels, it's a transaction ripe with
potential disaster. We probably all
know someone who bought a used
car—assured that "my grandmother
drove it once a week for ten years to
church and the grocery store"—only
to have it need $5,000 of work shortly
after bringing it home.

## How do I go about finding a used car?

It's best if you have some idea of the
make, model and year that you're
interested in. There are many good

sources to help you compare cars.
*Consumer Reports* magazine publishes
an annual car-buying issue, compar-
ing price, features, service histories,
resale values and reliability. Other
sources of information are *Motor Trend*
magazine and *Used Cars,* by Darrell
Parrish (Book Express). Once you've
made this preliminary decision, look
at the listings in your local newspaper. Don't forget weekly advertising
papers or local automobile publications as well. Call any mechanics that
you know and trust to see if they
know of any available vehicles. Finally, check with car dealers; they
often have used cars that people have
traded in.

## How much should I spend on a used car?

Check the wholesale and retail values
of the cars that interest you. Bookstores and libraries have copies of the
*Kelley Blue Book* (which lists wholesale
and retail prices), or you can find it
online at http://www.kbb.com. Lenders and insurance companies should
be able to give you the same information.

For a small fee (about $10), *Con-
sumer Reports* (http://
www.consumerreports.org or 800-
258-1169) will tell you how much a
particular car is worth, taking into
consideration the car's mileage, condition and additional equipment
(such as power windows or compact
disc player). The report also provides
information about the car's reliability.
You can also get most of this information from the *Kelley Blue Book* website
at http://www.kbb.com.

Once you know the vehicle's wholesale and retail values, you'll want to pay wholesale (the lower number) and the seller will want to charge retail (the higher number). You'll probably settle somewhere in between. Your final price will depend on a number of factors, including the condition of the car and the person from whom you buy it.

## The Buyers Guide

Federal law requires an automobile dealer to post a Buyers Guide in every used car it offers for sale (motorcycles and most recreational vehicles are exempt from this requirement). Among other things, the Buyers Guide tells you whether the vehicle is sold "as is" or with a warranty and describes the warranty. Be sure to get the Buyers Guide when you buy a used car and make sure it reflects any changes to warranty coverage that you negotiated with the dealer. The Buyers Guide becomes part of the sales contract—if the dealer refuses to make good on the warranty, you'll need it as proof of your original agreement.

### Obviously, price isn't the only factor to consider when buying a used car. What else do I need to know?

With used cars, reliability is as important as price. You should do the following:

- Have the car checked out by a mechanic you trust.
- Have the car inspected by a diagnostic center. These businesses will check virtually every aspect and component of a car. They're more expensive—but more thorough—than a mechanic.
- Ask for copies of the maintenance records for the life of the car.
- Ask your state motor vehicles department to tell you who has owned the car, the mileage each time it has been sold and all states (other than where you live) where the car has been registered.
- Do your own visual inspection—you'll want to look for oddities that might indicate damage (such as scratches or new paint).

Also, look at the vehicle identification number (VIN) on the lower left-hand side of the front windshield. If it shows any signs of tampering, the car may be stolen. And finally, if you're buying the car from a private party (as opposed to a car dealer), make sure the person selling the car actually holds title. Ask to see the seller's driver's license (or other form of ID) and the title certificate for the vehicle.

### Will a warranty protect me if I get a bad deal on a used car?

If you're buying a used car from a dealer, the dealer will probably offer you an extended warranty. Before buying, be sure you know exactly what is covered and what isn't, and for how long. You'll also need to know the type of problems the car has had in the past, and what types of problems that particular make of car is likely to have in the future. It makes no sense to buy an extended warranty that doesn't cover emissions, for example, if the type of car you're buying is likely to have emission problems in a year or so.

If you're buying a car from a private party, check to see if the car is still under a factory warranty or if the original owner purchased an extended warranty—and whether either of these warranties can be transferred to you as the new owner.

## *Used Car "Lemon Laws"*

Hawaii, Massachusetts, Minnesota, New Jersey, New York and Rhode Island have lemon laws for used cars. Connecticut requires dealers to provide express warranties on certain used cars, which gives buyers rights similar to lemon laws. If you're in one of these states and you buy a used car that turns out to be defective, contact your state attorney general or department of consumer affairs for the details of the law and how you can get redress under it.

# Financing a Vehicle Purchase

If you are like most people, you don't have a large sum of cash to plunk down for a new or used car. This means you'll have to finance your purchase. Of course, after you spend time shopping for a car and negotiat-

ing a good deal, the last thing you'll want to do is haggle over financing terms. But if you don't shop around for the best financing deal and read the finance contract carefully, you could end up paying lots more for a loan than you should.

## I want to buy a car, but I'm not sure how to finance my purchase. Do you have any general advice?

Clearly, if you can pay for the purchase outright you'll save money by not paying any interest charges. But if you don't happen to have $20,000 lying around and need to borrow money to buy your new car, consider the following sources:

- *The car dealer.* Many offer generous terms—for example, interest at 1.5% or 2%—especially in the early fall when dealers are anxious to clear out stock to make room for new models. Be careful that these low-interest loans don't require you to buy upgraded features—such as air conditioning or rust protection—or credit insurance. And don't assume you are getting the best deal around. Always compare dealer terms to those of banks and credit unions.

- *Banks you do business with.* Dealer financing isn't your only option. Before you buy, contact the banks where you have your savings, checking, credit card or business accounts. Ask about the going rate for car loans. Also ask about discount rates for loans tied to your other accounts.

- *Credit unions.* If you're a member of a credit union (or are eligible to join one), be sure to investigate its car loans. Historically, credit unions have offered some of the best loan terms.

Regardless of who finances the contract, if you want a good interest rate but have a poor credit history, you'll need to either put a substantial amount down or get a cosigner.

## Do You Need Credit Insurance?

Many dealers and lenders will ask you to buy credit insurance—insurance that will pay off your loan if you die or become disabled. Before you add this cost to your contract, consider whether you really need it. Remember, you can always sell the car and use the proceeds to pay off the loan. In fact, most financial experts say credit insurance is unnecessary and advise consumers not to buy it. If you do decide you want this protection, you can almost always buy this type of insurance from an outside source at a much better price.

### If I borrow money for the purchase, what should the lender tell me about my loan?

If you get a car loan from a bank, credit union or car dealer, the federal Truth in Lending Act requires that the lender disclose, in writing, impor-

tant information about your loan, including:

- your right to a written itemization of the amount borrowed
- the total amount of the loan
- the monthly finance charge
- the annual percentage rate (APR)
- the number, amount and due dates of all payments, and
- whether any late payment fee or penalty may be imposed.

# Insuring Your Car

*Certainly those so inclined can have lots of fun imagining possible needs for insurance.*

**—HAYDEN CURRY**

Most states require that every registered vehicle or licensed driver have some vehicle liability insurance. But even where it's not required by law, most drivers have some liability coverage. Before you buy auto insurance, you must decide how much coverage you need and what types of coverage are appropriate for you. And of course, you'll want to find ways to cut your insurance costs.

### Who is usually covered under an auto insurance liability policy?

An auto insurance liability policy usually covers the following people no matter what car they are driving:

- *Named insured*—the person or people named in the policy.
- *Spouse*—a spouse not named in the policy, unless he or she does not live with the named insured.
- *Other relative*—anyone living in the household with the named insured who is related by blood, marriage or adoption, usually including a legal ward or foster child.

Auto insurance liability policies also cover anyone driving the insured vehicle with permission. Someone who steals the car is not covered.

## Which vehicles are normally covered under an auto insurance liability policy?

- *Named vehicles*—an accident in a nonnamed vehicle is covered only if a named insured (see above) was driving.
- *Added vehicles*—any vehicle with which the named insured replaces the original named vehicle, and any additional vehicle the named insured acquires during the policy period (you may be required to notify the company of the new or different vehicle within 30 days after you acquire it).
- *Temporary vehicles*—any vehicle, including a rental vehicle, that substitutes for an insured vehicle that is out of use because it needs repair or service, or has been destroyed.

## What kinds of damage are covered under an auto insurance liability policy?

Liability insurance covers money owed when a driver is at fault for hurting another person or damaging her car. Coverage includes medical costs for diagnosis and treatment of injuries, property damage, loss of use of damaged property, expenses incurred (such as the cost of renting a replacement vehicle), lost income and costs of defending a lawsuit.

In addition, an injured person is entitled to a certain amount of "general damages," also referred to as pain and suffering.

## What is collision coverage?

Collision coverage pays for property damage to your vehicle resulting from a collision.

## What is comprehensive coverage?

Comprehensive coverage pays for property damage to your vehicle resulting from anything other than a collision, such as a theft or a break-in.

## What is uninsured motorist coverage?

If you have an accident with an uninsured vehicle or hit-and-run driver, the place to turn for compensation for your injuries is the uninsured motorist (UM) coverage of your own vehicle insurance policy. Normally, UM covers only bodily injury and not property damage to your vehicle. Vehicle damage caused would be covered by the collision coverage of your own policy.

## What are the limits on my ability to collect under an uninsured motorist provision?

UM coverage usually limits your ability to collect as follows:

- If your accident involves a hit-and-run driver, you must notify the police within 24 hours of the accident.
- If your accident involves a hit-and-run driver, the driver's car must have actually hit you—being forced off the road by a driver who disappears is not sufficient.
- Your UM coverage will be reduced by any amounts you receive under other insurance coverage, such as your personal medical insurance or any applicable workers' compensation coverage.
- If you or a relative are injured by an uninsured motorist while you are in someone else's car, your UM coverage will be secondary to the UM coverage of that other car's owner.

## What is no-fault automobile insurance?

Under no-fault coverage insurance, each person's own insurance company pays for his or her medical bills and lost wages—up to certain dollar amounts —regardless of who was at fault.

About half the states have some form of no-fault law, often referred to in policies as Personal Injury Protection (PIP). The advantage of no-fault insurance is prompt payment of medi-

cal bills and lost wages without any arguments about who caused the accident. But most no-fault insurance provides extremely limited coverage:

- No-fault pays benefits for medical bills and lost income only. It provides no compensation for pain, suffering, emotional distress, inconvenience or lost opportunities.
- No-fault coverage does not pay for medical bills and lost income higher than the PIP limits of each person's policy. PIP benefits often fail to reimburse fully for medical bills and lost income.
- No-fault often does not apply to vehicle damage; those claims are paid under the liability insurance of the person at fault, or by your own collision insurance.

## When No-Fault Benefits Aren't Enough

All no-fault laws permit an injured driver to file a liability claim, and lawsuit if necessary, against another driver who was at fault in an accident. The liability claim permits an injured driver to obtain compensation for medical and income losses above what the PIP benefits have paid, as well as compensation for pain, suffering and other general damages.

Whether and when you can file a liability claim for further damages against the person at fault in your accident depends on the specifics of the no-fault law in your state. In some states, you can always file a liability claim for all damages in excess of your PIP benefits. In others you must meet a monetary threshold, a serious injury threshold, or both, before you can file a liability claim.

## My auto insurance rates seem to keep going up. How can I cut some of the cost?

Here are a few suggestions for ways to reduce your premiums:

- Shop around for insurance. Just because your current company once offered you the best deal doesn't mean it's still competitive.
- Increase your deductibles.
- Reduce your collision or comprehensive coverage on older cars.
- Find out what discounts are available from your company (or from a different company). Discounts are often given to people who:
  - use public transit or carpool to work
  - take a class in defensive driving (especially if you are older)
  - own a car with safety features such as airbags or anti-lock brakes
  - install anti-theft devices
  - are students with good academic records
  - have no accidents or moving violations, or
  - have multiple insurance policies with the same company—such as automobile and homeowner's insurance.
- Find out which vehicles cost more to insure. If you're looking to buy a new car, call your insurance agent and find out which cars are expensive to repair, targeted by thieves or involved in a higher rate of acci-

dents. These vehicles all have higher insurance rates.
- Consolidate your policies. Most of the time you will pay less if all owners or drivers who live in the same household are on one policy or at least are insured with the same company.

### More Information About Insuring Your Car

*How to Insure Your Car*, by The Merritt Editors (Merritt Publishing), is a step-by-step guide to buying the right kind of auto insurance at a price you can afford.

# Your Driver's License

To a teenager, a driver's license seems magical—a ticket to freedom. For the rest of us, driver's licenses aren't much more than scraps of paper or plastic bearing bad pictures. But every now and then a question may arise about a license: Is it still good if I move to another state? What if I take a trip to a foreign country? And how do I know if I'm in danger of losing my license?

State laws governing how you can get, use and lose your driver's license vary tremendously. We can't answer every question here, but we do discuss some of the bigger issues that arise in connection with driving privileges.

## Is my driver's license good in every state?

If you have a valid license from one state, you may use it in other states that you visit. But if you make a permanent move to another state, you'll have to take a trip to the local department of motor vehicles to apply for a new license. Usually, you must do this within 30 days after moving to the new state. Most states will issue your new license without requiring tests, though some may ask you to take a vision test and a written exam covering basic driving rules.

In some situations, you may be unsure as to whether you need to apply for a new license. If you make frequent business trips to another state, or even if you attend school in a state away from home, there's no need to get another driver's license. But when you set up housekeeping in the new state and pay taxes there as well, it's time to apply.

## Young Drivers Who Cross State Lines

Adults who visit another state may rely on their driver's licenses, but the same may not be true for young drivers. The driving age varies significantly from state to state (from 15 to 21), and a state that makes people wait longer to drive may not honor a license from a state that issues licenses to younger folks. For example, New Jersey issues licenses to 17-year-olds, and will recognize a license from any other state if the driver is at least 17. But a 16-

year-old who is legally permitted to drive in New York may not be allowed to drive in New Jersey. A young driver who plans to drive in another state where the legal limit is above his or her age should call that state's department of motor vehicles to find out what the rules are.

## If I get a ticket in another state, will it affect my license?

Forty-five states belong to an agreement called the "Driver's License Compact." (The only states that don't belong are Georgia, Massachusetts, Michigan, Tennessee and Wisconsin.) When you get a ticket in one of these states, the department of motor vehicles will relay the information to your state—and the violation will add points to your driving record as if the ticket had been given at home.

## Can I use my license in a foreign country?

Many countries, including the United States, have signed an international agreement allowing visitors to use their own licenses in other nations. Before traveling to another country, contact its consulate office or embassy to find out whether your license will be sufficient. Look in the telephone book under the name of the country. Or, visit the U.S. State Department website at http://www.travel.state.gov.

In addition, you may want to obtain an International Driver's Permit, issued by the American Automobile Association. This document translates the information on your driver's license into ten languages. Many countries require the permit, not because it meets their requirements for a license, but because it is a ready-made copy of the important information on your American license.

Finally, if you intend to stay in another country for an extended period of time, you should check with the consulate to find out whether you'll need to apply for a license in that country. Every country will have its own rules about when a "visit" turns into something more permanent.

## When can my driver's license be suspended or revoked?

Driving a car is considered a privilege—and a state won't hesitate to take it away if a driver behaves irresponsibly on the road. A state may temporarily suspend your driving privileges for a number of reasons, including:

- driving under the influence of alcohol or drugs
- refusing to take a blood-alcohol test
- driving without liability insurance
- speeding
- reckless driving
- leaving the scene of an injury accident
- failing to pay a driving-related fine
- failing to answer a traffic summons, or
- failing to file an accident report.

In addition, many states use a "point" system to keep track of a driver's moving violations: Each moving violation is assigned a certain number of points. If a driver accumulates too many points within a given period of time, the department of motor vehicles suspends her license.

If you have too many serious problems as a driver, your state may take away (revoke) your license altogether. If this happens, you'll have to wait a certain period of time before you can apply for another license. Your state may deny your application if you have a poor driving record or fail to pass any required tests.

Finally, a few states revoke or refuse to renew driver's licenses of parents who owe back child support. (See Chapter 16, *Parents and Children*, for more information.)

## My elderly friend is becoming unsafe at the wheel. Will her license be taken away?

The number of drivers over 65 years old has more than doubled in the last 20 years. At present, there are 13 million older drivers; by the year 2020 there will be 30 million. Studies show that, as a group, older drivers drive less than younger drivers, but they have more accidents per mile.

Elderly, unsafe drivers who continue to drive despite the advice of family and friends often do not come to the attention of the state until the inevitable—the driver is stopped for erratic driving or, worse, he or she is involved in an accident. A few states try to screen out unsafe older drivers by requiring more frequent written tests. But the added tests are expensive and don't always identify unsafe driving habits.

All licensing departments accept information from police officers, families and physicians about a driver's abilities. If a licensing agency moves to cancel someone's license as the result of an officer's observations, an accident or the report of family members or a doctor, the driver usually has an opportunity to protest.

### What will happen if I'm caught driving with a suspended or revoked license?

You'll probably be arrested. Driving with a suspended or revoked license is usually considered a crime that carries a heavy fine and possibly even jail time. At worst, it may be a felony; you'll end up in state prison or with an obligation to perform many hours of community service. The penalties will probably be heaviest if the suspension or revocation was the result of a conviction for driving under the influence of alcohol or drugs (DUI).

## *The Whole Truth and Nothing but the Truth*

Many states will ask you specific questions regarding your health when you renew your driver's license. For example, you might receive a questionnaire that asks you whether you have ever had seizures, strokes, heart problems, dizziness, eyesight problems or other medical troubles. If you have medical problems and answer the questions truthfully, an examiner may question you further and may even deny you a license. If you

don't tell the truth, you may get your license—but you're setting yourself up for big legal trouble if you are in an accident caused by one of these impairments. It's not that different from driving a car when you know the brakes are bad: If you go out on the road with defective equipment that you know about (including the driver), you greatly increase the chance that you will be held responsible if the defect causes an accident.

# If You're Stopped by the Police

Most of us know the fear of being pulled over by the police. An officer may stop your car for any number of reasons, including an equipment defect (such as a burned-out headlight), expired registration tags, a moving violation or your car's resemblance to a crime suspect's car. You may also have to stop if you encounter a police roadblock or sobriety checkpoint.

### What should I do if a police officer pulls me over?

Remain as calm as possible, and pull over to the side of the road as quickly and safely as you can. Roll down your window, but stay in the car—don't get out unless the officer directs you to do so. It's a good idea to turn on the interior light, turn off the engine, put your keys on the dash and place your hands on top of the steering wheel. In short, make yourself visible and do nothing that can be mistaken for a dangerous move. For example, don't reach for a purse or backpack or open the glove box unless you've asked the officer's permission, even if you are just looking for your license and registration card. The officer may think you're reaching for a weapon.

When the officer approaches your window, you may want to ask (with all the politeness you can muster) why you were stopped. If you are at all concerned that the person who stopped you is not actually a police officer (for example, if the car that pulled you over is unmarked), you should ask to see the officer's photo identification along with her badge. If you still have doubts, you can ask that the officer call a supervisor to the scene or you can request that you be allowed to follow the officer to a police station.

## If an officer pulls me over for a traffic violation, can she search me or my car?

In most cases, no. Just because an officer has a justifiable reason for making a traffic stop—and even if she issues you a valid ticket for a traffic violation—that does not automatically give the officer authority to search you or your car. If the officer has a reasonable suspicion (based on

observable facts, and not just a "hunch") that you are armed and dangerous or involved in criminal activity, then the officer can do a "pat-down" search of you, and can search the passenger compartment of your car. The officer can also frisk any purses, bags or other objects within the car that might reasonably contain a weapon. The officer does have the authority, however, to ask you and any passengers to exit the car during a traffic stop.

## If my car is towed and impounded, can the police search it?

Yes. If your car is impounded, the police are allowed to conduct a thorough search of it, including its trunk and any closed containers that they find inside. This is true even if your car was towed after you parked it illegally, or if the police recover your car after it is stolen.

The police are required, however, to follow fair and standardized procedures when they search your car, and may not stop you and impound your car simply to perform a search.

## I was pulled over at a roadblock and asked to wait and answer an officer's questions. Is this legal?

Yes, as long as the police use a neutral policy when stopping cars (such as stopping all cars or stopping every third car) and minimize any inconvenience to you and the other drivers. The police can't single out your car unless they have good reason to believe that you've broken the law.

# Drunk Driving

If you're caught while driving drunk or under the influence of drugs, you'll face serious legal penalties. Many states will put you in jail, even for a first offense, and almost all will impose hefty fines. If you're convicted more than once, you may also lose your driver's license.

## How drunk or high does someone have to be before he can be convicted of driving under the influence?

In most states, it's illegal to drive a car while "impaired" by the effects of alcohol or drugs (including prescription drugs). This means that there must be enough alcohol or drugs in the driver's body to prevent him from thinking clearly or driving safely. Many people reach this level well before they'd be considered "drunk" or "stoned."

## How can the police find out whether a driver is under the influence?

Police typically use three methods of determining whether a driver has had too much to be driving:

- *Observation.* A police officer will pull you over if he notices that you are driving erratically—swerving, speeding, failing to stop or even driving too slowly. Of course, you may have a good explanation for your driving (tiredness, for example), but an officer is unlikely to buy your story if he smells alcohol on your breath or notices slurred words or unsteady movements.
- *Sobriety tests.* If an officer suspects that you are under the influence, he will probably ask you to get out of the car and perform a series of balance and speech tests, such as standing on one leg, walking a straight line heel-to-toe or reciting a line of letters or numbers. The officer will look closely at your eyes, checking for pupil enlargement or constriction, which can be evidence of intoxication. If you fail these tests, the officer may arrest you or ask you to take a chemical test.
- *Blood-alcohol level.* The amount of alcohol in your body is understood by measuring the amount of alcohol in your blood. This measurement can be taken directly, by drawing a sample of your blood, or it can be calculated by applying a mathematical formula to the amount of alcohol in your breath or urine. Some states give you a choice of whether to take a breath, blood or urine test—others do not. If you test at or above the level of intoxication for your state (.08 to .10 percent blood-alcohol concentration, depending on the state), you are presumed to be driving under the influence unless you can convince a judge or jury that your judgment was not impaired and you were not driving dangerously. In many states, this level is even lower for young drivers. (In california, the level is .05% for drivers under 21.) Defense attorneys often question the validity of the

conversion formula when driver's alcohol levels are based on breath or urine tests.

# The New National Drunk Driving Standard

On October 23, 2000, President Clinton signed a new law encouraging states to pass laws that define drunk driving as having a blood alcohol concentration (BAC) of .08%. Many states currently set the level for drunk driving at .10% BAC. States have until October 1, 2003 to change their laws to meet the federal standard. Otherwise, they'll lose a portion of their federal highway funds.

## Do I have to take a blood, breath or urine test if asked to do so by the police?

No, but it may be in your best interests to take the test. Many states will automatically suspend your license if you refuse to take a chemical test. And if your drunk driving case goes to trial, the prosecutor can tell the jury that you wouldn't take the test, which may lead the jury members to conclude that you refused because you were, in fact, drunk or stoned.

## Am I entitled to talk to an attorney before I decide which chemical test to take?

The answer depends on where you live. In California, for example, you don't have the right to speak with an attorney first. But many other states allow you to talk to your lawyer before you take a chemical test.

## If I am pulled over, does the officer have to read me my rights before he asks me how much I had to drink?

No. During a traffic stop, an officer does not have to read you your rights until you are under arrest. (See Chapter 18 for a description of Miranda rights.) Determining whether you are "under arrest" can be tricky—you can be under arrest even before a police officer says you are. But if an officer is just asking you questions at the side of the road or even if you are detained in the officer's car for a few minutes, you are probably not under arrest. Keep in mind that you don't have to answer an officer's questions, whether you are under arrest or not—and whether or not the officer has read your rights to you. Of course, sometimes it is wise to do so, as long as you don't say anything that can be used against you.

# When to Get a Lawyer

Defending against a charge of drunk driving is tricky business. Defenders need to understand scientific and medical concepts, and must be able to question tough witnesses, including scientists and police officers. If you want to fight your DUI charge, you're well advised to hire an attorney who specializes in these types of cases.

# Traffic Accidents

Anyone who drives or rides in a car long enough is likely to be involved in at least a minor fender-bender. Anyone who rides a bicycle or motorcycle knows the roads are even more dangerous for two-wheelers. And on our crowded streets, pedestrians, too, are often involved in accidents with buses, cars and bikes. Knowing a few laws of the road, and the best steps to take when an accident occurs, can help ease the pain of any accident that occurs—and help make any claims process involved less painful, too.

## What should I do if I'm involved in a traffic accident?

The most important thing to do is document the entire situation by taking careful notes soon after the accident. Good notes (rather than relying on your memory) will help with the claim process—and increase your chances of receiving full compensation for your injuries and damage to your vehicle.

Write things down as soon as you can: begin with what you were doing and where you were going, the people you were with, the time and the weather. Include every detail of what you saw, heard and felt. Be sure to include everything that others—those involved in the accident or witnesses—said about the accident.

Finally, make daily notes of the effects of your injuries. Always include pain, discomfort, anxiety, loss of sleep or other problems which are not as visible or serious as other injuries. You can still demand compensation for these things.

## Reporting to the DMV

In many states, you must report a vehicle accident resulting in physical injury or a certain amount of property damage to the state's department of motor vehicles. Check with your insurance agent or your local department of motor vehicles to find out the time limits for filing this report; you often have just a few days. Be sure to ask whether you'll need any specific form for the report.

If you must file a report, and the report asks for a statement about how the accident occurred, give only a very brief statement—and admit no responsibility for the accident. Similarly, if the official form asks what your injuries are, list every injury and not just the most serious or obvious. An insurance company could later have access to the report, and if you have admitted some fault in it, or failed to mention an injury, you might run into some trouble explaining yourself.

## What determines who is responsible for a traffic accident?

Figuring out who is at fault in a traffic accident is a matter of deciding who was careless. Each state has a set of traffic rules (which apply to automobiles, motorcycles, bicycles and pedestrians) that tell people how they are supposed to drive and provide guidelines for measuring liability.

Sometimes it is obvious that one driver violated a traffic rule which caused the accident—for example, one driver runs a stop sign and crashes into another. In other situations, whether or not there was a violation will be less obvious. A common example is a crash that occurs when drivers merge into a single lane of traffic. And at other times, neither driver violated a traffic rule, although one driver may still have been careless.

# Finding Your State's Traffic Rules

The traffic rules are contained in each state's Vehicle Code. You can usually obtain a simplified version of these rules—often called the "Rules of the Road"—from the department of motor vehicles (DMV). Most DMV offices also have the complete Vehicle Code. Or, you can find the Vehicle Code in a public library, law library or the Internet. (See this book's Appendix on Legal Research for more information on how to find state laws.)

## What if the cause of the accident is not clear?

It is sometimes difficult to say that one particular act caused an accident. This is especially true if what you claim the other driver did is vague or seems minor. But if you can show that the other driver made several minor

driving errors or committed several minor traffic violations, then you can argue that the combination of those actions caused the accident.

# Special Rules for No-Fault Policyholders

Almost half the states have some form of no-fault auto insurance, also called Personal Injury Protection. (See *Insuring Your Car*, above.)

In general, no-fault coverage eliminates injury liability claims and lawsuits in smaller accidents in exchange for direct payment by the injured person's own insurance company of medical bills and lost wages—up to certain dollar amounts—regardless of who was at fault for the accident. Usually, no-fault does not cover vehicle damage; those claims are still handled by filing a liability claim against the one who is responsible for the accident, or by looking to your own collision insurance.

## Who is liable if my car is rear-ended in a crash?

The driver who hit you from behind is almost always at fault, regardless of your reason for stopping. Traffic rules require that a driver travel at a speed at which she can stop safely if a vehicle stops suddenly. In rear-end accidents, the vehicle damage provides strong proof of liability. If the other car's front end and your car's rear end are both damaged, there is no doubt that you were struck from behind.

In some situations, both you and the car behind you are stopped when a third car runs into the car behind you, pushing it into the rear of your car. In that case, the driver of the third car is at fault and you should file a claim against her insurance.

### Are there any other clear patterns of liability in traffic accidents?

A car making a left turn is almost always liable to a car coming straight in the other direction. According to traffic rules, a car making a left turn must wait until it can safely complete the turn before moving in front of oncoming traffic. There may be exceptions to this rule if:

- the car going straight was going too fast (this is usually difficult to prove)
- the car going straight went through a red light, or
- the left-turning car began its turn when it was safe but something unexpected happened which made it have to slow down or stop its turn.

## Police Reports: Powerful Evidence

If the police responded to the scene of your accident, they probably made a written accident report (particularly if someone was injured).

Sometimes a police report will plainly state that a driver violated a specific Vehicle Code section and that the violation caused the accident. It may even indicate that the officer issued a citation. Other times, the report merely describes or briefly mentions negligent driving.

Any mention in a police report of a Vehicle Code violation or other evidence of careless driving will provide support for your claim that the other driver was at fault.

### http://www.nolo.com

*Nolo offers self-help information about a wide variety of legal topics, including what to do if you're in an accident.*

### http://www.kbb.com

*Kelley Blue Book can give you the resale and wholesale values of your vehicle, as well as new car prices.*

**http://www.edmunds.com**

*Edmund's offers information about buying a new car, including reviews, comparisons, prices and strategies.*

**http://www.bbb.org/library/newcar.html**

*The Better Business Bureau offers tips on buying a new car, including financing suggestions.*

**http://www.bbb.org/library/usedcar.html**

*The Better Business Bureau provides hints and checklists designed to help you through the process of buying a used car.*

**http://www.autopedia.com**

*Autopedia is an encyclopedia of automotive-related information. In addition to articles on many topics, it includes links to each state's lemon law.*

**http://www.consumerreports.org**

*Consumer Reports provides articles on how to buy or lease a car and, for a small fee, a price service for both new and used cars.*

**http://www.nhtsa.dot.gov/problems**

*The National Highway Traffic Safety Administration provides recall notices, service bulletins, defect investigations, consumer complaints and other data about vehicle problems.*

**http://www.leaseguide.com**

*Automobile Leasing: The Art of the Deal offers information about leasing a car, including frequently asked questions, an auto consumer's lease kit and tips for getting a good deal.*

**http://www.insure.com**

*The Insurance News Network provides information about choosing auto insurance, including an interactive experts forum.*

**http://www.dui.com**

*The Driver Performance Institutes provide information about driving under the influence.*

**http://www.motorists.org**

*This national organization for motorists offers lots of information on fighting traffic tickets.*

# **T**raveling

11.2    *Airlines*

11.9    *Rental Cars*

11.14   *Hotels and Other
        Accommodations*

11.19   *Travel Agents*

11.23   *Travel Scams*

*Travel is the frivolous part of
serious lives, and the serious
part of frivolous ones.*

**—MADAME SWETCHINE**

**E**ach year, Americans spend billions of dollars on traveling. And though most of us fondly recall our annual vacations—the trip to Europe after graduating from college or our children's faces the first time they visited a Disney theme park—we often share with one another the horror stories: The plane that took off

16 hours late, the rental company that charged $1,000 for returning the car with a slight scratch or the tour company that went out of business the night before the trip. The questions and answers in this chapter are designed to help your travels go more smoothly—and to let you know your rights should you encounter troubles along the way.

# Airlines

On any given day, over a million Americans take a trip by airplane. Major airlines have become some of the largest and most powerful businesses in the travel industry. Airline travel is subject to federal laws and regulations, although to a much lesser degree than 25 years ago. This deregulation has led to competition among airlines and a variety of benefits for passengers, including fare wars and frequent flyer programs.

### How do airlines calculate fares?

The price of most airfares is determined by complicated computer programs which calculate how many passengers are likely to book seats on any given flight. But rather than fly with empty seats, an airline might offer discount fares. Ticket prices may also be affected by competition with other airlines that offer discounted prices. The result is that passengers on the same flight could be paying as many as a dozen different fares.

## Benefits and Risks of E-Tickets

E-tickets aren't really tickets at all, but are reservations for air travel that are kept in the airline's computer system instead of being printed on paper. To get a boarding pass on the day of your flight, you simply present a photo ID and your credit card at the airport.

If you are booked on a single airline and are flying only in the United States, you will most likely have little trouble using your e-ticket. In fact, many find e-tickets to be convenient, since there's no paper ticket to keep track of or to lose.

E-tickets are not foolproof, however, especially if you are traveling internationally. Many countries require that you show some sort of ticket to gain access to a boarding area, and sometimes your e-ticket receipt and itinerary is not enough. In addition, some countries require that you present a roundtrip ticket at the point of entry—they want you to visit, but they don't want you to stay. If you have an e-ticket, you might have trouble convincing officials that you have booked passage out of their country. If you are traveling internationally by e-ticket, carry your itinerary and receipt with you.

On the domestic front, if your flight is canceled, your airline must first print a paper ticket before it can put you on another airline's flight. This can be time consuming. And, if your airline goes on strike, other airlines that might honor a paper ticket won't accept your e-ticket. If you have an e-ticket and an airline strike is imminent, exchange your e-ticket for a paper ticket as soon as possible.

## What's all that fine print on the back of my airline ticket?

The back of all standard airline tickets has at least 11 paragraphs of fine print under the heading "Conditions of Contract." In Paragraph 3 you'll find a statement that various "applicable tariffs" and the "Carrier's Conditions of Carriage and Related Regulations" are incorporated into the contract. This means that each airline has filed with the U.S. Department of Transportation a series of statements about its obligations to its passengers and its limitations of liability. These tariffs and conditions are the terms of your contract with the airline.

The Conditions of Carriage cover everything from the number of bags you can check to the type of compensation you receive if your flight is delayed or canceled. Boarding priority, check-in requirements and most of the other fine-print terms that describe an airline's rights and responsibilities to its passengers are set forth in the Conditions of Carriage.

Conditions of Carriage vary from airline to airline. Although most airline tickets look identical, the subtle differences in the hidden terms can make a substantial difference in your rights as a passenger. You can obtain a summary of the hidden terms and conditions of most major airlines' contracts by requesting a copy of *United States Air Carriers, Conditions of Contract, Summary of Incorporated Terms (Domestic Air Transportation)* from the Air Transport Association, Distribution Center, P.O. Box 511, Annapolis, MD, 20701. Enclose a $65 check payable to ATAA. You can also call the ATAA at 800-497-3326.

## Are there restrictions on my airline ticket?

Before the substantial deregulation of the airline industry in the 1980s, unused tickets were almost as good as cash—tickets could be cashed in, traded and even used on other airlines. This is still true for many full-fare, unrestricted tickets.

Most tickets, however, carry some sort of restrictions. Today, tickets usually have any or all of the following features:

- *Nontransferable.* A nontransferable ticket can be used only by the passenger whose name appears on the face of the ticket. If the names on the ID and the ticket do not match, the airline can confiscate the ticket. If a ticket is nontransferable but refundable, however, you may be able to cash in the old ticket and buy a new one with the new passenger's name.

- *Nonrefundable.* A nonrefundable ticket means you cannot get your money back if you decide not to travel. But each airline has exceptions. If you cannot make a flight for which you have a nonrefundable ticket, you may be able to apply the ticket toward a future flight or exchange it for credit toward future travel. If the fare has dropped on a flight for which you have a nonrefundable ticket, you may be able to get "re-ticketed." In either situation, you will probably have to pay a fee to make the change.
- *Penalties.* Often, there are penalties for canceling or making changes.

## Do airlines offer discounted tickets or let you change a ticket if you need to travel because of death or serious illness?

In certain exceptional cases, the airlines will allow nonrefundable tickets to be refunded if you need to cancel because of the illness or death of your traveling companion or a close relative. Similarly, an airline may offer a discounted fare (sometimes minor, sometimes generous) when a close relative becomes seriously ill or dies and you need to travel without any advanced planning. Who must be ill or have died for you to obtain a "bereavement fare" varies among airlines —for example, some airlines will give a discounted fare to attend the funeral of a parent, child, sibling, spouse or in-laws only, while other airlines include nonmarital partners and their immediate family members.

## What should I do if I lose my ticket?

Contact the airline immediately. You will be required to fill out a lost-ticket application. The airline will either issue a replacement ticket (after you sign an agreement to reimburse it for the cost of the replacement ticket if someone uses your lost ticket) or force you to purchase a replacement ticket at the currently available fare (often outrageously expensive because you don't get any advance purchase discounts). In addition, you usually have to pay some sort of service charge or penalty for issuing a replacement ticket.

After waiting three months to a year, the airline will issue you a refund for the price of your replacement ticket if your lost ticket was not used during that time.

## Am I entitled to be compensated if the airline overbooks and I get bumped off the flight?

If a flight is overbooked, the airline is required to ask passengers to volunteer to take a later flight. Normally, the airline will offer some kind of incentive such as a free domestic or international round-trip ticket. If an insufficient number of passengers volunteer to be bumped from a flight, the airline must begin involuntary bumping. Generally, passengers with the most recent reservations or those who checked in the latest are the first to be bumped.

If you are bumped, you are entitled to compensation if you have a confirmed reservation (your ticket has an "ok" or "hk" in the Status column) and the scheduled plane has a seating capacity of more than 60 passengers. Even if you meet both of these requirements, the airline might refuse to compensate you if any of the following is true:

- You did not comply with the airline's ticketing, check-in and reconfirmation requirements.
- You are not acceptable for transportation under the airline's usual rules and practices—for example, you are drunk.
- The entire flight was canceled.
- A smaller aircraft was substituted for safety or operational reasons.
- You refuse an offer to take a seat in a different section (class) of the aircraft at no extra charge.
- The airline offers to place you on another flight or flights scheduled to reach your final destination within one hour of the scheduled arrival of the original flight.

## Am I entitled to compensation if my flight is delayed, diverted or canceled?

A flight is considered on-time if it arrives at its destination within 15 minutes of the scheduled arrival time. Generally, a 15-minute delay will not affect your schedule very much. Longer delays can have serious consequences, particularly if you cannot make a connecting flight.

If your trip is delayed because of overbooking, the rules discussed in the previous question apply. If the delay is caused by any other reason, your rights depend on whether it's a domestic or international flight.

*Domestic flights.* Generally, airlines are not obliged to provide any compensation if the delay, diversion or cancellation was caused by factors outside of the airline's control, such as bad weather or air traffic congestion at a particular airport. On the other hand, airlines are required to compensate you for problems deemed in their control, such as mechanical difficulties or late-arriving crew members. The offered compensation can vary substantially among airlines—full-service airlines are likely to offer more generous terms, such as meals, hotels, alternate transportation or even emergency toiletries in the event of an overnight delay, while budget or no-frills airlines may offer little, if any, compensation.

*International flights.* Recovering damages for an international flight delay is very difficult if the delay was caused by anything other than the airline's overbooking. Under an international treaty called the Warsaw Convention, an airline can escape liability for damages caused by flight delay if it can show that it took all necessary measures to avoid the damage or that it was impossible to take such measures.

If your international flight is delayed, you may be able to persuade the airline that it should cover direct costs caused by the delay, such as meal, hotel or telephone expenses. To back up your argument, you can quote Article 19 of the Warsaw Convention which states: "The Carrier shall be liable for damages occasioned by delay in the transportation by air of passengers, baggage or goods."

## Compensation for Involuntarily Bumping

(Flights Within or Leaving U.S.)

| Scheduled Arrival of New Flight | Domestic Flights | International Flights (Departing From the U.S.) |
| --- | --- | --- |
| New flight scheduled to arrive less than one hour after original flight | No compensation | No compensation |
| New flight scheduled to arrive between one and two hours after original flight | Value of ticket segment, $200 maximum | Value of ticket segment, $200 maximum |
| New flight scheduled to arrive more than two hours after original flight (domestic only) | Twice the value of ticket segment, $400 maximum | N/A |
| New flight scheduled to arrive more than four hours after original flight (international only) | N/A | Twice the value of ticket segment, $400 maximum |

## Compensation for Involuntarily Bumping

(Flight Departing European Union Country)

| Scheduled Duration or Distance of Original Flight | Arrival at Destination | Compensation |
| --- | --- | --- |
| Less than two hours or 3,500 kilometers | Within two hours of originally scheduled arrival | 75 ECUs (approximately $50) |
| Less than two hours or 3,500 kilometers | More than two hours late | 150 ECUs (approximately $100) |
| Over two hours or over 3,500 kilometers | Within two hours of originally scheduled arrival | 150 ECUs (approximately $100) |
| Over two hours or over 3,500 kilometers | More than two hours late | 300 ECUs (approximately $200) |

## Am I entitled to compensation if my baggage is lost or damaged?

The airlines' treatment of baggage is a constant source of passenger complaints. At some point, nearly every airline passenger has waited for what seemed like an eternity for his or her baggage to show up on the baggage carousel. Many passengers can identify with the old suitcase commercial which showed a gorilla jumping up and down on the passenger's bags and throwing the passenger's suitcase around a room.

To be fair, most of the time baggage does arrive, in good shape, on the same flight you were on. When your luggage is damaged, delayed or lost, however, the results can be disastrous. The best way to protect yourself from the most serious losses is to follow one simple rule: *Never* put anything valuable or irreplaceable (such as jewelry), or that you might urgently need (such as medications), in checked baggage. Your compensation will rarely cover your actual loss.

*Domestic flights.* An airline can limit the amount it must pay if baggage is lost, damaged or delayed to $1,250 per passenger. You can get around this limit by declaring at check-in a higher value for the baggage, up to the airline's maximum, which is likely to be between $2,500 and $5,000. If you declare a higher value, the airline will charge you a fee based on a percentage of the declared value. The airline then becomes liable up to the declared value if it loses, damages or delays delivery of the baggage, un-

less the airline can prove that the actual loss was lower than the declared value.

*International flights.* The Warsaw Convention provides the rules under which liability for lost, delayed or damaged baggage is determined; these rules will not work to your advantage. Damages are calculated based on the weight of the baggage, regardless of the real value of the baggage or its contents. The Warsaw Convention states that the value for lost or damaged baggage is $9.07 per pound (or $20 per kilogram).

If your bag was weighed before the flight, then the value is determined by multiplying the weight of the bag times $9.07. For example, a 20-pound bag would be valued at $181.40. If your bags were not weighed, the airline will generally assume that all of your bags weighed a total of 70 pounds, and will reimburse you $634.90.

To add insult to injury, an airline can completely avoid responsibility for lost or damaged baggage if it can prove "that the damage was occasioned by error in piloting, in the handling of the aircraft or in navigation" and that, in all other respects, "the airline and its agents have taken all necessary measures to avoid the damage." It is difficult to understand why an airline should not be liable for your lost or damaged baggage if one of its pilots mishandles the airplane. On the other hand, if a pilot seriously mishandles the plane, your baggage may be the least of your concerns.

## Are there any legal protections for the credits I earn in a frequent flyer program?

While frequent flyer programs can provide you with some travel bargains, understand that there are few legal protections for the credits you earn. Under the rules of almost all frequent flyer programs, the airline can change award levels, have credits expire or even cancel the whole program without warning.

## Does it pay to belong to more than one frequent flyer program?

Some travelers will pay more for their tickets if they receive frequent flyer credit or will take an indirect or inconvenient flight on an airline in order to get frequent flyer credit. One way to avoid this frequent flyer trap is to join more than one program. Although you can get travel awards faster by concentrating your travel on one airline, you may get better fares and connections if you don't restrict yourself in that way. When you compare tickets, keep in mind that frequent flyer miles are worth approximately 2¢ per mile; use that figure to help calculate which option is best. The 2¢ per mile estimate was calculated by dividing the average cost of a domestic round trip ticket (approximately $500) by the number of frequent flyer miles needed for such a ticket (25,000 miles).

## Can I trade or sell my frequent flyer awards?

You can use your frequent flyer awards or give them to anyone you choose, but you cannot sell or trade them. Despite this clear limitation, frequent flyer awards are often bartered. Many of the deeply discounted tickets advertised in newspapers are actually tickets obtained by agents using purchased frequent flyer awards. Because airlines require you to present a photo ID when you check in and are traveling on a ticket obtained through a frequent flyer program, it is difficult to use these purchased coupons.

## I have a ticket on an airline that seems headed for bankruptcy. What can I do?

When an airline goes bankrupt, you technically become one of the airline's creditors in bankruptcy. If you file a claim in the bankruptcy court, there is a chance you will recover some very small percentage of the value of the ticket, but more likely you will recover nothing at all.

In the past, most airlines would honor a bankrupt airline's ticket and allow you on a substitute flight. But these days, given the competitive nature of the airline industry, this is rarely done. Sometimes, as a gesture of good will (and a way of luring new customers), an airline will offer a special discounted fare for passengers holding tickets on a bankrupt airline. If you have a ticket on a bankrupt airline and are a frequent flyer on another airline, try to negotiate free or discounted travel using the bankrupt airline's ticket. Trip cancellation or trip interruption insurance can sometimes cover the cost of a replacement ticket.

If you have an e-ticket, run fast to the nearest ticket counter for your airline and exchange it for a paper ticket. Any airline nice enough to accept passengers from a bankrupt airline will accept only those passengers with paper tickets.

# Rental Cars

A TOURIST IS A FELLOW WHO TRAVELS THOUSANDS OF MILES SO HE CAN BE PHOTOGRAPHED STANDING IN FRONT OF HIS CAR.

**—EMILE GANEST**

Whether on business or vacation, you may need to rent a car for at least part of your trip. This section outlines some of your basic rights as a renter. Most laws related to rental cars were enacted by state legislatures or derived from cases interpreting those state laws.

## Do I have any recourse if the rental car company doesn't provide me with the type of car I reserved?

If you have guaranteed payment and the company does not have the car you reserved available for you, the company must do everything it can to find you a different car from its fleet. Theoretically, the company must find you a car from another rental car company if it has no suitable substitute, but in practice this rarely happens. If the alternate car found for you is more expensive, you should not have to pay the difference.

If you haven't put down a deposit or guarantee, the company is still required to have a car available. But rental car companies often overbook to cover no-shows, which means that the class of car you reserved won't be available. The rental car company will usually provide you with a larger, more expensive car and tell you it is giving you a "free upgrade." Most renters are happy to accept the upgrade to a larger, more expensive car. If you accept a smaller, cheaper car than the one you reserved, the rental company is obliged to charge you the lower rate. If you refuse to accept a substitute car, you will probably have difficulty getting compensation afterward—you had a duty to reduce your damages by accepting a car that was a reasonable substitute for the car you reserved.

## What if the company fails to provide any car at all?

A company's overbooking may mean that no cars are available when you arrive. Your only real alternatives may be to find a substitute rental car at a different company or to take a taxi and seek reimbursement from the original car rental company. In addition, the rental car company may offer you future discounts.

## My son was told he couldn't rent a car because he's only 20. Is that legal?

Yes. Most major companies refuse to rent a car to someone who is under 21, or in some cases 25, unless that person is an employee using a corporate account or is military personnel traveling on orders. Companies that do rent to people as young as 21 usually charge an additional fee for drivers between 21 and 24.

This discrimination is not illegal. Rental car companies can do business with whomever they choose, as long as they do not discriminate based on race, religion, national origin, sex or other categories protected under civil rights laws.

## Do I need a credit card to rent a car?

Most rental car companies require a major credit card as a way to secure a deposit from you at the time of rental, although you can use the card or cash when you actually pay for the car. The company will check your credit limit and "freeze" an amount slightly greater than your estimated rental charges against your card, meaning that this amount is not available for you to charge. This freeze can last for several days after you return the car, even once the actual amount is charged or you pay with cash.

If you don't have a credit card, you can get a prepaid voucher through your travel agent by paying for the rental car first at the travel agency and bringing the voucher to the rental counter. The voucher may not cover taxes, surcharges, additional drivers, upgrades and other charges, so be sure to find out exactly what is included with the voucher before you pick up the car. Many companies require you to present a credit card or provide some other form of deposit even if you are using a voucher, so call ahead to find out.

## Can a rental car company charge a penalty if I don't show up or if I cancel my reservation?

Nearly all rental car companies charge penalties for four-wheel drives, minivans, convertibles and other specialty rentals if you fail to cancel a reservation in advance or are a no-show. Some companies are testing similar policies on their standard rental cars.

## Can a rental car company screen me based on my driving record?

Yes, and many companies now screen drivers when they rent in vacation-popular destinations such as Arizona, California, Florida, Nevada, New York, Virginia and Washington, DC. Sales agents conduct screening checks by entering your license number into a computer program that calls up your driver's record as reported by your state department of motor vehicles. If your record doesn't meet the screening criteria of the rental company, the agent will refuse to rent you a car.

Instead of screening you, some rental car companies may require you to sign a statement that you have an acceptable driving record. This shifts the responsibility for providing accurate information away from the company and to you. If you have an accident and signed a statement that turns out to be incorrect, the rental car company could use it against you by claiming that you acted in violation of the rental agreement.

## Screening Standards

Generally, a rental car company that screens drivers will deny you a vehicle if, during the past 36-month period, you:

- were caught driving with a suspended or invalid license
- had one instance of drunk driving, hit-and-run, driving a stolen car or other serious offense
- had three moving violations, or
- were at fault in two accidents.

The standards adopted by each rental car company vary and are subject to change, so you need to inquire about the specific rental screening standards of any company you are considering using.

If your driving record is questionable, do the following:

- Call your motor vehicle department to see if your state makes driver records available. If it doesn't, then relax and don't worry about being screened.
- If your state makes driver records available, when you call to reserve a rental car, ask if the company screens driving records and whether it maintains a nationwide blacklist.
- Get your driver record evaluated by a screening company. Several companies evaluate driving records to determine in advance whether drivers will be disqualified from renting. TML Information Services, the leading evaluator of vehicle records for rental car companies, operates a program for drivers from states that make driver record data available online. For around $11 (less for AAA members), you can get an evaluation of your driving record against the criteria for screening risky drivers used by six major rental car companies. You can reach TML on the Web at http://www.tml.com or by phone at 800-743-7891.
- If you don't want to pay for an evaluation, get a copy of your driving record from the motor vehicle agency in your state (allow plenty of time), obtain the screening criteria of the rental car companies you are considering and make an evaluation on your own.
- If you are traveling for business, rent from a company that has a liability agreement with your employer—the screening company may overlook items that would otherwise disqualify you.

Finally, if you are disqualified by a screening system, have someone you are traveling with rent the car and do the driving.

## How do rental car companies establish rental rates?

Car rental fees are set by each company and vary depending on the location of the rental office, time period the car will be rented, season, car model, special promotions or vacation packages, and your eligibility for discounts. In addition, because many rental car companies have franchises, the rates and policies of the central office may vary substantially from those of a local office. There is nothing illegal about these multiple prices, and there is nothing to stop you from asking about special fares when you rent or for a reduction after the rental if you learn that a better rate was available but was not offered to you. Although the company is not obligated to offer you the lower price, it may do so to maintain good customer relations.

## Can the rental car company tack on other fees?

Yes, but the company must tell you about the fees before you rent. Here are the most common fees you're likely to encounter:

- *Mileage charges* While many companies offer unlimited mileage, mileage charge policies change frequently, and you should ask each time you rent.
- *Fees for renting at an airport* Renting at an airport may be more expensive than renting at an urban or suburban location because airports and local governments often add surcharges and taxes to rental car rates.
- *Additional driver fees* Most rental car companies charge extra for anyone who drives the car other than the person who signs the rental agreement. Often, additional driver charges are waived for your spouse, immediate family member or business associate.
- *Young driver fees* As indicated above, many rental car companies add a daily surcharge for any driver aged 21 to 24.
- *Child safety seat fees* All states require children under a certain age to be placed in child car seats. If you don't bring your own seat, you will be required to rent one, usually at a cost of $3-$5 per day or $25 per week. You may be charged more for one-way rentals, and you may be required to make an extra deposit for the seat if you are paying cash for the car rental.
- *Vehicle drop-off fees* Many rental car companies charge high rates for dropping off a car at a location other than where you rented, unless the drop-off location is within the same

metropolitan area as where you picked up the vehicle. Charges for picking up the car in one city and dropping it off in another can be as high as $1,000.

- *Refueling charges.* Most companies require you to return the rental car with a full tank of gas. If you can't or you forget, you'll be forced to pay the company's inflated price per gallon.

## Do I have to take the rental car insurance offered to me?

No, and chances are you shouldn't. Each year, travelers in the U.S. spend more than $1 billion on rental car insurance, much of it unneeded or unwanted. A few states, including California, Texas and Indiana, require rental car companies to inform you that the rental car insurance may duplicate your personal automobile policy. But still, rental car insurance options are complex, confusing and rife with potential rip-offs.

When faced with a rental car insurance policy, adopt this basic strategy:

- determine what coverage you already have through your automobile insurance or credit cards—many gold cards issued by Visa and MasterCard provide rental car insurance coverage; American Express offers coverage as well
- find out what insurance options the rental car company offers, and
- don't fall prey to hardball sales tactics—buy only what you need.

## What is loss damage waiver? Is it insurance?

Loss damage waiver, or LDW (also known as collision damage waiver, or CDW), has gotten substantial press in recent years due primarily to its high cost and to complaints by consumers of pressure from rental car companies to purchase unnecessary LDW.

Rental car companies claim that they are not selling insurance, and that LDW is simply a waiver of the company's right to collect from you if the rental car is damaged or stolen while under your control. In most rental contracts, the rental company shifts all responsibility for collision damage or other loss to you; the effect of purchasing LDW is to shift responsibility back to the rental car company. But three aspects of LDW make its value suspect:

- the high pressure or deceptive sales tactics used to sell LDW
- the high price for LDW—especially when you may already be protected by your own insurance or credit card, and
- the number of exclusions (loopholes) in LDW coverage that allow the company to charge you even if you purchased LDW to protect yourself.

## Should You Purchase Loss Damage Waiver?

Purchasing loss damage waiver (LDW) may be a prudent choice for you if:

- You're in a foreign country and your auto insurance or credit card coverage does not include foreign rentals.

- You have no personal car insurance and do not want to rely on credit card coverage alone.
- Your personal auto insurance is insufficient to cover a rental vehicle.
- You can't afford to carry any credit charges until the credit card company reimburses you.
- Your rental car isn't covered under your insurance or your credit card coverage (this may be the case if you rent an antique or exotic car).

## What should I know before I rent a car in a foreign country?

Although the laws governing car rentals differ in every country, here are some general rules.

First, most countries will accept your valid state driver's license with another form of photo ID. Some countries may also require an International Driver's Permit (available through AAA offices). Check with an AAA travel office before you travel. You don't need to take a test to get an International Driver's Permit; all it does is explain (in a number of languages) the type of license you have, any limitations that apply and when it will expire.

Second, your personal automobile insurance policy may have restrictions or limitations on driving in foreign countries. Check your coverage, including the terms of your credit card policy, before you rent in a foreign country.

Third, in some countries, the police will take your license if you are in-

volved in an accident or stopped for a moving violation, and will not return it until you have paid any applicable fine. Get receipts for all payments you make, and report any mistreatment or apparent scams to the American embassy or consulate in that country.

Fourth, certain European countries track traffic violations with street cameras that photograph cars at intersections. The police trace the drivers using the license plate number of the car and request payment from the rental car company for the ticket. The rental car company is within its rights to collect the fine from you, even if the company is informed of the violation after you have returned and paid for the car.

# Hotels and Other Accommodations

When you travel, you have the choice of many different types of accommodations: hotels, motels, inns, bed and breakfasts, rental houses and other lodging. With some minor variations, the laws governing most types of accommodations are similar. To simplify matters, we use the term "hotel" to cover all types of accommodations. In addition, the following information only applies to hotels in the United States unless we indicate otherwise.

## Must a hotel provide me with a room, assuming there's a vacancy?

Generally, yes. The most basic legal principal concerning hotels is the "duty to receive." Created hundreds of years ago under the common law of England, the duty to receive required hotel keepers to accept and take care of any traveler who presented himself as a paying customer, as long as the inn had room. Although this basic duty to receive has been modified somewhat by state laws, it is still the basis for many of the fundamental obligations that a hotel has to its guests.

A hotel can say "no" only if it reasonably believes that you will:

- not pay for your room
- injure or annoy other guests, or
- physically damage or otherwise harm the hotel (including giving it a bad reputation).

If you arrive drunk and disorderly, threaten another guest or appear to want to use the room for prostitution, you'll probably be turned away.

## Must a hotel honor my prepaid or guaranteed reservation?

A prepaid or guaranteed reservation is one where you give the hotel a credit card number and the hotel promises to have a room for you no matter when you show up, even if it's midnight or 3:00 a.m. If you have a guaranteed reservation and the hotel does not hold a room for you, the hotel has breached a contract and must do everything it can to find you a room— even if that means sending you to another hotel. If you guaranteed your reservation with a credit or debit card, the hotel may be required under the terms of its agreement with the card issuer to:

- pay for your first night's stay at an alternate hotel
- provide free transportation to the alternate hotel
- pay for a three-minute phone call to let your family or office know where you'll be staying, and
- forward all incoming calls to your new hotel.

Be sure to request these services. In all cases, if your alternate lodging is more expensive, the hotel should pay the difference.

## Is a guaranteed reservation the same as a confirmed reservation?

If you have not paid for the reservation in advance or guaranteed it, but have received a "confirmed reservation" from the hotel, the hotel must keep a room for you unless you haven't met the conditions of the reservation. For example, it is common for a hotel to say, "We will hold the room for you until 6:00 p.m." or, "We will hold the room for you if we receive a written confirmation and deposit" by a certain date. If you do not fulfill these obligations, then the hotel does not have to hold the room for you. If you do meet your obligations and the hotel doesn't have a room for you, it must do its best to find you comparable lodging.

## Do I have the right to a particular room?

Generally, no. A hotel manager can put you anywhere or move you from one room to another, as long as it is not done in a discriminatory way. The only exception is if you've reserved a certain room, like the honeymoon suite for your honeymoon.

If it's crucial for you to have a particular room, make sure the hotel management knows in advance and that you receive written confirmation for your reservation of that particular room. If the room you reserved is occupied by other guests, the management may, but is not obligated to, move those guests to another room. (A hotel can satisfy its obligation to you simply by providing a room comparable to the one you reserved.) If the room is uninhabitable (say, a water pipe breaks), then the hotel is excused from providing that particular room.

## Do I have a right to privacy in my room?

If you are using your room in a normal way, not engaging in illegal acts or disturbing other guests, then you have a limited right of privacy in your room. But if the hotel management believes that you are carrying out illegal activities (such as dealing drugs), it is entitled to enter and search your room, even without your permission. The hotel management cannot, however, authorize the police to search your room without your permission or a search warrant.

The hotel management also has the right to enter your room to clean or perform needed maintenance, or if necessary, to stop you from disturbing other guests (for example, if you are playing the television very loudly) or destroying hotel property.

It is generally considered a violation of your privacy if the hotel tells an outside person the number of your room. The hotel can tell an inquirer whether you are a guest at the hotel and can connect any caller to your room. If you wish to maintain complete privacy, you must make it clear to the management that you are not to be contacted by anyone and that no one is to be told whether or not you are staying at the hotel.

## Why do hotel room rates vary so much?

There is no set formula for determining what amount a hotel can charge, although rates must be "reasonable." Many states require hotels to post the maximum charge for a room in a conspicuous place in each room (usually on the back of the door). Although the hotel may not charge more than this maximum rate (often referred to as the "rack rate"), it certainly may rent the room for less.

Always check your hotel bill to see whether it matches the rate you were quoted when you reserved the room. Frequently, additional charges will be tacked on. Some, such as visitor fees or "bed taxes," may be mandated by local or state law and are probably legitimate.

Other fees, such as service charges or telephone charges, may not be legitimate. A hotel cannot legally charge you more than the rate it quoted to you when you made your reservation, unless you approve the charges in advance. Many states have laws requiring that all additional charges be posted or approved in writing by guests.

## Ask About Discount Rates

When you reserve a hotel room, you may be able to get a reduced price simply by asking about discounts available to the following people:

- corporate employees—many hotels have negotiated rates with large corporations that are 10%-30% lower than their standard rates and these rates are generally available to anyone who asks for them (although an occasional desk clerk will ask for a business card or other ID)
- seniors
- families with children
- AAA members
- members of certain professional associations (like the American Medical Association or American Bar Association)
- guests paying with certain credit cards
- members of frequent flyer or frequent guest programs, or
- federal and state government employees.

## I paid a lot for a room that fell way short of my expectations. Is there anything I can do?

Sometimes you may find yourself in a hotel room that looks nothing like the one described to you or pictured in an advertisement or brochure. If the advertisement or description was intentionally deceptive, the hotel may be guilty of fraud. The law generally allows a limited amount of exaggeration or "puffing" in advertisements, but it does not allow intentional deception. When you find yourself in such a situation, your best bet is to talk to the manager immediately—he may be able to reduce your room charge or move you to a better room. If the problem is with the entire hotel, however (for example, it's in a very dangerous neighborhood), you're better off requesting a refund and finding other accommodations.

If your hotel room is unclean or unsanitary, report it to the manager and the housekeeping department immediately. If they are unable to clean your room to your satisfaction, request a new room or a refund. Should you end up in a serious dispute over the cleanliness of a room, the health

and safety codes for the city or state where the hotel is located may provide the best support for your argument. Report any serious violation to local health authorities, not only to bolster your claims, but as a service to future guests. Take photographs of the offending conditions if you can.

## I fell and hurt myself on a hotel's premises. Do I have any recourse against the hotel?

A hotel may be liable if you slip or trip and fall on the hotel premises—for example, on spilled food or drink in a hotel bar or restaurant, on snow and ice that has not been cleared from a walkway, or on moist tile floors or other slick surfaces. You might also be hurt because of a design or building flaw (such as steps that are too steep) or the hotel's failing to light an area properly.

## Does a hotel have any special obligation to protect its guests around the swimming pool?

Because swimming pools create a potentially dangerous situation, hotels must be especially vigilant in designing, maintaining and controlling access to them. Disclaimers such as "swim at your own risk" are unlikely to protect a hotel from liability if it didn't use sufficient care to protect its guests, such as failing to install a fence around a pool. This is true even if you are drunk. Most courts require hotels to anticipate that children, inebriated guests and others might find their ways into the pool if safeguards don't keep them out.

## Is the hotel responsible if I am the victim of a crime at or near the hotel?

A hotel cannot be held liable for crimes committed on or near the hotel unless it should have anticipated the crime (for example, the hotel is in a very high crime area) and could have prevented it, either by providing sufficient warnings or taking better security measures. In such situations, the hotel's general duty to warn you about dangerous conditions may extend to a duty to warn about crime in or around the hotel. Furthermore, the hotel's actions—such as failure to install proper locks on windows and doors, provide adequate lighting in parking areas or take adequate measures to ensure that passkeys are not used by criminals—may make the hotel at least partially liable.

## Is the hotel responsible if my belongings are stolen?

Traditionally, hotels were liable for virtually all loss or theft of a guest's property. Today, however, most states limit a hotel's liability if it takes certain steps to protect your belongings. For cash, jewelry and other valuables, a hotel is required to provide a safe. Most states require the hotel to tell you that the safe is available, that the hotel has limited liability for valuables left in the safe and that the hotel may have no liability if you do not place valuables in the safe.

The limitation of liability also includes a limitation for clothing and other personal goods you bring to the hotel. While you are not required to check expensive suits or mink stoles at the front desk as valuables, clothing and expensive luggage often exceed the amount of the hotel's maximum liability.

Generally, these limited liability laws were passed to protect hotels from forces beyond their control, such as fire or theft. If the hotel fails to use reasonable care to protect your valuables (for example, it leaves the safe unlocked), it will probably be liable for the full value of your loss.

### Is the hotel liable if my car is damaged, broken into or stolen?

Traditionally, hotels were strictly liable for protecting your means of transportation. This meant caring for your horses, saddles, tack and the rest. These days, hotels are required to use reasonable care to protect your car. Many state laws set a monetary limit for loss or damage to a vehicle or its contents. But even in these states, negligence by the hotel—including the valet—could make the hotel liable for damage it should have foreseen.

Whether the contents of a car parked at a hotel are the hotel's responsibility is not clear. They do not fall into the traditional categories of

goods within the hotel or transportation. The hotel is most likely to be liable when you pay for parking, a valet or other employee takes your car, retains the keys and is informed of the value of the contents of the car.

### What if I don't check out when I say I will?

In most states, renting a hotel room gives you what is called a "revocable license" to use the room. This right is much more limited than the rights a tenant has when renting an apartment. Formal eviction proceedings don't have to be brought if you overstay your welcome. The hotel can simply change the lock (easy to do today because hotels often use preprogrammed entry cards, not keys) and pack up your items.

# Travel Agents

*One of the most common disruptions of marital bliss is the choice of where to spend a vacation. What this country needs is an ocean in the mountains.*

**—PAUL SWEENEY**

At some point you're likely to rely on a travel agent—someone authorized to sell travel services to the public—to help you make decisions about where, when and how to travel. A travel agent's legal responsibilities vary de-

pending on the role the agent plays in helping with your plans.

## Does a travel agent work for me or for the travel industry?

A travel agent generally owes his highest duty to a travel supplier, such as an airline or tour operator, not you. This is because the travel supplier and the travel agent have an ongoing relationship—the agent represents the supplier and is compensated for providing business to the supplier.

You may feel that a travel agent should be "your" agent and should look out for your best interests, rather than the interests of travel suppliers. A good agent will take on this role, knowing that good customer service will lead to repeat business. In addition, the law is changing in this area, and sometimes a travel agent may be considered your agent as well. In most cases, however, the travel agent will owe you the normal duty owed by a salesperson to a customer, but no more.

## Does a travel agent have any special responsibility when making a reservation for me?

If a travel agent fails to make a reservation for you—or delays in making a reservation for you—and you lose money because of it, the agent is responsible to you if the failure to make the reservation or the delay was his fault. For example, if the flight you want to take has seats available when you call your agent, but the agent delays in making your reservation, the flight sells out and you have to take a more expensive flight, the agent would be liable to you for the difference. On the other hand, if the flight was already sold out when you called the agent, the agent is not liable because his inability to make a reservation is not his fault.

When making a reservation, a travel agent must do his best to match the reservation to your specific requirements and limitations. If your travel agent makes the wrong reservation and you have a ticket on a plane destined for somewhere you don't want to go, the agent is probably responsible for paying the additional cost of getting you to your proper destination. If the agent books you into the wrong hotel or reserves the wrong type of rental car, he should compensate you for the difference between the value you would have received had the agent made the reservation properly and what you did receive as a result of the agent's mistake.

## Is a travel agent responsible for confirming my reservation?

Generally, no. You must confirm your own reservations.

However, if your travel agent uses a tour operator or wholesaler who in turn makes your reservations, the agent probably has an obligation to verify your reservations with the various travel suppliers independently. The travel agent should not assume that a tour operator or wholesaler is reliable. Be sure to check with your travel agent about who is responsible for confirming your reservations.

## My travel agent charged me the wrong amount for my ticket. What should I do?

If you overpay because of a travel agent's mistake, the travel agent must reimburse you for the difference between the amount you paid and the actual fare. You must consider the proper fare at the time you reserved and paid for your ticket, not when a subsequent fare change was made.

If a travel agent charges you less than the actual cost of your ticket, you are not entitled to travel for less than the established fare. The travel supplier may require you to pay the additional amount due before you travel. Whether you can recover the difference from your travel agent depends on the circumstances. If you knew the correct price and agreed to it, and the travel agent simply hit the wrong key on the computer, you are not entitled to any compensation from the travel agent. On the other hand, if you didn't know the correct price and made your decision based upon what the agent told you, then you probably can recoup the difference if your reliance on the travel agent's statement was reasonable. (If you were told that a $999 flight was $799, your reliance would probably be reasonable. If, however, you were told that a $999 flight was $9.99, you'd be out of luck.)

## Is a travel agent responsible for researching airlines, hotels and other suppliers?

Travel agents do not have to thoroughly investigate suppliers. In general, they are required only to stay current with reasonably available information, such as what is in trade journals and magazines. The most important types of information are often the supplier's reputation, track record and financial condition. A travel agent must provide this type of information, as well as any specific experience that the travel agent has had with that supplier, if it would likely affect your decision to use the supplier.

If a travel agent books you on a flight that has already been canceled or in a hotel that has not been built, you have a fairly strong argument that the agent was negligent and failed to undertake a basic investigation. If, however, a tour operator suddenly goes out of business or a hotel closes between the time you make your reservation and the time you arrive, the agent's responsibility is less clear.

## Must a travel agent warn me of any travel risks?

If a travel agent knows of a substantial risk to you, such as an airline that is bankrupt but continuing to fly, the travel agent has an obligation to warn you of that risk, with the following limitations:

- A travel agent does not have to warn you about risks that are obvious and apparent, such as the risk that the car you rent from "Rent-a-Wreck" may not be in the best condition.
- A travel agent is not required to be a fortune teller, particularly concerning factors out of the agent's control. An agent might be liable for promoting a "sun and fun" vacation in India during monsoon season, but the agent does not have a duty to warn you about all possible conditions—such as unannounced strikes, political conditions or bad weather—that could affect your enjoyment of the journey.
- A travel agent does not have to point out disclaimers or other legal elements of an agreement between you and the travel supplier, although a helpful travel agent might do so.

## How are travel agents paid?

When a travel agent issues a ticket or makes other travel arrangements for you, he generally receives a commission from the travel supplier. This commission may range from 7% to 15% of the price you pay, but it is usually about 10%.

## Do any professional associations regulate travel agents?

No. Travel agents have to meet very few formal requirements. Most travel agents do belong to one or more professional associations, however, and each association has a code of ethics that requires its members to remain knowledgeable of developments within the travel industry and to refrain from engaging in misleading sales practices. Membership in a professional association is voluntary, however, and if an agent violates the code of ethics, you have little recourse within the association.

If you have a complaint about a travel agent, ask someone in his office if he belongs to a professional association. If he does, contact the association as follows:

American Society of Travel Agents (ASTA)
1101 King Street, Suite 200
Alexandria, VA 22314
703-739-2782
703-684-8319 (fax)
http://www.astanet.com

International Airlines Travel Agent Network (IATAN)
300 Garden City Plaza, Suite 342
Garden City, NY 11530
516-747-4716
516-747-4462 (fax)
http://www.iatan.org

Institute of Certified Travel Agents (ICTA)
148 Linden Street
Wellesley, MA 02482
800-542-4282
800-FAX-ICTA
http://www.icta.com

The association can tell you if the agent is a member in good standing. In some cases, an association may be able to help you if you have a complaint against one of their members. For example, ASTA has a mediation program to help resolve disputes between travel agents and their clients.

# Travel Scams

Each year, fraud costs American consumers over $100 billion. One out of every seven cases of fraud involves travel, with most travel scams being carried out over the telephone or by mail. Travel fraud knows no socioeconomic boundaries—scam artists ply their wares in every travel market. This section describes some common travel scams to help you avoid becoming part of these grim statistics.

## Are there any general rules to follow to avoid being the victim of a travel scam?

As with most things in life, if the offer sounds too good to be true, it probably is. That being said, here are some signs to watch out for:

- The solicitation says that you were "specially selected" or "awarded" a trip or prize, but you haven't entered any contest.
- You must make a payment to collect your prize.
- The salesperson uses high pressure sales tactics or insists on an immediate decision.
- You must disclose your income, Social Security number, bank account number or other private information.
- The company offers great bargains, but refuses to put the details in writing unless you pay first.
- The salesperson makes vague references to "all major airlines" or "all major hotels," without saying which ones you will use.
- You must wait more than 60 days before taking the trip or receiving the prize. (Most scam victims pay for their "prize" on their credit card; scam artists know that you must dispute any credit card charge within 60 days. If they force you to wait more than 60 days, you can't challenge the charge.)
- The caller asks for your credit card number over the phone.
- The company requests a direct bank deposit or certified check, or offers to send a courier to your home to pick up your check.
- The deal cannot be booked through a travel agent.
- You must call a 900 number.
- The company cannot provide the names of references, or the references you call repeat nearly verbatim the claims of the travel provider.

## Use a Credit Card Whenever Possible

Although using a credit card is not a surefire way to protect yourself, if you act quickly, you can dispute the charge and avoid paying for a scam. The Fair Credit Billing Act gives you 60 days from the date you receive your bill—not the date of your travel—to contest a charge. Some credit cards offer more extended coverage; a few even give members up to a year to contest a charge.

## Some kids at my daughter's college lost money when they signed up for a trip that was canceled at the last minute. How can my daughter avoid becoming the next victim?

Many fly-by-night travel operations pitch specifically to students through telemarketing and other hard-sell tactics, hoping to take advantage of inexperienced travelers on a tight budget who are looking to save money.

Students should find out whether the tour company meets the standards set by the Council on Standards for International Educational Travel (CSIET). To qualify, tour operators must submit a review signed by an independent certified public accountant as well as extensive documentation concerning government regulations for student exchanges, promotions and student insurance.

The *Advisory List of International Educational Travel and Exchange Programs*, an annually updated booklet listing companies that meet the standards, is available from CSIET by writing to 212 S. Henry Street, Alexandria, VA 22314. The booklet costs $15 for orders placed within the United States, and $20 for orders placed overseas. Call 703-739-9050 for more information or log onto the organization's website at http://www.csiet.org.

## We just returned from Hawaii, where we were constantly solicited to buy a timeshare. Are these deals as good as they sound?

Probably not. An estimated 94% of all timeshare owners never intended to buy in the first place; they are swept away by high pressure sales pitches and cleverly disguised promotions.

The idea behind a timeshare is simple: For a one-time price plus an annual maintenance fee, you can buy the right to use a given vacation property for a certain amount of time (typically one week) each year. What you may not be told is the extent to which the annual maintenance fee will increase over time—one timeshare owner in Hawaii saw her annual maintenance fees climb 76% in six years. Timeshare operators also may force owners to pay unexpected "special assessment fees," sometimes as high as $1,000. While a timeshare has the potential to be a satisfactory arrangement, it often yields a variety of pitfalls and frustrations for the unwary purchaser.

# A Typical Timeshare Sales Pitch

A new camera, a half-price parasail ride, a free day's rental car, a free gourmet meal—you name it, timeshare salespeople have offered it. Many timeshare developers lure tourists to sales presentations by selling tours and activities at highly discounted prices, but provide only vague disclosure of what is required to qualify for the discount deal.

In the usual scenario, the catch for the gift is that you must sit through a presentation about a timeshare vacation property. The presentations vary, but most include high-pressure sales pitches that drone on for hours and leave visitors desperate to get out. Timeshare salespeople frequently go over the advertised time allotted for their presentation and are not responsive if you complain. They sometimes refuse to give the promised gift or discount if you don't buy. Although it may be illegal to not give you the gift or discount, few consumers complain—they just want out.

## I've been told that I shouldn't buy a timeshare because it will be hard to sell it later. Is this true?

Very likely, yes. Timeshare owners face a couple of traps when they try to sell. The first hurdle is the lack of a strong resale market. Although statistics vary, all studies show that there are many more timeshare owners wanting to sell than there are buyers.

Another problem is the likelihood that you will lose money on the sale of a timeshare. The original price of a timeshare may have included premiums of up to 40% to cover sales costs. As a result, a resale will yield as little as 60% of the original purchase price—plus you will have to pay a commission to the broker (often as high as 20%) who sells the property for you.

## Is it possible to get out of a timeshare after signing a contract?

Maybe. Nearly 30 states have "cooling-off" laws; these let you get out of a timeshare contract if you act within a few days after signing (three to ten, depending on the state). If there is no cooling-off period, or you change your mind after the time has passed, your only recourse may be a formal lawsuit. Timeshare sellers are accustomed to handling claims from unhappy buyers and are unlikely to refund your money unless forced to do so.

# Suing a Timeshare Operator

There are several types of claims you might bring against a slippery timeshare seller. The first, breach of contract, involves promises explicitly made and set forth in the sales agreements. If the size, location, condition or some other important fact about the timeshare is materially different from what you agreed to in the sales contract, you may have a basis for claiming breach of the contract. But beware: These contracts are carefully drawn up by the timeshare sellers' attorneys and are likely to cover almost any contingency—scrutinize carefully before signing.

You may also bring claims based on tactics used and promises made before you agreed to purchase your timeshare. These claims may be covered under state laws prohibiting unfair business practices or those designed to prevent fraudulent inducement. In both cases, the idea is that the seller used unfair sales tactics or lies to get you to buy the timeshare. You will have to show:

- what the seller said or did
- why it was misleading
- that you wouldn't have bought the timeshare if the seller hadn't used the misleading tactics or promises, and
- that you suffered some monetary loss because of the purchase.

Timeshare sales contracts usually include clauses that disclaim any promises made during the sales pitch. The contract you sign will ask you to agree that you are making the purchase only on the basis of the representations in that contract. Prospective purchasers who notice differences between what is in the contract and what was promised by the salesperson are likely to be told that the contract is only "legal jargon." This is *not* true. If a timeshare salesperson will not put a promise in writing, don't go through with the sale. You will be forced to argue afterwards that you relied on that promise, even though you signed a contract that explicitly says you did not rely on any promises.

If you are the victim of a timeshare scam, you can ask for two things. First, you can ask to rescind the contract. You would get your money back, and the

seller would regain title to the timeshare. If the seller (or court) refuses this, you must prove monetary damages, the largest of which is the difference between the amount you paid for the timeshare and its actual value. As you can imagine, it can be quite difficult to determine the actual value of a timeshare, although the amount you could obtain by reselling it is one possible indicator.

## I received a vacation certificate in the mail. How can I figure out if it's legitimate?

First, review the tips at the beginning of this section. Then, if you note any of the following on a travel certificate, treat it with maximum skepticism and send it to the recycling bin:

- words such as "Certificate of Guarantee" and a spread-winged eagle or other prominent symbol designed to convey a sense of legitimacy
- a variety of possible vacation destinations, with no designated dates or price
- exciting descriptions of what you will do, such as "gala cruise," "glittering casino action," "moonlight dancing" or "resort accommodations," with no designated company names
- a phrase in the fine print indicating you were chosen "using credit and purchasing criteria to select individuals interested in the many benefits of travel," or
- fine print language stating that the receipt of one portion of the offer (for example, the airline ticket) is dependent on purchase of something else (such as hotel accommodations).

## How can I find out if a cheap airfare offered by a charter airline is legitimate?

Although many charter companies provide legitimate low-cost travel options, their reliability is far from uniform. Over the past few years, many charter operations have collapsed, leaving consumers in the lurch—and some that are still in business pose financial risks for current customers.

The Department of Transportation (DOT) regulates the manner in which charter operators must handle consumer funds. Among other things, the regulations require charter operators to post a bond or deposit consumer funds in an escrow account. Nonetheless, charter operators have found ways to shirk the rules; they may fail to deposit passenger funds into escrow accounts or divert funds that have already been deposited.

DOT regulations require sellers of charter flights to file a prospectus with the DOT, explaining how their business is organized. To find out whether a low-fare carrier has at least done this, call DOT's Consumer Affairs Office at 202-366-2220 and ask for the carrier's prospectus number.

### Where to Report a Travel Scam

If you are the victim of any kind of travel scam, contact one or more of the following agencies or associations:

**STATE AND LOCAL GOVERNMENT AGENCIES**

*State consumer protection office.* Call directory assistance in your state capital and ask for the number for your state attorney general, and the division or department of consumer affairs or consumer protection. *Local prosecutor.* Call the nearest district attorney or state attorney's office and ask whether there is a consumer fraud division. *State licensing board.* Some states are starting to license travel providers. Ask your state attorney general if travel providers are licensed in your state.

**FEDERAL GOVERNMENT AGENCIES**

*Federal Trade Commission.* One mission of the FTC is consumer protection. Although the agency generally does not involve itself in individual disputes, your complaint, comment, or inquiry can help the agency spot a pattern of law violations that requires action. Your input can also help the agency recognize and tell people about larger trends affecting consumers. You can file a complaint with the FTC by writing to FTC, CRC-240, Washington, D.C. 20580; by calling 202-326-2222; or by completing a complaint form online at http://www.ftc.gov/ftc/consumer.htm. The FTC also has a number of guides and resources that might assist you.

*Federal Communications Commission.* If you were defrauded by a telemarketer or phone solicitor, or sucked in when a travel service provider aired a fraudulent ad on radio or television, contact the FCC, 445 12th St. SW, Washington, DC 20554, 202-225-5322, http://www.fcc.gov.

*U.S. Department of Justice, Criminal Division, Fraud Section.* The Fraud Section directs the federal law enforcement effort against fraud and white collar crime. You can reach the Fraud Section by phone at 202-514-7023, by fax at 202-514-7021 or online at http://www.usdoj.gov/criminal/fraud.html.

*U.S. Department of Transportation.* If you have a consumer concern or complaint regarding air services, you can contact the U.S. Department of Transportation's Aviation Consumer Protection Division at U.S. Department of Transportation, Room 4107, C-75, Washington, DC 20590; 202-366-2220; http://www.dot.gov/airconsumer.

*U.S. Postal Service.* If you were cheated by anyone who used the U.S. mail, file a complaint with the U.S. Postal Inspection Service. To do so, contact your local inspector's office or complete a complaint form online at http://www.framed.usps.com/postalinspectors.

**PRIVATE ORGANIZATIONS**

*National Fraud Information Center.* NFIC can help you file a complaint with the appropriate federal agency, give you tips on how to avoid becoming the victim of a scam or send you consumer publications. You can reach NFIC as follows: 800-876-7060 (voice), 202-835-0767 (fax), 202-347-3189 (electronic bulletin board), 202-737-5084 (TTD) or http://www.fraud.org. Or you can write to NFIC, c/o National Consumer's League, 1701 K Street, NW, Suite 1201, Washington, DC 20006.

*American Society of Travel Agents (ASTA).* If you have a complaint concerning an ASTA member, contact ASTA, 1101 King Street, Alexandria, VA 22314, 703-739-2782, 703-684-8319 (fax), http://www.astanet.com. You can also request a free copy of *Avoiding Travel Problems.*

*United States Tour Operators Association (USTOA).* If you have a complaint concerning a USTOA member or a question about USTOA's consumer protection plan, contact USTOA, 342 Madison Avenue, Suite 1522, New York, NY 10173, 212-549-6599, 212-599-6744 (fax), http://www.ustoa.com.

*Better Business Bureau (BBB).* You can provide a public service to other travelers by filing a complaint with all offices of the BBB where the scammer operates. In addition, the National Council of Better Business Bureaus operates a nationwide system for settling consumer disputes through mediation and arbitration. So, if you can find the company, you might be able to get some recourse through a BBB. Check http://www.bbb.org.

## How can I tell whether a deeply discounted airfare is legitimate?

Deceptive airline advertising is so frequent that you may have already learned to read between the lines and scan the fine print to get the real picture. If you are not so savvy, watch out for the following:

- Deceptive two-for-one offers. The airline promises two tickets for the price of one, but then requires you to buy a ticket in a class that costs the same, if not more, than two tickets at some other published fare.

- Misleading discounts. Some airfare promotions advertise drastic price reductions in airfares without specifying the base fare from which the discounts are calculated. Furthermore, airlines usually advertise ticket prices at half their true cost. The fine print explains that the fare is "each way, based on round-trip purchase," despite the fact that you cannot buy a one-way ticket at the price shown.

- Phantom "sale" seats. The classic airline bait-and-switch tactic is to promote low airfares for a given route and then fail to disclose the strict limitations on the availability of seats. The airline may try to sell you a higher-priced seat or may offer a reasonable number of low-fare seats for the first few days of the promotion, and then retract the seats for the duration of the ad campaign.

- Frequent flyer deceptions. Airlines continue to severely limit the number of seats that they allocate to frequent flyers, especially for business and first class seats. As a result, frequent flyer customers may have a difficult time getting the seats they've earned.

### More Information About Your Rights as a Traveler

*Trouble-Free Travel … and What to Do When Things Go Wrong*, by Attorneys Stephen Colwell and Ann Shulman (Nolo), helps you anticipate and avoid hassles while traveling, and shows you how to deal with airlines, tour operators, rental car companies, hotels and other travel providers should problems arise.

**http://www.nolo.com**
Nolo offers self-help information about a wide variety of legal topics, including travel law.

**http://www.dot.gov**
The U.S. Department of Transportation offers information and tips for resolving travel problems.

**http://www.travelocity.com**
Travelocity can help you plan your entire trip, from finding the cheapest airfare to choosing your activities.

**http://www.bbb.org**
The Better Business Bureau provides information on resolving disputes through mediation and arbitration.

**http://www.air-transport.org**
The Air Transport Association of America allows you to order most major airlines' conditions of contract, the hidden terms of your ticket.

**http://travel.state.gov**
The Bureau of Consular Affairs provides extensive information on travelers' security, applying for a passport, foreign countries' entry requirements, international adoptions and how U.S. consulates can help you overseas.

**http://www.cdc.gov/travel**
The Centers for Disease Control and Prevention offers travel information on health risks in foreign countries and appropriate precautions to take.

**http://www.faa.gov**
The Federal Aviation Administration provides information and tips on air travel, including a fact sheet called Fly Smart.

**http://www.sath.org**
The Society for the Advancement of Travel for the Handicapped offers information to assist disabled people preparing to take a trip.

**http://www.customs.ustreas.gov**
The U.S. Customs Service provides publications including guides for returning U.S. residents and import restrictions.

# **12**

# **W**ills and Estate Planning

12.2    *Wills*

12.8    *Probate*

12.9    *Executors*

12.13   *Avoiding Probate*

12.15   *Living Trusts*

12.18   *Estate and Gift Taxes*

12.22   *Funeral Planning and Other Final Arrangements*

12.25   *Body and Organ Donations*

*It's not that I'm afraid to die. I just don't want to be there when it happens.*

**—WOODY ALLEN**

**T**he first thing that comes to many people's minds when they think of estate planning is property: Who gets what you own when you die? But estate planning encompasses much more—for example, minimizing probate court costs and estate taxes, deciding who will care for your minor children if you can't, appointing people to handle your medical and financial affairs if necessary, and expressing your wishes regarding memorial services and burial. While none of us relish the thought of thinking about these things, taking some time to do so now can save your loved ones a great deal of money, pain and confusion later on.

This chapter answers often-asked questions about estate planning, from basic wills to organ donation. Along the way we consider probate and the many ways to avoid it, methods for eliminating or reducing death taxes, and funeral planning. For information about arranging for someone to make your medical and financial decisions should you become unable to handle them yourself, see the next chapter, *Living Wills and Powers of Attorney*.

# Wills

Though most Americans are aware that they need a will, the majority—about 70% of us—don't have one. There are lots of reasons we put off making our wills, from fear of lawyers' fees to fear of death. But writing a will doesn't have to be expensive, or even terribly complicated. And once it's done, you can rest a little easier, knowing that your wishes are known and will be followed after your death.

## What happens if I die without a will?

If you don't make a will or use some other legal method to transfer your property when you die, state law will determine what happens to your property. (This process is called "intestate succession.") Your property will be distributed to your spouse and children or, if you have neither, to other relatives according to a statutory formula. If no relatives can be found to inherit your property, it will go into your state's coffers. Also, in the absence of a will, a court will determine who will care for your young children and their property if the other parent is unavailable or unfit.

## Do I need a lawyer to make my will?

Probably not. Making a will rarely involves complicated legal rules, and most people can draft their own will with the aid of a good self-help book or software program. If you know what you own and whom you care about, and you have a good self-help resource to guide you, it's hard to make a mistake.

But you shouldn't approach the task of will drafting absolutely determined not to consult a lawyer. If you have questions that aren't answered by the resource you're relying on, a lawyer's services are warranted. Even so, you don't have to turn over the whole project; you can simply ask your questions and then finish making your own will.

For example, you may want to consult a lawyer if:

- You have questions about your will or other options for leaving your property.
- You expect to leave a very large amount of assets—over $1 million—that will be subject to estate taxes unless you engage in tax planning. (But first look at a good self-help resource that discusses tax-saving strategies.)
- You own a small business and have questions as to the rights of surviving owners or your ownership share.
- You must make arrangements for long-term care of a beneficiary—for example, a disabled child.
- You fear someone will contest your will on grounds of fraud, or claim that you were unduly influenced or weren't of sound mind when you signed it.
- You wish to leave no property, or very little property, to your spouse. It's usually not possible to do this unless you live in a community property state where your spouse already owns half of most assets acquired after marriage. (See *Can I disinherit relatives I don't like?*, below.) But a lawyer can explain exactly what your spouse is entitled to claim from your estate.

Also, some people simply feel more comfortable having a lawyer review their will, even though their situation has no apparent legal complications.

## I don't have much property. Can't I just make a handwritten will?

Handwritten wills, called "holographic" wills, are legal in about 25 states. To be valid, a holographic will must be written, dated and signed in the handwriting of the person making the will. Some states allow will writers to use a fill-in-the-blanks form if the rest of the will is handwritten and the will is properly dated and signed.

If you have very little property, and you want to make just a few specific bequests, a holographic will is better than nothing if it's valid in your state. But generally, we don't recommend them. Unlike regular wills, holographic wills are not usually witnessed, so if your will goes before a probate court, the court may be unusually strict when examining it to be sure it's legitimate. It's better to take a little extra time to write a will that will easily pass muster when the time comes.

## Making Your Will Legal

Any adult of sound mind is entitled to make a will. (And if you're reading this book, you're of sound mind.) Beyond that, there are just a few technical requirements:

- The will must be typewritten or computer generated (unless it is a valid handwritten will, as discussed above).
- The document must expressly state that it's your will.
- You must date and sign the will.
- The will must be signed by at least

two, or in some states three, witnesses. They must watch you sign the will, though they don't need to read it. Your witnesses must be people who won't inherit anything under the will.

You don't have to have your will notarized. In many states, though, if you and your witnesses sign an affidavit (sworn statement) before a notary public, you can help simplify the court procedures required to prove the validity of the will after you die.

## Do I need to file my will with a court or in public records somewhere?

No. A will doesn't need to be recorded or filed with any government agency, although it can be in a few states. Just keep your will in a safe, accessible place and be sure the person in charge of winding up your affairs (your executor) knows where it is.

## Can I use my will to name somebody to care for my young children, in case my spouse and I both die suddenly?

Yes. If both parents of a child die while the child is still a minor, another adult—called a "personal guardian"—must step in. You and the child's other parent can use your wills to nominate someone to fill this position. To avert conflicts, you should each name the same person. If a guardian is needed, a judge will appoint your nominee as long as he or she agrees that it is in the best interest of your children.

The personal guardian will be responsible for raising your children until they become legal adults. Of course, you should have complete confidence in the person you nominate, and you should be certain that your nominee is willing to accept the responsibility of raising your children should the need actually arise.

## I'm raising a child on my own. Do I have to name the other biological parent as personal guardian, or can I name someone who I think will do a better job of caring for her?

If one parent dies, the other usually takes responsibility for raising the child. But if you and the other parent have parted ways, you may feel strongly that he or she shouldn't have custody if something happens to you. A judge will grant custody to someone else only if the surviving parent:
- has legally abandoned the child by not providing for or visiting the child for an extended period, or
- is clearly unfit as a parent.

In most cases, it is difficult to prove that a parent is unfit, absent serious problems such as chronic drug or alcohol use, mental illness or a history of child abuse.

If you honestly believe the other parent is incapable of caring for your child properly, or simply won't assume the responsibility, you should write a letter explaining why and attach it to your will. The judge will take it into account, and may appoint the person you choose as guardian instead of the other parent.

# How to Leave Property to Young Children

Except for property of little value, the law requires that an adult manage property inherited by children until they turn 18. You can use your will to name someone to manage property inherited by minors, thus avoiding the need for a more complicated court-appointed guardianship. There are many ways to structure a property management arrangement. Here are four of the simplest and most useful:

## Name a custodian under the Uniform Transfers to Minors Act

The Uniform Transfers to Minors Act (UTMA) is a law that has been adopted in almost the same form in every state except South Carolina and Vermont. Under the UTMA, you can choose someone, called a custodian, to manage property you are leaving to a child. If you die when the child is under the age set by your state's law—18 in a few states, 21 in most, 25 in several others— the custodian will step in to manage the property. An UTMA custodianship must end by the age specified by your state's law (18, 21 or up to 25). At that time, your child receives what's left of the trust property outright. If, however, you want to extend property management beyond the age set by your state, you may want to use one of the next three methods.

## Set up a trust for each child

You can use your will to name someone (called a trustee) who will handle any property the child inherits until the child reaches the age you specify. When the child reaches the age you specified, the trustee ends the trust and gives whatever is left of the trust property to the child.

## Set up a pot trust for your children

If you have more than one child, you may want to set up just one trust for all of them. This arrangement is usually called a pot trust. In your will, you establish the trust and appoint a trustee. The trustee doesn't have to spend the same amount on each child; instead, the trustee decides what each child needs, and spends money accordingly. When the youngest child reaches a certain age, usually 18, the trust ends. At that time, any property left in the trust will be distributed as you direct in the trust document.

## Name a property guardian

If you wish, you can simply use your will to name a property guardian for your child. Then, if at your death your child needs the guardian, the court will appoint the person you chose. The property guardian will manage whatever property the child inherits, from you or others, if there's no other mechanism (a trust, for example) to handle it.

## Can I disinherit relatives I don't like?

It depends on whom you want to disinherit. If it's anyone other than your spouse or child, the rule is very simple: Don't mention that person in your will, and he or she won't receive any of your property. Rules for spouses and children are somewhat more complex.

*Spouses.* It is not usually possible to disinherit your spouse completely. If you live in a community property state (Arizona, California, Idaho, Louisiana, Nevada, New Mexico, Texas, Washington or Wisconsin), your spouse automatically owns half of all the property and earnings (with a few exceptions) acquired by either of you during your marriage. You can, however, leave your half of the community property, and your separate property (generally considered to be all property you owned before marriage or received via gift or inheritance during marriage), to anyone you choose.

In all other states, there is no rule that property acquired during marriage is owned by both spouses. To protect spouses from being disinherited, these states give your spouse a legal right to claim a portion of your estate, no matter what your will provides. But keep in mind that these provisions kick in only if your spouse challenges your will. If your will leaves your spouse less than the statutory share and he or she doesn't object, the document will be honored as written.

If you don't plan to leave at least half of your property to your spouse in your will and have not provided for him or her generously outside your will, you should consult a lawyer—unless your spouse willingly consents in writing to your plan.

*Children.* Generally, it's legal to disinherit a child. Some states, however, protect minor children against the loss of a family residence. For example, the Florida Constitution prohibits the head of a family from leaving his residence to anyone other than a spouse if he is survived by a spouse or minor child.

Most states have laws—called "pretermitted heir" statutes—to protect children of any age from being accidentally disinherited. If a child is neither named in your will or specifically disinherited, these laws assume that you accidentally forgot to include that child. In many states, these laws apply only to children born after you made your will, but in a few states they apply to any child not mentioned in your will. The overlooked child has a right to the same share of your estate as he or she would have received if you'd left no will. The share usually depends on whether you leave a spouse and on how many other children you have, but it is likely to be a significant percentage of your property. In some states, these laws apply not only to your children, but also to any of your grandchildren by a child who has died.

To avoid any legal battles after your death, if you decide to disinherit a child, or the child of a deceased child, expressly state this in your will. And if you have a new child after you've made your will, remember to make a new will to include, or specifically disinherit, that child.

## What happens to my will when I die?

After you die, your executor (the person you appointed in your will) is responsible for seeing that your wishes are carried out as directed by your will. He or she may hire an attorney to help wind up your affairs, especially if probate court proceedings are required. Probate and executors are discussed in more detail in the next three sets of questions.

## Make Your Will and Records Accessible

Your executor's first task is to locate your will, and you can help by keeping the original in a fairly obvious place. Here are some suggestions:

• Store your will in an envelope on

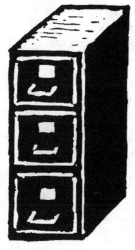

which you have typed your name and the word "Will."
• Place the envelope in a fireproof metal box, file cabinet or home safe. An alternative is to place the original in a safe deposit box. But before doing that, learn the bank's policy about access to the box after your death. If, for instance, the safe deposit box is in your name alone, the box can probably be opened only by a person authorized by a court, and then only in the presence of a bank employee. An inventory may even be required if any person enters the box or for state tax purposes. All of this takes time, and in the meantime, your document will be locked away from those who need access to it.

Finally, wherever you choose to keep your will, make sure your executor (and at least one other person you trust) knows where to find it.

## What if someone challenges my will after I die?

Very few wills are ever challenged in court. When they are, it's usually by a close relative who feels somehow cheated out of his or her rightful share of the deceased person's property.

Generally speaking, only spouses are legally entitled to a share of your property. Your children aren't entitled to anything unless you unintentionally overlooked them in your will. (See *Can I disinherit relatives I don't like?*, above.)

To get an entire will thrown out as invalid, someone must go to court and prove that it suffers from a fatal flaw: the signature was forged, you weren't of sound mind when you made the will or you were unduly influenced by someone.

### More Information About Wills

*Quicken Lawyer Personal Deluxe* (Nolo) (software), lets you create a valid will and many other important estate planning documents.

*The Quick and Legal Will Book*, by Denis Clifford (Nolo), contains forms and instructions for creating a basic will.

*Nolo's Will Book*, by Denis Clifford (Nolo), contains a detailed discussion of wills and all the forms you need to create one.

*Nolo's Law Form Kit: Wills* (Nolo), contains a simple fill-in-the-blanks will.

# Probate

THERE IS ONLY ONE WAY YOU CAN

BEAT A LAWYER IN A DEATH CASE.

THAT IS TO DIE WITH NOTHING.

THEN YOU CAN'T GET A LAWYER

WITHIN TEN MILES OF YOUR HOUSE.

—WILL ROGERS

When a person dies, someone must step in to wind up the deceased person's affairs. Bills must be paid, property must be accounted for and items must be passed on to the people chosen by the deceased person. If state law requires that all this be handled through court proceedings, the process can take many months.

## What is probate?

Probate is a legal process that includes:

- proving in court that a deceased person's will is valid (usually a routine matter)
- identifying and inventorying the deceased person's property
- having the property appraised
- paying debts and taxes, and
- distributing the remaining property as the will directs.

Typically, probate involves paperwork and court appearances by lawyers, who are paid from estate property that would otherwise go to the people who inherit the deceased person's property. Property left by the will cannot be distributed to beneficiaries until the process is complete.

Probate rarely benefits your beneficiaries, and it certainly costs them money and time. Probate makes sense only if your estate will have complicated problems, such as many debts that can't easily be paid from the property you leave.

## Property That Avoids Probate

Not all property has to go through probate. Most states allow a certain amount of property to pass free of probate, or through a simplified probate procedure. In California, for example, you can pass up to $100,000 of property without probate, and there's a simple transfer procedure for any property left to a surviving spouse.

In addition, property that passes outside of your will—say, through joint tenancy or a living trust—is not subject to probate. For a discussion of the most popular probate-avoidance methods, see *Avoiding Probate*, below.

## Who is responsible for handling probate?

In most circumstances, the executor named in the will takes this job. If there isn't any will, or if the will maker fails to name an executor, the probate court names someone (called an administrator) to handle the process—most often the closest capable relative, or the person who inherits the bulk of the deceased person's assets.

If no formal probate proceeding is necessary, the court does not appoint an estate administrator. Instead, a close relative or friend serves as an informal estate representative. Normally, families and friends choose this person, and it is not uncommon for several people to share the responsibilities of paying debts, filing a final income tax return and distributing property to the people who are supposed to get it.

# Executors

An executor is the person you name in your will to handle your property after death. The executor must be prepared to carry out a long list of tasks, prudently and promptly.

## How do I choose an executor?

The most important factor in naming an executor is trust. The person you choose should be honest, with good organizational skills and the ability to keep track of details. If possible, name someone who lives nearby and who is familiar with your financial matters; that will make it easier to do chores like collecting mail and locating important records and papers.

Many people select someone who will inherit a substantial amount of their property. This makes sense, because a person with an interest in how your property is distributed is likely to do a conscientious job of managing your affairs after your death. He or she may also come equipped with knowledge of where your records are kept and an understanding of why you want your property left as you have directed.

Whomever you select, make sure the person is willing to do the job. Discuss the position with the person you've chosen before you make your will.

## Are there restrictions on whom I may choose as my executor?

Your state may impose some restrictions on who can act as executor. You can't name a minor, a convicted felon or someone who is not a U.S. citizen. Most states allow you to name someone who lives in another state, but some require that out-of-state executors be a relative or a primary beneficiary under your will. Some states also require that nonresident executors obtain a bond (an insurance policy that protects your beneficiaries in the event of the executor's wrongful use of your estate's property) or an in-state resident to act as the executor's representative. These complexities underscore the benefits of naming someone who lives nearby. If you feel strongly about naming an executor who lives out of state, be sure to familiarize yourself with your state's rules.

## Is it difficult to serve as executor?

Serving as an executor can be a tedious job, but it doesn't require special financial or legal knowledge. Common sense, conscientiousness and honesty are the main requirements. An executor who needs help can hire lawyers, accountants or other experts and pay them from the assets of the deceased person's estate.

Essentially, the executor's job is to protect the deceased person's property until all debts and taxes have been paid, and see that what's left is transferred to the people who are entitled to it. The law does not require an executor to be a legal or financial expert or to display more than reasonable prudence and judgment, but it does require the highest degree of honesty, impartiality and diligence. This is called a "fiduciary duty"—the duty to

act with scrupulous good faith and candor on behalf of someone else.

## Does the person named in a will as executor have to serve?

No. When it comes time, an executor can accept or decline this responsibility. And someone who agrees to serve can resign at any time. That's why many wills name an alternate executor, who takes over if necessary. If no one is available, the court will appoint someone to step in.

## Does the executor get paid?

Obviously, the main reason for serving as an executor is to honor the deceased person's request. But the executor is also entitled to payment. The exact amount is regulated by state law and is affected by factors such as the value of the deceased person's property and what the probate court decides is reasonable under the circumstances. Commonly, close relatives and close friends (especially those who are inheriting a substantial amount anyway) don't charge the estate for their services.

## Is a lawyer necessary?

Not always. An executor should definitely consider handling the paperwork without a lawyer if he or she is the main beneficiary, the deceased person's property consists of common kinds of assets (house, bank accounts, insurance), the will seems straightforward and good self-help materials are at hand. Essentially, shepherding a case through probate court requires shuffling a lot of papers. In the vast majority of cases, there are no disputes that require a decision by a judge. So the executor may never see the inside of a courtroom, but will certainly become familiar with the court clerk's office. The executor may even be able to do everything by mail. Doing a good job requires persistence and attention to tedious detail, but not necessarily a law degree.

If, however, the estate has many types of property, significant tax liability or potential disputes among inheritors, an executor may want some help.

There are two ways for an executor to get help from a lawyer:

- Hire a lawyer to act as a "coach," answering legal questions as they come up. The lawyer might also do some research, look over documents before the executor files them or prepare an estate tax return.

- Turn the probate over to the lawyer. If the executor just doesn't want to deal with the probate process, a lawyer can do everything. The lawyer will be paid out of the estate. In most states, lawyers charge by the hour ($150–$200 is common) or charge a lump sum. But in a few places, including Arkansas, California, Delaware, Hawaii, Iowa, Missouri, Montana and Wyoming, state law authorizes the lawyer to take a certain percentage of the gross value of the deceased person's estate unless the executor makes a written agreement calling for less. An executor can probably find a competent lawyer who will agree to a lower fee.

## If an executor doesn't want to hire a lawyer, is there any other way to get help?

Lawyers aren't the only source of information and assistance. Here are some others:

- *The court*. Probate court clerks will probably answer basic questions about court procedure, but they staunchly avoid saying anything that could possibly be construed as "legal advice." Some courts, however, have lawyers on staff who look over probate documents; they may point out errors in the papers and explain how to fix them.

- *Other professionals*. For certain tasks, an executor may be better off hiring an accountant or appraiser than a lawyer. For example, a CPA may be a big help on some estate tax matters.

- *Paralegals*. In many law offices, lawyers delegate all the probate paperwork to paralegals (nonlawyers who have training or experience in preparing legal documents). Now, in some areas of the country, experienced paralegals have set up shop to help people directly with probate paperwork. These paralegals don't offer legal advice; they just prepare documents as the executor instructs them, and file them with the court. To find a probate paralegal, an executor can look in the Yellow Pages under "Typing Services," "Legal Document Preparers," or "Attorney Services." The executor should hire someone only if that person has substantial experience in this field and provides references that check out.

## An Executor's Duties

Executors have a number of duties, depending on the complexity of the deceased person's estate. Typically, an executor must:

Decide whether or not probate court proceedings are needed. If the deceased person's property is worth less than a certain amount (it depends on state law), formal probate may not be required.

Figure out who inherits property. If the deceased person left a will, the executor will read it to determine who gets what. If there's no will, the administrator will have to look at state law (called "intestate succession" statutes) to find out who the deceased person's heirs are.

Decide whether or not it's legally permissible to transfer certain items immediately to the people named to inherit them, even if probate is required for other property.

If probate is required, file the will (if any) and all required legal papers in the local probate court.

Find the deceased person's assets and manage them during the probate process, which may take up to a year. This may involve deciding whether to sell real estate or securities owned by the deceased person.

Handle day-to-day details, such as terminating leases and credit cards, and notifying banks and government agencies—such as Social Security, the post office, Medicare and the Department of Veterans Affairs—of the death.

Set up an estate bank account to hold money that is owed to the deceased person—for example, paychecks or stock dividends.

Pay continuing expenses—for example, mortgage payments, utility bills and homeowner's insurance premiums.

Pay debts. As part of this process, the executor must officially notify creditors of the probate proceeding, following the procedure set out by state law.

Pay taxes. A final income tax return must be filed, covering the period from the beginning of the tax year to the date of death. State and federal estate tax returns may also be required, depending on how much property the deceased person owned at death and to whom the property was left.

Supervise the distribution of the deceased person's property to the people or organizations named in the will.

## More Information About Executors and Probate

*The Executor's Handbook,* by Theodore E. Hughes and David Klein (Facts On File), is a general but useful guide to an executor's duties. It's not a how-to book, but it discusses many aspects of the executor's job, including funerals, wills, the probate court process, simplified procedures for small estates and managing assets.

*Social Security, Medicare and Pensions,* by Joseph Matthews (Nolo), explains how to make claims for survivors benefits from the Social Security Administration, Federal Civil Service and the Veterans Administration.

*How to Probate an Estate in California,* by Julia Nissley (Nolo), leads you through the California probate process step by step. It contains tear-out copies of all necessary court forms, and instructions for filling them out. Although the forms are used only in California, the book contains much information that would be valuable background in any state.

# Avoiding Probate

Because probate is time-consuming, expensive and usually unnecessary, many people plan in advance to avoid it. There are a number of ways to pass property to your inheritors without probate. Some of these probate-avoidance methods are quite simple to set up; others take more time and effort.

## Should I plan to avoid probate?

Whether to spend your time and effort planning to avoid probate depends on a number of factors, most notably your age, your health and your wealth. If you're young and in good health, a simple will may be all you need—adopting a complex probate avoidance plan now may mean you'll have to redo it as your life situation changes. And if you have very little property, you might not want to spend your time planning to avoid probate. Your property may even fall under your state's probate exemption; most states have laws that allow a certain amount of property to pass free of probate, or through a simplified probate procedure.

But if you're older (say, over 50), in ill health or own a significant amount of property, you'll probably want to do some planning to avoid probate.

## How to Avoid Probate

No one probate-avoidance method is right for all people. Which methods, if any, you should use depends on your personal and financial situation. Here are some common techniques to consider:

### Pay-on-death designations

Designating a pay-on-death beneficiary is a simple way to avoid probate for bank accounts, government bonds, individual retirement accounts and, in most states, stocks and other securities. In a few states, you can even transfer your car through such an arrangement. All you need to do is name someone to inherit the property at your death. You retain complete control of your property when you are alive, and you can change the beneficiary if you choose. When you die, the property is transferred to the person you named, free of probate.

### Joint tenancy

Joint tenancy is a form of shared ownership where the surviving owner(s) automatically inherits the share of the owner who dies. Joint tenancy is often a good choice for couples who purchase property together and want the survivor to inherit. (Some states also have a very similar type of ownership, called "ten-

ancy by the entirety," just for married couples.) Adding another owner to property you already own, however, can create problems. The new co-owner can sell or borrow against his or her share. Also, there are negative tax consequences of giving appreciated property to a joint tenant shortly before death.

### A living trust

A revocable living trust is a popular probate-avoidance device. You create the trust by preparing and signing a trust document. Once the trust is created, you can hold property in trust, without giving up any control over the trust property. When you die, the trust property can be distributed directly to the beneficiaries you named in the trust document, without the blessing of the probate court. Living trusts are discussed in more detail in the next set of questions.

### Insurance

If you buy life insurance, you can designate a specific beneficiary in your policy. The proceeds of the policy won't go through probate unless you name your own estate as the beneficiary.

### Gifts

Anything you give away during your life doesn't have to go through probate. Making nontaxable gifts (up to $10,000 per recipient per year, or to a tax-exempt entity) can also reduce eventual federal estate taxes. So if you can afford it, a gift-giving program can save on both probate costs and estate taxes.

*More Information
About Avoiding Probate*

*8 Ways to Avoid Probate*, by Mary Randolph (Nolo), explains eight simple and inexpensive methods of sparing your family the hassle and expense of probate after your death.

*Plan Your Estate*, by Denis Clifford and Cora Jordan (Nolo), offers an in-depth discussion of almost all aspects of estate planning, including probate avoidance.

# Living Trusts

If you're considering setting up a living trust to avoid probate, there's no shortage of advice out there—much of it contradictory. Personal finance columnists, lawyers, your Uncle Harry—everybody's got an opinion.

Whether or not a living trust is right for you depends on exactly what you want to accomplish and how much paperwork you're willing to put up with. Living trusts work wonderfully for many people, but not everyone needs one.

## What is a living trust?

A trust is an arrangement under which one person, called the trustee, holds legal title to property on behalf of another. You can be the trustee of your own living trust, keeping full control over all property held in trust.

There are many kinds of trusts. A "living trust" (also called an "inter vivos" trust by lawyers who can't give up Latin) is simply a trust you create while you're alive, rather than one that is created at your death under the terms of your will.

All living trusts are designed to avoid probate. Some also help you save on death taxes, and others let you set up long-term property management.

## Why do I need a living trust?

If you don't take steps to avoid probate, after your death your property will probably have to detour through probate court before it reaches the people you want to inherit it. In a nutshell, probate is the court-supervised process of paying your debts and distributing your property to the people who inherit it. (For more information see *Probate* and *Executors*, above.)

The average probate drags on for months before the inheritors get anything. And by that time, there's less for them to get: In many cases, about 5% of the property has been eaten up by lawyer and court fees. The exact amount depends on state law and the rates of the lawyer hired by the executor.

## Don't Forget Your Will!

Even if you make a living trust, you still need a will. Here's why:

A will is an essential back-up device for property that you don't transfer to your living trust. For example, if you acquire property shortly before you die, you may not think to transfer ownership of it to your trust—which means that it won't pass under the terms of the trust document. But in your back-up will, you can include a clause that names someone to get any property that you don't leave to a particular person or entity.

If you don't have a will, any property that isn't transferred by your living trust or other probate-avoidance device (such as joint tenancy) will go to your closest relatives in an order determined by state law. These laws may not distribute property in the way you would have chosen.

## How does a living trust avoid probate?

Property held in a living trust before your death doesn't go through probate. The successor trustee—the person you appointed to handle the trust after your death—simply transfers ownership to the beneficiaries you named in the trust. In many cases, the whole process takes only a few weeks, and there are no lawyer or court fees to pay. When the property has all been transferred to the beneficiaries, the living trust ceases to exist.

## Is it expensive to create a living trust?

The expense of a living trust comes up front. Lawyers have figured out that they can charge high fees—much higher than for wills, documents usually of comparable complexity—for living trusts. They commonly charge upwards of $1,000 to draw up a simple trust. If you're going to hire a lawyer to draw up your living trust, you might pay as much now as your heirs would have to pay for probate after your death—which means the trust offers no net savings.

But you don't have to pay a lawyer to create a living trust. With a good self-help book or software program, you can create a valid Declaration of Trust (the document that creates a trust) yourself. If you run into questions that a self-help publication doesn't answer, you may need to consult a lawyer, but you probably won't need to turn the whole job over to an expensive expert.

## Isn't it a hassle to own property in a trust?

Making a living trust work for you does require some crucial paperwork. For example, if you want to leave your house through the trust, you must sign a new deed showing that you now own the house as trustee of your living trust. And in a few states, you may need to use special language in your trust document to avoid wrinkles in your state's income tax laws. This paperwork can be tedious, but the hassles are fewer these days because living trusts are becoming quite commonplace.

## Is a trust document ever made public, like a will?

A will becomes a matter of public record when it is submitted to a probate court, as do all the other documents associated with probate—inventories of the deceased person's assets and debts, for example. The terms of a living trust, however, need not be made public.

## Does a trust protect property from creditors?

Holding assets in a revocable trust doesn't shelter them from creditors. A creditor who wins a lawsuit against you can go after the trust property just as if you still owned it in your own name.

After your death, however, property in a living trust can be quickly and quietly distributed to the beneficiaries (unlike property that must go through probate). That complicates matters for creditors; by the time they find out about your death, your property may already be dispersed, and the creditors have no way of knowing exactly what you owned (except for real estate, which is always a matter of public record). It may not be worth the creditor's time and effort to try to track down the property and demand that the new owners use it to pay your debts.

On the other hand, probate can offer a kind of protection from creditors.

During probate, known creditors must be notified of the death and given a chance to file claims. If they miss the deadline to file, they're out of luck forever.

## I'm young and healthy. Do I really need a trust now?

Probably not. At this stage in your life, your main estate planning goals are probably making sure that in the unlikely event of your early death, your property is distributed how you want it to be and, if you have young children, that they are cared for. You don't need a trust to accomplish those ends; writing a will, and perhaps buying some life insurance, would be simpler.

## Can a living trust save on estate taxes?

A simple probate-avoidance living trust has no effect on taxes. More complicated living trusts, however, can greatly reduce your federal estate tax bill. Federal estate taxes are collected only from large estates—so few people need to worry about them. (See *Estate and Gift Taxes*, below.)

One tax-saving living trust is designed primarily for married couples with children. It's commonly called an AB trust, though it goes by many other names. This type of trust can save up to hundreds of thousands of dollars in estate taxes, money that will be passed on to the couple's final inheritors. For more information about how an AB trust works, see the next set of questions, *Estate and Gift Taxes.*

### More Information About Living Trusts

*Quicken Lawyer Personal Deluxe* (Nolo) (software), lets you make a basic probate-avoidance trust or tax-saving AB trust using your computer.

*Make Your Own Living Trust*, by Denis Clifford (Nolo), contains forms and instructions for preparing two kinds of living trusts: a basic probate avoidance trust and a tax-saving AB trust.

*Plan Your Estate*, by Denis Clifford and Cora Jordan (Nolo), is a detailed guide to estate planning, including information about living trusts.

# Estate and Gift Taxes

*In this world nothing can be said to be certain, except death and taxes.*

—BENJAMIN FRANKLIN

It's a universal truth that you can't take it with you. But will your inheritors have to pay for what you leave behind? Most people who consider estate planning are understandably concerned with death taxes (also called estate and inheritance taxes). The good news is that most people's estates won't have to pay any death taxes—federal or state.

## Will my estate have to pay taxes after I die?

Most don't. The federal government imposes estate taxes only if your property is worth more than a certain amount at your death. All property left to a spouse is exempt from the tax, as long as the spouse is a U.S. citizen. And estate taxes won't be assessed on any property you leave to a tax-exempt charity.

Currently, the amount that you can leave that is exempt from estate tax is scheduled to rise steadily until 2010, at which time the estate tax will no longer be imposed at all. But unless Congress extends the estate tax repeal, the tax will pop up again in 2011 (with a $1 million exemption).

### THE ESTATE TAX EXEMPTION

| YEAR | AMOUNT |
|------|--------|
| 2001 | $675,000* |
| 2002, 2003 | $1 million* |
| 2004, 2005 | $1.5 million |
| 2006, 2007, 2008 | $2 million |
| 2009 | $3.5 million |
| 2010 | Estate tax repealed |
| 2011 | $1 million unless Congress extends repeal |

*There is a special $1.3 million exemption for family farms and other businesses that stay in the family; it will become superfluous when the individual exemption hits $1.5 million in 2004.

## Don't some states also impose death taxes?

A handful of states impose death taxes. These taxes are of two types: inheritance taxes and estate taxes.

Inheritance taxes are paid by your inheritors, not your estate. Typically, how much they pay depends on their relationship to you. For example, Nebraska imposes a 15% tax if you leave $25,000 to a friend, but only 1% if you leave the money to your child. But tax rates vary from state to state. If you live in Connecticut, your child wouldn't owe any taxes on a $25,000 inheritance, but your friend would owe 9%.

## States That Impose Inheritance Taxes

| | |
|---|---|
| Connecticut (phased out by 2005) | Michigan |
| | Nebraska |
| Indiana | New Hampshire |
| Iowa | New Jersey |
| Kentucky | Oklahoma |
| Louisiana (phased out by 2004) | Pennsylvania |
| | Tennessee |
| Maryland | |

State estate taxes are similar to the estate tax imposed by the federal government. Your estate must pay this tax no matter who your beneficiaries are. The good news is that every state except Ohio has abolished these taxes,

at least in effect. In the rest, the state takes part of the money that you owe to the feds; it's a matter for accountants and tax preparers, but doesn't increase the tax bill.

You can find a listing of your state's death tax laws in Nolo's *Plan Your Estate*, by Denis Clifford and Cora Jordan.

## What are the rates for federal estate taxes?

The estate tax rate starts at 37%. The maximum rate is 55% for property worth over $3 million. That top rate is 50% in 2002 and will drop to 45% in 2009, the year before the estate tax is repealed.

## Are there ways to avoid federal estate taxes?

Yes, although there are fewer ways than many people think, or hope, there are.

The most popular method is frequently used by married couples with grown children. It's called an **AB trust**, though it's sometimes known as a "credit shelter trust," "exemption trust," "marital life estate trust" or "marital bypass trust." Spouses put their property in the trust, and then, when one spouse dies, his or her half of the property goes to the children—with the crucial condition that the surviving spouse gets the right to use it for life and is entitled to any income it generates. When the second spouse dies, the property goes to the children outright. Using this kind of trust keeps the second spouse's taxable estate half the size it would be if the property were left entirely to the spouse, which means that estate taxes may be avoided altogether.

Unlike a probate-avoidance revocable living trust, an AB trust controls what happens to property for years after the first spouse's death. A couple who makes one must be sure that the surviving spouse will be financially and emotionally comfortable receiving only the income from the money or property placed in trust, with the children as the actual owners of the property.

## How an AB Trust Works: An Example

Ellen and Jack have been married for nearly 50 years. They have one grown son, Robert, who is 39. Ellen and Jack create an AB trust and transfer all their major items of property to it. They name each other as life beneficiaries, and Robert as the final beneficiary.

Ellen dies first. The trust splits into two parts: Trust A, which is irrevocable, contains Ellen's share of the property. Trust B is Jack's trust, and it stays revocable as long as he is alive.

The property in Trust A legally belongs to Robert, but with one very important condition: His father, Jack, is entitled to use the property, and collect any income

it generates, for the rest of his life. When Jack dies, the property will go to Robert free and clear.

Now let's take a look at the tax savings: Ellen's half of the trust property is worth $600,000 when she dies.

*At Ellen's death*

Taxable estate .................. $600,000

Estate tax ...................................... $0

*(because of the personal exemption)*

*At Jack's death*

Taxable estate .................. $600,000

Estate tax ...................................... $0

If Ellen had left all her property to Jack outright, his estate would have been worth $1.2 million at his death—which would have resulted in thousands of dollars of estate tax if they died before 2004.

## Are there other ways to save on estate taxes?

Yes. Common ones include what's called a "QTIP" trust, which enables a surviving spouse to postpone estate taxes that would otherwise be due when the other spouse dies. And there are many different types of charitable trusts, which involve making a sizable gift to a tax-exempt charity. Some of them provide both income tax and estate tax advantages.

## Can I avoid paying state death taxes?

If your state imposes death taxes, there probably isn't much you can do. But if you live in two states—winter here, summer there—your inheritors may save on death taxes if you can make your legal residence in the state with lower, or no, death taxes.

## Can't I just give all my property away before I die and avoid estate taxes?

No. The government long anticipated this one. If you give away more than $10,000 per year to any one person or noncharitable institution, you are assessed federal "gift tax," which applies at the same rate as the estate tax. There are, however, a few exceptions to this rule. You can give an unlimited amount of property to your spouse, unless your spouse is not a U.S. citizen, in which case you can give away up to $101,000 per year free of gift tax. Any property given to a tax-exempt charity avoids federal gift taxes. And money spent directly for someone's medical bills or school tuition is exempt as well.

The federal gift tax will not be repealed in 2010 with the estate tax. Instead, it will survive, but with a $1 million exemption. In other words, you'll still be able to give away $1 million in taxable gifts (and most ordinary gifts aren't taxable) without owing any tax.

## But I've heard that people save on estate taxes by making gifts. How?

You can achieve substantial estate tax savings by making use of the $10,000 annual gift tax exclusion for gifts to people and nonexempt organizations. If you give away $10,000 for four years, you've removed $40,000 from your taxable estate. And each member of a couple has a separate $10,000 exclusion. So a couple can give $20,000 a year to a child free of gift tax. If you have a few children, or other people you want to make gifts to (such as your sons- or daughters-in-law), you can use this method to significantly reduce the size of your taxable estate over a few years.

Consider a couple with combined assets worth $1.2 million and three children. Each year they give each child $20,000 tax free, for a total of $60,000 per year. In seven years, the couple has given away $420,000 and has reduced their estate to $600,000, far below the federal estate tax threshold.

Of course, there are risks with this kind of gift-giving program. The most obvious is that you are legally transferring your wealth. Gift giving to reduce eventual estate taxes must be carefully evaluated to see if you can comfortably afford to give away your property during your lifetime.

### *More Information About Estate and Gift Taxes*

*9 Ways to Avoid Estate Taxes*, by Mary Randolph and Denis Clifford (Nolo), presents the major methods you can use to avoid or reduce federal estate taxes.

*Plan Your Estate*, by Denis Clifford and Cora Jordan (Nolo), is a detailed guide to estate planning, including all major methods of reducing or avoiding estate and gift taxes.

# Funeral Planning and Other Final Arrangements

Many of us are squeamish when it comes to thinking and talking about death, particularly our own. But there are many good reasons to spend some time considering what you want to have happen to your body after death, including any ceremonies and observances you'd like.

## Why should I leave written instructions about my final ceremonies and the disposition of my body?

Letting your survivors know your wishes saves them the difficulties of making these decisions at a painful time. And many family members and friends find that discussing these matters ahead of time is great relief—especially if a person is elderly or in poor health and death is expected soon.

Planning some of these details in advance can also help save money. For many people, death goods and services cost more than anything they bought during their lives except homes and cars. Some wise comparison shopping in advance can help ensure that costs will be controlled or kept to a minimum.

## Why not leave these instructions in my will?

A will is not a good place to express your death and burial preferences for one simple reason: Your will probably won't be located and read until several weeks after you die—long after decisions must be made.

A will should be reserved for directions on how to divide and distribute your property and, if applicable, who should get care and custody of your children if you die while they're still young.

## What happens if I don't leave written instructions?

If you die without leaving written instructions about your preferences, state law will determine who will have the right to decide how your remains will be handled. In most states, the right—and the responsibility to pay for the reasonable costs of disposing of remains—rests with the following people, in order:

- spouse
- child or children
- parent or parents
- the next of kin, or
- a public administrator, who is appointed by a court.

Disputes may arise if two or more people—the deceased person's children, for example—share responsibility for a fundamental decision, such as whether the body of a parent should be buried or cremated. But such disputes can be avoided if you are willing to do some planning and to put your wishes in writing.

## What details should I include in a final arrangements document?

What you choose to include is a personal matter, likely to be dictated by custom, religious preference or simply your own whims. A typical final arrangements document might include:

- the name of the mortuary or other institution that will handle burial or cremation
- whether or not you wish to be embalmed
- the type of casket or container in which your remains will be buried or cremated, including whether you want it present at any after-death ceremony
- the details of any ceremony you want before the burial or cremation
- who your pallbearers will be if you wish to have some
- how your remains will be transported to the cemetery and gravesite
- where your remains will be buried, stored or scattered
- the details of any ceremony you want to accompany your burial, interment or scattering, and
- the details of any marker you want to show where your remains are buried or interred.

## What services can I expect from a mortuary?

Most mortuaries or funeral homes are equipped to handle many of the details related to disposing of a person's remains. These include:

- collecting the body from the place of death
- storing the body until it is buried or cremated

- making burial arrangements with a cemetery
- conducting ceremonies related to the burial
- preparing the body for burial, and
- arranging to have the body transported for burial.

## Where can I turn for help in making final arrangements?

From an economic standpoint, choosing the institution to handle your burial is probably the most important final arrangement that you can make. For this reason, many people join memorial or funeral societies, which help them find local mortuaries that will deal honestly with their survivors and charge reasonable prices.

Society members are free to choose whatever final arrangements they wish. Most societies, however, emphasize simple arrangements over the costly services often promoted by the funeral industry. The services offered by each society differ, but most societies distribute information on options and explain the legal rules that apply to final arrangements.

If you join a society, you will receive a form that allows you to plan for the goods and services you want—and to get them for a predetermined cost. Many societies also serve as watchdogs, making sure that you get and pay for only the services you choose.

The cost for joining these organizations is low—usually from $20 to $40 for a lifetime membership, although some societies periodically charge a small renewal fee.

To find a funeral or memorial society near you, look in the YellowPages of your telephone book under Funeral Information and Advisory Services, or contact the Funeral and Memorial Societies of America, 800-458-5563, or http://www.funerals.org/famsa.

If you don't want to join a society, you can look for a mortuary or funeral home on your own. You'll have to shop around to find the institution that best meets your needs in terms of style, proximity and cost.

## Beware of Prepayment Plans

Shopping around for the most suitable and affordable funeral goods and services is a wise idea. Be extremely cautious, however, about paying in advance—often called prepaying—for them.

Although there are a number of legal controls on how the funeral industry can handle and invest funds earmarked for future services, there are many reported instances of mismanaged or stolen funds. A great many other abuses go unreported by family members too embarrassed or too grief-stricken to complain.

There are additional pitfalls. When mortuaries go out of business, the consumer who has prepaid is often left without funds and without recourse. Also, many individuals who move to a new locale during their lifetimes are dismayed to find that their prepayment funds are nonrefundable or that there is a substan-

tial financial penalty for withdrawing or transferring them. In addition, money paid now may not cover inflated costs of the future, meaning that survivors will be left to cover the substantially higher costs.

If you are interested in setting aside a fund of money to pay for your final arrangements, a more prudent approach for most people is to set up a trust or savings account earmarked to pay for your final arrangements. Most banks and savings institutions will do so for a very slight charge. You can easily withdraw or transfer the funds during your life, if need be. At your death, the trusted individual or institution you name in the bank documents can take over and spend the money as you have directed.

### More Information About Final Arrangements

Funeral and Memorial Societies of America—Funeral Consumers Alliance can help you locate a funeral or memorial society near you. Call 800-458-5563 or reach FAMSA-FCA online at http://www.funerals.org/famsa.

*Quicken Lawyer Personal Deluxe* (Nolo) (software) lets you use your computer to create a final arrangements document, in addition to a valid will, living trust, healthcare directives, a durable power of attorney for finances, and other documents.

# Body and Organ Donations

In addition to making other arrangements for your funeral and burial or cremation, you may want to arrange to donate some or all of your body organs. You must make these arrangements separately and document your wishes on a special form.

## How can I arrange to donate my body for scientific research or study after my death?

Arrangements for whole body donations must usually be made while you are alive, although some medical schools will accept a cadaver through arrangements made after death.

The best place to contact to arrange a whole body donation is the nearest medical school. If you live in a state with no medical school or one that has very strict requirements for whole body donations, you may wish to find out more about your body donation options from the National Anatomical Service at 800-727-0700.

## How can I arrange to donate my body organs for others to use after my death?

The principal method for donating organs is by indicating your intent to do so on a uniform donor card. Once signed, this card identifies you to medical personnel as a potential organ donor. You can get a donor card or form from most hospitals, the county or state office of the National Kidney Foundation or a community eye bank.

In most states, you can also obtain an organ donation card from the department of motor vehicles. Depending on where you live, you can check a box, affix a stamp or seal or attach a separate card to your license, indicating your wish to donate one or more organs.

Even if you have not signed a card or other document indicating your intent to donate your organs, your next of kin can approve a donation after you die. If you fill out an organ donor card, make sure you tell family members you have done so. Even if you have indicated an intent to donate your organs, an objection by your next of kin will often defeat your intention; medical personnel usually do not proceed in the face of an objection from relatives. The best safeguard is to discuss your wishes with close friends and relatives, emphasizing your strong feelings about donating your body for research or teaching.

### http://www.nolo.com

*Nolo offers extensive self-help information about wills and estate planning.*

### http:// www.estateplanninglinks.com

*This site contains a very thorough list of websites that cover almost every imaginable estate planning issue.*

# **H**ealthcare Directives and Powers of Attorney

13.2     *Healthcare Directives*

13.7     *Durable Powers of Attorney for Finances*

13.10    *Conservatorships*

*There is no mortal whom sorrow and disease do not touch.*

**—EURIPIDES**

**M**any of us fear that we may someday become seriously ill and unable to handle our own affairs. Who would act on our behalf to pay bills, make bank deposits, watch over investments and deal with the paperwork that accompanies collecting insurance and government benefits? Who would make arrangements for our medical care and see that our wishes for treatment are carried out?

Preparing a few simple documents—healthcare directives and a durable power of attorney for finances—can ease these worries by ensuring that your affairs will stay in the hands of the trusted people you choose. This chapter answers your questions about these documents and how they work, as well as what happens if a court appoints a conservator—that is, the person who will manage your affairs if you haven't drafted legally valid instructions naming someone to take over.

# Healthcare Directives

Nearly 80% of Americans die in a hospital or other care facility. The doctors who work in these facilities are generally charged with preserving a patient's life through whatever means are available. This may or may not be what you would like in the way of treatment. Healthcare directives give you the opportunity to write out your wishes in advance and ensure some legal respect for them if ever you are unable to speak for yourself.

## What is a healthcare directive?

A healthcare directive is a straightforward legal document that sets out your wishes about what medical treatment should be withheld or provided if you become unable to communicate those wishes. Depending upon the state, your healthcare directive may go by one of several different names: Medical Directive, Directive to Physicians, Declaration Regarding Healthcare, Designation of Healthcare Surrogate or Patient Advocate Designation. A healthcare directive may also be called

a "living will," but it bears no relation to the conventional will or living trust used to leave property at death.

The directive creates a contract with the attending doctor. Once the doctor receives a properly signed and witnessed directive, she is under a duty either to honor its instructions or to make sure you are transferred to the care of another doctor who will.

Many people mistakenly believe that healthcare directives are used only to instruct doctors to withhold life-prolonging treatments. In fact, some people want to reinforce that they would like to receive all medical treatment that is available—and a healthcare directive is the proper place to say so.

## What is a durable power of attorney for healthcare? Doesn't that do the same thing as a healthcare directive?

A durable power of attorney for healthcare—called a healthcare proxy in some states—gives another person authority to make medical decisions for you if you are unable to make them for yourself. Unlike a healthcare directive, this document doesn't necessarily state what type of treatment you want to receive. You can leave those decisions to your proxy if you feel comfortable doing so. Depending on the requirements imposed by your state law, you may need to make one or two documents to express your wishes for medical care. For example, your healthcare directive may contain a clause appointing a proxy (sometimes called an attorney-in-fact, agent or representative) to be certain your wishes are carried out as you've directed. Or you may create two separate documents: a directive explaining the treatment you wish to receive, and a durable power of attorney appointing someone to oversee your directive.

If you don't know anyone you trust enough to name as your healthcare proxy, it is still important to complete and finalize a healthcare directive recording your wishes. That way, your doctors will still be obligated to give you the medical care you want.

## What happens if I don't have any healthcare documents?

If you have not completed a healthcare directive to express your wishes or a durable power of attorney to appoint someone to make healthcare decisions on your behalf, the doctors who attend you will use their own discretion in deciding what kind of medical care you will receive.

When a question arises about whether surgery or some other serious procedure is authorized, doctors may turn for consent to a close relative—spouse, parent or adult child. Friends and unmarried partners, although they may be most familiar with your wishes for your medical treatment, are rarely consulted, or are purposefully left out of the decision-making process.

Problems arise when partners and family members disagree about what treatment is proper. In the most complicated scenarios, these battles over medical care wind up in court, where a judge, who usually has little medical knowledge and no familiarity with you, is called upon to decide the future of your treatment. Such legal battles—

which are costly, time consuming and usually painful to those involved—are unnecessary if you have the foresight to use a formal document to express your wishes for your healthcare.

## When Your Healthcare Directive Takes Effect

Your healthcare directive becomes effective when three things happen:
- you are diagnosed as close to death from a terminal condition or permanently comatose—or, in a few states, if you have a number of other serious conditions
- you cannot communicate your own wishes for your medical care—orally, in writing or through gestures, and
- the medical personnel attending you are notified of your written directions for your medical care.

In most instances, your directive becomes part of your medical record when you are admitted to a hospital or other care facility. But to ensure that your wishes will be followed if your need for care arises unexpectedly or while you are out of your home state or country, it is best to give copies of your completed documents to several people, including your regular physician, your healthcare proxy and another trusted friend.

## Whom should I choose as a healthcare proxy?

The person you name as your healthcare proxy should be someone you trust—and someone with whom you feel confident discussing your wishes. While your proxy need not agree with your wishes for your medical care, you should believe that he respects your right to get the kind of medical care you want.

The person you appoint to oversee your healthcare wishes could be a spouse or partner, relative or close friend. Keep in mind that your proxy may have to fight to assert your wishes in the face of a stubborn medical establishment—and against the wishes of family members who may be driven by their own beliefs and interests, rather than yours. If you foresee the possibility of a conflict in enforcing your wishes, be sure to choose a proxy who is strong willed and assertive.

While you need not name someone who lives in the same state as you do, proximity may be an important factor. The reality is that the person you name may be called upon to spend weeks or months near your bedside, making sure medical personnel abide by your wishes for your healthcare. If you name someone who lives far away, make sure that person is willing to travel and stay with you a while. The job of proxy may demand it.

You should not choose your doctor or an employee of a hospital or nursing home where you receive treatment. In fact, the laws in many states prevent you from naming such a person. In a

few instances, this legal constraint may frustrate your wishes. For example, you may wish to name your spouse or partner as your representative, but if he or she works as a hospital employee, that alone may bar you from naming that person. If the law in your state bans your first choice, you will have to name another person to serve.

## What if I really don't know anyone I trust to supervise my medical care?

Naming a healthcare proxy is an optional part of completing your healthcare directive. It is better not to name anyone than to name someone who is not comfortable with the directions you leave—or who is not likely to assert your wishes strongly.

Medical personnel are still technically bound to follow your written wishes for your healthcare—or to find someone who will care for you in the way you have directed. It is far better to put your wishes for final healthcare in writing than to let the lack of a representative stand in the way.

## What types of medical care should I consider when completing my healthcare documents?

Technological advances mean that currently unfathomable procedures and treatments will become available, and treatments that are now common will become obsolete. Also, the treatments that are available vary drastically with region, depending on the sophistication and funding levels of local medical facilities.

While putting together your healthcare directive, the best that you can do is to become familiar with the kinds of medical procedures that are most commonly administered to patients who are seriously ill. These include:

- blood and blood products
- cardiopulmonary resuscitation (CPR)
- diagnostic tests
- dialysis
- drugs
- respirators, and
- surgery.

## Can I provide instructions in my healthcare documents about pain medication, or about food and water?

The laws of most states assume that people want relief from pain and discomfort and specifically exclude pain-relieving procedures from definitions of life-prolonging treatments that may be withheld. Some states also exclude food and water (commonly called nutrition and hydration) from their definitions of life-prolonging treatments.

But there is some controversy about whether providing food and water, or drugs to make a person comfortable, will also have the effect of prolonging life. Some people are so adamant about not having their lives prolonged when they are comatose or likely to die soon that they choose to direct that all food, water and pain relief be withheld, even if the doctor thinks those procedures are necessary. Under the U.S. Constitution, you are allowed to leave these instructions even if your state's law is restrictive; your doctors are legally bound to follow your wishes.

On the other hand, some people feel concerned about how much pain or discomfort they may experience during a final illness; these people are willing to have their lives prolonged rather than face the possibility that discomfort or pain would go untreated. Obviously, it's a very personal choice; you're free to leave the instructions that feel right for you.

## Where can I get a healthcare directive—and who can help complete it?

Many people first realize the need for healthcare documents when they're being admitted to a hospital. But hospital admission time is probably not the best time to learn about your options in directing healthcare or to reflect on your wishes. It's better to get information and complete your documents when you're under less stress.

Local senior centers may be good resources for help. Many of them have trained healthcare staff on hand who will be willing to discuss your health-care options. The patient representa-tive at a local hospital may also be a good person to contact for help. And if you have a regular physician, you can discuss your concerns with him or her.

Local special interest groups and clinics may provide help in obtaining and filling out healthcare directives—particularly organizations set up to meet the needs of the severely ill, such as AIDS groups or cancer organiza-tions. Check your telephone book for a local listing—or call one of the group's hotlines for more information or a possible referral.

There are also a number of seminars offered to help people with their healthcare documents. Beware of groups that offer such seminars for a hefty fee, however. Hospitals and se-nior centers often provide them free of charge.

### More Information About Healthcare Directives

*Quicken Lawyer Personal Deluxe* (Nolo) (software) walks you step by step through the process of writing your own healthcare directives, in addition to your will, durable power of attorney for finances and a document setting out your final arrangements.

## Make Your Documents Legal

There are a few requirements you must meet to make a valid healthcare directive. In most states, you must be 18 years old, though a few states allow parents to make healthcare directives for their minor children. All states require that the person making a healthcare directive be able to understand what the document means, what it contains and how it works.

Also, every state requires that you sign your documents. If you are physically unable to sign them yourself, you can direct another person to sign them for you.

You must sign your documents, or have them signed for you, in the presence of witnesses or a notary public—sometimes both, depending on your state's law. The purpose of this additional formality is so that there is at least one other person who can con-firm that you were of sound mind and of legal age when you made the documents.

# Durable Powers of Attorney for Finances

A durable power of attorney for finances is a simple, inexpensive and reliable way to arrange for someone to make your financial decisions should you become unable to do so yourself. It's also a wonderful thing to do for your family members. If you do become incapacitated, the durable power of attorney will likely appear as a minor miracle to those close to you.

## How does a durable power of attorney work?

When you create and sign a power of attorney, you give another person legal authority to act on your behalf. This person is called your attorney-in-fact or, sometimes, your agent. The word attorney here means anyone authorized to act on another's behalf; it's most definitely not restricted to lawyers.

A "durable" power of attorney stays valid even if you become unable to handle your own affairs (incapacitated). If you don't specify that you want your power of attorney to be durable, it will automatically end if you later become incapacitated.

## When does a durable power of attorney take effect?

A durable power of attorney can be drafted so that it goes into effect as soon as you sign it. That is appropriate if you face a serious operation or incapacitating illness—or even if you're not incapacitated but want your attorney-in-fact to start helping with financial tasks right away.

You can also specify that the durable power of attorney does not go into effect unless a doctor certifies that you have become incapacitated. This is called a "springing" durable power of attorney. It allows you to keep control over your financial matters unless and until you become incapacitated, when it springs into effect.

## How do I create a durable power of attorney for finances?

To create a legally valid durable power of attorney, all you need to do is properly complete and sign a fill-in-the-blanks form that's a few pages long. Some states have their own forms.

After you fill out the form, you must sign it in front of a notary public. In some states, witnesses must also watch you sign the document. If your attorney-in-fact will have authority to deal with your real estate, you must put a copy on file at the local land records office. (In just two states, North and South Carolina, you must record your power of attorney for it to be durable.)

Some banks, title companies, insurance companies, brokerage companies and other financial institutions have their own durable power of attorney forms. If you want your attorney-in-fact to have an easy time with these institutions, you may need to prepare two (or more) durable powers of attorney: your own form and forms provided by the institutions with which you do business.

## What happens if I don't have a durable power of attorney for finances?

If you become incapacitated and you haven't prepared a durable power of attorney for finances, a court proceeding is probably inescapable. Your spouse, closest relatives or companion will have to ask a court for authority over at least some of your financial affairs.

If you are married, your spouse does have some authority over property you own together—to pay bills from a joint bank account, for example. There are significant limits, however, on your spouse's right to sell property owned by both of you.

If your relatives go to court to get someone appointed to manage your financial affairs, they must ask a judge to rule that you cannot take care of your own affairs—a public airing of a very private matter. And like any court proceeding, it can be expensive if your relatives must hire a lawyer. Depending on where you live, the person appointed is called a conservator, guardian of the estate, committee or curator. When this person is appointed, you lose the right to control your own money and property.

The appointment of a conservator is usually just the beginning of court proceedings. Often the conservator must:

- post a bond—a kind of insurance policy that pays if the conservator steals or misuses property
- prepare (or hire a lawyer or accountant to prepare) detailed financial reports and periodically file them with the court, and
- get court approval for certain transactions, such as selling real estate or making slightly risky investments.

A conservatorship isn't necessarily permanent, but it may be ended only by the court. Conservatorships are discussed in more detail in the next set of questions.

## The Attorney-in-Fact's Duties

Commonly, people give an attorney-in-fact broad power over their finances. But you can give your attorney-in-fact as much or as little power as you wish. You may want to give your attorney-in-fact authority to do some or all of the following:

- use your assets to pay your everyday

expenses and those of your family

- buy, sell, maintain, pay taxes on and mortgage real estate and other property
- collect benefits from Social Security, Medicare or other government programs or civil or military service
- invest your money in stocks, bonds and mutual funds
- handle transactions with banks and other financial institutions
- buy and sell insurance policies and annuities for you
- file and pay your taxes
- operate your small business
- claim property you inherit or are otherwise entitled to
- represent you in court or hire someone to represent you, and
- manage your retirement accounts.

Whatever powers you give the attorney-in-fact, the attorney-in-fact must act in your best interests, keep accurate records, keep your property separate from his or hers and avoid conflicts of interest.

## I have a living trust. Do I still need a durable power of attorney for finances?

A revocable living trust can be useful if you become incapable of taking care of your financial affairs. That's because the person who will distribute trust property after your death (the successor trustee) can also, in most cases, take over management of the trust property if you become incapacitated.

Few people, however, transfer all their property to a living trust, and the successor trustee has no authority over property that the trust doesn't own. So a living trust isn't a complete substitute for a durable power of attorney for finances.

## Can my attorney-in-fact make medical decisions on my behalf?

No. A durable power of attorney for finances does not give your attorney-in-fact legal authority to make medical decisions for you.

You can, however, prepare a durable power of attorney for healthcare, a document that lets you choose someone to make medical decisions on your behalf if you can't. In most states, you'll also want to write out your wishes in a "living will" (also called a healthcare directive or directive to physicians), which will tell your doctors your preferences about certain kinds of medical treatment and life-sustaining procedures if you can't communicate your wishes.

Healthcare documents are discussed in more detail in the previous section of this chapter.

## When does the durable power of attorney end?

It ends at your death. That means that you can't give your attorney-in-fact authority to handle things after your death, such as paying your debts, making funeral or burial arrangements or transferring your property to the people who inherit it. If you want your attorney-in-fact to have authority to wind up your affairs after your death, use a will to name that person as your executor.

Your durable power of attorney also ends if:

- You revoke it. As long as you are mentally competent, you can revoke a durable power of attorney at any time.
- A court invalidates your document. This happens rarely, but a court may declare your document invalid if it concludes that you were not mentally competent when you signed it, or that you were the victim of fraud or undue influence.
- You get a divorce. In a handful of states, including Alabama, California, Colorado, Illinois, Indiana, Minnesota, Missouri, Pennsylvania, Texas and Wisconsin, if your spouse is your attorney-in-fact and you divorce, your ex-spouse's authority is automatically terminated. In any state, however, it is wise to revoke your durable power of attorney after a divorce and make a new one.
- No attorney-in-fact is available. A durable power of attorney must end if there's no one to serve as attorney-in-fact. To avoid this problem, you can name an alternate attorneys-in-fact in your document.

*More Information About Durable Powers of Attorney for Finances*

*Quicken Lawyer Personal Deluxe* (Nolo) (software) walks you step by step through the process of writing your own will, durable power of attorney for finances, healthcare documents and a document setting out your final arrangements.

# Conservatorships

A conservatorship is a legal arrangement in which an adult has the court-ordered authority and responsibility to manage another adult's financial affairs. Many states use the terms "conservator" and "guardian" interchangeably, or use other terms such as "custodian" or "curator." In this book, we use the term "guardian" for a person who makes personal decisions for a child, and "conservator" for someone who takes care of financial matters for an incapacitated adult. The adult who needs help is called the "conservatee."

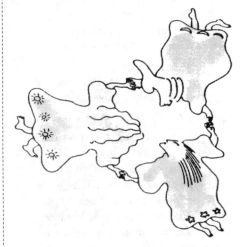

If you need information about guardianships for children, see Chapter 16, *Parents and Children*.

## When is a conservatorship necessary?

A conservatorship is permitted only when someone is so incapacitated that he cannot manage his own financial affairs. Generally, conservatorships are established for people who are in comas, suffer from advanced stages of Alzheimer's disease or have other serious illnesses or injuries.

Conservatorships are rarely needed for people who have made—or can knowingly sign—financial documents, such as a durable power of attorney for finances. (See the previous set of questions.)

## What are the advantages of a conservatorship?

Conservatorships are subject to court supervision, which provides a powerful safeguard for an incapacitated adult's property. To prevent a conservator from mismanaging the property of the person she is helping (the conservatee), most courts require the conservator to provide periodic reports and accountings that give details about the conservatee's assets and how the conservatee's money was spent. Many courts also require the conservator to seek permission before making major decisions about the conservatee's property, such as whether to sell real estate.

## What are the downsides to a conservatorship?

Conservatorships are time consuming and expensive; they often require court hearings and the ongoing assistance of a lawyer. The paperwork can also be a hassle because, as mentioned above, the conservator must keep detailed records and file court papers on a regular basis.

In addition, a conservator must usually post a bond (a kind of insurance policy that protects the conservatee's estate from mishandling). The bond premiums are paid by the conservatee's estate—and are an unnecessary expense if the conservator is competent and trustworthy.

Occasionally, however, a conservator will mismanage a conservatee's assets. Common abuses range from reckless handling of the conservatee's assets to outright theft. Although each state has rules and procedures designed to prevent mishandling of assets, few have the resources to keep an eye on conservators and follow through if they spot trouble. Many cases of incompetence or abuse go unnoticed.

Finally, a conservatorship can be emotionally trying for the conservatee. All court proceedings and documents are public records, which can be embarrassing for someone who values independence and privacy.

## How are conservators compensated for their services?

The conservatee's estate must reimburse the conservator for necessary expenses and must usually pay for the conservator's services—if these payments are "reasonable" in the eyes of a court. Generally, payments are made to professional or public conservators, but a family member who has been appointed conservator may also seek compensation by making a request to the court.

## Are there ways to block a conservatorship?

Before a court approves a conservatorship, notice must be given to the proposed conservatee and his close family members. Anyone—including the proposed conservatee, family members and friends—may object to the conservatorship in general, or to the specific choice of conservator. The person who wants to block the conservatorship must file papers with the court, inform all interested parties (the proposed conservatee, family members and possibly close friends) and attend a legal hearing. The final decision is up to a judge.

The best way to avoid a conservatorship is to prepare a durable power of attorney for finances before a health crisis occurs. That way, someone you've hand-picked will be able to step in and make decisions for you if necessary. (For information about preparing a durable power of attorney, see the previous set of questions.)

## How does a judge choose a conservator?

When a conservatorship petition is filed in court, a judge must decide whom to appoint. Often, just one person is interested in taking on the role of conservator—but sometimes several family members or friends vie for the position. If no one suitable is available to serve as conservator, the judge may appoint a public or other professional conservator.

When appointing a conservator, a judge follows certain preferences established by state law. Most states give preference to the conservatee's spouse, adult children, adult siblings or other blood relatives. But a judge has some flexibility; he may use his discretion to pick the person he thinks is best for the job. Without strong evidence of what the conservatee would have wanted, however, it is unlikely that a nonrelative would be appointed over a relative. Because of this, conservatorship proceedings may cause great heartache if an estranged relative is chosen as conservator over the conservatee's partner or close friend.

## Who financially supports the conservatee?

If the conservatee has the means, money for his support will come from his own assets. But a conservator should seek all financial benefits and coverage for which the conservatee may qualify. These benefits may include Social Security, medical insurance, Veterans Administration benefits, pension and retirement benefits, disability benefits, public assistance and Supplemental Security Income. When needed, close family members (including the conservator) often contribute their own money to help support a conservatee.

## When does a conservatorship end?

A conservator must care for the conservatee's finances until the court issues an order relieving her from responsibility. This ordinarily happens when:

- the conservatee dies
- the conservatorship estate is used up
- the conservatee regains the ability to handle her own finances, or
- the conservator becomes unable or unwilling to handle the responsibilities. In this situation, the conservatorship itself does not end, but someone else takes over the conservator's duties.

### *More Information About Conservatorships*

*The Conservatorship Book*, by Lisa Goldoftas & Carolyn Farren (Nolo), contains forms and instructions for getting a conservator appointed in California, without a lawyer. For information about conservatorships in other states, visit your local law library.

### http://www.nolo.com

*Nolo offers self-help information on a wide variety of legal topics, including healthcare directives, powers of attorney and conservatorships.*

### http://www.choices.org

*Choice In Dying offers information and publications about healthcare directives, as well as state-specific forms that you can download for free.*

*Many sites offer state-specific information about durable powers of attorney for finances and conservatorships. If you need more information about your state's laws, you can use an online search engine to hunt for a site that will help you. See the Legal Research Appendix for more information on how to do this.*

# Older Americans

14.2    *Social Security*

14.8    *Medicare*

14.13   *Pensions*

14.20   *Retirement Plans*

*To be seventy years young is some-times far more cheerful and hopeful than to be forty years old.*

**—OLIVER WENDELL HOLMES, JR.**

**F**or many older Americans, the final years are no longer the Golden Years. Worries over limited incomes—and the real threat of being financially ruined by any extended bout with the medical system—crowd out thoughts of leisure and fulfillment.

There is help available for supplementing limited incomes and covering medical care in your later years, but you have to take some initiative to find it. It also helps if you have the good fortune and foresight to do some early planning.

# Social Security

Social Security is the general term that describes a number of related programs —retirement, disability, dependents and survivors benefits. These programs together provide workers and their families with some money when their normal flow of income shrinks because of retirement, disability or death.

Unfortunately, the government's original goal of providing financial security through these programs is becoming increasingly remote. The combination of rapidly rising living costs, stagnating benefit amounts and penalties for older people who continue to work make the amount of support offered by Social Security less adequate with each passing year. This shrinking of the Social Security safety net makes it that much more important that you know how to get the maximum benefits to which you are entitled.

## How much can I expect to get in Social Security benefits?

There is no easy answer to this question. The amount of benefits to which you are entitled under any Social Security program is not related to need, but is based on the income you have earned through years of working. In most jobs, both you and your employer have paid Social Security taxes on the amounts you earned. Since 1951, Social Security taxes have also been paid on reported self-employment income. Social Security keeps a record of these earnings over your working lifetime, and pays benefits based upon the average amount earned.

## Who is eligible to collect benefits?

The specific requirements vary depending on the type of benefits, the age of the person filing the claim and, if you are claiming as a dependent or survivor, the age of the worker. There is a general requirement, however, that everyone must meet to receive one of these Social Security benefits: The worker on whose earnings record the benefit is to be paid must have worked in "covered employment" for a sufficient number of years —that is, earned what Social Security calls work credits—by the time he or she claims retirement benefits, becomes disabled or dies. To find out about your eligibility, call the Social Security Administration, 800-772-1213, or visit the Seocial Security website at http:// www.ssa.gov.

Note that Social Security eligibility rules have recently changed for some specific types of workers, including federal, state and local government workers; workers for nonprofit organizations; members of the military; household workers; and farm workers. If you have been employed for some time as one of these types of workers, check with the Social Security Administration for special rules that may affect your eligibility.

## Social Security Benefits: A Guide to the Basics

Four basic categories of Social Security benefits are paid based upon the record of your earnings: retirement, disability, dependents and survivors benefits.

**Retirement benefits.** You may choose to begin receiving retirement benefits at any time after you reach age 62; the amount of benefits will increase for each year you wait until age 70. The increase in delayed benefits varies from 2% to 8%, depending on the year in which you were born. But no matter how long you wait to begin collecting benefits, the amount you receive will probably be only a small percentage of what you were earning.

Because so many variables are thrown into the mix in computing benefit amounts—some of them based on your individual work record and retirement plans, some of them based on changes and convolutions in Social Security rules—it is impossible to give you what you want most: a solid estimate of the amount that will appear on your retirement benefit check. For a 65-year-old single person first claiming retirement benefits in 2000, the average monthly benefit is about $800; $1,350 for a couple. But these numbers are just averages. Benefits change yearly as the cost of living changes.

**Disability benefits.** If you are under 65 but have met the work requirements and are considered disabled under the program's medical guidelines, you can receive benefits roughly equal to what your retirement benefits would be.

**Dependents benefits.** If you are the spouse of a retired or disabled worker who qualifies for retirement or disability benefits, you and your minor or disabled children may be entitled to benefits based on the worker's earning record. This is true whether or not you actually depend on your spouse for your support.

**Survivors benefits.** If you are the surviving spouse of a worker who qualified for retirement or disability benefits, you and your minor or disabled children may be entitled to benefits based on your deceased spouse's earnings record.

## How are my benefit amounts calculated?

The amount of any benefit is determined by a formula based on the average of your yearly reported earnings in covered employment since you began working. To further complicate matters, Social Security computes the average of earnings differently depending on your age. If you reached age 62 or became disabled on or before December 31, 1978, the computation is simple: Social Security averages the actual dollar value of your total past earnings—and bases the amount of your monthly benefits on that amount.

If you turned 62 or became disabled on or after January 1, 1979, Social Security divides your earnings into two categories: earnings from before 1951 are credited with their actual dollar amount, up to a maximum of $3,000 per year; and from 1951 on, yearly limits are placed on earnings credits, no matter how much you actually earned in those years.

## How can I find out what I've earned so far?

The Social Security Administration keeps a running computer account of your earnings record and work credits, tracking both through your Social Security number. The Administration mails out copies of individual Social Security records on a Personal Earnings and Benefit Estimate Statement. The statement is mailed to everyone age 40 and over who is not currently receiving Social Security benefits.

If you are age 40 or over but have not received your statement, or you are under age 60 and want to check your statement now, you can request a copy by filing out a simple form, SSA 7004, called a Request for Earnings and Benefit Estimate Statement, available at your local Social Security office. If you cannot easily get to your local office, you can request a copy of the form, in either Spanish or English, by calling 800-772-1213.

## Request Your Earnings and Benefit Statement Online

You can request your Personal Earnings and Benefits Estimate Statement through the Social Security Administration's website, without having to fill out and request a written form. The Administration reportedly responds to online requests much more quickly than it does to mailed requests, so using this format may shave weeks off the time it takes to get your estimate.

If you have access to the Internet, you can find the Social Security Administration's site at http://www.ssa.gov. Once you get to the site, look for the headings listed under Online Direct Service. Click *Request a Personal Earnings and Benefits Statement.*

## If You Find an Error

Some government-watchers estimate that the Social Security Administration makes mistakes on at least 3% of the total official earnings records it keeps. It is always wise for you to check the SSA's work. Make sure that the Social Security number noted on your earnings statement is your own. Also make sure the earned income amounts listed on the agency's records mesh with your own records of earnings as listed on your income tax forms or pay stubs.

When you have evidence of your covered earnings in the year or years for which you think Social Security has made an error, call Social Security's helpline at 800-772-1213, Monday through Friday from 7 a.m. to 7 p.m. This is the line that takes all kinds of Social Security questions and it is often swamped, so be patient. It is best to call early in the morning or late in the afternoon, late in the week or late in the month. Have all your documents handy when you speak with a representative.

If you would rather speak with someone in person, call your local Social Security office and make an appointment to see someone there, or drop into the office during regular business hours. If you drop in, be prepared to wait, perhaps as long as an hour or two, before you get to see a representative. Bring with you two copies of your benefits statement and the evidence that supports your claim of higher income. That way, you can leave one copy with the Social Security worker. Write down the name of the person with whom you speak so that you can reach the same person when you follow up.

The process to correct errors is slow. It may take several months to have the changes made in your record. And once Social Security confirms that it has

corrected your record, go through the process of requesting another benefits statement to make sure the correct information is in your file.

## Can I collect more than one type of benefit at a time?

No. You may qualify for more than one type of Social Security benefit, but you can collect just one. For example, you might be eligible for both retirement and disability, or you might be entitled to benefits based on your own retirement as well as on that of your retired spouse. You can collect whichever one of these benefits is higher, but not both.

## Can I claim spousal benefits if I'm divorced?

You are eligible for dependents benefits if both you and your former spouse have reached age 62, your marriage lasted at least ten years and you have been divorced for at least two years. This two-year waiting period does not apply if your former spouse was already collecting retirement benefits before the divorce.

You can collect benefits as soon as your former spouse is eligible for retirement benefits. He or she does not actually have to be collecting those benefits for you to collect your dependents benefits.

If you are collecting dependents benefits on your former spouse's work record and then marry someone else, you lose your right to those benefits. You may, however, be eligible to collect dependents benefits based on your new spouse's work record. If you divorce again, you can return to collecting benefits on your first spouse's record, or on your second spouse's record if you were married for at least ten years the second time around.

## Can I keep a job even after I start collecting retirement benefits?

Yes—and many people do just that. But if you plan on working after retirement, be aware that the money you earn may cause a reduction in the amount of your Social Security benefits. Until you reach age 65, Social Security will subtract money from your retirement check if you exceed a specific amount of earned income for the year.

If you are age 62 to 64 and you earn income over the year's limit, your Social Security retirement benefits are reduced by one dollar for every two dollars over the limit. In 2000, the limit on earned income was $10,000 per year.

## How do I claim my Social Security benefits?

Start by contacting your local Social Security office. Most sizable cities have at least one Social Security office; in major urban areas, there will be several. You can find the address and telephone number of the office closest to you in your telephone directory under the listing for United States Government, Social Security Administration, or sometimes under United States Government, Department of Health and Human Services, Social

Security Administration. If you have trouble finding an office nearby, call the Social Security Administration at 800-772-1213, or use the agency's website at http://www.ssa.gov.

Social Security workers should be able to answer general questions about benefits and rules over the phone—including what type of paperwork must be completed and what documentation is required to claim each kind of benefit. It is generally best to get the benefit application process started by paying a personal visit to the nearest office. If illness or disability prevents this, however, call for accommodations. The most important thing is to act promptly and apply for the benefits to which you are entitled.

## What do I do if I feel I've been wrongly denied my benefits?

If your application for benefits is denied, you may not be completely out of luck. A substantial percentage of decisions are changed on appeal. For example, almost half of all disability appeals, which are by far the most common, are favorably changed during the appeal process.

There are four possible levels of appeal following any Social Security decision. The first is called reconsideration; it is an informal review that takes place in the local Social Security office where your claim was filed. The second level is a hearing before an administrative law judge; this is an independent review of what the local Social Security office has decided, made by someone outside the local office. The third level is an appeal to the Social Security national appeals council in Washington, DC. And the final level is filing a lawsuit in federal court.

Appealing a Social Security claim need not be terribly difficult. In many situations, the appeal will require little more from you than taking another opportunity to explain why the information you already presented should qualify you for a benefit. In other cases, it will simply involve presenting one or two more pieces of information that better explain your situation to Social Security personnel.

Begin your appeal by completing a simple, one-page form you can get from the Social Security office. It is called a Request for Reconsideration. Most of the form is easy to fill out; you'll be asked for basic information such as your name and Social Security number. Then you will need to state, very briefly, the reasons why you think you were unfairly denied benefits or were allotted lower benefits than you believe you earned. When you submit your form, you can attach other material you want the administrators to consider, such as recent medical records or a letter from a doctor or employer about your ability to work. You must send in the completed Request for Reconsideration within 60 days after you of receive written notice of Social Security's decision denying you benefits.

## Sign Up Three Months Before Your Birthday

If you need to receive benefit payments at the youngest eligibility age, file your claim three months before the birthday on which you will become eligible. This will give Social Security time to process your claim so that you will receive the benefits on time. If you file a claim later, you cannot get benefits retroactively for months during which you were eligible but before you applied.

Anyone who is eligible for Social Security benefits is also eligible for Medicare coverage at age 65. (For more information about Medicare, see the next series of questions.) Even if you are not going to claim Social Security benefits at age 65—because your benefit amount will be higher if you wait—you should sign up for Medicare coverage three months before your 65th birthday. There is no reason to delay signing up for Medicare, and waiting until after your 65th birthday will delay coverage.

### More Information About Social Security

*Social Security, Medicare and Pensions,* by Joseph Matthews with Dorothy Matthews Berman (Nolo), explains Social Security rules and offers strategies for dealing with the Social Security system.

The Social Security Administration, 800-772-1213, answers general questions about eligibility and applications over the phone. It also operates a helpful Website that provides information about Social Security benefits and regulations. You can reach it at http://www.ssa.gov.

In every state, there is a department or commission on aging that gives information and provides advice about problems with Social Security claims. Check the phone book under Aging or Elderly for the service in your state.

# Medicare

*Give me health and a day and I will make the pomp of emperors ridiculous.*

**—RALPH WALDO EMERSON**

Over the last several decades, Medicare has been carving an inroad into the mountain of consumer health care costs. At present, the Medicare system provides some coverage for almost 40 million people, most of them seniors. Medicare pays for most of the cost of hospitalization and much other medical care for older Americans—about half of all medical costs for people over 65.

Despite its broad coverage, Medicare does not pay for many types of medical services, and pays only a portion of the costs of other services. To take maximum advantage of the benefits Medicare does provide, to protect yourself against the gaps in Medicare coverage and to understand the current political debate about the program's future, you must become well informed about how the Medicare system works.

## What is Medicare?

Medicare is a federal government program that helps older and some disabled people pay their medical bills. The program is divided into two parts: Part A and Part B. Part A is called hospital insurance and covers most of the costs of a stay in the hospital, as well as some follow-up costs after time in the hospital. Part B, medical insurance, pays some of the cost of doctors and outpatient medical care.

## Medicare, Medicaid: What's the Difference?

People are sometimes confused about the differences between Medicare and Medicaid. Medicare was created in an attempt to address the fact that older citizens have medical bills significantly higher than the rest of the population, while it is much more difficult for most seniors to continue to earn enough money to cover those bills. Eligibility for Medicare is not tied to individual need. Rather, it is an entitlement program; you are entitled to it because you or your spouse paid for it through Social Security taxes.

Medicaid, on the other hand, is a federal program for low-income, financially needy people, set up by the federal government and administered differently in each state.

Although you may qualify and receive coverage from both Medicare and Medicaid, there are separate eligibility requirements for each program; being eligible for one program does not necessarily mean you are eligible for the other. Also, Medicaid pays for some services for which Medicare does not.

## Who is eligible for Medicare Part A coverage?

There are two types of eligibility for Medicare Part A hospital insurance. Most people age 65 and over are covered for free, based on their work records or on their spouse's work records. People over 65 who are not eligible for free Medicare Part A coverage can enroll in it and pay a monthly fee for the same coverage—at least $166 per month according to current rules. The premium increases by 10% for each year after your 65th birthday during which you are not enrolled.

If you enroll in paid Part A hospital insurance, you must also enroll in Part B medical insurance, for which you pay an additional monthly premium.

## Inpatient Care Generally Covered by Part A

The following list gives you an idea of what Medicare Part A does, and does not, cover during your stay in a participating hospital or skilled nursing facility. Remember, though, even when Part A pays for something, there are significant financial limitations on its coverage.

Medicare Part A hospital insurance covers:

- a semi-private room (two to four beds per room); a private room if medically necessary
- all meals, including special, medically required diets
- regular nursing services
- special care units, such as intensive care and coronary care
- drugs, medical supplies and appliances furnished by the facility, such as casts, splints or a wheelchair
- hospital lab tests, X-rays and radiation treatment billed by the hospital
- operating and recovery room costs
- blood transfusions; you pay for the first three pints of blood, unless you arrange to have them replaced by an outside donation of blood to the hospital, and
- rehabilitation services, such as physical therapy, occupational therapy and speech pathology provided while you are in the hospital or nursing facility.

Medicare Part A hospital insurance does not cover:

- personal convenience items such as television, radio or telephone

- private duty nurses, or
- a private room, unless medically necessary.

## How much of my bill will Medicare Part A pay?

All rules about how much Medicare Part A pays depend on how many days of inpatient care you have during what is called a benefit period or spell of illness. The benefit period begins the day you enter the hospital or skilled nursing facility as an inpatient—and continues until you have been out for 60 consecutive days. If you are in and out of the hospital or nursing facility several times but have not stayed out completely for 60 consecutive days, all your inpatient bills for that time will be figured as part of the same benefit period. Medicare Part A pays only certain amounts of a hospital bill for any one benefit pe-

riod—and the rules are slightly different depending on whether the care facility is a hospital, psychiatric hospital, skilled nursing facility or care received at home or through a hospice.

## What kinds of costs does Medicare Part B cover?

Part B is medical insurance. It is intended to help pay doctor bills for treatment in or out of the hospital. It also covers many other medical expenses you incur when you are not in the hospital, such as the costs of necessary medical equipment and tests.

The rules of eligibility for Part B medical insurance are much simpler than for Part A: If you are age 65 or over and a citizen of the United States, or you are a resident of the United States who has been here lawfully for five consecutive years, you are eligible to enroll in Medicare Part B medical insurance. This is true whether or not you are eligible for Part A hospital insurance.

## *Types of Services Covered by Medicare Part B*

Part B medical insurance is intended to cover basic medical services provided by doctors, clinics and laboratories. The lists of services specifically covered and not covered are long, and do not always make a lot of common sense. Making the effort to learn what is and is not covered can be important—you may get the most benefits by fitting your medical treatments into the covered categories whenever possible.

Part B insurance pays for:

- doctors' services (including surgery) provided at a hospital, doctor's office or your home
- some screening tests, such as colorectal cancer screening, mammograms and PAP smears
- medical services provided by nurses, surgical assistants or laboratory or X-ray technicians
- services provided by pathologists or radiologists while you're an inpatient at a hospital
- outpatient hospital treatment, such as emergency room or clinic charges, X-rays and injections
- an ambulance, if required for a trip to or from a hospital or skilled nursing facility
- drugs or other medicine administered to you at a hospital or doctor's office
- medical equipment and supplies, such as splints, casts, prosthetic devices, body braces, heart pacemakers, corrective lenses after a cataract operation, oxygen equipment, wheelchairs and hospital beds
- some kinds of oral surgery
- some of the cost of outpatient physical and speech therapy
- manual manipulation of out-of-place vertebrae by a chiropractor, and
- part-time skilled nursing care, physical therapy and speech therapy provided in your home.

## How much of my bill will Medicare Part B pay?

When all your medical bills are added up, you will see that Medicare pays, on average, for only about half the total. There are three major reasons why Part B medical insurance pays for so little.

First, Medicare does not cover a number of major medical expenses, such as routine physical examinations, medications, glasses, hearing aids, dentures and a number of other costly medical services.

Second, Medicare only pays a portion of what it decides is the proper amount—called the approved charges—for medical services. When Medicare decides that a particular service is covered and determines the approved charges for it, Part B medical insurance usually pays only 80% of those approved charges; you are responsible for the remaining 20%.

Note, however, that there are now several types of treatments and medical providers for which Medicare Part B pays 100% of the approved charges rather than the usual 80%. These categories of care include: home health care, clinical laboratory services and flu and pneumonia vaccines.

Finally, the approved amount may seem reasonable to Medicare, but it is often considerably less than what doctors actually charge. If your doctor or other medical provider does not accept assignment of the Medicare charges, you are personally responsible for the difference.

## Free Prescription Drugs

You may be able to avoid the outrageous cost of prescription drugs by asking your doctor for samples of the drugs. Pharmaceutical companies, in an effort to push their particular brand of drugs, send free samples to doctors, and many doctors are willing to dispense those drugs to you free of charge instead of forcing you to buy the drugs on your own.

But many doctors forget what they have in the way of samples, or simply do not offer samples unless asked. It will usually help if you ask your doctor if he or she has samples of the drug you need, explaining that it will be very hard on your pocketbook if you have to purchase them.

## States With Limits on Billing

Several states—Connecticut, Massachusetts, Minnesota, New York, Ohio, Pennsylvania, Rhode Island and Vermont—have passed balance billing or charge-limit laws. These laws forbid a doctor from billing patients for the balance of the bill above the amount Medicare approves. The patient is still responsible for the 20% of the approved charge not paid by Medicare Part B.

The specifics of these patient protection laws vary from state to state: Some forbid balance billing to any Medicare patient, others apply the restriction only to patients with limited incomes or assets. To find out the rules in your state, call the following agencies:

Connecticut Medical Assignment Program: 800-443-9946

Massachusetts Office of Elder Affairs: 800-882-2003

Minnesota Board of Aging, Ombudsman: 800-657-3591

New York State Office for the Aging: 800-342-9871

Ohio State Department of Health: 800-899-7127

Pennsylvania State Department of Aging: 717-783-8975

Rhode Island Department of Elderly Affairs: 800-322-2880

Vermont Department of Aging and Disabilities: 800-642-5119

### More Information About Medicare

*Social Security, Medicare and Pensions* by Joseph Matthews with Dorothy Matthews Berman (Nolo), further explains Medicare rules and offers strategies for dealing with the Medicare system.

*The Medicare Handbook,* available from the Social Security Administration, 800-772-1213, provides a complete list of Medicare benefits.

# Pensions

Some employers set up pension plans for employees as part of compensation for work. Although no law requires employers to offer these retirement funds, they are a crucial part of many labor negotiations and individual job decisions.

Since the 1980s, however, the number and scope of pension plans—and the number of workers covered by them—have been steadily shrinking. Workers are far more frequently laid off or let go, and as they lose their jobs, they also lose the pension benefits that go with longtime employment.

## What is a pension plan?

A pension is an agreement between you, your employer and, sometimes, your union. Under the agreement, your employer contributes a certain amount of money to a retirement fund during the years you work. With some plans, you must contribute as well. Then, when you retire, you begin to receive money from the fund. Most people begin to collect retirement money at age 65, but many pension plans pay a smaller amount at younger ages.

Pensions come in several shapes and sizes, but most plans can be divided into two basic categories: defined benefit and defined contribution plans.

## What's the difference between "defined benefit" and "defined contribution" plans?

Under a defined benefit plan, you receive a definite, predetermined amount of money when you retire or become disabled. The amount you receive is based on your years of service with a particular employer. Most often, your monthly benefit is a fixed amount of money for each year of service. For example, a plan may pay $20 per month for each year of service. If you worked 20 years for that company, your pension would be $400 per month until you die or payments end, as specified in your individual plan.

Payments under a defined benefit plan may also be calculated on a percentage of your salary over the years. In such plans, the benefit is figured by taking your average salary over all the years you worked, multiplying that average by the fixed percentage established by the pension plan, and then multiplying that total by the number of years you worked for the company.

### EXAMPLE

*Bob's average salary over 20 years' employment with one employer was $20,000 per year. The company's pension plan used 1% of yearly salary as the pension base. Bob's pension would be calculated by taking 1% of his average salary of $20,000, which is $200. That amount would then be multiplied by Bob's 20 years of service, for a yearly pension of $4,000.*

Defined contribution plans, on the other hand, do not guarantee any particular pension amount upon retirement. They guarantee only that the employer will pay into the pension fund a certain amount every month, or every year, for each employee. The employer usually pays a fixed percentage of an employee's wages or salary, although sometimes the amount is a fraction of the company's profits, with the size of each employee's pension share depending on the amount of wage or salary. Payments end at the employee's death, or as specified in the individual plan. Some plans, for example, pay benefit amounts to survivors for a specified number of years.

## Who is entitled to pension benefits?

If your employer offers a pension, you must be permitted to participate in that plan if you are age 21 or older and have worked for the company for at least one year. One year means a total of 1,000 hours at work in a 12-month period beginning your first day of work; that is an average of 20 hours a week for 50 weeks.

To participate in a plan simply means that your time at the job will be counted toward qualifying for retirement benefits, and the employer must begin paying into your pension account if the plan requires ongoing employer contributions. But this does not necessarily mean that you will receive a pension; that question is governed by a different set of rules.

## What does it mean to have "vested" pension benefits?

Every pension plan establishes a level of accumulated benefits—years of employment—after which you have a legal right to receive a pension at retirement. This is true whether or not you continue to work for that employer up to retirement age. When your accumulated benefits reach this level, they are called vested benefits.

There are good reasons to understand how and when your benefits become vested. Before retiring or changing jobs, you will want to know whether your pension rights have vested. Also, in many pension plans there are different levels of vesting, so you must learn what those levels are to know how much of a pension to count on, and when is the best time to leave the job.

## Can I collect a private pension and Social Security retirement benefits at the same time?

Not always. Some pension plans—known as integrated plans—are dependent on Social Security retirement benefits. In these plans, the pension benefit is reduced by all, or some percentage of, the retiree's Social Security check. Since 1988, however, the law has required that the plan leave you with at least half of your pension. Unfortunately, Social Security benefits can wipe out your entire integrated pension plan earnings for pensions earned before 1988, if those benefits are greater than the pension amount.

Integrated pension plans work in one of two ways:

*Benefit goals.* Some integrated plans set up what is called a benefit goal for your retirement—the amount of money you should have from a combination of pension and Social Security retirement income. The plan's benefit goal is usually a percentage of your average pre-retirement income. Your pension amount is then only what is needed to make up the difference between your Social Security benefits and this predetermined benefit goal.

## EXAMPLE

*Roberto worked for a company that had an integrated pension plan that set a benefit goal of 40% of the retiree's final salary. Roberto was making $28,000 a year when he retired, so his benefit goal was $11,200 (40% of $28,000) a year, or $933 a month.*

*Based on his years of service, the company's plan would have owed him $500 a month, without integration. But Roberto also received $650 a month in Social Security retirement benefits, bringing his total Social Security and pension benefits to $1,150 a month. This is $217 more than the benefit goal of $933 a month. So Roberto's pension would be reduced by $217, from $500 to $283 a month.*

*Offset plans.* Another common variety of integrated pension is the offset plan, which reduces or offsets pension benefits by a certain percentage of Social Security benefits. For example, an offset plan might reduce your pension benefits by 50% of your Social Security benefits. If you had earned $250 monthly in pension benefits before the offset, but you receive $400 a month from Social Security, your pension would be reduced by $200—50% of the $400 Social Security benefit. In the end, you would only receive $50 a month from the pension fund.

## Do I sacrifice my pension rights if I take early retirement?

Many pension plans allow you to choose reduced benefits if you have not quite reached retirement age. Full retirement benefits are usually offered at age 65, although a very few plans still offer full benefits earlier. Early retirement age is usually between 60 and 65.

If your pension plan offers early retirement, it must also offer an early retirement survivor annuity. The annuity gives your spouse, or in some plans another named survivor, a right to collect pension money if you die before normal retirement age. For your survivor to collect this annuity, you must have reached either the company's early retirement age, or have reached an age ten years before the plan's normal retirement age, whichever is later. In practical terms, this means you must have reached at least age 55.

## Can I lose pension benefits if the company I work for changes hands?

When a company is sold or reorganized, it often changes the rules of its pension plan. But if your pension benefits have vested under an existing plan, you cannot legally be deprived of any of those benefits when the plan's rules change. The law does not

## The Envelope, Please: Will I Get All the Money at Once?

Pension plans pay retirement benefits in a number of different ways. Frequently, a single plan will offer several payment options. The form of payment not only determines when you receive benefits, but also how much in total you receive and whether your spouse or other survivor can continue to get benefits after you die.

Lump-sum payment. Many defined contribution plans offer to pay you the entire amount accumulated in your pension account at retirement. If you need the money immediately to meet living expenses, this is an obvious choice. Also, this entire pension amount can serve as, or add to, an investment in a business, home or other property. Or, if you are investment savvy, you may feel that you can get a greater return on the money than the alternatives offered by your pension plan.

Simple life annuity. Annuities pay a fixed amount of benefits every year (although most annuities actually pay monthly) for the life of the person who is entitled to them. In a simple life annuity, when the person receiving the annuity dies, the benefits stop. There is no final lump sum payment and no provision to pay benefits to a spouse or other survivor. If you are relatively healthy when you claim your retirement, a simple life annuity may pay you more over the years than a lump sum pension plan.

Continuous annuity. Some plans offer an annuity that pays monthly installments for the life of the retired worker, and also provide a smaller continuing annuity for the worker's spouse or other survivor after the worker's death. If the worker dies within a specified time after retiring—usually five or ten years—the annuity will be paid to the surviving spouse or other beneficiary for the rest of the period set out in the annuity plan. A retiring worker who chooses this option will receive less in monthly pension benefits—usually about 10% less—than would be paid under a simple life annuity.

Joint and survivor annuity. A pension plan that pays benefits in any annuity form is required to offer a worker the choice of a joint and survivor annuity in addition to whatever other form of annuity is offered. This form of annuity pays monthly benefits as long as the retired worker is alive, and then continues to pay the worker's spouse for life. Some pension plans also permit a survivor annuity to be paid to a nonspouse beneficiary, but the law does not require that such a benefit be offered. A worker who chooses the joint and survivor annuity will receive slightly less in pension benefits than under a simple annuity plan; how much less is determined by the age of the worker's spouse or other named beneficiary. The younger the beneficiary—that is, the longer the pension is likely to be paid—the lower the benefits. The amount the survivor receives is usually half of the retired worker's pension amount, although a few plans provide for larger survivor payments.

protect you, however, if your pension rights have not yet vested at the time of the change.

Under federal law, if the company you work for is taken over by a new company which keeps the existing pension plan, your years of service continue to accumulate and the benefits you receive must at least equal the benefits you would have received under the old plan. The law does not, however, obligate a new company to continue paying into the existing pension plan. If the existing plan is discontinued, your benefits under that plan will not increase even though you continue to work. If the new company institutes its own pension plan, however, your continued work may accumulate credits under that plan, eventually entitling you to a second pension. These rules do not protect you from changes in a pension plan which occurred prior to 1974.

## Know Your Rights

Your employer must provide a Summary Plan Description that explains how your pension plan works and describes your benefit choices. You must receive this information within 90 days after qualifying as a participant in the plan, usually one year after the first day as a full-time employee. Your plan description should explain rules regarding participation, benefit accrual, vesting, pay-out options, retirement ages and claim procedures. If the plan changes, you are entitled to an updated Summary Plan Description from the personnel or pension plan administrator's office where you work, or from your union's pension office.

In addition to the general plan description, you are entitled to a statement of your personal benefit account that explains the benefits you have accrued and tells you what benefits have vested, or when they will vest. Not all employers provide this statement regularly; you may have to make a written request for it. You are also entitled to a copy of your benefit statement if you leave your job.

Each pension plan must make a yearly report to the federal government about the investments of the money in the plan fund. You should be able to see a copy of the latest annual report or to obtain a copy at minimal expense from your pension plan administrator's office.

And any time you have a question about your pension plan, you may make a written request for clarification to the plan administrator. If the administrator's office does not give you a satisfactory answer, direct your questions to the local area office of the federal government's Labor-Management Services Administration. You can find its number in the government listings of the white pages of the telephone book under United States Government, Department of Labor.

## Do I have any rights to a spouse's pension if we divorce?

The answer depends on what state you live in and what agreement you and your spouse reach. Because pension benefits are deferred compensation for work already done, in community property states (Arizona, California, Idaho, Louisiana, Nevada, New Mexico, Texas, Washington and Wisconsin) and many other states, the portion of the pension earned during marriage is considered marital property and is subject to division at divorce.

Valuing a pension in order to divide it before the pension holder retires is not easy. Pensions are evaluated by people called actuaries, who figure out what a pension is worth by estimating the following:
- when the pension holder will retire
- when the pension holder will die
- what salary the pension holder will have at retirement, and
- what inflation and interest rates are likely to do between now and when the pension holder retires.

Divorcing couples have several options when dividing pension rights. You can:
- *Agree to keep rights to your own pension plans.* This eliminates the need to value the pensions and minimizes your future financial ties.
- *Give up your individual interest in your spouse's pension plan in exchange for receiving money or some other property of equal value.* This requires that you value the pension, but minimizes your future financial ties.
- *Divide the value of your pension rights so that each takes a future share.* This requires that you value the pension. Furthermore, you stay financially tied to your ex-spouse because you won't get your share of the benefits until your ex-spouse is eligible to retire. You run the risk of your ex-spouse leaving the job before vesting or before the pension builds up.

## Do I have any legal protection if my pension fund is mismanaged?

Since 1974, when the Employee Retirement Income Security Act (ERISA) was passed, at least some of the worst sorts of disappearing pension acts have been halted. To protect pension rights, ERISA:
- sets minimum standards for pension plans, guaranteeing that pension rights cannot be unfairly denied or taken from a worker
- provides some protection for workers in the event certain types of pension plans cannot pay the benefits to which workers are entitled, and
- requires that employers provide full and clear information about employees' pension rights, including the way pension benefits accumulate, how the company invests pension funds and when and how pension benefits can be collected.

## What if the pension fund simply runs out of money?

Under ERISA, there is some protection against such pension fund collapse. The Pension Benefit Guaranty Corporation (PBGC), a public, nonprofit insurance fund, provides some limited coverage against bankrupt pension funds. Should a pension fund be unable to pay all its obligations to its retirees, the PBGC may pay some of the pension fund's unfulfilled obligations.

If you have a question about termination of benefits because of failure of your pension plan or the sale or end of your employer's company, write or call the Pension Benefit Guaranty Corporation, 1200 K Street, NW, Washington, DC 20005-4026, 202-326-4000, 800-400-7242, 800-877-8339 (TDD). You can also use the PBGC website at http://www.pbgc.gov.

## How do I claim my pension benefits?

Although ERISA does not spell out one uniform claim procedure for all pension plans, it does establish some rules which must be followed when you retire and want to claim your benefits. All pension plans must have an established claim procedure and all participants in the plan must be given a summary of the plan which explains that procedure. When your claim is filed, you must receive a decision on the claim, in writing, within a "reasonable time." The decision must state specific reasons for the denial of any claimed benefits and must explain the basis for

determining the benefits which are granted.

## What do I do if my claim is denied or if I disagree with the amount I receive?

If you disagree with either the amount of your benefits or the method in which they are to be paid, you have 60 days from the date you receive a written notice of the amount and method to file a written appeal. Your plan summary explains where and how to file the appeal. If you are considering an appeal, or have filed one, you have the right to examine the pension plan's files and records regarding your pension account, and you can present written materials that correct or contradict information in those files.

Within 60 days of filing your appeal, the pension plan administrators must file a written response to your claim. If your appeal is denied, you have a legal right to press your claim in either state or federal court.

### *More Information About Pension Plans*

*Social Security, Medicare and Pensions*, by Joseph L. Matthews with Dorothy Matthews Berman (Nolo), contains detailed information about pension plans and shows you how to maximize your pension benefits.

*Get a Life: You Don't Need a Million to Retire Well,* by Ralph Warner (Nolo), discusses strategies for creating a satisfying and enjoyable retirement, including pension plans.

*Divorce and Money,* by Violet Woodhouse (Nolo), guides you through the difficult process of dividing retirement funds in the event of a divorce.

You can also get information and assistance regarding your rights under pension plans from the independent, nongovernment Pension Rights Center, 918 16th Street, NW, Suite 704, Washington, DC 20006-2902, 202-296-3778, 202-833-2472 (fax).

# Retirement Plans

In decades past, most Americans relied on retirement income from pension plans and Social Security benefits. However, that is changing rapidly. Today, the Social Security program is weaker than ever before, and many employers offer retirement plans such as 401(k)s instead of pensions. In addition, many Americans are turning to other devices, such as individual retirement accounts (IRAs), to save for the future.

## Why should I set up a retirement plan?

The obvious reason to create a retirement plan is so that you'll have enough income to support yourself when you're no longer working. But retirement plans offer other important benefits as well.

Retirement plans were created by the U.S. Congress several decades ago to encourage working people to save for their later years—and they come with significant tax incentives. Contributions to most types of retirement plans are tax deductible.

Also, if you have the opportunity to participate in a retirement plan—such as a 401(k) plan—at work, your employer may make contributions to the plan in addition to your own contributions. A decision not to participate may mean that you're turning down a gift of additional investment dollars.

But of course it's not all good news. Retirement plans carry some restrictions, too. For example, there are limits on how much you or your employer can contribute to a retirement plan each year. And there are often penalties if you withdraw money before retirement.

## What is a qualified retirement plan?

A qualified plan is simply one that is described in Section 401(a) of the Tax Code. A qualified plan must be established by an employer or a self-employed individual. The most common type of qualified plan is a profit sharing plan. Profit sharing plans include 401(k)s. Most likely, if you are covered by a retirement plan at work, it is a qualified plan.

In general, contributions to qualified plans are not taxed until you withdraw money from the plan. In addition, any contributions an employer makes on an employee's behalf are tax deductible for the employee. Employee contributions are also tax deductible.

## What is a 401(k) plan?

401(k) plans are deferred compensation savings and investment programs—financial structures into which employees can place a certain amount of their wages and defer the taxes on them until retirement. An employee makes contributions by diverting a portion of his or her salary into the plan. Employers can, but do not have to, contribute a set amount per year to the employee's account. Contributions to the plan are tax deductible. The income and profits that come from investing the contributions are not taxed either. However, when the employee starts making withdrawals (usually at retirement), the money is subject to income tax.

## Why are 401(k) plans so popular?

Employers like 401(k) plans because they are less expensive to fund than other types of retirement plans. This is because, usually, all or most of the plan contributions are made by the employee, not the employer.

Employees like 401(k) plans because they can save for retirement while simultaneously reducing their current income tax bill. And, because 401(k) plans allow employees to contribute more each year than do individual retirement plans, such as IRAs, the savings can be substantial. The ability to withdraw money early in certain circumstances is also an attractive feature for many employees. In addition, 401(k) plans offer a certain amount of flexibility. For example, an employee can usually change the amount of salary deferred into the plan if his or her circumstances change. And employees can typically make their own investment decisions.

## What is an Individual Retirement Account (IRA)?

An IRA, or Individual Retirement Account, is a retirement plan governed by Section 408 of the Tax Code. The rules are different than those for qualified plans. The most significant difference is that, unlike qualified plans, which must be established by employers, some IRAs (such as traditional and Roth IRAs) can only be established by individuals. However, this doesn't hold true for all IRAs. Other types, such as SEPs and SIMPLE IRAs, are for businesses only and must be established by an employer.

## What is the difference between a traditional and Roth IRA?

There are two big differences between traditional and Roth IRAs. Those differences determine who can contribute to the plan and what type of tax benefit you receive.

Anyone can establish a traditional IRA, regardless of income. For most people, the money deposited into a traditional IRA each year is tax deductible. (People who earn very high salaries can't deduct the value of their contributions.) For anyone who opens an IRA, the income and profits earned on contributions is not taxed. But when you withdraw money from your account, those funds are subject to income taxes.

The Roth IRA, created by the 1997 Taxpayer Relief Act, is a whole different animal. Workers who earn high incomes cannot contribute to Roth IRAs. For those who can establish a Roth IRA, contributions are not tax deductible. Income accumulates tax free, however, as long as the contributions stay in the account for at least five years. Most important, withdrawals are not taxed.

## I am self-employed. Can I set up a retirement plan?

Although self-employed people cannot open 401(k) accounts, they can take advantage of many other types of retirement plans. These fall into three broad categories: individual plans, employer IRAs and Keogh plans.

- *Individual plans.* Self-employed workers can always establish and contribute to a traditional or Roth IRA.

- *Employer IRAs.* Self-employed workers can take advantage of a category of IRAs designed for employers: SIMPLE IRAs and SEPs. SEPs and SIMPLE IRAs permit larger contributions (and, therefore, bigger tax deductions) than do traditional and Roth IRAs.

- *Keogh plans.* A Keogh plan is a qualified plan for self-employed individuals. Keoghs differ somewhat from qualified plans established by companies. For example, contribution limits for Keoghs are lower than for other qualified plans. And, self-employed individuals can never borrow from a Keogh, whereas employees can often borrow from their corporate retirement plans.

## Can I contribute to a traditional or Roth IRA if I am already contributing to another retirement plan?

Usually, yes. Anyone can contribute to a traditional or Roth IRA, even if they are already contributing to another retirement plan. For example, if you contribute to a 401(k) plan at work, you can also establish a traditional or Roth IRA. Or, if you are self-employed and contribute to a Keogh, you can also set up a traditional or Roth IRA. The rules for SIMPLE IRAs and SEPs are more complicated, however. Whether you can contribute to one along with another retirement plan depends, in part, on whether you work for an employer in addition to being self-employed.

## What does it mean to be "vested" in my retirement plan?

If you are vested in your company's retirement plan, you can take it with you when you leave your job. If you are 50% vested, you can take 50% of it with you when you go. In the case of a 401(k) plan, you are always 100% vested in the salary you contribute to the plan.

## Is my retirement plan protected from creditors?

Most employer plans are safe from creditors, thanks to the Employee Retirement Income Security Act of 1974, commonly known as ERISA. ERISA requires all plans under its control (generally, qualified plans) to include provisions that prohibit the assignment of plan assets to a creditor. The U.S. Supreme Court has also ruled that ERISA plans are protected from creditors even when you are in bankruptcy.

Unfortunately, Keogh plans that cover only you—or you and your partners, but not employees—are not governed or protected by ERISA. Neither are IRAs, whether traditional, Roth, SEP or SIMPLE.

But even though IRAs are not automatically protected from creditors under federal law, many states have put safeguards in place that specifi-

cally protect IRA assets from creditors' claims, whether or not you are in bankruptcy. Also, some state laws contain protective language that is broad enough to protect single-participant Keoghs, as well.

### *More Information About Retirement Plans*

*IRAs, 401(k)s and Other Retirement Plans: Taking Your Money Out* , by Twila Slesnick and John C. Suttle (Nolo), explains the different types of retirement plans—including 401(k)s and other profit-sharing plans, self-employed plans (Keoghs), IRAs and tax-deferred annuities—and the taxes and penalties that can deplete your nest egg.

*Creating Your Own Retirement Plan: IRAs and Keoghs for the Self-employed,* by Twila Slesnick and John Suttle (Nolo), provides self-employed people with the information they need to choose, establish and administer a retirement plan.

*Avoid Taxes on Early Retirement Distributions,* by Twila Slesnick (Nolo). This eGuide tells you everything you need to know if you want to withdraw money from your retirement plan before the age of 59 1/2.

## http://www.nolo.com

*Nolo offers self-help information about a wide variety of legal topics, including issues affecting older Americans.*

## http://www.aarp.org

*The American Association of Retired Persons offers helpful information on a range of issues for older people—including family, health, money matters, housing and crime prevention.*

## http://www.aoa.dhhs.gov/ elderpage.html

*The Administration on Aging's ElderPage provides directories of resources that can help with aging issuues—along with a host of articles covering topics such as retirement planning, housing alterations and Medicare fraud.*

## http://www.pbgc.gov

*The Pension Benefit Guaranty Corporation (PBGC) was established to protect pension benefits, primarily by giving financial assistance to some types of plans that have become insolvent. Its site provides information on pension rights and benefits, including what to expect if your pension plan changes hands and how to appeal an adverse pension decision.*

# **15**

# **S**pouses and Partners

Love is love's reward.

**—JOHN DRYDEN**

15.2    *Living Together—
        Gay and Straight*

15.6    *Premarital
        Agreements*

15.8    *Marriage*

15.14   *Divorce*

15.24   *Domestic Violence*

15.27   *Changing Your Name*

**W**e all know how the story goes: Boy meets girl, boy and girl fall in love, get married and live happily ever after. And sometimes boy meets boy or girl meets girl—but the fairy tale hopes remain largely unchanged.

What we often don't see are the details: Where do boy and girl get a marriage license, and do they need blood tests first? What should girl and girl do if they can't get married, but they want to buy a house together? And what if the fairy tale turns into a nightmare, and one partner wants to end it?

Our intimate relationships aren't always the stuff of childhood tales, and there are a lot of real-world concerns—emotional and practical—that need attention every day. The questions and answers in this chapter are designed to help you with some of the legal tasks and troubles that may surface during the course of your relationship. Keep in mind that the laws in this area vary, sometimes dramatically, from state to state. We've put together a good overview to get you started, but be certain to confirm your state's law before you act on any of the information given here.

# Living Together —Gay & Straight

Many laws are designed to govern and protect the property ownership rights of married couples. But no such laws exist for unmarried couples. If you and your partner are unmarried, you must take steps to protect your relationship and define your property rights. You will also face special concerns if you are raising children together.

## My partner and I don't own much property. Do we really need a written contract covering who owns what?

If you haven't been together long and don't own much, it's really not necessary. But the longer you live together, the more important it is to prepare a written contract making it clear who owns what—especially if you begin to accumulate a lot of property. Otherwise, you might face a serious (and potentially expensive) battle if you split up and can't agree on how to divide what you've acquired. And when things are good, taking the time to draft a well-thought-out contract helps you clarify your intentions.

## My partner makes a lot more money than I do. Should our property agreements cover who is entitled to her income and the items we purchase with it?

Absolutely. Although each person starts out owning all of his or her job-related income, many states allow this to be changed by an oral contract or even by a contract implied from the circumstances of how you live. These types of contracts often lead to misunderstandings during a breakup. For example, absent a written agreement stating whether income will be shared or kept separate, one partner might falsely claim the other promised to split his income 50-50. Although this can be tough to prove in court, the very fact that a lawsuit can be brought creates a huge problem. For obvious reasons, it's an especially good idea to make a written agreement if a person with a big income is living with and supporting someone with little or no income.

## What is palimony? And should we make any agreements about it?

Palimony is a phrase coined by journalists—not a legal concept—to describe the division of property or alimony-like support paid to one partner in an unmarried couple by the other after a break up. Members of unmarried couples are not legally entitled to such payments unless they have an agreement. To avoid a cry for palimony, it's best to include in a written agreement whether or not one person will make payments to the other.

## Buying a House? Make an Agreement

It's particularly important to make a written property agreement if you buy a house together; the large financial and emotional commitments involved are good reasons to take extra care with your plans.

Your contract should cover at least four major areas:

**How is title (ownership) listed on the deed?** One choice is as "joint tenants with rights of survivorship," meaning that when one of you dies, the other automatically inherits the whole house. Another option is "tenants in common," meaning that when one of you dies, that share of the house goes to whomever is named in a will or trust, or goes to blood relatives if the deceased partner left no estate plan.

**How much of the house does each of you own?** If it's not 50-50, is there a way for the person who owns less than half to increase his share—for example,

by fixing up the house or making a larger share of the mortgage payment?

**What happens to the house if you break up?** Will one of you have the first right to stay in the house (perhaps to care for a young child) and buy the other out, or will the house be sold and the proceeds divided?

**If one of you has a buyout right, how will the house be appraised and how long will the buyout take?** Most people agree to use the realtor they used to buy the house to appraise it, and then give the buying partner one to five years to pay off the other.

## My partner and I have a young son, and I'm thinking of giving up my job to become a full-time parent. How might I be compensated for my loss of income?

This is a personal—not a legal—question. If you and your partner decide that compensation is fair, there are many ways to arrange it. For example, you could make an agreement stating that if you break up while you're still providing childcare, your partner will pay an agreed-upon amount to help you make the transition to a new situation. Or, you might agree in writing that your partner will pay you a salary during the time you stay at home, including Social Security and other required benefits.

## Am I liable for the debts of my partner?

Not unless you have specifically undertaken responsibility to pay a particular debt—for example, as a cosigner or if the debt is charged to a joint account. By contrast, husbands and wives are generally liable for all debts incurred during marriage, even those incurred by the other person. The one exception for unmarried couples applies if you have registered as domestic partners in a city where the domestic partner ordinance states that you agree to pay for each other's "basic living expenses" (food, shelter and clothing).

## If one of us dies, how much property will the survivor inherit?

Nothing, unless the deceased partner made a will or used another estate planning device such as a living trust or joint tenancy agreement, or, if under the terms of a contract (such as a contract to purchase household furnishings together), the survivor already owns part of the property. This is unlike the legal situation married couples enjoy, where a surviving spouse automatically inherits a major portion of a deceased spouse's property. The bottom line is simple: To protect the person you live with, you must specifically leave her property using a will, living trust or other legal document.

## If I am injured or incapacitated, can my partner make medical or financial decisions on my behalf?

Not unless you have executed a document called a "durable power of attorney" giving your partner the specific authority to make those decisions. Without a durable power of attorney, huge emotional and practical problems can result. For example, the fate of a severely ill or injured person could be in the hands of a biological relative who disapproves of the relationship and who makes medical decisions contrary to what the ill or injured person wants. It is far better to prepare the necessary paperwork so the loving and knowing partner will be the primary decision-maker. For more information about durable powers of attorney, see Chapter 13, *Living Wills and Powers of Attorney*.

## If my partner and I live together long enough, won't we have a common law marriage?

Probably not. A common law marriage can occur only when:
- a straight couple (common law marriages don't apply to same-sex couples) lives together in one of the few states that still recognize common law marriages
- for a significant period of time (not defined in any state)
- holding themselves out as a married couple—typically this means using the same last name, referring to the other as "my husband" or "my wife" and filing a joint tax return, and
- intending to be married.

Unless all four are true, there is no common law marriage. When one exists, the couple must go through a formal divorce to end the relationship.

## Parenting Concerns of Unmarried Couples

All unmarried couples face unique concerns when they raise children together.

- Straight couples who have children together should take steps to ensure that both are recognized as the legal parents. Both parents should be listed on the birth certificate, and at a minimum the father should sign a statement of paternity. Even better, both parents should sign a statement of parentage acknowledging the father's paternity.

- All unmarried couples face potential obstacles when adopting together because all states favor married couples as adoptive parents.

For more information about adoption by unmarried couples, see Chapter 16, *Parents and Children*.

- Members of unmarried couples who have children from former marriages face the potential prejudice of an ex-spouse or a judge called on to make a custody determination. In most states, this is a much greater concern for lesbian and gay parents than for straight ones, as judges (with the exception of a few states which also come down hard on unmarried couples) tend to be more tolerant of opposite-sex cohabitation than same-sex cohabitation. Many judges prefer to place children with a parent who is heterosexual and married, if that's an option.

## States That Recognize Common Law Marriage

| | |
|---|---|
| Alabama | Oklahoma |
| Colorado | Pennsylvania |
| District of Columbia | Rhode Island |
| Iowa | South Carolina |
| Kansas | Texas |
| Montana | Utah |
| New Hampshire* | |

*For inheritance purposes only.

### More Information About Living Together

*Living Together: A Legal Guide for Unmarried Couples,* by Attorneys Ralph Warner, Toni Ihara & Frederick Hertz (Nolo), explains the legal rules that apply to unmarried couples and includes sample contracts governing jointly owned property.

*A Legal Guide for Lesbian and Gay Couples,* by Hayden Curry, Denis Clifford, Robin Leonard and Frederick Hertz (Nolo), sets out the law and contains sample agreements for same-sex couples.

# Premarital Agreements

*Love reasons without reason.*

**—WILLIAM SHAKESPEARE**

Before a couple marries, the parties may make an agreement concerning certain aspects of their relationship. This agreement might cover their responsibilities and property rights during marriage—for example, how the mortgage gets paid and who will stay home to take care of the kids. But more likely it will determine how property will be divided, and whether alimony will be paid, in the event the couple later divorces. These agreements are also called antenuptial or prenuptial agreements.

## Are premarital agreements legal?

Courts usually uphold premarital agreements unless one person shows that the agreement:

- promotes divorce (for example, by providing for a large award of alimony in the event of divorce),
- was written and signed with the intention of divorcing, or
- was created unfairly (for example, one spouse giving up all of the rights in his spouse's future earnings without the advice of an attorney).

Nor will courts uphold agreements of a nonmonetary nature. For example, you can't sue your spouse for failure to take out the garbage, even if your premarital agreement says that he or she must do so every Tuesday night.

## Should my fiancé and I make a premarital agreement?

Whether you should make a premarital agreement depends on your circumstances and on the two of you as individuals. Some couples choose to make a premarital agreement as a way of clarifying their intentions and expectations, as well as their rights should they later split up.

On the other hand, some couples make premarital agreements to circumvent what a court might decide in the event of a divorce. Often this happens when one partner has property that he or she wishes to keep if the marriage ends—for example, a considerable income or a family business. Perhaps most frequently, premarital agreements are made by individuals who have children or grandchildren from prior marriages. In this case, a partner may use a premarital agreement to ensure that the bulk of his or her property passes to the children or grandchildren, rather than the current spouse.

## Are there rules about what can or cannot be included in a premarital agreement?

A law called the Uniform Premarital Agreement Act provides legal guidelines for people who wish to make agreements prior to marriage regarding the following: ownership, management and control of property;

property disposition on separation, divorce and death; alimony; wills; and life insurance beneficiaries.

States that haven't adopted the Act (or which have made some changes to it) have other laws, which often differ from the Act in minor ways. One important difference is that a few states, including California, do not allow premarital agreements to modify or eliminate the right of a spouse to receive court-ordered alimony at divorce. Other states have their own quirky laws—Maine, for example, voids all premarital agreements one and one-half years after the parties to the contract become parents, unless the agreement is renewed.

In every state, whether covered by the Act or not, couples are prohibited from making binding provisions about child support payments.

## States That Have Adopted the Uniform Premarital Agreement Act

| | |
|---|---|
| Arizona | Montana |
| Arkansas | Nebraska |
| California | Nevada |
| Connecticut | New Jersey |
| Delaware | New Mexico |
| District of Columbia | North Carolina |
| Hawaii | North Dakota |
| Idaho | Oregon |
| Illinois | Rhode Island |
| Indiana | South Dakota |
| Iowa | Texas |
| Kansas | Utah |
| Maine | Virginia |

## Can my fiancé and I make our premarital agreement without a lawyer?

You can look up the laws for your state and write your agreement yourselves. Unfortunately, however, there's no good self-help resource for writing premarital agreements, and if you make a mistake, a court may find your agreement unenforceable. If you'd like to draft a contract on your own, we recommend that you have an attorney skilled in family or contract law (preferably both) look it over to make sure you've followed the law to the letter.

## I've been living with someone for several years and we've decided to get married. Will our existing property agreement be enforceable even after we are married?

Probably not. To be enforceable, contracts made before marriage must be made in contemplation of marriage. This means that unless your living together contract is made shortly before your marriage, when you both plan to be married, a court will disregard it.

If you want to convert your living together contract into a premarital agreement, follow these steps:

- Use your upcoming marriage as an opportunity to take another look at your agreement, and make any agreed-upon updates and changes.
- Rewrite your agreement. Call it a premarital or prenuptial agreement, and state that it is made in contem-

plation of marriage and does not take effect until you marry.
- Because there is no good self-help resource in this area, and because even a small mistake can result in your agreement later being held unenforceable, have your agreement checked out by a lawyer.
- Sign the document in front of a notary.

# Marriage

THERE IS MORE OF GOOD NATURE

THAN OF GOOD SENSE AT THE BOTTOM

OF MOST MARRIAGES.

**—HENRY DAVID THOREAU**

Marriage is the legal union of two people. When you are married, your responsibilities and rights toward your spouse concerning property and support are defined by the laws of the state in which you live. The two of you may be able to modify the rules set up by your state, however, if you desire to do so.

Your marriage can only be terminated by a court granting a divorce or an annulment.

## What are the legal rights and benefits conferred by marriage?

Marriage entails many rights and benefits, including the rights to:
- file joint income tax returns with the IRS and state taxing authorities

- create a "family partnership" under federal tax laws, which allows you to divide business income among family members (this will often lower the total tax on the income)
- create a marital life estate trust (this type of trust is discussed in Chapter 12—see *Estate and Gift Taxes*)
- receive spouse's and dependent's Social Security, disability, unemployment, veterans', pension and public assistance benefits
- receive a share of your deceased spouse's estate under intestate succession laws
- claim an estate tax marital deduction
- sue a third person for wrongful death and loss of consortium
- sue a third person for offenses that interfere with the success of your marriage, such as alienation of affection and criminal conversation (these lawsuits are available in only a few states)
- receive family rates for insurance
- avoid the deportation of a noncitizen spouse
- enter hospital intensive care units, jails and other places where visitors are restricted to immediate family
- live in neighborhoods zoned for "families only"
- make medical decisions about your spouse in the event of disability, and
- claim the marital communications privilege, which means a court can't force you to disclose the contents of confidential communications between you and your spouse during your marriage.

## Requirements for Marriage

You must meet certain requirements in order to marry. These vary slightly from state to state, but essentially require that you:

- are one man and one woman
- are at least the age of consent (usually 18, though sometimes you may marry younger with your parents' consent)
- are not too closely related to your intended spouse
- have the mental capacity—that is, you must understand what you are doing and what consequences your actions may have
- are sober at the time of the marriage
- are not married to anyone else
- get a blood test, and
- obtain a marriage license.

## What's the difference between a "marriage license" and a "marriage certificate"?

A marriage license is the piece of paper that authorizes you to get married and a marriage certificate is the document that proves you are married.

Typically, couples obtain a marriage license, have the wedding ceremony and then have the person who performed the ceremony file a marriage certificate in the appropriate county office within a few days. (This may be the office of the county clerk, recorder or registrar, depending on where you live.) The married couple will be sent a certified copy of the marriage certificate within a few weeks after the ceremony.

Most states require both spouses, the person who officiated and one or two witnesses to sign the marriage certificate; often this is done just after the ceremony.

## Where can we get a marriage license?

Usually, you may apply for a marriage license at any county clerk's office in the state where you want to be married. (In some circumstances, you must apply in the county or town where you intend to be married—this depends on state law.) You'll probably have to pay a small fee for your license, and you may also have to wait a few days before it is issued.

In some states, even after you get your license you'll have to wait a short period of time—one to three days—before you tie the knot. Often, this waiting period can be waived in special circumstances. Licenses are good for 30 days to one year, depending on the state. If your license expires before you get married, you can apply for a new one.

For more specific information about marriage license laws in your state, see *Marriage Licenses and Blood Tests*, below.

## Do all states require blood tests? And why are they required?

Many states—but not all—require blood tests for couples planning to marry (see the chart below). But the trend is to eliminate these tests. Keep this in mind as you check the chart

below. Your state's requirements may have changed since the publication of this book.

Blood tests are to find out whether either partner has a venereal disease or rubella (measles). The tests may also disclose the presence of genetic disorders such as sickle cell anemia or Tay-Sachs disease. You will not be tested for HIV, but in some states, the person who tests you will provide you with information about HIV and AIDS. In most states, the blood test may be waived for people over 50 and for other reasons, including pregnancy or sterility.

If either partner tests positive for a venereal disease, what happens depends on the state where you are marrying. Some states may refuse to issue you a marriage license. Other states may allow you to marry as long as you both know that the disease is present.

## MARRIAGE LICENSES AND BLOOD TESTS

| State | Blood tests required | Waiting period between applying for and receiving license | How soon you can marry after receiving license | When license expires |
|---|---|---|---|---|
| Alabama | Yes | None | Immediately | 30 days |
| Alaska | No | 3 days | Immediately | 3 months |
| Arizona | No | None | Immediately | 1 year |
| Arkansas | No | None | Immediately | No provision |
| California | No | None | Immediately | 90 days |
| Colorado | No | None | Immediately | 30 days |
| Connecticut | Yes | None | Immediately | 65 days |
| Delaware | No | None | 24 hours; 96 hours if both spouses are nonresidents | 30 days |
| District of Columbia | Yes | 3 days | Immediately | No provision |
| Florida | No | None | Immediately | 30 days |
| Georgia | Yes | None | Immediately | No provision |
| Hawaii | No | None | Immediately | 30 days |
| Idaho | No | None | Immediately | No provision |
| Illinois | No | None | 1 day | 60 days |
| Indiana | Yes | None | Immediately | 60 days |
| Iowa | No | 3 days | Immediately | No provision |
| Kansas | No | 3 days | Immediately | 6 months |
| Kentucky | No | None | Immediately | 30 days |
| Louisiana | Yes | None | 3 days | 30 days |
| Maine | No | 3 days | Immediately | 90 days |
| Maryland | No | None | Immediately | 6 months |
| Massachusetts | Yes | 3 days | Immediately | 60 days |
| Michigan | No | 3 days | Immediately | 33 days |
| Minnesota | No | 5 days | Immediately | 6 months |
| Mississippi | Yes | 3 days | Immediately | No provision |
| Missouri | No | 3 days | Immediately | No provision |

15.11

## MARRIAGE LICENSES AND BLOOD TESTS

| State | Blood tests required | Waiting period between applying for and receiving license | How soon you can marry after receiving license | When license expires |
|---|---|---|---|---|
| Montana | Yes | None | Immediately | 180 days |
| Nebraska | No | None | Immediately | 1 year |
| Nevada | No | None | Immediately | 1 year |
| New Hampshire | No | 3 days | Immediately | 90 days |
| New Jersey | No | 72 hours | Immediately | 30 days |
| New Mexico | Yes | None | Immediately | No provision |
| New York | No | None | 24 hours | 60 days |
| North Carolina | No | None | Immediately | 60 days |
| North Dakota | No | None | Immediately | 60 days |
| Ohio | No | 5 days | Immediately | 60 days |
| Oklahoma | Yes | 72 hours if either applicant is under 18 | Immediately | 30 days |
| Oregon | No | 3 days | Immediately | 60 days |
| Pennsylvania | No | 3 days | Immediately | 60 days |
| Rhode Island | No | None | Immediately | 3 months |
| South Carolina | No | 24 hours | Immediately | No provision |
| South Dakota | No | None | Immediately | 20 days |
| Tennessee | No | 3 days if either applicant is under 18 | Immediately | 30 days |
| Texas | No | None | 3 days | 31 days |
| Utah | No | None | Immediately | 30 days |
| Vermont | No | None | Immediately | 60 days |
| Virginia | No | None | Immediately | 60 days |
| Washington | No | None or up to 3 days | Immediately | 60 days |
| West Virginia | No | None | Immediately | 60 days |
| Wisconsin | No | 5 days | Immediately | 30 days |
| Wyoming | No | None | Immediately | No provision |

## Who can perform a marriage ceremony?

Nonreligious ceremonies—called civil ceremonies—must be performed by a judge, justice of the peace or court clerk who has legal authority to perform marriages, or by a person given temporary authority by a judge or court clerk to conduct a marriage ceremony. Religious ceremonies must be conducted by a clergy member—for example, a priest, minister or rabbi. Native American weddings may be performed by a tribal chief or by another official, as designated by the tribe.

## Are there requirements about what the ceremony must include?

Usually, no special words are required as long as the spouses acknowledge their intention to marry each other. Keeping that in mind, you can design whatever type of ceremony you desire.

It is customary to have witnesses to the marriage, although they are not required in all states.

## What is a common law marriage?

In twelve states and the District of Columbia, heterosexual couples can become legally married if they:

- live together for a long period of time
- hold themselves out to others as husband and wife, and
- intend to be married.

These marriages are called common law marriages. Contrary to popular belief, even if two people cohabit for a certain number of years, if they don't intend to be married and hold themselves out as married, there is no common law marriage.

When a common law marriage exists, the spouses receive the same legal treatment given to formally married couples, including the requirement that they go through a legal divorce to end the marriage.

To find out whether your state recognizes common law marriages, see the list on page 15.6.

## Does any state yet recognize same-sex marriages?

In a word, no. Hawaii came close in 1993 when a court ruled that denying same-sex marriages violated the state's constitution. But the Hawaii legislature changed that by passing a constitutional amendment banning same-sex marriages.

The tide may be turning, however, at least in Vermont. In December 1999, in *Baker v. State, 744 A.2d 864 (Vermont 1999)*, the Vermont Supreme Court ordered its state legislature to provide same-sex couples with traditional marriage benefits and protections.

In response to the Supreme Court's mandate, the Vermont Civil Union law went into effect on July 1, 2000. While this law doesn't legalize same-sex marriages, it does provide gay and lesbian couples with many of the advantages of marriage, including:

- use of family laws such as annulment, divorce, child custody, child support, alimony, domestic violence, adoption and property division

- the right to sue for wrongful death, loss of consortium and any other tort or law related to spousal relationships
- medical rights such as hospital visitation, notification and durable power of attorney
- family leave benefits
- joint tax filing, and
- property inheritance without a will.

*The Vermont Guide to Civil Unions*, published by the Vermont Secretary of State, has a complete list of these rights and benefits. It is available online at http://www.sec.state.vt.us/pubs/civilunions.htm.

What if—like most people—you don't live in Vermont? You can go to Vermont and participate in a civil union ceremony. But, because no other state recognizes Vermont civil unions, the rights and benefits listed above won't be available to you in your state. In fact, several states, including Georgia, South Dakota, Texas and Utah have laws designed to thwart same-sex marriages. In addition, the federal Defense of Marriage Act bars the federal government from recognizing same-sex marriages and permits states to ignore same-sex marriages performed in other states.

For more information about same-sex marriage, you can contact the Vermont Freedom to Marry Task Force, P.O. Box 1312, Middlebury, VT 05753, 802-388-2633, http://www.vtfreetomarry.org. You may also want to contact the Marriage Project of the Lambda Legal Defense and Education Fund, 212- 809-8585, http://www.lambdalegal.org.

# Divorce

THERE IS NO DISPARITY

IN MARRIAGE LIKE UNSUITABLILITY

OF MIND AND PURPOSE.

**—CHARLES DICKENS**

Divorce is the legal termination of a marriage. In some states, divorce is called dissolution or dissolution of marriage. A divorce usually includes division of marital property and, if necessary, arrangements for child custody and support. It leaves both people free to marry again.

## How does an annulment differ from a divorce?

Like a divorce, an annulment is a court procedure that dissolves a marriage. But an annulment treats the marriage as though it never happened. For some people, divorce carries a stigma, and they would rather their marriage be annulled. Others prefer an annulment because it may be easier to remarry in their church if they go through an annulment rather than a divorce.

Grounds for annulment vary slightly from state to state. Generally, an annulment may be obtained for one of the following reasons:

- *misrepresentation or fraud*—for example, a spouse lied about the capacity to have children, stated that she had reached the age of consent or failed to say that she was still married to someone else
- *concealment*—for example, concealing an addiction to alcohol or drugs, conviction of a felony, children from a prior relationship, a sexually transmitted disease or impotency
- *refusal or inability to consummate the marriage*—that is, refusal or inability of a spouse to have sexual intercourse with the other spouse, or
- *misunderstanding*—for example, one person wanted children and the other did not.

These are the grounds for civil annulments; within the Roman Catholic church, a couple may obtain a religious annulment after obtaining a civil divorce, in order for one or both spouses to remarry.

Most annulments take place after a marriage of a very short duration—a few weeks or months, so there are usually no assets or debts to divide or children for whom custody, visitation and child support are a concern. When a long-term marriage is annulled, however, most states have provisions for dividing property and debts, as well as determining custody, visitation, child support and alimony. Chil-

dren of an annulled marriage are *not* considered illegitimate.

## When are married people considered separated?

Many people are confused about what is meant by "separated"—and it's no wonder, given that there are four different kinds of separations:

*Trial separation.* When a couple lives apart for a test period, to decide whether or not to separate permanently, it's called a trial separation. Even if they don't get back together, the assets they accumulate and debts they incur during the trial period are usually considered jointly owned. A trial separation is a personal choice, not a legal status.

*Living apart.* Spouses who no longer reside in the same dwelling are said to be living apart. In some states, living apart without intending to reunite changes the spouses' property rights. For example, some states consider property accumulated and debts incurred between living apart and divorce to be the separate property or debt of the person who accumulated or incurred it.

*Permanent separation.* When a couple decides to split up, it's often called a permanent separation. It may follow a trial separation, or may begin immediately when the couple starts living apart. In most states, all assets received and most debts incurred after permanent separation are the separate property or responsibility of the spouse incurring them. In some states, assets and debts are joint until the divorce papers are filed, regardless of when you separate.

*Legal separation.* A legal separation results when the parties separate and a court rules on the division of property, alimony, child support, custody and visitation—but does not grant a divorce. The money awarded for support of the spouse and children under these circumstances is often called separate maintenance (as opposed to alimony and child support). You can get a legal separation in all but 12 states: Delaware, Florida, Georgia, Maryland, Mississippi, New Hampshire, New Jersey, Ohio, Pennsylvania, Texas, Vermont and Washington.

## What is a "no-fault" divorce?

"No-fault" divorce describes any divorce where the spouse suing for divorce does not have to prove that the other spouse did something wrong. All states allow divorces regardless of who is at "fault."

To get a no-fault divorce, one spouse must simply state a reason recognized by the state. In most states, it's enough to declare that the couple cannot get along (this goes by such names as "incompatibility," "irreconcilable differences" or "irremediable breakdown of the marriage"). In nearly a dozen states, however, the couple must live apart for a period of months or even years in order to obtain a no-fault divorce.

## Is a no-fault divorce the only option even when there has been substantial wrongdoing?

In 18 states, yes. The other states allow a spouse to select either a no-fault divorce or a fault divorce. Why choose a fault divorce? Some people don't want to wait out the period of separation required by their state's law for a no-fault divorce. And in some states, a spouse who proves the other's fault may receive a greater share of the marital property or more alimony.

The traditional fault grounds are:
- cruelty (inflicting unnecessary emotional or physical pain)—this is the most frequently used ground
- adultery
- desertion for a specified length of time
- confinement in prison for a set number of years, and
- physical inability to engage in sexual intercourse, if it was not disclosed before marriage.

## What happens in a fault divorce if both spouses are at fault?

Under a doctrine called "comparative rectitude," a court will grant the spouse least at fault a divorce when both parties have shown grounds for divorce. Years ago, when both parties were at fault, neither was entitled to a divorce. The absurdity of this result gave rise to the concept of comparative rectitude.

## Can a spouse successfully prevent a court from granting a divorce?

One spouse cannot stop a no-fault divorce. Objecting to the other spouse's request for divorce is itself an irreconcilable difference that would justify the divorce.

A spouse can prevent a fault divorce, however, by convincing the court that he or she is not at fault. In addition, several other defenses to a divorce may be possible:

- *Collusion*. If the only no-fault divorce available in a state requires that the couple separate for a long time and the couple doesn't want to wait, they might pretend that one of them was at fault in order to manufacture a ground for divorce. This is collusion because they are cooperating in order to mislead the judge. If, before the divorce, one spouse no longer wants a divorce, he could raise the collusion as a defense.
- *Condonation*. Condonation is someone's approval of another's activities. For example, a wife who does not object to her husband's adultery may be said to condone it. If the wife sues her husband for divorce, claiming he has committed adultery, the husband may argue as a defense that she condoned his behavior.
- *Connivance*. Connivance is the setting up of a situation so that the other person commits a wrongdoing. For example, a wife who invites her husband's lover to the house and then leaves for the weekend may be said to have connived his adultery. If the wife sues her husband for divorce, claiming he has committed adultery, the husband may argue as a defense that she connived—that is, set up—his actions.
- *Provocation*. Provocation is the inciting of another to do a certain act. If a spouse suing for divorce claims that the other spouse abandoned her, her spouse might defend the suit on the ground that she provoked the abandonment.

Keep in mind that although these defenses exist, most courts will eventually grant the divorce. This is because of the strong public policy against forcing people to stay married against their will.

## GROUNDS FOR DIVORCE

| State | Fault grounds | No-fault grounds (other than separation) | Separation | Length of separation |
|---|---|---|---|---|
| Alabama | x | x | x | 2 years |
| Alaska | x | x | | |
| Arizona | | x | | |
| Arkansas | x | | x | 18 months |
| California | | x | | |
| Colorado | | x | | |
| Connecticut | x | x | x[1] | 18 months |
| Delaware | x | x[2] | | |
| District of Columbia | x | | x | 6 months if both parties agree; otherwise 1 year |
| Florida | | x | | |
| Georgia | x | x | | |
| Hawaii | | x | x | 2 years |
| Idaho | x | x | x | 5 years |
| Illinois | x | x[3] | x[3] | 2 years |
| Indiana | | x | | |
| Iowa | | x | | |
| Kansas | x | x | | |
| Kentucky | | x[4] | | |
| Louisiana | x | | x | 180 days |
| Maine | x | x | | |
| Maryland | x | | x | 12 months if both agree; otherwise 2 years |
| Massachusetts | x | x | | |
| Michigan | | x | | |
| Minnesota | | x | | |
| Mississippi | x | x | | |
| Missouri | | x | | |
| Montana | | x | x | 180 days |

| State | Fault grounds | No-fault grounds (other than separation) | Separation | Length of separation |
|---|---|---|---|---|
| Nebraska | | x | | |
| Nevada | | x | x | 1 year |
| New Hampshire | x | x | | |
| New Jersey | x | | x | 18 months |
| New Mexico | x | x | | |
| New York | x | | x | 1 year |
| North Carolina | x | | x | 1 year |
| North Dakota | x | x | x | 2 years |
| Ohio | x | x[5] | x | 1 year |
| Oklahoma | x | x | | |
| Oregon | | x | | |
| Pennsylvania | x | x | x | 2 years |
| Rhode Island | x | x | x | 3 years |
| South Carolina | x | | x | 1 year |
| South Dakota | x | x | | |
| Tennessee | x | x | x[6] | 2 years |
| Texas | x | x | x | 3 years |
| Utah | x | x | x | 3 years |
| Vermont | x | | x | 6 months |
| Virginia | x | | x[7] | 1 year |
| Washington | | x | | |
| West Virginia | x | x | x | 1 year |
| Wisconsin | | x | x | 12 months |
| Wyoming | | x | | |

[1] Separation-based divorce must also allege incompatibility.

[2] No-fault requires a 6-month separation.

[3] Must allege irretrievable breakdown and separation for no-fault; if parties consent, two years may be reduced to six months.

[4] No-fault requires a 60-day separation.

[5] Divorce will be denied if one party contests ground of incompatibility.

[6] Separation-based divorce allowed only if there are no children.

[7] May be reduced to six months if there are no children.

## Do you have to live in a state to get a divorce there?

All states except Alaska, South Dakota and Washington require a spouse to be a resident of the state for a certain length of time (30 days to one year, depending on the state) before filing for a divorce there. Someone who files for divorce must offer proof that he has resided there for the required length of time.

## Can one spouse move to a different state or country to get a divorce?

If one spouse meets the residency requirement of a state or country, a divorce obtained there is valid, even if the other spouse lives somewhere else. The courts of all states will recognize the divorce.

Any decisions the court makes regarding property division, alimony, custody and child support, however, may not be valid unless the nonresident spouse consented to the jurisdiction of the court or later acts as if the foreign divorce was valid—for example, by paying court-ordered child support.

I'M A GREAT HOUSEKEEPER.

I GET DIVORCED. I KEEP THE HOUSE.

**—ZSA ZSA GABOR**

## How is property divided at divorce?

It is common for a divorcing couple to decide about dividing their property and debts themselves, rather than leave it to the judge. But if a couple cannot agree, they can submit their property dispute to the court, which will use state law to divide the property.

Division of property does not necessarily mean a physical division. Rather, the court awards each spouse a percentage of the total value of the property. Each spouse gets items whose worth adds up to his or her percentage.

Courts divide property under one of two schemes: equitable distribution or community property.

- *Equitable distribution.* Assets and earnings accumulated during marriage are divided equitably (fairly). In practice, often two-thirds of the assets go to the higher wage earner and one-third to the other spouse. Equitable distribution principles are followed everywhere except the community property states listed just below.
- *Community property.* In Arizona, California, Idaho, Louisiana, Nevada, New Mexico, Texas, Washington and Wisconsin, all property of a married person is classified as either community property, owned equally by both spouses, or the separate property of one spouse. At divorce, community property is generally divided equally between the spouses, while each spouse keeps his or her separate property (that property which is accumulated prior to the divorce or acquired by gift or inheritance. In Alaska, couples can agree in writing to have their property treated as if they lived in a community property state.

## DURATIONAL RESIDENCY REQUIREMENTS FOR DIVORCE

The durational residency requirement is the length of time a person filing for divorce must live in that state before he or she can file court papers.

| State | No Statutory Provision | 30 days | 6 Weeks | 60 Days | 3 Months or 90 Days | 6 Months or 180 Days | 12 Months or 1 year |
|---|---|---|---|---|---|---|---|
| Alabama | | | | | | x | |
| Alaska | x | | | | | | |
| Arizona | | | | | x | | |
| Arkansas | | | | x | | | |
| California | | | | | | x | |
| Colorado | | | | | x | | |
| Connecticut | | | | | | | x |
| Delaware | | | | | | x | |
| District of Columbia | | | | | | x | |
| Florida | | | | | | x | |
| Georgia | | | | | | x | |
| Hawaii | | | | | | x | |
| Idaho | | | x | | | | |
| Illinois | | | | | x | | |
| Indiana | | | | | | x | |
| Iowa | | | | | | | x |
| Kansas | | | | x | | | |
| Kentucky | | | | | | x | |
| Louisiana | | | | | | x | |
| Maine | | | | | | x | |
| Maryland | | | | | | | x |
| Massachusetts | | | | | | | x |
| Michigan | | | | | | x | |
| Minnesota | | | | | | x | |
| Mississippi | | | | | | x | |
| Missouri | | | | | x | | |
| Montana | | | | | x | | |
| Nebraska | | | | | | | x |
| Nevada | | | x | | | | |
| New Hampshire | | | | | | | x |
| New Jersey | | | | | | | x[1] |
| New Mexico | | | | | | x | |
| New York | | | | | | | x |

| State | No Statutory Provision | 30 days | 6 Weeks | 60 Days | 3 Months or 90 Days | 6 Months or 180 Days | 12 Months or 1 year |
|---|---|---|---|---|---|---|---|
| North Carolina | | | | | | x | |
| North Dakota | | | | | | x | |
| Ohio | | | | | | x | |
| Oklahoma | | | | | | | |
| Oregon | | | | | | x | |
| Pennsylvania | | | | | | x | |
| Rhode Island | | | | | | | x |
| South Carolina[2] | | | | | x | | |
| South Dakota | x | | | | | | |
| Tennessee | | | | | | x | |
| Texas | | | | | | x | |
| Utah | | | | | x | | |
| Vermont | | | | | | x | |
| Virginia | | | | | | x | |
| Washington | x | | | | | | |
| West Virginia | | | | | | | x[1] |
| Wisconsin | | | | | | x | |
| Wyoming | | | | x | | | |

[1]Required for all grounds but adultery.

[2]If only one spouse is a resident of South Carolina, the requirement is one year.

Very generally, here are the rules for determining what's community property and what isn't:

Community property includes all earnings during marriage and everything acquired with those earnings. All debts incurred during marriage, unless the creditor was specifically looking to the separate property of one spouse for payment, are community property debts.

Separate property of one spouse includes gifts and inheritances given just to that spouse, personal injury awards received by that spouse and the proceeds of a pension that vested (that is, the pensioner became legally entitled to receive it) before marriage. Property purchased with the separate funds of a spouse remain that spouse's separate property. A business owned by one spouse before the marriage remains his or her separate property during the marriage, although a portion of it may be considered community property if the business increased in value during the marriage or both spouses contributed to its worth.

Property purchased with a combination of separate and community funds is part community and part separate property, so long as a spouse is able to show that some separate funds were used. Separate property mixed together with community property generally becomes community property.

## My spouse and I are thinking of using a divorce mediator. Is there anything we should know before we begin the process?

More and more couples are turning to mediation in order to negotiate divorce agreements. Mediation almost always takes less time, is less expensive and results in a more solid agreement than using a lawyer to take the case to court. Of course, every divorcing spouse should know and understand his or her legal rights before agreeing to a settlement, even one reached through mediation. You might want to consult a lawyer or do some independent legal research early in the process and then have a lawyer review the agreement before signing. (See Chapter 17, *Courts and Mediation*, for general information on mediation and Chapter 16, *Parents and Children*, for more information on mediating disputes about child custody and visitation.)

### *More Information About Divorce*

*How to Do Your Own Divorce in California*, by Charles Sherman (Nolo Occidental), contains step-by-step instructions for obtaining a California divorce without a lawyer.

*How to Do Your Own Divorce in Texas*, by Charles Sherman (Nolo Occidental), contains step-by-step instructions for obtaining a Texas divorce without a lawyer.

*Do Your Own Divorce in Oregon*, by Robin Smith (Nolo), provides easy-to-use forms and step-by-step instructions for handling a non-contested divorce in Oregon.

*Using Divorce Mediation: Save Your Money and Your Sanity*, by Katherine E. Stoner (Nolo), provides divorcing couples with all the information they need to work with a neutral third party to resolve differences and find solutions.

*Divorce and Money: How to Make the Best Financial Decisions During Divorce*, by Violet Woodhouse with Dale Fetherling (Nolo), explains the financial aspects of divorce and how to divide property fairly.

*Nolo's Pocket Guide to Family Law*, by Robin Leonard and Stephen Elias (Nolo), explains legal concepts you may run across if you're involved in a divorce, adoption or other family law matter.

*Annulment: Your Chance to Remarry Within the Catholic Church*, by Joseph P. Zwack (Harper & Row), explains how to get a religious annulment.

# Domestic Violence

Domestic violence occurs more often than most of us realize. Those who are abused range in age from children to the elderly, and come from all backgrounds and income levels. The majority of those subjected to domestic violence are women abused by men, but women also abuse other women, men abuse men and women abuse men. If you're being hurt at home, the first rule of advice is to get away from the abuser and go to a safe place where he or she cannot find you. Then, find out about your options for getting help.

## What kind of behavior is considered domestic violence?

Domestic violence can take a number of forms, including:

- physical behavior such as slapping, punching, pulling hair or shoving
- forced or coerced sexual acts or behavior such as unwanted fondling or intercourse, or jokes and insults aimed at sexuality
- threats of abuse—threatening to hit, harm or use a weapon on another, or to tell others confidential information, and
- psychological abuse—attacks on self-esteem, controlling or limiting another's behavior, repeated insults and interrogation.

Typically, many kinds of abuse go on at the same time in a household.

## Finding a Safe Place

Many communities have temporary homes called battered women's shelters where women and their children who are victims of domestic violence may stay until the crisis passes or until they are able to find a permanent place to relocate. The best way to find these shelters is to consult the local police, welfare department, neighborhood resource center or women's center. You can also look in your phone book under Crisis Intervention Services, Human Service Organizations, Social Service Organizations, Family Services, Shelters or Women's Organizations. In some states, the police are required to provide an apparent battering victim a list of referrals for emergency housing, legal services and counseling services.

If you're having trouble finding resources in your area, you can contact the National Domestic Violence Hotline, 800-799-SAFE (7233), 800-787-3224 (TTY), http://www.ndvh.org.

## If I leave, how can I make sure the abuser won't come near me again?

The most powerful legal tool for stopping domestic violence is the temporary restraining order (TRO). A TRO is a decree issued by a court that requires the perpetrator to stop abusing you. The order may require, for example, that the perpetrator stay away from the family home, where you work or go to school, your children's school and other places you frequent (such as a particular church). The order will also prohibit further acts of violence.

Many states make it relatively easy for you to obtain a TRO. In New York, California and some other states, for example, the court clerk will hand you a package of forms and will even assist you in filling them out. In other areas, nonlawyers may be available to help you complete the forms. When you've completed your forms, you'll go before a judge to show evidence of the abuse, such as hospital or police records. Judges are often available to issue TROs after normal business hours because violence certainly occurs at times other than between 9 a.m. and 5 p.m.

## Programs for Abusive Men

A number of programs have been established to help abusive men change their behavior. You can get more information from the following organizations:

Men Overcoming Violence (MOVE)
54 Mint Street, Suite 300
San Francisco, CA 94103
415-626-6683

Abusive Men Exploring New Directions
(AMEND)
2727 Bryant Street, Suite 350
Denver, CO 80211
303-832-6363
http://www.amend-co.org

Men Stopping Violence
1020 DeKalb Avenue, Suite 25
Atlanta, GA 30307
404-688-1376
http://www.menstoppingviolence.org

## In my community, judges don't issue TROs after 5 p.m. How can I get protection?

Contact your local police department. In many communities, the police can issue something called an emergency protective order when court is out of session. An emergency protective order usually lasts only for a brief period of time, such as a weekend or a holiday, but otherwise it is the same as a temporary restraining order. On the next business day, you will need to go to court to obtain a TRO.

## Are TROs and emergency protective orders only available when the abuser is a spouse?

No, in most states, the victim of an abusive live-in lover, even of the same sex, can obtain a TRO or emergency protective order. In a few states, the victim of any adult relative, an abusive lover (non-live-in) or even a roommate can obtain such an order. In some states, if non-romantic victims and abusers do not live in the same household, the domestic violence laws do not apply. However, in this situation, other criminal laws may come into play. To learn about your state's rule, contact a local crisis intervention center, social service organization or battered women's shelter.

### Help for Abused Gay Men and Lesbians

The following organizations provide information and support for battered gay men and lesbians:

Community United Against Violence (CUAV)
973 Market Street, Suite 500
San Francisco, CA 94103
415-777-5500
415-333-4357 (Crisis Hotline)
http://www.xq.com/cuav/

Advocates for Abused and Battered Lesbians
P.O. Box 85596
Seattle, WA 98105-9998
206-547-8191
http://www.aabl.org

## What should I do once I have a TRO?

Register it with the police located in the communities in which the abuser has been ordered to stay away from you—where you live, work, attend school or church and where your children go to school. Call the appropriate police stations for information about how to register your order.

## What if the abuse continues even if I have a TRO?

Obviously, a piece of paper cannot stop an enraged spouse or lover from acting violent, although many times it is all the deterrent the person needs.

If the violence continues, contact the police. They can take immediate action and are far more willing to intervene when you have a TRO than when you don't. Of course, if you don't have a TRO or it has expired, you should also call the police—in all states, domestic violence is a crime and you don't have to have a TRO for the police to investigate.

The police should respond to your call by sending out officers. In the past, police officers were reluctant to arrest abusers, but this has changed in many communities where victims' support groups have worked with police departments to increase the number of arrests. You can press criminal charges at the police department, and ask for criminal prosecution. Documentation is crucial if you want to go this route. Be sure to insist that the officer responding to your call makes an official report and takes photographs of any bodily injuries, no matter how slight. Also, get the report's prospective number before the officer leaves the premises.

If you do press charges, keep in mind that only the district attorney decides whether or not to prosecute. If you don't press charges, however, the chance is extremely low that the district attorney will pursue the matter.

## Getting Legal Help

If you want to take legal action against your abuser or you need other legal help related to domestic abuse, the following organizations can refer you to assistance programs in your area:

The National Coalition Against Domestic Violence (NCADV), 303-839-1852, http:www.ncadv.org.

The National Domestic Violence Hotline, 800-799-SAFE (7233), 800-787-3224 (TTY).

# Changing Your Name

You may be thinking of changing your name for any number of reasons —perhaps you're getting married or divorced, or maybe you just don't like the name you've got, and you want one that suits you better. Whatever the reason, you'll be glad to know that name changes are common—and usually fairly easy to carry out.

## I'm a woman who is planning to be married soon. Do I have to take my husband's name?

No. When you marry, you are free to keep your own name, take your husband's name or adopt a completely different name. Your husband can even adopt your name, if that's what you both prefer. Give some careful thought to what name feels best for you. You can save yourself consider-able time and trouble by making sure you are happy with your choice of name before you change any records.

## Can my husband and I both change our names—to a hyphenated version of our two names or to a brand new name?

Yes. Some couples want to be known by a hyphenated combination of their last names, and some make up new names that combine elements of each. For example, Ellen Berman and Jack Gendler might become Ellen and Jack Berman-Gendler or, perhaps, Ellen and Jack Bergen. You can also pick a name that's entirely different from the names you have now, just because you like it better.

## What if I do want to take my husband's name? How do I make the change?

If you want to take your husband's name, simply start using the name as soon as you are married. Use your new name consistently, and be sure to change your name on all of your iden-tification, accounts and important documents. To change some of your identification papers—your Social Security card, for example—you'll need a certified copy of your marriage certificate, which you should receive within a few weeks after the marriage ceremony.

For a list of people and institutions to contact about your name change, see *Changing Identification and Records*, below.

## I took my husband's name when I married, but now we're getting divorced, and I'd like to return to my former name. How do I do that?

In most states, you can request that the judge handling your divorce make a formal order restoring your former or birth name. If your divorce decree contains such an order, that's all the paperwork you'll need. You'll probably want to get certified copies of the order as proof of the name change—check with the court clerk for details. Once you have the necessary documentation, you can use it to have your name changed on your identification and personal records.

If your divorce papers don't show your name change, you can still resume your former name without much fuss. In most states, you can simply begin using your former name consistently, and have it changed on all your personal records (see *Changing Identification and Records*, below). If you're returning to a name you had before marriage, you're not likely to be hassled about the change. A few states have more stringent laws, however, and you'll have to apply to a court for an order approving your name change. Contact your local court clerk's office to find out whether you'll need a court order.

## After my husband and I are divorced and I return to my former name, can I change the last name of my children as well?

Traditionally, courts ruled that a father had an automatic right to have his child keep his last name if he continued to actively perform his parental role. But this is no longer true. Now a child's name may be changed by court petition when it is in the best interest of the child to do so. When deciding to grant a name change, courts consider many factors, such as the length of time the father's name has been used, the strength of the mother-child relationship and the need of the child to identify with a new family unit (if the change involves remarriage). The courts must balance these factors against the strength and importance of the father-child relationship. What this all boils down to is that it's up to a judge to decide which name is in the child's best interest.

Keep in mind that even if you do change your children's last name, you won't be changing the paternity—that is, the court's recognition that he is their father, and the rights and obligations that come with that recognition. Nor will a name change affect the rights or duties of either parent regarding visitation, child support or rights of inheritance. Changes such as these occur only if the parental roles are altered by court order—for example, a new custody decree or a legal adoption.

## I just don't like my birth name and I want to change it. Can I choose any name I want?

There are some restrictions on what you may choose as your new name. Generally, the limits are as follows:

- You cannot choose a name with fraudulent intent—meaning you intend to do something illegal. For example, you cannot legally change your name to avoid paying debts, keep from getting sued or get away with a crime.
- You cannot interfere with the rights of others, which generally means capitalizing on the name of a famous person.
- You cannot use a name that would be intentionally confusing. This might be a number or punctuation—for example, "10," "III" or "?".
- You cannot choose a name that is a racial slur.
- You cannot choose a name that could be considered a "fighting word," which includes threatening or obscene words, or words likely to incite violence.

## That's "Mr. Three" to You

Minnesota's Supreme Court once ruled that a man who wanted to change his name to the number "1069" could not legally do so, but suggested that "Ten Sixty-Nine" might be acceptable (*Application of Dengler,* 287 N.W.2d. 637 (1979)).

## Do I have to file forms in court to change my birth name?

Maybe not. In all but a handful of states, you can legally change your name by usage only. A name change by usage is accomplished by simply using a new name in all aspects of your personal, social and business life. No court action is necessary, it costs nothing and it is legally valid. (Minors and prison inmates are generally exceptions to this rule.)

Practically speaking, however, an official court document may make it much easier to get everyone to accept your new name. Because many people and agencies do not know that a usage name change is legal, they may want to see something in writing signed by a judge. Also, certain types of identification—such as a new passport or a birth certificate attachment—are not readily available if you change your name by the usage method.

If it's available in your state, you may want to try the usage method and see how it goes. If you run into too many problems, you can always file a court petition later.

You can find out whether your state requires a court order by contacting your local clerk of court. Or, if the court clerk doesn't give you enough information, you can look at your state's statutes in a local law library—start in the index under

"Name" or "Change of Name," or ask the reference librarian for help.

## How do I implement my name change?

Whether you have changed your name by usage or by court order, the most important part of accomplishing your name change is to let others know you've taken a new name. Although it may take a little time to contact government agencies and businesses, don't be intimidated by the task—it's a common procedure.

The practical steps of implementing a name change are:

- *Advise officials and businesses.* Contact the various government and business agencies with which you deal and have your name changed on their records. See *Changing Identification and Records*, below.
- *Enlist help of family and friends.* Tell your friends and family that you've changed your name and you now want them to use only your new one. It may take those close to you a while to get used to associating you with a new sound. Some of them might even object to using the new name, perhaps fearing the person they know so well is becoming someone else. Be patient and persistent.
- *Use only your new name.* If you are employed or in school, go by your new name there. Introduce yourself to new acquaintances and business contacts with your new name.

If you've made a will or other estate planning document (such as a living trust), it's best to replace it with a new document using your new name. Your beneficiaries won't lose their inheritances if you don't, but changing the document now will avoid confusion later.

Finally, remember to change your name on other important legal papers—for example, powers of attorney, living wills and contracts.

## Changing Identification and Records

To complete your name change, you'll need to tell others about it. Contact the people and institutions you deal with and ask what type of documentation they require to make your name change official in their records. Different institutions may have very different rules; some may need only your phone call, others may require special forms or a copy of a court document.

It's generally recommended that you first acquire a driver's license, then a Social Security card in your new name. Once you have those pieces of identification, it's usually fairly simple to acquire others or have records changed to reflect your new name.

Here are the people and institutions to notify of your name change:

- friends and family
- employers
- schools
- post office
- Department of Motor Vehicles
- Social Security Administration
- Department of Records or Vital

Statistics (issuers of birth certificates)

- banks and other financial institutions
- creditors and debtors
- telephone and utility companies
- state taxing authority
- insurance agencies
- registrar of Voters
- passport office
- Public Assistance (welfare) office, and
- Veterans Administration.

Many government agencies provide instructions on how to register a name change with the agency via their websites. (For information on how to find government websites, see the Legal Research Appendix.) For example, you can download the form for changing your name on your Social Security card at http://www.ssa.gov/online/ss-5.html.

## What should I do if I have a hard time getting my new name accepted?

Some people and institutions may be reluctant to accept your new name— particularly if you've changed it without a court order. If you live in a state where no court order is required, however, you should be able to persuade them to make the change.

Start by providing documentation that shows both the old and new names. If you've recently obtained a passport, it may be helpful because it can show your old name as well as the new name as an AKA ("also known as").

If you're stonewalled, you may want to gently, but forcefully, give a rundown of state law that supports your position. (You can research the law for your state at your local law library or on the Internet. See the Le-

gal Research Appendix.) If the person with whom you are dealing remains uncooperative, ask to speak to his or her supervisor. Be confident that you have the legal right to change your name, even if the people you're dealing with don't know your rights. Keep going up the ladder until you get results. If you have trouble at the local office of a government agency, contact the main office. If you come up against a seemingly impossible situation, get the help of your local elected official.

Finally, if you run into more trouble than you're prepared to deal with, consider going to court and getting a signed order from a judge. It costs more and will take a little time, but an official document will certainly make it easier to handle people and institutions who refuse to accept your new name.

### *More Information About Changing Your Name*

*How to Change Your Name in California*, by David Ventura Loeb and David W. Brown (Nolo), provides complete information on how to change your name in California.

Local law libraries are good sources of information for name changes. Look under "Name" or "Change of Name" in the index of your state's statutes, or ask the reference librarian for help. You can also research state laws on the Internet. See the Legal Research Appendix for more information.

### http://www.nolo.com
*Nolo offers self-help information about a wide variety of legal topics, including relationships between spouses and partners.*

### http://samesexlaw.com
*Same Sex Law provides information affecting lesbian and gay couples.*

### http://www.lectlaw.com
*The 'Lectric Law Library's Lawcopedia on Family Law offers articles and other information on a wide variety of family law issues, including articles about living together.*

### http://divorceonline.com
*The American Divorce Information Network provides FAQs, articles and information on a wide range of divorce issues.*

### http://www.ncadv.org
*The National Coalition Against Domestic Violence offers help, information and links for those affected by domestic violence.*

# 16

# **P**arents and Children

16.2   *Adopting a Child*

16.11  *Stepparent Adoptions*

16.13  *Adoption Rights: Birthparents, Grandparents and Children*

16.17  *Child Custody and Visitation*

16.24  *Child Support*

16.30  *Guardianship of Children*

*A child of five could understand this.*
*Fetch me a child of five.*

**—GROUCHO MARX**

**R**aising children is a big job, and an emotional subject even when family relationships are well established and running smoothly. An adoption, divorce or guardianship proceeding adds extra stress, requiring us to juggle law, economics and our highly charged feelings. Be reassured, however, that there are many people who can help you find your way through family law proceedings, including knowledgeable lawyers, mediators, counselors and therapists. In this chapter, we get you started by answering many of your questions about the laws that affect parents and their children.

# Adopting a Child

Adoption is a court procedure by which an adult legally becomes the parent of someone who is not his or her biological child. Adoption creates a parent-child relationship recognized for all purposes—including child support obligations, inheritance rights and custody. The birthparents' legal relationship to the child is terminated, unless a legal contract allows them to retain or share some rights or the adoption is a stepparent adoption, in which case only the parent without custody loses parental rights.

This section discusses the general legal procedures and issues involved in adopting a child, including the advantages and disadvantages of various types of adoption and some of the special concerns of single people or unmarried couples (gay and straight) who want to adopt a child. Stepparent adoptions and the rights of relatives are discussed later in this chapter.

## Who can adopt a child?

As a general rule, any adult who is found to be a "fit parent" may adopt a child. Married or unmarried couples may adopt jointly, and unmarried people may adopt a child through a procedure known as a single-parent adoption.

Some states have special requirements for adoptive parents. A few of these require an adoptive parent to be a certain number of years older than the child. And some states require the adoptive parent to live in the state for a certain length of time before they are allowed to adopt. You will need to check the laws of your state to see whether any special requirements apply to you. And keep in mind that if you're adopting through an agency, you may have to meet strict agency requirements in addition to any requirements under state law.

Even if you find no state or agency barriers to adopting a child, remember that some people or couples are likely to have a harder time adopting than others. A single man or a lesbian couple may not legally be prohibited from adopting, but may have a harder time finding a placement than would a married couple. This is because all states look to the "best interests of the child" as their bottom line, and will judge the various characteristics of the parent or couple—often factoring in biases about who makes a good parent—when making a placement determination.

## I'm single, but I'd like to adopt a child. What special concerns will I face?

As a single person, you may have to wait longer to adopt a child, or be flexible about the child you adopt. Agencies often "reserve" healthy infants and younger children for two-parent families, putting single people at the bottom of their waiting lists. And birthparents themselves often want their children to be placed in a two-parent home.

If you're a single person wishing to adopt, you should be prepared to make a good case for your fitness as a parent. You can expect questions from case workers about why you haven't married, how you plan to support and care for the child on your own, what will happen if you do marry and other questions that will put you in the position of defending your status as a single person. To many single adoptive parents, such rigorous screening doesn't seem fair, but it is common.

Agencies serving children with special needs may be a good option for singles, as such agencies often cast a wider net when considering adoptive parents. Of course, you shouldn't take a child unless you feel truly comfortable with the idea of raising him or her—but being flexible will make the obstacles to single-parent adoptions easier to overcome.

## My long-term partner and I prefer not to get married, but we'd like to adopt a child together. Will we run into trouble?

There is no specific prohibition against unmarried couples adopting children—sometimes called two-parent adoptions. Like singles, however, you may find that agencies are biased towards married couples. You may have a longer wait for a child, or you may have to expand your ideas about what kind of child you want.

## Is it still very difficult for lesbians and gay men to adopt children?

Only Florida, Utah and Mississippi specifically prohibit lesbians and gay men from adopting children. But that doesn't mean it's easy to adopt in other states. Connecticut, for example, allows judges to consider the sexual orientation of the adoptive parent in determining whether an adoption should take place. The same is true in other states—even if a state adoption statute does not specifically mention sexual orientation, it may become an issue in court, and some judges will use it to find a prospective adoptive parent to be unfit.

On the other hand, many gay men and lesbians have been able to adopt children, and an increasing number of states are allowing gay and lesbian couples to adopt jointly. Beginning in Alaska in 1985, joint adoptions by gay and lesbian couples have been granted in California, Colorado, the District of Columbia, Illinois, Indiana, Massachusetts, Michigan, Minnesota,

New Jersey, New York, Oregon, Pennsylvania, Texas, Vermont and Washington.

Keep in mind that the legal landscape in all areas affecting gays and lesbians is changing rapidly. Just as a legislature might make it easier for gays and lesbians to adopt, a court decision to the contrary might provide quite a different result. Lesbians and gay men will need an experienced attorney to handle an adoption. But you can do your own homework: The National Center for Lesbian Rights (address and phone number listed below) provides information for gay men and lesbians who want to adopt.

### Can I adopt a child whose race or ethnic background is different from mine?

Usually, yes. You do not need to be the same race as the child you want to adopt, although some states do give preference to prospective adoptive parents of the same race or ethnic background as the child. Adoptions of Native American children are governed by federal law—the Indian Child Welfare Act—which outlines specific rules and procedures that must be followed when adopting a Native American child.

### Whose consent is needed for an adoption to take place?

For any adoption to be legal, the birthparents must consent to the adoption unless their parental rights have been legally terminated for some other reason, such as a finding that he or she is an unfit parent. All states

prohibit birthparents from giving their consent to an adoption until after the child's birth, and some states require even more time—typically three to four days after the birth—before the parents are allowed to consent. This means that birthparents can legally change their minds about putting their child up for adoption at any point before the child is born.

## Types of Adoption

**Agency Adoptions.** Agency adoptions involve the placement of a child with adoptive parents by a public agency, or by a private agency licensed or regulated by the state. Public agencies generally place children who have become wards of the state because they were orphaned, abandoned or abused. Private agencies are often run by charities or social service organizations. Children placed through private agencies are usually brought to an agency by parents that have or are expecting a child that they want to give up for adoption.

**Independent Adoptions.** In an independent or private adoption, a child is placed with adoptive parents without the assistance of an agency. Some independent adoptions consist of direct arrangement between the birthparents and the adoptive parents, while others are arranged through an intermediary such as a lawyer, doctor or clergyperson. Whether or not an intermediary is used, a lawyer is essential because of the legal complexities involved. Most states allow independent adoptions, though many regulate them quite carefully. Independent adoptions are not allowed in Connecticut, Delaware, Massachusetts or Minnesota.

**Identified Adoptions.** An identified, or designated, adoption is one in which the adopting parents locate a birthmother (or the other way around) and then ask an adoption agency to handle the rest of the adoption process. In this way, an identified adoption is a hybrid of an independent and an agency adoption. Prospective parents are spared the waiting lists of agencies by finding the birthparents themselves, but reap the other benefits of agencies, such as their experience with legal issues and their counseling services. Identified adoptions provide an alternative to parents in states that ban independent adoptions.

**International Adoptions.** In an international adoption, the adoptive parents take responsibility for a child who is a citizen of a foreign country. In addition to satisfying the adoption requirements of both the foreign country and the parents' home state in the U.S., the parents must obtain an immigrant visa for the child through the U.S. Immigration and Naturalization Service. The INS has its own rules for international adoptions, such as the requirement that the adoptive parents be either married or, if single, at least 25 years old. The INS also requires adoptive parents to complete several forms and submit a favorable home study report. Finally, you must apply for U.S. citizenship for the child; it is not granted automatically.

**Relative Adoptions.** When a child is related to the adoptive parent by blood or marriage, the adoption is a relative adoption. The most common example of

this type of adoption is a stepparent adoption, in which a parent's new spouse adopts a child from a previous partner. Grandparents often adopt their grandchildren if the parents die while the children are minors. These adoptions are usually easier and simpler than nonrelative adoptions.

## What are some of the advantages and disadvantages of an agency adoption?

Using an agency to manage your adoption can be helpful for a number of reasons. Agencies are experienced in finding children, matching them with parents and satisfying the necessary legal requirements. Agencies will do most of the legwork of an adoption, from finding a birthparent to finalizing the papers, and they'll walk

adoptive parents through many of the crucial steps in between, such as conducting the home study, obtaining the necessary consents and advising parents on the state's specific legal requirements.

One key advantage of an agency adoption is the extensive counseling that agencies provide throughout the process. Typically, counseling is available for adoptive parents, birthparents and the children (if they are older). Careful counseling can help everyone involved weather the emotional, practical and legal complexities that are likely to arise during the adoption.

Finally, many agencies specialize in certain kinds of children; this may be helpful if you want, for example, to adopt an infant, a child of a different race from yours or a child with special medical needs. Some agencies also offer international adoption services.

On the down side, private agencies are often extremely selective when choosing adoptive parents. This is because they have a surplus of people who want to adopt and a limited number of available children. Most agencies have long waiting lists of prospective parents, especially for healthy, white infants. Agencies weed out parents using criteria such as age limits, marital status, income, health, religion, family size, personal history (including criminal conduct) and residency requirements.

Additionally, agencies often wait to place the child in the adoptive home until all necessary consents have been given and become final. Because of this, a child may be placed in foster care for a few days or weeks, depend-

ing on the situation and the state's law. This delay concerns many adoptive parents who want the child to have a secure, stable home as soon as possible. Some agencies get around this by placing infants immediately through a type of adoption known as a "legal risk placement": If the birthmother decides she wants her child back before her rights have been legally terminated, the adoptive parents must let the child go.

Public agencies often have many children ready to be adopted, but they often specialize in older or special needs children. If you want a newborn, a public agency might not be able to help you. Also, public agencies often do not provide many other services such as the much-needed counseling that private agencies offer. Generally, they don't have as many resources as private agencies.

## How do I find an adoption agency?

There are an estimated 3,000 adoption agencies in the United States, public and private. If you live in a state like California or New York, you'll have more options than if you live in a less populated state. But wherever you live, you'll probably have to do some searching to find an agency that meets your needs and is able to work with you. You can call a national adoption organization for referrals to get you started. The addresses and phone numbers of several organizations are listed at the end of this section.

Be persistent with the agencies you contact. If they tell you that there are no children, ask whether there is a waiting list. Then ask other questions such as: Is the waiting list for child placement or a home study? How do they determine who may file an application? Can you fill out an application now? If not, when can you? Do they hold orientation meetings? If so, when will the next one be held? Ask if you can speak with other parents in circumstances similar to yours who have adopted through the agency. These parents may provide valuable information about the service they received from the agency, how long the process took and whether they were ultimately happy with the outcome. Screen the agencies as much as they screen you.

## How can I check on the reputation of an adoption agency?

As discussed above, you can and should speak with other parents who have adopted through the agency. In addition, you should check out the agency's accreditation. Start with the licensing department of your state. It can tell you whether the agency has been cited for licensing violations, or whether the licensing office has received any complaints about the agency. You can also request a copy of the state's rules governing agencies so that you understand the standards to which your agency is held.

The staff at your state's department of social services may also be able to give you information about the agency. Finally, you can check your state or local department of consumer affairs to see if it handles complaints about adoption agencies.

## Are agency adoptions very expensive?

They can be. Agencies charge fees to cover the birthmother's expenses as allowed by state law; these expenses may include medical costs, living expenses during the pregnancy and costs for counseling. Add to this the agency's staff salaries and overhead—and charges can mount up quickly.

Many agencies charge a flat fee for adoptions, while others add the birthmother's expenses to a fixed rate for the agency's services. Some agencies use a sliding scale that varies with adoptive parents' income levels, usually with a set minimum and maximum fee. You can expect to pay between $1,000 and $6,000 to adopt a young child, and $10,000 or more to adopt a newborn. Some agencies charge a lower rate for handling special needs adoptions.

Public agencies generally do not charge fees for placing children in adoptive homes.

## What are the costs involved in an independent adoption?

Because each situation is unique, fees for independent adoptions vary widely. Prospective parents must generally cover the costs of finding a birthmother, all costs related to the pregnancy and birth, and the legal costs involved in the adoption process. Some states also include the birthmother's living expenses during the pregnancy. Expenses such as hospital bills, travel costs, phone bills, home study fees, attorneys' fees and court costs can often surpass $10,000.

# You Can't Buy a Baby

It is illegal in all states to buy or sell a baby. All states, however, allow adoptive parents to pay certain "reasonable" costs that are specifically related to the adoption process. Each state has its own laws defining the expenses that may be paid by adoptive parents in any kind of adoption proceeding—agency or independent. If you pursue an independent adoption, you must adhere to these laws when you give any money to the birthmother. And agencies are regulated to make sure that they charge adoptive parents only for the costs that the state allows.

Most states allow the adoptive parents to pay the birthmother's medical expenses, counseling costs and attorney fees. Some states allow payments to cover the birthmother's living expenses such as food, housing and transportation during pregnancy. Most states require all payments to be itemized and approved by a court before the adoption is finalized. Be sure to know and understand your state's laws, because providing or accepting prohibited financial support may subject you to criminal charges. Furthermore, the adoption itself may be jeopardized if you make improper payments.

## What should I keep in mind when deciding whether to pursue an independent adoption?

Birth and adoptive parents are sometimes attracted to independent adoptions because they allow control over the entire adoption process. Rather than relying on an agency as a go-between, the birthparent and adoptive parents can meet, get to know each other and decide for themselves whether the adoption should take place. Independent adoptions also avoid the long waiting lists and restrictive qualifying criteria that are often involved in agency adoptions. Plus, independent adoptions usually happen much faster than agency adoptions, often within a year of beginning the search for a child.

One major drawback to independent adoptions is that they are illegal in some states, currently Connecticut, Delaware, Massachusetts and Minnesota. States that do allow independent adoptions sometimes regulate them in other ways—for example, by prohibiting adoptive parents from advertising for birthmothers. Be sure to check your state's laws before you proceed.

Another concern is that birthparents might not receive adequate counseling during the adoption process. This may leave your agreement more vulnerable to unraveling. Furthermore, some states extend the period in which birthparents may revoke their consent for independent adoptions; this places your agreement at additional risk.

Finally, independent adoptions are a lot of work. Adoptive parents often spend enormous amounts of time—and money—just finding a birthmother, not to mention the efforts required to follow through and bring the adoption to a close. Some parents decide afterwards that the energy and expense needed to adopt independently are just too much, and they hire an agency to do the work for their next adoption.

## Open Adoptions

An open adoption is one in which there is some degree of contact between the birthparents and the adoptive parents—often this includes contact with the child as well. There is no one standard for open adoptions; each family works out the arrangement that works best for them. Some adoptive parents consider meeting the birthparents just once before the birth of the child, while others form ongoing relationships which may include written correspondence or visits.

Open adoptions often help reduce stress and worry by eliminating the power of the unknown: Rather than fearing the day that a stranger will come knocking on their door to ask for the child back, adoptive parents are reassured by knowing the birthparents personally and dealing with them directly. This openness can be beneficial to the child as well, who will grow up with fewer questions—and misconceptions—than might a child of a "closed" adoption.

If you want your adoption to be open and decide to use an agency, be sure to find out their policies on open placements. Some agencies offer only closed or "semi-open" adoptions, and will not provide identifying information about birth or adoptive parents even if both families want the adoption to be open. On the other hand, independent adoptions—where allowed—permit any degree of openness desired by the birth and adoptive families.

## What's a home study?

All states require adoptive parents to undergo an investigation to make sure that they are fit to raise a child. Typically, the study is conducted by a state agency or a licensed social worker who examines the adoptive parents' home life and prepares a report that the court will review before allowing the adoption to take place. Some states do not require a report to be submitted to a court. These states allow the agency or social worker to decide whether the prospective parents are fit to adopt. Common areas of inquiry include:

- financial stability
- marital stability
- lifestyles
- other children
- career obligations
- physical and mental health, and
- criminal history.

In recent years, the home study has become more than just a method of investigating prospective parents: It serves to educate and inform them as well. The social worker helps to prepare the adoptive parents by discussing issues such as how and when to talk with the child about being adopted, and how to deal with the reaction that friends and family might have to the adoption.

## Can I adopt a child from another country?

You can adopt a foreign child through an American agency which specializes in intercountry adoptions—or you can adopt directly. If you prefer a direct adoption, you will have to adhere not only to the adoption laws of your state, but also to U.S. immigration laws and the laws of the country where the child is born. It will be a complex process, so be prepared for some tangles. Do as much research as you can before you fly off to find a child; the more you know about the chosen country's adoption system ahead of time, the better off you'll be when you get there.

U.S. immigration laws require that prospective adoptive parents be married or, if single, at least 25 years old. The adoptive parents must file a Petition to Classify Orphan as an Immediate Relative (INS form I-600) with the Immigration and Naturalization Service which shows either that the child's parents have died, disappeared or have abandoned the child, or that one remaining parent is not able to care for the child and consents to the child's adoption and immigration to the U.S. If there are two known parents, the child will not qualify as an orphan under any circumstances.

Along with the I-600, you will need to submit a number of other documents, including a favorable home study report. If the INS approves the petition, and there are no disqualifying factors such as a communicable disease, the child can be issued an immigrant visa.

Much of the paperwork for an intercountry adoption can be completed even before you have identified a specific child to adopt. Advance preparation is a valuable option because the INS paperwork often takes a long time to process, and may hold up the child's arrival in the U.S. even after all foreign requirements have been met.

Finally, be sure to check your own state laws for any preadoption requirements. Some states, for instance, require you to submit the written consent of the birthmother before they approve the entry of the child into the state. Some experts recommend that parents who adopt overseas readopt the child in their own state in order to make sure that the adoption fully conforms to state law.

For more information about intercountry adoptions, see the resource list at the end of this section.

## What should my adoption petition say?

A standard adoption petition will generally include five pieces of information:

1) the names, ages and address of the adoptive parents
2) the relationship between the adoptive parents and the child to be adopted
3) the legal reason that the birthparents' rights are being terminated (usually that they consented to the termination)
4) a statement that the adoptive parents are the appropriate people to adopt the child, and
5) a statement that the adoption is in the child's best interests.

Typically, the written consent of the birthparents or the court order terminating their parental rights is also filed along with the petition. Adoptive parents also often include a request for an official name change for the child.

## Do I need an attorney to handle the adoption of my child?

If you do not use an agency, yes. And even if you do use an agency, you will probably need to hire a lawyer to draft the adoption petition and to represent you at the hearing. Although there is no legal requirement that a lawyer be involved in an adoption, the process can be quite complex and should be handled by someone with experience and expertise. When seeking a lawyer, find out how many adoptions he or she has handled, and whether any of them were contested or developed other complications.

## When is an adoption considered final?

All adoptions—agency or independent—must be approved by a court. The adoptive parents must file a petition to finalize the adoption proceeding; there will also be an adoption hearing.

Before the hearing, anyone who is required to consent to the adoption must receive notice. Usually this includes the biological parents, the adoption agency, the child's legal representative if a court has appointed one and the child himself if he is old enough (12 to 14 years in most states).

At the hearing, if the court determines that the adoption is in the child's best interest, the judge will issue an order approving and finalizing the adoption. This order, often called a final decree of adoption, legalizes the new parent-child relationship and usually changes the child's name to the name the adoptive parents have chosen.

# Stepparent Adoptions

The majority of adoptions in the United States are stepparent adoptions, in which the biological child of one parent is formally adopted by that parent's new spouse. This type of adoption may occur when one biological parent has died or has left the family after a divorce, and the remaining parent remarries. While most stepparents do not formally adopt their stepchildren, if they do, they obtain the same parental rights as biological parents. This section discusses some of the issues that arise when a stepparent adopts a stepchild.

## My new spouse wants to adopt my son from a previous marriage. Are there special adoption rules for stepparents?

Generally speaking, a stepparent adoption is much easier to complete than a nonrelative adoption. The procedure is generally the same as for any adoption, but specific steps are sometimes waived or streamlined. For instance, waiting periods, home studies and even the adoption hearing are sometimes dispensed with in a stepparent adoption.

In all stepparent adoptions, however, your ex-spouse will need to consent to the adoption because she is the other legally recognized parent of the child. If your former spouse refuses to consent, the adoption will not be allowed unless his or her parental rights are terminated for some other reason—abandonment or unfitness, for example.

## My new husband has a great relationship with my 10-year-old son and wants to adopt him. My son communicates about once or twice a year with his real father, who will consent to the adoption. Is adoption the right thing to do?

Stepparent adoptions can be complicated when the noncustodial biological parent is still alive and in contact with the child. There may be no legal reason why the adoption cannot take place, but the emotional impact of the adoption also needs to be considered.

If an adoption will bring stability to your new family and help your son feel more secure, it may be the right choice. But no matter how well your son gets along with your new husband, he may feel conflicting loyalties between his adoptive father and his real father, and this may be hard for him to handle. Generally speaking, the less contact your son has with his real father, the more sense it makes for an adoption to take place.

Besides the impact on the child (which should be of primary importance), also make sure your ex-husband understands that giving consent to the adoption means giving up all parental rights to his son, including any right to visit him or make decisions for him regarding issues such as medical treatment or education. In addition, he would no longer be responsible for child support once his parental rights were terminated.

In addition, your new husband should be aware that if he adopts your son, and you and he divorce, he will be responsible for paying child support. Of course, he will also be entitled to visitation or custody.

## I had my daughter when I was unmarried, and we haven't heard from her father for several years. I'm now married to another man, and he wants to adopt my daughter. Do I have to find her biological father and get his consent to the adoption before it can take place?

As in any adoption, the adoption cannot take place until the absent parent either gives consent or has his parental rights terminated for some other reason. That being said, there are a few specific ways to proceed with an adoption when one biological parent is out of the picture.

First, it is possible to go forward without a biological parent's consent if you can prove that the absent parent has not exercised any parental rights and convince the court that it's appropriate to legally terminate that parent-child relationship. Most states' laws allow parental rights to be terminated when a parent has willfully failed to support the child or has abandoned the child for a period of time, usually a year. Generally, abandonment means that the absent parent hasn't communicated with the child or supported the child financially.

If the absent parent is a father, another common way to terminate his parental rights is to show that he is not, legally speaking, the presumed father of the child. Most states have statutes establishing who the presumed father of a child is in certain situations. In this case, you won't have to prove that the father has abandoned the child. You simply must show that he does not meet the legal definition of presumed father. For instance, in all states, a man who is married to a woman at the time she gives birth is legally presumed to be the child's father. Another way of establishing presumed fatherhood in many states is by marrying the mother after the child has been born and being named as the father on the child's birth certificate.

If you can show that the father doesn't meet any of the tests in your state for presumed fatherhood, the court may terminate his rights and allow you to proceed without his consent. If, however, the father meets one of the state's tests for presumed fatherhood, you'll need either to obtain the father's consent to the adoption, or to have his rights terminated by proving abandonment, willful failure to support the child or parental unfitness.

# Adoption Rights: Birthparents, Grandparents and Children

The rights of parents to raise and care for their children have traditionally received strong legal protection. Courts have long recognized that the bond between parents and children is a profound one, and the law will not interfere with that bond except in the most carefully defined circumstances. Since adoption generally involves creating a parent-child relationship where there previously was none—and sometimes negating someone's parental rights in the process—balancing the legal rights of the parties involved can sometimes be difficult. This section discusses how the legal rights of birthparents, grandparents and children can be affected by the adoption process.

## Are birthparents allowed to change their minds and take children back even after they've been placed in the adoptive parents' home?

Even after the birthparents have consented to an adoption and the child is living in the adoptive home, many states set aside a period of time during which the birthparents can change their minds. Depending on the state, the birthparents have the right to withdraw consent weeks or even months after the placement. Though it can be nervewracking—and sometimes devastating—for the adoptive parents who have begun to care for the child, it's important that they understand that birthparents have this right. Adoptive parents should find out how long their state allows for birthparents to legally withdraw consent.

## The birthmother of the baby we were going to adopt just decided she wants to keep her child. She's eight months pregnant, and we've paid all of her medical bills during her pregnancy. Can we get our money back?

Unless the mother agrees to pay you back, you're probably out of luck. Especially with independent adoptions, paying a birthmother's allowable costs is a risk for adoptive parents. Birthparents often change their minds, and courts will not force them to pay back the expenses paid by the adoptive parents.

## My girlfriend is pregnant and I'm the father. I want to keep the baby, but she wants to give it up for adoption. Can she do that?

No. If you acknowledge that you're the father of the child, your consent is needed before the baby can be adopted. The rights of fathers have gotten much more attention in recent years and are now more strongly protected by the law. Some court rulings have held that father's homes must be strongly considered as best for the child. It's important to understand, however, that fathers' rights vary greatly from state to state, and the law in this area is far from settled. If you don't want to see your baby adopted, you should be sure to acknowledge paternity and make it clear to the mother that you won't allow your parental rights to be terminated.

## My husband and I found an expectant mother who wants us to adopt her baby. But her mother is trying to talk her out of giving up the child. Can a grandparent legally object to an adoption?

No. The parents of a birthmother don't have any legal right to stop her from giving up the baby. Also, grandparents won't necessarily be favored as adoptive parents over nonrelative parents. (One big exception to this rule is the adoption of Native American children, where a special federal law applies.)

That said, however, grandparents often hold a lot of sway over birthparents, and in many cases have convinced them at the last minute not to give up their babies. If you know that the grandparents are actively trying to talk the birthmother out of the adoption, you should know that there's an increased risk that the adoption might fall through. In this situation, it's especially important to keep in close touch with the birthmother and make extra efforts to encourage open communication. You'll have to judge for yourself how confident you feel about proceeding with a birthmother whose family is opposed to the adoption.

### I was adopted as a baby. Now I'm 25 and I want to find my birthparents. Do I have a legal right to obtain my birth records?

In most adoptions, the original birth records and other case documents are "sealed" by the court that finalizes the adoption, which means that no one can see them without the court's permission. But as attitudes toward adoption have become more open, states have adopted a variety of ways for adopted children to find their birthparents, some of which do not require the unsealing of records.

Only a few states offer adult adopted children open access to original birth certificates. More popular is a system called "search and consent," in which an adopted child has an agency contact the birthparent, who then indicates whether or not he or she agrees to be identified. If the birthparent consents, then the agency provides the information to the child. The most common system is a mutual consent registry, used in about 25 states, in which birthparents and

adopted children provide identifying information about themselves to the registry. If a birthparent and his or her adopted child both appear within a register, the agency in charge of the register will share the information with each of them, enabling them to contact each other.

If one of these options isn't available or doesn't work for you, it may be possible to obtain your birth records. Generally, a court will unseal a record for "good cause," such as a need for medical or genetic information.

The best way to start your search is to contact a local adoption agency that knows your state's laws and procedures for contacting birthparents. The National Adoption Information Clearinghouse and the North American Council on Adoptable Children are good sources for referrals to local agencies. (See the end of this section for contact information.)

Another useful tool in searching for birthparents is the Internet. Dozens of organizations and services designed to help adopted children find their birth families have cropped up on the Web. A good place to start is Yahoo!'s adoption category, located at http:// www.yahoo.com/Society_and_Culture/ Families/Parenting/Adoption.

## More Information About Adopting a Child

*The Adoption Resource Book*, by Lois Gilman (HarperPerennial), is a comprehensive guide for anyone considering adoption.

The Committee for Single Adoptive Parents, P.O. Box 15084, Chevy Chase, MD 20825, is a clearinghouse for single people seeking information about adoption. The Committee publishes *The Handbook for Single Adoptive Parents*.

The National Adoption Information Clearinghouse, P.O. Box 1182, Washington, DC 20012-1182, 703-352-3488, 888-251-0075 (toll-free), naic@calib.com (e-mail), http://www.calib.com/naic. NAIC provides free information about adoption as well as referrals to local agencies and support groups.

*Adoption and Parenting: Legal Issues for Lesbians and Gays,* by Attorneys Denis Clifford, Robin Leonard and Frederick Hertz, is a Nolo eGuide that provides an overview of the major legal issues involved with lesbian and gay parenting, including adoptions, foster parenting and guardianships.

The National Center for Lesbian Rights, Adoption & Foster Parenting Project, 870 Market Street, Suite 570, San Francisco, CA 94102, 415-392-6257, http://www.nclrights.org/, provides help to gay men and lesbians who want to adopt.

The National Federation for Open Adoption Education, c/o The Independent Adoption Center, 391 Taylor Boulevard, Suite 100, Pleasant Hill, CA 94523, 925-827-2229, can refer you to agencies with expertise in open adoptions.

The North American Council on Adoptable Children (NACAC), 970 Raymond Ave., Suite 106, St. Paul, MN 55114, 651-644-3036, can provide you with information about adoption resources in your local area.

*Adopt International: Everything You Need to Know to Adopt a Child from Abroad*, by O. Robin Sweet & Patty Bryan (Noonday Press), is a good source of information for prospective parents considering an international adoption.

*How to Adopt Your Stepchild in California*, by Frank Zagone & Attorney Mary Randolph (Nolo), explains everything you need to know and do in order to adopt a stepchild in California.

The United States Immigration and Naturalization Service, 425 I Street, Washington, DC 20536, http://www.ins.usdoj.gov publishes a pamphlet called *The Immigration of Adopted and Prospective Adoptive Children* (M-249N), as well as other forms you will need for an international adoption.

*U.S. Immigration Made Easy*, by Laurence Canter & Martha Siegel (Nolo), contains a chapter on international adoptions, including the necessary INS forms.

# Child Custody and Visitation

YOU CAN'T SHAKE HANDS

WITH A CLENCHED FIST.

**—INDIRA GHANDI**

When parents separate or divorce, the term "custody" often serves as shorthand for "who gets the children" under the divorce decree or judgment. In many states, custody is split into two types: physical custody and legal custody. Physical custody refers to the responsibility of taking care of the children, while legal custody involves making decisions that affect their interests (such as medical, educational and religious decisions). In states that don't distinguish between physical and legal custody, the term "custody" implies both types of responsibilities.

For information on finding your state's law, see the Legal Research Appendix. Also, the Legal Information Institute, at http:www.cornell.edu/topics/child_custody.html, has an excellent summary of child custody laws, cases and resources.

## Does custody always go to just one parent?

No. Courts frequently award at least some aspects of custody to both parents, called "joint custody." Joint custody usually takes at least one of three forms:

- joint physical custody (children spend a relatively equal amount of time with each parent)
- joint legal custody (medical, educational, religious and other decisions about the children are shared), or
- both joint legal and joint physical custody.

In every state, courts are willing to order joint legal custody, but about half the states are reluctant to order joint physical custody unless both parents agree to it and they appear to be sufficiently able to communicate and cooperate with each other. In New Hampshire and New Mexico, courts automatically award joint legal custody unless the children's best interests—or a parent's health or safety—would be compromised. Many other states expressly allow their courts to order joint custody even if one parent objects to such an arrangement.

## Can someone other than the parents have physical or legal custody?

Sometimes neither parent can suitably assume custody of the children, perhaps because of substance abuse or a mental health problem. In these situations, others may be granted custody of the children or be given a temporary guardianship or foster care arrangement by a court.

## What factors do courts take into account when deciding who gets custody of the children?

A court gives the "best interests of the child" the highest priority when deciding custody issues. What the best interests of a child are in a given situation depends upon many factors, including:

- the child's age, gender, mental and physical health
- the mental and physical health of the parents
- the lifestyle and other social factors of the parents, including whether the child is exposed to secondhand smoke and whether there is any history of child abuse
- the love and emotional ties between the parent and the child, as well as the parent's ability to give the child guidance
- the parent's ability to provide the child with food, shelter, clothing and medical care
- the child's established living pattern (school, home, community, religious institution)
- the quality of the schools attended by the children
- the child's preference, if the child is above a certain age (usually about 12), and
- the ability and willingness of the parent to foster healthy communication and contact between the child and the other parent.

Assuming that none of these factors clearly favors one parent over the other, most courts tend to focus on which parent is likely to provide the children a stable environment. With younger children, this may mean awarding custody to the parent who has been the child's primary caregiver. With older children, this may mean giving custody to the parent who is best able to foster continuity in education, neighborhood life, religious institutions and peer relationships.

## Are mothers more likely to be awarded custody over fathers?

In the past, most states provided that custody of children of "tender years" (about five and under) had to be awarded to the mother when parents divorced. This rule is now rejected in most states, or relegated to the role of tie-breaker if two fit parents request custody of their preschool children. Most states require their courts to determine custody on the basis of what's in the children's best interests without regard to the sex of the parent.

As it turns out, most divorcing parents agree that the mother will have custody after a separation or divorce, and that the father will exercise reasonable visitation. This sometimes happens because fathers presume that mothers will be awarded custody or because the mother is more tenacious in seeking custody. In still other situations, the parents agree that the mother has more time, a greater inclination or a better understanding of the children's daily needs.

## Are there special issues if a gay or lesbian parent is seeking custody or visitation rights?

Only the District of Columbia has a law on its books stating that a parent's sexual orientation cannot be the sole factor in making a custody or visitation award. In a few states—including Alaska, California, New Mexico and Pennsylvannia—the highest court has ruled that a parent's homosexuality, in and of itself, cannot be grounds for an automatic denial of custody. But trial courts in many other states—including Alabama, Arizona, Connecticut, Delaware, Florida, Illinois, Indiana, Iowa, Kentucky, Maine, Maryland, Massachusetts, Michigan, New Jersey, New York, North Dakota, Ohio, Oregon, South Carolina, Utah, Vermont, Washington, West Virginia, Wisconsin and Wyoming—have ruled that judges must find that a parent's sexual orientation would harm the child before it can be used as the basis for denying custody or visitation.

In reality, a lesbian or gay parent faces a difficult struggle when trying to gain custody in most American courtrooms, especially if that parent lives with a partner. The trend in the late 1990s—particularly in southeastern states—has been to deny many lesbian mothers and gay fathers custody of their children. It is fair to say that many, if not most, judges are ignorant about, prejudiced against, or suspicious of, gay and lesbian parents. Only a few judges understand that a parent's sexual orientation, alone, does not effect the best interests of the children. But judges often use the best-interests standard to deny a gay or lesbian parent custody.

## Is race ever an issue in custody or visitation decisions?

The U.S. Supreme Court has ruled it unconstitutional for a court to consider race when a noncustodial parent petitions for a change of custody. In that case, a white couple had divorced, and the mother had been awarded custody of their son. She remarried an African-American man and moved to a predominantly African-American neighborhood. The father filed a request for modification of custody based on the changed circumstances. A Florida court granted the modification, but the U.S. Supreme Court reversed, ruling that societal stigma, especially a racial one, cannot be the basis for a custody decision. (*Palmore v. Sidoti*, 466 U.S. 429 (1984)).

When a court awards physical custody to one parent and "visitation at reasonable times and places" to the other, who determines what's reasonable?

The parent with physical custody is generally in the driver's seat regarding what is reasonable. This need not be bad if the parents cooperate to see that the kids spend a maximum amount of time with each parent. Unfortunately, it all too often translates into very little visitation time with the noncustodial parent, and lots of bitter disputes over missed visits and inconvenience. To avoid such problems, many courts now prefer for the parties to work out a fairly detailed parenting plan (known as a parenting agreement) which sets the visitation schedule and outlines who has responsibility for decisions affecting the children.

## The judge in my divorce case has mentioned a parenting agreement. What is that?

A parenting agreement is a detailed, written agreement between a divorcing couple that describes how they will deal with visitation, holiday schedules, vacation, religion, education and other issues related to their child. More and more, courts are encouraging the use of parenting agreements during divorce proceedings. Often, if couples have discussed and agreed upon how to deal with issues affecting their children—rather than having the judge make an independent ruling on those issues—they are more likely to stick to the terms of the agreement.

## I have sole custody of my children. My ex-spouse, who lives in another state, has threatened to go to court in his state and get the custody order changed. Can he do that?

All states and the District of Columbia have enacted a statute called the Uniform Child Custody Jurisdiction Act (UCCJA), which sets standards for when a court may make a custody determination and when a court must defer to an existing determination from another state. Having the same law in all states helps standardize how custody decrees are treated. It also helps solve many problems created by kidnapping or disagreements over custody between parents living in different states.

In general, a state may make a custody decision about a child only if it meets one of these tests (in order of preference):

- The state is the child's home state. This means the child has resided in the state for the six previous months, or was residing in the state but is absent because a parent took the child to another state. (A parent who wrongfully removed or retained a child in order to create a "home state" will be denied custody.)

- The child has significant connections in the state with people such as teachers, doctors and grandparents and, in the words of the UCCJA, "substantial evidence in the state concerning the child's care, protection, training and personal relationships." (A parent who wrongfully removed or retained a child in order to create "significant connections" will be denied custody.)

- The child is in the state and either has been abandoned or is in danger of being abused or neglected if sent back to the other state.
- No other state can meet one of the above three tests, or a state that can meet at least one test has declined to make a custody decision.

If a state cannot meet one of these tests, the courts of that state cannot make a custody award, even if the child is present in the state. In the event more than one state meets the above standards, the law specifies that only one state may make custody decisions. This means that once a state makes a custody award, any other state must keep its hands off the matter.

## Under what circumstances can custody and visitation orders be changed within the state where they were obtained?

After a final decree of divorce or other order establishing custody and visitation (such as a paternity decree) is filed with a court, parents may agree to modify the custody or visitation terms. This modified agreement (also called a "stipulated modification") may be made without court approval. If one parent later reneges on the agreement, however, the other person may not be able to enforce it unless the court has approved the modification. Thus, it is generally advisable to obtain a court's blessing before relying on such agreements. Courts usually approve modification agreements

unless it appears that they are not in the best interests of the child.

If a parent wants to change an existing court order and the other parent won't agree to the change, he or she must file a motion (a written request) asking the court that issued the order to modify it. Usually, courts will modify an existing order only if the parent asking for the change can show a "substantial change in circumstances." This requirement encourages stability of arrangements and helps prevent the court from becoming overburdened with frequent and repetitive modification requests. Here are some examples of a substantial change in circumstances:

- *Geographic move.* If a custodial parent makes a significant move, or the move will seriously disrupt the stability of the child's life, the move may constitute a changed circumstance that justifies the court's modification of a custody or visitation order. Some courts switch custody from one parent to the other, although the increasingly common approach is to ask the parents to work out a plan under which both parents may continue to have significant contact with their children. If no agreement is reached, what the court will do depends on where you live. Courts in some states will permit the move unless it is shown that the child will be adversely affected. In other states, the court will carefully examine the best interests of the child and make a decision about which parent should have custody.

• *Change in lifestyle.* Changes in custody or visitation orders may be obtained if substantial changes in a parent's lifestyle threatens or harms the child. If, for example, a custodial parent begins working at night and leaving a nine-year-old child alone, the other parent may request a change in custody. Similarly, if a noncustodial parent begins drinking heavily or taking drugs, the custodial parent may file a request for modification of the visitation order (asking, for example, that visits occur when the parent is sober, or in the presence of another adult). What constitutes a lifestyle sufficiently detrimental to warrant a change in custody or visitation rights varies tremendously depending on the state and the particular judge deciding the case.

## Custodial Interference

In most states, it's a crime to take a child from his or her parent with the intent to interfere with that parent's physical custody of the child (even if the taker also has custody rights). This crime is commonly referred to as "custodial interference." In most states, the parent deprived of custody may sue the taker for damages, as well as get help from the police to have the child returned.

If a parent without physical custody (who may or may not have visitation rights) removes a child from—or refuses to return a child to—the parent with physical custody, it is considered kidnapping or child concealment in addition to custodial interference. Federal and state laws have been passed to prosecute and punish parents guilty of this type of kidnapping, which is a felony in over 40 states.

In many states, interfering with a parent's custody is a felony if the child is taken out of state. Many states, however, recognize good-cause defenses, such as where the taker acted to prevent imminent bodily harm to herself or himself, or to the child. In addition, some states let a parent take a child out of state if the parent is requesting custody in court and has notified the court or police of the child's location.

## I've heard that mediation is the best approach to solving disagreements about child custody and visitation. Is this true?

Mediation is a nonadversarial process where a neutral person (a mediator) meets with disputing persons to help them settle a dispute. The mediator does not have power to impose a solution on the parties, but assists them in creating an agreement of their own. (In a few states, however, the mediator may be asked by the court to make a recommendation if the parties cannot reach an agreement.)

There are several important reasons why mediation is a superior method to litigation for resolving custody and visitation disputes:

• Mediation usually does not involve lawyers or expert witnesses (or their astronomical fees).

• Mediation usually produces a settlement after five to ten hours of mediation over a week or two. (Child custody litigation can drag on for months or even years.)

- Mediation enhances communication between the couple and makes it much more likely that they will be able to cooperate after the divorce or separation when it comes to raising their children. Experts who have studied the effects of divorce on children universally conclude that when divorcing or separating parents can cooperate, the children suffer far less.

## How to Find a Family Law Mediator

Several states require mediation in custody and visitation disputes and a number of others allow courts to order mediation. In these situations, the court will direct the parents to the mediator and will pay for the services. Parents can also find and pay for the mediator themselves. With increasing frequency, family law attorneys are offering mediation services for child custody and other divorce-related disputes, as are a number of nonlawyer community mediators. Two resources for finding a family law mediator in your area are:

Academy of Family Mediators
5 Militia Drive
Lexington, MA 02421

718-674-2663
718-674-2690 (fax)
http://www.mediators.org

Society of Professionals in Dispute Resolution (SPIDR)
1527 New Hampshire Avenue, NW
Third Floor
Washington, DC 20036
202-667-9700
202-265-1968 (fax)
http://www.spidr.org

## Things are so bitter between my ex and me that it's hard to see us sitting down together to work things out. How can mediation possibly work?

Mediators are very skilled at getting parents who are bitter enemies to cooperate for the sake of their children. The more parents can agree on the details of separate parenting, the better it will be for them and their children. And mediators are skilled at getting the parents to recognize this fact and then move forward towards negotiating a sensible parenting agreement. If there is a history of abuse or if the parents initially cannot stand to be in the same room with each other, the mediator can meet with each parent separately and ferry messages back and forth until agreement on at least some issues is reached. At this point, the parties may be willing to meet face to face.

*More Information
About Child Custody*

*Child Custody: Building Parenting Agreements That Work,* by Mimi Lyster (Nolo), shows separating or divorcing parents how to create a win-win custody agreement.

National Center for Lesbian Rights, 870 Market Street, Suite 570, San Francisco, CA 94102, 415-392-6257, http://www.nclrights.org, provides legal information, referrals and assistance to lesbian and gay parents.

National Congress for Fathers and Children, 9454 Wilshire Boulevard, Suite 207, Beverly Hills, CA 90212, 800-733-3237 or 310-247-6051, http://com.primenet.com/ncfc, provides information and assistance for fathers.

# Child Support

*Children have more need
of models than of critics.*

**—JOSEPH JOUBERT**

Child support is an emotional subject. Parents who are supposed to receive it on behalf of their children often do not. Parents who are supposed to pay it often cannot, or choose not to for a variety of reasons that are not legally recognized. It is the children who suffer the most when child support levels are inadequate or obligations are not met. Therefore, the trend in all states is to increase child support levels and the ways child support obligations can be enforced.

## How long must parents support their children?

Biological parents and adoptive parents must support a child until:
- the child reaches the age of majority (and sometimes longer if the child has special needs or is in college)
- the child is on active military duty
- the parents' rights and responsibilities are terminated (for example, when a child is adopted), or
- the child has been declared emancipated by a court. (Emancipation can occur when a minor has demonstrated freedom from parental control or support and an ability to be self-supporting.)

## How are child support obligations affected by a divorce or separation?

When one parent is awarded sole custody of a child, the other parent typically is required to fulfill his or her child support obligation by making payments to the custodial parent. The custodial parent, however, meets his or her support obligation through the custody itself. When parents are awarded joint physical custody in a divorce, the support obligation of each is often based on the ratio of each parent's income to their combined incomes, and the percentage of time the child spends with each parent.

## Are fathers who never married the mother still required to pay child support?

The short answer to this question is yes. When a mother is not married, however, it's not always clear who the father is. An "acknowledged father" is any biological father of a child born to unmarried parents for whom paternity has been established by either the admission of the father or the agreement of the parents. Acknowledged fathers are required to pay child support.

Additionally, a man who never married may be presumed to be the father of a child if he welcomes the child into his home and openly holds the child out as his own. In some states, the presumption of paternity is considered conclusive, which means it cannot be disproved, even with contradictory blood tests.

The obligation to pay child support does not depend on whether a court ordered it. Where most unmarried fathers encounter this principle is when the mother seeks public assistance. Sooner or later the welfare department will ask the court to order the father to reimburse it, based on his support obligation and income during the period in question. Sometimes this happens many years later, and the father is required to pay thousands of dollars in back support that he never knew he owed.

## Do fathers have the same right to child support as mothers?

Yes. If you're a father with custody, you have the right to ask for child support. Each parent has a duty to support his or her children, and that duty doesn't discriminate between genders.

## Is a stepparent obligated to support the children of the person to whom he or she is married?

No, unless the stepparent legally adopts the children.

## Calculating Child Support

Each state has guidelines for calculating child support, based on the parents' incomes and expenses. These guidelines vary considerably from state to state. In addition, in some states judges have considerable leeway in setting the actual amount, as long as the general state guidelines are followed. But an increasing number of states impose very strict guidelines that leave the judges very little latitude.

In most states, the guidelines in effect specify factors which must be considered in determining who pays child support, and how much. These factors usually include:

- the needs of the child—including health insurance, education, day care and special needs
- the income and needs of the custodial parent
- the paying parent's ability to pay, and
- the standard of living of the child before divorce or separation.

## How does the court determine the amount I am able to pay for child support?

When determining your ability to pay child support, the court looks at your net income. This is your gross income from all sources—such as wages, investment income, rents from real property or public benefits—less any mandatory deductions. Mandatory deductions include income taxes, Social Security payments and healthcare costs. In most states, courts don't consider other types of automatic deductions from your paycheck (such as wage attachments or credit union payments) or debt obligations (such as loan or credit card payments) when figuring net income. This is because the law places a high priority on child support. Courts would rather see other debts go unpaid than have a child suffer from inadequate support. One

exception is other child support obligations. In some states, courts allow you to deduct the amount of child support you pay for other children from your gross income.

Some courts consider reasonable expenses you incur for the necessaries of life—for example, rent, mortgage, food, clothing and healthcare. But, this usually does not include costs for tuition, eating in restaurants or entertainment. Again, the theory is that support of your children should come before these types of personal expenses. In a growing number of states, courts will not consider any personal expenses when determining your ability to pay support.

## Can the court base its child support order on what I am able to earn as opposed to what I'm actually earning?

In most states, the judge is authorized to examine a parent's ability to earn as well as what she is actually earning, and order higher child support if there is a discrepancy. Actual earnings are an important factor in determining a person's ability to earn, but are not conclusive where there is evidence that a person could earn more if she chose to do so.

For example, assume a parent with an obligation to pay child support leaves his current job and enrolls in medical or law school, takes a job with lower pay but good potential for higher pay in the future or takes a lower-paying job that provides better job satisfaction. In each of these situations, a court may base the child support award on the income from the original job (ability to earn) rather than on the new income level (ability to pay). The basis for this decision would be that the children's current needs take priority over the parent's career plans and desires.

On the other hand, several courts have ruled that a parent's imprisonment entitles the parent to a reduction or suspension of child support where there is no showing that the imprisonment resulted from an attempt to avoid paying the support.

## What happens if a parent falls behind on his or her child support payments?

Each installment of court-ordered child support is to be paid according to the date set out in the order. When a person does not comply with the order, the overdue payments are called arrearages or arrears. Judges have become very strict about enforcing child support orders and collecting arrearages. While the person with arrears can ask a judge for a downward modification of future payments, the judge will usually insist that the arrearage be paid in full, either immediately or in installments. In fact, judges in most states are prohibited by law from retroactively modifying a child support obligation.

### EXAMPLE
*Joe has a child support obligation of $300 per month. Joe is laid off of his job, and six months pass before he finds another one with comparable pay. Although Joe could*

*seek a temporary decrease on the grounds of diminished income, he lets the matter slide and fails to pay any support during the six-month period. Joe's ex-wife later brings Joe into court to collect the $1,800 arrearage; Joe cannot obtain a retroactive ruling excusing him from making the earlier payments.*

In addition, back child support cannot be cancelled in a bankruptcy proceeding. This means that once it is owed, it will always be owed, until paid.

## My ex-spouse is refusing to pay court-ordered child support. How can I see to it that the order is enforced?

Under the Child Support Enforcement Act of 1984, the district attorneys (or state's attorneys) of every state must help you collect the child support owed by your ex. Sometimes this means that the D.A. will serve your ex with papers requiring him to meet with the D.A. and arrange a payment schedule, and telling him that if he refuses to meet or pay, he could go to jail. If your ex has moved out of state, you or the D.A. can use legal procedures to locate him and seek payment. Federal and state parent locator services can also assist in locating missing parents.

Federal laws permit the interception of tax refunds to enforce child support orders. Other methods of enforcement include wage attachments, seizing property, suspending the business or occupational license of a payer who is behind on child support or—in some states—revoking the payer's driver's license. Your state's D.A. may employ any one of these methods in an attempt to help you collect from your ex.

If you and your ex live in different states, you may use the Revised Uniform Reciprocal Enforcement of Support Act (RURESA) to seek payment. Under that law, the court in the state where you live contacts a court in your ex-spouse's state, which in turn requires him to pay. This procedure will be provided to you free of charge. Unfortunately, however, it often falls short of its stated goals due to the complexity of the process and the low priority frequently assigned to these cases by the courts and law enforcement officers which are involved.

In 1992, Congress passed the Child Support Recovery Act (CSRA) which makes it a federal crime for a parent to willfully refuse to make support payments to a parent who lives in another state. This statute has been challenged on constitutional grounds (beyond the authority of Congress), and its enforcement is spotty.

As a last resort, the court that has issued the child support order can hold your ex in contempt and, in the absence of a reasonable explanation for the delinquency, impose a jail term. This contempt power is exercised sparingly in most states, primarily because most judges would rather keep the payer out of jail where he has a chance of earning the income necessary to pay the support.

## I think our existing child support order is unfair. How can I change it?

You and your child's other parent may agree to modify the child support terms, but even an agreed-upon modification for child support must be approved by a judge to be legally enforceable.

If you and your ex can't agree on a change, you must request the court to hold a hearing in which each of you can argue the pros and cons of the proposed modification. As a general rule, the court will not modify an existing order unless the parent proposing the modification can show changed circumstances. This rule encourages stability of arrangements and helps prevent the court from becoming overburdened with frequent and repetitive modification requests.

Depending on the circumstances, a modification may be temporary or permanent. Examples of the types of changes that frequently support temporary modification orders are:
- a child's medical emergency
- the payer's temporary inability to pay (for instance, because of illness or an additional financial burden such as a medical emergency or job loss), or
- temporary economic or medical hardship on the part of the recipient parent.

A permanent modification may be awarded under one of the following circumstances:
- either parent receives additional income from remarriage

- changes in the child support laws
- job change of either parent
- cost of living increase
- disability of either parent, or
- needs of the child.

A permanent modification of a child support order will remain in effect until support is no longer required or the order is modified at a later time—again, because of changed circumstances.

## Do I have to pay child support if my ex keeps me away from my kids?

Yes. Child support should not be confused with custody and visitation. Every parent has an obligation to support his or her children. With one narrow exception, no state allows a parent to withhold support because of disputes over visitation. The exception? If the custodial parent disappears for a lengthy period so that no visitation is possible, a few courts have ruled that the noncustodial parent's duty to pay child support may be considered temporarily suspended.

No matter what the circumstances, if you believe that your ex is interfering with your visitation rights, the appropriate remedy is to go back to court to have your rights enforced or modified rather than stop making support payments.

*More Information About Child Support*

*Nolo's Pocket Guide to Family Law*, by Robin Leonard and Stephen Elias (Nolo), explains legal concepts you may run across if you're involved in a divorce, custody dispute, adoption or other family law matter.

In addition, the following organizations can give you information about enforcing child support orders:

National Child Support Enforcement Association
Hall of the States
444 N. Capitol Street, Suite 414
Washington, DC 20001-1512
202-624-8180
ncsea@sso.org
http://www.ncsea.org

Administration for Children and Families
Child Support Enforcement
Mail Stop: OCSE/DCS/NRC
370 L'Enfant Promenade, SW
Washington, DC 20447
202-401-9383
http://www.acf.dhhs.gov

# Guardianship of Children

A guardianship is a legal arrangement in which an adult has the court-ordered authority and responsibility to care for a child (someone under 18 in most states) or an incapacitated adult. This section focuses on guardianships of children.

A guardianship may be necessary if a child's parents die, or if the child has been abandoned, is not receiving adequate care or is being abused in some way.

## What does a guardian do?

Typically, a guardian takes care of a child's personal needs, including shelter, education and medical care. A guardian may also provide financial management for a child, though sometimes a second person (often called a "conservator" or "guardian of the estate") is appointed for this purpose.

## What is the difference between a guardianship and an adoption?

An adoption permanently changes the relationship between the adults and child involved. The adopting adults legally become the child's parents. The biological parent (if living) gives up all parental rights and obligations to the child, including the responsibility to pay child support. If a biological parent dies without a will, the child has no right to inherit.

Although a guardianship establishes a legal relationship between a child and adult, it does not sever the legal relationship between the biological parents and the child. For example, the biological parents are legally required to provide financial support for the child. And if a biological parent dies without a will, the child has certain automatic inheritance rights.

## May I be appointed guardian if the child's parents object?

It depends on how a judge sees the situation. You'll need to start by filing guardianship papers in court. A court investigator will likely interview you, the child and his or her parents and make a recommendation to the judge. The judge will then review the case and decide whether to appoint you. As a general rule, guardianships are not granted unless:
- the parents voluntarily consent
- the parents have abandoned the child, or
- a judge finds that it would be detrimental to the child for his or her parents to have custody.

## If a child lives with me, do I need a guardianship?

You won't need a guardianship if the child is only staying with you for a few weeks or months. But anyone who anticipates caring for a child for a period of years will probably need a legal guardianship. Without this legal arrangement, you may have trouble registering the child in school, arranging for medical care and obtaining benefits on the child's behalf. In addition, you'll have no right to keep the child if his parents want him back—even if you think they're not capable of caring for him properly.

# If You Want to Avoid a Formal Guardianship

An adult who has physical custody of a child may have strong reasons to avoid becoming a legal guardian—for example:

- The caretaker expects that the child's parents will not consent to a legal guardianship.
- Dynamics between family members are such that filing for a guardianship might set off a battle for legal custody. (This would be especially likely where a stepparent and one natural parent care for a child.)
- The caretaker doesn't want his or her personal life scrutinized in court or by a court-appointed investigator.

Some adults try to slide by and raise children (often grandchildren or other relatives) without any legal court authorization. If you go this route, you could run into problems with institutions that want authority from a parent or court-appointed legal guardian. Some communities and institutions are, however, very accommodating of people who are bringing up someone else's children. California, for example, has created a form that gives a nonparent permission to enroll a child in school and make medical decisions on his or her behalf without going to court. Research the laws for your state,

or talk to a knowledgeable family law attorney, to find out whether there are ways for you to care for a child short of becoming a legal guardian.

## When does a guardianship end?

A guardianship ordinarily lasts until the earliest of these events:

- the child reaches legal age
- the child dies
- the child's assets are used up—if the guardianship was set up solely for the purpose of handling the child's finances, or
- a judge determines that a guardianship is no longer necessary.

Even if a guardianship remains in force, a guardian may step down from his or her role with permission from the court. In that case, a judge will appoint a replacement guardian.

## Who financially supports a child under a guardianship?

Unless a court terminates the biological parents' rights (uncommon in most guardianship situations), the parents are responsible for supporting their child. In practice, however, financial support often becomes the guardian's responsibility. The guardian may choose to pursue financial benefits on the child's behalf, such as public assistance and Social Security.

Any funds the guardian receives for the child must be used for that child's benefit. Depending on the amount of money involved, the guardian may be required to file periodic reports with a court showing how much money was received for the child and how it was spent.

# Are You Prepared to Be a Guardian?

An obvious but important question to ask yourself before you take any steps to establish a guardianship is whether you're truly prepared for the job.

- Do you want the ongoing responsibilities of a legal guardianship—including potential liability for the child's actions?
- If you're managing the child's finances, are you willing to keep careful records, provide a court with periodic accountings and go to court when you need permission to handle certain financial matters?
- What kind of personal relationship do you have with the child? Do you want to act as the legal parent of this child for the duration of the guardianship?
- Will the guardianship adversely affect you or your family because of your own children, health situation, job, age or other factors?
- Do you have the time and energy to raise a child?
- What is the financial situation? If the child will receive income from Social Security, public assistance programs, welfare, a parent or the estate of a deceased parent, will this be enough to provide a decent level of support? If not, are you able and willing to spend your own money to raise the child?
- Do you anticipate problems with the child's relatives—including parents—who may suddenly reappear and contest the guardianship? (This is rare, but it can happen.)

- What kind of relationship do you have with the child's parents? Will they support the guardianship, or will they more likely be hostile, antagonistic or interfering?

It's smart to consider your options carefully before initiating a guardianship proceeding. After honestly answering the questions above, you may need to rethink your plans.

## Is it true that parents may need a guardianship of their own child?

It's strange but true: Sometimes parents need to establish a particular type of guardianship—called a "guardianship of the estate"—to handle their own child's finances—even if the child lives with them. This situation usually arises when significant amounts of property (at least $5,000 in most states) are given directly to a child.

Understandably, institutions and lawyers are reluctant to turn assets over to parents when they were intended for a child. A guardianship of the estate relieves the institution from liability, and the parents are directly accountable to a court to show how funds are spent and invested.

**EXAMPLE**

*The Thompsons lived next door to an elderly widow, who was extremely fond of their small daughter. When the widow died, she left her house to little Suzy Thompson. The lawyer handling the widow's estate suggests that Suzy's parents go to court to establish a guardianship of their child's estate. The house is then transferred into the name of Suzy's guardianship estate, which her parents manage until she reaches adulthood.*

While this system is effective in protecting children's assets from unscrupulous parents, setting up a formal guardianship of the estate involves time and money that well-meaning parents sometimes find burdensome. For this reason, all states have passed laws to make it easier to give money or property to children. These laws provide simple, inexpensive procedures by which gifts to minors (typically up to $10,000) can be managed by their parents without setting up a formal guardianship of the estate. The gift-giver must simply name, in his or her will or in a trust document, someone to manage the gift until the child reaches adulthood. No court involvement is required. (For more information about leaving property to children, see Chapter 12, *Wills and Estate Planning*.)

## I have young children, and I'm worried about who will care for them if something happens to me. How can I name a guardian?

You can use your will to name a guardian for your children. The specifics are discussed in Chapter 12 of this book, *Wills and Estate Planning*.

### More Information About Guardianships

*The Guardianship Book for California*, by Lisa Goldoftas and David Brown (Nolo), contains all forms and instructions necessary to become a child's guardian in California.

For information about guardianships in other states, visit your local law library.

### http://www.nolo.com

*Nolo offers self-help information about a wide variety of legal topics, including laws that affect parents and their children.*

### http://www.calib.com/naic

*The National Adoption Information Clearinghouse provides information about adoption as well as referrals to local agencies and support groups.*

### http://www.adoption.com

*This site provides information about adoption agencies, international adoption and many other adoption issues.*

### http://www.divorceonline.com

*Divorce Online provides general information, including articles about mediation and child custody. The site also gives answers to frequently asked family law questions.*

### http://www.law.cornell.edu/topics/topic2.html#family#law

*The Legal Information Institute at Cornell Law School provides links to many of the family laws available on the Web, including laws governing adoption, child custody and children's rights.*

# Courts and Mediation

17.2     *Representing Yourself in Court*

17.13     *Small Claims Court*

17.21     *Mediation*

17.27     *Dealing With Your Lawyer*

NINETY PERCENT OF OUR LAWYERS SERVE

TEN PERCENT OF OUR PEOPLE. WE ARE

OVER-LAWYERED AND UNDER-REPRESENTED.

**—JIMMY CARTER**

The average citizen's ability to gain access to the American justice system has long been determined by economic status. The wealthy can afford experienced lawyers—the legal system's gatekeepers— while most others are frozen out. Fortunately, a number of initiatives are being developed to level the legal playing field. Although still too few, and often too limited in the size and types of disputes they can consider, mediators, expanded small claims courts and family courts that make nonlawyers welcome are all part of the changing landscape. So, too, are Internet-based legal information sites, which increasingly provide legal information as well as low-cost forms and instructions necessary to complete routine legal tasks. Together they give hope that all Americans will have improved access to our legal system in the years ahead.

# Representing Yourself in Court

IN THE SPRING OF 1988,
A MAN WAS ARRESTED IN NEW YORK
FOR IMPERSONATING A LAWYER OVER
A LENGTHY PERIOD OF TIME.
ASSISTANT MANHATTAN DISTRICT
ATTORNEY BRIAN ROSNER SAID ONE
JUDGE TOLD HIM:

*"I should have suspected he wasn't a lawyer. He was always so punctual and polite."*

With lawyers' fees often running in excess of $200 an hour, it often makes sense to represent yourself in a small civil (noncriminal) lawsuit. The task may seem daunting, but if you have a good self-help resource to guide you and, if possible, someone who knows the ropes to coach you when you need help, you really can act as your own lawyer—safely and efficiently.

## Is it ever truly sensible to appear in court without a lawyer?

When it comes to small claims court, which is designed to be accessible to nonlawyers—yes, of course. But sometimes it's also a good idea to represent yourself in a more formal court pro-ceeding. Hiring a lawyer rarely makes economic sense for disputes that involve less than $50,000 and often costs more than it's worth for disputes in the $50,000–$100,000 range. In these dollar ranges, representing yourself may be your only reasonable option.

## Are you saying that for small cases, the cost of hiring a lawyer is too high, given the amount at stake?

With most lawyers charging hefty hourly fees, and any contested court case racking up at least dozens of hours of attorney time, it is obvious that attorney fees can quickly dwarf what is at stake in many disputes. But the problem is really more fundamental: No matter what the size of the case, many people don't have the kind of money it takes to pay a lawyer's hourly rate in the first place. This means that unless the case is for a personal injury or another type of dispute that lawyers will handle for a contingency fee (a percentage of the total recovery)—or the lawyer quotes a reasonable fixed fee to deal with the dispute from start to finish—the person will either have to go it alone or give up the lawsuit altogether.

## Free Legal Help

Before you decide to represent yourself, you may want to explore the possibility of getting help at no cost to you. Here are several instances in which you may be able to get an attorney to represent you for free. If none of these matches your situation, or if you simply wish to represent yourself, you'll also want to explore whether your court offers pro per assistance either in person or on the Internet.

### If you face criminal charges.

If you've been charged with a crime and cannot afford to hire your own lawyer, you have a constitutional right to an attorney at government expense. At your request, an attorney, often from a public defender's office, can be appointed to represent you when you are formally charged in court with a criminal offense.

### If you've been injured.

If you have been significantly injured and it appears that someone else is at least partially at fault, many lawyers will agree to represent you on a "contingency fee" basis. This means that you pay attorney's fees only when and if the attorney recovers money for you, in which case the attorney takes an agreed-upon percentage of that total as fees. Be aware, however, that even if a lawyer takes your case on a contingency fee basis, you still have to agree to pay costs, which can

add up to several thousand dollars. Costs, which will sometimes be advanced by a lawyer, include court filing fees, court reporters' fees, expert witness fees and jury fees. The good news is that if you win your case, the judge will usually order your adversary to pay you back for these costs.

### If you qualify for legal aid.

If you can't afford an attorney, you may qualify for free legal assistance. Legal aid lawyers are government-funded lawyers who represent people with low incomes in a variety of legal situations, including eviction defense, denial of unemployment compensation or other benefits, and consumer credit problems. If you think you might qualify, look in your telephone directory or ask a local attorney, lawyer referral service or elected representative for the nearest legal aid office.

### If your claim involves an issue of social justice.

If your dispute involves a social justice issue, an attorney or nonprofit organization with an interest in that issue may represent you on a free or "pro bono" (for the public good) basis. For example, if your claim involves sexual harassment by an employer, abuse by a spouse or partner, discrimination in housing or employment, freedom of speech or religion or environmental pollution, you may find an attorney or nonprofit organization willing to represent you pro bono. Help is much more likely to be forthcoming if your claim raises new and important issues of law. Call a local bar association or a private organization that deals with the kind of problem you face, such as the American Civil Liberties Union, the NAACP Legal Defense Fund, the Natural Resources Defense Council, the National Women's Law Center or the Lambda Legal Defense and Education Fund (gay and lesbian rights).

***If your claim involves a divorce, child custody or support, domestic violence or other family law problem.***

Increasingly, family courts are providing plain English information and simplified forms to self-represented litigants. Many have established comprehensive family law centers right at the courthouse, where trained staff help nonlawyers successfully achieve their goals.

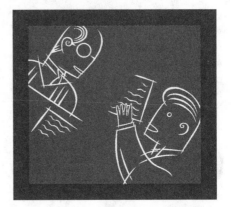

## Court Information Online

Courts in all 50 states have begun posting legal information and useful forms and instructions on the Internet. Generally, small claims and family (divorce) courts provide the most helpful information, but in some areas all courts are striving to become more accessible. Here's how to find court websites:

- Nolo's Legal Research Center (http://www.nolo.com/research/index.html) links to federal, state and local courts around the country. It also provides access to information about small claims court in many states.

- The National Center for State Courts (http://www.ncsc.dni.us/court/sites/courts.htm) lists state and local court websites.

- The Federal Judiciary's website (http://www.uscourts.gov/links.htm) lists federal court websites.

If I do decide to represent myself, how can I possibly cope with all the picky procedural rules and complex legal language?

Essentially, you have two choices. Get the dispute diverted to mediation (see Mediation, below), where things are done in plain English and procedural rules are kept to a minimum, or take the time to learn how to navigate a formal court proceeding. As with learning any other bureaucratic process, doing this will take some effort, but it is far from impossible. Fortunately, Nolo publishes an excellent primer, *Represent Yourself in Court*, by Paul Bergman and Sara Berman-Barrett, which covers all the basics.

## Will I really be able to learn everything I need to know to represent myself competently?

Again, the basics of how to bring or defend a case aren't difficult. But trying to get on top of every nuance of procedure and strategy is tricky. That's why Nolo suggests a two-pronged approach: learn how to handle routine representation tasks yourself while hiring a lawyer as a self-help law coach to provide advice on strategy and tactics as needed. In many situations, hiring a lawyer to coach your self-help efforts will cost only about 10%-20% of what it would cost to hire the lawyer to do the entire job.

## How to Find a Lawyer Coach

Ten years ago, trying to find a lawyer who would help you find your own way through the legal system was next to impossible. Today, given the surplus of personal service lawyers and a gradual change for the better in the profession's attitude towards self-helpers, it's much easier. Because law is an increasingly specialized field, however, you'll want to find someone who is knowledgeable about your type of problem—not just any lawyer. Try to get a referral from someone else who has recently worked with lawyers in the area of your legal concern. For example, if you're opening a small business and want to find an appropriate lawyer to provide occasional guidance, you might talk to the owners of excellent local businesses to see whom they work with. Once you have a few names, make and pay for a first appointment (lawyers will respect you far more if you don't beg for a free consultation). Come right out and ask the lawyer if she is prepared to help you help yourself. If you're persistent, you're likely to find a lawyer who meets your needs. Another approach is to use one of several Internet sites, such as LegalOpinion.com, which for a reasonable fee allow you to ask a lawyer questions without obligating yourself to full-scale representation.

I'm trying to decide whether to sue someone—for example, a contractor who goofed up my expensive remodeling project. What are my first steps?

You need to be able to answer yes to three fundamental questions in order to decide whether it's worthwhile to go forward:

• Do I have a good legal case?
• Can I prove my case?
• Can I collect when I win?

If the answer to any of these questions is no, you probably won't want to sue.

## How hard is it to collect a court judgment?

That depends on your opponent. Most reputable businesses and individuals will pay you what they owe. But if your opponent tries to stiff you, collecting what you are owed can be a costly time-consuming struggle. Unfortunately, the court won't collect your money for you or even provide much help; it will be up to you to identify the assets you can grab.

Normally, if an individual is working or owns valuable property—such as land or investments—collection is less difficult; you can instruct your local law enforcement agency (usually the sheriff, marshal or constable) to garnish her wages or attach her non-exempt property. The same is true of a successful business, especially one which receives cash directly from customers; you can authorize your local sheriff or marshal to collect your judgment right out of the cash register. And in many states, if you are su-

ing a contractor or other business person with a state license, you can apply to have the license suspended until the judgment is paid.

But if you can't identify any collection source—for example, you're dealing with an unlicensed contractor of highly doubtful solvency—think twice before suing. A judgment will be of no value to you if the business or individual is insolvent, goes bankrupt or disappears.

## How do I decide if I have a good case?

Lawyers break each type of lawsuit ("cause of action," in attorney-speak) into a short list of required elements. As long as you know what the elements are for your type of lawsuit, it's usually fairly easy to determine whether your case is legally sound. For example, a lawsuit against a contractor for doing substandard construction would be for breach of contract (the contractor agreed either orally or in writing to do the job properly). The legal elements for this type of lawsuit are:

*Contract formation.* You must show that you have a legally binding contract with the other party. If you have a written agreement, this element is especially easy to prove. Without a written contract, you will have to show that you had an enforceable oral (spoken) contract, or that an enforceable contract can be implied from the circumstances of your situation.

*Performance.* You must prove that you did what was required of you under the terms of the contract. Assuming you have made agreed-upon payments and otherwise met the terms of the agreement, you'll have no problems with this element.

*Breach.* You must show that the party you plan to sue failed to meet her contractual obligations. This is usually the heart of the case—you'll normally need to prove that the contractor failed to do agreed-upon work or did work of poor quality.

*Damages.* You must show that you suffered an economic loss as a result of the other party's breach of contract. Assuming the work must be redone or finished, this element is also easy to prove.

The legal elements for other types of lawsuits are different. You can find outlines for most in *Represent Yourself in Court,* by Attorneys Paul Bergman and Sara J. Berman-Barrett (Nolo).

## Is it difficult to prepare the paperwork to initiate a lawsuit?

Actually, it's often fairly easy—especially if you learn how to do the necessary legal research and prepare drafts of the papers, restricting your lawyer's role to that of checking your work. Initiating a lawsuit is especially straightforward in states such as California and Michigan, where court clerks provide preprinted fill-in-the-blanks forms for many types of lawsuits. But even in states where lawsuits are filed the old-fashioned way, using paragraphs of appropriate legal jargon on numbered legal paper, the actual wording you'll need is almost always available word for word from lawyer "forms books" or CD-ROMs.

These information sources, which are routinely used by lawyers, are available at most larger law libraries and are usually fairly easy for the nonlawyer to understand.

## I've filed my lawsuit. What do I need to do next?

Before a case gets scheduled for trial, a number of things need to happen, including meetings with your opponent and paperwork designed to reduce or narrow disputed issues. Court rules that cover many of these—for example, whether and when a settlement conference must take place, when papers must be filed and how to place a case on the court's trial calendar—should be available from the court clerk and, increasingly, on the Web (see Court Information Online, above). Unfortunately, many clerks are not willing to provide help beyond handing out a copy of often confusing written rules. To get a plain English overview of the pretrial process, see Nolo's *Represent Yourself in Court,* by Attorneys Paul Bergman & Sara J. Berman-Barrett.

In addition to procedural maneuverings, most larger lawsuits involve a search for information about the facts of the case, called "discovery." This process is left largely up to you and the other parties to the lawsuit. For example, one type of discovery consists of your taking the deposition (oral statement) of the other party or one or more witnesses to find out what he or she is likely to say at trial. Additional types of discovery consist of interrogatories (written questions to the other party), a request to produce documents or a request that the other party admit certain facts (stipulations).

## What are the advantages and disadvantages of taking a deposition?

Depositions, which normally consist of face-to-face questioning of the other party or a witness before trial, have several big advantages as compared to the other types of discovery mentioned above:

- You can learn a great deal about your adversary's case, so as to avoid surprise in the courtroom.
- You can offer a deposition transcript into evidence at trial if the deponent (the person questioned) is unavailable to give live testimony. This rule explains why you might consider deposing a helpful witness who may not be available to testify at the time of trial.
- If an adversary's witness whose deposition you have taken testifies significantly differently at trial than at the deposition, you can read the inconsistent deposition testimony into the trial record to impeach (attack) the deponent's credibility.

### EXAMPLE

*You have sued your former employer for violating state law by firing you for missing work because you served on a jury in a lengthy trial. Before trial you take the deposition of your former supervisor, Paul Chepick. At the deposition, Chepick testified that your work performance had been* *satisfactory before you took off for jury duty. At trial, Chepick testifies that you were fired not because of your jury service, but because of a number of work-related problems. Because Chepick's deposition testimony contradicts his trial testimony, you could read the deposition testimony into the record at trial to call his believability into question.*

- As compared to conducting discovery by asking written questions (interrogatories), depositions allow for more flexibility in questioning because you hear a deponent's answer before you ask the next question. For example, assume that a deponent unexpectedly refers to an important business meeting that you had no idea had taken place. In a deposition, you can immediately follow up the remark with questions about what took place during this meeting.
- You can take anyone's deposition. You can depose your adversary, an employee who works for your adversary, a bystander who witnessed a key event, an expert witness hired by your opponent—or even your opponent's attorney! By contrast, you can send written questions (interrogatories) only to your opponent, not to witnesses.
- You elicit the testimony of an individual deponent. While your adversary's lawyer will probably attend the deposition and can consult with the deponent during recesses (breaks in the testimony), it is the deponent who has to answer the questions. By contrast, attorneys often play a major role in preparing

the answers to written interrogatories and usually advise clients how to answer them in a way that provides you with as little information as possible.

- You can use a deposition to learn and ask about documents (or other tangible items) by simply using a Notice of Deposition (to depose your opponent) or a subpoena duces tecum (to depose a nonparty witness). In either case you can list items you want the deponent to bring to the deposition.

Unfortunately, deposing an adversary or a witness who supports your adversary also has some disadvantages. Weigh these considerations very carefully before you decide to take a deposition:

- Depositions are the most expensive discovery tool. Even if you are representing yourself (and therefore not paying an attorney to take or attend a deposition), you must pay a court reporter to transcribe the testimony and prepare a written transcript. While costs vary somewhat by locality, it's not unusual for a court reporter to charge up to $5.00 per page of transcript. A day of deposition testimony fills up about 150 pages, meaning that a day-long deposition may cost you around $750. If you win your case, however, the judge may order your adversary to pay your deposition costs.

- If you are involved in a lawsuit against a good-sized business or governmental entity and haven't investigated thoroughly enough to know which witnesses are most likely to have important information, you may end up paying dearly to depose a witness whose main answers are, "I don't know." By contrast, written interrogatories give you access to "corporate knowledge." This means that when you send interrogatories to an adversary that is a business or other entity, any employee with knowledge has to contribute to the answers.

- Effective deposition questioning is a difficult skill, even for many attorneys. You have to pose questions carefully in order to be confident that you know how adverse witnesses will testify at trial. If questions are vague or you forget to cover a topic, you won't be prepared for your opponent's evidence at trial or be able to show that a witness has changed a story and therefore should not be believed.

- Your adversary's lawyer can be present at a deposition. The attorney may throw you off track by objecting to your questions. Also, an adversary's attorney can help witnesses "refresh their recollections" during recesses. Finally, seeing you in action will allow the attorney to estimate your own credibility, and by listening to your questions often learn as much about your case as you learn about your adversary's.

- If you depose an adverse witness who becomes unavailable for trial, you enable the adversary to offer the deposition transcript into evidence at trial.

## How do I take a deposition?

Start by checking your local court rules (see Court Information Online, above). Then read *Nolo's Deposition Handbook*, by Paul Bergman and Albert Moore, which contains detailed instructions on how to ask and answer questions. Pay particular attention to the time window for taking depositions and understand exactly how to notify a person whose deposition you want to take. Under all rules, you'll need to select a date and location for the deposition, arrange and pay for a court reporter's presence (many are listed in phone books), and give the deponent and opposing counsel (or your self-represented adversary) at least ten days' written notice. Even better, as a courtesy, talk to all the necessary people ahead of time to try to arrange a mutually convenient date and location.

If you want to depose a "non-party witness" (someone other than your adversary), you'll probably have to serve the witness with an official court form called a "Subpoena re Deposition." If you want the non-party witness to bring documents to the deposition, use instead a form carrying the fancy title "Subpoena Duces Tecum re Deposition." (These forms should be available from a court clerk.) List the documents you want the witness to bring along, and state briefly how they pertain to the case.

Once the deposition has been scheduled, follow these tips to learn as much information as you can:

- Prepare a list of questions before you take a witness's deposition. You need not slavishly follow the list, but having one to refer to should prevent you from forgetting important topics.

- Bring (or subpoena) copies of any written statements about the case that the deponent has previously given. For example, bring the police report if the witness gave a statement to a police officer who included it in the report, or the witness's own declaration (statement under oath) if one was attached to a document filed in court. Ask the deponent to amplify on and fill any holes in a statement's contents, then check to see if the deponent in any way contradicts a prior statement. If so, you might ask the witness to repeat the contradictory statement. That way, if you impeach (attack the credibility of) the witness at trial, the witness cannot easily wriggle out by saying, "I made a careless mistake during my deposition."

- Bring copies of any other documents about which you want to question the witness, regardless of whether the witness wrote the document or has any connection to it. For example, you may want to know whether the witness ever saw a document, the date on which the witness saw it or whether the witness is aware of the information in the document.

- Review and bring along all paperwork relating to the case organized chronologically, including the complaint, answer and any motions or court rulings. These documents can help if an issue arises concerning the relevance of your questions.

## When my case finally makes it to the courtroom, I'm afraid I won't know what to say, when to say it or even where to stand. How can I learn what to do?

It's not hard to learn how to conduct yourself in court. This is especially true if your trial is before a judge without a jury, because when dealing with a self-represented person many judges make an effort to simplify jargon and procedure. And there are several practical steps you can take to learn the ropes:

- Attend a few trials involving similar issues. You'll see that it won't be that difficult to present your story and evidence to a judge.
- Carefully read a self-help book such as Nolo's *Represent Yourself in Court*, by Attorneys Paul Bergman and Sara J. Berman-Barrett, which explains what you'll need to do in great detail. For example, you'll want to prepare and practice a brief but thorough opening statement to tell the judge what your case is about.
- Prepare a Trial Notebook which outlines each major aspect of your trial and what you need to do and say at each point. For example, based on taking the other side's deposition or asking written questions (interrogatories), you probably have a pretty good idea what she will say when she testifies. Clearly, it's a good idea to use your Trial Notebook to prepare a carefully

crafted outline of what you plan to ask her in court. Similarly, because you will know before trial who else will testify for the other side, your Trial Notebook should contain a well-organized list of points you want to cover when you have a chance to question (cross-examine) them.

## A Typical Trial

Allowing for many possible variations, most trials begin with each side making an opening statement—each party presents an overview of his case, including what he expects to prove. The next stage is direct examination, during which the plaintiff (the person who filed the suit) presents her testimony about what happened and supports it with witnesses' statements and other relevant evidence. After each of the plaintiff's witnesses testifies, the defendant gets a chance to cross-examine them. In doing so, the defendant attempts to produce testimony favorable to his version of events and to cast doubt on the reliability or credibility of the plaintiff's witnesses. Finally, each side gets to make a closing argument explaining to the judge or jury why they should win.

## What types of evidence win trials?

As mentioned above, in addition to having a legally sound case, you need to be able to prove it before a judge or jury. Technically, this means establishing each required legal element of your cause of action by a preponderance (more than 50%) of the evidence. (See above, "How do I decide if I have a good case?") Practically, it usually means focusing on one or two disputed elements of a case (did your remodeling contractor breach the contract by using substandard materials, doing poor work or installing equipment not called for in the contract?). Unfortunately, too many self-represented litigants try to rely primarily on their own oral rendition of events and overlook the need to back this up with tangible evidence. Depending on the key issues that must be proved, this normally means presenting things like photos, contracts, cost estimates to redo the work or government records. In addition, it typically involves presenting witnesses who either saw or heard what happened (overheard a boss demanding sex with a subordinate) or are qualified to render an expert opinion on a key aspect of the case (a master tile layer who will testify that the installation of the tile floor in your kitchen was botched).

## What about actually examining (presenting) witnesses? I'm more than a little intimidated by having to act like Perry Mason.

And well you should be. It's not easy being an actor, especially one who died years ago. But fortunately, appearing in a routine court proceeding isn't that difficult, as long as you know the basic rules. For instance, when you present the testimony of eyewitnesses or expert witnesses, you do so by asking a series of questions.

First you need to establish that your eyewitness has personal knowledge of the event in question, or that an expert witness is qualified to render an opinion on the issues in dispute. This normally means you must show that your eyewitness personally observed, heard, smelled, touched or tasted whatever he is testifying to—for example, that your witness was on the spot and overheard the contractor you are suing talking to someone about the details of your garage job. Or in the case of an expert witness, her opinion is based on a careful and accurate review of the facts of the case. Second, you must learn to ask questions that allow that person to explain whatever it is he knows that supports your case without putting words into his mouth (called "leading the witness"). You can learn the basic techniques of how to question a witness and how to object to any improper questions asked by reading a good self-help book.

## You've said a lot about trials before judges. Don't I have a right to have my civil case heard by a jury?

For some types of cases, such as those involving child support or custody, or a request for an injunction (to stop the city from cutting down a tree, for example), you are not entitled to a jury trial. And in some courts, the parties in all small civil cases must first try to resolve the case between themselves via mediation before initiating any type of trial. But in most civil cases, including those involving personal injury, breach of contract, professional malpractice, libel or slander, you are entitled to a jury trial if you want one.

You may, however, want to think twice before you request a jury trial; it will be more complicated and harder to handle a case before a jury on your own than it would be to represent yourself before a judge. Not only can it be tricky to participate in the jury selection process, but formal procedural and evidentiary rules will almost surely be more rigorously enforced when a jury is involved. In short, most who go it alone are better off avoiding this added level of complexity by trying their case in front of a judge. But, of course, the other party has a say, too, and if that person demands a jury, so be it.

*More Information About Representing Yourself in Court*

*Represent Yourself in Court: How to Prepare and Try a Winning Case,* by Paul Bergman and Sara J. Berman-Barrett (Nolo). We have mentioned this book a number of times because it is quite simply the only publication that competently explains all aspects of a civil court trial, including how to determine if you have a good case, line up persuasive witnesses, present effective testimony in court, cross-examine opponents and even pick a jury.

*Nolo's Deposition Handbook,* by Paul Bergman and Albert Moore (Nolo), thoroughly covers the deposition process. Whether you are represented by a lawyer or self-representing, it explains how to prepare for your deposition, how to respond to questions and how to cope with the tricks lawyers may use to influence your testimony. It also contains an excellent chapter on deposing expert witnesses.

*The Criminal Law Handbook,* by Paul Bergman and Sara J. Berman-Barrett (Nolo), tells you what you'll want to know if you or someone you love has been charged with a crime.

# Small Claims Court

Small claims court judges resolve disputes involving relatively modest amounts of money. The people or businesses involved normally present their cases to a judge or court commissioner under rules that encourage a minimum of legal and procedural formality. The judge then makes a decision (a judgment) reasonably promptly. Although procedural rules dealing with when and where to file and serve papers are established by each state's laws and differ in detail, the basic approach to properly preparing and presenting a small claims case is remarkably similar everywhere.

## How much can I sue for in small claims court?

The limit is normally between $2,000 and $10,000, depending on your state. For instance, the maximum is

$5,000 in California, $7,500 in Minnesota, $3,000 in New York and $3,500 in Vermont. (See the chart below for your state's limit.)

## Can any kind of case be resolved in small claims court?

No. Small claims courts primarily resolve small monetary disputes. In a few states, however, small claims courts may also rule on a limited range of other types of legal disputes, such as evictions or requests for the return of an item of property (restitution). You cannot use small claims court to file a divorce, guardianship, name change or bankruptcy, or to ask for emergency relief (such as an injunction to stop someone from doing an illegal act).

When it comes to disputes involving money, you can usually file in small claims court based on any legal theory that would be allowed in any other court—for example, breach of contract, personal injury, intentional harm or breach of warranty. A few states do, however, limit or prohibit small claims suits based on libel, slander, false arrest and a few other legal theories.

Finally, suits against the federal government or a federal agency, or even against a federal employee for actions relating to his or her employment cannot be brought in small claims court. Suits against the federal government normally must be filed in a federal District Court or other federal court, such as Tax Court or the Court of Claims. Unfortunately, there are no federal small claims procedures available except in federal Tax Court.

## Are there time limits in which a small claims court case must be filed?

Yes. States establish rules called "statutes of limitations" which dictate how long you may wait to initiate a lawsuit after the key event giving rise to the lawsuit occurs or, in some instances, is discovered. Statutes of limitations rules apply to all courts, including small claims.

You'll almost always have at least one year to sue (measured from the event or, sometimes, from its discovery). Often, you'll have much longer. But if you're planning to sue a state or local government agency, however, you'll usually need to file a formal claim with that agency within three to six months of the incident. Only after your initial timely complaint is denied are you eligible to file in small claims court.

## SMALL CLAIMS COURT LIMITS FOR THE 50 STATES

| | |
|---|---|
| Alabama | $3,000 |
| Alaska | $7,500 |
| Arizona | $2,500 (Small Claims Division); $5,000 (Regular Justice Court) |
| Arkansas | $5,000 |
| California | $5,000 (A plaintiff may not file a claim over $2,500 more than twice a year. The limit for suits involving a surety company is $4,000.) |
| Colorado | $5,000 |
| Connecticut | $3,500 (No limit for landlord-tenant cases involving security deposit claims) |
| Delaware | $15,000 |
| District of Columbia | $5,000 |
| Florida | $5,000 |
| Georgia | $15,000 |
| Hawaii | $3,500 |
| Idaho | $4,000 |
| Illinois | $5,000 (Small Claims); ($2,500 Cook County Pro Se Branch) |
| Indiana | $3,000 ($6,000 in Marion and Allen Counties) |
| Iowa | $4,000 |
| Kansas | $1,800 |
| Kentucky | $1,500 |
| Louisiana | $3,000 ($2,000 for movable property) |
| Maine | $4,500 |
| Maryland | $2,500 |
| Massachusetts | $2,000 |
| Michigan | $3,000 |
| Minnesota | $7,500 |
| Mississippi | $2,500 |
| Missouri | $3,000 |
| Montana | $3,000 |
| Nebraska | $4,000 |
| Nevada | $5,000 |

| | |
|---|---|
| **New Hampshire** | $5,000 |
| New Jersey | $2,000 (Small Claims Court); $10,000 (Special Civil Part, Superior Court) |
| **New Mexico** | $7,500 |
| New York | $3,000 |
| **North Carolina** | $4,000 |
| North Dakota | $5,000 |
| **Ohio** | $3,000 |
| Oklahoma | $4,500 |
| **Oregon** | $5,000 |
| Pennsylvania | $8,000 (Small Claims Court); $10,000 (Philadelphia Municipal Court) |
| **Rhode Island** | $1,500 |
| South Carolina | $7,500 |
| **South Dakota** | $8,000 |
| Tennessee | $15,000 ($25,000 in counties where population is over 700,000; no limit in a suit to recover personal property) |
| **Texas** | $5,000 |
| Utah | $5,000 |
| **Vermont** | $3,500 |
| Virginia | $1,000 (Small Claims Court); $3,000 (General District Court); $15,000 (Circuit Court); no limits on eviction suits in General District Court |
| **Washington** | $4,000 |
| West Virginia | $5,000 |
| **Wisconsin** | $5,000 (no limit on eviction suits) |
| Wyoming | $3,000 (Small Claims Court); $7,000 (County Circuit Court) |

If some time has passed since the incident giving rise to your lawsuit occurred—for example, after the breach of a written contract or a personal injury—you may need to do a little research to determine whether you can still file your claim. Check your state's legal code under the index heading "statute of limitations." See the Legal Research Appendix for information on how to do this in the library or online.

## Where should I file my small claims lawsuit?

Assuming the other party lives or does business in your state, rules normally require that you sue in the small claims court district closest to that person's residence or headquarters. In some instances, you also may be able to sue in the location (court district) where a contract was signed or a personal injury occurred (such as an auto accident). Check with your small claims clerk for detailed rules.

If a defendant has no contact with your state, you'll generally have to sue in the state where the defendant lives or does business. Because most major corporations operate in all states, it's easy to sue most of them almost anywhere. But small businesses typically only conduct business in one or a few states, meaning you have to sue there.

## If You Want to Avoid Going to Court

If you are anxious to recover what's owed to you, but you want to avoid the

trouble of bringing a lawsuit, you have a couple of options to consider. First, even if you've been rudely turned down in the past, ask for your money at least once more. This time, make your demand in the form of a straightforward letter that briefly reviews the key facts of the dispute and concludes with the statement that you'll file in small claims court in ten days unless payment is promptly received. Unlike a conversation, where the other party may assume you'll never follow up, a polite but direct demand letter is like tossing a cup of cold water in his or her face in that it lets the person know you're serious about getting paid. Because many individuals and small business people have a strong aversion to appearing at a public trial (including the time and inconvenience it will take), making it clear you are prepared to file a lawsuit can be effective in getting the other party to talk settlement.

If your letter does cause your adversary to offer a settlement, be ready to agree to reasonable compromise. There are three reasons for this advice. First, studies show that in small claims cases, the prevailing party rarely gets everything she sues for. Second, by compromising, you save the time and anxiety inherent in preparing and presenting your case in court. And finally, when cases are settled, payment is normally made or forthcoming, meaning that you avoid potential collection problems.

Many states offer, and a few require, community- or court-based mediation designed to help parties who have not already settled their small claims dispute on their own. Mediation works best where the parties have an interest in staying on good terms, as is generally the case with neighbors, family members or small business people who have done business together for many years. This type of dispute resolution procedure can be remarkably successful. In Maine, for example, where mediation is required before a small claims suit may be resolved in a courtroom, over half of the cases settle. For more information about mediation, see the next series of questions.

## Will I get paid if I win the lawsuit?

Not necessarily. The court may decide in your favor, but it won't handle collection for you. So before you sue, always ask, "Can I collect if I win?" If not, think twice before suing.

Worrying about whether or not you can get paid is reasonable, because some people and businesses are "judgment proof"—that is, they have little money or assets and aren't likely to acquire much in the foreseeable future. In short, if they don't pay voluntarily, you may be out of luck. Ask yourself whether the person you're suing has a steady job, valuable real property or investments. If so, it should be reasonably easy to collect by garnishing his wages if you win. If not, try to identify another collection source, such as a bank account, before going forward. For people who seem to have no job or assets, ask whether they are likely to be more solvent in the future, since court judgments are good for 10 to 20 years in many states and can usually be renewed for longer periods. Consider whether the person

might inherit money, graduate from college and get a good job, or otherwise have an economic turn around not too far down the road.

## If I'm sued in small claims court but the other party is really at fault, can I countersue?

In some states, you can and must countersue if your claim arises out of the same event or transaction, or risk forever waiving that claim. In other states, "counterclaims" are not mandatory and you can sue separately later. No matter what the technical rules, you'll normally want to countersue promptly.

If the amount you sue for is under the small claims limit, your case will probably remain in that court. If, however, you want to sue for more, check with your small claims clerk for applicable rules. Often, you'll need to have the case transferred to a different court that has the power to handle cases where more money is at stake.

## What should I do to prepare my small claims case?

Whether you are a plaintiff (the person suing) or the defendant (person being sued), the key is to realize that it's often what you bring with you to court to back up your story—not what you say—that determines whether you'll win or lose. This makes sense if you understand that the judge has no idea who you are and whether your oral (spoken) testimony is reliable. After all, your opponent is likely to claim that the "true story" is exactly the reverse of your version.

It follows that your chances of winning will greatly increase if you carefully collect and present convincing evidence. Depending on the facts of your case, a few of the evidentiary tools you can use to convince the judge you are right include eyewitnesses, photographs, letters from experts, or an advertisement you relied on which falsely hyped a product or service and written contracts.

## What's the best way to present my case to a judge?

First, understand that the judge is busy and has heard dozens of stories like yours. To keep the judge's attention, get to the point fast by describing the event that gave rise to your claim. Immediately follow up by stating how much money you are requesting. To be able to do this efficiently, it's best to practice in advance. Here is an example of a good start: "Your Honor, my car was damaged on January 10, 2001, when the defendant ran a red light at Rose and Hyacinth Streets in the town of Saginaw and hit my front fender. I have a canceled check to show it cost me $1,927 to fix the fender."

After you have clearly stated the key event and the amount of your loss, double back and tell the judge the events that led up to your loss. For example, you might next explain that you were driving below the speed limit and had entered the intersection when the light was green, and when the defendant came barreling through the red light, you did your best to avoid her car. Then it would be time

to present any eyewitnesses, police reports or other evidence that backs up your version of events.

## A Court Without Lawyers?

In a handful of states, including California, Michigan and Nebraska, you must appear in small claims court on your own. In most states, however, you can be represented by a lawyer if you like. But even where it's allowed, hiring a lawyer is rarely cost-efficient. Most lawyers charge too much given the relatively modest amounts of money involved in small claims disputes. Happily, several studies show that people who represent themselves in small claims cases usually do just as well as those who have a lawyer.

## Will witnesses need to testify in person?

If possible, it's best to have key witnesses speak their piece in court. But if this isn't convenient, a clearly written memo or letter will be allowed under the rules of most small claims courts. (Be sure to check your state's rules—the Legal Research Appendix explains how.) Have the witness start the statement by establishing who he or she is. ("My name is John Lomax. I've owned and managed Reo's Toyota Repair Service for the last 17 years.") In clear, unemotional language, the witness should explain what he or she observed or heard. ("I carefully checked Mary Wilson's engine and found that it has been rebuilt improperly, using worn-out parts.") Finally, the witness should try to anticipate any questions a reasonable person might ask and provide the answers. ("Although it can take a few days to get new parts for older engines, such as the one Mary Wilson owned, it is easy and common practice to do so.")

## If I lose my case in small claims court, can I appeal?

The answer depends on the state in which you live. In some, either party may appeal within a certain period of time, usually between 10 and 30 days, and obtain a complete new trial in a formal court. In other states, appeals must be based solely on the contention that the small claims judge made a legal mistake, and not on the facts of the case. And some states have their own unique rules. In California, for example, a defendant may appeal to the Superior Court within 30 days. A plaintiff may not appeal at all, although she can make a motion to correct clerical errors or to correct a decision based on a legal mistake.

To find the appeals rules for your state, call your local small claims court clerk or refer to the Legal Research Appendix for information on how to get them in the library or online.

### More Information About Small Claims Court

*Everybody's Guide to Small Claims Court*, by Ralph Warner (Nolo), explains how to evaluate your case, prepare for court and convince a judge you're right. It also contains a useful section on trying to negotiate or mediate a compromise with the other party without going to court. Best of all, it explains the most useful courtroom techniques and tactics to convincingly present evidence, witnesses and your own testimony.

*Collect Your Court Judgment*, by Gini Graham Scott, Stephen Elias and Lisa Goldoftas (Nolo), explains 19 legal ways to collect after you win a lawsuit in California. It also shows you how to locate debtors and their assets.

# Mediation

*I'd rather jaw, jaw, jaw, than war, war, war.*

**—WINSTON CHURCHILL**

If you're involved in a legal dispute, you may be able to settle it without going to court. One way to do this is to work out a solution with the help of a mediator—a neutral third person. Unlike a judge or an arbitrator, a mediator will not take sides or make a decision, but will help each party evaluate goals and options in order to agree on a solution that works for everyone. One exception to this rule is made for child custody mediations in a few states such as California, where a mediator has the power to recommend a solution to a judge if the parties cannot agree.

When you reach an agreement with an opposing party through mediation, you can make it legally binding by writing down your decisions in the form of an enforceable contract.

## What kinds of cases can be mediated?

Most civil (noncriminal) disputes can be mediated, including those involving contracts, leases, small business ownership, employment and divorce. For example, a divorcing couple might engage in mediation to work out a mutually agreeable child custody agreement. Similarly, estranged business partners might choose mediation to work out an agreement to divide their business. Nonviolent criminal matters, such as claims of verbal or other personal harassment, can also be successfully mediated.

Finally, you may want to consider mediation if you get into a scrape with a neighbor, roommate, spouse, partner or co-worker. Mediation can be particularly useful in these areas because it is designed to identify and cope with divisive interpersonal issues not originally thought to be part of the dispute. For example, if one neighbor sues another for making outrageous amounts of noise, the court will usually deal with only that issue—and by declaring neighbor A the winner and neighbor B a loser, may worsen long-term tensions. In mediation, however, each neighbor will be invited to present all issues in dispute. It may turn out that overly loud neighbor B was being obnoxious in part because neighbor A's dog constantly pooped on his lawn or A's son's pickup blocked a shared driveway. In short, since mediation is designed to surface and solve all problems, it's a far better way to restore long-term peace to the neighborhood, home or workplace.

## How long does mediation take?

Typical cases such as consumer claims, small business disputes or auto accident claims are usually resolved after a half day or, at most, a full day of mediation. Cases with multiple parties often last longer: Add at least an hour of mediation time for each additional party. Major business disputes—those involving lots of money, complex contracts or ending a partnership—may last several days or more.

Private divorce mediation, where a couple aims to settle all the issues in their divorce—property division and alimony, as well as child custody, visitation and support—may require half a dozen or more mediation sessions spread over several weeks or a couple of months.

## How is mediation different from arbitration?

A mediator normally has no authority to render a decision; it's up to the parties themselves—with the mediator's help—to work informally toward their own agreement. An arbitrator, on the other hand, conducts a contested hearing between the parties and then, acting as a judge, rends a legally binding decision. The arbitrator's decision-making power may, however, be limited based on a written agreement between the parties. For example, the parties may agree in advance that the arbitrator is limited to making an award of monetary damages of between $200,000 and $500,000. Arbitration, which has long been used to resolve commercial and labor disputes, typically resembles a court hearing—with witnesses called and evidence taken.

# The 6 Stages of Mediation

While mediation is a less formal process than going to court, it is more structured than many people imagine. A full-scale mediation typically involves at least six distinct stages, as discussed below. However, in some small claims, child custody and other publicly funded mediation procedures, time constraints mean that some of these stages end up being combined.

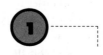

### Mediator's Opening Statement

After the disputants are seated at a table, the mediator introduces everyone, explains the goals and rules of the mediation and encourages each side to work cooperatively toward a settlement.

### Disputants' Opening Statements

Each party is invited to tell, in his or her own words, what the dispute is about and how he or she has been affected by it, and to present some general ideas about resolving it. While one person is speaking, the other is not allowed to interrupt.

## Joint Discussion

The mediator may try to get the parties talking directly about what was said in the opening statements. This is the time to determine what issues need to be addressed.

## Private Caucuses

Often considered the guts of mediation, the private caucus is a chance for each party to meet privately with the mediator (usually in a nearby room) to discuss the strengths and weaknesses of his or her position, and propose new ideas for settlement. The mediator may caucus with each side just once, or several times, as needed. In mediation procedures sponsored by small claims courts and other public agencies, where time is short, this step may be shortened or skipped, with the parties encouraged to move on to joint negotiation.

## Joint Negotiation

After caucuses, the mediator may bring the parties back together to negotiate directly.

## Closure

This is the end of the mediation. If an agreement has been reached, the mediator may put its main provisions in writing as the parties listen. The mediator may ask each side to sign the written summary of agreement or suggest they take it to lawyers for review. If the parties want to, they can write up and sign a legally binding contract. If no agreement was reached, the mediator will review whatever progress has been made and advise everyone of their options, such as meeting again later, going to arbitration or going to court.

## Why should I consider having my case mediated?

If you've given up on negotiating a settlement of your dispute directly with the other party, mediation may be the most painless and efficient way to solve it. Compared to a lawsuit, mediation is swift, confidential, fair and low cost. Mediation sessions are usually scheduled within a few weeks or, at most, a couple of months from the time of a request—and most sessions last only a few hours or a day, depending on the type of case. In contrast, lawsuits often take many months, or even years, to resolve. Another advantage of mediation is confidentiality. With very few exceptions (for example, where a criminal act or child abuse is involved), what you say during mediation cannot legally be revealed outside the mediation proceedings or used later in a court of law.

Another huge advantage of mediation is that it will nearly always save you money. In many parts of the country, nonprofit community mediation centers handle relatively minor consumer, neighborhood, workplace and similar disputes for free or for a nominal charge. Private dispute resolution companies tackle more complex cases for a fraction of the cost of bringing a lawsuit. A half-day mediation of a personal injury claim, for example, may cost each side about $500-$1,000. By comparison, a full-scale court battle could cost $50,000 or more, sometimes much more.

Finally, consider that agreements reached through mediation are more likely to be carried out than those imposed by a judge. When folks go to court, the losing party is almost always angry and often prone to look for ways to violate the letter or spirit of any judgment. In contrast, a number of studies show that people who have freely arrived at their own solutions through mediation are significantly more likely to follow through.

## What Will It Cost?

In nearly all cases, mediating is far less expensive than going to court. Actual fees will vary depending on the type of case and who does the mediating. Here are some examples to consider.

**Neighborhood dispute.** Three neighbors are involved in a dispute over disruptive children. Mediation is provided by hundreds of nonprofit community mediation centers in the United States.

*Typical length of mediation:* full day
*Typical fees per party:* $10-$50 (fees usually waived for financial hardship)

**Personal injury claim.** A passenger in a car suffers leg and spine fractures when the driver hits a telephone pole. The passenger and the driver's insurance company cannot agree on the amount of compensation for these injuries. Mediation is conducted by a private dispute resolution company.

*Typical length of mediation:* half day
*Typical fees per party:* $600-$1,000

**Business contract dispute.** Ace Computer Supply sues Big Computer, Inc. for $5 million when Big C rejects parts which Ace claims conform to contract specifications. Just before the trial is to begin, the parties decide to try mediation. Mediation is provided by a private dispute resolution company.

*Typical length of mediation:* four days
*Typical fees per party:* $8,000

**Divorce mediation.** A divorcing couple with a house, two cars, bank accounts, pension plans and three minor children are trying to reach an agreement out of court as to the division of their property and the custody and visitation of their children. Mediation is provided by an independent divorce mediator in private practice.

*Typical length of mediation:* six two-hour sessions over two months, plus five hours to prepare a written agreement

*Typical cost for couple:* $2,000-$3,000 (split 50-50)

## How can I be sure mediation will produce a fair result?

Remember that in mediation, you and the opposing parties will work to craft a solution to your own dispute. Unless you freely agree, there will be no final resolution. This approach has several advantages over going to court:

- Obscure legal precedents or the whim of a judge will not dictate the solution.
- If your dispute harbors undiscovered or undisclosed issues, mediation, unlike a structured court battle, offers the opportunity and flexibility to ferret them out.
- Because mediation does not force disputants to undergo the fear and sometimes paranoia of the courtroom—where a judge or jury can stun either party with a big loss—people who choose mediation tend to be more relaxed and less defensive, making it far easier to arrive at a compromise.

*A piece of paper,*

*blown by the wind*

*into a law court may in the end*

*only be drawn out by two oxen.*

**—CHINESE PROVERB**

## How can I find a good mediator?

Much depends on the type of dispute you're involved in. Many cities have community mediation centers which do an excellent job of handling most types of routine disputes (consumer problems, neighbor disputes, landlord-tenant fights). For more complicated disputes (business termination, personal injury, breach of contract) it is often better to turn to a private mediation center. Two good online sources of information are the American Arbitration Association, http://www.adr.org and the Mediation Information and Resource Center, http://www.mediate.com. Private divorce mediations are usually handled by sole practitioners or small local mediation groups. Get a list from the phone book and check references carefully.

## Are there some cases that should not be mediated?

All parties to a dispute must agree to mediate, so if one party refuses or isn't competent to participate, a dispute cannot be mediated. In addition, mediation may also not be the best choice if:

- One of the parties is attempting to set a legal precedent that interprets or defines the law according to its own point of view. Legal precedents cannot be set in mediation because mediation agreements do not establish who is "right" or "wrong," and are usually not made public.
- A person believes he or she can win a huge verdict against a big company (or even a small company with a big bank account or plenty of insurance). Because of the tendency toward compromise in mediation, hitting a legal "jackpot" is more likely in a jury trial.
- One person feels intimidated or intellectually overwhelmed by the other, in which case it's hard to arrive at a true meeting of the minds. It's often possible, however, to remedy a "power imbalance" by arranging for the more vulnerable person to participate with an advisor—perhaps a lawyer.

## If I choose mediation, will I still need a lawyer?

In most mediations, it's not necessary to have a lawyer participate directly. This is because the parties are trying to work together to solve their problem—not trying to convince a judge or arbitrator of their point of view—and because mediation rules are few and straightforward. If your case involves substantial property or legal rights, however, you may want to consult with a lawyer before the mediation to discuss the legal consequences of possible settlement terms. You may also want to condition any

agreement you make on a lawyer's approval.

### More Information About Mediation

*How to Mediate Your Dispute,* by Peter Lovenheim (Nolo), thoroughly explains the mediation process and shows you how to choose a mediator, prepare a case and conduct yourself during a mediation.

*Using Divorce Mediation: Save Your Money and Your Sanity,* by Katherine E. Stoner (Nolo), provides divorcing couples with all the information they need to work with a neutral third party to resolve differences and find solutions. By choosing mediation, couples can avoid court battles, save money, get through a divorce quickly and minimize negative effects on children.

*Child Custody: Building Agreements That Work,* by Mimi Lyster (Nolo), provides a step-by-step method for overcoming obstacles and putting together a practical parenting agreement that everyone—especially the children—can live with.

*When Push Comes to Shove: A Practical Guide to Resolving Disputes,* by Karl Slaikeu (Jossey-Bass), is a how-to mediation guide for lawyers, managers and human resource professionals.

# Dealing With Your Lawyer

*May your life be filled*
*with lawyers.*

—MEXICAN CURSE

For any number of reasons, you may be frustrated with a lawyer you hired to do legal work for you. Perhaps your lawyer has failed to keep you informed about your case, to meet deadlines, to do what you believe is quality work or to involve you in decision making. Maybe your lawyer has sent you a bill for far more than you believe is reasonable. Or perhaps nothing specific is wrong, but you have simply concluded that you and your lawyer are not a good fit. The questions below look at the reasons for most complaints against attorneys and offer suggestions as to what you can do about them.

## I've lost confidence in my lawyer. Can I fire him?

You have the right to end a relationship with a lawyer at any time. If you are paying for the lawyer's services, by all means insist on working with someone in whom you have full confidence. But if the lawyer you don't like is representing you on a contingency fee basis (for a percentage of any recovery), it is often better not to fire him unless his services really are substandard and you have a better lawyer lined up or feel you can handle the

case yourself. That's because unless lots of money is involved it can often be hard to find a second lawyer who will agree to pick up your case in the middle. Changing lawyers under a contingency fee arrangement usually means any eventual fee will have to be split between the two lawyers—and may mean the second lawyer has to clean up after the first.

## I fired my lawyer, but I need my file. How do I get it?

Ask, or sign an authorization allowing any new attorney to get it. Even if you have a fee dispute with your former lawyer or you simply have not paid him, you are entitled to your file. If you have decided to represent yourself, demand that the lawyer turn your file over to you. If the lawyer refuses, contact your state's bar association for help.

## I'm pretty sure my lawyer screwed up my case. Can I sue her for malpractice?

Unfortunately, it is very hard to win a malpractice case. Malpractice means that the lawyer failed to use the ordinary skill and care that would be used by other lawyers in handling a similar problem or case under similar circumstances.

To win a malpractice case against an attorney, you must prove four basic things:

- duty—that the attorney owed you a duty to act properly
- breach—that the attorney breached the duty, was negligent, made a

mistake or did not do what she agreed to do

- causation—that this conduct caused you damages, and
- damages—that you suffered financial losses as a result.

Causation may be your biggest hurdle. To win a malpractice case, you must prove not only that your lawyer made a mistake, but that you would have won the underlying case that the lawyer mishandled. (This second part is not required in Ohio.) Then, you will have to show that if you had won the underlying case, you would have been able to collect from the defendant. For example, let's say you were hit by a car when you were walking across the street, and you hired a lawyer who didn't file the lawsuit on time, with the result that your claim was legally dead. You sue for malpractice and can easily prove the lawyer's negligence and the driver's liability. But to win the malpractice case against your lawyer, however, you'd also have to show that the driver had the ability to pay your claim. If you can't show that the driver had assets which could have been used to pay the judgment, you won't win your malpractice case, even though the lawyer clearly blew it and the driver was clearly at fault.

# My Lawyer Won't Call Me Back!

If your lawyer fails to return phone calls, it isn't malpractice, but it's a sure sign of trouble. Try to find out why your lawyer isn't calling you back. (He may be busy, rude, sick or procrastinating.) As you do this, examine the possibility that your lawyer may be avoiding you for a good reason—you may be too demanding. A good way to deal with this situation is to write or fax the lawyer a polite but straightforward letter explaining your difficulty in communicating and asking for a phone call or meeting to re-establish or restore your relationship. If this doesn't work, consider firing the lawyer and/or filing a formal complaint with your state's attorney regulatory agency.

## My lawyer seems to have stopped working on my case. Is this malpractice?

The longer your attorney ignores you and your case, the more likely it is to amount to malpractice. You should act quickly to see that your case is properly handled and get another lawyer if necessary. Writing or faxing a letter expressing your concerns and asking for a meeting is a good first step.

## My case was thrown out of court because my lawyer did no work. Is this grounds to sue my lawyer?

Maybe. Your lawyer is responsible for whatever money you could have won had the case been properly handled. Your difficulty will be in proving not only that your lawyer mishandled the case, but that if handled correctly, you could have won and collected a judgment.

## My lawyer originally said my case was worth six figures and now suggests that I settle for peanuts. Can I sue the lawyer for the difference?

No. It's possible that newly discovered facts mean your case is worth less than first thought. Or, your lawyer may have initially given you an optimistic estimate of the value of your case to encourage you to hire her. In either case, this does not amount to malpractice. To find out, get your file from your lawyer and get a second opinion as to the value of your case. If another reputable lawyer believes you are being advised to settle for too little, consider changing lawyers.

## Can I sue my lawyer for settling my case without my authorization?

Yes, but you would have to prove that the settlement your lawyer entered into was for less than your case was worth.

## Big Bills

If you receive an unexpectedly large bill, your lawyer may have overcharged you. In this situation, you have six options:

- You can pay the entire bill and vow not to go near that attorney again.
- You can pay the part of the bill you think is reasonable with a letter explaining why you are refusing to pay the rest.
- You can refuse to pay any of the bill until the lawyer agrees to accept less as full payment.
- In most states and situations, you can request fee arbitration from a state or local bar association, usually before a panel made up of local lawyers and perhaps one or two nonlawyers. Arbitration is a process where a supposedly neutral decisionmaker resolves your fee dispute. But when it comes to disputes over legal fees, you will normally want to follow this approach only if it is "nonbinding," meaning that you are free to reject the arbitrator's decision. That's because whenever an arbitration is conducted by a panel dominated by lawyers, you are likely to get a biased result.
- You can pay the bill and file a complaint with your state attorney disciplinary agency.
- You can pay the bill and sue your attorney for a refund.

While weighing these options, keep in mind that a lawyer who has not been paid has far more motive to settle for a reasonable amount than does a lawyer who has already received half of your fee. So, even if you believe your attorney is entitled to part of the big bill, it often makes sense to try to arrive at a mutually acceptable compromise before you pull out your checkbook.

## I saw my lawyer playing tennis with the opposing lawyer. Is this a breach of attorney ethics?

No. There is nothing ethically wrong with opposing attorneys playing tennis, bridge, golf or enjoying other common social interactions. If they talk about your case (on the tennis court or anywhere else), however, and your lawyer lets slip something that you said in confidence, that would be a clear violation of your attorney's duty to you.

Even though socializing with the opposing counsel isn't a violation of ethical rules, in the real world it can obviously make a big difference how you found out about it. If your lawyer told you he occasionally played tennis with the opposing attorney when you first discussed your case, you clearly had a chance to hire another lawyer if it bothered you. But you'll likely feel differently if you head to the tennis court to relax with a friend after being grilled by the opposing attorney at your deposition, only to run into your lawyer playing tennis with the same "barracuda" who just tried to eat you for lunch. But instead of firing your lawyer on the spot, it makes more sense to make an appointment to clarify his relationship with your adversary's lawyer.

## I'm worried that my lawyer may have misused money I paid as a retainer. What should I do?

If you seriously suspect your lawyer has misused any money he holds for you in trust, complain to your state's attorney regulatory agency right away. Although regulation of lawyers is lax in most states, complaints about stealing clients' money are almost always taken seriously, so you should get a prompt response. All states except Maine and New Mexico have funds to reimburse clients when lawyers are caught stealing.

### More Information About Dealing With Your Lawyer

*Mad at Your Lawyer,* by Attorney Tanya Starnes (Nolo), is a comprehensive guide on what to do if you have a problem with your lawyer.

*Attorney Fee Disputes: What to Do When Your Lawyer Charges Too Much,* by Attorney Tanya Starnes (Nolo), is an eGuide which explains all your options if you've got a gripe about a lawyer's billing practices.

*Firing Your Lawyer: When and How to Do It,* by Attorney Tanya Starnes (Nolo), is an advice-packed eGuide which discusses when it's time to fire your lawyer and explains how to do the deed.

*Suing Your Former Lawyer,* by Attorney Tanya Starnes (Nolo), is an eGuide which provides valuable advice on when and how to sue your lawyer.

*Taming the Lawyers: What to Expect in a Lawsuit and How to Make Sure Your Attorney Gets Results,* by Kenneth Menendez (Silver Lake Publishing), is a guide to choosing and managing a lawyer through various stages of a civil lawsuit.

### http://www.nolo.com

*Nolo offers self-help information about a wide variety of legal topics, including representing yourself in court, small claims court, mediation and how to handle problems with your lawyer.*

### http://www.nolo.com/research/index.html

*Nolo's Legal Research Center links to federal, state and local courts around the country. It also provides access to information about small claims court in many states.*

### http://www.legalethics.com/states.html

*The Internet Ethics Site provides links to all states' rules of professional conduct and some states' ethics opinions.*

### http://www.ncsc.dni.us/court/sites/courts.htm

*The National Center for State Courts' website provides links to state and local court websites. These sites often contain helpful legal information, court forms and instructions.*

### http://www.uscourts.gov/links.htm

*The Federal Judiciary's website provides links to federal court websites.*

# 18

# Criminal Law and Procedure

18.2    *Criminal Law and Procedure: An Overview*

18.9    *If You Are Questioned by the Police*

18.10   *Searches and Seizures*

18.14   *Arrests and Interrogations*

18.17   *Bail*

18.20   *Getting a Lawyer*

IT IS A LESS EVIL THAT SOME CRIMINALS

SHOULD ESCAPE THAN THAT THE GOVERNMENT

SHOULD PLAY AN IGNOBLE PART.

**—OLIVER WENDELL HOLMES**

**T**he word "criminal" reflects our society's belief that certain acts are unacceptable and that people who commit these acts should be punished. Because we place a high value on freedom, however, our state and federal constitutions make it difficult for the government to take that freedom away from us. As a result—and perhaps as a price—the court system often appears to protect the criminal rather than the victim, and to unduly favor defendants who are blessed with clever attorneys. On the other hand, if the system doesn't place a heavy burden on government prosecutors, we risk sending innocent people to jail and we make it easier for our government to slide into totalitarian practices. One thing is sure: No matter what type of system we have for prosecuting and punishing people who commit crimes, it will always be a matter of great controversy.

## Caution!

The material in this chapter is designed to give you a general overview of several important criminal law topics. As you read, keep in mind that the criminal justice system differs in many small but important ways from state to state, county to county and even court to court. This means that some of the material in this chapter may not be applicable in your area.

In addition, the many different players in the criminal justice system—police, prosecutors, defense attorneys and judges—frequently adapt the law to their own uses and contexts. What this gap between theory and practice may mean in a particular case can only be understood by someone who knows the players and who is familiar with how they go about their jobs. Usually, this person would be a local private criminal defense attorney or public defender.

Because we cannot precisely describe the law in your state and what is likely to happen in your case, consider this chapter a place to get started. To get more specific and reliable information, do some research or consult a knowledgeable criminal defense attorney. For a more in-depth treatment of the topics addressed here as well as other aspects of the criminal justice system—including lineups, arraignments, defenses, plea bargains and sentencing—see *The Criminal Law Handbook: Answers to Everyday Questions About Our Criminal Justice System*, by Paul Bergman and Sara Berman-Barrett (Nolo).

# Criminal Law and Procedure: An Overview

A crime is any behavior that is punishable by imprisonment or fine (or both). State legislatures have an almost unlimited ability to decide which behaviors are considered crimes, and often their decisions do more than simply define socially unacceptable behaviors—they also reflect the values and judgments of the legislators. For example, most state legislatures define welfare fraud as a crime, and welfare recipients who cheat can end up in jail. On the other hand, no state legislature defines deliberate overcharging by an attorney or other professional as a crime.

While state legislatures have broad powers to decide what constitutes crime, Congress can define behavior as a crime only if the U.S. Constitution authorizes Congress to regulate that type of behavior in the first place. For example, the Constitution gives Congress the power to "regulate commerce . . . among the several States." Congress, therefore, can make many activities—such as racketeering—illegal, if the actions cross state lines or affect commerce that does.

## Who decides how the criminal justice system works?

Though legislators have relatively unfettered power to decide whether a certain behavior should be a crime, many rules limit the ways in which the state or federal government can prosecute someone for a crime. These restrictions start with the U.S. Constitution's Bill of Rights, which provides basic protections—such as the right to refuse to testify against oneself, the right to confront one's accusers and the right to a trial by jury—for people charged with crimes. State constitutions may increase (but not take away from) the federal protections. Federal and state legislatures can pass laws governing how criminal procedures work in their jurisdictions, but these laws cannot reduce the protections offered by the federal and state constitutions.

The interplay between constitutional provisions and legislative enactments is regulated by our courts. Courts decide whether or not a particular legislative rule, court practice or police action is permissible under federal and state constitutional law. What may seem like a slight variation from one case to another can be, in the eyes of a court, the determining factor that leads to a vastly different result. For example, a police officer is frisking a suspect on the street and feels a hard object in the suspect's pocket. Suspecting that the object is a possible weapon, the officer reaches into the pocket and finds both a cardboard cigarette box and a packet of heroin. This action by the police officer—reaching into the pocket—would be deemed a permissible search under the rulings of most courts (to protect the officer's safety), and the heroin could be admitted into court as evidence. However, if the object felt by the officer was soft and obviously not a weapon, then reaching into the suspect's pocket might be deemed an illegal search, in which case the heroin couldn't be used as evidence.

## What's the difference between a felony and a misdemeanor?

Most states break their crimes into two major groups—felonies and misdemeanors. Whether a crime falls into one category or the other depends on the potential punishment. If a law provides for imprisonment for longer than a year, it is usually considered a felony. If the potential punishment is for a year or less, then the crime is considered a misdemeanor. In some states, certain crimes, called "wobblers," may be considered either a misdemeanor or a felony, because under some conditions the punishment may be imprisonment for less than a year, and in other situations, the criminal may go to prison for a year or more.

Behaviors punishable only by fine are usually not considered crimes at all, but infractions—for example, traffic tickets. But a legislature may on occasion punish behavior only by fine and still provide that it is a misdemeanor—such as possession of less than an ounce of marijuana for personal use in California.

## How can I tell from reading a criminal statute whether I'm guilty of the crime it defines?

All criminal statutes define crimes in terms of required acts and a required state of mind, usually described as the actor's "intent." These requirements are known as the "elements" of the offense. A prosecutor must convince a judge or jury that the person charged with the crime (the defendant) did the acts and had the intent described in the statute. For example, commercial burglary is commonly defined as entering a structure (such as a store) belonging to another person, with the intent to commit petty or grand theft (that is, to steal) or any felony. To convict a person of this offense, the prosecutor would have to prove three elements:

1. The defendant entered the structure.
2. The structure belonged to another person.
3. At the time the defendant entered the structure, he intended to commit petty or grand theft or any felony.

You will have to do the same when you read the law. Parse the crime into its required elements to see if each applies in your situation.

## What is the presumption of innocence?

All people accused of a crime are legally presumed to be innocent until they are convicted, either in a trial or as a result of pleading guilty. This presumption means not only that the prosecutor must convince the jury of the defendant's guilt, but also that the defendant need not say or do anything in his own defense. If the prosecutor can't convince the jury that the defendant is guilty, the defendant goes free.

The presumption of innocence, coupled with the fact that the prosecutor must prove the defendant's guilt beyond a reasonable doubt (see below), theoretically makes it difficult for the government to put people behind bars.

## What does it mean to prove guilt "beyond a reasonable doubt"?

The prosecutor must convince the judge or jury hearing the case that the defendant is guilty "beyond a reasonable doubt." This standard is meant to be hard to meet. (By contrast, in noncriminal cases, such as an accident or breach of contract, a plaintiff has to prove her case only by a preponderance of the evidence—just over 50%.) As a practical matter, the high burden of proof in criminal cases means that judges and jurors are supposed to resolve all doubts about the meaning of the evidence in favor of the defendant. With such a high standard imposed on the prosecutor, a defendant's most common defense is often to argue that there is reasonable doubt—that is, that the prosecutor hasn't done a sufficient job of proving that the defendant is guilty.

## If I'm accused of a crime, am I guaranteed a trial by a jury?

Yes. The U.S. Constitution gives the right to be tried by a jury to a person accused of any crime where the maximum punishment is 6 months or more in jail. Some states (for example, California) guarantee a right to a jury trial for any misdemeanor or felony charge, even where the maximum possible sentence is less than 6 months. This right has long been interpreted to mean a 12-person jury that must arrive at a unanimous decision to convict or acquit. (In most states, a lack of unanimity is called a "hung jury" and the defendant will go free unless the prosecutor decides to retry the case. In Oregon and Louisiana, however, juries may convict or acquit on a vote of ten to two.) The potential jurors must be selected randomly from the community, and the actual jury must be selected by a process which allows the judge and lawyers to screen out biased jurors. In addition, a lawyer may eliminate several potential jurors simply because he feels that these people would not be sympathetic to his side—but these decisions may not be based on the juror's personal characteristics, such as race, sex, religion or national origin.

## Can a jury acquit me even if I broke the law?

The jury has the ultimate power to decide whether a person is guilty of a crime. As the "conscience of the community," jurors can free a defendant even if they think the defendant actually committed the crime charged. The name for this power is "jury nullification." It has always been a part of our judicial system.

When jurors nullify a law by acquitting a defendant who has obviously broken that law, judges and prosecutors can do nothing about it. A jury's not guilty verdict is final. Jury nullification rarely occurs, but when it does, it most often involves cases that have a political component (such as the refusal to convict draft dodgers during the Vietnam War) or that have harsh punishments the jury does not want to impose on that particular defendant.

## If I do not have any witnesses who will testify on my behalf, can I still win at trial?

Yes. Defendants often go to trial without having anyone testify for them. This strategy allows the defendant's lawyer to focus on cross-examining the prosecution witnesses in order to poke holes in the prosecutor's case—thereby creating reasonable doubt. Defense attorneys rely on a variety of arguments to discredit the prosecutor's witnesses. Some common arguments include:

- Prosecution witnesses are biased against the defendant and therefore are lying or grossly exaggerating.
- Prosecution witnesses are mistaken in their observations because the lighting was bad, they were under the influence of drugs or alcohol or they were too far away.
- Evidence from police laboratories is unreliable because the machines were not properly maintained or the technicians were not properly trained.
- Prosecution witnesses are lying to get a good deal on the criminal charges they themselves are facing (witnesses are often criminals who have been offered a deal if they testify against the defendant).

What these arguments have in common is that they do not depend on defense evidence. Rather, they rely on the presumption of innocence and prosecutor's failure to overcome it by proving guilt beyond a reasonable doubt.

## I am confused about why a defendant would choose to not testify. If I were innocent, why wouldn't I want to take the stand and tell my story?

A criminal defendant has a right not to testify, and jurors will be told that they cannot assume anything negative if the defendant decides to keep quiet. Of course, some jurors do make assumptions—and they cast their votes accordingly. On the other hand, there are some excellent reasons why a defendant might remain silent in court:

- If the defendant has previously been convicted of a crime, the prosecutor may be able to bring this fact out— but only if the defendant testifies. Evidence of a previous crime may cause some jurors to think that the defendant is guilty of the current crime, too.
- If the defendant testifies, the prosecutor may be able to bring out other information that tarnishes the defendant's reputation and discredits his testimony.
- Some defendants have a poor demeanor when speaking in public. A judge or jury may not believe a defendant who, though telling the truth, is a nervous witness and makes a bad impression.
- The defendant may have a perfectly good story which would nevertheless sound fishy to the average jury in that particular locale.

## What is self-defense—and how can a defendant prove it?

Self-defense is a common defense asserted by someone charged with a crime of violence, such as battery (striking someone), assault with a deadly weapon or murder. The defendant admits that she did in fact commit the crime, but claims that it was justified by the other person's threatening actions. The core issues in most self-defense cases are:

- Who was the aggressor?
- Was the defendant's belief that self-defense was necessary a reasonable one?
- If so, was the force used by the defendant also reasonable?

Self-defense is rooted in the belief that people should be allowed to protect themselves from physical harm. This means that a person does not have to wait until she is actually struck to act in self-defense. If a reasonable person would think that she is about to be physically attacked, she has the right to strike first and prevent the attack. But she cannot use more force than is reasonable—if she does, she may be guilty of a crime even though some force was justifiable.

## When can a defendant win an acquittal on grounds of insanity?

The insanity defense is based on the principle that punishment is justified only if the defendant is capable of controlling his or her behavior and understanding that what he or she has done is wrong. Because some people suffering from a mental disorder are not capable of knowing or choosing right from wrong, the insanity defense prevents them from being criminally punished.

Despite its ancient origins (England, 1505), the insanity defense remains controversial. Victim-oriented critics point out that a person killed by an insane person is just as dead as a person killed by someone who is sane, and argue that people should be punished for the harm they cause regardless of their mental state. Critics also question the ability of psychiatrists, judges and jurors to determine whether a person suffers from a mental disorder, and to link mental disorders to the commission of crimes.

The insanity defense is an extremely complex topic; many scholarly works are devoted to explaining its nuances. Here are some major points of interest:

- Despite popular perceptions to the contrary, defendants rarely enter pleas of "not guilty by reason of insanity." On the few occasions that the defendant does raise it, judges and jurors rarely support it.
- Because neither the legal system nor psychiatrists can agree on a single meaning of insanity in the criminal law context, various definitions are employed. The most popular definition is the "McNaghten rule," which defines insanity as "the inability to distinguish right from wrong." Another common test is known as "irresistible impulse": A person who acts out of an irresistible impulse knows that an act is wrong, but because of mental illness, cannot control his actions.

- Defendants found not guilty by reason of insanity are not automatically set free. They are usually confined to a mental institution, and not released until their sanity is established. These defendants can spend more time in a mental institution than they would have spent in prison had they been convicted.

- An insanity defense normally rests on the testimony of a psychiatrist, who testifies for the defendant after examining him and his past history, and the facts of the case. Courts appoint psychiatrists at government expense to assist poor defendants who cannot afford to hire their own psychiatrists. The prosecution will normally hire another psychiatrist, who may offer an opinion different from the defense psychiatrist.

## Competency to Stand Trial

Aside from insanity as a defense to criminal charges, the question may arise as to whether a defendant is mentally capable of facing a trial. Defendants cannot be prosecuted if they suffer from a mental disorder that prevents them from understanding the proceedings and assisting in the preparation of their defense. Based on a defendant's unusual behavior, a judge, prosecutor or defense attorney may ask that trial be delayed until the defendant has been examined and her ability to understand the proceedings has been determined in a court hearing. If a judge finds that a defendant doesn't understand what's going on, the defendant will probably be placed in a mental institution until her competence is re-established. At that time, the trial will be held.

## Can a defendant go free because he was drunk or high on drugs when he committed a crime?

Defendants who commit crimes under the influence of drugs or alcohol sometimes argue that their mental functioning was so impaired that they cannot be held accountable for their actions. Generally, however, voluntary intoxication does not excuse criminal conduct. People know (or should know) that alcohol and drugs affect mental functioning, and thus they should be held legally responsible if they commit crimes as a result of their voluntary use.

Some states allow an exception to this general rule. If the defendant is accused of committing a crime that requires what's known as "specific intent" (intending the precise consequences, as well as intending to do the physical act that leads up to the consequences), the defendant can argue that he was too drunk or high to have formed that intent. This is only a partial defense, however, because it doesn't entirely excuse the defendant's actions. In this situation, the defendant will usually be convicted of another crime that doesn't require proof of a specific intent—for example, assault with a deadly weapon instead of assault with the intent to commit murder.

# If You Are Questioned by the Police

*There is plenty of law at the end of a nightstick.*

**—GROVER A. WHALEN**

If a police officer wants to stop and question you, whether or not you must comply depends on the circumstances and the reasons the officer has for questioning you. This section explores some of the common questions people have about their rights and responsibilities when approached by a law enforcement officer.

## If an officer wants to stop me while I'm walking on the street and I know I've done nothing wrong, should I comply?

A police officer may interfere with your freedom of movement only if he has observed unusual activity suggesting that criminal activity is afoot and that you are involved. Even if the officer is mistaken, however, you do not have the right to keep walking. As long as the officer has a good faith belief in your connection to criminal activity, he is allowed to detain you. Stopping you is one thing, however. It doesn't mean that you must answer all of his questions. (See below.)

## If You Run Away

It is not unusual for people who are approached by the police to run away. Some courts have recognized that people of color, in particular, have a well-founded fear of unfair treatment at the hands of the police, and that many people will avoid contact with the police not because they are guilty of a crime, but because they reasonably believe that they may be mistreated or unjustly accused. Other courts view evasive behavior as evidence of guilt, however, and allow the police to rely on the attempt to run away as grounds for a detention.

## If I am legally stopped by a police officer on the street, can he search me?

Yes and no. A police officer is permitted to briefly frisk your outer clothing for weapons if the officer reasonably fears for his safety. If a frisk is later challenged in court as being unreasonable, a judge will usually uphold it.

A frisk is different than a search in that a search may be conducted for evidence of a crime or contraband (an illegal item), and may be much more intrusive than a frisk. An officer who frisks you may not search you unless he has good cause to believe that you committed a crime or that you're hiding an illegal item. (See *Searches and Seizures,* below.)

18.9

## How a Frisk Becomes a Legal Search—And Possibly an Arrest

When frisking a person for weapons, the police are attuned not only to the feel of possible weapons under clothing, but also to the feel of packaged drugs. Although a frisk may not turn up a weapon, it may turn up a suspicious package which the officer knows is commonly used to carry illegal drugs or some other illegal substance. A discovery like that may create sufficient cause for a more intensive search of the person's clothing. The lesson here is that a frisk often leads to a search. And if a search produces an illegal substance, it may result in an arrest.

### If I am questioned by a police officer after being stopped on the street, do I have to respond to the questions?

The general rule is that you don't have to answer any questions that the police ask you. This rule comes from the Fifth Amendment to the U.S. Constitution, which protects you against self-incrimination. As with all rules, however, there is an exception. Many local and state governments have anti-loitering laws that require people to account for their presence if the police have a reasonable suspicion that they are loitering. Once the police have asked all of their questions about loitering, however, you don't have to answer any others—such as

questions about a crime in the neighborhood.

A defense lawyer's most sacred piece of advice is this: Don't talk to the police about a crime unless you clearly weren't involved and you want to help the police solve it.

# Searches and Seizures

Most people instinctively understand the concept of privacy. It's the freedom to decide which details of your life are public and which are not. At the same time, most of us acknowledge that society is served when the police, in appropriate circumstances, are allowed to look for and seize contraband, stolen goods and evidence of a crime.

In an attempt to balance our desires for privacy against the legitimate needs of the police, the Fourth Amendment of the U.S. Constitution prohibits "unreasonable" searches and seizures by state or federal law officers. Generally, this means that the police may conduct a search of your home, barn, car, boat, office, personal or business documents, bank account records, trash barrel or any other property if:

- the police can show that it is more likely than not that a crime has occurred and that if they are allowed to search, they will probably find evidence or contraband (this requirement is called "probable cause"), and

- a judge agrees there is probable cause and issues a search warrant, or the police are permitted to search without a warrant because of the particular circumstances involved (the warrant requirement).

So, for a search to be legal under the constitution, the police must have both probable cause to conduct the search and a search warrant (although the warrant requirement has many exceptions, some of which are discussed below).

## When is a police investigation considered a search?

A police investigation is not a search unless it intrudes on a person's privacy. In other words, if a person did not have a "legitimate expectation of privacy" in the place or thing searched, no "search" has occurred, at least not for the purpose of determining whether the Fourth Amendment has been violated.

Courts ask two questions to determine whether a person had a legitimate expectation of privacy in the place or things searched:

- Did the person expect some degree of privacy?
- Is the person's expectation reasonable—that is, one that society is willing to recognize?

For example, a person who uses a public restroom expects that no one will spy on her, and most people—including judges and juries—would consider that expectation to be reasonable. Therefore, if the police install a hidden video camera in a public restroom, the action is considered a

search and must meet the Fourth Amendment's requirement of reasonableness.

On the other hand, if the police glance into a car and see a weapon on the front seat, it is not a search because it is unlikely that a person would think that the front seat of a car is a private place. And even if he did, society is not generally willing to extend the protections of privacy to the front seat of an automobile.

## How Private Is Your Property?

Generally, if the police are able to view contraband or evidence on your property without actually entering it, they have not conducted a search. In other words, you cannot have a reasonable expectation of privacy in an area that can legitimately be seen from outside your property. This means that the police can use what they have seen as the basis for getting a warrant to come in and take a closer look. Or, if the situation calls for prompt action (the need to stop a drug deal, for instance), they may enter without a warrant.

Law enforcement officers are allowed to take aerial photographs or come close enough to overhear your conversations—these actions are not considered searches. On the other hand, without a warrant or an exception to the rule requiring a warrant, officers are probably not allowed to use sophisticated equipment to discover what is on your property or to eavesdrop on your conversations. In general, if the investigation method is highly artificial and high-tech, it's likely to be considered a search. Where the line is drawn, however, is not clear or consistent from state to state.

## What is a search warrant?

A search warrant is a kind of permission slip, signed by a judge, that allows the police to enter private property to look for particular items. It is addressed to the owner of the property, and tells the owner that a judge has decided that it is reasonably likely that certain contraband, or evidence of criminal activities, will be found in specified locations on the property.

As a general rule, the police are supposed to apply for a warrant before conducting a search of private property; any search that is conducted without a warrant is presumed to be unreasonable—even if there was "probable cause" to conduct the search. This means that the police officers will later have to justify the search—and why a warrant wasn't obtained first—if the defendant challenges it in court.

## What does it take to get a search warrant?

A judge will issue a search warrant after the police have convinced her that:

- it is more likely than not that a crime has taken place, and
- items connected to the crime are likely be found in a specified location on the property.

To convince the judge of these facts, the police tell the judge what they know about the situation. Usually, the information given to the judge is based either on the officers' own observations or on the secondhand observations of an informant.

The police are limited in their ability to use secondhand information. As a general rule, the information must be reliable given the circumstances. Generally, information is reliable if it is corroborated by police observation. For example, a citizen's tip that a suspect regularly delivers drugs to a certain location would be corroborated if an officer observes that suspect's routine. But corroboration is not necessary in every case. Sometimes a judge will issue a warrant if the source of the information is known to the police and has provided trustworthy information in the past.

## What are the police allowed to do after they obtain a search warrant?

Once the police have a search warrant, they are entitled to enter the designated property to search for the items listed on the warrant. Legally, the search is supposed to be confined to the specific areas described in the warrant. For example, if the search warrant includes only the living room, the search should not extend into the kitchen, bathroom or bedroom. But there are exceptions to this limitation which are frequently used to justify broader searches. For example, the police may search beyond the terms of the warrant in order to:

- ensure their safety and the safety of others

- prevent the destruction of evidence
- discover more about possible evidence or contraband that is in plain view elsewhere on the property, or
- hunt for evidence or contraband that, as a result of their initial search, they believe exists in another location on the property.

For instance, although a warrant might be issued for the search of a house, the sound of a shotgun being loaded in the backyard would justify expanding the search to the yard in order to protect the officers; similarly, a search limited to the ground floor might legitimately expand to the upstairs if the police, searching for illegal drugs, hear toilets being flushed above. And the police can always seize evidence or illegal items if they are in plain view or are discovered while the officers are searching for the items listed in the warrant.

## Do the police always need a warrant to conduct a search?

No. In many situations, police may legally conduct a search without first obtaining a warrant.

- *Consent searches.* If the police ask your permission to search your home, purse, briefcase or other property, and you agree, the search is considered consensual, and they don't need a warrant. The police typically obtain a person's consent by threatening to detain her while they obtain the warrant.
- *Searches that accompany an arrest.* When a person is placed under arrest, the police may search the

person and the immediate surroundings for weapons that might be used to harm the officer. If the person is taken to jail, the police may search to make sure that weapons or contraband are not brought into the jail. (This is called an inventory search.) Inventory searches also frequently involve a search of the arrested person's car (if it is being held by the police) and personal effects on the theory that the police need a precise record of the person's property to avoid claims of theft.

- *Searches necessary to protect the safety of the public.* The police don't need a warrant if they have a reasonable fear that their safety, or that of the public, is in imminent danger. For example, an officer who suspected a bomb-making operation while walking his beat might be justified in entering immediately and seizing the ingredients. And in the famous O.J. Simpson case, the police justified their entry onto O.J. Simpson's property on the grounds that they feared for the safety of other family members.
- *Searches necessary to prevent the imminent destruction of evidence.* A police officer does not need to obtain a warrant if she has observed illegal items (such as weapons or contraband) and believes that the items will disappear unless the officer takes prompt action. This exception arises most frequently when the police spot contraband or weapons in a car. Because cars are moved so frequently, the officer is justified in searching the entire vehicle, includ-

ing the trunk, without obtaining a warrant—if the officer has probable cause. On the other hand, if the police learn about a marijuana-growing operation from a neighbor, they usually would need a warrant, as it is unlikely that the growing plants and other evidence of the operation will disappear quickly enough to justify a warrantless search.

- *"Hot pursuit" searches.* Police may enter private dwellings to search for criminals who are fleeing the scene of a crime.

### Can my roommate—or my landlord—give the police permission to search my apartment?

The police may search your apartment if the person in charge of the premises gives permission. If you and your roommate share common areas (such as the kitchen and living room), your roommate can authorize a search of those areas. But your roommate cannot give permission to search your separate bedroom.

Similarly, your landlord cannot give permission to search your apartment. Although the landlord owns the property, your monthly check guarantees your privacy at home. This is true even if you are behind in your rent or your landlord has sued to evict you. Until the landlord has a court order that permits him to enter and retake the premises, he cannot enter without your permission. (But keep in mind that many states allow a landlord to enter for inspections, which

usually require advance notice of a day or two.) If the police can point to circumstances that would justify immediate entry, however—such as the sound of a ferocious fight or the smell of burning marijuana—they may enter without permission from anyone.

# Arrests and Interrogations

I HAVEN'T COMMITTED A CRIME.

WHAT I DID WAS FAIL TO COMPLY

WITH THE LAW.

**–DAVID DINKINS**

An arrest occurs when a police officer armed with an arrest warrant utters the magic words "you're under arrest," or when a police officer's actions cause you to believe that you are not free to leave. The restraint must be more than a mere detention on the street (discussed above). Although in most situations the police will take you to the police station for booking (photographs and fingerprinting), it is also possible for an officer to arrest and book you at the crime scene, and then release you when you give a written promise to appear in court at a later time.

After the police arrest you, they will often question you in order to find out more about the crime, your role in it and whether there may be other suspects. There are several Constitutional protections that you may invoke during police interrogations.

## When do the police need a warrant to make an arrest?

As long as the police have good reason (called "probable cause") to believe that a crime has been committed and that the person they want to arrest committed the crime, they can, with just one exception, make an arrest without asking a judge for a warrant.

The exception? There are few places where the adage "a man's home is his castle" still applies, and an arrest at home is one of them. The police must have a warrant to arrest a person at home if the arrest is for a nonserious offense—such as a simple assault—and there is no fear that the person they want to arrest will destroy evidence or cause harm to the public.

## How do the police obtain an arrest warrant?

An officer must present sworn evidence to a judge that a crime has occurred and that the police have probable cause to believe that the crime was committed by the person they want to arrest. If the judge agrees, she will issue a warrant. The police are then entitled to seize the person wherever they can find him.

## If the police make an illegal arrest, is the arrested person set free?

No. But if a search of the person or her immediate surroundings is conducted during the arrest and turns up incriminating evidence, the evidence may be kept out of the person's trial on the grounds that it is "fruit of the poisonous tree"—that is, the evidence was found as the result of an improper arrest. Also, if the illegally arrested person makes any statements to the police after being arrested, the statements may not be used as evidence. This is true whether or not the arrested person was "read their rights." (See below.)

## Can a person who is charged with a crime be forced to give bodily samples?

Yes. You might think that being forced to give bodily samples—such as blood, hair or fingernail clippings—is a violation of the U.S. Constitution's protection against self-incrimination, found in the Fifth Amendment. But the U.S. Supreme Court thinks otherwise. It has ruled that the Fifth Amendment protects communications only, and that bodily samples are physical evidence and therefore not covered by the Constitution.

## If I'm arrested, do the police have to "read me my rights"?

No. However, if they don't read you your rights, they can't use anything you say as evidence against you at trial. What are these rights? Popularly known as the *Miranda* warning (ordered by the U.S. Supreme Court in *Miranda v. Arizona*), your rights consist of the familiar litany invoked by T.V. police immediately upon arresting a suspect:

- You have the right to remain silent.
- If you do say anything, what you say can be used against you in a court of law.
- You have the right to consult with a lawyer and have that lawyer present during any questioning.
- If you cannot afford a lawyer, one will be appointed for you if you so desire.
- If you choose to talk to the police officer, you have the right to stop the interview at any time. (This part of the warning is usually omitted from the screenplay.)

It doesn't matter whether an interrogation occurs in a jail or at the scene of a crime, on a busy downtown street or in the middle of an open field: If you are in custody (deprived of your freedom of action in any significant way), the police must give a *Miranda* warning if they want to question you and use your answers as evidence at trial. If you are not in police custody, however, no *Miranda* warning is required. This exception most often comes up when the police stop someone on the street to question them about a recent crime and the person blurts out a confession before the police have an opportunity to deliver the warning.

## Will a judge dismiss my case if I was questioned without a *Miranda* warning?

No. Many people mistakenly believe that a case will be thrown out of court if the police fail to give *Miranda* warnings to the arrested person. What *Miranda* actually says is that a warn-ing is necessary if the police interrogate a suspect and want to use any of her responses as evidence. If the police fail to give you a *Miranda* warning, nothing you say in response to the questioning can be used as evidence to convict you. In addition, under the "fruit of the poisonous tree" rule, if the police find evidence as a result of an interrogation that violates the *Miranda* rule, that evidence is also inadmissible at trial. For example, if you tell the police where a weapon is hidden and it turns out that you gave this information in response to im-proper questioning, the police will not be able to use the weapon as evidence unless the police can prove that they would have found the weapon without your statements. If there is sufficient other evidence to convict you beyond any statements you made to the police, you can still be con-victed even when the police don't give *Miranda* warnings.

## What's the best way to assert my right to remain silent if I am being questioned by the police?

If you're taken into custody by the police, you don't have to use any magic words to let police officers know that you want to remain silent. You can simply say nothing in re-sponse to police questions. Or, after an officer gives you a *Miranda* warn-ing, you can stop the questioning by saying something like:
- I want to talk to an attorney.
- I won't say anything until I talk to an attorney.
- I don't have anything to say.

- I don't want to talk to you anymore.
- I claim my *Miranda* rights.

If the police continue to question you after you have asserted your right to remain silent, they have violated *Miranda*. As a result, anything you say after that point—and any evidence gleaned from that conversation—should not be admissible at your trial. Once you've invoked your right to silence, however, the best course is to remain silent, instead of counting on a judge to keep out your statements further down the line.

## How heavy handed can the police get when asking questions?

Information that you voluntarily disclose to a police officer (after you have been properly warned) is generally admissible at trial. The key word is "voluntary." Police officers are not allowed to use physical force or psychological coercion to get you to talk to them. The days of the rubber hose, protracted grilling under bright lights and severe sleep deprivation are pretty much over. If police officers obtain information through any of these illegal means, the information cannot be used by the prosecutor at trial. In addition, under the rule known as "the fruit of the poisonous tree," any evidence that the police obtain as the result of a coerced statement is equally inadmissible.

### Reality Check: Cops Usually Win a Swearing Contest

Defendants often claim that police officers coerced them into talking. And it's just as common for police officers to say that the defendants spoke voluntarily. If the police physically coerce a defendant into talking, the defendant can support his coercion claims with photos of marks and bruises. But actual police brutality is unusual, and a defendant cannot usually offer independent evidence to support his claims of psychological coercion. Judges, believing that defendants have a greater motivation to lie than do police officers, usually side with the police and conclude that no coercion took place.

## Bail

*Those who expect to reap the blessings of freedom must . . . undergo the fatigue of supporting it.*

**—THOMAS PAINE**

Many people, especially those arrested for minor misdemeanors, are given citations at the scene of an arrest telling them when to appear in court, and are immediately released. Others, however, are put in jail. Often, a person's first thought upon landing in jail is how to get out—and fast. The usual way to do this is to "post bail." This section answers common questions about the bail system, including its version of Monopoly's "Get Out of Jail Free" card—called release O.R.

## What does it mean to "post bail"?

Bail is cash or a cash equivalent that an arrested person gives to a court to ensure that he will appear in court when ordered to do so. If the defendant appears in court at the proper time, the court refunds the bail. But if the defendant doesn't show up, the court keeps the bail and issues a warrant for the defendant's arrest.

Bail can take any of the following forms:
- cash or check for the full amount of the bail
- property worth the full amount of the bail
- a bond—that is, a guaranteed payment of the full bail amount, or
- a waiver of payment on the condition that the defendant appear in court at the required time, commonly called "release on one's own recognizance" or simply "O.R."

## Who decides how much bail I have to pay?

Judges are responsible for setting bail. Because many people want to get out of jail immediately and, depending on

when you are arrested, it can take up to five days to see a judge, most jails have standard bail schedules which specify bail amounts for common crimes. You can get out of jail quickly by paying the amount set forth in the bail schedule.

## Are there are restrictions on how high my bail can be?

The Eighth Amendment to the U. S. Constitution requires that bail not be excessive. This means that bail should not be used to raise money for the government or to punish a person for being suspected of committing a crime. The purpose of bail is to give an arrested person her freedom until she is convicted of a crime, and the amount of bail must be no more than is reasonably necessary to keep her from fleeing before a case is over.

So much for theory. In fact, many judges set an impossibly high bail in particular types of cases (such as those involving drug sales or rape) to keep a suspect in jail until the trial is over. Although bail set for this purpose—called preventative detention—is thought by many to violate the Constitution, no court has stopped the practice.

## What can I do if I can't afford to pay the bail listed on the bail schedule?

If you can't afford the amount of bail on the bail schedule, you can ask a judge to lower it. Depending on the state, your request must be made either in a special bail-setting hearing or when you appear in court for the first time, usually called your arraignment.

## How soon can I appear before a judge?

In federal court, a person taken to jail must be brought "without unnecessary delay before the nearest available . . . magistrate." Most states have similar rules. In no event should more than 48 hours elapse (not counting weekends and holidays) between the time of booking and bringing you to court. Unfortunately, these rules are rarely enforced because the police can simply release the suspect when the time is up and then immediately re-arrest him.

## How do I pay for bail?

There are two ways to pay your bail. You may either pay the full amount of the bail or buy a bail bond. A bail bond is like a check held in reserve: It represents your promise that you will appear in court when you are supposed to. You pay a bond seller to post a bond (a certain sum of money) with the court, and the court keeps the bond in case you don't show up. You can usually buy a bail bond for about 10% of the amount of your bail; this premium is the bond seller's fee for taking the risk that you won't appear in court.

A bail bond may sound like a good deal, but buying a bond may cost you more in the long run. If you pay the full amount of the bail, you'll get that money back (less a small administrative fee) if you make your scheduled court appearances. On the other hand, the 10% premium you pay to a bond seller is nonrefundable. In addition,

the bond seller may require "collateral." This means that you (or the person who pays for your bail bond) must give the bond seller a financial interest in some of your valuable property. The bond seller can cash in this interest if you fail to appear in court.

Nevertheless, if you can't afford your bail and you don't have a friend or relative that can help out, a bond seller may be your only option. You can find one by looking in the Yellow Pages; you're also likely to find bond sellers' offices very close to any jail.

Finally, be ready to pay in cash, a money order or a cashier's check. Jails and bond sellers usually do not take credit cards or personal checks for bail.

## Is it true that a defendant who proves his reliability can get out of jail on his word alone?

Sometimes. This is generally known as releasing someone "on his own recognizance," or "O.R." A defendant released O.R. must simply sign a promise to show up in court. He doesn't have to post bail. A defendant commonly requests release on his own recognizance at his first court appearance. If the judge denies the request, he then asks for low bail.

In general, defendants who are released O.R. have strong ties to a community, making them unlikely to flee. Factors that may convince a judge to grant an O.R. release include the following:

- The defendant has other family members (most likely parents, a spouse or children) living in the community.

- The defendant has resided in the community for many years.
- The defendant has a job.
- The defendant has little or no past criminal record, or any previous criminal problems were minor and occurred many years earlier.
- The defendant has been charged with previous crimes and has always appeared as required.

# Getting a Lawyer

JUSTICE OFT LEANS TO THE SIDE

WHERE YOUR PURSE HANGS.

**—DANISH PROVERB**

If you are accused of a crime, you will probably face the possibility of going to jail. This fact alone will most likely drive you to look for a good lawyer. Unfortunately, private criminal defense lawyers don't come cheap, and you may not be able to afford one. This doesn't mean you'll be completely at the mercy of the government, however. The U.S. Constitution provides that you are entitled to be represented by an attorney if the state is trying to deprive you of your liberty. This means that a court may be required to appoint a lawyer to represent you for free—or for a fee you can afford. This section discusses the role of private and court-appointed attorneys in the criminal process and offers suggestions for finding a private attorney if you can afford one.

## How can I get a court to appoint a lawyer for me?

Normally, if you want a court to appoint a lawyer for you at government expense, you must:

- ask the court to appoint a lawyer, and
- provide details about your financial situation.

Typically, your first opportunity to ask the court to appoint a lawyer for you will be at your first court appearance, normally called your arraignment or bail hearing. The judge will probably ask you whether you are represented by a lawyer. If you're not, the judge will then ask whether you want to apply for court-appinted counsel. If you say yes, some courts will appoint a lawyer right on the spot and finish your arraignment. Other courts will delay your case and appoint a lawyer only after reviewing and approving your economic circumstances.

Each state (or even county) makes its own rules as to who qualifies for a free lawyer. Also, the seriousness of the charge may affect a judge's decision as to whether you are eligible for free legal assistance. For example, a judge may recognize that a wage-earner can afford the cost of representation for a minor crime, but not for a crime involving a complicated and lengthy trial.

If you don't qualify for free help but can't afford the full cost of a private lawyer, you may still obtain the services of a court-appointed attorney. Most states provide for "partial indigency," which means that at the conclusion of the case, the judge will require you to reimburse the state or county for a portion of the costs of representation.

## Do I need a lawyer at my arraignment?

In most criminal courts the arraignment is where you first appear before a judge and enter a plea of guilty or not guilty to the offense charged. Assuming you enter a plea of not guilty, which almost every defendant does at this early stage, the court will then:

* set a date for the next procedural event in your case
* consider any bail requests that you or the prosecutor make
* appoint your lawyer, and
* ask you to waive time—that is, give up your right to have the trial or other statutory proceedings occur within specified periods of time.

Most people can handle this proceeding without a lawyer. However, if you can get the court to appoint a lawyer for you without postponing the arraignment, or you are able to arrange for private representation before your arraignment, it's always better to have a lawyer.

## If I'm poor, will a judge appoint a public defender to represent me?

Because most criminal defendants are unable to afford their own attorneys, many states have Public Defender's Offices. Typically, each local office has a Chief Public Defender and a number of Assistant Public Defenders (P.D.s). P.D.s are fully-licensed lawyers whose sole job is to represent poor defendants in criminal cases. Because they appear daily in the same courts, P.D.s can gain a lot of experience in a short period of time. And because they work daily with the same cast of characters, they learn the personalities (and prejudices) of the judges, prosecutors and local law enforcement officers—important information to know when assessing a case and conducting a trial.

## My county doesn't have a public defender's office. How will the court provide an attorney for me?

In areas that don't have a public defender's office, the court maintains a list of attorneys and appoints them on a rotating basis to represent people who can't afford to hire their own lawyers.

## Do public defenders provide the same quality of representation as regular lawyers?

Despite the increasingly severe financial constraints on their offices, public defenders often provide representation that is at least as competent as that provided by private defense attorneys. A 1992 study conducted by the National Center for State Courts concluded that P.D.s and private lawyers achieve approximately equal results. For example, in the nine counties surveyed in the study, 76% of P.D.

clients were convicted, compared to 74% of clients with private lawyers.

Despite these good points, public defenders are often asked to perform too much work for not enough money, which can cut into their abilities to be effective.

## How can I get a second opinion on my public defender's advice?

Like all attorneys, public defenders are ethically obligated to vigorously defend their clients' interests. Undoubtedly, most lawyers live up to their ethical duties. But defendants who think that their court-appointed attorneys are not representing them adequately can buy advice from a private defense attorney. Even a low-income person may be able to pay for a short "second opinion" consultation.

## How can I find a private defense lawyer?

Recently arrested people often need to talk to a lawyer as soon as possible. The most urgent priority is often getting a lawyer to help arrange release and provide some information about what's to come in the days ahead.

If you have been represented by a criminal defense lawyer in the past, that is usually the lawyer to call—as long as you were satisfied with his services. If you have no previous experience with criminal defense lawyers, you can look to the following sources for a referral:

- *Lawyers you know.* Most lawyers do civil (noncriminal) work, such as divorces, drafting wills, filing bankruptcies or representing people

hurt in accidents. If you know any attorney that you trust, ask him to recommend a criminal defense lawyer. (Some lawyers who do civil work can also represent clients in criminal matters, at least for the limited purpose of arranging for release from jail following an arrest.)

- *Family members or friends.* Someone close to you may know of a criminal defense lawyer or may have time to look for one.
- *Martindale-Hubbell.* Martindale-Hubbell directories identify lawyers according where they work and the type of law they practice. The directories even rate lawyers for competency. All law libraries have Martindale-Hubbell books; many general public libraries have them as well. If you have computer access to the World Wide Web, you can also find Martindale-Hubble online at http://www.martindale.com/.
- *Courthouses.* You can visit a local courthouse and sit through a few criminal hearings. If a particular lawyer impresses you, ask for her card after the hearing is over, and then call for an appointment.

## Should I expect a lawyer to guarantee a good result?

Toasters come with guarantees; attorneys don't. Steer clear of lawyers who guarantee satisfactory outcomes. A lawyer who guarantees a good result may simply be trying a hard-sell tactic to induce you to hire her.

## What is a private lawyer likely to cost?

It's impossible to give a definitive answer. Attorneys set their own fees, which vary according to a number of factors:

- *The complexity of a case.* Most attorneys charge more for felonies than for misdemeanors because felonies carry greater penalties and are likely to involve more work for the attorney.
- *The attorney's experience.* Generally, less experienced attorneys set lower fees than their more experienced colleagues.
- *Geography.* Just as gasoline and butter cost more in some parts of the country than others, so do lawyers.

According to a survey of readers reported in the February, 1996 issue of *Consumer Reports*, the median legal fee charged by lawyers in criminal cases was $1,500. Many defendants can expect to pay more than this, however. A defendant charged with a misdemeanor should not be surprised by a legal fee in the neighborhood of $3,000-$5,000; an attorney may want $15,000-$25,000 in a felony case. And most attorneys want all or a substantial portion of the fee paid up front.

## Can I arrange for a contingency fee in a criminal case?

No. A contingency fee is an arrangement where the lawyer gets paid only if he wins the case. These arrangements are not allowed in criminal cases.

## Can I change lawyers if I'm unhappy with the one I hired?

Generally, defendants who hire their own attorneys have the right to fire them at any time, without court approval. A defendant doesn't have to show "good cause" or even justify the firing. After firing a lawyer, a defendant can hire another lawyer or perhaps even represent herself. Of course, changing lawyers will probably be costly. In addition to paying the new lawyer, the defendant will have to pay the original lawyer whatever portion of the fee the original lawyer has earned.

## Limits on Your Right to Change Lawyers

Your right to change lawyers is limited by the prosecutor's right to keep cases moving on schedule. If you want to change attorneys on the eve of trial, for example, your new attorney is likely to agree to represent you only if the trial is delayed so she can prepare. The prosecutor may oppose delay, possibly because witnesses won't be available to testify later on. In these circumstances, the judge is likely to deny your request to change lawyers.

## What if I'm not happy with my court-appointed lawyer? Can I get a new one?

Probably not. Defendants with court-appointed lawyers often ask for new ones. Sometimes the problems are the same as those that would be encountered with any retained lawyer: inability to communicate, personality conflicts or dissatisfaction with the strategy. In addition, clients who are represented by court-appointed lawyers often assume that the representation is substandard.

Requests for a new court-appointed lawyer are rarely granted. A defendant would have to prove that the representation is truly incompetent.

## Why do some defendants choose to represent themselves?

Defendants choose to represent themselves for a variety of reasons:

- Some defendants can afford to hire a lawyer, but don't do so because they think the likely punishment is not severe enough to justify the expense.
- Some defendants believe (often mistakenly) that an attorney who represented them previously was ineffective, and figure they can do just as well on their own.
- Some defendants believe that lawyers are part of an overall oppressive system and seek to make a political statement by representing themselves.
- Some defendants want to take responsibility for their own destiny.
- Some defendants who are in jail can gain privileges through self-representation, such as access to the jail's law library. Also, not bound by lawyers' ethical codes, self-represented defendants can delay proceedings and sometimes wreak havoc on an already overloaded system by repeatedly filing motions.

## How can I tell whether I should represent myself or not?

The most obvious rule is that the less severe the charged crime, the more sensible it is to represent yourself. Defendants charged with minor traffic offenses should rarely hire an attorney, while defendants charged with serious felonies should rarely be without one. The most difficult decisions involve misdemeanors such as drunk driving, possession of drugs or shoplifting. Hiring an attorney in these situations may be wise because jail time and a fine are possibilities, and convictions may carry hidden costs, such as more severe punishment for a second conviction or vastly increased insurance rates. On the other hand, first time offenders charged with nonviolent crimes are not usually sentenced to jail, and judges and prosecutors often offer standard deals to all defendants, whether or not they are represented by an attorney. Thus, the most critical piece of information that defendants should try to learn before deciding whether to hire an attorney is what the punishment is likely to be if they are convicted.

## How to Find Out What Your Punishment Is Likely to Be

It can be difficult to learn about judges' common sentencing practices. Typical sentences aren't usually listed in statutes or court rules, unless you're being sentenced in federal court (and even in that case, the federal sentencing code is incredibly technical, so likely punishment can be difficult to figure out). If you want to find out what your punishment is likely to be if you're convicted, you might take the following steps:

• Pay a private defense attorney for an hour of consultation. An experienced defense attorney can often make accurate predictions as to likely punishment.

• Ask a relative or close friend who is or who knows an attorney for informal, unpaid advice.

• Call the public defender's office, and ask if they have an "attorney of the day" who can answer your questions.

## Can I represent myself and pay a lawyer to advise me as I go?

Yes. If you're thinking about representing yourself, you might want to seek out an attorney willing to serve as a "legal coach." The goal of hiring a legal coach is to combine a lawyer's knowledge with your own time. Because you pay for the lawyer's help only occasionally, the cost of a legal coach can be far less than turning the entire case over to a private attorney.

Not all attorneys are willing to serve as legal coaches. Some are worried about their liability if they give wrong advice based on incomplete information; others do not want to be involved with a case unless they are in control of it. Thus, if you're considering going it alone and you think you'll want a lawyer's help, you should try to line up your legal coach before you make your final decision.

### More Information About Crimes and Criminal Procedure

There are many books and publications devoted to the explanation of state and federal criminal law and procedure. Although most of them are written for lawyers, nonlawyers will find them useful, too. Since the practice of criminal law is so intimately tied to state and local laws, we cannot list every resource here. Your best bet is to go to your local law library and ask for practice manuals or digests on the subject. See the Appendix on Legal Reseach for more information on finding state law and practice manuals and digests.

### http://nolo.com

*Nolo offers self-help information about a wide variety of legal topics, including criminal law and procedure.*

### http://www.findlaw.com

*Most states have put their statutes, including their criminal and criminal procedure codes, on the Internet.*

Glossary

**401(k) plan** A deferred compensation savings program in which employees invest part of their wages, sometimes with added employer contributions, to save on taxes. Income taxes on the amounts invested and earned are not due until the employee withdraws money from the fund, usually at retirement.

**AB trust** A trust that allows couples to reduce or avoid estate taxes. If property is held in an AB trust, when the first spouse dies, his or her half of the property goes to the beneficiaries named in the trust with the condition that the surviving spouse has the right to use the property for life and is entitled to any income it generates. This keeps the property out of the surviving spouse's estate, reducing the likelihood that estate tax will be due when the surviving spouse dies.

**acquittal** A decision by a judge or jury that a defendant in a criminal case is not guilty of a crime.

**adjustable rate mortgage (ARM)** A mortgage loan with an interest rate that fluctuates in accordance with a designated market indicator—such as the weekly average of one-year U.S. Treasury Bills—over the life of the loan.

**administration (of an estate)** The court-supervised distribution of a deceased person's property.

**adoption** A court procedure by which an adult becomes the legal parent of someone who is not his or her biological child.

**annuity** A purchased policy that pays a fixed amount of benefits every year for the life of the person who is entitled to those benefits under the policy.

**annulment** A court procedure that dissolves a marriage and treats it as if it never happened.

**appeal** A written request to a higher court to modify or reverse the judgment of a trial court or intermediate level appellate court.

**appellate court** A higher court that reviews the decision of a lower court when a losing party files an appeal.

**arbitration** A procedure for resolving disputes out of court using one or more neutral third parties—called the arbitrator or arbitration panel.

**arraignment** A court appearance in which a criminal defendant is formally charged with a crime and asked to respond by entering a plea, most commonly guilty, not guilty or "nolo contendere."

**arrest** A situation in which the police detain someone in a manner that would lead any reasonable person to believe that he or she is not free to leave.

**arrest warrant** A document issued by a judge or magistrate that authorizes the police to arrest someone.

**articles of incorporation** A document filed with state authorities to form a corporation.

**assault** The crime of attempting to physically harm another person in a way that makes the person under attack feel immediately threatened. Actual physical contact is not necessary.

**attorney-in-fact** A person named in a written power of attorney document to act on behalf of the person who signs the document, called the principal.

**audit** An examination of the financial records of a person, business or organization, typically undertaken to clean up careless or improper bookkeeping, or to verify that proper records are being kept. Audits are also conducted by the IRS in order to determine whether a person or business owes taxes.

**B**

**bail** The money paid to the court, usually at arraignment or shortly thereafter, to ensure that an arrested person who is released from jail will show up at all required court appearances.

**bail bond** Money posted for a defendant who cannot afford bail. The defendant pays a certain portion, usually 10%. If the defendant fails to appear at a court hearing, the defendant may lose the money.

**balloon payment** A large final payment due at the end of a loan, typically a home or car loan, to pay off the amount your monthly payments didn't cover.

**bankruptcy trustee** A person appointed by a bankruptcy court to oversee the case of a person or business that has filed for bankruptcy.

**battery** The crime of making physical contact with someone with the intention to harm him or her. Unintentional harmful contact is not battery, no mater how careless the behavior or how severe the injury.

**beneficiary** A person or organization that is legally entitled to receive benefits through a legal device, such as a will, trust or life insurance policy.

**bylaws** The rules that govern the internal affairs or actions of a corporation.

**C corporation** Common business slang to describe a corporation whose profits are taxed separately from its owners under Subchapter C of the Internal Revenue Code.

**capital gains** The profit on the sale of a capital asset, such as stock or real estate.

**capitalized interest** Accrued interest that is added to the principal balance of a loan while you are not making payments or when your payments are insufficient to cover both the principal and interest due.

**case** A term that most often refers to a lawsuit—for example, "I filed my small claims case." "Case" also refers to a written decision by a court.

**certification mark** A name, symbol or other device used by an organization to vouch for the quality of products and services provided by others.

**child support** Money paid by a parent to support his or her children until the children reach the age of majority or become emancipated—usually by marriage, by entry into the armed forces or by living independently.

**circuit court** In many states, the name used for the principal trial court. In the federal system, the name for the appellate courts, which are organized into thirteen circuits.

**civil case** A noncriminal lawsuit in which an individual, business or government entity sues another to protect, enforce or redress private rights. There are hundreds of varieties of civil cases. A few examples include lawsuits involving breach of contract, probate, divorce, negligence and copyright violations.

**collateral** Property that guarantees payment of a secured debt.

**collection agency** A company hired by a creditor to collect a debt.

**collective mark** A name, symbol or other device used by members of a group or organization to identify the goods or services it provides.

**collision damage waiver** See "loss damage waiver."

**collision insurance coverage** A component of car insurance that pays for damages to the insured vehicle that result from a collision with another vehicle or object.

**common law** The system of rules that is established by court decisions and not by statutes, regulations or ordinances.

**community property** A method used in some states for defining the ownership of property acquired and the responsibility for debts incurred during marriage. Generally, all earnings during marriage and all property acquired with those earnings are considered community property. Likewise, all debts incurred during marriage are community property debts.

**common law marriage** In some states, a type of marriage in which couples can become legally married by living together for a long period of time, representing themselves as a married couple and intending to be married.

**conservator** Someone appointed by a judge to oversee the affairs of an incapacitated person. A conservator may also be called a guardian, committee or curator.

**constitution** The system of fundamental laws and principals that lay down the nature, functions and limitations of a government body. The United States Constitution is the supreme law of the United States. States also have constitutions. State constitutions can give people *more* rights than does the U.S. Constitution, but cannot give people *fewer* rights than those found in the U.S. Constitution.

**contingency fee** A method of paying a lawyer for legal representation by which, instead of an hourly or per job fee, the lawyer receives a percentage of the money his or her client obtains after settling or winning the case.

**cooling-off rule** A rule that allows you to cancel certain contracts within a specified time period (typically three days) after signing.

**copyright** A legal device that provides the owner the right to control how a creative work is used.

**corporation** A legal structure authorized by state law that allows a business to organize as a separate legal entity from its owners, thereby shielding them from personal liability from business debts and obligations, and allowing the business to take advantage of corporate tax rules.

**counterclaim** A defendant's court papers that claim that the plaintiff—not the defendant—committed legal wrongs, and that as a result it is the defendant who is entitled to money damages or other relief. In some states, a counterclaim is called a cross-complaint.

**covenants, conditions & restrictions (CC&Rs)** Restrictions governing the use of real estate, usually enforced by a homeowners' association and passed on to the new owners of property.

**credit bureau** A private, profit-making company that collects and sells information about a person's credit history.

**credit insurance** Insurance that pays off a loan if the person who owes the money dies or becomes disabled.

**credit report** An account of your credit history, prepared by a credit bureau.

**creditor** A person or entity (such as a bank) to whom a debt is owed.

**crime** A type of behavior that has been defined by the state or federal government as deserving of punishment. The punishment for a crime may include imprisonment.

**custody (of a child)** The legal authority to make decisions affecting a child's interests (legal custody) and the responsibility of taking care of the child (physical custody).

**cybersquatting** Buying a domain name that reflects the name of a business or famous person with the intent of selling the name back to the business or celebrity for a profit.

# D

**death taxes** Taxes levied at death, based on the value of property left behind. Federal death taxes are called estate taxes. Some states also levy death taxes, sometimes called inheritance taxes, on people who inherit property.

**debit card** A card issued by a bank that can be used to withdraw cash at a bank like an ATM card, and can be used at stores to pay for goods and services in place of a check. A debit card automatically deducts money from your checking account at the time of the transaction.

**debtor** A person or entity (such as a bank) who owes money.

**deductible** Something that is taken away or subtracted. Under an insurance policy, for example, the deductible is the maximum amount that an insured person must pay toward his own losses before he can recover from the insurer.

**deed** A document that transfers ownership of real estate.

**deed in lieu of foreclosure** A method of avoiding foreclosure where the lender accepts ownership of the property in place of the money owed on the mortgage.

**default** The failure to perform a legal duty. For example, a default on a mortgage or car loan happens when a borrower fails to make the loan payments on time, fails to maintain adequate insurance or violates some other provision of the agreement.

**defendant** The person against whom a lawsuit is filed. In certain states, and in certain types of lawsuits, the defendant is called the respondent.

**defined benefit plan** A type of pension plan that pays a definite, predetermined amount of money when the worker retires or becomes disabled. The amount received is based on length of service with a particular employer.

**defined contribution plan** A type of pension plan that does not guarantee any particular pension amount upon retirement. Instead, the employer pays into the pension fund a certain amount every month, or every year, for each employee.

**dependents benefits** A type of Social Security benefit available to the spouse and minor or disabled children of a retired or disabled worker who qualifies for either retirement or disability benefits under the program's rigorous qualification guidelines.

**design patent** A patent issued on a new design, used for purely aesthetic reasons, that does not affect the functioning of the underlying device.

**deposition** A tool used in pretrial case investigation (called "discovery") where one party questions the other party or a witness in the case. All questions be answered under oath and be recorded by a court reporter, who creates a deposition transcript.

**disability benefits** Money available from Social Security to benefit those under 65 who qualify because of their work and earnings record and who meet the program's medical guidelines defining disability.

**dischargeable debts** Debts that can be erased by going through bankruptcy.

**discovery** A formal investigation—governed by court rules—that is conducted before a trial. Discovery allows one party to question other parties and sometimes witnesses and to force others to disclose documents or other physical evidence.

**district court** In federal court and, in some states, the name of the main trial court.

**dissolution** A term used instead of divorce in some states.

**divorce** The legal termination of marriage.

**doing business as (DBA)** A situation in which a business owner operates a company under a name different from his or her real name.

**domain name** A combination of letters and numbers that identifies a specific website on the Internet, followed by an identifier such as .com or .org.

**down payment** A lump sum cash payment made by a buyer when he or she purchases a major piece of property, such as a car or house.

**durable power of attorney** A power of attorney that remains in effect if the maker becomes incapacitated. If a power of attorney is not specifically made durable, it automatically expires upon incapacity.

**durable power of attorney for finances** A legal document that gives someone authority to manage the maker's financial affairs if he or she becomes incapacitated.

**durable power of attorney for healthcare** A legal document that names someone to make medical decisions if the person who makes the document is unable to express his or her wishes for care.

# E

**emergency protective order** Any court-issued order meant to protect a person from harm or harassment. This type of order is a stop-gap measure, usually lasting only for a weekend or holiday.

**escrow** A document (such as a grant deed to real property) or sum of money that, by agreement of parties to a transaction, is held by a neutral third party until certain conditions are met. Once the conditions are met, the third party releases the funds or document from escrow.

**estate** Generally, all the property a person owns when he or she dies.

**estate taxes** Taxes imposed by the federal government on property as it passes from the dead to the living. Some states also impose "death taxes" or "inheritance taxes."

**eviction** Removal of a tenant from rental property by a law enforcement officer.

**evidence** The many types of information presented to a judge or jury designed to convince them of the truth or falsity of the key facts in a case. Evidence may include testimony of witnesses, documents, photographs, items of damaged property, government records, videos or laboratory reports.

**executor** The person named in a will to handle the property of someone who has died.

**exempt property** The items of property you are allowed to keep if a creditor wins a lawsuit against you or if you file for Chapter 7 bankruptcy.

**express warranty** A guarantee made by a seller about the quality of goods or services provided. An express warranty is explicitly stated, either orally or in writing.

**extended warranty contract** Warranty coverage on an item that takes effect after the warranty coverage provided by the manufacturer or seller expires.

**federal court** A branch of the United States government with power derived directly from the U.S. Constitution. Federal courts decide cases involving the U.S. Constitution, federal law and some cases where the parties are from different states.

**felony** A serious crime, usually punishable by a prison term of more than one year or, in some cases, by death.

**fictitious business name** The name under which a business operates or by which it is commonly known. See also "doing business as."

**fixed rate mortgage** A mortgage loan that has an interest rate that remains constant throughout the life of the loan, so that the amount you pay each month remains the same over the entire mortgage term.

**for sale by owner (FSBO)** A type of house sale in which the owner acts alone, without a real estate broker.

**forbearance** Voluntarily refraining from doing something, such as asserting a legal right. For example, a creditor may forbear on its right to collect a debt by temporarily postponing or reducing the borrower's payments.

**foreclosure** The forced sale of real estate to pay off a home loan on which the owner of the property has defaulted.

**garnishment** A court-ordered process that takes property from a person to satisfy a debt. For example, a creditor may garnish a debtor's wages if the debtor loses a lawsuit filed by the creditor.

**general partnership** A business that is owned and managed by two or more people (called partners or general partners) who are personally liable for all business debts.

**gift taxes** Federal taxes assessed on any gift, or combination of gifts, from one person to another that exceeds $10,000 in one year. There are some exceptions to this tax.

**grace period** A period of time during which you are not required to make payments on a debt.

**grant deed** A deed containing an implied promise that the person transferring the property actually owns the title and that it is not encumbered in any way, except as described in the deed.

**guarantor** A person who makes a legally binding promise to either pay another person's debt or perform another person's duty if that person defaults or fails to perform.

**guardian** An adult who has been given the legal right by a court to control and care for someone known as a "ward." The ward may be either a minor child or an incapacitated adult. The guardian may make personal decisions on behalf of the ward (a "personal guardian"), manage the ward's property (a "property guardian" or "guardian of the estate"), or both.

**guardian of the estate** See "guardian."

**guardianship** A legal relationship created by a court between a guardian and his ward—either a minor child or an incapacitated adult. The guardian has a legal right and duty to care for the ward.

**healthcare directive** A legal document that allows the maker to set out written wishes for medical care—and to name a person to make sure those wishes are carried out. A healthcare directive may also be called a living will, advance directive or directive to physicians.

**healthcare proxy** A person named in a healthcare directive or durable power of attorney for healthcare to make medical decisions for the person who signed the document, called the principal. A healthcare proxy may also be known as an attorney-in-fact, agent or patient advocate.

**holographic will** A will that is completely handwritten, dated and signed by the person making it. Holographic wills are generally not witnessed.

**home warranty** A service contract that covers a major housing system—for example, plumbing or electrical wiring—for a set period of time from the date a house is sold. The warranty guarantees repairs to the covered system and is renewable.

**homeowners' association** An organization of neighbors concerned with managing the common areas of a subdivision or condominium complex. The homeowners' association is also responsible for enforcing any covenants, conditions and restrictions that apply to the property.

**hung jury** A jury unable to come to a final decision, resulting in a mistrial.

# I

**implied warranty** A guarantee about the quality of goods or services purchased. An implied warranty is not written down or explicitly spoken, but is provided to consumers by law.

**implied warranty of fitness** An implied warranty that applies when you buy an item for a specific pur-

pose. If you notify the seller of your specific needs, this warranty guarantees that the item will function to meet those needs.

**implied warranty of habitability** A legal doctrine that requires landlords to offer and maintain livable premises for their tenants.

**implied warranty of merchantability** An implied warranty that a new item will work for its specified purpose.

**independent contractor** A self-employed person, as defined by the IRS. The key to the definition is that, unlike employees, independent contractors retain control over how they do their work. The person or company paying the independent contractor controls only the outcome—the product or service.

**individual retirement account (IRA)** A savings or brokerage account to which a person may contribute up to a specified amount of earned income each year. There are several types of IRAs. The most common are traditional contributory IRAs and Roth IRAs. With a traditional contributory IRA, contributions and interest earned are not taxed until the participant withdraws funds at retirement. With Roth IRAs, contributions are taxed, but most distributions (investment returns and withdrawals at retirement) are not.

**infraction** A minor violation of the law that is punishable only by a fine—for example, a traffic or parking ticket.

**infringement (of copyright, patent or trademark)** The violation of a patent, copyright or trademark owner's rights. Usually, this occurs when someone uses or benefits from a patented or copyrighted work or a trademark or servicemark, without the owner's permission.

**inheritance taxes** See "death taxes."

**interrogatories** Written questions that one party to a lawsuit asks an opposing party. Interrogatories are designed to discover key facts about an opponent's case, and are a common part of pretrial case-investigation.

**interest** A commission that a borrower pays to a bank or other creditor for lending the borrower money or extending credit. An interest rate represents the annual percentage that is added to the balance of a loan or credit line. This means that if your loan has an interest rate of 8%, the creditor adds 8% to the balance each year.

**intestate succession** The method by which property is distributed when a person dies without a valid will. Usually, the property is distributed to the closest surviving relatives.

**irrevocable trust** A permanent trust. Once the trust is created, it cannot be revoked, amended or changed in any way.

**J**

**joint custody** An arrangement by which parents who do not live together share the upbringing of a child. Joint custody can be joint legal custody (in which both parents have a say in decisions affecting the child) joint physical custody (in which the child spends a significant amount of time with both parents) or both.

**joint tenancy** A way for two or more people to share ownership of real estate or other property. When property is held in joint tenancy and one owner dies, the other owners automatically receive the deceased owner's share.

**judgment** A final court ruling resolving the key questions in a lawsuit and determining the rights and obligations of the opposing parties.

**judgment-proof** A term used to describe a person from whom nothing can be collected because he or she has little income and no property, or is protected from collection of the judgment by law—for example, a law preventing the collection of exempt property.

**jury** A group of people selected to apply the law, as stated by a judge, to the facts of a case and render a decision, called the verdict.

**jury nullification** A decision made by a jury to acquit a defendant who has violated a law that the jury believes is unjust or wrong.

# L

**landlord** The owner of any real estate, such as a house, apartment building or land, that is leased or rented to another person, called the tenant.

**lease** An oral or written agreement between two people concerning the use by one of the property of the other. A person can lease either real estate (such as an apartment or business property) or personal property (such as a car or a boat).

**legal custody** The right and obligation to make decisions about a child's upbringing, including schooling and medical care. Compare "physical custody."

**legislature** The branch of government that has the responsibility and power to make laws. A state legislature makes state laws and the federal legislature (the U.S. Congress) makes federal laws.

**lemon** A car that gives you serious trouble soon after you buy it.

**liability** (1) The state of being liable—that is, legally responsible for an act or omission. (2) Something for which a person is liable. For example, a debt is often called a liability.

**liability insurance** A contract that provides compensation to third parties who are injured or whose property is damaged due to the fault of the insurance policyholder.

**license (of invention, copyright or trademark)** A contract giving written permission to use an invention, creative work or trademark.

**lien** The right of a secured creditor to take a specific item of property if the borrower doesn't pay a debt.

**life estate** A property interest that provides the right to live in or use, but not own, a specific piece of real estate until death.

**life insurance** A contract under which an insurance company agrees to pay money to a designated beneficiary upon the death of the policyholder. In exchange, the policyholder pays a regularly scheduled fee, known as the insurance premiums.

**limited liability** The maximum amount a business owner can lose if the business is subject to debts, claims or other liabilities. One of the primary advantages of forming a corporation or limited liability company (LLC) is that the business owners stand to lose only the amount of money invested in the business—creditors can't come after an owner's personal assets.

**limited liability company (LLC)** A business ownership structure that offers limited personal liability for business obligations and a choice of how the business will be taxed: either as a separate entity or as a partnership-like structure in which profits are taxed on the owners' personal income tax returns.

**limited liability partnership (LLP)**
A type of partnership recognized in a majority of states that protects a partner from personal liability for negligent acts committed by other partners or by employees not under his or her direct control.

**limited partnership** A business structure that allows some partners (called limited partners) to enjoy limited personal liability for partnership debts while other partners (called general partners) have unlimited personal liability. Limited partners are usually passive investors; they are not allowed to make day-to-day business decisions.

**living trust** A trust created during the trustmaker's life to avoid probate after death. Property transferred into the trust during life passes directly to the trust beneficiaries after death, without probate.

**living will** See "healthcare directive."

**loan broker** A person who specializes in matching home buyers with appropriate mortgage lenders.

**loan consolidation** Combining a number of loans into a single new loan.

**loss damage waiver (LDW)**
Rental car insurance that makes the rental car company responsible for damage to or theft of a rental car. Also called a "collision damage waiver."

# M

**malpractice (by an attorney)** The delivery of substandard services by a lawyer. Generally, malpractice occurs when a lawyer fails to provide the quality of service that should reasonably be expected in the circumstances, with the result that the lawyer's client is harmed.

**marital property** Most of the property accumulated by spouses during a marriage, called "community property" in some states.

**marriage license** A document that authorizes a couple to get married, usually available from the county clerk's office in the state where the marriage will take place.

**marriage certificate** A document that provides proof of a marriage, typically issued to newlyweds a few weeks after they file for the certificate in a county office.

**mediation** A dispute resolution method designed to help warring parties resolve their dispute without going to court. In mediation, a neutral third party (the mediator) meets with the opposing sides to help them find a mutually satisfactory solution.

**Medicare** A federal program that provides health insurance to elderly and disabled people.

**Medicaid** A federal program that provides health insurance program for financially needy people. The program is administered by each state.

**meeting of creditors** A meeting held with a bankruptcy trustee about a month after a debtor files for bankruptcy.

**Miranda warning** A warning that the police must give to suspect before conducting an interrogation; otherwise, the suspect's answers may not be used as evidence in a trial. Also known as "reading a suspect his rights."

**misdemeanor** A crime, less serious than a felony, punishable by no more than one year in jail.

**mortgage** A loan in which the borrower puts up the title to real estate as security (collateral) for the loan. If the borrower doesn't pay back the debt on time, the lender can foreclose on the real estate and have it sold to pay off the loan.

**no-fault divorce** Any divorce in which the spouse who wants to split up does not have to accuse the other of wrongdoing, but can simply state that the couple no longer gets along.

**no-fault insurance** Car insurance laws that require the insurance company of each person involved in an accident to pay for the medical bills and lost wages of its insured, up to a certain amount, regardless of who was at fault.

**nolo contendere** A plea entered by the defendant in response to being charged with a crime. A defendant who pleads nolo contendere neither admits nor denies that he or she committed the crime, but agrees to a punishment (usually a fine or jail time).

**nondischargeable debts** Debts that cannot be erased by filing for bankruptcy.

**nondisclosure agreement** A legally binding contract in which a person or business promises to treat specific information as a trade secret and not disclose it to others without proper authorization.

**nonexempt property** The property that a debtor risks losing to creditors when he or she files for Chapter 7 bankruptcy or when a creditor sues the debtor and wins a judgment.

**nonprofit corporation** A business structure that allows people to come together to obtain support for an organization (such as a club) or for some public purpose (such as a hospital or environmental organization). Nonprofits receive benefits—for instance, reduced filing fees and tax exemptions—that are not available to regular corporations.

**nonrefundable ticket** An airline ticket for which you cannot get your money back if you decide not to travel.

**nontransferable ticket** An airline ticket that can be used only by the passenger whose name appears on the ticket.

**notarize** The act of certification by a notary public that establishes the authenticity of a signature on a legal document.

**notary public** A licensed public officer who administers oaths, certifies documents and performs other specified functions.

**nuisance** Something that interferes with the use of property by being irritating, offensive, obstructive or dangerous. Nuisances include a wide range of conditions, from a chemical plant's noxious odors to a neighbor's dog barking.

**O**

**open adoption** An adoption in which there is some degree of contact between the birthparents and the adoptive parents and sometimes with the child as well.

**order** A decision issued by a court. It can be a simple command—for example, ordering a recalcitrant witness to answer a proper question during a trial—or it can be a complicated and reasoned decision made after a hearing, directing that a party either do or refrain from some act.

**ordinance** A law passed by a county or city government.

**own recognizance (OR)** A way for a criminal defendant to get out of jail, without paying bail, by promising to appear in court when next required to be there. Only those defendants with

strong ties to the community, such as a steady job, local family and no history of failing to appear in court, are good candidates for "OR" release.

**parenting agreement** A detailed written agreement between a divorcing couple that describes how they will deal with visitation, holiday schedules, vacation, education, religion and other issues related to their child.

**partnership** When used without a qualifier such as "limited" or "limited liability," this term usually refers to a legal structure called a general partnership: a business that is owned and managed by two or more people who are personally liable for all business debts.

**party** A person, corporation or other legal entity that files a lawsuit (a plaintiff or petitioner) or defends against one (a defendant or respondent).

**patent** A legal monopoly, granted by the U.S. Patent and Trademark Office (PTO), for the use, manufacture and sale of an invention.

**pay-on-death (POD) designation** A way to avoid probate for bank accounts, government bonds, individual retirement accounts and, in many states, securities or a car. A pay-on-death designation is created when the property owner names someone on the ownership document—such as the registration card for a bank account—to inherit the property at the owner's death.

**pension** A retirement fund for employees paid for or contributed to by some employers as part of a package of compensation for the employees' work.

**personal property** All property other than land and buildings attached to land. Cars, bank accounts, wages, securities, a small business, furniture, insurance policies, jewelry, patents, pets and season baseball tickets are all examples of personal property.

**petition** A formal written request made to a court, asking for an order or ruling on a particular matter.

**petitioner** A person who initiates a lawsuit. The term is a synonym for plaintiff, and it is used almost universally in some states and in others for certain types of lawsuits, most commonly divorce and other family law cases.

**physical custody** The right and obligation of a parent to have his child live with him. Compare "legal custody."

**plaintiff** The person, corporation or other legal entity that initiates a lawsuit. In certain states and for some types of lawsuits, the term "petitioner" is used instead of "plaintiff."

**plant patent** A patent issued for new strains of asexually reproducing plants.

**plea** The defendant's formal answer to criminal charges. Typically defendants enter one of the following pleas: guilty, not guilty or nolo contendere.

**plea bargain** A negotiation between the defense and prosecution (and sometimes the judge) that settles a criminal case. The defendant typically pleads guilty to a lesser crime (or fewer charges) than originally charged, in exchange for a guaranteed sentence that is shorter than what the defendant could face if convicted at trial.

**pocket part** The paper supplement found in the front or back of a book of laws—such as state statutes—that contains annual changes to the law that are not included in the hardcover version of the book.

**pot trust** A trust for children—typically established in a will or living trust—in which the trustee decides how to spend money on each child, taking money out of the trust to meet each child's specific needs.

**power of attorney** A document that gives another person (called the "attorney-in-fact" or "agent") legal authority to act on behalf of the person who makes the document, called the principal.

**premarital agreement** An agreement made by a couple before marriage that controls certain aspects of their relationship, usually the management and ownership of property, and sometimes whether alimony will be paid if the couple later divorces.

**preponderance of the evidence**
A legal "standard of proof" in which a jury is instructed to find for the party that, on the whole, has the stronger evidence, however slight that edge may be. This standard is used in most civil cases.

**private mortgage insurance (PMI)** Insurance that reimburses a mortgage lender if the buyer defaults on the loan and the foreclosure sale price is less than the amount owed the lender (the mortgage plus the costs of the sale).

**pro per** A term derived from the Latin in propria, meaning "for one's self," used in some states to describe a person who handles her own case without a lawyer. In other states, the term "pro se" is used.

**pro se** See "pro per."

**probable cause** The amount and quality of information a judge must have before she will sign a warrant allowing the police to conduct a search or arrest a suspect. If the police have presented reliable information that convinces the judge that it's more likely than not that a crime has occurred and the suspect is involved, the judge will conclude that there is "probable cause" and will issue the warrant.

**probate** The court process following a person's death that includes: proving the authenticity of the deceased person's will, appointing someone to handle the deceased person's affairs, identifying and inventorying the deceased person's property, paying debts and taxes, identifying heirs and distributing the deceased person's property.

**property guardian** See "guardian."

**prosecutor** A lawyer who works for the local, state or federal government to bring and litigate criminal cases.

**provisional patent application (PPA)** An interim patent application that has the legal effect of providing the inventor with an early filing date for her invention. The PPA does not take the place of a regular patent application, but it does confer patent pending status on the underlying invention.

**public defender** A lawyer appointed by the court and paid by the county, state, or federal government to represent clients who are charged with violations of criminal law and are unable to pay for their own defense.

**QTIP trust** A marital trust for wealthy couples designed to reduce estate taxes. The surviving spouse receives only a "life estate" in the trust property, which passes to the trust's final beneficiaries after the surviving spouse's death. No estate taxes are assessed on the trust property until surviving spouse dies.

**quitclaim deed** A deed that transfers whatever ownership interest the transferor has in a particular property. The deed does not guarantee anything about what is being transferred.

**real estate agent** A foot soldier of the real estate business who shows houses and does most of the other nitty-gritty tasks associated with selling real estate in exchange for a commission on the sale.

**real estate broker** A real estate professional one step up from a real estate agent. A broker has more training and can supervise agents.

**real property** Another term for real estate. It includes land and things permanently attached to the land, such as trees, buildings, and stationary mobile homes.

**recording** The process of filing a copy of a deed or other document concerning real estate with the land records office for the county in which the land is located. Recording creates a public record of changes in ownership for all property in the state.

**regulation** A law issued by a state or federal administrative agency for the purpose of implementing and enforcing a statute.

**rent control** Laws that limit the amount of rent landlords may charge, and that state when and by how much the rent can be raised. Most rent control laws also require a landlord to provide a good reason, such as repeatedly late rent, for evicting a tenant.

**rental agreement** A contract, either oral or written, between a landlord and tenant that sets forth the terms of a tenancy.

**renter's insurance** Insurance that covers those who rent residential property against losses to their belongings that occur as a result of fire or theft.

**repossession** A creditor's taking of property that has been pledged as collateral for a loan. Lenders most often repossess cars when the buyer has missed loan payments and has not attempted to work with the lender to resolve the problem.

**request for admissions** A procedure in which one party to a lawsuit asks the opposing party to admit that certain facts are true. This occurs in the pretrial case-investigation phase of a lawsuit, known as "discovery."

**request to produce (documents or things)** A procedure in which one party to a lawsuit asks an opposing party to turn over certain documents or physical objects. Like a "request for admissions," this procedure is part of the pretrial case-investigation phase of a lawsuit, called "discovery."

**respondent** A term used instead of "defendant" in some states—especially for divorce and other family law cases—to identify the party who is being sued.

**restraining order** A court order directing a person not to do something, such as make contact with another specified person, enter the family home or remove a child from the state.

**Roth IRA** See "individual retirement account."

**ruling** Any decision a judge makes during the course of a lawsuit.

# S

**S corporation** A term that describes a corporation organized under Subchapter S of the Internal Revenue Code in which shareholders enjoy limited liability status but are taxed on their individual tax returns in the same way as sole proprietors or owners of a partnership.

**search warrant** An order signed by a judge that directs the owners of private property to allow the police to enter and search for items named in the warrant.

**secret warranty program** A program under which a car manufacturer will make repairs for free on vehicles with persistent problems, even after the warranty has expired, in order to avoid a recall and the accompanying bad press.

**secured debt** A debt on which a creditor has a lien. The creditor can initiate a foreclosure or repossession to take the property identified by the lien, called the collateral, to satisfy the debt if the borrower defaults.

**security deposit** A payment required by a landlord to ensure that a tenant pays rent on time and keeps the rental unit in good condition.

**sentence** Punishment in a criminal case. A sentence can range from a fine and community service to life imprisonment or death.

**separate property** In community property states, property owned and controlled entirely by one spouse in a marriage.

**service mark** A word, phrase, logo, symbol, color, sound or smell used by a business to identify a service and distinguish it from those of its competitors.

**service contract** Another term for "extended warranty contract."

**settlement** An agreement resolving a dispute between the parties in a lawsuit without a trial.

**severance pay** Funds, usually amounting to one or two months' salary, frequently offered by employers to workers who are laid off.

**sexual harassment** Unwelcome sexual advances or conduct on the job that creates an intimidating, hostile or offensive working environment.

**shared custody** See "joint custody."

**shareholder** An owner of a corporation whose ownership interest is represented by shares of stock in the corporation. Also called a "stockholder."

**short sale (of a house)** The sale of a house in which the proceeds fall short of what the owner still owes on the mortgage. Many lenders will agree to accept the proceeds of a short sale and forgive the rest of what is owed on the mortgage if the owner cannot make the mortgage payments.

**sick leave** Time off work for illness.

**small claims court** A state court that resolves disputes involving relatively small amounts of money. Adversaries usually appear without lawyers—in fact, some states forbid lawyers in small claims court.

**Social Security** The general term that describes a number of related programs administered by the federal government, including retirement, disability, dependents and survivors benefits. These programs operate together to provide workers and their families with some monthly income when their normal flow of income shrinks because of the retirement, disability or death of the person who earned that income.

**sole custody** An arrangement in which only one parent has physical and legal custody of a child and the other parent has visitation rights.

**sole proprietorship** A business owned and managed by one person—or, in some circumstances, a husband and wife. Business profits are reported and taxed on the owner's personal tax return and the owner is personally liable for all business debts.

**state court** A court that decides cases involving state law or the state constitution. State courts have jurisdiction to consider disputes involving individual defendants who reside in that state or have minimum contacts with the state, such as using its highways, owning real property in the state or doing business in the state.

**statute** A written law passed by Congress or a state legislature and signed into law by the President or a state governor.

**statute of limitations** The legally prescribed time limit in which a lawsuit must be filed.

**subpoena** A court order that requires a witness to appear in court. Subpoenas may be issued at the request of a party to a lawsuit. Also spelled "subpena."

**subpoena duces tecum** A type of subpoena, usually issued at the request of a party to a lawsuit, by which a court orders a witness to produce certain documents at a deposition or trial.

**Supreme Court** The United States Supreme Court is this country's highest court, which has the final power to decide cases involving the interpretation of the U.S. Constitution, certain legal areas set forth in the Constitution (called federal questions) and federal laws. It can also make final decisions in certain lawsuits between parties from different states. Most states also have a supreme court, which is the final arbiter of the state's constitution and state laws. In several states, this court uses a different name.

**surviving spouse** A widow or widower.

**survivors benefits** An amount of money available to the surviving spouse and minor or disabled children of a deceased worker who qualified for Social Security retirement or disability benefits.

**temporary restraining order (TRO)** An order that tells one person to stop harassing or harming another, issued after the aggrieved party appears before a judge.

**tenant** Anyone, including a corporation, who rents real property, with or without a house or structure, from the owner (called the landlord). A tenant may also be called the "lessee."

**timeshare** The right to use a given vacation property for a certain amount of time. Usually, a person with a timeshare pays a one-time lump sum and annual maintenance fees.

**trade dress** The distinctive packaging or design of a product that promotes the product and distinguishes

it from other products in the marketplace.

**trade name** The official name of a business, the one it uses on its letterhead and bank account when not dealing with consumers.

**trade secret** In most states, a formula, pattern, physical device, idea, process, compilation of information or other information that provides a business with a competitive advantage, and that is treated in a way that can reasonably be expected to prevent the public or competitors from learning about it.

**trademark** A word, phrase, logo, symbol, color, sound or smell used by a business to identify a product and distinguish it from those of its competitors. Compare "trade dress," "service mark," "certification mark" and "collective mark."

**treatise** An extensive book or series of books written about a particular legal topic.

**trial court** The first court to hear the issues of fact and law presented by the parties to a lawsuit.

**trust** A legal device used to manage property—whether real or personal—established by one person for the benefit of another. A third person, called the trustee, manages the trust.

**trust deed** The most common method of financing real estate purchases in California (most other states use mortgages). The trust deed transfers title to the property to a trustee—often a title company—who holds it as security for a loan. When the loan is paid off, the title is transferred to the borrower.

**trustee** The person who manages assets owned by a trust under the terms of the trust document. A trustee's purpose is to safeguard the trust and distribute trust income or principal as directed in the trust document.

**unemployment insurance (UI)** A program run jointly by federal and state governments that provides money benefits for a specified time—usually 26 weeks—after an employee has been laid off or fired from a job for reasons other than serious misconduct. In some instances, an employee who quits a job for a good reason (for example, because she was being sexually harassed at work) can also collect unemployment insurance benefits.

**uninsured motorist coverage** The portion of car insurance that provides compensation for any injuries resulting from an accident with an uninsured motorist or a hit-and-run driver.

**unlawful detainer** An eviction lawsuit.

**utility patent** A patent issued for inventions that perform useful functions. Most patents issued by the U.S. Patent and Trademark Office (PTO) are utility patents.

**visitation rights** The right to see a child regularly, typically awarded by a court to the parent who does not have physical custody of his or her child.

# W

**warranty** A guarantee by a seller to stand by its product or services by making repairs or offering replacements if something goes wrong. See "express warranty" and "implied warranty."

**warranty deed** A seldom-used type of deed that contains express assurances about the legal validity of the title being transferred.

**will** A document in which a person specifies what is to be done with his or her property at death, names an executor to oversee the distribution of that property and names a guardian for his or her young children.

**witness** A person who testifies under oath at a deposition or trial, providing firsthand or expert evidence. In addition, the term also refers to someone who watches another person sign a document and then adds his name to confirm that the signature is genuine; this is called "attesting."

**workers' compensation** A program that provides replacement income and medical expenses to employees who are injured or become ill due to job duties.

# Z

**zoning** The laws dividing cities into different areas according to use, from single-family residences to industrial plants. Zoning ordinances control the size, location, and use of buildings within these different areas.

# **A**ppendix: Legal Research

**A.2**  **Learning About a Particular Area of the Law**

**A.4**  **Finding a Specific Law**

**A.8**  **Finding Answers to Specific Legal Questions**

**A.10**  **Finding Legal Forms**

**L**egal research is how you learn about the law. It is not a skill reserved exclusively for lawyers; you can find the answers to your legal questions if you are armed with a little bit of patience and a good road map.

The best legal research method depends on what you need to find out. Usually, people want to research the law in order to accomplish one of the following things:

- understand a particular area of the law
- find and read a statute, regulation, ordinance, court decision or piece of pending legislation (usually called a bill)
- find the answer to a specific legal question, or
- find a legal form.

This appendix explains how to do legal research in each of these situations.

# Learning About a Particular Area of the Law

Many people need to understand an area of the law before making an important decision. For example, you might want to know:

- What laws are involved when selling a business?
- What's the difference between a living trust and a living will?
- What effect does divorce have on pensions earned during marriage?

Questions like these can be answered without regard to your specific circumstances; they involve a general understanding of the law. To find this type of information about a legal topic, you should turn to legal background materials.

Legal background materials are books, pamphlets, articles and encyclopedia entries in which experts summarize and explain the basic principles of a legal subject area, such as bankruptcy, landlord-tenant law or criminal law. These materials come in many forms and can be found in law libraries or, sometimes, on the Internet.

## How to Find a Law Library

Most counties have law libraries in the government buildings or courthouses at the county seat. These libraries are open to the public. County libraries are a good place to go if you're looking for your state's laws.

Law schools also maintain libraries for their students and staff. Although public access to some law school libraries is restricted, many are willing to extend help to non-students. If you are looking for material from other states or countries, a law school library is the best place to start.

Finally, don't limit yourself to law libraries. Most major public libraries in urban areas contain both local and state laws.

Here are a number of legal background resources that you may find useful:

- *Self-help Law Books.* Self-help law books, such as those published by Nolo, are written in plain English for a non-lawyer audience. They are an excellent starting point for cracking any legal area that is new to you. Law libraries, public libraries and bookstores (including Nolo's online bookstore at http://www.nolo.com) often carry self-help law books.

- *Organizations and Advocacy Groups.* Many non-profit and professional organizations or advocacy groups—such as tenants' rights groups, the American Association of Retired People (AARP) and local business groups—publish pamphlets on particular legal topics. Think about what groups might have the information you need and then look for them in the Yellow Pages or on the Web.

- *Legal Encyclopedias.* You can often find a good introduction to your topic in a legal encyclopedia. The legal encyclopedias most commonly found in law libraries are *American Jurisprudence* and *Corpus Juris.* Many states have legal encyclopedias that are state-specific—for example, *Texas Jurisprudence.*

- *The "Nutshell" Series.* Another good introduction to legal topics is the "Nutshell" series, as in *Torts in a Nutshell* and *Intellectual Property in a Nutshell,* published by West Group. These books are available in most law libraries.

- *Treatises.* If you have the time and patience to delve deeply into a subject, you can find comprehensive books—generally known as treatises—on virtually every legal topic. For example, if you want to know about some aspect of trademark law, you could use *McCarthy on Trademarks,* a multi-volume treatise on all aspects of trademark law.

- *West's Legal Desk Reference.* This book, by Statsky, Hussey, Diamond and Nakamura, lists background materials both by state and legal topic. In addition, *West's Legal Desk Reference* provides keywords and phrases that will help you use the indexes to other resources you may need during your research.

- *Internet Resources.* Nolo's Legal Encyclopedia, available free at http://www.nolo.com, explains many common legal issues in plain English. The other major legal websites (listed below) also provide helpful information and links to specific areas of the law. Finally, many government agency sites provide legal information, such as state marriage license requirements or downloadable pamphlets on different legal topics. For example, if you visit the Federal Judiciary's website at http://www.uscourts.gov, you can download Bankruptcy Basics, a pamphlet providing a good overview of bankruptcy. To find government agencies online, see Finding Court and Government Agency Websites, below.

## The Best Legal Websites

In addition to our own website at http://www.nolo.com, Nolo's favorite legal websites are:

- **Findlaw**
  http://www.findlaw.com
- **The National Federation of Paralegal Associations** http://www.paralegals.org/LegalResources/home.html
- **The World Wide Web Virtual Library** http://www.law.indiana.edu/v-lib/index.html
- **American Association of Law Libraries: Legal Research Links** http://www.aallnet.org/research/
- **Law Library of Congress** http://lcweb2.loc.gov/glin/worldlaw.html
- **The Legal Information Institute at Cornell Law School** http://www.law.cornell.edu

# Finding a Specific Law

There are many reasons why you might need to find a specific statute, regulation, ordinance or court decision. For example, you might learn from the newspaper about new state laws governing overtime wages and want to read the laws themselves. Or perhaps the city building department has referred you to a particular city ordinance that covers zoning laws in your neighborhood. Whatever the

reason, the research involved in finding a specific law or court decision is relatively straightforward. The steps depend on what type of law you seek.

## City or County Laws

You can usually get copies of city or county laws (often called "ordinances") from the office of the city or county clerk. The main branch of your public library is also likely to have a collected set of these laws. Once you get there, ask the reference librarian for help.

Many local ordinances are also available on the Web. The best place to start is Municipal Codes Online, maintained by the Seattle Public Library at http://www.spl.org/govpubs/municode.html.

## State or Federal Statutes and Regulations

Rules established by state and federal governments are called statutes and regulations. Federal statutes are passed by the United States Congress, while state statutes are passed by state legislatures. Regulations are issued by state or federal administrative agencies (such as the U.S. Department of Transportation or the State Department of Health) for the purpose of implementing and enforcing statutes.

You can find statutes and regulations in the library or on the Internet. You can also use legal background materials to point the way to the statute or regulation you seek.

**Finding statutes and regulations at the library.** State and federal statutes and regulations can be found at a law library or the main branch of a public library. Depending on the state, statutes are compiled in books called codes, revised statutes, annotated statutes or compiled laws. For example, the federal statutes are contained in a series called *United States Code*, and the Vermont statutes are found in a series called *Vermont Statutes Annotated*. (The term "annotated" means that the statutes are accompanied by information about their history and court decisions that have interpreted them.) Once you've located the books you need, search for the specific statute by its citation (if you know it) or by looking up keywords in the index.

And after you find a law in the statute books, it's important to look at the update pamphlet in the front or back of the book (called the "pocket part") to make sure your statute hasn't been amended or deleted. Since pocket parts are published only once per year, brand new statutes often have not yet made it to the pocket part. Law libraries subscribe to services and periodicals that update these books on a more frequent basis than the pocket parts. You can ask the law librarian to point you toward the materials you need.

Most federal regulations are published in the *Code of Federal Regulations* (*C.F.R.*), a well-indexed set of books organized by subject. If you don't have a citation for the regulation you seek, check the index. To make sure

the regulation is current, look at the monthly pamphlet that accompanies the books, called *C.F.R.-L.S.A. (List of C.F.R. Sections Affected)*.

State regulations are harder to find. If you know which agency publishes the regulation you want, call or visit to get copies. Many states also keep a portion of their regulations in a series of books called the "Administrative Code." Check the table of contents. If the regulation is not in an Administrative Code, look for loose-leaf manuals published by the individual agency. If you find a regulation in the Administrative Code or loose-leaf manual, you should still call the agency to make sure the regulation hasn't recently changed.

**Finding statutes and regulations online.** You can find federal statutes, the entire *Code of Federal Regulations* and most state statutes by visiting Nolo's Legal Research Center at http://www.nolo.com/research/index.html. Your best bet for state regulations is Findlaw at http://www.findlaw.com. Findlaw also offers federal statutes and regulations, and state statutes.

If you are looking for a brand-new statute online, you may have to search for recently enacted legislation (see below), since there is often a delay between the time a statute is passed and the time it is included in the overall compilation of laws. The good legal websites listed earlier in this appendix also offer state and federal statutes.

Almost every state maintains its own website for pending and recently enacted legislation. These sites contain not only the most current version of a bill, but also its history. To find your state's website, see Finding Court and Government Agency Websites, below. Finally, the United States Congress maintains a website at http://thomas.loc.gov that contains all pending federal bills.

**Using background materials to find statutes and regulations.** When looking for a particular statute or regulation (whether it be state or federal), you may want to consult background materials, which often include relevant laws. For example, *Collier on Bankruptcy*, the leading bankruptcy treatise, contains a complete set of the federal bankruptcy laws. Even if the background resource does not include the text of the statutes or regulations, it will provide citations to the relevant laws and the books in which they are found.

# Finding Court and Government Agency Websites

Many courts and government agencies provide statutes and case law, plus other useful information such as forms, answers to frequently asked questions and downloadable pamphlets on various legal topics. To find to your state's website, open your browser and type in http://www.state.<your state's postal code>.us. (Your state's postal code is the two-letter abbreviation you use for mailing addresses. For example, NY is the postal code for New York.)

Nolo's Legal Research Center (http://www.nolo.com/research/index.html) provides links to courts across the country and access to small claims court information for most states. You can also find local, state and federal court websites on the National Center for State Courts' website at http://www.ncsc.dni.us/court/sites/courts.htm. The Federal Judiciary's website at http://www.uscourts.gov/links.htm/ lists federal court websites.

## State Case Law

State case law consists of the rules established by courts in court decisions (or "court opinions"). Court decisions do one of two things. First, courts interpret statutes, regulations and ordinances so that we know how they apply in real-life situations. Second, courts make rules that are not found in statutes, regulations or ordinances. These rules are called the "common law."

**Finding state cases in the library.** State cases are found in a series of books called reports or reporters. For example, California cases are contained in the *California Reporter* and *California Reports*. You can also find state cases in books known as "regional reporters." These volumes contain cases from several states in a geographical region. For example, the *Atlantic Reporter* contains cases from states such as Delaware and Maryland.

If you have a case citation, which is the number of the volume and page where the case appears (for example,

21 Cal.App.3d 446), you simply locate the correct series of books (in the above example, it would be the California Appellate Reports, 3rd Series), select the appropriate volume (here it's volume 21) and open the book to the indicated page (in the example, page 446). If you don't have a citation but know the name of one or both of the parties in the case—for instance, in the case named *Jones v. Smith*, Jones and Smith are the names of the parties—you can use a "case digest." Look for the parties' names in the digest's Table of Cases. If you don't know the name of the case or the citation, then it will be very difficult to find the case in the law library.

**Finding state cases on the Web.** If the case is recent (within the last few years), you may be able to find it for free on the Internet. A good place to start is FindLaw at http://www.findlaw.com. Also, many state websites now publish recent cases. See Finding Court and Government Agency Websites, above, for information on how to find your state's website.

If the case is older, you can still find it on the Internet, but you will probably have to pay a private company for access to its database. Versuslaw at http://www.versuslaw.com maintains an excellent library of older state court cases. You can do unlimited research on Versuslaw for $6.95 per month. You can also get state cases online through the Lexis and Westlaw databases. (For more information, see Using Westlaw and Lexis to Do Legal Research on the Web, below.)

## Federal Case Law

Federal case law consists of the rules established by federal courts. Like state cases, you can find federal case law in both the library and on the Web.

**Finding federal cases in the library.** Cases decided by the U.S. Supreme Court are published in three different series of reporters. All three contain the same cases. The names of these series are:

- *United States Reports*
- *Supreme Court Reporter*; and
- *Supreme Court Reports: Lawyers' Edition.*

Well-stocked law libraries also have cases from other federal courts, including the Federal Circuit Courts of Appeal (federal appellate courts), U.S. District Courts (federal trial courts) and specialized courts such as bankruptcy or tax court.

To find a case in the Supreme Court reporters or any of the volumes containing other federal cases, follow the guidelines for finding state cases by citation or case name, above.

**Finding U.S. Supreme Court cases on the Web.** Nolo's Legal Research Center, available at http://www.nolo.com/research/index.html, provides U.S. Supreme Court cases decided within the last hundred years.

**Finding other federal cases on the Web.** FindLaw, at http://www.findlaw.com, contains cases decided by the Federal Circuit Courts of Appeal within the last four or five years, some bankruptcy opinions and very recent tax court cases. The Cornell Law School Legal Information

Institute at http://www.law.cornell.edu provides access to all federal appellate court cases, some District Court cases and some bankruptcy opinions. VersusLaw (explained above) also has some U.S. District Court cases and some bankruptcy opinions. If you can't find the case you're looking for on one of these websites, your best bet is to use Westlaw or Lexis.

## Using Lexis and Westlaw to Do Legal Research on the Web

Lexis and Westlaw are the chief electronic legal databases which contain the full text of many of the legal resources found in law libraries, including almost all reported cases from state and federal courts, all federal statutes, the statutes of most states, federal regulations, law review articles, commonly used treatises and practice manuals.

Although Westlaw and Lexis databases are available over the Internet, subscriptions are pricey. However, both offer some free and some fee-based services to non-subscribers that are both helpful and reasonably priced (between $9 and $10 per document). To find out more about these services, visit Westlaw at http://www.westlaw.com or Lexis at http://www.lexis.com.

# Finding Answers to Specific Legal Questions

It's one thing to track down information on a recent case or statute or to read up on general information about a legal topic. It's quite another to confidently answer a question about how the law might apply to your own situation, such as:

- I live in North Carolina, and I've been charged with second offense drunk driving. My passenger was injured as a result of the accident. What penalties do I face?
- My brother is the executor of our parents' estate, and I don't like how he's handling things. What can I do?
- Can I run a home school in my state (North Dakota) if I've been convicted of a felony?

These are the types of questions that people have traditionally asked lawyers. To answer such questions, you often need to look at all the legal resources we have mentioned thus far. You must also make sure that the law you find is current. If you want to undertake this type of legal research on your own, we recommend that you use a comprehensive legal research guide that wallks you through the process step-by-step. (See the list of resources at the end of this appendix.) Here, we can provide just a brief overview of what you'll need to do.

When seeking the answer to a specific legal question, your ultimate goal is to predict, as near as possible, how a judge would rule if presented with the issues and facts of your case. The closer your facts are to the facts in previous cases or the more directly a statute applies to your situation, the more likely you'll be able to predict what a judge would decide. Sometimes, your question is so basic that the answer is easy to find. But often, a statute won't address each facet of your situation and the facts of other cases won't match up 100%. Because of this, legal research cannot always provide a definitive answer, although it can often give you a good idea of what the answer will be. (That's why lawyers often hem and haw when asked a legal question.)

## Basic or Common Legal Questions

It should be fairly easy to find an answer if your legal question is a common one—such as "What is the filing fee for a Chapter 7 bankruptcy?" or "Can the state garnish my wages if I fall behind on child support payments?" These types of questions usually rely on general legal information—rather than the nuances of your particular circumstances. You should begin your research by consulting one or more of the background resources discussed in Section A, above. You might focus on organizations, advocacy groups or government agencies that are likely to have the answer you need. For example, a local tenants' rights group might provide pamphlets with frequently asked questions about evictions. Or, the Association of American Retired Persons (AARP) may be able to tell you what the current estate tax rate is. You can often find this kind of information online.

## Complex Legal Questions

If you can't get an answer to your legal question from a background resource—usually because your question involves unique facts related to your situation—you'll need to do more detailed research. But don't forget what the background materials have taught you. Remember that background resources can give you an important overview of your legal topic and also provide cites to relevant statutes and cases.

To proceed further, first search for statutes, regulations or ordinances that address your question. If you find relevant statutes, look for cases that have interpreted them. To do this at a law library, you can:

- look at case notes that follow the statute in an annotated code book
- use *Shepard's Citations for Statutes* (a book that provides a complete list of cases that mention a particular statute, regulation or constitutional provision), and
- search for cases in "case digests" (books that list cases by subject).

If you can't find a relevant statute or other legislative enactment, you need to look for case law only. To do this at a law library, you can:

- read any relevant cases mentioned in the background materials

- search in case digests by subject area or keywords
- if you find a relevant case, read the cases that it mentions, and
- if you find a relevant case, use *Shepard's Citations for Cases* to find more cases on point. (*Shepard's* provides a complete list of cases that mention your case.)

## Making Sure the Law is Up to Date

Because law changes rapidly, you must make sure that the principles stated in your cases and statutes are still valid. A case may no longer be helpful to you if a more recent case has questioned its reasoning, ruled a different way or expressly stated that your case is no longer good law. Likewise, you should check to make sure your statute has not been changed or eliminated.

**Updating your research in the library.** If you are using the law library, there are a few things you should do to make sure your research is up to date.

- *Background Resources.* If you use background materials, be sure to check the pocket part; it contains changes and new developments in the law.
- *Statutes.* Books containing statutes and regulations also contain pocket parts. Be sure to check these as well. Also check law library periodicals that contain more recent statutory updates.
- *Cases.* You can check the validity of every case you find by using *Shepards' Citations for Cases. Shepards'* will list every case that mentions your case, and tell you the reasons

why it was mentioned. For example, it might show that a later case overruled your case, which means your case is no longer valid.

**Updating your research on the Web.** On the Internet, the updating process is easier, but often more expensive.

- *Statutes.* If you're checking a state statute, visit your state's website for current legislative developments. (See Finding Court and Government Agency Websites, above.) If you need federal information, track Congress' legislative developments through Nolo's website at http://www.nolo.com/research/index.html or by visiting http://thomas.loc.gov. You can also get the most recent version of a statute for a fee through Westlaw or Lexis. (See Using Westlaw and Lexis to Do Legal Research on the Web, above.)
- *Cases.* You can check the validity of cases through fee-based services. Try KeyCite at http://www.keycite.com/ or VersusLaw at http://www.versuslaw.com.

# Finding Legal Forms

If you must take care of a legal matter, chances are good that you'll need to use a form of some sort—that is, a pre-formatted document that contains standard ("boilerplate") language addressing your specific situation. Leases, wills, trusts, sales agreements and employment contracts are just a few examples of the thousands of legal forms that are used in the course of our daily personal and business affairs.

## What Form Do You Need?

Figuring out what form you need is usually simple—someone will tell you. For example, suppose you are handling your own divorce and when you try to file the papers, the clerk says you are missing a "disclosure" form. If the court can't give it to you, you'll have to find it on your own. Or, suppose you are trying to sell your car and the buyer says she wants a bill of sale. Again, you'll have to track one down.

If you haven't been directed toward a particular form, but want to undertake a procedure and suspect that it requires forms, you should find a resource that explains the procedure or transaction. Many of these resources will provide the necessary forms and explain how to fill them in.

Keep in mind that some forms used by courts and government agencies are "mandatory." This means that you have to use their form, and not a similar form that you or someone else has designed, even if your version contains the same information. If you need a form for a court or government agency, it's wise to ask the clerk whether the court has a mandatory form.

## Finding the Form You Need

Fortunately, forms are readily available from many sources. Here are the best ways to get them.

- *Stationery Stores.* Many large stationery stores sell legal forms. However, these forms usually don't come with legal instructions, so you may need some help filling them in.
- *Self-help Legal Materials.* Self-help legal materials, including those published by Nolo, are a good place to find legal forms. Because self-help law materials are written for non-lawyers, the forms are usually accompanied by detailed instructions in plain English. You can find self-help legal materials in bookstores, law libraries and on the Internet.
- *Law Libraries.* Most law libraries have a large collection of books that contain forms for almost every legal transaction imaginable. They usually contain step-by-step instructions for completing the forms and highlight areas where the boilerplate language might not be appropriate.
- *Government Forms on the Web.* Many federal, state, county and municipal courts offer forms on their websites. (See Finding Court and Government Agency Websites, above.) Often, these forms are accompanied by instructions and an overview of the relevant law. Also, Findlaw at http://www.findlaw.com/ provides lists of government forms, specific subject matter forms, form collections and indexes. Many of these forms are not accompanied by instructions. So, unless you already know what you are doing, you may have to search for additional information to assist you in filling them out.

## More Information About Legal Research

*Legal Research: How to Find and Understand the Law*, by Stephen Elias and Susan Levinkind (Nolo), is an easy-to-read book that provides step-by-step instructions on how to find legal information, both in the law library and online. It includes examples, exercises (with answers) and sample legal memos.

*Gilbert's Legal Research*, by Peter Honigsberg (Harcourt Brace Legal and Professional Publications), is a no-nonsense guide to commonly used law library resources.

### http://www.nolo.com/research/index.html

*Nolo's Legal Research Center provides links to courts across the country and access to small claims information in many states. It also contains U.S. Supreme Court cases and federal and state statutes.*

### http://www.spl.org/govpubs/municode.html

*Municipal Codes Online, maintained by the Seattle Public Library, provides the text of many local ordinances around the country.*

### http://www.ncsc.dni.us/court/sites/courts.htm

*The National Center for State Courts provides links to local, state and federal court websites.*

### http://www.uscourts.gov/links.htm

*The Federal Judiciary's website provides links to federal court websites.*

### http://www.versuslaw.com

*Versuslaw allows you to search online for state and federal statutes and cases for a low monthly fee of $6.95.*

### http://findlaw.com

*Findlaw's extensive database allows you to search for state and federal statutes and cases and provides links to many courts around the country.*

# Index

## A

AB trust, 12/19–20

Accident reporting to DMV, 10/23

Accommodation under the ADA, 4/26–28

ADA. *See* Americans with Disabilities Act (ADA)

ADEA. *See* Age Discrimination in Employment Act (ADEA)

Adjustable rate mortgage (ARM), 1/4

Adopting a child, 16/2–11

  agency adoptions, 16/4, 16/5–7

  by stepparent, 16/11–13

  identified adoptions, 16/5

  independent adoptions, 16/4–5, 16-/7–9

  international adoptions, 16/5, 16/9–10

  open adoptions, 16/9

  relative adoptions, 16/5

  types of adoption, 16/4–5

Adoption rights, 16/13–15

Advertisements for jobs, legal guidelines, 5/30

Age Discrimination in Employment Act (ADEA), 4/18–19

Agency adoptions, 16/4, 16/5–7

Airlines, 11/2–9

  baggage problems and compensation, 11/7

  bankrupt airline and tickets, 11/8–9

  bereavement fares, 11/4

  charter companies, 11/27

  Conditions of Carriage, 11/3

  delayed, diverted or canceled flights, 11/5

  discount tickets, 11/29

  e-tickets, 11/2–3

  frequent flyer programs, 11/8

  lost tickets, 11/4

  overbooked flights and compensation, 11/4–5, 11/6

  ticket restrictions, 11/3–4

Americans with Disabilities Act (ADA), 4/26–29

  employers and, 5/35–36

  medical record disclosure rules, 5/34

  recovering addicts and, 5/32

Amortizing versus deducting capital assets, 5/21–22

Annuities, pension plans, 14/16

Annulments, 15/14–15

Anticybersquatting Consumer Protection Act (ACPA), 8/16

Antidilution statutes, 8/9

Appraising a home's value, 1/10–11

Arbitration

  lemon law relief, 10/5–6

  mediation compared to, 17/22

ARM (adjustable rate mortgage), 1/4

Arraignments and lawyers, 18/21

Arrests and interrogations, 18/14–17

Arrest warrants, 18/15

Asbestos exposure, landlord liability, 2/15

"As is" product and warranty, 9/3

Asking price for home, 1/10–11

Assignment of rights, 7/6

ATM or debit cards, 9/10–12

Attorney-in-fact, duties of, 13/8–9

Audits by the IRS, 9/21–22
Autos. *See* Cars

**B**
BAC (blood-alcohol concentration),
    10/21–22
Background checks and privacy, 5/32
Baggage problems and compensation,
    11/7
Bail, 18/17–20
Bankruptcy, 9/25–28
    airline tickets from bankrupt airline,
        11/8–9
Bankruptcy Reform bill, 9/28
Barking dogs, 2/10–11
Bereavement fares, 11/4
Berne Convention, 7/7
BFOQ (bona fide occupational qualifica-
    tion), 4/18
Birthparents, adoption rights, 16/13–15
Blood-alcohol concentration (BAC),
    10/21–22
Blood tests for marriage licenses,
    15/10–12
Bodily samples, giving after arrest, 18/15
Body and organ donations, 12/25
Bona fide occupational qualification
    (BFOQ), 4/18
Books. *See* Reference books
Bouncing a check, 9/17
Boundaries of property, 2/2–3
Boundary tree, 2/5
Breaking a long-term lease, 3/3
Business methods, patent protection, 6/4
Business plans, 5/6
Buydown of mortgage, 1/6
Buyers Guide for used cars, 10/11
Buying a house, 1/2–9
Bypass trust (AB trust ), 12/19–20

**C**
Canceled flights, 11/5

Capital assets, amortizing versus
    deducting, 5/21–22
Car dealers, negotiating with, 10/2–3
Cars
    business expenses, 5/20
    buying a new car, 10/2–7
    buying a used car, 10/10–12
    canceling sales contract, 10/4
    financing, 10/12
    hotel parking and, 11/19
    insurance for, 10/13–16
    leasing, 10/7–10
    lemon laws, 10/5–7
    lemon laws for used cars, 10/12
    missing a payment, 9/12–13
    rental cars, 11/9–14
    repossession, 9/13
    "secret warranties," 10/6–7
    *See also* Driving
Cash advance fees, 9/10
Cash refunds, 9/6–7
CC&Rs (covenants, conditions and
    restrictions), 1/7
    home-based business restrictions, 5/26
    view regulations, 2/7
Certification mark, 8/3
    *See also* Trademarks
Changing your name, 15/27–31
Chapter 7 and 13 bankruptcy, 9/25–28
Chapter 11 and 12 bankruptcy, 9/25
Charge cards, 9/7–10
Charter companies, 11/27
Cheating on taxes, 9/19–20
Checks, writing a bad check, 9/17
Child custody and visitation, 16/17–24
Children. *See* Parents and children
Child support, 16/24–29
Child Support Enforcement Act, 16/27
Child Support Recovery Act (CSRA),
    16/28
Civil Rights Act, sexual harassment, 4/21
Claim filing. *See* Filing

Closing (transfer of home ownership), 1/13

COBRA and health insurance, 4/32

Collecting court judgments, 17/6

Collection agencies, 9/22–25

Collective mark, 8/3
*See also* Trademarks

Collective works, copyright, 7/5

Collision coverage, cars, 10/14

Common law marriage, 15/4, 15/6, 15/13

Community property, 15/20, 15/22–23

Comparative rectitude, 15/16

Compensation
baggage problems, 11/7
delayed, diverted or canceled flights, 11/3
overbooked flights, 11/4–5, 11/6

Compensatory time, 4/4

Competency to stand trial, 18/8

Complaint filing. *See* Filing

Comprehensive coverage, cars, 10/14

Comps and asking price for house, 1/10–11

Comp time instead of overtime pay, 4/4

Computer software, patent protection, 6/4

Conditions of Carriage, 11/3

Confirmed reservations at hotels, 11/15–16

Consent searches, 18/13

Conservatorships, 13/10–13

Consignment, selling goods and services on, 5/6–7

Consolidated Omnibus Budget Reconciliation ACT (COBRA), 4/32

Consumer protection laws, small businesses and, 5/6

Contingencies in offers, 1/8

Continuous annuity, pension plans, 14/16

"Cooling Off Rule" for contracts, 9/5
auto sales contracts, 10/4
timeshare contracts, 11/25

Copyright, 7/1–12
collective works, 7/5
copyright notice, 7/6–7
enforcement, 7/10–11
exclusive rights granted by, 7/5–6
fair use, 7/8–9
international protection, 7/7
Internet material, 7/9
joint works, 7/5
length of, 7/3–4
overview, 7/2–4
ownership, 7/4–6
patents compared to, 6/14
protections, 7/6–9
public domain material, 7/7–8
registration, 7/10
trademarks compared to, 8/18
transfer of rights, 7/6

Corporations, 5/12–15

Counterclaims, in small claims court, 17/18

Counteroffers, 1/11

Couples. *See* Gays and lesbians; Spouses and partners; Unmarried couples

Courts
collecting judgments, 17/6
depositions, 17/8–11
evidence in, 17/11–12
free legal help, 17/2–4
good case requirements, 17/6–7
representing yourself, 17/2–13
small claims court, 17/13–20
witness examination, 17/12
*See also* Criminal law and procedure

Covenants, conditions and restrictions. *See* CC&Rs

Credit
landlords and tenant's credit, 3/8
and loan approval, 1/2–3
rebuilding credit, 9/29–32

Credit and charge cards, 9/7–10
rental car companies and, 11/10

Credit bureaus, 9/30

Credit insurance for car purchase, 10/13

Credit reports
errors, correcting, 9/30–31
obtaining, 9/30

Criminal acts and activities
hotel liability, 11/18
landlord's liability, 3/12–14

Criminal law and procedure, 18/1–26
arrests and interrogations, 18/14–17
bail, 18/17–20
competency to stand trial, 18/8
court-appointed attorneys, 18/20–22
felony, 18/4
guilt "beyond a reasonable doubt,"
18/5
insanity defense, 18/7–8
lawyers and, 18/20–25
misdemeanor, 18/4
overview, 18/2–8
police questioning, 18/9–10
police searches and seizures, 18/10–14
presumption of innocence, 18/4
punishment, likely sentences, 18/25
right to an attorney, 17/3
self-defense, 18/7
self-representation, 18/24, 18/25
See also Courts

CSRA (Child Support Recovery Act),
16/28

Custodial interference, 16/22

Custody and visitation, 16/17–24

Cybersquatters, 8/16

**D**

Debit or ATM cards, 9/10–12

Debt collections, 9/22–25

Debt counseling, 9/12

Debtor's prisons, 9/17

Debt repayment strategies, 9/12–18

Debts, nondischargeable debts in
bankruptcy, 9/26–27

Deductible business expenses, 5/19–22

Deeds, 1/14–15
deed in lieu of foreclosure, 9/14

Defined benefit and defined contribution
plans, 14/13–14

Delayed flights, 11/5

Dependents benefits, Social Security,
14/3

Depositions, 17/8–11

Design patents, 6/2, 6/3

Disability benefits, Social Security,
4/14–15, 4/33, 14/3

Disability discrimination, 4/25–29
See also Americans with Disabilities
Act (ADA)

Disclosures by home seller, 1/7
obligations, 1/11–12

Discount airline tickets, 11/29

Discount rates for hotels, 11/17

Discrimination
age discrimination, 4/17–21
disability discrimination, 4/25–29
housing discrimination, 3/4–6
sexual harassment, 4/21–25

Dispute resolution, landlord-tenant,
3/17–18

Diverted flights, 11/5

Divorce, 15/14–23
child custody and visitation, 16/17–24
and child support, 16/25
grounds for by state, 15/18–19
mediation, 15/23
no-fault, 15/16
pension plan benefits, 14/18
preventing a fault divorce, 15/17
property distribution, 15/20, 15/22–23
residency requirements, 15/20,
15/21–22
separation, types of, 15/15–16
Social Security spousal benefits,
14/5–6

Doctors and workers' compensation, 4/15

Dog barking, 2/10–11

Domain names
for business, 5/3
cybersquatters, 8/16
searching for, 8/13
trademark conflicts with, 8/16–17
and trademark protection, 8/7–8

Domestic violence, 15/24–27

Driver's license, 10/16–19

Driving
driver's license, 10/16–19
drunk driving, 10/21–22
foreign countries, 10/17–18
police stops, 10/19–20
tickets from other states, 10/17
traffic accidents, 10/23–25
young drivers in other states, 10/17
*See also* Cars

Drug-dealing tenants, landlord liability,
3/13–14

Drunk driving, 10/21–22

Durable powers of attorney
for finance, 13/7–10
for healthcare, 13/2–3

**E**

EEOC. *See* Equal Employment Opportunity Commission (EEOC)

Eight-hour workday, 4/5

Employee evaluations, 5/33

Employee Retirement Income Security
Act (ERISA), 14/18–19

Employers' rights and responsibilities,
5/29–42
ADA compliance, 5/35–36
advertisements for jobs, 5/30
background checks, 5/32
copyright and employees, 7/4–6
employee evaluations, 5/33
independent contractors, 5/41–42
interviewing guidelines, 5/30–31
inventor-employees and patents,
6/13–14

laying off employees, 5/39
obligations after employee leaves, 5/40
paid time off, 5/34–35
personnel files, 5/33–34
references for former employees,
5/40–41
religious discrimination complaint
handling, 5/38
sexual harassment complaint handling, 5/36–38
smoking issues, 5/38–39
trade secret protections, 5/39–40
unpaid leave requirements, 5/35

Employment rights. *See* Workplace
rights

Encroachment on your property, 2/2

Entering rental property, 3/8

Entertainment expenses for business, 5/20

Equal Employment Opportunity
Commission (EEOC)
ADA enforcement by, 4/28–29
age discrimination, 4/19
sexual harassment, 4/22

ERISA (Employee Retirement Income
Security Act), 14/18–19

Errors
on ATM or debit card statement, 9/11
on credit card billing statement,
9/9–10
on credit report, 9/30–31
on Social Security earnings records,
14/4–5

Estate planning, 12/1–26
avoiding probate, 12/13–15
body and organ donations, 12/25
funeral and final arrangements
planning, 12/22–24
living trusts, 12/15–18
probate, 12/8–9
taxes, 12/18–21
wills, 12/2–13

E-tickets, 11/2–3

Evidence
    searches to prevent destruction of,
        18/13–14
    in trials, 17/11–12
Executors, 12/9–13
    duties of, 12/12
Expenses, deductible business expenses,
    5/19–22
Expressed warranty, 9/3
Extended warranties, 9/4

**F**

Failure to file tax return, 9/19
Fair Debt Collection Practices Act
    (FDCPA), 9/23, 9/24
Fair Labor Standards Act (FLSA), 4/2–3
    independent contractors and, 4/6–7
Fair pay and time off, 4/2–9
Fair use, copyright, 7/8–9
Family and Medical Leave Act (FMLA),
    4/7–8
FDCPA (Fair Debt Collection Practices
    Act), 9/23, 9/24
Felony, 18/4
Fence regulations, 2/3–4
Filing
    age discrimination complaints,
        4/19–20
    housing discrimination complaints,
        3/5–6
    OSHA complaints, 4/10
    sexual harassment claims, 4/25
    workers' compensation claims, 4/14
Final arrangements and funerals,
    12/22–24
Final paycheck, time for receiving, 4/7
Finances, 9/1–33
    ATM or debit cards, 9/10–12
    bankruptcy, 9/25–28
    car purchases, 10/12
    "Cooling Off Rule" for contracts, 9/5
    credit and charge cards, 9/7–10

debt collections, 9/22–25
    debt repayment, 9/12–18
    fraud complaints, 9/4–5
    purchasing goods and services, 9/2–7
    rebuilding credit, 9/29–32
    taxes and, 9/18–22
    three-day right to cancel contract, 9/6
    unordered merchandise, 9/5
    warranties, 9/2–4
Fired from job, 4/29–31
Fixed rate mortgage, 1/4
Fizzbo. See FSBO (For Sale By Owner)
FLSA. See Fair Labor Standards Act
    (FLSA)
FMLA. See Family and Medical Leave
    Act (FMLA)
Foreclosure on house, 9/13
Forms of life, patent protection, 6/4
For Sale By Owner, 1/5, 1/9–10
401(k) plans, 14/21
Fraud complaints
    products and services, 9/4–5
    reporting travel scams, 11/27–28
    travel scams, 11/23–29
Free legal help, 17/2–4
Frequent flyer programs, 11/8
Frisks by police, 18/9–10
FSBO (For Sale By Owner), 1/5, 1/9–10
Funeral or memorial societies, 12/23–24
Funeral planning, 12/22–24

**G**

Garnishing of wages, 9/16–17
GATT treaty, copyright protection, 7/7
Gays and lesbians
    and adopting a child, 16/3–4
    custody or visitation rights, 16/19
    domestic violence support groups,
        15/26
    living together, 15/2–6
    same-sex marriages, 15/13–14
    sexual harassment protections, 4/22

*See also* Spouses and partners

General Agreement on Tariffs and Trade. *See* GATT treaty

General partnerships, 5/9

Gifts
   to avoid probate, 12/14
   gift taxes, 12/21

Government-guaranteed house loans, 1/2–3–4

Grandparents, adoption rights, 16/13–15

Grant deed, 1/15

Guaranteed reservations at hotels, 11/15–16

Guardianship for children, 16/30–33
   in will, 12/4

Guardianship of the estate, 16/32–33

## H

Handwritten wills, 12/3

Health and safety, in the workplace, 4/9–12

Healthcare directives, 13/2–6
   legal requirements, 13/6
   medical procedures covered by, 13/5
   proxy appointment, 13/4
   when it takes effect, 13/3

Health insurance, after losing job, 4/32

Health Insurance Act, 4/32

Height restrictions on fences, 2/3

Holographic wills, 12/3

Home-based businesses, 5/24–29
   insurance for, 5/27
   part-time business, 5/28–29
   tax deduction, 5/23, 5/27, 5/28–29
   zoning issues, 5/25–26

Home closing, 1/13

Home inspections, 1/7–8

Home inventory, 1/17–18

Homeowners' associations, 1/6–7
   *See also* CC&Rs

Homestead exemption for bankruptcy, 9/27

Home study for adoption, 16/9

Home warranties, 1/12–13

Hotels and other accommodations, 11/14–19
   crime victims and hotel liability, 11/18
   discount rates, 11/17
   injuries and hotel liability, 11/18
   privacy in rooms, 11/16
   reservations, 11/15–16
   stolen belongings, 11/8–19

"Hot pursuit" searches, 18/14

Houses
   agreement for unmarried couples, 15/3
   buying, 1/2–9
   deeds, 1/14–15
   foreclosure proceedings, 9/13
   homestead exemption for bankruptcy, 9/27
   IRS seizure of, 9/21
   lien on, 9/17
   safety issues, 1/16–18
   selling, 1/9–14
   tips for buying, 1/8

Housing discrimination, 3/4–6

## I

Identified adoptions, 16/5

Implied warranty, 9/2–3

Incapacitation, and conservatorships, 13/11

Independent contractors
   copyright and, 7/4–5
   employer's obligations to, 5/41–42
   Fair Labor Standards Act and, 4/6–7
   status and home-based business, 5/27

Individual Retirement Accounts (IRAs), 14/21–22

Infractions, 18/4

Infringement
   of copyright, 7/10–11
   of a patent, 6/9–10
   of a trademark, 8/9–10

Inherently distinctive marks, 8/5–6
Injuries
    hotel liability, 11/18
    job-related and workers' compensa-
        tion, 4/12–17
    prevention of, 4/10–11
    on rental property and landlord's
        liability, 3/10–11
Insanity defense, 18/7–8
Inspections of home, 1/7–8
Insurance
    to avoid probate, 12/14
    car insurance, 10/13–16
    credit insurance for car purchase, 10/13
    home-based businesses, 5/27
    homeowner's insurance, 1/18
    private mortgage insurance (PMI), 1/6
    reducing auto premiums, 10/16
    rental car insurance, 11/13–14
    rental property, 3/15–16
    renter's insurance, 3/16–17
Intent-to-use (ITU) trademark registra-
    tion application, 8/8
    enforcement, 8/9–10
International adoptions, 16/5, 16/9–10
International travel
    compensation for baggage problems,
        11/7
    compensation for delayed flight, 11/5
    compensation for overbooked flight,
        11/6
    e-tickets and, 11/2–3
    renting a car, 11/14
Internet
    copyright and, 7/9
    *See also* Domain names; Resources
Interrogations by police, 18/14–17
Interviewing guidelines, for employers,
    5/30–31
Inter vivos trusts. *See* Living trusts
Intestate succession, 12/2
Inventions. *See* Patents

Inventory. *See* Home inventory
IRAs, 14/21–22

**J**
Joint and survivor annuity, pension
    plans, 14/16
Joint tenancy, to avoid probate, 12/14
Joint works, copyright, 7/5
Jury trial right, 18/5

**K**
Keogh plans, 14/22

**L**
Labor regulations. *See* Workplace rights
Landlord liability
    asbestos exposure, 2/15
    criminal acts and activities, 3/12–14
    injuries on rental property, 3/10–11
    lead poisoning, 3/14–15
Landlord-tenant laws, 3/2–21
Late rent, 3/6
Law libraries, A/2
Laws. *See* Statutory codes
Lawyers
    changing lawyers in criminal cases,
        18/23–24
    coaching by, 17/5
    contingency fee basis, 17/3
    court-appointed, 18/20–22
    criminal law and procedure, 18/20–25
    dealing with, 17/27–31
    for DUI charges, 10/22
    fees for criminal cases, 18/23
    firing, 17/27
    large bills from, 17/29–30
    locating criminal defense lawyers,
        18/22
    malpractice case against, 17/27–28
    pro bono representation by, 17/4
    wills and, 12/2–3
    for workers' compensation cases, 4/16
LDW (loss damage waiver), 11/13–14

Lead-based paint and hazards disclosure, 1/12

Lead poisoning, landlord liability, 3/14–15

Leases (rental property), 3/2–3

Leasing a car, 10/7–10

Legal aid, 17/3

Legal forms, A/10–11

Legal research, A/1–12
  background materials, A/2–4
  finding a law, A/4–8
  finding answers to specific questions, A/8–10
  forms, sources of, A/10–11
  law libraries, A/2

Legal separation, 15/15–16

Lemon laws, 10/5–7
  for used cars, 10/12

Lesbians. *See* Gays and lesbians

Lexis, A/8

Liability insurance, cars, 10/13–14

Licensing
  copyright and, 7/6
  an invention, 6/13

Lien on house, 9/17

Limited liability, for businesses, 5/9–10

Limited liability companies (LLCs), 5/14

Liquidation bankruptcy (Chapter 7), 9/25–28

Living apart, 15/15

Living trusts, 12/15–18
  to avoid probate, 12/14
  durable power of attorney for finances and, 13/9

LLCs, 5/14

Loans and mortgages, 1/2–4, 1/6

Location for a business, 5/5

Lodging. *See* Hotels and other accommodations

Losing or leaving your job, 4/29–33

Loss damage waiver (LDW), 11/13–14

Lost airline tickets, 11/4

Lost ATM or debit cards, liability for charges, 9/11

Lost credit cards, liability for charges, 9/9

Lump-sum payments, pension plans, 14/16

**M**

Maintenance
  of fence on the property line, 2/4
  of rental property, 3/9–11

Marriage, 15/8–14
  blood test requirements by state, 15/11–12
  changing your name, 15/27–28
  requirements for, 15/9
  rights conferred by, 15/8–9

Marriage certificate, 15/9

Marriage license, 15/9–12

Martindale-Hubbell directories, 18/22

Mediation, 17/21–26
  about child custody and visitation, 16/22–23
  arbitration compared to, 17/22
  costs of, 17/24–25
  divorce agreements, 15/23
  landlord-tenant disputes, 3/17
  locating a mediator, 17/25
  stages of, 17/22–23

Medicaid, 14/8–9

Medical records, ADA and limited disclosure rules, 5/34

Medicare, 14/8–12
  Part A coverage, 14/9–10
  Part B coverage, 14/10–11
  prescription drugs, 14/12
  states with limits on patient billing, 14/12

Memorial or funeral societies, 12/23–24

Men, sexual harassment protections, 4/22

Minimum payments for credit cards, 9/8

Minimum wage, 4/3

and tips, 4/5

Miranda rights
  police and, 18/15–16
  traffic stops and, 10/22
Misdemeanor, 18/4
MLS (multiple listing service), 1/5
Money. *See* Finances
Mortgages and loans, 1/2–4, 1/6
  missing payments, 9/13
  walking away from house, 9/14
Mortuaries, services offered by, 12/23
Motels. *See* Hotels and other accommo-
  dations
Multiple listing service (MLS), 1/5

## N

Names, changing your name, 15/27–31
Naming a business, 5/3–5, 8/4
NDA. *See* Nondisclosure agreement
  (NDA)
Neighbors, 2/1–11
New homes, buying tips, 1/6
No-fault car insurance, 10/15–16, 10/24
No-fault divorce, 15/16
Noise problems, 2/8–11
Nondischargeable debts, 9/26–27
Nondisclosure agreement (NDA), for
  trade secret protection, 5/39–40
Nonobvious invention, 6/5–6
Nonprofit corporations, 5/15–18
Nonrefundable tickets, 11/3
Nontransferable tickets, 11/3
Notarization, of deeds, 1/15
Notice, of entry by landlord, 3/8
Novel invention, 6/5
Nuisance, trees as, 2/6

## O

Occupational Safety and Health Act
  (OSHA), 4/9–10, 4/12
Offers and counteroffers, 1/11
Older Americans, 14/1–24
  age discrimination, 4/17–21

driver's licenses, 10/18–19
  Medicare, 14/8–12
  pensions, 14/13–20
  retirement plans, 14/20–23
  Social Security, 14/2–8
Older Workers Benefit Protection Act,
  4/19
On-call time regulations, 4/6
Open adoptions, 16/9
Organ donations, 12/25
O.R. releases, 18/19–20
OSHA, 4/9–10, 4/12
Overbooked flights and compensation,
  11/4–5, 11/6
Overtime regulations, 4/3–5
  comp time instead of, 4/4

## P

Palimony, 15/2–3
Parenting agreement, 16/20
Parents and children, 16/1–34
  adopting a child, 16/2–11
  adoption rights, 16/13–15
  child custody and visitation, 16/17–24
  child support, 16/24–29
  disinheriting children, 12/6–7
  guardianship of children, 16/30–33
  leaving property to children, 12/5
  personal guardians for children, 12/4
  stepparent adoptions, 16/11–13
  unmarried couples and parenting,
    15/5
Partnerships, 5/9
Part-time home-based business, 5/28–29
Patents, 6/1–16
  applying for, 6/7–9
  capitalizing on, 6/12–14
  copyrights compared to, 6/14
  enforcing, 6/9–12
  length of protection, 6/10–11
  protections abroad, 6/9
  Provisional Patent Application (PPA),
    6/8

qualifying for, 6/2–7

trademarks compared to, 6/15, 8/18–19

Pay-on-death designations, 12/14

PBGC (Pension Benefit Guaranty Corp.), 14/19

P.D.s (public defenders), 18/21–22

Pension Benefit Guaranty Corp. (PBGC), 14/19

Pensions, 14/13–20

divorce and, 14/18

mismanagement or loss of funds, 14/18–19

older workers and, 4/19

Social Security benefits and, 14/14–15

Summary Plan Description requirement, 14/17

types of payments, 14/16

vested benefits, 14/14

Permanent disability, Social Security benefits, 4/14–15

Permanent separation, 15/15–16

Personal estate tax exemption, 12/18

Personal guardians for children, 12/4

Personal injury lawsuits, filed by tenant, 3/11

Personal Injury Protection (PIP), 10/15–16, 10/24

Personnel files, 5/33–34

Phone numbers. *See* Resources

PIP (Personal Injury Protection), 10/15–16, 10/24

Plant patents, 6/2, 6/3

PMI (private mortgage insurance), 1/6

POD accounts, 12/14

Police

frisks, 18/9–10

questioning by, 18/9–10

searches and seizures, 18/10–14

searches during traffic stops, 10/20

searches of impounded cars, 10/20

traffic stops, 10/19–20

Police investigation, and expectation of privacy, 18/11

Police reports for traffic accidents, 10/25

Posting bail, 18/18

Pot trusts, 12/5

Power of attorney. *See* Durable powers of attorney

PPA (Provisional Patent Application), 6/8

Premarital agreements, 15/6–8

Prescription drugs, Medicare, 14/12

Presumption of innocence, 18/4

Privacy rights

in hotel rooms, 11/16

and IRS files, 9/19

police searches and, 18/11–12

screening prospective employees, 5/32

of tenants, 3/8

Private mortgage insurance (PMI), 1/6

Prizes and travel scams, 11/23

Probate, 12/8–9

avoiding, 12/13–15

Property boundaries, 2/2–3

Property guardians, for children, 12/5

Property managers, 3/14

Provisional Patent Application (PPA), 6/8

Proxy appointment, for healthcare directive, 13/4

Public defenders (P.D.s), 18/21–22

Public domain material, copyright, 7/7–8

Public safety and searches, 18/13

**Q**

QTIP trust, 12/20

Qualified retirement plans, 14/20–21

Questioning by police, 18/9–10

Quiet Enjoyment clauses, noise problems, 2/9

"Quiet hours," 2/9

Quitclaim deed, 1/14–15

as deed in lieu of foreclosure, 9/14

## R

Real estate agents and brokers, 1/5
  working with on a limited basis, 1/10
Rear-end accident liability, 10/24–25
Reasonable accommodation under the
  ADA, 4/27–28
Rebuilding credit, 9/29–32
Recording, deeds, 1/15
Recordkeeping
  for small businesses, 5/19
  tax record retention period, 9/18–19
Recovering addicts, ADA protections,
  5/32
Reference books
  adopting a child, 16/16
  bankruptcy, 9/28
  buying a house, 1/9
  cars, insuring, 10/16
  cars, lemon laws, 10/5, 10/7
  cars, negotiating with dealers, 10/3
  changing your name, 15/31
  child custody, 16/24
  child support, 16/29
  conservatorships, 13/13
  copyright, 7/11
  credit, rebuilding, 9/32
  debt collections, 9/25
  debt management, 9/12
  debt repayment, 9/17–18
  divorce, 15/23
  durable power of attorney for finance,
    13/10
  employers' rights and responsibilities,
    5/42
  estate and gift taxes, 12/21
  executors, 12/13
  gays and lesbians, 15/6
  guardianships, 16/33
  home businesses, 5/29
  insurance for cars, 10/16
  IRS and taxes, 9/22
  landlord-tenant law, 3/20–21
  about lawyers, 17/30–31
  legal background materials, A/3
  lemon laws, 10/5, 10/7
  living together, 15/6
  living trusts, 12/18
  mediation, 17/26
  Medicare, 14/12
  neighbor law, 2/11
  nonprofit corporations, 5/18
  patents, 6/15
  pensions, 14/19–20
  personal injury lawsuits, 3/11
  probate, 12/13
  probate, avoiding, 12/15
  representing yourself in court, 17/13
  retirement plans, 14/23
  selling your home yourself, 1/10
  sexual harassment, 4/25
  small business, 5/7–8
  small business legal structures, 5/14–15
  small business taxes, 5/24
  small claims court, 9/7, 17/20
  Social Security, 14/7
  tax exempt organizations, 5/18
  trademarks, 8/19
  traveling, 11/29
  unmarried couples, 15/6
  wills, 12/8
  workers' compensation, 4/17
  *See also* Resources
References for former employees, 5/40–41
Refund policies, 9/6–7
Registered trademark, 8/10
Relative adoptions, 16/5
Release (waiver not to sue), older
  workers and, 4/20
Rent, 3/6
Rental agreements, 3/2–3
Rental cars, 11/9–14
Rent control, 3/7
Renter's insurance, 3/16–17
Reorganization bankruptcy, 9/25–28

Repairs. *See* Maintenance

Repossession of car, 9/13

Representing yourself in court, 17/2–13
  criminal cases, 18/24, 18/25

Request for Earnings and Benefit
  Estimate Statement, 14/4

Reservations at hotels, 11/15–16

Resources
  for abused gays and lesbians, 15/26
  for abusive men, 15/25
  adopting a child, 16/16
  age discrimination, 4/20–21
  bankruptcy, 9/28
  body donations, 12/25
  buying and selling homes, 1/19–20
  cars, 10/25–26
  cars, buying a new car, 10/2, 10/3
  cars, buying a used car, 10/10
  cars, leasing, 10/10
  cars, "secret warranties," 10/7
  child custody, 16/24
  child support, 16/29
  Conditions of Carriage, 11/3
  conservatorships, 13/13
  consumer protection laws, 5/6
  copyright, 7/12
  copyright clearinghouses, 7/9
  court information online, 17/4, 17/31
  court websites, A/6
  credit, charge, ATM and debit cards,
    9/12
  credit bureaus, 9/30
  credit bureaus, phone numbers, 9/31
  credit repair, 9/32
  criminal law, 18/25–26
  debt collections, 9/25
  debt counseling, 9/12
  debt repayment, 9/18
  defense lawyers, locating, 18/22
  disability discrimination, 4/29
  domain name searches, 8/13

  domestic violence, 15/24, 15/25,
    15/26, 15/27
  driving record evaluation service, 11/11
  durable power of attorney, 13/13
  durable power of attorney for finance,
    13/10
  EEOC, 4/20, 4/22, 4/29
  estate planning, 12/26
  Fair Housing Information Clearing-
    house (HUD), 3/5
  family law mediators, 16/23
  finances, 9/33
  fraud complaints, 9/5
  funerals and final arrangements, 12/24
  gays and lesbians, 4/22
  government agency websites, A/6
  government-guaranteed house loans,
    1/2–3–4
  healthcare directives, 13/6, 13/13
  home-based businesses, 5/43
  homeowner's insurance, 1/18
  independent contractors, 5/43
  IRS and home offices, 5/28
  IRS and selling a home, 1/14
  Job Accommodation Network, 4/27
  landlord-tenant law, 3/21
  legal forms, A/11
  legal websites, A/4, A/12
  lemon laws, 10/5
  Lexis, A/8
  mediators, 17/25
  minimum wage, 4/3
  National Fraud Information Center,
    9/5
  National Lead Information Center,
    1/12, 3/15
  Newspapers Association of America,
    1/5–6
  nonprofit corporations, 5/43
  nonsmokers rights, 4/11
  for older Americans, 14/24
  OSHA, 4/12

OSHA complaint filing, 4/10

parenting, 16/34

Patent and Trademark Depository Libraries (PTDLs), 6/7

patents, 6/16

patent searches, 6/6–7

Pension Benefit Guaranty Corp. (PBGC), 14/19

pensions, 14/20

purchasing goods and services, 9/7

Request for Earnings and Benefit Estimate Statement, 14/4

same-sex marriages, 15/14

"secret warranties" for cars, 10/7

selling your home yourself, 1/10

sexual harassment, 4/25

small business sites, 5/43

Social Security Administration, 14/2, 14/8

spouses and partners, 15/32

student loan servicers, 9/15

student loan status, 9/16

student travel, 11/24

trademarks, 8/19–20

trademark searches, 8/12–14

travel agent associations, 11/22

traveling, 11/20

travel scam reporting, 11/27–28

U.S. Copyright Office, 7/10

U.S. Patent and Trademark Office, 6/6

Vermont Civil Unions, 15/14

wages, hours and time off, 4/9

Westlaw, A/8

workplace rights, 4/33–34

*See also* Reference books

Retention period for tax records, 9/18–19

Retirement, early retirement and age discrimination, 4/19

Retirement benefits, Social Security, 14/3

Retirement plans, 14/20–23

Returning security deposits, 3/7

Revised Uniform Reciprocal Enforcement of Support Act (RURESA), 16/28

Revoking driver's license, 10/18, 10/19

Roth IRAs, 14/22

RURESA (Revised Uniform Reciprocal Enforcement of Support Act), 16/28

**S**

Safety for the home, 1/16–18

Same-sex marriages, 15/13–14

Scams. *See* Fraud complaints

Screening practices, rental car companies, 11/10–11

Searches

domain name searches, 8/13

patent searches, 6/6–7

trademark searches, 8/11–14

Searches by police, 18/10–14

during traffic stops, 10/20

of impounded cars, 10/20

search warrants, 18/12–13

warrantless searches, 18/13–14

Section 179 business deductions, 5/21–22

Security deposits, 3/7

Seizure of assets by IRS, 9/21

Self-defense, 18/7

Self-representation in court, 17/2–13

criminal cases, 18/24, 18/25

Selling goods and services on consignment, 5/6–7

Selling your home, 1/9–14

Separation, types of, 15/15–16

SEPs, 14/22

Servicemarks, 8/2–3

business name as, 5/4

*See also* Trademarks

Severance pay, 4/32

Sexual harassment, 4/21–25

employer's handling of complaints, 5/36–38

Shelters, domestic violence, 15/24

Shipping delays and goods ordered by mail or phone, 9/6

Shop rights, 6/13–14
Short sales, 9/13
Sick time, 4/7–8
SIMPLE IRAs, 14/22
Simple life annuity, pension plans, 14/16
Single people and adopting a child, 16/3
Small business, 5/1–43
    employers' rights and responsibilities,
      5/29–42
    hiring independent contractors or
      employees, 5/23
    home-based businesses, 5/24–29
    legal structures and taxes, 5/22–23
    legal structures for, 5/8–15
    location for, 5/5
    naming, 5/3–5, 8/4
    nonprofit corporations, 5/15–18
    start-up considerations, 5/2–3
    tax issues, 5/18–24
Small claims court, 17/13–20
    appeals, 17/20
    avoiding, 17/17–18
    counterclaims, 17/18
    limits by state, 17/15–16
Sobriety tests, 10/21
Social Security, 14/2–8
    benefits, 14/3
    claiming benefits, 14/6, 14/7
    disability benefits, 4/14–15, 4/33
    errors on earnings records, 14/4–5
    pension plans and, 14/14–15
    Request for Earnings and Benefit
      Estimate Statement, 14/4
    working while collecting benefits,
      14/6
Sole proprietorship, 5/8–9
Spite fence, 2/4
Spouses and partners, 15/1–32
    changing your name, 15/27–31
    disinheriting a spouse, 12/6
    domestic violence, 15/24–27
    marriage, 15/8–14

    premarital agreements, 15/6–8
    unmarried couples, 15/2–6
    *See also* Divorce; Gays and lesbians
Springing durable power of attorney,
    13/7
State-imposed inheritance taxes, 12/19
Statutory codes
    antidilution statutes, 8/9
    finding a specific law, A/4–8
    landlord-tenant law, 3/18–19
Stepparent adoptions, 16/11–13
Stolen ATM or debit cards, liability for
    charges, 9/11
Stolen belongings and hotel liability,
    11/18–19
Stolen credit cards, liability for charges,
    9/9
Student loans, 9/15–16
Student travel, 11/24
Summary Plan Description requirement,
    14/17
Surveying costs, 2/2
Survivor benefits
    joint and survivor annuity, 14/16
    Social Security, 14/3
Suspension of driver's license, 10/18,
    10/19
Swimming pools, hotel liability, 11/18

**T**
Tax issues
    audit tips, 9/21–22
    avoidance schemes, 9/20
    cheating on taxes, 9/19–20
    corporations and, 5/13–14
    dealing with the IRS, 9/18–22
    debt settlement and, 9/14
    estate and gift taxes, 12/18–21
    exemptions for 501(c)(3) nonprofits,
      5/17
    failure to file return, 9/19
    home office deduction, 5/23, 5/27,
      5/28–29

negotiating payments to IRS, 9/20–21

personal estate tax exemption, 12/18

privacy and IRS files, 9/19

record retention period, 9/18–19

seizure of assets by IRS, 9/21

selling a home, 1/13–14

small business, 5/18–24

state-imposed inheritance taxes, 12/19

Teaser rates for credit cards, 9/8

Telephone numbers. *See* Resources

Temporary restraining order (TRO),
domestic violence and, 15/24–26

Tenants

landlord-tenant laws, 3/2–21

noise problems, 2/9

privacy rights, 3/8

renter's insurance, 3/16–17

selecting, 3/4

Three-day right to cancel contract, 9/6

Tickets (driving), from other states, 10/17

Time for selling a home, 1/9

Timeshares, 11/24–26

Tips and minimum wage, 4/5

Title X. *See* Lead-based paint and hazards
disclosure

Tobacco smoke in the workplace, 4/11–12

employer's responsibilities, 5/38–39

Trade dress, 8/3

*See also* Trademarks

Trademarks, 8/1–20

benefits of registration, 8/15–16

business name as, 5/4, 8/4

copyright compared to, 8/18

inherently distinctive marks, 8/5–6

length of registration, 8/16

notice marks, 8/10

patents compared to, 6/15, 8/18–19

protections, 8/5–8

registered trademark, 8/10

registering, 8/14–18

reserving for future use, 8/8–9

searching for, 8/11–14

state-level registration, 8/17

types of, 8/2–4

using, 8/8

Trade secret protections, 5/39–40

Traffic accidents, 10/23–25

Traffic stops, 10/19–20

Transfer of rights, copyright, 7/6

Travel, 11/1–30

airlines, 11/2–9

business expenses, 5/23–24

fraud, 11/23–29

hotels, 11/14–19

rental cars, 11/9–14

travel agents, 11/19–22

Travel agents, 11/19–22

Trees

as fences, 2/3

regulations about, 2/4–6

view problems and, 2/6–7

Trial separation, 15/15

Trimming a tree, 2/5

TROs and domestic violence, 15/24–26

Trust deed, 1/15

Trusts

AB trust, 12/19–20

for children, 12/5

QTIP trust, 12/20

*See also* Living trusts

Truth in Lending Act, three-day right to
cancel contract, 9/6

**U**

UCCJA (Uniform Child Custody
Jurisdiction Act), 16/20–21

Ugly fences, 2/4

UM. *See* Uninsured motorist coverage

Unemployment insurance, 4/33

Uniform Child Custody Jurisdiction Act
(UCCJA), 16/20–21

Uniform Premarital Agreement Act,
15/7

Uniform Transfers to Minors Act
(UTMA), 12/5

Uninsured motorist coverage, 10/14–15

Unmarried couples, 15/2–6

and adopting a child, 16/3

Unordered merchandise, 9/5

"Urgency payment" options to avoid, 9/23

Used cars, buying, 10/10–12

Utility bills, 9/15

Utility patents, 6/2–3

UTMA (Uniform Transfers to Minors Act), 12/5

**V**

Vacation certificates, legitimacy of, 11/26

Vacations and employers, 4/7

Vermont Civil Union law, 15/13–14

Vested benefits, 14/14

Vested in retirement plan, 14/23

View ordinance, 2/6–7

View problems, 2/6–8

Visitation and custody, 16/17–24

**W**

Wages

garnishing of, 9/16–17

minimum wage, 4/3

rules about, 4/2–3

Waivers not to sue, older workers and, 4/20

Warranties

for goods or services, 9/2–4

for homes, 1/12–13

"secret warranties" for cars, 10/6–7

Warranty deed, 1/15

Websites. *See* Resources

Westlaw, A/8

Wills, 12/2–13

challenges to, 12/7

disinheriting relatives, 12/6–7

executors, 12/9–13

handwritten, 12/3

leaving property to children, 12/5

legal requirements, 12/3–4

living trusts and, 12/16

personal guardians for children, 12/4

probate, 12/8–9

Witness examination, 17/12

"Wobblers," 18/4

Workers' compensation, 4/12–17, 4/33

Workplace rights, 4/1–34

age discrimination, 4/17–21

copyright and employees, 7/4–6

disability discrimination, 4/25–29

fair pay and time off, 4/2–9

health and safety, 4/9–12

inventor-employees and patents, 6/13–14

losing or leaving your job, 4/29–33

sexual harassment, 4/21–25

workers' compensation, 4/12–17

Works made for hire, 7/4–5

**Z**

Zoning issues

and business location, 5/5

home-based businesses, 5/25–26

## An Important Message to Our Readers

This product provides information and general advice about the law. But laws and procedures change frequently, and they can be interpreted differently by different people. For specific advice geared to your specific situation, consult an expert. No book, software or other published material is a substitute for personalized advice from a knowledgeable lawyer licensed to practice law in your state.